JOURNEYS OF THE MIND

JOURNEYS OF THE MIND

A LIFE IN HISTORY

PETER BROWN

PRINCETON UNIVERSITY PRESS

PRINCETON AND OXFORD

Published by Princeton University Press
41 William Street, Princeton, New Jersey 08540
99 Banbury Road, Oxford OX2 6JX

press.princeton.edu

Library of Congress Cataloging-in-Publication Data

Names: Brown, Peter, 1935– author.
Title: Journeys of the mind : a life in history / Peter Brown.
Description: Princeton : Princeton University Press, [2023] |
    Includes bibliographical references and index.
Identifiers: LCCN 2022020395 (print) | LCCN 2022020396 (ebook) |
    ISBN 9780691242286 (hardback) | ISBN 9780691242293 (ebook)
Subjects: LCSH: Brown, Peter, 1935– | Historians—United States—Biography. |
    BISAC: BIOGRAPHY & AUTOBIOGRAPHY / General | RELIGION /
    Christianity / History
Classification: LCC E175.5.B798 A3 2023 (print) | LCC E175.5.B798 (ebook) |
    DDC 930/.5092 [B]—dc23/eng/20221206
LC record available at https://lccn.loc.gov/2022020395
LC ebook record available at https://lccn.loc.gov/2022020396

British Library Cataloging-in-Publication Data is available

Editorial: Rob Tempio and Chloe Coy
Production Editorial: Lauren Lepow
Text and Jacket Design: Heather Hansen
Production: Erin Suydam
Publicity: Alyssa Sanford and Carmen Jimenez

Jacket photograph: © Robert MacLennan

This book has been composed in Arno Pro

Printed on acid-free paper. ∞

Printed in the United States of America

10 9 8 7 6 5 4 3 2 1

CONTENTS

PREFACE

THE BOOK

The study of late antiquity (roughly from AD 200 to 700) is a daunting and exhilarating enterprise. It involves a reassessment of almost every aspect of the history of Europe, North Africa, and the Middle East from the last centuries of the Roman Empire to the early Middle Ages. The birth and expansion of Christianity, the emergence of rabbinic Judaism, the fall of Rome, and the rise of Islam all happened in this crucial half millennium.

This book is about my engagement with this remarkable period of history. It is not a conventional autobiography; nor is it an impersonal history of the field of late antiquity. It is somewhere in between: the story of my life as a scholar; of the intellectual world in which I moved; of the institutions where I have studied and taught in England and America; and of the many scholars whom I have known and admired.

It was inspired by many years of conversations with graduate students and younger colleagues in America and elsewhere. I noticed that, although they had followed diligently the stream of publications in the field of late antiquity, they often had little idea of the social and institutional settings from which this field had emerged. I was sometimes left feeling that it was easier to explain to young Americans and Europeans the institutions of Dark Age Europe than the workings of Oxford in the 1950s and 1960s, and the often tenuous relationship between English and Continental scholarship in the postwar period.

Some of the questions were about myself. Many assumed that I was English. "Near miss," I would say politely; "I am Irish." "So you are Catholic?" "No," I would say, "I am Protestant." Traveling in more militant regions in the Middle East, I have occasionally had to stretch my language skills to the utmost so as to explain that, although I was Irish, I was not a member of the IRA.

So I had to explain myself by becoming a historian of myself.

BACKGROUND

I was also inspired by my dissatisfaction with brisk historiographical surveys that presented scholars purely as products of academe, as if they had begun to think and feel only when they entered their first graduate seminar. A sensitivity to what might be called background—to region, religion, family, and early education—is a necessary counterweight to this one-dimensional approach.

For this reason, I would like the reader to follow (and at a leisurely pace) the development within me of a historical sense. This is a precious gift that cannot be taken for granted. It may be fostered and disciplined in schools and in the universities. But it depends on the mobilization of a wider range of sensibilities and enthusiasms than those contained within the narrow confines of any campus.

The reader may also wonder why I have lingered, in the first few chapters, on my family's background. I did this partly out of loyalty to my parents; and partly because, in themselves, the Protestants of Ireland merit the historian's attention as a minority frequently overlooked by outsiders. But there was more to it than that. The ambiguities of the Protestant presence in Ireland ensured that I grew up with complex memories that recalled many aspects (both positive and negative) of the last centuries of Rome.

FRIENDS IN THE FIELD

In 1956, I graduated from Oxford and decided to specialize in late antiquity. Since then the field has grown exponentially, and scholars have had to widen their view of the world in ways that were barely imaginable in the middle of the last century. Faced by such rapid growth, any account of the development of one scholar in the field must, first and foremost, be an exercise in gratitude to all the others who have shared in this grand adventure.

As my account progresses, I have mentioned many names, well known to historians of late antiquity and of other periods, who have inspired and instructed me: my mentor, Arnaldo Momigliano; my hero, Henri-Irénée Marrou; my friends, Robert Markus, Mary Douglas, Pierre Hadot, Évelyne Patlagean, Lellia Ruggini, Ian Wood, and Averil Cameron—to mention only a few among the array of well-known scholars who have contributed to the expansion of the field. I had many such distinguished colleagues; and it is only for lack of space that I have not discussed them all. For each of them, each in a different way, did more than provide me with information or teach me a methodology: they also inspired me by their example and gave me the courage to continue in a difficult endeavor.

I have also gone out of my way to mention scholars who are less well known to present-day readers—teachers, to begin with, and then, in later years, students and colleagues from all over the world. Each deserves to be remembered as a contributor to an ever-expanding field. Many of their names now lie silently (if there at all) in modern footnotes. Some of the best of them are now deemed out-of-date. They are snowed under by more recent bibliography, much of it published in International English, and are often (to our shame) no longer read because they wrote in foreign languages.

Networks in a Changing World

In 1956, late antiquity (like any other period of the ancient world) was a field pursued in an old-fashioned manner. The modes of scholarly interchange in Europe and America were not so very different from what they had been when Edward Gibbon embarked on his monumental *History of the Decline and Fall of the Roman Empire* in 1776. Most of us (apart from specialists, such as archaeologists, epigraphers, and papyrologists) knew the field of late antiquity, as Gibbon did, mainly from print alone. Books and articles were read at home (in well-worn armchairs, in pubs, and even, at times, in my English days, in the bath) or in great libraries—the Bodleian Library and the Ashmolean Library in Oxford, the library of the Warburg Institute in London, the Biblioteca Marciana in Venice, Dow Library and the library of the Graduate Theological Union in Berkeley, Firestone Library and the library of the Theological Seminary in Princeton. Each of these had its own distinctive atmosphere that communicated, discreetly but effectively, what a scholar in the field of late antiquity could hope to do with the peculiar riches of each of them: creaking volumes of the Fathers of the Church in Venice; state-of-the-art archaeology in the Ashmolean and in the Institute for Advanced Study in Princeton; row after row of journals of New Testament studies in all languages and from every denomination, in the GTU in Berkeley and the PTS in Princeton.

In these conditions, educated persons were, paradoxically, both more cosmopolitan and more parochial than they are today. They had fewer contacts across national borders. Instead, they traveled through print. It was taken for granted that scholars of the ancient world and late antiquity read foreign literature—French, German, and Italian—to a high standard, as well as Latin and Greek. But this was reading and writing knowledge only: many of the most distinguished among them claimed (often somewhat assertively) to be reluctant to speak a word of a foreign tongue.

Hence a contrast between my wide access, through books, to the overarching macrocosm, appropriately spoken of in German as *gelehrtes Europa*—"learned Europe": the Europe of the Learned—and my limited personal contacts with scholars outside Britain. The pattern of these contacts shifted over the years, following both my own interests and the changing shape of Europe itself. In the 1960s, my foreign friends and colleagues were mainly French, connected with my work on Saint Augustine. In the 1970s, as my own work widened to embrace the world of late antiquity as a whole, the French were joined by Americans, and, later, by Italians.

This pattern of widening friendships, region by region, reflected the slow but sure growth of interconnectivity throughout Europe itself in the years before and after the formation of the Common Market. To begin with—in a time of postwar currency restrictions—travel on the Continent was not easy for Irish and English nationals; while to cross the Iron Curtain, as I did to Czechoslovakia, in 1966 and 1969, was a major undertaking.

Academic meetings, also, were much less frequent than nowadays. They were limited to major gatherings at international congresses. The rapid to-and-fro of transglobal seminars and workshops, which now plays such an important role in the career of young scholars, was largely absent. It was, perhaps, easier for an English student from Oxford or Cambridge to wander at will through Europe in the fourteenth century than in the 1950s. Hence the great importance for me of the Oxford Patristics Conference of 1963, when I first met so many of my foreign colleagues face-to-face, after I had known them for so many years from the printed page.

By the 1970s, things had changed for the field. Currency restrictions had gone, and travel was easier. British academe had grown closer both to Europe and to America. Things had also changed for me. I reached out to the Middle East, traveling through Iran in 1974 and 1976, only a few years before the Iranian Revolution. Those weeks of travel in Iran have marked me ever since.

A Portrait of an Age

Last but not least, the reader should know that this book was not meant to be only a story of my life and a reconstruction of my own intellectual genealogy. It was also intended to be, in part, a portrait of an age—of the remarkable half century after the end of World War II in which the study of late antiquity in its present form came into its own in England, America, and Europe. That age is past. Many of us sensed that it had begun to pass already in the late 1980s, with clear signs of the imminent revolution that led to the fall of the Berlin Wall.

Hence my decision to end this book in 1987. This was not an arbitrary date. A sense of strangeness had begun to settle even on so close a past: much of the work of previous decades had come to seem somehow dated, both to ourselves and to a younger generation of scholars. The past was no longer like the present. It had become possible to ask the historian's eternal question: "What was it like?"—what was it like when the study of late antiquity got underway?

As for myself, the thirty-five years after 1987 have been filled with further journeys of the mind. To narrate them would require an entire new book. But I hope that the journeys that are recorded here will give, at least, a touch of the thrill of exploring, in those now-distant days, the long-neglected last centuries of the ancient world.

Autobiography is not like straight history. In writing *Journeys of the Mind*, I have had to learn new skills, and to be more than usually grateful for the criticism and advice of others. The list of those who read through the book in many drafts is a testimony to the bonds of friendship that make the academic enterprise worthwhile: Ra ʿanan Boustan, Averil Cameron, Emily Chesley (a much-needed technical assistant), Angela Creager, John Dillon, Andrew Feldherr, Kyle Harper and Judith Herrin (both readers for Princeton University Press), Jamie Kreiner, Harry Liebersohn and Dorothee Schneider, Bob and Jane MacLennan, Dave Michelson, Helmut Reimitz, Christian Sahner, Jack Tannous, and Ian Wood. By sending me a digitalized version of *The Salopian*—the magazine of Shrewsbury School—Dr. Robin Brooke-Smith, Taylor Librarian and Archivist—brought back to me the feel of a remarkable institution in the early years of postwar Britain. Despite the dislocation of COVID-19 in its many forms, Rob Tempio, the acquisitions editor, kept an alert eye on the progress of this somewhat idiosyncratic experiment in writing and steered it toward Princeton University Press, placing it in the hands of Lauren Lepow—the most exact, the most cultivated, and the least intrusive copy editor that I have ever had the pleasure to know. Above all else, Betsy, my wife and friend, truly *dimidium animae meae*, half of my soul, read and reread every word of it; and researched, corrected, and improved it every time. It is dedicated to her.

PART I

IRELAND TO
SHREWSBURY

HOME AND ABROAD

THE PROTESTANT IRISH

After my mother's death in 1987, I returned to Ireland to sort out her house. There, in a bureau in the attic, I found clippings from two very different newspapers from two very different places: the *Irish Times* in Dublin and the *Khartoum Times* in Sudan. Apart from noting my arrival on July 26, 1935, at Hatch Street Hospital in Dublin, I found on the back of each clipping various items of news. In an interview with the *Khartoum Times*, Air Marshal Italo Balbo (1896–1940), the creator of the Italian air force, insisted that air power was the best guarantee of world peace. No nation would dare to go to war, knowing that its women and children, its wives and mothers, would face destruction from the air. And, in a speech reported in the *Irish Times*, Éamon de Valera (1882–1975), the great nationalist leader, declared that within fifty years the Irish people would all be speaking Irish. They would have forgotten whether they were Catholics or Protestants.

Balbo died in 1940, in the first year of the Second World War, shot from the sky outside Tobruk, but not before suffocating entire villages with poison gas in the course of Mussolini's conquest of Ethiopia. He did not live to know of the London Blitz, still less to know of the dropping of the atomic bomb. As for de Valera: relations between Protestants and Catholics have, indeed, improved in the Republic; but little Irish is spoken in the streets of Dublin.

Sitting in the empty attic of my mother's house, in 1987, fifty-two years after my birth, I was touched by the primal sadness of all historians. I was reading about people who knew as little of their future as I knew of my own.

HOME AND ABROAD

As the two birth announcements showed, at the time of my birth and for many years afterward, the life of my parents was divided between two places: "home," in Ireland, and "abroad," in Sudan, where my father, James Lamont Brown, worked as a traffic manager in the Sudan Railways from 1930 to 1947.

As a small child I lived between two worlds, spending the summer in Ireland and the winter in Sudan. A little later, during the war, from 1939 to 1944 (until the Mediterranean was opened again to civilian traffic) my mother and I lived in Ireland while my father stayed at his job abroad. Our only links to him were airmail letters, bearing exotic stamps of camel-riders and date palms, silhouetted against a sepia desert dawn, calculated to fire the imagination of a young boy. This experience established "abroad"—Egypt and Sudan—as a strong imaginative pole for me and my family.

"OUR CROWD": THE PROTESTANT IRISH

We were a Protestant family. This meant that I grew up in Ireland very aware that I was a member of a religious minority. Foreigners often assume that the Republic of Ireland is an entirely Catholic country, and that Protestantism is limited to the British enclave in Ulster, known as Northern Ireland. But we were there in the South. Reduced to a minority of about 5 percent by the 1940s, Protestants were well established in Dublin, though they were no longer a presence in much of the countryside. In a society where religious differences still mattered, Protestants thought of themselves as a group apart, clearly defined against the Catholic majority. Walking around Dublin as a boy, I was expected to know, instinctively, to which people I should take off my cap: well-to-do or distinctly seedy, they were "our crowd."

This meant that Protestant society in Dublin (as I viewed it through the memories of my parents and my aunts) was surprisingly interconnected. Among other links, its members shared a respect for books. Literary talent was appreciated and was often set to work in eloquent letters to the editor of the *Irish Times* on topics as diverse as the evils of censorship (a constant grievance) and the proper care of dogs. Until his very last days, my father would always cut out these letters, as specimens of homegrown rhetoric, to send to me, alongside any mention of any achievement by any Irish man or woman anywhere in the world.

My aunts remembered that W. B. Yeats (1865–1939)—the cousin of a cousin—would sit in the front row at their school performance of *Deirdre of the Sorrows* by John Millington Synge (1871–1909). Another cousin of Yeats, William Monk Gibbon (1896–1987)—known to us schoolboys as Gubb-Gubb—notably failed to teach me Latin at school. He later rose to fame as the Grand Old Man of Irish Letters, and was, perhaps, best known for his perpetual grudge against Yeats for having refused to include any of his poems in the famous *Oxford Book of Modern Verse*.

Emily and Ellen Synge, first cousins of the dramatist John Millicent Synge, were friends (maybe even distant relatives) of my mother's mother. They would occasionally come to Dublin from Annamoe in the Wicklow Mountains to attend the opera. They would bring a large box of chocolates, which they opened, with much rustling of paper, as the overture began, to the great annoyance of their neighbors. "Ada," Emily would say in a loud stage whisper, "If looks could kill!"

Most of these people had limited means. They did not own many books—but they read what they had. Works of poetry, fiction, and scholarship were expected to resonate among "our crowd." There was a strong sense that high ideas and serious learning did not need to be confined to academe. As a writer, I have always felt an obligation to "the folk of few books"—to use the phrase of Yeats. To write well, to spread knowledge, and to widen sympathies by the use of the pen has always been a top priority for me.

AFFINITIES

This background may explain certain affinities between what I picked up in the Ireland of my boyhood and the issues on which I have concentrated in the study of late antiquity.

Respect for the power of religion was the most obvious of them. I remember being puzzled, in my first years at school in England and in subsequent years as an undergraduate and teacher at Oxford, by the polite indifference of so many of my English friends to the role of religion as a social force. Such indifference was unthinkable in Ireland. In a world characterized by dignified poverty, both Protestant and Catholic churches offered to their members something to be proud of. This confessional mentality provided a social map with clearly delineated boundaries. Altogether, I expected religious ideas to be powerful and to have an impact on society—often, alas, in the form of intolerance: a sad topic that I came to study early in my life as a scholar.

A Past without a Future

I am also struck by the way in which I appear to have been drawn to study unfamiliar tracts of history, often buried beneath a mound of modern prejudice. To rehabilitate lost centuries has been my particular joy. This is not, perhaps, so surprising: after all, I grew up in a country that, for centuries, had been denied a future. Its Golden Age lay in the distant past, in the "Isle of Saints and Scholars" of the early Middle Ages, followed by tragic centuries of invasion and submission to alien rule.

By contrast, when I went to school in England as a boy, the history textbooks that I used still radiated confidence, even in a battered postwar Britain. Firm lines of progress seemed to run from the distant past—from Magna Carta and the origins of Parliament, through the Glorious Revolution of 1688, the Reform Bill of 1832, the expansion of the British Empire, and—it was now hoped by many—the new Britain of the welfare state. The history books that I read and the teaching that I received for much of the time stressed, with admirable robustness, the power of progressive institutions and the supreme virtue of common sense.

But where were those virtues to be seen in the history of Ireland? Where were they during the Irish Famine of 1845 to 1849? Charles Trevelyan (1807–1886), the English minister in charge of relief for the famine, was a pillar of progressive views. He was a Cornishman, who praised his countrymen as improved Celts—"Celts who by long habits of intercourse with the Anglo-Saxons have learned at last to be practical men."[1] His first notion of practical measures was to leave Ireland to its fate, so as to allow "the operation of natural causes" to rectify the shortage of food according to strict laws of laissez-faire commerce.[2] As a result, one million Irish men, women, and children died of starvation. Trevelyan, the "practical man," the free-market economist and impeccable administrator, had no regrets. The Irish, the unimproved Celts, were to blame:

> The great evil with which we have to contend [is] not the physical evil of the famine, but the moral evil of the selfish, perverse and turbulent character of the people.[3]

---

1. Cecil Woodham-Smith, *The Great Hunger* (New York: Harper and Row, 1962), 59.
2. Woodham-Smith, *Great Hunger*, 374.
3. Woodham-Smith, *Great Hunger*, 156.

Not surprisingly with such a past, a growing boy in Ireland (whether Protestant or Catholic) did not pick up the respect for common sense and for the beneficent power of institutions that was taken for granted, across the sea, in England.

Altogether, the history of Ireland could not be presented as a steady progress. It was punctuated by catastrophes and by all too many examples of decline and fall. In the past four centuries, Ireland had witnessed the collapse not of one ruling class, but of two. The traditional Irish aristocracy had been ruthlessly pushed aside by Protestant adventurers in the sixteenth and seventeenth centuries, largely (though not invariably) newcomers from Britain. But no sooner were these families established than they also began to decline. The agricultural depression after 1815, the catastrophe of the Great Famine of the 1840s, and the mobilization of the Land League of the 1880s scythed their income and severed their links to the land. By 1940, their fine houses littered the countryside as empty shells, some of them burned out in times of civil war.

So I grew up among people dressed in shabby tweed coats. Many of them, and their families, had seen better times. But most of them lived with good cheer and a sense of dignity. Even as a boy, I picked up a prevailing mood. I learned that a lively and imaginative culture could coexist with constrained political and economic circumstances. It was, perhaps, a good start with which to approach the world of late antiquity—a period of history that seemed, at first sight, to be going nowhere, but which would prove, on closer inspection, to be the making of both Europe and the Middle East.

EMPIRE

THE GREYS

The Double World of Neil Grey

The Irish Protestant gentry had lived for generations in narrow worlds backed by immense horizons. Many of them depended for their survival on a connection with the military that took them out of Ireland and spun them, like the particles that make up the rings of Saturn, around the prodigious mass of the British Empire at the time of its expansion.

They formed an ambiguous class: for all their fierce loyalty to the empire, they never thought of themselves as English. They have always reminded me of the provincials from the frontiers of the Roman Empire in its last centuries (Moors in Africa; Illyrians and Pannonians along the Danube)—men of war who had never seen Rome, but whose loyalty to a worldwide empire remained unshaken. The strong imaginative polarity between "home" and "abroad" with which I grew up was only the last, most modern version of an ancient ambiguity.

My mother's mother was born Ada Grey. According to *Burke's Landed Gentry of Ireland*, "The tradition of this family is that they descend from Lord Leonard Grey (beheaded in 1541) . . . great uncle of the famous and unfortunate Lady Jane Grey (beheaded in 1554)."[1]

Lord Leonard Grey had come to Ireland as lord deputy (the English governor of the island). He ruled for several tumultuous years before he ran into trouble. After the fall of his patrons in England, he was recalled and summarily executed.

---

1. *Burke's Landed Gentry of Ireland* (London: Burke's Peerage Limited, 1954), 320.

He left a son in Ireland—Neil Grey—who summed up in his own person the ambiguities of the English presence. Neil's mother was a daughter of the great Conn O'Neill, and he was brought up among the O'Neills, the dynasty that controlled a good part of Ulster. A boy with a double background, fluent both in English and in Irish, he was used by the O'Neills as an envoy to the current lord deputy, the truculent Earl of Sussex.

Sussex was a sworn enemy of Sean O'Neill, Neil Grey's uncle and now the head of the O'Neill clan. In 1561, he tried to enlist Neil—a young man caught between two worlds—to get rid of his uncle. We know this from a secret report of the earl to Queen Elizabeth, preserved in the *Calendar of State Papers*:

> I entered talk with Neil Grey. . . . I swore him upon the Bible to keep secret what I should say unto him, and assured him if it were ever known . . . it should cost him his life.
>
> I used long circumstance in persuading him to serve you to benefit his country. . . . *In fine* [finally] I brake with him to kill Shane [Sean] and bound myself by oath to see him have a hundred marks of land by the year to him and his heirs for reward.

It was a risky business: Neil "seemed desirous to serve your Highness, and to have the land but fearful to do it, doubting his own escape after with safety."[2]

Not surprisingly, Neil decided not to murder his uncle. Undeterred, Sussex tried again to get rid of Sean by sending him a barrel of poisoned wine. But the wine had no more effect than to give Sean—a notable drinker—a heavier hangover than usual.[3] Eventually, in 1567, he was killed by a rival Ulster clan.

CONNECTIONS

Neil Grey's descendants soon sank from view. They survived as minor land-owners west of the river Shannon. (Some branches of them spelled their name as Grey, with an *e*, others as "Gray"). I knew little about them, until, about

---

2. *Burke's Landed Gentry of Ireland*, 320, taken from J. A. Froude, *The Reign of Elizabeth and James* (London: Dent, 1911), 1:396–397. See now Ciaran Brady, *Shane O'Neill* (Dublin: University College of Dublin Press, 2015), 44–62.

3. Brady, *Shane O'Neill*, 66.

thirty years ago, I inherited a cache of letters, most of them from the early nineteenth century. They offered a glimpse of an Irish Protestant family in the days of Nelson and Wellington.

The letters are about the six grandsons of Hugh Grey. He was the poor relation of a powerful family—the Wynnes of Sligo. In an age when connections mattered, the Greys knew that they owed much to their link to the Wynnes. For almost two centuries, they adopted Wynne as their second name in honor of their patrons: even my mother, born in 1903, was christened Sheila *Wynne* Warren.

Hugh Grey had two sons. The older son, John Grey, was editor of the *Sligo Journal*—a publication entirely controlled by the Wynnes. The younger son, Captain Owen Wynne Grey of the Sixth Inniskilling Dragoons, may well have got his military commission through the Wynnes. It proved to be his passport to a wider world for himself and his children. In 1792, he was on campaign in Flanders under the Duke of York. He even brought his son, George, with him, although the boy was only fourteen. Young George's horse was shot from under him, and the duke, who had noticed the boy's courage, immediately promoted him to cornet—the junior officer who carried the battle flag of his cavalry troop.

The Six Sons of Owen Wynne Grey

Captain Grey faced a common dilemma. A second son, he had little land and a large family: two sons and two daughters from his first marriage, to Elizabeth O'Neill, and four sons and three daughters by his second marriage, to Elizabeth Philpott.

I learned about this dilemma from the family letters that had come my way. Most of them were written in 1805 by George Grey—the brave cornet of the Flanders campaign, and now a seasoned officer—to his stepmother, Elizabeth Philpott Grey. The most striking aspect of this correspondence was George's loyalty to the family as a whole. While making arrangements for his younger half brother, Philpott Grey, he reassured Elizabeth that he was looking out for all his other brothers and half brothers:

> I assure you that I have their interests at heart as much as a man can have and my pride will be to raise them in life—as much as it is mine to get to the head of my profession. (George Grey to Elizabeth Grey, March 13, 1805)

George would serve under the Duke of Wellngton during the Peninsular War. In April 7, 1812, the British stormed the highly fortified city of Badajoz and suffered terrible casualities. Wellington reported: "The list of killed and wounded will show that the officers . . . put themselves at the head of the attacks. . . . I must likewise mention Lieutenant-Colonel Grey of the 30th who was unfortunately killed."[4]

Elizabeth was a shrewd woman, plainly the brains of the family. Her priorities were conventional: to find husbands for the girls, and commissions in the army (or their equivalent in the navy) for the boys. In both respects she succeeded completely.

Young women with exiguous dowries, living in Gort, a village in the far West of Ireland, would have found it hard to find suitable husbands. Yet all five sisters got married, three of them to army officers, perhaps introduced by their father and brothers. For them, quite as much as for their brothers, the British army offered an escape from rural stagnation.

The Grey brothers joined either the army or the navy. They had little option. Short of land, they had to earn a living; and only three professions were considered suitable for a gentleman—the law, the church, or the armed forces. Individuals needed personal connections to enter any profession, and the connections enjoyed by the Greys (through the Wynnes) steered them toward the army. The brothers were part of a massive influx of Irishmen into the British forces. In 1780, one-third of the officers' commissions were held by members of the Irish gentry, and the disproportion continued throughout the nineteenth century.[5]

Most of the surviving letters concerned the advancement of the brothers. All six had fighting careers. William, the eldest, lost an eye in 1812, fighting the Americans at Lundy's Landing near Niagara Falls, and eventually died from the lingering complications of this injury. George—the second son and the writer of most of the letters—was killed at Badajoz. Owen Wynne Grey (Elizabeth Philpott Grey's first son) ended up in Travancore, as the commander in chief of the army of an Indian maharani. Elizabeth's second son, Matthew Philpott Grey, joined the navy. The next son, John, having fought in the Afghan

---

4. *The Dispatches of Field Marshal the Duke of Wellington from 1799 to 1818*, ed. Lieutenant Colonel Gorwood (London: John Murray, 1838), 9:39 and 41.

5. T. Bartlett and K. Jeffery, *A Military History of Ireland* (Cambridge University Press, 1996), 7.

War, moved to New Zealand in 1847. The youngest, Hugh, died in the Burmese war of 1826.

Philpott's War

The letters mainly concerned George's younger half brother, Matthew Philpott Berry Grey (usually known as Philpott). They show very clearly the mechanisms that launched a twelve-year-old boy on a career of war. On February 17, 1805, George Grey wrote from England to his stepmother, Elizabeth Philpott Grey, in Gort. He had good news concerning Philpott. George had found that an admiral (Admiral Montagu, an intimate acquaintance of George's, who was sitting beside George as he wrote) was willing to ask a friend to take young Philpott aboard his ship. Seeing that Philpott was only twelve years old at the time, this was a remarkable stroke of good fortune. But, George warned, it would be costly:

> My admiral further desires me to say that you allow him £30 a year as he means to send him on board a ship where he will meet nothing but the sons of Noblemen or Gentlemen's sons of Rank in this Country.

Above all, Philpott must come immediately to England:

> No time is to be lost as consider his chance of prize money. (George Grey to Elizabeth Grey, February 17, 1805)

Prize money was in the air. The British navy was assembling for the campaign that would end with Nelson's victory at Trafalgar, on October 21, 1805, and a massive distribution of loot from the captured ships, where even midshipmen were entitled to a share.

George reassured Elizabeth that Philpott would get his war: "there is plenty of fighting which is the only thing to do him good in his profession and give him a claim hereafter. The more he sees of it the better" (George Grey to Elizabeth Grey, April 7, 1805).

So Philpott, aged twelve, was sent off to join the British navy. Even to get him to his ship had been no small matter. Gort was not exactly at the center of the world. Philpott was passed with great care along a network of servants and clients known to Elizabeth from Gort to Dublin, Dublin to Liverpool, and then to London. On his arrival, George was able to reassure Elizabeth: "Philpott is well and in great spirits—you see he is a famous traveller" (George Grey to Elizabeth Grey, April 7, 1805). Our "famous traveller" brought with him from Dublin twelve half-pound canisters of Ladyfoot Snuff, either for George or as *douceurs* for the gentlemen officers he would meet on board his ship (George Grey to Elizabeth Grey, March 13, 1805).

There the letters cease; but I could follow Philpott's naval career. In 1807, he was on board HMS *Brilliant*, "actively engaged on the coast of France, where besides blocking the ports of Cherbourg and St Malo, he joined in many cutting out affairs, contributed much to the obstruction of the enemy's coasting trade, and assisted at the capture of a privateer." In 1809, now promoted to midshipman, he was on HMS *Thallia*, chasing two French frigates along the west coast of Greenland as far north as Baffin Bay. A few months later, "while in attendance on the King off Weymouth," he "assisted in saving the royal barge" during a storm. For the next few years, he served mainly in the Caribbean, where "he was thrice placed in charge of prizes of great value, the whole of which he succeeded in conducting through the difficult and dangerous navigation"—caused by strong currents and abundant coral reefs—"which leads into Nassau, New Providence [in the Bahamas]."

In 1814, now a sublieutenant, he was sent to fight the Americans. He was put in charge of an "advice-vessel," a sort of patrol boat, and was soon leading a "squadron down the Potomac, and effecting the destruction, during the descent, of one of the enemies' forts." (This was the campaign where the British failed to capture Baltimore—an event commemorated in "The Star Spangled Banner"—but succeeded in capturing the new capital at Washington and in burning down the White House.) He "was next employed in covering a foraging party at Windmill Point," on the Chesapeake Bay, "where he landed and, with only 24 men, defeated a large detachment of American militia, but not without receiving a slight sword-wound on the elbow and two buckshot in the leg." A few days later, on September 3, Admiral Cochrane promoted him to lieutenant, in recognition of his "zeal, diligence, and activity." By 1816, the wars with France and America were over, and Philpott, like many other naval officers, retired on half pay. He was only twenty-three years old. He would live until 1863.[6]

Philpott was the grandfather of Ada Grey, my grandmother on my mother's side. I have his portrait, painted when he was an older man. It is rather grim. He has already become a Victorian. By contrast, the portrait of his mother, Elizabeth Grey, belongs to an earlier age—with powdered hair, a turban, and features that are recognizably those of my mother and myself.

---

6. William O'Byrne, *A Naval Biographical Dictionary. Comprising the Life and Services of Every Living Officer in Her Majesty's Navy* (London: John Murray, 1849), 1:425.

Of all the Grey brothers, only Philpott returned to Ireland and lived there until his death. The others died and were buried abroad. It was Philpott who preserved the letters written to his mother that enabled me to glimpse—as if through a crack in the wall of time—a generation saved from penury by an empire at war.

India: Owen Wynne Grey

With the ending of the Napoleonic Wars in Europe, Philpott's older brother, Owen Wynne Grey, looked to India. In a letter that he wrote to his mother, the ever-vigilant Elizabeth, in 1819, he made plain that he would not return to Ireland in the near future:

> I wish none more than I ever did to get home, but it would be the height of folly at the moment to think of abandoning a situation where I am likely to pay my debts, assist my family and put by something to educate my children and home with. Mrs Grey [his wife] will go to Bath. . . . It's the finest place in the world to educate girls . . . and economically.

Then he went on:

> The appointment I at present have is the command of the Troops of Her Highness the Ranee of Travancore, they consist of a Troop of Cavalry, a Brigade of 6 pounders [cannon], and two Battalions of 1000 men each. In a few years, should I remain they will be something like soldiers. (Owen Wynne Grey to Elizabeth Grey, postmarked 1819)

Owen Wynne became, for the next twenty years, the *killahdar*—the commander in chief—of the army of the maharani (the mother regent) of Travancore. The maharani, Gowri Parvati Bayi, who ruled as regent from 1815 to 1829, was a remarkable women, as was her charge, her nephew Swathi Thirumai Rama Varma (1813–1846), a gifted musician and a progressive administrator. Owen Wynne was plainly no footloose mercenary captain. He was a professional soldier, serving a model court.

The family memorabilia included an ivory-framed miniature in the Mughal style that Owen Wynne had sent to his mother, Elizabeth, on the occasion of his thirty-fifth birthday.

> My dear Mother,
> With this you will receive my Picture which I beg your acceptance of as one of the strongest proofs of my love for you. (Owen Wynne Grey to Elizabeth Grey, April 9, 1824)

The miniature showed Owen Wynne, with ginger-orange hair, a plump and ruddy face, small gray eyes, and a scarlet uniform jacket—the typical Irish soldier viewed through Indian eyes. He spent the rest of his life in India, as did his children. He had traveled a long way from Gort.

THE ROMANCE OF A PROCONSUL:
SIR GEORGE GREY OF NEW ZEALAND (1812–1898)

The children, grandchildren, great-grandchildren and great-great-grandchildren of the six sons of Owen Wynne Grey continued to serve the British Crown—mainly in the army, but also in the navy and in the colonial administration—in places as far apart as Baluchistan and Lemnos, Khorasan and Penang. But my mother remembered only one of them: Sir George Grey (1812–1898), the posthumous son of Lieutenant Colonel George Grey, who had died at Badajoz.

Sir George belonged to a different generation from Philpott and his brothers. He was not a career soldier, but an empire-builder in full Victorian style. He was twice governor of New Zealand (in 1845–1853 and 1862–1868) and then became its first prime minister (in 1877–1878). He had been governor, also, of South Australia (1841–1845) and of Cape Colony, in South Africa (in 1854–1861). An adulatory biography entitled *The Romance of a Proconsul* was prominently displayed on my mother's bookshelf.[7]

There was a lot that *The Romance of a Proconsul* did not tell. In the modern historiography of British imperialism, Sir George appears as "a strange hybrid of legend and counter-legend." To use the carefully weighed words of the *Oxford Dictionary of National Biography*: "The humane, reserved, intellectual gentleman co-existed with a racialist and imperialist zealot." He ended his life in angry isolation in his splendid residence at Kawau, north of Auckland, dismissed as a crank and an ideologue—a Prospero on his magic island at the bottom of the world.[8] When I visited Kawau in 1991, I was astonished to find, at the bottom of the main staircase, a white marble bust whose high forehead and distinctive droop of the eyes could have been my mother's.

---

7. James Milne, *The Romance of a Proconsul. Being the Personal Life and Memories of the Right Hon. Sir George Grey* (London: Chatto and Windus, 1899).

8. See J. Rutherford, *Sir George Grey* (London: Cassell, 1961), with James Belich, *The Victorian Interpretation of Racial Conflict: The Maori, the British and the New Zealand Wars* (Montreal: McGill-Queen's University Press, 1989), and Belich, s.v. "Grey, Sir George," *The Oxford Dictionary of National Biography* (Oxford University Press, 2004).

But among the Greys, Sir George was an exception. Most were soldiers. They lived between two worlds—home and abroad. They were fiercely loyal to the British Empire and to the British armed forces. But England itself was a blank on their map, and even Ireland seemed a narrow place compared with the wide spaces of the empire.

That world has now vanished. I was born in its last years. Ireland was independent and neutral during World War II. And yet most of my older male cousins fought for Britain, and several of them died. I was even told, with pride, that an uncle by marriage in the Royal Air Force had helped to plan the famous raid on the Mohne Dam. This pattern, of being Irish but looking beyond Ireland to the British Empire, had lasted for generations and was still potent during my childhood. As a result, "abroad" was always charged for me with associations of adventure in distant places and tinged with the possibility of death.

DECLINE AND FALL

The Wynnes of Hazelwood

The men of the Grey family entered new horizons through service in the British Empire. It had a cost: three out of the six sons of Owen Wynne Grey were killed in war. Yet they plainly preferred the risks of service in distant lands to remaining in Ireland. Those of their cousins who stayed in Ireland did not fare well. Their land would vanish from under them in the course of the nineteenth century. Hence a cluster of family memories of loss and dereliction.

As we have seen, the Greys had been the poor relations of a powerful family—the Wynnes of Sligo. But the power of the Wynnes steadily declined throughout the nineteenth century. They lost their pocket borough. They lost their right to collect tolls. They were forced to sell their land to their tenants. Yet, for many years, they continued to live in Hazelwood House, the first Palladian house to be built in Ireland (in 1730) by Richard Cassels, the country's leading architect. They still presided over local society at regattas and polo matches, and surrounded the house with gardens, "plainly the outcome of unstinted outlay and exquisite taste."[1]

The house was named after an ancient hazel wood, where the poet W. B. Yeats used to walk:

I went out to the hazel wood,
Because a fire was in my head,
And cut and peeled a hazel wand,
And hooked a berry to a thread. . . . [2]

---

1. Terrence O'Rorke, *The History of Sligo: Town and Country* (Dublin: James Duffy, 1889), 1:337.
2. "The Song of Wandering Aengus," *The Wind among the Reeds*, in *The Collected Poems of W. B. Yeats* (New York: Macmillan, 1956), 57.

The Wynnes finally left Hazelwood in 1923, just after the Irish Civil War. The beautiful Palladian house is now boarded up, on the grounds of a whiskey distillery. But the hazel wood remains.

A BRAWLING SQUIREEN

Other cousins in the Sligo area, the Ormsbys of Castle Dargan, were ruined by the Irish Famine of 1845–1847. John Ormsby tried to help by founding a Famine Relief Committee; but the famine cost him much of his land. In the 1850s, large tracts of his property were sold off to pay arrears in rates and taxes. A little later, after John's death in 1870, his grandson, John Robert Ormsby, delivered the coup de grâce to the family fortune.

W. B. Yeats, a cousin of John Robert's wife, often visited Ormsby during these years of decline:

> Sometimes I would ride to Castle Dargan, where lived a brawling squireen. . . . It was, I daresay, the last household where I could have found the reckless Ireland of a hundred years ago in final degradation. . . .
>
> The first day I came there he gave my cousins a revolver . . . and to show off, . . . he shot a passing chicken; and half an hour later, at the lake's edge under his castle, now but the broken corner of a tower with a rising stair, he fired at or over an old countryman walking on the far edge of a lake. The next day I heard him settling the matter with the old countryman over a bottle of whiskey, and both were in good humour.

Yeats told another story about John Robert "shooting in the pride of his marksmanship, at his own door with a Martini-Henry rifle until he had shot the knocker off." Eventually (Yeats concludes), "having now neither friends nor money, he made off to Australia or Canada."[3] Father O'Rorke, the genial historian of Sligo, was less severe:

> The present representative of this branch [of the Ormbys] . . . resides now in America, where he is very popular, as he always was in Ireland before his emigration.[4]

Yeats remained haunted by the memory of Castle Dargan in its glory days. A few years before his death, he wrote:

---

3. W. B. Yeats, *Autobiographies* (London: Macmillan, 1955), 54–55.
4. O'Rorke, *The History of Sligo*, 1:350.

O but I saw a solemn sight
Said the rambling shambling travelling man
Castle Dargan's ruins all lit
Lovely ladies dancing in it
What though they danced those days are gone.[5]

VIOLENCE

In 1864, Philpott Grey's daughter, Anna Maria, married her distant cousin, Captain St George Grey. His branch of the Grey family had been more prosperous than the Greys of Sligo and Gort. In the first half of the nineteenth century, they had remained comfortably in Ireland, often attending Trinity College Dublin, and sometimes practicing law or marrying heiresses. They were not dependent, as the other Greys had been, on powerful relatives, such as the Wynnes.

Yet by the middle of the nineteenth century the family had begun to drift away from the Irish countryside. Captain Grey had five brothers: two emigrated to America; one joined the Indian Medical Service; another had a long and happy career at Trinity College Dublin. Only one chose to remain on the land: William Henry Grey (1828–1887), who managed 1,421 acres at Dorrington House in county Westmeath. In the 1850s, he built a model farm, with barns, milking sheds, and up-to-date brick piggeries. He saw himself as a progressive landowner. But the change from wheat to pigs and cattle meant a less labor-intensive farming and fewer jobs.[6] Hence, perhaps, the death threat that he received in 1869 and duly passed over to the local police station, from whence it eventually found its way into the National Archives. It showed a man holding a rifle above his head:

Gray
    Look at your deadly weapon, here it is. This will be your doom if you don't alter your way of going. . . . I have the same gun, eye, and hand that took down [Captain Roland] Tarleton.[7]

5. W. B. Yeats, "The Wicked Hawthorn Tree," in *The Collected Work of W. B. Yeats X: Later Articles and Reviews*, ed. Colton Johnson (New York: Scribner, 2000), 278.

6. D. S. Jones, *Graziers, Land Reform and Political Conflict in Ireland* (Washington, DC: Catholic University of America Press, 1995), 10

7. https://www.thejournal.ie/Westmeath-ribbonism-2550096-Jan2016.

William held on; but all five of his sons emigrated. His daughter, Mary Emily, became a military nurse in India; in 1908 she received a medal for her devoted care of the wounded during a British army expedition into Afghanistan. Dorrington House has vanished. Only the barns and the state-of-the-art piggeries survive, duly recorded in the *National Inventory of Architectural Heritage* as "an integral part of the architectural heritage of Westmeath."[8]

As I look back, these stories of great houses abandoned bear a troubling resemblance to the fate of many villas in the last days of the Roman Empire—splendid affairs, often larger and more brilliant than at any other time; but then suddenly deserted, as if their clock had stopped.

8. www.buildingsofireland.ie.

SQUIREENS

THE WARRENS FROM COUNTY MEATH TO DUBLIN

"Drummin"

In 1897, my mother's parents—Ada Grey (the granddaughter of Philpott) and Robert Gibson Warren—were married. The Warrens were different from the Greys. They were an Anglo-Norman family, descended from the first wave of settlers who arrived in Ireland with the Normans in the twelfth century. They had lived for centuries in county Meath, just north of Dublin. Unlike the Greys, they had few connections with the empire and the British armed forces. My mother always regarded them as somehow less grand and more comfortably "Irish."

In around 1770, John Grant Warren built a family seat called "Drummin" near Duleek in county Meath:

> a substantial stone house and offices, suitable for a gentleman farmer. It was of the old style, with walls at least 30 inches thick, and the woodwork in proportion. The windows in the rear were protected against burglars or other enemies and the front windows by stout shutters on the inside.[1]

"Drummin" was not like Hazelwood House. It was as much a little fortress as a gentleman's residence. I saw it once, in a thoroughly dilapidated state. Recently, I learned that it was on sale, optimistically described as "a country house of exceptional merit." An aerial photograph showed it sitting comfortably

---

1. Revd. Thomas Warren, *A History and Genealogy of the Warren Family, A.D. 912–1902* (Printed for Private Circulation, 1902), 303–304.

in the middle of a group of fields that may have been the "two hundred Irish acres of which twenty was peat bog" of John Grant Warren's original estate. He was what would be called a "squireen"—halfway between a farmer and a country gentleman.

There was nothing grand about "Drummin," but it was cherished in the memory of my older relatives. To them, it was home: the place where they had been born, and where their parents and grandparents had died and been buried in the nearby Protestant churchyard. Judging by old photographs, it was a place where people played croquet, not polo, and wore sensible shawls and jackets.

Not all Warrens had been loyal to the Crown. According to family tradition, John Grant Warren's son, Mervyn, was hanged for taking part in the Great Rebellion of 1798—the famous "Year of the French," when a major uprising, aided by French troops, threatened to drive the English out of Ireland.[2] In later generations, a number of Warren boys were named Mervyn, presumably in his memory.

When Warrens left Ireland, as many of them did, they did not seek glamorous careers as soldiers and colonial administrators in the British Empire, as the Greys had done. Rather, they found low-profile jobs as doctors, engineers, and businessmen in Toronto, Chicago, and Kansas City. I even traced one Warren as far as Alabama, where he was blown up in the explosion of a steamboat in 1867. In Ireland itself, there were slim pickings. Mervyn Warren's younger brother, William, became a revenue official—not the most popular of occupations. He was "drowned in Lough Foyle, when on duty."

Meanwhile, at "Drummin," the family continued to multiply at a rate of about nine children in every generation. It seemed to be a predictable story of the slow decline of a gentry family eroded by its own fertility. But in 1859, John Grant's grandson, Henry Warren, saved the family by looking for a wife outside his usual circle. He married Anna, the daughter of Edward Atkinson, a rich doctor from the nearby port of Drogheda.

THE ATKINSONS OF DROGHEDA

Anna's family was different from the Warrens in almost every respect: they came from Ulster; they were clever, energetic, and, sometimes, extremely ruthless. Dr. Atkinson had studied medicine at Glasgow University, and then

---

2. *Genealogy: A Journal of American Ancestry* 1 (1912): 89.

he settled in Drogheda in the 1840s, where he plainly prospered. In 1851, only a few years after the Great Famine, he was able to purchase Glenwilliam Castle near Limerick. He may have bought it at a cut rate, at a bankruptcy sale of the property of landowners ruined by the famine. Local legend was kinder: it was said that he had won it at cards.[3]

Much of Edward's wealth came from his wife, Rosetta McCullough. Her family was descended from a Scotsman named James Shaw who had built a grim little castle at Ballygally on the coast of Antrim (Northern Ireland) in 1625. It is now a luxury hotel, complete with legends of ghosts, making it "one of the most haunted hotels" in Ireland. The ghosts include Shaw's unhappy wife, allegedly starved to death by her husband.

In the 1780s the castle and its rich estate had belonged to John Shaw, an elderly and childless man, who planned to leave it to his nephew. But John's brother-in-law, Dr. William McCullough, had other ideas. According to the account in the *Ulster Journal of Archaeology*, McCullough "did all he could to turn his brother-in-law against his nephew." Eventually he persuaded old Mr. Shaw to visit him, "professedly to stay for one night." But the next morning, Mr. Shaw was "so ill that he could not be moved." His nephew and other friends "called at Dr. McCullough's house to inquire after him but were never allowed to see him." Five or six weeks later, the old man was secretly "buried at midnight in the churchyard of Cairncastle, with no persons at his funeral but those that were necessary to inter him." Dr. McCullough "produced a will, which he alleged had been made by the late Mr. Shaw and by which the gentleman's entire property of every kind was left to him." At the castle, he installed a guard "who kept constant watch and ward at one of the windows with a loaded blunderbuss" to block the entry of the rightful heir.[4]

After a prolonged lawsuit, Dr. McCullough had to surrender the castle, but not before stripping the estate of its assets, and making himself bitterly unpopular in the neighborhood. His granddaughter, Rosetta, married Dr. Atkinson; and it was their daughter, Anna Atkinson, who married Henry Warren of "Drummin" in 1859. Her inheritance saved Henry's children from genteel poverty.

3. Mark Bence-Jones, *A Guide to Irish Country Houses* (London: Constable,1988), 140.

4. C. Porter and J. Bigger, "Ballygally Castle," *Ulster Journal of Archaeology*, ser. 2, 7 (1901): 65–77, at 72–73.

John Atkinson (1844–1932)

The marriage to Anna Atkinson brought more than money to the Warrens. She had useful connections. Her brother, John, was "unquestionably the ablest man at the Irish bar, as well as its leader."[5] He was queen's counsel in 1880, solicitor general in 1889, and attorney general for Ireland in 1892, an office based in Dublin. From 1895 to 1905, he was Conservative MP for Londonderry North. In 1905, he was made a life peer and entered the House of Lords as one of the four lords of appeal ordinary—that is, one of the judges at the highest level of the British judiciary. He moved to England, where he stayed for the rest of his life.

Atkinson's legal career was a success; but his political career ended in ruin. Before 1905, he had been an active politician in Dublin. He was a Unionist—that is, he wanted to keep Ireland within the United Kingdom, and he wanted to do this through reform. He was legal adviser for the Land Act of 1896, which offered funds to enable tenants to buy the lands they worked on, and for the Government Act of 1898, which effectively took local government out of the hands of the great landlords. These acts broke the power of the Protestant Ascendancy in Ireland. Some regarded Atkinson as a traitor to his class. His promotion to the House of Lords, which took him out of Ireland for good, may have come as a relief. But he lived until 1932—long enough to see the Irish War of Independence and the end of his hopes for a peaceful union of Britain and Ireland.

In his Dublin days, before he moved to England, Atkinson seems to have taken his nephew, my grandfather Robert Warren (Bob Warren to his friends and admirers), under his wing. He pushed Bob in the direction of the law and ensured that he went to Dublin to follow the career of a solicitor rather than attempting to maintain the life of a country gentleman at "Drummin" in county Meath.

Though I heard little about him, Atkinson must have been a looming presence in the early stages of my grandfather's career. Newspaper cuttings, carefully placed in an album by Bob Warren's daughters—by my mother and my aunt Freda—traced the rise of the Atkinsons, husband and wife, in Dublin society of the 1890s.

---

5. H. Montgomery-Hyde, *Carson: The Life of Sir Edward Carson, Lord Carson of Duncairn* (London: Heinemann, 1953), 209.

Thus when Bob Warren married Ada Grey, the occasion was reported as a "Fashionable Wedding." The *Irish Times* reporter went out of his way to add that the Atkinsons attended. "Mrs Atkinson's dress was finished with a fichu of old lace." It also recorded, among an impressive list of silverware, that the attorney general (John Atkinson) had contributed a check. I suspect that it was a big one.

The wedding was in 1897. A generation earlier, Atkinson might have encouraged my grandfather to follow in his steps as a politician. But now it was too late. Undermined by the reforms that Atkinson himself had helped to frame, the Protestant Ascendancy was broken. Outside Ulster, Protestants were seldom elected to Parliament. There was no room for a bright young Dublin lawyer to make a career in that direction. Bob Warren had to find other interests and other ambitions.

RUGBY FOOTBALL

BOB WARREN

"He Played a Perfect Game"

Bob Warren seems to have made little use of the support provided by his famous uncle. His heart was elsewhere. He began his career in Dublin as a sports idol. At the age of twenty-one, in 1887, he was captain of the Irish Rugby Football team that beat England for the first time ever. The match took place in the newly built Lansdowne Road rugby football stadium. It was a spectacular event:

> The spectators were fairly demented . . . hats went flying all over the place and handkerchiefs [waved by the women] were largely on display. . . . Saxon prestige in the football field was at length lowered, and the Rose had to bow down to the Shamrock.[1]

It takes some effort of the imagination to enter into the sheer excitement of the game in a major city such as Dublin. Rugby football was a game in the making. It had begun as ritual tussles in English boys' schools. By the 1880s, it had gone public in a grand way; but it remained an elite game, played by amateurs only. Many of them were like Bob Warren—former landed gentry who had moved to Dublin. For this urban gentry, now established in the professions, the Saturday match replaced the hunt.

But these gentlemanly amateurs now performed in front of ten thousand spectators in the newly built stadium at Lansdowne Road. And Bob Warren

---

1. *Sport*, February 12, 1887, cited in P. Rouse, *Sport and Ireland: A History* (Oxford University Press, 2015), 187–188.

gave them the excitement that they needed. He was a little man. He usually played half-back, close to the scrum formed by the forwards. The scrum would hunker down to push each other like a great crab made up of human bodies, slowly rotating, advancing, and retreating, until the ball came loose between their legs. Then Bob Warren would make the ball fly, carrying it in spectacular, cunning dashes, ducking tackles and wrong-footing his opponents. He kept the game open, for all in the stands to watch.

This was what they had come to see. Here was no muscular deadlock, but a nimble figure, weaving in and out of the thick of bulky opponents. Bob Warren was said to have always worn a bandana around his neck. Those who attempted to stop him by grabbing his shirt collar would be left with the silken cloth in their hands. That was the style that made him, for a time, the talk of Dublin. In the words of a reporter, carefully pasted into the Warren family scrapbook, "he played a perfect game."

"You Don't Shoot Bob Warren"

Bob Warren died in 1940, in a world that had changed profoundly since his glory days in Dublin. I have a vague memory of a little man with a ginger, almost golden moustache, sitting bolt upright in a high chair. He would be delighted when I ran round the table, chanting, "Run Rabbit, Run Rabbit, Run, Run, Run" on the days when we would eat rabbit stew (often the only meat available in wartime).

All that I was told about Bob Warren concerned his fame as a sportsman. His legal career was barely mentioned, still less the patronage of John Atkinson. This may be because Atkinson's patronage had led to a dead end. In any case, politics do not seem to have engaged Bob Warren. What mattered for him was his reputation as the doyen of rugby football. This was undiminished, even though his legal career may have suffered many disruptions as Ireland made its way to independence.

The first of these shocks was the Easter Rising of April 24–30, 1916. When the rising happened, the family was caught on holiday in Skerries, a beachside resort a little north of Dublin. I found a letter from this time written by Ada Warren (Bob's wife, my grandmother) to her eldest daughter, my aunt Vivyenne.

My darling Vy,

I don't know if this will ever reach you but I must risk it [so that] you can let all know how we are going on here as I expect the papers say [only] a "small row in Ireland". Here we are likely to remain. The Sinn Feiners (Shin Finners) have Dublin. . . .

We are here in Skerries now under martial law. All in their houses at 8 pm and lights out. . . . As I write a cart of ammunition has gone by guarded by soldiers with fixed bayonets. . . . Fancy an armoured train patrols the railway and we were actually talking to soldiers on it. . . . Artillery yesterday swept Westmorland street. This is all true. You will not hear it in England. It is Asquith and his pals [who caused all this, by advocating Home Rule]. Thousands of the S[inn] F[einer]s paraded the streets of Dublin a month ago and nothing was said. Skerries now has no butter. Its too awful.

Best love from all

Your loving mother

Yet the coming of the Republic and the years of bitter fighting that preceded it seem to have left Bob Warren with his reputation as a popular Dublin figure largely intact. At some time at the very end of British rule in Ireland (possibly through the support of Atkinson), he became crown solicitor for county Wicklow. I still have the dress sword, with the crown on its hilt, with which he must have attended the viceroy's receptions at Dublin Castle. But the office of crown solicitor did not deal with criminal cases or anything else that was politically charged. It was not a danger-post. He was unlikely to be assassinated. In later years, however, his daughters liked to believe that an order had gone out to the IRA: "You Don't Shoot Bob Warren." He had been the toast of Dublin. His portrait had appeared on matchboxes. He was untouchable. I suspect that this was how he thought of himself. Politics were of little interest to him. He remained first and foremost a sportsman.

Indeed, it is a remarkable sign of the strength of the sports-based networks of Dublin that Bob Warren lived on to be the Grand Old Man of the Irish Rugby Football Union, long after any hope of a political career had been blocked by the departure of Atkinson and, later, by the foundation of an independent Irish Republic. His heart was in the rugby field, not in politics. He was on the board of the International Rugby Football Union from 1887 to 1938, where, according to family rumor, he gloried in expelling France for violent play (those neck tackles that he himself had avoided so adroitly) and for the ultimate taboo in a sport for gentlemen—for "professionalism": the highly charged issue of payments to members of their international team.

In his will, Bob Warren left me a great silver salver, covered with the signatures of his friends and fellow players, presented to him, in 1938, on his retirement from the Irish Rugby Football Union. But he had no illusions about me. I am told that, when I was first shown to him by my mother, a few days after my birth, he declared, "That child does not have the hands of a rugby player." I have only now learned (through the internet) that an eccentric donor still pays for flowers to be left on Bob Warren's grave in Enniskerry, near Bray, on behalf of the Rugby Union.

Altogether, I learned from the experience of both sides of my mother's family much that was of use to a historian of the Roman Empire in its last centuries. From the Greys, I learned about the magnetic draw of a worldwide empire in its glory days—in its Golden Age, like the Rome in the age of the Antonines (138–180) with which Edward Gibbon began his melancholy narrative in the *Decline and Fall of the Roman Empire*. From the Warrens, I learned something more sad but more challenging for a historian: how to understand what it was like to face the end of empire on the ground—in the small world of the little big men of the provinces—and to do so with dignity and good nature. John Atkinson and Bob Warren, each in his own way, bowed out of the active politics of Ireland—Atkinson to become a judge in England, Bob Warren to be a Grand Old Man of rugby football—much as Roman senators had detached themselves, discreetly, from a world they could no longer call their own.

DUBLINERS

THE LAMONT BROWNS

The Lamonts

My father's family, the Lamont Browns, felt no need for florid ancestors. It was dignity enough for them to have been Scots and Presbyterians, and, now, to be Dubliners. They were part of a sept (a subdivision) of a displaced clan, the Lamonts, which had been gradually driven off their land to the west of Glasgow (behind Dunoon, in Strathclyde) by the Campbells.

Recently, I was interested to learn that the bulk of the Lamonts had remained Catholic. The head of the clan is alive and well—and not quite the person one would expect. He is Father Peter Lamont, a Catholic parish priest in the suburbs of Sydney, Australia. On the clan's website, Father Peter reassured his fellow clansmen that the chieftainship would pass to his married brother and to his nephews.

A Republican Printer

The Lamont Browns, however, had settled into Dublin as staunch Presbyterians. They were not members of the established Church of Ireland, which was a branch of the Anglican Church and, for that reason, was intimately identified with the Protestant Ascendancy. By remaining Presbyterian, the Lamont Browns placed clear water between themselves and the core of English rule in Ireland. My father's grandfather was a successful color printer—a craft in which Protestants predominated in Dublin at that time.[1] He was also said to

---

1. Mary E. Daly, *Dublin: The Deposed Capital. A Social and Economic History 1860–1914* (Cork: Cork University Press, 1984), 125.

have been a political radical: an antimonarchist and an advocate for an Irish Republic.

I remember that once, when I was having lunch with my father at Bewley's in Westmoreland Street (a favored meeting place for businessmen), an elderly historian of the Irish labor movement came over to tell us that he had found something about my grandfather's support for the Dublin workers' unions. But that was all. It saddens me to know so little about the Lamont Browns. I suspect that Lamont ancestors would have offered me a very different set of family memories from those that had gathered around the Greys and the Warrens. But, alas, in Victorian Dublin, no one thought of writing *The Romance of a Republican Printer*.

My father's father was known as the Bear. We knew little about him. It was said that, having run through the fortune made by his father, he had retired to a back room to read paperback novels, leaving the management of the house and family to my grandmother, always known by the archaic, Latin title of "the Mater." He died in 1937, before I could know him. But he gave one clear indication of his religious loyalties. Once, in his glory days, the Bear had owned a yacht. He had called the yacht *Ziska*. The yacht was long gone; but the silver toast rack that he had made from the letters *ZISKA* was always on the breakfast table at "Number Sixty"—the family home at no. 60 Lansdowne Road.

Much later, I realized that the strange name belonged to the hero of the Hussite Wars, Jan Žiška. Jan Žiška z Trocnova (ca. 1360–1424) was the one-eyed leader of the Hussite armies and a proto-Protestant hero. It is strange to think that this fragment of Protestant hagiography should come to rest in a bourgeois terrace house in Dublin, among silverware that spoke of better days.

Worlds Apart

As I look back, it strikes me that the Dublin in which my father grew up, and even the Dublin that I knew as a boy, was a silently fragmented place. Central Dublin was a world of its own—a world of stately squares and of slums that were among the worst in Europe. The gap between this Dublin and the newly developed, middle-class suburbs was unusually wide. The occupants of the suburbs lived "privileged lives"—to borrow the title of a penetrating recent study.[2]

2. Tony Farmar, *Privileged Lives: A Social History of Middle-Class Ireland 1882–1989* (Dublin: A. and A. Farmar, 2010).

But they lived in a world patterned by any number of unspoken boundaries and social no-go areas.[3]

These divisions caused greater suffering than I, as a growing boy, was ever allowed to know. The deepest and most cruel of these was the division between Catholics and Protestants. Like a huge, chill iceberg, seemingly at rest on a bright, calm sea, a map of Irish society irremediably divided between two faiths lay quietly at the back of the minds of almost every member of the Dublin middle class. In his book *Dublin Made Me*, Christopher Andrews (an exact contemporary of my parents) describes the attitude to Protestants of his well-to-do Catholic family:

> From childhood, I was aware that there were two separate and immiscible kinds of citizens: the Catholics, of whom I was one, and the Protestants who were as remote and different from us as if they had been blacks and we whites.[4]

Sitting in no. 60 Lansdowne Road, the Lamont Browns—the Bear and the Mater—thought the same, word for word. It was very definitely in Ireland that I learned the power of religious intolerance. In later life, this was a theme that I would follow closely in all my work on the rise of Christianity and the end of the Roman Empire. Indeed, my very first published work would consist of articles on religious conflict and on the theory and practice of religious coercion in Roman North Africa in the time of Saint Augustine.

Where Love Was Murdered

I have come to realize that this intolerance was by no means uniform and omnipresent in the Ireland of my grandparents. In certain circles, class counted for more than religion, as was often the case also in the later empire: something that I came to learn in my own work on the Roman aristocracy. Mixed marriages were often less of a charged issue among gentry families than they were in the suburbs of Dublin. The gentry, I suspect, were less afraid of losing their identity through such marriages, and were less affected by the growing emphasis on confessional divisions in Dublin middle-class society. In August 1897, my grandmother Ada Grey married Bob Warren; in July 1897, her sister Anna

---

3. Daly, *Dublin: The Deposed Capital*, 239.

4. C. S. Andrews, *Dublin Made Me* (Dublin, 1979), 9, cited in Daly, *Dublin: The Deposed Capital*, 151.

had married Captain Bernard Daly of the Royal Irish Rifles. The two marriages were recorded in identical terms:

> Robert Gibson Warren, son of Henry Warren of Drummin House, Duleek, Co. Meath. . . .

> Capt. Bernard Daly, JP [Justice of the Peace], of Old Hall, Tullamore, King's Co. [now county Offaly], High Sheriff [in] 1897.[5]

Bernard Daly was Catholic, from an old county family. The religious difference worried neither set of in-laws. Bernard was immediately welcomed by the Greys. My mother would always speak with affection of "Uncle Bernie," and his son, Brian, was her favorite cousin.

In the very different world of the expanding suburbs of Dublin, intolerance had usually been held in check by the silent fragmentation of society. Protestants and Catholics went their own ways—to different schools, to different businesses, and to different marriages. Everything seemed to work smoothly, provided that both sides kept their distance.

But such separation was not as easy in the 1930s as it had once been. The Dublin bourgeoisie (Catholic and Protestant alike) had become more comfortable. There were motorcars for jaunts, cinemas for a night out, and an ever-greater number of tennis clubs. On these occasions, young men and women mixed with relative indifference to their religious backgrounds. Boundaries weakened. For a moment, the chill breath off the iceberg of confessional intolerance seemed to have died down. Friendships developed that might turn into love. And that, of course, was the problem. Love meant marriage; and, for many families of the young couple, a mixed marriage meant the end of the world.

This is what happened to my youngest aunt. At roughly the age of eighteen, she fell in love—with a Catholic boy. They had shared in all the pastimes of the well-to-do. They had played tennis together. They had gone on walks together. They had gone to the pictures together. He had given her a pet spaniel as a present.

Unfortunately, they fell in love. They told their parents that they intended to marry. Both families exploded. A mixed marriage of this kind was the dread of both religions. It simply could not happen. The Mater was trenchant: "It would kill your father." (I suspect that she was the most resolute opponent

---

5. *Burke's Landed Gentry of Ireland* (London: Burke's Peerage Limited, 1958), 322.

of the marriage.) Much the same must have been said in the Catholic family. All the gifts and letters that the couple had exchanged were returned. Only the spaniel was allowed to remain. My aunt was sent to relatives in Africa and eventually found a husband there.

Alas, this tragedy was only one of many in the dangerously fluid world of suburban Dublin. Bill Beckett, the father of the famous writer Samuel Beckett (1906–1989), had been heartbroken in the same way. He was a Protestant boy. He and his sister had both of them fallen in love with the daughter and the son of a well-to-do Catholic family. William Martin Murphy (1845–1919), the head of that family and a distinguished Dubliner, was adamant in breaking up the two young couples. In Sam Beckett's words:

It ruined both their lives. Bill never got over it, never.

Neither did Bill's sister. Years later, Bill Beckett would occasionally take his sister and her daughter out for a drive.

As they drove past a castellated mansion near Rathgar, [the sister would] announce angrily that this was "where the murder took place." "What murder?" asked her daughter. . . .

"William Martin Murphy's house. He murdered love, didn't he Bill?"[6]

One could have said the same of "Number Sixty."

My poor aunt was never so open. Indeed, the true horror of the story is that I knew nothing of it. The entire incident was buried in silence. It was seventy years later that I first heard of it. At the age of eighty-seven, she told the story to my wife. She spoke without bitterness or self-pity. It was all very simple. The love of her life had been taken from her at the age of eighteen. Nothing was quite the same ever since. "My mother," she said, "was a very good woman. But she was terribly wrong about a few things."

6. James Knowlson, *Damned to Fame: The Life of Samuel Beckett* (New York: Grove Press, 1996), 32–33.

7

SUDAN

NORTH AND SOUTH

A Job Abroad

My father, James Lamont Brown, was the eldest son of the Bear and the Mater. Born in 1900, he had studied engineering at Trinity College Dublin. In the newly independent, deeply poor Ireland of the twenties there were few jobs in his field. So as soon as he graduated, in 1924, he went to England to work in the traffic department of the Great Western Railway.

He remained in England for six years. Then his brother-in-law, Leonard Bayley, the husband of his eldest sister, my aunt Norah, took the matter in hand. Uncle Leonard was a Lancashire man, who had already established himself in the Sudan Railways, where he was known to his colleagues as "Buggins" Bayley. He had firm views. No man should marry on less than seven hundred pounds sterling a year. And "Buggins" knew of a job for seven hundred pounds in the Sudan Railways. My father took it. Or that was how the story was told.

A year later, he met my mother, Sheila Wynne Warren, at Skerries, the seaside resort north of Dublin where the Warrens had once been stranded, in 1916, by the Easter Rising. It was on his first year's leave from Sudan. My father was impressed by how neat and trim she looked. My mother would tell me that she was struck by his courtesy and good nature when he reassured the waitress who had accidentally poured a pot of tea on the lap of his brother, Billy. They married in 1931. I was born in 1935.

Until war was declared in 1939, my mother and I would join my father in Sudan in the cooler months of the year, by sailing from England to Egypt through the Mediterranean. From 1939 to 1944 we could not be with him, as the Mediterranean was closed to all civilian traffic. We stayed at home in a self-consciously neutral Ireland while he faced the risks of war. He would later tell me how he would be up at dawn as a volunteer observer for the antiaircraft batteries that protected Atbara from the occasional raid of Italian Cassini bombers—Air Marshal Balbo's air force based in conquered Ethiopia.

Like so many men on my mother's side of the family, my father had found a career abroad and not at home. But there was a difference. My father did not go to Sudan as an empire-builder—as a soldier or a colonial administrator. The "Romance of a Proconsul" was not for him. He went as a technician. His job was to administer trains, not to rule people. Both his profession and his Irish citizenship kept him at a distance from the solidly English core of the Sudan Political Service, who were the true rulers of the country. Rather, he belonged to a service class of experts. The English spoke of them, always somewhat condescendingly, as "boffins"—backroom boys. This meant that he had less day-to-day contact in the workplace with the English colonial government than he did with the Egyptian Copts, the Christian Lebanese, and the Sudanese who were also part of the expert administration of the railways. He helped to "run the railways"; the English "ran the show."

He settled in Atbara, two hundred miles north of Khartoum, where he eventually rose to the rank of deputy traffic manager of the Sudanese Railways. There was a lot of traffic for him to manage. Atbara was called the "Crewe Junction" of Sudan (after the legendary railway junction in the British Midlands). A single railway line, passing north–south through Atbara along the valley of the Nile, held Sudan together. It joined the scorching deserts of the North to the great, green swamps of the southern Nile. I was proud to grow up with a daddy whose realm seemed to stretch for thousands of miles along rails and river steamers, from the deserts of the North, through wide savannas, where the long necks of giraffes frequently became entangled with his telegraph wires, to the deep South, where the riverside stations of his steamboats would, on occasion, be trampled to matchwood by lovesick hippopotami.

"Fighting Dervishes"

So what was Sudan like in the early 1930s? The naval *Handbook of the Anglo-Egyptian Sudan* (a manual for administrators and army officers) told us that there were two Sudans: an overwhelmingly Muslim northern Sudan and a pagan South, where Christian missions were active. The North had to be treated with care. In northern Sudan, the end of the Mahdiyya was less than forty years in the past. It had been led by Mohammad Ahmad (1844–1885) who had been acclaimed as the *Mahdi*—that is, as the figure whose coming was to precede the Second Coming of Jesus and the Last Judgment. He raised an army from the camel-riding tribes of northern Sudan, known to the British as "fighting dervishes." Between 1881 and 1885 he drove all foreign armies (British and Egyptian alike) out of the country, and killed the charismatic General Gordon in Khartoum. Ten years later the independent state maintained by the *Mahdi*'s successor, the "Khalifa" Abdallahi ibn Mohammad, was invaded by General Kitchener, and the dervishes were mowed down with industrial precision (or so it was claimed, with indecent satisfaction) by the Maxim guns of Kitchener's army at the Battle of Omdurman, outside Khartoum in 1898. This massacre was the beginning of joint British and Egyptian rule in Sudan.

The Mahdiyya was a drama that the naval *Handbook* encouraged its readers to forget as quickly as possible: "in endeavoring to understand the Arab peoples of the Sudan it is necessary to clear one's mind of the associations connected with the words 'fighting dervishes.'"[1]

This was easier said than done. "Fighting dervishes" were not the sort of people that a growing boy was likely to forget. Indeed, the front hall of "Number Sixty" contained an entire stand of ferocious spears, along with a bulletproof buffalo-hide shield as hard as steel. In my more exuberant moods, I would jump into the hall, swinging around the bottom post of the ample staircase that led to the upper floor, so as to land with a heavy thump that brought a loud clang from those deadly spears.

THE HARDNESS OF ISLAM

Altogether, the naval *Handbook* insisted that, rather than fill our minds with such romantic and anxiety-provoking images, we should think of the "good" nomads and the solid peasantry of the Nile valley:

> The Arab of the Sudan, who has in varying degrees the blood and tradition of the pure Arab races, is proud, tenacious, and intelligent, although curiously unappreciative of time, not generally well educated, and prone to bigotry.[2]

1. *A Handbook of the Anglo-Egyptian Sudan* (Naval Staff Intelligence Division, 1922), 200.
2. *Handbook*, 191.

"Prone to bigotry" was a description calculated to set off alarm bells in some English readers. It implied that the natives were as obdurate and dangerous as were the Catholics of Ireland. They were represented as the adherents of a rigid faith, fearsome in its warlike intolerance, but, fortunately, on its way to extinction. This was the clear view of Sir Harold MacMichael, the civil secretary (the effective head of the administration) of Sudan:

> The religion of the Arab [of the northern Sudan] is the fruit of centuries of discipline and dogma, and it appears now to have reached a stage of worldwide stagnation periodically rippled by political restlessness.[3]

Islam, indeed, was frequently presented as the Roman Catholicism of the East—as the dried-out corpse of a religion, waiting to collapse into dust at the first touch of a Protestant Reformation, brought by the missionaries and (if with more caution and less overt religious zeal) by the progressive administration of the colonial powers. Much as the Reformation was believed—at least, by Protestants—to have superseded rigid Catholicism in Europe, so now it was the time for Christianity and Western values to supersede the "essential hardness of Islam" in Sudan and the Middle East.[4]

All I can say about my parents is that they were not involved in these toxic attitudes, largely because they were not part of the colonial administration. I never heard them speak a word against Muslims or against Islam at any time. Indeed, I was surprised to find from his notebooks that my father had learned considerably more Arabic than he revealed to me. He also kept a copy of *Sudanese Courtesy Customs: A Foreigner's Guide to Polite Phrases*. This was a carefully prepared volume, complete with Arabic sentences, that represented a sincere attempt to establish a common etiquette between well-to-do Sudanese and English.[5] In my teens, with the help of my father and a *Teach Yourself Arabic* book, I would attempt to learn its many gracious greetings. In this way,

---

3. Harold MacMichael, October 25, 1928, in Robert O. Collins, *Shadows in the Grass: Britain in the Southern Sudan, 1918–1956* (New Haven, CT: Yale University Press, 1983), 172.

4. Dr. Lloyd to the Church Missionary Society, November 3, 1922, in Jack Bermingham and Robert O. Collins, "The Thin White Line," in *The British in the Sudan, 1898–1956: The Sweetness and the Sorrow*, ed. Robert O. Collins and Francis M. Deng (London: Macmillan, 1984), 193.

5. V. L. Griffiths and Abdel Rahman Ali Taha, *Sudanese Courtesy Customs: A Foreigner's Guide to Polite Phrases in Common Use among the Sophisticated Arabic-Speaking Population of the Northern Sudan* (Sudan Government, 1936).

my parents' days in Sudan, though strangely encapsulated in many ways, kept open a space in my imagination for the world of Islam.

THE SOUTH

Over a thousand miles below Atbara, there stretched a vast, green world of swamps, called by Arabic-speakers al-Sudd—the Barrier. This region was inhabited by stateless, largely pagan tribes scattered among the infinitely divided capillary system of waterways that fed into the southern Nile. At a time when the Islam of the North seemed immovable, even still threatening, many English colonial officers throve on the wide-open frontiers of the South.

These were the district commissioners. A mystique surrounded them. They were held to represent the colonial venture at its most daring and (so it was hoped) its most successful. In reality, they were an odd lot. Unlike applicants for the Indian Civil Service, they did not have to pass any exams. It was not for them to be brainy, but to be tough, sociable, and resourceful. They came overwhelmingly from Oxford and Cambridge, where almost all of them had been outstanding sportsmen. As far as I can tell, there was not a single Irishman among them all the time that my father was in Sudan.

My father knew the "D.C.s" only by reputation. As a railway man stationed in the North and unconnected with the business of government, he had little to do with them except for the occasional visit to check the steamer service that extended the reach of the railways into the deep South.

As for myself, the nearest that I ever came to the watery South was the Khartoum Zoo. It was one of the first zoos to be designed as a safari park. I still remember the sight of giraffes, their preternaturally long necks swaying against the sky as they walked down an avenue of jacaranda trees. In a pool in one corner of the zoo there was a large hippopotamus taken straight from the deep South. At the age of three, I offered the hippo one of my most prized possessions—a Mickey Mouse handkerchief. I remember how the courteous beast chumbled it, with apparent satisfaction, before swallowing it with an impressive opening and closing of its great pink mouth.

Yet it was at this time, and in southern Sudan, that one of the major breakthroughs in our modern understanding of the beliefs and practices of tribal societies took place. As this breakthrough affected me deeply when I came to work on religion and society in late antiquity, I trust that the reader will allow me to sketch out the context in which it occurred.

The Bog Barons: "Chunky" Willis (1881–1975)

Those who found themselves in charge of the vast swamps of the southern Nile were called "Bog Barons." They were little emperors in their own vast realms. But how much did they actually know of the world to which they had come? The answer is, in many (but by no means all) cases—very little. While a thick wall of overt prejudice stood between the British and Islam in the northern Sudan, a screen of fantasies, as light but as opaque as the rustling man-high grasses of the region, often stood between the district commissioners and the realities of tribal life in southern Sudan.

Take the case of Charles Armine Willis—"Chunky" Willis. "Chunky" was so called because he had the stalwart legs of a great rower. He had rowed twice for Oxford. He had gone down from Magdalen with a third class degree. An Old Etonian, he was a great snob, proud to be the member of seven London clubs.

"Chunky" became governor of the Upper Nile in 1927. He had a favorite obsession. He was convinced that the cattle-raising Nuer of his province were in thrall to witch doctors—the *kujurs*—who acted as "prophets." For him, the *kujurs* were the potential *Mahdis* of the pagan South. He thought that they held the tribes in the grip of religious terror; and that, at any moment, they might unleash a pagan holy war against British rule, as the *Mahdi* had once done in the North. After failing to hunt down the principal "prophet" of the region, "Chunky" decided that the Nuer had to be cowed. The RAF was consulted. A few bombs would do the trick. He wanted to test what would be "the moral effect of the mere presence of airplanes on this primitive people." The next bombing raid was devoted to an attempt (only partially successful) to flatten the great pyramid raised in the 1890s by Ngundeng, the ancestor of the most impressive of the "prophets." It had been an astonishing monument, made of packed mud, sixty feet high and visible from five miles away—like the spire of a great cathedral—as it rose above the dead flat plain.[6]

"The Poet": Evans-Pritchard (1902–1973)

Fortunately, "Chunky" was not representative of all Bog Barons. But he did carry to extremes ideas that circulated largely unchallenged among them. It was these entrenched certainties that were undermined by a British anthropologist

---

6. Robert O. Collins, *Shadows in the Grass: Britain in the Southern Sudan* (New Haven, CT: Yale University Press, 1983), 129 and 152

usually known as "E.-P."—Edward Evans-Pritchard. Evans-Pritchard would soon emerge as the brilliant founder of the British school of social anthropology. A young man of only twenty-five, he was summoned to clear up the mess created by the heated imaginations of persons like "Chunky."

In many ways, Evans-Pritchard was as magnificently idiosyncratic as any Bog Baron. He did things his way. This was his first venture in anthropological inquiry. He went in among the tribes. He drew his own conclusions from months of meticulous fieldwork. From 1927 onward he flickered in and out of the world of the governors and the district commissioners. They called him "the Poet." His relations with "Chunky" were, predictably, abysmal: "he could speak of Willis only in four-letter words."[7]

WITCHCRAFT DEMYSTIFIED

E.-P., "the Poet," was the great demystifier of the South. His study of the Azande (the neighbors of the Nuer) showed that witchcraft was not a menace. As we will see, he proved that it was a banal matter, part of the undramatic, day-to-day pattern of life among a highly intelligent and hardheaded people. It was not the object of craven fears on the part of mentally undeveloped "primitives," as was believed by people like "Chunky" and, indeed, by most of the reading public of that time.[8]

This was Evans-Pritchard's decisive contribution. He, quite simply, removed a barrier of prejudice, to show a world in its full humanity, delivered, at last, from the imagined nightmares of those who sought to govern it.

Little did I know, as I fed my Mickey Mouse handkerchief to the resident hippopotamus in the Khartoum Zoo, that, within a quarter of a century, I would be sitting opposite Evans-Pritchard (by then professor of social anthropology in Oxford) in the lunchroom of All Souls College, Oxford. I owe to E.-P.'s book, *Witchcraft, Oracles and Magic among the Azande,* an exhilarating breakthrough in my own study of sorcery in the later Roman Empire. But the book did more than that. It removed a screen for me, much as it was intended to remove a screen of ignorant fear among the Bog Barons of southern Sudan.

7. Douglas H. Johnson, "E.-P., the Nuer and the Sudan Political Service," *African Affairs* 81 (1982): 231–246, at 234.

8. E. E. Evans-Pritchard, *Witchcraft, Oracles and Magic among the Azande* (Oxford: Clarendon Press, 1937). See chapter 49: "History and Anthropology."

Reading E.-P. for the first time (in 1967) revived in me trace memories of a great fear that affected all Europeans in Sudan and elsewhere. Scattered by the chance of empire in lands whose inhabitants remained dangerously opaque to them, they constantly had to ask themselves, "What do the Natives think?" even "How do they think?" I now realize that there was a basis in the experience of my family and those around them for one of the driving forces of my work as a historian. This has been to remove such screens of prejudice wherever I found them—to explain practices and beliefs in the distant past that seemed, at first sight, to be as irrational and often as repugnant as the imagined witchcraft practices of the southern Sudan. In this way, by a strange detour through a masterpiece generated in the swamps of the southern Nile, I gained a new respect for the poise and cunning with which ancient and medieval persons—for all the world like the Nuer and the Azande, and just as much the objects of adverse modern prejudices—faced the problems of good and evil in ages very different from our own.

ATBARA

LIFE ABROAD

"An Uninspired Place": Atbara

My father had little contact with the southern Sudan. He was based in At-bara, two hundred miles north of Khartoum, in a very different world from the South. In any case, that wider world was closed to him by the extreme compartmentalization of English society in Sudan. The Political Service (the colonial government) was an English, almost an Oxford and Cambridge, pre-serve. Railway personnel did not count as part of that world. They were held to be rather boring persons, who would insist on talking "shop" about en-gines, gradients, and culverts. So my father was doubly excluded. He was both an engineer and an Irishman.

Even the system of honors in which the staff of the Sudanese Railways were included (and which meant much in the intensely hierarchical world of government service) passed him by. As an Irish citizen he could not receive the OBE—the Order of the British Empire—that was the accustomed honorific "handshake" to departing railway personnel. My father's brother-in-law and the sponsor of his career in early days, "Buggins" Bayley, was an Englishman who duly received *his* OBE. As a child, I was reminded to be very careful to write "Leonard Bayley, Esquire, O.B.E." in all my letters to him.

In a manner characteristic of English rule in the colonies, my father was slotted into a compartment from which he was not expected to move. To the best of my memory, he never offered any opinion on the politics of Sudan when he returned to Ireland. He had done his job. That was enough.

We lived in Atbara. Atbara was what one would call a "company town": it existed because of the railways. It lacked the imperial tone of Khartoum. In the words of an administrator:

> Atbara was not highly regarded by the colonial service proper. It gave to outsiders the impression of a local patriotism and a guild fidelity jealous of interference. No doubt it was all the romantic stuff about the desert which made Atbara seem an uninspired place with its rows of neat bungalows and tidy gardens.[1]

Even in the hubbub of modern Sudan, Atbara has retained that quality. The Bradt Travel guidebook speaks of the Railway Quarter (where my father would have lived) with approval:

> Full of neat bungalows of café au lait brick and red roof tiles along quiet tree-lined avenues, giving it a distinctly provincial air . . . you could almost imagine yourself in Surrey, or the cantonment of some Indian colonial town.[2]

I suspect that my parents liked it that way. Yet this orderly world was, in some ways, strangely insecure. The bungalows were owned by the Sudan Railways. In the total absence of hotels, their occupants were frequently called upon to put up strangers. One of the advantages of bridge, which they played all the time, was that they did not have to talk while playing, either to unknown guests or to persons they knew only too well.

The Cost of Abroad

Most important of all, travel to and from home was in the hands of the Sudan government. My mother's diary for 1946 (the only one that has survived from her days in Sudan) gives a glimpse of what this meant. It tells a story of extreme dependence on arbitrary schedules that must have been agonizing for those who wanted to enjoy as much as possible of their leave safely back at home.

On the first stage of the long journey back to Ireland, my parents arrived by train in Cairo on March 26. My mother wrote in her diary:

1. J. E. Frost, "Memories of the Sudan Civil Service," in *The British in the Sudan, 1898–1956: The Sweetness and the Sorrow*, ed. Robert O. Collins and Francis M. Deng (London: Macmillan, 1984), 87.

2. Sophie Ibbotson and Max Lovell-Hoar, *Sudan*, 3rd ed., Bradt Travel Guides (Chalfont St. Peter, Berks: Bradt Tourist Guides, 2012), 153.

Arrived at Cairo at last.

Demonstration at station, but all went well. Checked into Hotel Victoria—breakfast, bath.

Tea at Groppi's

What my mother omitted to mention was that the "Demonstration" was one of the greatest ever anti-British demonstrations of the time. Ramses Square, outside the station, must have been a heaving sea of protesters. To go on to tea at Groppi, the world-famous café and center of Cairo society, was grand enough. But I notice that, when in Cairo, my parents—maybe, I suspect, short of money—always spoke of tea, but never of actually dining out. And then the long, uncertain wait began. They lost over a month of their leave time stranded in Cairo until a ship was available to take them to England. My mother's entries in the diary show rare self-control:

April 2 Sunday. Tea at Groppi's. Most amusing watching the crowd. Still no news of passage.

April 10 Tea at Groppi's. Still no word of getting passage.

May 1 Went round to Sudan agency. Rumours of a ship on 9th but nothing definite.

May 2 Hear we may be out on 9th!!!

By May 13 my parents' ship had reached Malta:

Very interesting, and, though it was hard to see bomb damage at first—you could see it through glasses. Saw 2 submarines. Took on a Malta contingent for V [Victory Day] parade [the great parade in London in that year]. All ships in harbor have flags.

At last, after six weeks of hanging around, the journey from abroad back to home was under way. They arrived in Ireland on May 21, having spent almost half of their leave in transit.

And what of the "little death" of parting when my father had to go back again to Sudan in August, at the end of his leave, leaving my mother and me at home?

August 7 Had bad night as Peds couldn't sleep and we took him in with us. Poor Jimsie went off on early train [to catch the mailboat from Dún Laoghaire to Holyhead, and from there to a ship from an English port].

My mother hardly ever used this affectionate diminutive for my father—he was always Jim or J. "Abroad" had its cost. It demanded of ordinary people, like my mother and father, a constant, quiet courage—a stoicism imposed by the sheer size of empire. A month later she joined my father, having left me off at Aravon (the boys' school in Bray where I was a boarder):

> hated leaving Peds, but he seemed alright with the other boys, poor wee scrap . . . got bus home and did [luggage] labels.

MEMORIES

That was in 1946. By then, I had been away from Sudan for seven years. I had been there three times—in the winter seasons between November and April in 1936/37, 1937/38, and 1938/39. I have snatches of memory: of the huge sound of ship's sirens; of bright overhead lights in passageways and dining rooms on board ship; of a dried gecko resting among flowers in my parents' garden in Atbara; of a camel being pulled out of a ditch beside a dusty road; and of my father, looking up from a veranda into a sky weighed down with stars.

Occasionally, memories would return with surprising intensity. In 1974, when I was in Iran, and stranded at the end of a bus line in the middle of the inner desert, I remember that I woke up at dawn to the noise of the grumbling of camels. I had a momentary sense of perfect ease. It was a reassuring trace memory of dawn in Atbara. The same thing happened in Cairo, a few years later, when I used to go to a fleapit theater patronized by Nubians and Sudanese. Among these very large men, with their scarred faces and wide, white *jibbas*, I had, for a moment, a child's sense of utter security. My mother's snapshots show Abdu and Mursi, two Sudanese servants, hovering above me as surrogate nannies: perhaps I had remembered them.

Somehow, I always feel that my life began with a band of sunshine on warm earth. Both through my own trace memories and through the memories of my parents I grew up with a constant sense of the presence of the Middle East that would add an intimate dimension, a sense of affinity, to my work on the East Roman Empire and the rise of Islam.

MARTHA

The figure from abroad whom I remember best was Martha, a stately Ethiopian refugee who was my nanny in Sudan. In October 1935, soon after Air Marshal Balbo had delivered his reassuring message to the *Khartoum Times*, the Italians invaded Ethiopia. Balbo's air force bombed the towns and villages of the country, dropping poison gas. By May 1936 it was all over. Emperor Haile Selassie (1892–1975) fled to Jerusalem and then to England. Ethiopian refugees, many from the Amhara upper class, streamed into Khartoum and Atbara. The local Anglican church did what it could to help them. Aged three, I was sent to bed as a punishment for refusing to yield my stuffed panda to be donated to a church rummage sale in aid of the Ethiopian refugees.

This was why, in my very last stay in Sudan, from late 1938 to early 1939, I had Martha as my nanny. Martha—alas, I do not even know her full name— came from the Amhara elite of Ethiopia. When in Khartoum, she had been lodged with Mr. and Mrs. Hamilton, a couple of African American Baptist missionaries, to whom she later referred, with great affection, as "my mummy and daddy." The snapshots of her show a tall young woman of remarkable beauty. I have a memory of her, standing in the veranda, tall and thin, cutting pastry for a pie. Then, in 1939, I left for Ireland, never to return. My mother and I were cut off from Sudan and my father by the outbreak of the war: he stayed "abroad," in Atbara and Port Sudan; my mother and I returned to Ireland and made the best we could of a long absence from him.

Only after the war did my parents receive a letter from Martha, written on December 13, 1945. She wrote that she had returned from a liberated Ethiopia to Khartoum. There she was told that my father had been drowned at sea, on a boat returning home. Alas, this was an all-too-credible story. She soon learned that this was not so, and received a letter from my mother. It is good to end an account of life abroad, with its many complexities and rigid barriers, with extracts from her reply:

Dear Mrs. Brown,

Your letter came to me today, bringing much joy to my anxious heart. Your news of Peter is very encouraging. It is hard for me to express my joy in writing. The picture of dear Peter is wonderful; he has grown a nice big boy. I wonder if he remembers Martha?

You asked what I did. Well, I just served my country. After your departure, [in 1939] I too bought medicine with the money daddy [Mr. Hamilton] saved for me over £30 including your last gift of £8 for which I never had the opportunity to thank you. Please accept my thanks now. I purchased medicine and all necessary things, joined a band of Patriots, and went by train. Then at Gedaref southeast of Khartoum, on the Sudanese side of the frontier, on the way that led up into the mountains of Gondar] we left secretly for Doka, from thence we travelled until we reached the

Italian Guard. About midnight we crossed their frontier and entered Ethiopia behind the Italians and there for 9 months we carried on a campaign of encouraging, healing and looking for [after] the Patriots. My clinic was in the deep forest where the Italian planes could not spot us. I suffered.

[She later received from Haile Selassie himself three medals and the title "Arbanya," "Patriot".]

I often think of little Peter, who used to tell me that he would grow up and fight the Italians. What I have seen of war and its bitterness I do pray that our dear Peter may never have to do this job over again.

TIME OF WAR

HOME AND ABROAD IN TIME OF WAR

"Abroad" in Time of War

From September 1939 to 1945 the war closed down the regular traffic between home and abroad (based on a system of annual home leaves) that had been one of the attractions of my father's job. For five years I did not see my father. He was caught in Sudan, while my mother and I were stranded in Ireland, since wives and children were not allowed on the boats that sailed through the Mediterranean to Sudan. We settled in Bray, a seaside town south of Dublin where my mother's father, Bob Warren, the rugby footballer, still lived. And so I grew up in wartime Bray as an only child with a lonely mother on a lonely island.

I remember those years in Bray as gray and anxious in a strange sort of way. They were dominated by a sharp sense of incongruity. For here we were, my mother and I, in a neutral Ireland, at a time when the hearts of all my family were still "abroad"—deeply implicated in the fate of an empire at war.

"A Sweet Boy": Brian St George Daly (1908–1941)

The coming of war in 1939 revealed the extent of the social and emotional ties that bound thousands of Irishmen—Catholics and Protestants alike—to the British armed forces. While my father had gone to a civilian job in Sudan, many members of my mother's family (especially on her mother's—the Grey—side) had followed the path that led directly to a career in the British army, navy, or RAF. This was the case with my mother's first cousin, Brian St George Daly.

Brian Daly ("Cousin Brian") was a favorite relative of the Warren family. His father, Bernard Daly (known to my mother as "Uncle Bernie"), was the stuff of family gossip. He had inherited from his father the distillery of Tullamore Dew whiskey. But he proved to be more a sportsman than a businessman. He had a passion for the turf—for polo, horses, and horse racing. It was said that he had once wagered the distillery on a horse from Tullamore (which, fortunately, won). He was also rumored to have been disqualified from the Royal Dublin Society Dog Show for having burnished the hair of his favorite dog with black boot polish.

Bernie's son, my mother's cousin, Brian Daly, shared his father's sense of derring-do. At the Birmingham Oratory—an English school for Catholic boys—Brian and the Duke of Norfolk (who had inherited the title at the age of nine!) were said to have made their way around the great baroque dome of the Oratory on a bet, spread-eagled on its surface at a dizzying height above the ground.

More impressive yet, Brian made a name for himself as a rugby football player in England. He was acclaimed as the hero of the day by a sports journalist reporting the game between the two Catholic public schools, Beaumont and the Oratory:

> Daly's second try [goal] was the outcome of a remarkable run . . . but he is no mere runner. He knows the game. . . .
>
> He is well-built, tall and lithe. His home, I am told, is in one of the suburbs of Dublin. . . . He is the best public school player I have seen this season.

Here was a cousin after the heart of Bob Warren.

For my mother and her sisters, Brian Daly was always the favorite cousin. Freda pasted into her scrapbook the newspaper cutting that had praised his feats as a rugby football player. My mother always spoke of him as "a sweet boy." But the empire claimed him. As soon as war was declared, Brian joined the Lancashire Fusiliers, as a pilot in the RAF squadron attached to the regiment during the Battle of France. He was killed on February 4, 1941, flying one of the slow and heavy Blenheim bombers (veritable flying coffins) in a raid on Brest.

I found touching tributes to Brian and to his father in the "Irishman's Diary" of the *Irish Times* glued into a family album. Brian's father, Bernard—"Uncle

Bernie"—had died only nine months before his son: he was praised as "an exemplar of the virtues both of the gentry and the people of Ireland. He was kindly, . . . possessed a great sense of humour, was completely devoid of class-consciousness, and was a great horseman." Now Brian too was dead, at the age of thirty-one. "A friend who met him about twelve months ago . . . found the same charming, unaffected . . . young man, still thoroughly Irish despite his long years in an un-Irish environment."

DEATH AND EMPIRE

The tragedies of war were shared by Catholics and Protestants alike. But Irish Protestants experienced them in a distinctive way. The Protestantism of families committed to the British armed forces was a religion greatly concerned with the commemoration of the war dead. The Roll of Honor for the war dead of 1914–1918 in Christ Church, Bray, bore thirty-nine names and a Latin inscription:

Qui ante diem perierunt sed milites, sed pro Patria

Who died before their time—but as soldiers; but for their Country.

Then came an English phrase: "Called to a higher service."

I remember how, in Aravon, the Protestant preparatory school to which I would be sent, the walls of the dormitories and of the principal halls were paneled. Each panel bore the name of an Old Aravonian—a boy who had passed through the school. Those who served in the British armed forces added the names of their regiment, ship, or squadron. Those who died in action would be further distinguished. Their regimental badge would be attached to the panel above their name. Only too soon, the panels became studded with these badges. It was considered bad luck if any one of us found himself assigned to a bed close to panels where the badges clustered too thickly. In this, and in so many other different ways, war was right beside us in the midst of the strange, self-conscious peace of a neutral country.

Altogether, death and memory were close to me as a boy, all the more poignantly for being experienced in a country that was not, itself, at war. Many years later, when I came to study the rise of the cult of saints in early Christianity, I was always touched by the huge sadness of great cemeteries—the catacombs of Rome and the sprawling cities of the dead outside every Roman town—and by the heroic effort, shown in thousands of late Roman gravestones, to overcome, by memory, the cruel face of death.

A TIME OF FEAR

For my mother, these years at Bray were sad years. Not only was she separated by war from my father. She also resumed the role of the unmarried youngest daughter. She returned to "Glendair," the family house, and took care of her father, Bob Warren. "Glendair" had a magnificent view to the west, to the Wicklow Mountains and the exquisitely shaped volcanic cones of the Big Sugarloaf and the Little Sugarloaf. The mountains brought a touch of wild, barbarian beauty—a hint of Dark Age Ireland, of forest, bog land, and steep slopes covered with purple heather and golden, prickly gorse, often caught in a haunting storm light—that formed the backdrop to a stolid seaside town.

When Bob died, in 1941, "Glendair" was sold, and we moved into a succession of rented houses. I remember accompanying my mother, cycling vigorously beside her on my tricycle, ringing my bell, and proudly telling all passersby that my mummy and I were moving house.

We finally settled into "Sidmonton Lodge," a fine house with a garden and, even, an air-raid shelter—a sign of emergency—tastefully covered by a heavy growth of bright nasturtians. "Sid. Lodge" also had a water barrel fed from the roof gutter by a downpipe. It was there that I played at naval war. I once reenacted with too much enthusiasm the Japanese sinking of the *Prince of Wales* in 1941 (a chilling victory of new airpower over the old-fashioned British navy). I sent a cigar box to the bottom of the water barrel under a stream of well-aimed pebbles. When I accompanied the sinking with shouts of triumph, I was rebuked by my mother with a flash of anger that showed the fears of the time. A Japanese victory was no joke.

"Abroad" was, indeed, a dangerous place. The British Empire in East Asia had suddenly folded under Japanese attack. Hong Kong and Singapore had fallen. Entire civilian populations had ended up "in the bag"—the dry term used by my aunts for the horrors of internment by the Japanese. If this could happen in East Asia, it might yet happen to my daddy in the Middle East.

It was a time of fear. Occasionally, at night, I would hear the heavy thud of the German Condor bombers, as they made their way northward over the Irish Sea to strike Belfast and Liverpool. Some German bombs did fall on Dublin, and the sinister thing was that we never knew whether this happened on purpose or by accident. On the night of May 30–31, 1941, a stick of bombs fell on the crowded tenement houses of Summerhill. The raid (if it was a raid, and not some pilot's error) was all the more frightening as it was totally unexpected. If it happened once, it could happen again. For a moment the Blitz came to Dublin.[1]

But I remember the raids somewhat differently. The shadows on the curtains that would frighten me on those dark nights, as the Dorniers passed by, were not, for me, the shadows of Germans—I imagined them to be the shadows of my fellow Irishmen, the gunmen of the IRA. In many ways, I picked up from those around me the sense that I was abroad and in danger in my own land. We could never know for sure who might be anti-British and pro-German. My mother would send me out alone to the barber's with instructions:

> Ask for short back and sides. Give the man a sixpence tip. Be sure not to talk about the war. You never know what side he's on.

A Speech Defect

It was at this time that my stammer began to develop in a way that added to my poor mother's anxieties. To be tongue-tied in a verbal culture, such as Ireland—not to be able to answer questions, or even greetings, instantly, politely, and with wit—caused embarrassment and shame all round. In 1943, the Christmas report for elocution in my primary school was firm:

> Peter works hard but is greatly worried by his speech defect, and really needs medical attention.

"Medical attention" was forthcoming. In the robust, all-male manner of the time, the doctors declared that I was an anxious child, who had been too long alone with my mother. I needed a tougher and more manly regime. And what could be tougher or more manly than to be sent as a boarder to Aravon Preparatory School for Boys in Bray, presided over by Arthur Craig, known to us all as "the Boss"?

I suspect that the doctor often gave this advice to worried parents. He was not entirely wrong. Aravon was a preparatory school in the British (not the American) sense: a privately owned boarding school for boys between seven and thirteen. It was widely considered one of the few outstanding schools for young Protestant boys in Ireland.

---

1. For an eyewitness account of this incident, see Alec King in Kevin C. Kearns, *Dublin Voices: An Oral Folk History* (Dublin: Gill and Macmillan, 1998), 16–21.

This took place in 1943. I have an airgraph letter (a smaller photographic copy of an original letter, reduced in size so as to take up less space in the mail) in which my father endeavored to hearten me in my first weeks at Aravon:

> I'm sure you have a very good time, and even if <u>everything</u> isn't just as good as you have been used to, well, that is the way of the world and those people are happiest who can find some good even in things that are largely dull or unpleasant.
>
> I am glad to hear you were at the punch ball, learning how to sock any-one who has to be socked.
>
> I'm sure you'll like the steamer I'm on at the moment, for there is a magnificent big engine room with two great diesel engines going "thump, thump," in a very powerful way, as well as other smaller engines going about their job too.

The combination of gentle, reflective advice with concrete exhortations and descriptions calculated to appeal to a young boy was characteristic of my father. I wonder whether he was not, in part, addressing such consolation to himself. I also wonder whether he knew that I would need all the consolation I could get when confronted with the Boss.

THE BOSS

It is not often that the headmaster of a small school for boys in Ireland should emerge, over half a century later, in the pages of the *London Review of Books*, as the living incarnation of all that was most horrific in the educational system of a cruel and distant age. Yet, discussing the brutal educational methods of Tudor England, the literary critic Michael Neill allowed himself a flashback to his own days at Aravon under the Boss—Arthur Craig (1890–1955).

I grew up in postwar Northern Ireland and at the age of eight . . . I was loaded on to a train at Belfast Central and was shunted across the border to Aravon, a dismal institution . . . where Latin . . . was taught, as befitted his station, by the headmaster. A tall gaunt figure with a lividly scarred cheek-bone and glittering, oddly-skewed eyes, A. B. Craig bore a disconcerting resemblance to the bird of prey that punningly [A Raven: for Aravon] adorned the school coat of arms. Along with his twin brother, whose name we could see high up on the roll of honour, Craig had fought in the Somme: according to school legend a shell had landed on their platoon killing his twin brother and blowing the right side of Craig's own face away. By the grace of God an ingenious surgeon had managed to patch this wound with the dead brother's cheek. The prosthesis, however, was said to be held in place with a metal plate which would heat up when the old man became annoyed, causing him excruciating pain—hence the rage triggered by the most trivial error in Latin grammar. Craig would begin his classes in a jovial mood, often tempting us to relax with a jokey mnemonic ("Every family has its little *soror*"); but it would not be long before the scar would redden dangerously; a bungled ablative would excite roars of outrage; the strings of the piano behind his desk would begin to vibrate in horrified sympathy; and the blows would start to fall. "Stupid, *stupid* boys."[1]

I confess that my memory also stirred, in a similar manner, at the thought of the Boss. In 1990, I visited the graves of the Warren family in the little Protestant cemetery at Enniskerry just outside Bray. Walking among the graves, I saw a massive tombstone with the simple inscription: A.B. Craig. I instantly cried out to my wife, "Under at last!" A few days later, at a dinner at Trinity College Dublin, my wife sat beside the registrar. Learning that he also had been to Aravon, she asked him, "Is it really true what people say about the Boss?" The registrar put down his knife and fork and turned to her with a serious look.

I can assure you, Mrs. Brown, that everything your husband has told you about the Boss is true—absolutely true.

The registrar was a scientist. Even as a boy, he had observed these terrifying outbursts of rage with cool, analytic eyes. He had figured out the Boss. The story of the Battle of the Somme was a myth. Craig's brother had indeed been killed. But he was an airman—shot down in Mesopotamia. Craig himself had also been in Mesopotamia and had brought back with him, from the marshes of southern Iraq, a lingering malarial fever. This recurrent fever accounted for the violent swings of his mood. The registrar continued:

But did your husband tell you about the Hoo-Doo page?

Apparently, the registrar explained, there were pages in the mathematics textbook that were particularly difficult to explain. They were known to insiders as "Hoo-Doo pages." When a Hoo-Doo page coincided with a new bout of malarial fever, a perfect storm of rage would ensue. On those occasions, his yells could be heard emerging from the main building of the school like the bellowing of a wounded bull.

Yet it was not the physical violence of the Boss, or even his rages, that hurt me. It was the sarcasm with which he made the boys feel small and stupid. He insisted that mathematics was all a matter of common sense. Only babies and spoiled weaklings could fail to unravel its manly, grown-up certitudes. These exhortations had the effect on me of giving me a lasting suspicion of common sense. It was the weapon of bullies.

---

1. Michael Neill, "Wilderness of Tigers," *London Review of Books* 37, no. 6 (March 19, 2015): 41–44: a review of Colin Burrow, *Shakespeare and Classical Antiquity* (Oxford University Press, 2013).

I think that the Boss is best seen as a tragic product of the First World War. He was at his happiest showing lantern slides of the Gallipoli campaign. He enjoyed telling us how the British troops had made hand grenades out of empty bully-beef tins filled with dynamite to lob at the Turks. Little warriors ourselves, we loved him for that.

The Boss was one of those many veterans of the First World War for whom church, army, and death came together in a painful knot. To lead school worship on Armistice Day (a day heavy with notions of the Higher Calling and the Supreme Sacrifice) was the high point of his religious life. What we never learned was that his own mother, at the age of sixty-seven, had enlisted as a voluntary ambulance driver. She had been killed near Boulogne in the same year as his twin brother had died.

Conkers

Looking back, I am less surprised by the psychotic behavior of the Boss than by the fact that it had far less effect on the outlook and morale of the school than one might have expected. The reason is that the Boss, though outrageous, summed up important features of our education. We were not at Aravon to be nice. We were there to become little barbarians who throve on toughness and conflict. Every autumn we would stand beneath the row of great chestnut trees beside the school yard, throwing sticks and cricket bats up into the branches to dislodge the great chestnuts. These would then be hardened and pitted against each other in "conker-bashing" competitions. The hardest chestnut— the most compact and gnarled conker—won.

And we ourselves wished to be little conkers. We wanted tough bodies to pit against each other in fistfights and in rugby scrums. The worst insult was "flab"—and, even worse, "flab baby." In such an atmosphere, rugby football emerged less as a game of skill than as a test of conker-hood. Victory went to the tough. Teams that allowed themselves to be beaten in too ignominious a manner were put on compulsory boxing for the remainder of the year. This happened notably when we were beaten by Catholic schools—such as the local Presentation College: a legendary bunch of little toughs, given to brutal neck tackles. (Defeat at the hands of the more gentlemanly Catholic school, St. Gerard's, never incurred such punishment.)

We of Aravon were convinced that we owed our victories to absence of "flab." By contrast, Castlepark School (north of Bray, in Sandycove) was seen as a veritable sink of "flab." It was known to us as "Curly Pigs," from its initials,

C. P. "Curly Pigs" boys were allowed to see their mummies, aunts, and sisters every weekend. The Boss permitted this indulgence only once a month. He spoke of weekend visits with ill-veiled contempt. He called them "C.C. and C.": "Cream Cakes and Cuddles." No wonder that the Aravon XV—hard as conkers and uncorrupted by female endearments—trashed the "Curly Pigs" in every rugby game that I remember.

It is, perhaps, poetic justice on the Boss that his predictions proved him right in part. In later years, flab won out. Castle Park became coeducational. When I visited the school in 2014, charming and well-bred mothers from the Dublin bourgeoisie were picking up their little girls in front of the school. So that was what Cream Cakes and Cuddles led to! It would have confirmed the worst suspicions of the Boss. But the Boss would not have been pleased to learn that Aravon, also, became coeducational and has now closed its doors— but not before producing Miss World for 2003!

SENIOR TEASING

Yet with all this cult of masculine toughness, there was little or no bullying at Aravon. The reason was one that students of the Nuer of the southern Sudan or of Dark Age Europe would understand: the entire fabric of the school was held together by carefully engineered, perpetual feuds. Insult, teasing, and wisecracks were never the monopoly of a small group of school bullies, directed against a few unlucky victims. Everybody was doing it to everybody else, all the time. I was amazed, on rereading my letters to my parents, at how much space I devoted to recounting with pride my achievements in S.T.—"Senior Teasing." Seeing that I was, at that time, only nine and most seniors were boys of eleven or twelve, I would have thought that "Senior Teasing" was a most unadvisable activity. But no. We were always at it.

More than that, we were organized for it. We had an "anti-Senior General." I myself headed a group known as the J.M.P.—"The Junior Military Police." We worked in many different ways. We engineered diversionary actions and, at times, direct confrontations. I kept my parents informed of these feats of strategy:

> If you shout or even say "Waore!" he'll get waxy [angry], and to get them waxy is the whole point of the fighting. Another way is to dash across the Fives Court while they're playing fives. That makes them really waxy. The Seniors were beaten yesterday. . . . Well, the J.M.P. took a ball off two

Seniors playing fives and they got angry and whacked an officer [of the J.M.P. no less!] with a racquet, but we were not beaten. I was chased a bit but escaped, we use air-guns [BB guns], of course not real ones but small shoots of bamboo you put one wad of <u>wet brown</u> paper at each end, then you push one down the hole and the strength of the compressed air shoots one piece out with super force

Looking back, I am struck by this prevalence of low-level feuding without outright bullying, and also by our zest for forming oppositional groups— subversive militias staffed by ranked officers, committed to bringing off carefully planned operations. Maybe there was something in the air of postin- dependence Ireland that added an extra frisson to the little wars of little boys. The model of the competing militias of the Irish War of Independence and the Irish Civil War lay somewhere in the background of our imagination.

"BROWNUS HITS CORNISHUM": LEARNING LATIN FROM A POET

Despite its many idiosyncrasies, Aravon was a serious academic establishment. It prepared boys for the Common Entrance Examination. This was a test for entrance to the public schools of the United Kingdom and Ireland, taken at the age of eleven. (American readers must bear with me if I stick to English usage: by "public schools" I mean long-established, private boarding schools for boys over thirteen.) Preparation started early and the pace was intense. I came to Aravon at the age of eight as a total illiterate. In my first spelling test, I could spell only one word—JAM.

Little did I know it, but this spelling test was the first of a succession of exami- nations that would determine every step of my career until the age of twenty-one. By the age of ten, I was already deep into Latin, French, history, and geography (but no science), all in preparation for the Common Entrance Examination. From then onward, from exam to exam, the pace never slackened.

The teachers who guided us in this brisk forced march of learning were a mixed bunch. Private schools such as Aravon were human bird sanctuaries. Some teachers were local figures. They held part-time teaching assignments as a form of outdoor relief (welfare). Mr. Monk Gibbon (known as "Gubb-Gubb") was one such gentleman down on his luck. He was a travel writer, who later wrote a Batsford travel book on the baroque churches of Austria. He was also a poet; and not only was he a poet—he was also a cousin of W. B. Yeats. As we have seen, he was permanently aggrieved that his distinguished relative had not included any of his poems in the famous *Oxford Book of Modern Verse*.

Monk Gibbon made a point of coming to Aravon only on Fridays. It was known why he did so. As a Protestant school, we refused to eat fish on Fridays, as the Catholics did. Instead, Irish stew was served for lunch. And the Friday Irish stew was the best meat dish of the week. Well-fed, Monk Gibbon would then proceed to conduct what he considered to be a Latin lesson.

> Latin [he told us] is all about endings. Yes: that's it . . . endings. Nominative ending and accusative ending.
> Brown! Hit Cornish!

This was a bad turn for the lesson to take. Cornish, who sat beside me, was a boy of conker toughness. Such a blow would not remain unavenged after class. Knowing that I would sign my own death warrant by striking him, I gave Cornish a hesitant tap.

> There you are! [Monk Gibbon continued] Brownus hits Cornishum. That's it. Nominative Brownus. Accusative Cornishum. There you have it!

Wherewith the poet wrapped his thick tweed coat more tightly around him, placed his feet on the stove that warmed the classroom, and settled down into his armchair as if for a good sleep. It was not, perhaps, the best introduction to a classical tongue.

The Border and the Uses of Geography

Cyril Ward, our geography teacher, was very different. With a thin, white face and a bushy, almost Edwardian, jet-black moustache, and the upper pocket of his light-green tweed jacket stuffed with colored pens, he seemed the model teacher. But he, too, had his eccentricities. He came from county Down in Northern Ireland. That is, he came from the wrong, the northern, side of the border that separated an enclave of British rule from the free republic of the South.

That was how Mr. Ward saw it. He was a fierce Irish nationalist. He was even said to have learned Irish—a rare achievement for a teacher in a Protestant private school. The heavy-handed insistence on the compulsory teaching of Irish in the state schools of the Republic made Irish repugnant to most of us. Ignorance of Irish was a sign of our independence, as a private school, to which we clung with a stubbornness that I now regret. His reputed knowledge of Irish cast an aura of difference around Cyril Ward.

Ward was not allowed to teach Irish. Instead, he taught The Border by teaching geography. In his opinion, the border between the republican South and the Six Counties of the North, where British rule prevailed, was no ordinary frontier. It was an open wound inflicted on the natural unity of the island. So we would learn to trace the exact shape of that wound. Armed with two pens—one green, for the side of the South; and one bright red—an English red: the red of Redcoats—for the side of the North—we would draw The Border in its full, complex iniquity. It was important to know where was where: that Armagh was in the North, while Monaghan was in the South; that the iniquitous thing (no respecter of natural boundaries) snaked through the middle of Lough Melvin and Lough Macnean; and that, paradoxically, county Donegal, the northernmost county of the island, was in the South. Taught by Cyril Ward, geography was a lesson in civic virtue, seen through southern Irish eyes.

COLONEL BLIMP—ARAVON STYLE

The massive demobilization of 1945 brought yet stranger human flotsam to Aravon. Colonel Lockhart—we never knew his Christian name—came from India. He had served in the Indian army. Given the fact that many of the boys' parents were still abroad, working in the territories of the empire, the arrival of an authentic representative of the British Raj was more than welcome. And Colonel Lockhart looked the part. With bristling moustache and plump features, he was set to be the Colonel Blimp of Aravon.

But things were not quite as they appeared. Colonel Lockhart was no Colonel Blimp. He had returned from India a convinced Marxist and an ardent supporter of Mahatma Gandhi. We soon realized that we had yet another odd man out among us. We boys might have shrugged Colonel Lockhart off as a bit of a crank. Except for one thing. He knew all about tigers. He had seen them. He had hunted them. He had brought with him from India the works of James Corbett, the great spinner of tales about tigers. He would hold us spellbound at bedtime, reading *The Man-Eaters of Kumaon*.

MITTELEUROPA . . . OR WORSE

But, among the rare birds that came our way, Colonel Lockhart was quite outshone by Mr. Bowlby. Charles Bowlby (1911–1959) was the most mysterious of the new arrivals. Apparently, he had emerged from Admiral Horthy's Hungary. He brought with him a tantalizing whiff of *Mitteleuropa*—of Central

Europe. He was multilingual. When he read to us *The Three Musketeers* of Alexandre Dumas, he would pronounce the names of the protagonists with a perfect French accent. These alien sounds rolled off his tongue, with hypnotic ease, while Colonel Lockhart—for all his tiger lore—mangled the names of heroes and villains alike whenever he read the works of Dumas to us.

Bowlby was handsome and ferociously athletic. He could kick a rugger ball like a cannon shot. He later lived up to this prowess as a sportsman by founding the Leprechauns—a cricket club devoted to raising the standard of amateur cricket throughout Ireland, which is still active today.

And Mr. Bowlby knew his European history. He covered the blackboard with beautifully drawn maps and genealogical trees, drawn in different colored chalks, conjuring up empires and dynasties of which we knew little from our English textbooks.

Most important of all, Bowlby set my imagination alight. He did this not only by opening the door to wider worlds. He also treated me as a mind. For all his athletic commitment, he was uncompromisingly intellectual. Even if I was not an athlete, he told me, I did not need to worry about being a "flab." I did not have to be good at games. I did not even have to worry about my stammer. It didn't matter. "You have a brain."

Bowlby lived up to his challenge to me to use my brain. He made sure that I enrolled to compete for the Townsend Warner Prize in 1947. This was a prize to be won by an examination in British history. The competitors came from all the preparatory schools in Britain and Ireland. I was the only Irish boy to receive mention. It was Bowlby who ensured that I emerged from Aravon with confidence that I had a brain.

But I also emerged with something of a problem. The more we paid attention to Mr. Bowlby's history lessons, the more we realized that, somehow, Mr. Bowlby's modern Europe was not our modern Europe. He seemed strangely unmoved by the certitudes for which my parents had fought in the past six years. He suggested that the war was started by the obstinacy of the Poles over Danzig. He reminded us that concentration camps were invented by the British during the Boer War. These occasional throwaway remarks struck a strange note. But, if anything, they served only to heighten Mr. Bowlby's charisma as a historian and a connoisseur of Europe.

Looking back, I had thought (too charitably, it now appears) that Bowlby must have been one of those young men whose romanticism had drawn him to Eastern European and Balkan countries, with their fascist and anti-Semitic elements. But then my wife discovered on the internet an article on

Bowlby written by Charles Lysart in "An Irishman's Diary" in the *Irish Times* of February 16, 2009.

What I read put an entirely different and more sinister face on the whole story. Bowlby had arrived in Ireland one step ahead of the hangman. He had been a colleague of William Joyce (1906–1946)—the odious "Lord Haw-Haw"—who had regularly broadcast propaganda for Hitler's Germany. Having hanged Joyce, who claimed to have been born in Galway—and so to be exempt from British justice—the British were no longer interested in Bowlby. In Lysart's words, they "had no stomach for a wrangle" on the liability of Irish citizens to British justice. To hang one putative Irishman was enough. The sooner Bowlby was forgotten, the better.

It turns out that the Boss had learned about Bowlby's past from an article in the *Daily Mail*. He was appalled. He did the right thing, by going straight to Sir John Maffey—the British representative to Ireland. He was told to do and say nothing; and that he should keep Bowlby. The Boss did so willingly. For Bowlby was an inspired teacher: I was only one of those many who had been turned on to the study of history by him. His shady wartime past was kept a total secret from parents and pupils alike.

The saga of Bowlby continued. It was a sad one. He left Aravon to found a new school. It failed, amid noxious tales of embezzlement and sexual harassment. He died of Hodgkin's disease in London in 1959. The Leprechauns, however, had taken off. None other than Sir John Maffey (who must have known about Bowlby's past from the Boss's visit to him) signed up as a member. Shameless to the last, Bowlby even suggested that the Leprechauns should celebrate the coronation of Elizabeth II in 1953, by displaying the colors red, white, and blue on their fixture card. His fellow members overruled him.

We knew little or nothing of this in 1945. But what I had picked up would stand me in good stead as a historian. To listen to Colonel Lockhart's Marxist take on the British Raj, juxtaposed with the insidious fascist vision of Mr. Bowlby, had already laid the foundations for me of a robust sense of historical relativism. I saw that it was possible to look at the same historical events from very different angles. This was a lesson that I would carry with me, after 1945, when I left Bray for the less sheltered, more troubled world of Dublin.

DUBLIN DAYS

"NUMBER SIXTY"

"Number Sixty"

In April 1945, my mother joined my father in Sudan. I moved from Bray to Dublin, to live at no. 60 Lansdowne Road—"Number Sixty"—with my father's mother and sister. There I stayed for two years.

Number Sixty was a tall terrace house. It stood next to the end of the terrace. Then came the railway line, and then the great rugby football stadium of Lansdowne Road, the site of the glories of Bob Warren. Vast crowds would converge to watch major matches, both national and international, filling the house with huge, excited noise every Saturday.

But the railway that ran between "Number Sixty" and the stadium was equally exciting. It was the line along which the Cork Express would hurtle at night. Every evening, Rory the dog (of whom more anon) would jump up from the fireside with a premonitory woof. Bursting through the kitchen, he would hurl himself headlong down the steep staircase into the garden, all four paws raising a clatter like a machine gun as he slid down the wooden steps, so as to rush up and down the garden barking wildly. Then, honor satisfied, he would return with self-satisfied panting. Once again, he had seen the monster off his premises.

The house was full of memories. It was reassuring to find that there was no misdeed that a little boy of ten might commit that had not been committed before him, in this very house, by his father and uncle. Jessie Brown, my father's mother (the Mater) was a quiet but resolute presence. She seemed to spend most of her time in the kitchen, making soda bread by hand alone—throwing the ingredients together without the use of a single measuring cup.

Large mutton roasts would appear on Sundays. We would have cold meat for the rest of the week, served with delicious chutneys. The Mater would distribute huge lumps of fat—pure white, like alabaster—with the exhortation "Fat. Food for angels!" (When later I recounted this anecdote to diet-conscious friends in California, they broke out into helpless laughter.)

AUNTIE MAI

Auntie Mai was granite. Her rough complexion (she may have suffered from a skin disease when young) was all of a piece with her gruff voice and rugged opinions. She was an unflappable and deeply reassuring presence. Her demands were precise and mercifully delimited. I should write immediately to answer letters and to thank for birthday presents. I should wash my teeth in hot water. Above all, I should "mind my p's and q's." When out for a walk or in Dublin, I should raise my cap to those to whom I should raise my cap. Who these were, she never made plain. She just took for granted that I would know. In fact, I did know, instinctively, which of the unpretentiously dressed ladies and gentlemen (whom I encountered anywhere: in the middle of a Dublin bookshop, on top of a bus, or along the banks of the river Dodder) were known to "Number Sixty." Apart from this, my conscience was free.

Her remedies, also, were straightforward. Milk of magnesia was a sure answer to the ills of the heart. When my stammer distressed me, or when I felt weepy, Auntie Mai was unperturbed. Milk of magnesia and a good rest would see me through. I spent happy years at "Number Sixty," unburdened by anxiety. Milk of magnesia was there, in a medicine cupboard in a bathroom where hot water streamed from large brass taps, and the wooden walls of the bath smelled more strongly of disinfectant ammonia and health-giving pine than any bathroom I have ever known.

Auntie Mai's Christmas parties were the crowning achievement of her benevolent despotism. Coming from Bray and an only child, I had no friends in Dublin. So Mai would summon friends. I would be presented with a list of suitable boys and girls, most of whom were totally unknown to me: "Linette Sinclair. A nice girl. I play bridge with her mother."

The parties were invariably successful. Jellies of rare shades were served. Sweets appeared, made from tinned peaches ingeniously disguised as poached eggs. The side rooms of the great entrance hall were perfect for hide-and-seek. The darkness into which the stairs led upward to the bedrooms formed a spooky backdrop to the game of "Murder."

The secret of all this was Aunt Mai's trifle. The daughter of a stern teetotaler, Mai did not drink. But she would lace her trifles with so generous a dose of sherry that all of us, children and attendant grown-ups alike, soon became voluble and pink with pleasure.

Aunt Mai was very much the product of a Victorian family. The unmarried daughter, she had stayed at home to look after her parents. Her father—the Bear—had died in 1937; but the Mater continued to rule her with a quiet but indomitable will. Mai loved music. She would listen on the radio to Beethoven—whom she resolutely pronounced "Beat-oven"—for long periods and very loud, for the benefit of the Mater, who was hard of hearing. Indeed, I always remember her as surrounded with magnificent, classical noise. Amid Mai, Beethoven, and the Mater, I needed no elocution lessons to teach me to "speak up" or to fill my lungs. Instead of having to break silence with uncertain words, I found myself bawling like a ship's captain on the high seas. It did my stammer a world of good.

Mai was not a great reader. But she respected books. She ran the patients' library at Sir Patrick Dun's Hospital. She encouraged me to sink into reading matter of every kind. When, in later years, I was asked for whom I wrote, I would answer immediately, "For my aunts." This was not a flippant answer. I wanted to write for Auntie Mai—for persons like her, who had received a good high school education but had not continued to the university. This was as true for men as for women. My father was the only member of his family who had gone on from school to university—to Trinity College Dublin. But such people knew good books when they saw them (just as, like Mai, they knew good music). In the distinctive atmosphere of Dublin, books and the writing of books were constantly talked about; and the role of teachers and authors as spreaders of useful knowledge was respected even in the most seedy of individuals. As a result, the idea of writing for an imagined public came naturally to me from this time onward.

TEEDAH

No two aunts could have been more different than my aunt Mai and my aunt Teedah—Freda Warren, my mother's sister. Freda was the middle sister, and my mother the youngest. The oldest, Vivyenne—Aunt Vivy—had vanished abroad. She had married Walter Revell, an able and courageous British officer in the Engineer Corps, who had earned the DSO (the Distinguished Service Order) in the First World War. Vivy was good for an annual letter, usually accompanied by a hilarious poem. A strident woman and more English than the English, she frightened my mother.

Teedah, by contrast, was the sweet and worldly-wise aunt. She had opted early for independence. She trained as a secretary. Her skills placed her at the center of an entire network of well-placed and diverse persons in Dublin. She supported the well-known Dublin doctor Tom Wilson (1901–1969) as his appointment secretary. "Miss Warren" was a name to conjure with. She was even mentioned and praised in the annual pantomime at the Gaiety Theatre by none other than the great Dublin comic Jimmie O'Dea (1899–1965). He was the cameo Irishman—rather, the Irishwoman: for he played Biddie Mulligan of Ballygobackwards on *Irish Hour* on the BBC. But at the Gaiety he was the authentic voice of Dublin. He would often come up with a witty "call out" for Teedah.

Teedah, also, was the tolerant aunt. Her move to Dublin had taken her out of the narrow cubicles in which the Warrens of Bray and the Browns of Lansdowne Road were both, in their different ways, enclosed. She was pointedly loyal to her Jewish doctor, Dr. Abrahams. She kept in close contact with the family of her Catholic cousin Brian Daly. Her very best friend was a lady from Athlone who had converted to Catholicism. Not only did Teedah serve for years in the Society for Distressed Gentlefolk. She also did good by stealth to many families. When I attended her funeral on an icy day in February 1984, I was astonished to find, at the back of the church, a weeping woman. She had been one of the many recipients, over the years, of "Miss Warren's kindnesses."

For me she was the indulgent aunt. While Mai was of granite, Teedah was "Cream Cakes and Cuddles" incarnate. Every month, Teedah would drive down from Dublin to Aravon in her little Austin Mini to take me out for a Sunday lunch and tea. We would park by the seaside, immune to the rain in the comfortable leather upholstery of the Mini. She would read to me the wickedly ironic short stories of "Saki" (H. H. Munro).

Above all, Teedah had the gift for encouraging men of all ages to show off unashamedly in her presence. She drew me out—a little boy full of news and views from Aravon and Lansdowne Road. I remember her now: with a cigarette in one hand and a glass of sherry in the other, her legs crossed with a hint (to which my mother drew attention, with a certain envy) of French silk lingerie. The chair in which she sat—a low chair, suited to her rather dumpy figure—is the one that I still use to read and take notes on a board placed across its two long arms, close enough to the floor to enable me to reach down for the books piled at its feet.

A Totemic Dog: Rory

Rory was my aunt Mai's dog. For me he was more than a dog. He was a sibling and a totemic beast. He was a mongrel, the result of an amorous encounter between a pedigree spaniel and a Labrador. That meant, in Irish terms, that Rory was the product of that most charged of liaisons—a mixed marriage. He was, indeed, a striking mixture. His ears went up, and then drooped softly. His tail was as covered with fine hair as a fly whisk. He had a beard like a Chinese dragon. He had bandy legs that combined soft, woolly flanks with robust, gnarled forelegs. He was more than a dog to me. He was a link to the rough earth of Ireland. But what was that Ireland like?

WHO'S WHAT?

IDENTITIES

"You Know Where He Is . . ."

On April 30, 1945, Adolf Hitler committed suicide. That same morning, I had lost my front tooth while roller skating, and on the next day, May 1, my aunt Freda (Teedah to me) took me to the dentist in Dublin.

We took the number 8 bus, which passed the German embassy at 58 Northumberland Road. On that day, the huge black swastika, set in a white circle on a great crimson drape, was flying at half-mast above the door of the embassy. We were on the top of the bus, so we passed this obscene thing at eye level. There were murmurs all around the bus. But my aunt Freda was cautious. In neutral Ireland, one never quite knew what others thought about Britain and the Reich. It was safer not to show too much jubilation. Freda leaned toward me and whispered to me in a low voice, "You know where *he* is, Peds." I answered, "Indeed I do, Auntie." It was my first lesson in spiritual geography: Hitler was in Hell.

Neutrality

My aunt Freda had better reasons than I knew to have lowered her voice on that bus. She had been directly involved in a serious breach of neutrality on behalf of British airmen. She was secretary to Dr. Thomas Wilson, a notable eye, ear, and throat doctor who played a major role in setting up an "underground railway." British airmen who had been forced to land in Ireland were interned (as part of the neutrality policy of states such as Ireland, Switzerland, and

Sweden during the war). Tom helped these airmen to escape from the internment camp in the Curragh, and to make their way back to British territory by
crossing the border into Northern Ireland. He was discovered and convicted
in 1942.

While under threat of a jail sentence (which was later suspended), he finished a biography of the famous Dublin physician Sir William Wilde, who was
the father of Oscar Wilde. It was called *Victorian Doctor* and was illustrated by
copper engravings made by Tom himself. Always something of a mystery man,
Tom was rumored to be the illegitimate son of Oscar Wilde. Freda had a copy
of *Victorian Doctor*. In it, Tom Wilson had written,

> To Freda Warren, My friend in adversity.

As his secretary, Freda had loyally kept his practice going in those difficult
years, and may well have had a hand in helping the escape of the British
airmen.

Where Did I Belong?

By 1945, at the age of ten, I was already affected by the tension between my
father's involvement in the war in Sudan and the strangely sheltered atmosphere of a neutral Ireland. It made me wonder where I was and who I was.
Many young children have these feelings. But the form they took was specific
to my own situation.

For instance, I now learned that I was a "native" of Ireland. But I had read
that "natives" were dangerous creatures, and prone to "risings." The *Handbook
of the Anglo-Egyptian Sudan* of 1922 listed thirteen such risings between 1901
and 1916, and added ten more recent ones in an appendix.

> The number of these fanatics, petty as many of the "risings" seem, justifies
> the unsleeping vigilance of the government.[1]

But we in Ireland had mounted any number of "risings" against British rule.
These had culminated in *the* Rising—the "Easter Rising" of 1916; and we were,
by and large, almighty proud of it. I needed only to travel on the top of a bus
past the General Post Office, which had been the center of the famous Easter
Rising of 1916, to be impressed (as small children tended to be) by the bullet
holes that riddled the great allegorical figures in bronze which flanked the

---

1. *A Handbook of the Anglo-Egyptian Sudan* (Naval Staff Intelligence Division, 1922), 178.

monument to Daniel O'Connell, making their ample bosoms look like colanders.

So where did I belong? And, above all, *how much* did I belong and to what? The notion of "fidelity to the nation" (a catchword in nationalist circles in Ireland at this time) seemed to imply a disturbingly open-ended commitment. What did it really mean? For members of the Protestant minority in the Republic (that self-conscious 5 percent) it always posed a problem. How Irish did we have to be to be authentically "Irish"? Did we have to speak Irish (or at least attempt to learn it)? Did we have to have an authentic "Irish" accent? Last of all, did we even have to abandon our Protestant religion in order to be accepted, by our fellow countrymen, as "real" Irish—that is, as Catholics?

Every time I got on a bus, I faced these issues in miniature. When I wanted to get to the center of the city, would I ask for a ticket to "Nelson's Pillar" (the original English name of the high pillar that bore a statue of Lord Nelson) or simply to "the Pillar"? Would I be able to ask for it in a homely, flat Dublin accent? Or would my attempts to avoid a stammer by speaking slowly and with careful enunciation come out as a high-pitched, "hoity-toity" English voice? I found myself as if walking on stilts, perched above the "real" soil of Ireland, confined by my squeaky voice and the cramp across the chest caused by my stammer. I was a permanent "not quite."

"Are Cowboys Catholics?"

Altogether, I grew up in a world where religion was still a primary identity. My map of society was structured with all-embracing precision around the binary of Catholic and Protestant. Every person had to be fitted onto that map. So what about cowboys? My mother had presented me, at the age of four, with a box of tin cowboys. I, in turn, dropped her a heavy hint: would she, perhaps, like a cowboy outfit for her next birthday? I wanted to be a cowboy; but, before I could fully identify with these wild men, I had to know one thing: were they Catholics or Protestants? Nobody could tell me.

The binary also passed through the animal world. The dog in the family mill in Dublin, which my father came to manage after his return from Sudan, was known as "the Protestant dog." For it would howl when the bells of the neighboring Catholic church tolled the Angelus at midday. Not even our cat was immune from suspicion. It would come in to us after its long sleep among the warm pine needles of a neighboring wood, smelling suspiciously of incense. Had the cat gone to Mass?

Such anecdotes make good stories. But it was just as well that I knew nothing of the tragedy of my poor aunt. Like the granite outcrops washed by the waves along the coast of Dublin, the religious prejudices of Ireland seemed, most of the time, to be reassuring rather than oppressive. They were rock firm. You knew where you stood. But the warm stone dropped into chill depths, where seaweed and slime gathered in a bitter sea. For both sides, active intolerance, rather than simply separation, was always just round the corner.

My sense of the power of religion in society dates from those Dublin days. Coming to England as a schoolboy and later as a student, I was surprised by the genteel oblivion to religion that seemed to be widespread at the time, in contrast to the ethos of Ireland. I remained puzzled, and increasingly frustrated, by finding a similar underestimating of religion as a social force in many of the teachers of history in Oxford. It was against what struck me as this cozy attitude that I would direct much of my work in later years.

13

THE MODERN WORLD

The Modern World

On August 8, 1945, Japan surrendered, after the dropping of atomic bombs on Hiroshima and Nagasaki. The news came when I was in the stadium of the Royal Dublin Society Horseshow, watching the horse-jumping competitions. It takes some effort to remember what it was like when news was tied so closely to place. Those away from their home radio depended on the evening newspapers for news of the day.

At the end of the afternoon, as the events were about to wind down, there was a sudden murmur at the bottom end of the stadium. The evening newspapers had arrived with the news of Japan's surrender. A wave of sound started from that one corner and spread, like a gust of the wind across a wheat field, until it engulfed the entire stadium.

It was a memorable moment. Looking back, I realize that I had witnessed one of the last examples of a phenomenon that reached back to Rome and Byzantium—the sudden swell of human sound across a gathering assembled in a hippodrome. For the remainder of the summer, I would stand on the rocks at the edge of the sea, satisfying a small boy's zest for big bangs, by dropping flat stones into the water, in the hope of producing mushroom-shaped splashes.

Like many persons of the time, I thought that, with the surrender of Japan, a bucolic peace would descend on the world. The sports news would move to the front page of the newspapers. Instead, the newspapers came to be filled with gray news, particularly disturbing to those with a stake in the world "abroad." From Hong Kong to India, the British Empire rapidly unraveled. Strange peoples, led by leaders with strange names, pushed their way into the headlines.

For Christmas 1947, my parents gave me a subscription to *The Sphere*, a weekly photojournal of a new sort. With its high quality black-and-white photographs, *The Sphere* was my entry point to the modern world. It caught the ambiguities of the immediate postwar period. Sinister blurred photos of emergent Communist dictators in Eastern Europe ran side by side with group portraits of the royal family still shining in full regalia, and with images of the most modern of modern objects: streamlined cars; airplanes on the threshold of the jet age; buildings with curved walls, their façades consisting of portholes and sheets of glass.

My absorption of *The Sphere* marked a change for me. I was less a schoolboy and more a solitary reader. Classes continued. The Boss still roared. Bowlby still inspired. But what I remember best was settling into my bed, now in the attic bedroom at the very top of "Number Sixty," looking out on the lights of central Dublin and the Liffey Dockland, and reading, with a torch beneath the blankets, long after lights were supposed to be off, sad tales of the modern world: *Germany Puts the Clock Back* by Edgar Mowrer and *Hiroshima* by John Hershey.

Entirely to one side of my Aravon curriculum (where no science was taught), I became a little scientist. When my cousins, Jennifer and Alison, visited us from Scotland, we would share our knowledge of dangerous substances:

> Jennifer, I, and Alison do lots of chemistry, we are trying to make gunpowder and are trying hard to make gunpowder and are <u>not</u> being successful. Auntie Mai hopes we aren't and we hope we are.

Alas, we were. We burned a hole into the hearth rug of the drawing room.

This change of interest owed much to my father. He could now return on yearly leave from Sudan. I loved the engineer in him. He would explain the workings of his railway lines, and how the old piston engine differed from the modern diesel. He had seen the very first jet planes being tested in the desert in Sudan. He showed me his plans for complex railroad constructions drawn up with exquisite draftsmanship. He was, indeed, an engineer's engineer.

Altogether, my father now came to sum up for me another side of Irish Protestant culture—the rational, Enlightenment side that had produced great scientists. For instance, there was the famous mathematician Sir Rowan Hamilton (1805–1865), the director of Dunsink Observatory in Dublin and discoverer of Hamiltonian mechanics. We could still see where Hamilton had carved the formula for quaternion equations on Portobello Bridge, when it came to him on a walk along the Dublin Canal. (He was said to have intuited the mathematics necessary to predict the trajectory of moving objects—a mathematics that proved crucial to the development of antiaircraft gunnery in the Second Word War—by watching the young ladies of Dublin playing the daring new game of tennis.)

ASTRONOMY

Most important of all, my father lent me his binoculars to do stargazing when on holiday at Portsalon, in Donegal. For the first time, I viewed the moons of Jupiter. It was an extraordinary experience. I was no longer looking *at* Jupiter. With the aid of a pair of eight-magnification binoculars, I was looking *into* the satellite system of the planet. I could almost feel the distances on which Jupiter and its moons floated in the depths of space.

I read *The Stars in Their Courses*, a history of modern astronomy, by Sir James Jeans (1877–1946). I also discovered, in the hotel at Portsalon, older books of astronomy. In them, the new discoveries of the immensity of the universe and complexity of the galaxies were still presented, in a thoroughly Victorian manner, as evidences of the majesty of God's Creation. By 1950 I was reading far more daring stuff. *The Nature of the Universe*, by Fred Hoyle (1915–2001), delivered on the famous BBC Radio 4 (the cultural and scientific program, which was very much the voice of rationalist, progressive England), took me to the edge. Could I really imagine (as Hoyle encouraged me to do, in his last pages) that our universe itself was only one of many? Could I accept that it differed in no way from the newly discovered mini-universes of atomic particles? Indeed, our own galaxy might be just that. I speculated that it might even be an atomic particle in the leg of a very big dog, barking (I presumed, like Rory) in outer space. Seen in this way, from the viewpoint of the universe, the vertigos of difference that separated natives from residents abroad, neutral Irish from British and Germans, and even Protestants from Catholics, suddenly appeared to be mercifully insignificant.

Little did I know it, but I was on the edge of a decision that would have altered the entire course of my future career. I had intended to opt for science when I went on to my next school on leaving Aravon. Science had the additional attraction for me that it seemed to be an easier career for me, given my stammer: it did not demand public speaking to such an extent as would law, teaching, or membership of the clergy. Given the rigidity of the school systems in Ireland and England, this choice would have led to almost immediate specialization in science at the expense of arts subjects, such as languages or history. But my low performance in mathematics exams—for I had been lamentably taught by the Boss—ruled this out. Astronomy would remain a hobby for me, and not the way into a scientific career.

INVALIDED OUT

Looking back on the years immediately after the war, I am a little uncertain as to the exact chronology of important events. My parents and I were more often together, and so there was no need for the regular correspondence that I can now use to date events in the wartime years. But the reason for this blurring was deeper. Developments were taking place that were totally hidden from me by my parents. After years of strain in wartime, my father's health had collapsed.

During the war, my father was responsible for maintaining the crucial link between Port Sudan and Atbara, and equally the link between Atbara and the rest of Sudan. It was a new burden for him. As long as the Mediterranean was closed by the German and Italian occupation of much of North Africa, Port Sudan—hitherto a rather small port—replaced Suez. The flow of soldiers and matériel between Britain and India had to pass through Africa, via Port Sudan and Atbara.[1]

Partly as a result of the strain of work, my father developed a kidney disease, anemia, and cutaneous leishmaniasis—a peculiarly draining and painful form of skin infection, all too well known in the Middle East under various names, such as "Jericho Boil." In 1947, he underwent treatment for the skin infection, as well as an operation that removed one kidney, leaving him dependent, for the rest of his life, on a little bottle of hydrochloric acid. Characteristically, he took great pride in having this bottle always available, tucked away neatly in a special little travel case. Keeping himself alive was yet another job for him to do well.

But my father's Sudan days were over. On October 8, 1948, he sent a telegram to Teedah from London:

INVALIDED OUT AS FROM TODAY PROBABLY BAYLERYS CONSIDER BEST THING SQUAIRES DEFINITELY THINK THAT I AM WISE. SPLENDID TRIP. ALL LOVE = JIM

---

1. R. C. Hill, *Sudan Transport: A History of Railway, Marine and River Services in the Republic of the Sudan* (Oxford University Press, 1965), 209.

The telegram referred to a final interview with the Sudan Government Agency in London, in which he was signed off and retired as a result of a medical report.

This final visit to London took place immediately after my parents had left me off at Shrewsbury School, in Shropshire. For my father had planned an abroad for me. I would not stay in Ireland. Although public schools on an English model existed there—Saint Columba's in Dublin; Portora in the North—he plainly wanted something else for me. As early as 1946, he and my mother visited Shrewsbury for a day, when at home from Sudan, as part of a lightning tour of relatives in England. He was given a Shrewsbury School Prospectus at that time. It is revealing that the only passage which he marked up in the margin was that which concerned Entrance Scholarships. These were worth about eighty pounds a year, and were awarded on the basis of the results of an examination that took place at the school in early June of every year, for entrance in the winter.

And so, in early June 1948, I traveled to Shrewsbury with my parents to take the scholarship examination. Of this, I remember only two things. The first was the extraordinary quietness and beauty of the tree-lined plateau on which the school was set; and the song of the cuckoo in the early morning. The second was the winding blow of the mathematics papers. Framed in the most beguiling manner, with deliberately comic problems to be solved, they were utterly opaque to me. I handed in, literally, a clean sheet. By contrast, I enjoyed the history and English papers so much that, although I did not receive a scholarship, I was urged to come to Shrewsbury and to try again. The Boss had let me down. Bowlby had done me proud.

At this time, I already knew that my father was ill. I had visited him in 1947, after his kidney had been removed, at Portobello Nursing Home—a splendid Georgian building, near the bridge over the Dublin Canal where Sir Rowan Hamilton had written his famous equations. We talked seriously about the nature of jet propulsion. He explained the virtues and the working of hydrochloric acid. He was sitting up, with a little smile on his lips, making the best of a hospital meal. He explained to me how to make a surgical incision—a "Lane-like incision," he called it, from the name of Dr. Lane, the surgeon who had just removed his kidney—across the soft surface of a poached egg. He loved skill of any kind.

At the time, I had no idea that this illness had caught his plans for me in a cruel scissor cut. Just as he had begun to commit himself to a future for me in an English public school, his income dropped suddenly. Had he been able to stay on in Sudan until 1952, he could have retired on a full pension. Invalided out before his time, he could count on only half that amount.

I discovered this just a few years ago, when I found the letters that my father had written to J. M. Peterson, the headmaster of Shrewsbury School, in July 1952. They did not concern my fees at Shrewsbury. He had paid those regularly and uncomplainingly, on his limited income. What worried him was whether he could now send me to Oxford. He had been told that Shrewsbury awarded Leaving Scholarships, to support some of their best scholars at the universities. Peterson had asked him for a full statement of his finances. Here it is:

I do not know what information exactly might be required, but the facts of my position are that when Peter was entered for Shrewsbury I was in a senior post in the Traffic Department of the Sudan Railways. I had the prospect of occupying the post of Traffic Manager during the last three years of my service, with a considerable step in pay and consequent on that, a substantial increase in pension also. Then when I was Assistant Traffic Manager I was sent home ill, and, after having had a diseased kidney removed and being found to be suffering from a type of pernicious anemia caused by tropical conditions (for which I must have treatment for the rest of my life) I was invalided out of Sudan Government Service. Since then I have also been found to have a form of arthritis affecting the lower part of my spine.

A Sudan Government pension is calculated with relation to, partly, length of service and, secondly, to the pay drawn during the final two years of full service, and just before the final two years of service. Any one such as I, compelled to retire some years short of full service, and just before receiving the greatly increased pay of a post such as that of Traffic Manager, is entitled to a much smaller pension than he would have received if able to serve through to the normal retiring age.

As a result, instead of leaving the Sudan this year (1952) after Peter had completed his career at Shrewsbury, while I was in a well-paid post, and with a good pension to look forward to I had to face the whole period of Peter's time at Shrewsbury and at a University on a pension very much smaller than it would have been if my career had gone ahead normally.

My fitness [was sufficient to enable me to] to take up a Directorship and Managerial post that I was given in a small family firm manufacturing animal feeding stuffs. But conditions in that industry have been far from good, and I have never been able to draw more than a small salary and, at the moment, prospects for a continuance of the business at all are not very good.

As regards my annual income from pension is just over £621 and from my salary and fees £410. I am receiving (and will receive until 1955) £100 a year from an Educational Endowment Insurance. I have no private means.

I was appalled when I read this many years after his death. It meant that my parents had returned to Ireland to face a considerably more cramped life than they had expected. They had enough to "maintain their estate"—as Tudor gentry had once said. They bought a house in Glenageary: "Summerland," at the top of Castle Park Road. Glenageary was halfway between the two worlds of Bray and Dublin. It was within easy walking distance of Dalkey Hill—with its splendid view across Killiney Beach and the Vale of Shanganagh to Bray Head in the south. To walk down Castle Park Road was to come out onto the coastal road that led straight to Dublin, and Sandycove Harbor (well known for the Martello tower associated with James Joyce and the writing of his *Ulysses*) and the Forty Foot—a famous Gentleman's Bathing Place.

In this house (a house without central heating, it goes without saying), good family furniture decorated the rooms. Silver and china from their wedding gifts appeared on the tables on special occasions. My father ran a car. We even had a maid for a short time. But the frills of life that give an extra space to the retired, just as their lives seem to be closing in, were denied them. My father would have dearly loved to be a member of a golf club, even of a yachting club. A polite and witty man, he would have thriven on that extra dimension to his life. As it was, he was effectively housebound as he grew older, except for visits to Dublin for the occasional good gossip with his brother Billy at Bewley's Café in Westmoreland Street.

But of all this I heard nothing—no complaints, not the slightest emphasis on the sacrifices that my father had made for my education. It is a tribute to my father's quiet, stoic courage, and to my mother's loyalty to him, that not a word of this was breathed to me when they set out with me, in early October 1948, on the mail boat to Holyhead, and then by train to Shrewsbury, to leave me in the new "abroad" that they had planned for me.

TO BE A TWEAK

SHREWSBURY SCHOOL

I had not been altogether wrong in my first impressions of Shrewsbury School when I came from Ireland to take my scholarship examination in early June of 1948. It was a stunningly beautiful site. The school buildings and the Houses (where the boys slept, ate, and lived: each a fine mansion of its own) lay around a great sea of green grass, framed by avenues of ancient trees. The steep drop from the plateau down to the river Severn made the school seem to hover above the town.

It was a quiet place. Aravon had been full of noise—from the spasmodic roars of the Boss to the constant monkey-chatter of "Senior Teasing." In Shrewsbury, it was as if the soundtrack had been turned off. I found myself surrounded by quiet, polite voices, speaking in perfectly pitched tones. The Boss no longer roared. Even the mathematics master, Mr. Hadland—who had to teach me a subject that, at the hands of the Boss at Aravon, had been a source of constant terror—struck me at once (despite a gruff voice and gnarled face) as a gentle man. The only time he roared was when he was prevailed upon by the boys to treat us to a dramatic rendering, in the original Aramaic, of the story of Daniel in the Lions' Den. Not surprisingly, my math progressed in leaps and bounds.

As for the boys, they were soft-spoken little gentlemen. They worked by words. In Aravon, by contrast, fistfighting had been normal. We were little squireens, given to furious brawling. But the tongues of these little English gentlemen could be as wounding as the fist. When first subjected to well-aimed verbal "ragging"—on my stammer and on my Irish-ness—by fellow members of my study room, I found myself living down to the stereotype of the "wild Irishman." I swung a chair at my tormentors. This was deemed to be a social faux pas. But it cleared the air.

Unknowingly, I had stumbled against the sharp edge of what was a totally new phenomenon to me—the English class system. Here, in Shrewsbury, boys were molded by smooth words. The control of speech (along with the control of manners) was the secret of what an acute Sudanese observer of this time had seen in English public school men: "a soft, gentle superiority."

> There are people who tell you that they are your lords. With the English you know it by yourself.[1]

This was all new to me: I had not encountered a class system of this kind in Ireland. I came from a more archaic, "tribal" world. Whether brutish or well-groomed, whether rich or as poor as church mice, Protestants were "our crowd." That was all the identity they needed. The English boys, by contrast, seemed less sure of their position in society. As I came to know them, over the years, they increasingly struck me as if they were always attempting to climb a greasy pole, inching ever farther up, and always afraid that they might slip down. They seemed to be constantly measuring their position against others by their accents, by their manners, by innumerable unspoken acts of adaptation to the speech, ways, and interests of their betters. Successful mimesis was the way to the top.

Fortunately, these aspects of the English class system were not as oppressive in Shrewsbury as in the public schools of southern England. David Gee, the historian of Shrewsbury, has rightly said that the school fostered "a 'northern' (or, at least, non-metropolitan) individualism."[2] It was, indeed, a surprisingly diverse school. My parents had chosen Shrewsbury, in large part, because it had the reputation for taking in Irish boys.

Shrewsbury had begun as a grammar school, housed in an elegant Tudor building in the middle of town. In the 1940s, it still preserved something of the embedded quality of a local school. Many pupils came from the neighboring

1. Francis M. Deng, "In the Eyes of the Ruled," in *The British in the Sudan, 1898–1956*, ed. Robert O. Collins and Francis M. Deng (London: Macmillan, 1984), 216–243, at 229.

2. *The Salopian*, no. 150 (Summer 2010): 5.

gentry or were the sons of well-to-do farmers. A friend of mine was allowed to take Thursdays off every week. This was so that he could help his father bring his cows into the weekly cattle market.

To add to the mix, Wales was close. Shrewsbury was a "Marcher" town. It lay on the frontier between England and Wales. And Wales was a Celtic country. When I arrived at Holyhead, I had to communicate to the railway porters that my precious trunk should be put on the Chester train, and then to change for Shrewsbury. This meant approaching large men, who spoke a mellifluous Welsh. When the effort to communicate my wishes proved too much for my stammer, they would gather round me, chanting encouragement in English: "Sing it, sonny! Sing it!" To take the train from Holyhead, skirting the mountains of Snowdonia in the dawn light, was to travel through another Ireland.

But Shrewsbury also reached out to the very different England of Liverpool and the industrial northern Midlands. Liverpool boys, the sons of industrialists, added a splash of raw color to the House. Their fathers would appear at inter-House soccer matches. They and their Liverpool cronies were used to the free-spoken manners of the professional soccer stadium. They notably lacked sportsmanship. They would barrack vigorously, with shouts of "Specs Ref!!" whenever the team of their offspring was penalized. It was said that our housemaster (the most gentlemanly of men) had been insulted in this way, when acting as a referee. He bore a permanent grudge against Liverpool boys. But Liverpool boys stood for urban sophistication. They brought from home copies of the *News of the World*—a newspaper notorious for its spicy reportage of sexual misdemeanors.

Altogether, arriving at Shrewsbury was a pleasant surprise. In my very first letter, I reassured my parents that I was safe among the English. They were not as arrogant or abrasive as my parents had feared they might be. I had fallen among the right sort of gentlemen. For all their insidious sense of class, most of them were polite and good-natured. Such mildness even puzzled me. By Irish standards, they appeared to be softies. They raised neither their voices nor their fists. But this softness came as a welcome relief. It was the equivalent of the wide and quiet prospects of the plateau on which the school was placed.

To Be a Tweak: Hierarchy and Ambition

Though spared many of the nastier aspects of the English class system, Shrewsbury School made up for this by creating its own complex hierarchies. Within a week, I was memorizing "The Colour Book." This book itemized, in

Byzantine detail, an entire structure of privileges and forms of dress that distinguished every category of boys from every other: who could wear silk handkerchiefs in their jacket front pockets; who must wear their jackets tightly buttoned, who could wear them on one button only; who—what immortals!—could allow their jackets to flap open, as they strode across lawns forbidden to lesser beings.

Yet I do not remember finding this intricate system oppressive or conformist. For (as in Byzantium) it did not erect a series of barriers to achievement so much as provide a map of the routes that led to the top. And it also showed that the top could be reached by more than one route. Inevitably, given public school attitudes to games, sportsmen were privileged. They were known to the less sporting as "thicks." They were creatures of brawn, not of brain. But they were not the only ones at the top. The route map of privileges showed other, less conventional paths.

Indeed, to a remarkable degree, the structure and ethos of Shrewsbury encouraged each of us to "customize" his own excellence. Despite a heavy prejudice in favor of sportsmen, there was a remarkable amount of freedom in the choice of personae in which to excel. It was the race to the top that mattered. A constant, headlong search for distinction made the life of the school as electric and as all-absorbing as the politics of any ancient Greek *polis* or medieval Italian city-state.

Hence the weight of the word "tweak." This word—tweak—was so deeply embedded in the consciousness of the school that I have not, so far, been able to trace its origin. But its meaning was clear. It meant that you could get away with doing anything as long as you did it well, with a certain epic *démesure*—and made sure that others knew that you were doing it. To be a tweak showed that you were fully engaged, in your own way, in the race to the top. You could be a tweak in many surprising things. Dull dogs and thicks could be tweaks in soccer, rowing, and cricket. But you could also be a tweak in dirty jokes—a veritable rhapsode of smut. It didn't matter, as long as you did it with flair and energy.

My very first contact at Shrewsbury was with one such tweak. Seamus Finn was an older boy who had been assigned to me as my "guardian angel" when I first arrived. (His name betokened an Irish background: he was probably chosen to be my guide for that reason.) Plump, with tight, frizzy, light ginger (almost albino) hair and gold-rimmed spectacles, he was already a tweak. And to my delight, he was a tweak in history. At the age of fourteen, he had provided the *Round Britain Quiz* on the BBC with questions as to the titles of little-known rulers: What was the name, for instance, of the ruler of Swat? (The "Akhoond," of course!):

> he's a wonder at royal genealogy and can make a tree of the Spanish Succession from Maximilian to Louis XIV in a minute.

Now *that* was a tweak after my own heart! Like a rare bird treading delicately across a pool of crocodiles, Seamus held to his reputation as a "Super Nerd" throughout his time at Shrewsbury. He suffered no disturbance or opprobrium from the "thicks" and the sportsmen. He was accepted as a tweak among tweaks. What sort of tweak would I try to be?

15

YOU SHALL DO GREEK

CLASSICS SIDE

I had come to Shrewsbury with every intention of becoming a scientist. This is easily explained by a long-delayed identification with my father, an engineer who had just returned from six years of absence. My choice was also linked to my passion for astronomy, and to what I had sensed of the robust attitudes of the Irish Protestant Enlightenment. Science meant Progress in the face of bigotry and superstition. Despite my bad performance in mathematics in the Shrewsbury entrance exam, I was determined to enter the modern age by opting for science.

The powers that be in Shrewsbury thought otherwise. I was summoned by my housemaster, W. E. "Willy" Matthews. On this occasion he resembled an English schoolmaster straight out of central casting—corduroy trousers, tweed jacket, pipe, and all. He addressed me in between puffs. "Brown," he said, "[puff] ... you have done too well in your Entrance Scholarship ... [puff] ... to do [puff] ... Science. You shall do ... [puff] ... *Greek*."

And so I did. For all the coming year, I joined the prestigious Classics Side. It was as a classical scholar, versed in Latin and Greek, that I resat the scholarship examination, gaining an award of eighty pounds, and also passed the Britain-wide School Certificate. At the end of the year, I opted for history rather than classics. But I never went back to science.

Little did I know at the time that this would prove to be an irrevocable step. It takes some leap of the imagination (especially for those used to an American system of education) to realize the degree of specialization from an early age that my choice implied. The range of topics taught to me narrowed dramatically, year by year, as I concentrated more and more on a single chosen subject. By the age of fourteen I was already doing ten periods of history a week, eight of French—and only three of geography and two of physics. My commitment to history would grow higher and higher like a mesa, leaving sheer precipices of ignorance on every side—no science, no economics, very little English.

I was not the only one whose field of vision had narrowed. Scientists were equally locked into their chosen field. They virtually abandoned the humanities. By the age of fifteen, I found myself running a thriving business. In exchange for Mars bars (made doubly precious currency by postwar candy rationing) I would ghostwrite the English essays of members of the Science VIth. I was fully complicit in the division between "the two cultures" (that of science and that of the humanities) which Lord Snow (1905–1980) would soon come to lament in a memorable pamphlet.

As I look back, the degree of specialization in the education offered in the English public schools leaves me aghast. But how else could I be a "tweak"? How else could Shrewsbury come to shine? This brutal narrowing of focus was due to an overpowering ambition, shared by every public school in England: that some of their students should excel in exams. In each school, bright boys were singled out and trained like pedigree racehorses to do one thing and one thing only—to succeed in a succession of examinations on their core subject: Entrance Scholarship; School Certificate; State Scholarship; and, finally—like the bull's-eye on a target waiting for an arrow to strike home—the supreme victory of a scholarship at Oxford or Cambridge. That Willy M. directed me toward Greek meant that I was to aim at the most prestigious scholarship of all—a scholarship in classics.

The culture of examinations, which already reached back to when I first wrote "JAM" for my spelling test in Aravon, now closed in around me. From the age of thirteen (in 1948) to the time that I took the All Souls Fellowship Exam at twenty-one (in 1956), my fate was decided at every step in this way.

In order to understand the schools and universities of Britain at this time, one must remember the omnipresence and the rigidity of that basic system. We did not receive grades in our courses: there were no report cards filling up the years with a continuous assessment of my progress, on the American model. My fate would be determined by a few, crucial examinations. Even if I did not spend my entire time "swotting" for exams, I knew that they were there. I knew that I would have to face a small number of high moments—each as lonely, as exalted, and as inexorable as a public execution or a medieval ordeal. On each occasion, I would sit down in front of a carefully printed page (the number of questions to be answered and the time allowed always shown in bold type) and would begin to write, hoping to score—in a series of three-hour papers, spread over a few days—those marks in arcane Greek (alpha plus, alpha, alpha minus, alpha/beta, and so on down) on which the entire course of my academic career would depend. I was a "scholarship boy" through and through.

"Ferny"

It was just as well that I knew nothing at the time of these forbidding implications. As it was, Greek and Latin opened my heart. The master in charge of the Junior Classics form was the school chaplain, the Reverend Cuthbert Guy Furnival. He was known to his charges as "Ferny." He was the best sort of romantic Hellenist. He would tell us, with unalloyed pleasure, that, in Greece, the modern word for motorcar—*avtokiníton*—derived directly from classical Greek. I last met Ferny in Athens, in 1958, as happy as a child, bathed in sunlight and on his way to the Parthenon.

Ferny plainly loved what he taught. He somehow managed to reach down to deeper levels than the usual stone-breaking exercise in "Construe"— "construction": the dogged, word-by-word translation and grammatical analysis of classical texts—that made up most of our classical reading. As we read book 6 of Vergil's *Aeneid*, a change in the tone of Ferny's usual, somewhat bleating, clerical voice ensured that we would feel with him the magic of Aeneas's descent into the underworld. He chanted the lines. He communicated that Latin was not all about grammar. It was also about feeling. Locked away in a majestic, pre-Christian past, a pagan world of shifting shapes and ambiguous desires was there to be entered. I wrote to my parents, "Doing dash good 'Stru' about Orpheus and Eurydice, about caligentem nigram horridine fauces of which Ferny is very fond." Then I added, by way of more manly, less scholarly validation, "Found out that he was an excellent Rugger player."

At this time, the golden mists of a distant age (like the fog that rose on winter's evenings from the river Severn and mingled in a golden glow with the lights of the school Houses) began to swirl around me. It blocked out the clear, cold spaces of the stars. Within a term, along with the upsurge of so many new emotions at the beginning of my teens, I passed, irrevocably, from science to the humanities, with Ferny's Vergil as my guide.

Greek opened other worlds to me. It had begun as a slog. My very first act of conscious impiety was to decide, on a strict cost-opportunity basis, to devote my attention in school chapel not to the Psalms but to the silent recitation of Greek irregular verbs. But even this grind added a further dimension to my heart. When muttering verbs, I would stare at the stained glass windows of the school chapel. These were classic examples of what could be called "Anglican Hellenism." Here was an idealized ancient world, in which Apostles and Fathers of the Church were dressed in impeccable togas. In scenes of the life of Saint Martin or of the confrontation between Saint Ambrose and Theodosius I, holy persons in pure classical garb appeared before emperors and their soldiers, who were dressed in uniforms taken straight from our textbooks of Roman history. Eventually, Greek and Latin would open up for me not only the road back to Athens and Rome, but also (and just as importantly) the road to Galilee and to Saint Paul.

MODERN SIDE

THE MODERN SIDE

In 1949, I decided to join what was known as the Modern Side as distinct from the Classics Side and the Science Side. In other words, I would try to become a tweak in history. What surprises me, on looking back, is the extent to which I was left on my own in these years, to do it my way. One would have thought that so determined an effort to encourage boys to excel as specialists would lead to heavy class schedules. But this was not so. Shrewsbury boys were encouraged to become pensive readers quite as much as they were expected to shine in examinations. What I remember best were delicious stretches of free time even in my first year. As I wrote to my parents:

> hardly any of us had been set work to do, so I learnt off a few Greek adjectives, completed a well composed summary of Roman expansion, 220–133 B.C. by P.R.L. Brown, then spent a blissful 2½ more periods designing a model rocket jet and the jet plane to fly with it and then working out the weight of the earth by logs [logarithms] and the weight of iron, I was only a 1000 tons out, and then drew a few models of cars, a picture of Charles II and some characters from "Twelfth Night", the book we're doing for School Cert.

I soon found my way to the school library. Known as the Moser Library, it was a gem. A capacious bow window in Tudor style looked out over the river and the town. I would sit there, working my way through the entire run of copies of *Punch*—the humorous and political journal that stretched from the 1840s to the present. I looked principally at the political cartoons for which *Punch* was famous. These cartoons provided a memorable, visual commentary on the politics of the day. Mr. Punch, I noticed, had no love for my compatriots. Irishmen would regularly appear with long upper lips and bandy legs, like noxious apes. Most chilling of all, in 1916, was the drawing of a gallows rising into lowering clouds, above a scene of utter destruction that evoked the carnage of the Battle of the Somme. It bore the title "For Traitors!" This was *our* Easter Rising—the beginning of Irish independence—seen from across the sea.

More decisive still, it was through the Moser Library that I learned to look at the stars with a historian's eyes. In modern terms, I "historicized" my passion for astronomy. When writing a long (eighteen-and-a-half-page) essay entitled "Science in the Seventeenth Century—Was There a Scientific Revolution?" I stumbled on a shelf that contained the earliest publications of the Royal Society (the society of scientists founded by Charles II). I read the account by Robert Hooke (1635–1703) of his attempt to observe, through a Gregorian telescope, the moons of Mars and Jupiter. I realized that Hooke was using a telescope of roughly the same resolution as my father's binoculars. Hooke and I both peered into space with the same equipment, to scan the same planet. But what was it like to be Hooke: to see those dancing spots of light with the eyes of a man of the seventeenth century? This was my first serious attempt to enter the *minds* of people in the past. And these were not kings, generals, or politicians. They were my own heroes—astronomers like myself, looking up at the same stars, but at a distance of three centuries.

"Inclined Towards Ideas of Freedom and . . . Utopias"

An English public school was a total society if ever there was one. It locked me into a febrile world shot through with strivings for distinction alternating with moments of deep peace, and set against a perpetual background noise of sexual gossip. It is hard to realize that I spent more than half the year back home with my parents in Ireland. Yet, each time, the journey to Holyhead, and then across the sea to Dún Laoghaire, seemed to bring down a glass wall between myself and Shrewsbury.

At that time, I had no friends of my own age in Ireland. The decision to send me to Shrewsbury took me out of the loop of the Protestant boys who had gone on from Aravon to Irish schools. I was on my own. What was I doing and thinking? Hence my surprise when I recently discovered the beginnings of a diary.

I wrote the diary for only three days—from January 5 to January 8, 1951. Then I abandoned it in order to write, in the following pages, the opening chapter of a science fiction novel. Let me linger for a moment on the diary. It is not often that an octogenarian can look into the heart of a fifteen-year-old boy who happens to be himself.

The diary shows that at home, at least, the scientist in me was alive and well. I regularly trained my binoculars on the night sky and planned the making of a telescope. I devoured the science fiction novels of H. G. Wells (1866–1946). Inspired by Wells, my imagination strained toward Utopia: "It was a nice clear day and I felt in a nice clear mood, specially inclined towards ideas of freedom and the Utopias of H.G. Wells." Such high thoughts mingled with reassuring family routines. Traveling by bus with my aunt Norah, I "talked about cats, and signals to the moon." Walking Rory with my beloved aunt Mai, I was still at it: "We talked about equality and the morality of the Sweepstakes." This was the famous Irish Sweepstake, a lottery whose principal office, alight with green neon shamrocks of the most garish kind, faced the austere, classical façade of the Royal Dublin Society in Ballsbridge—the society devoted to the progress of science, which housed a rich library that I would soon come to use.

Clutching a precious sheaf of book tokens, I would make my way to the A.P.C.K. bookstore (the major Protestant bookstore, run by the Association for the Propagation of Christian Knowledge), duly doffing my cap to the many "right people" who shuffled in shabby overcoats along its shelves. But it was not Christian Knowledge that I was after. It was Utopia. I bought two books, both in the Teach Yourself History series—models of scholarly outreach to a general public. These were *Lenin and the Russian Revolution* by Christopher Hill and *Lorenzo de' Medici and Renaissance Italy* by Cecilia Ady. They dealt with the two faces of Utopia. Hill's *Lenin* struck me as "the story of the ultimately stupid, cruel, futile, horrible story [of the attempt] to create another Utopia."

Ady's *Renaissance* was marvelously different: "what a wonderful period! What Freedom . . . Of course, only feasible in small communities. . . . If only one could destroy this horrid, smoky, grimy, hustling ganglion of modern civilization. . . . And yet was not modern life caused by this Spring of Mankind? . . . Then I had tea, beans on toast, bread and butter, Xmas cake, etc. . . . Then to a bath . . . like the Renaissance, pure, free and cleansing."

I still remember the occasion. I should add that it took some imagining to equate that bath with the new birth of Europe. Baths in Glenageary were Spartan affairs. The electric heater soon ran out of hot water. I would lie in two inches of it, watching the steam of the bath form into thick clouds as it hit the cold draft coming in from the window.

For all its effusions, the diary shows a young boy at a crossroads. In Ireland, the scientist dreaming Utopias was still very present. In Shrewsbury, however, I had already become the worldly-wise teenager, fascinated by the human scene. My letters to my parents took apart the micropolitics of the school as if I were taking apart the mechanisms of a Greek city-state or following the ins and outs of an eighteenth-century oligarchy. This meant, in fact, that I had reached the History Sixth, and was being taught to do just that by "the Duke"—by J.R.M. Senior, the head of the History Side.

THE DUKE

HISTORY WITH "THE DUKE"

THE DUKE

Murray Senior was called "the Duke." Tall, with a hatchet face and upright bearing, he did, indeed, resemble the Duke of Wellington. He was an institution. He had taught history at Shrewsbury since 1932. Above all, he had founded the History Library in the classroom of the History Sixth, on the corner of the second floor of the Schoolhouse, where it enjoyed a splendid view across the river on to Shrewsbury town. The library installed by the Duke was well stocked. It was not filled with textbooks. Rather, it emphasized the fact that modern English history—above all, the history of the eighteenth and nineteenth centuries—was accessible to us through original documents: through memoirs, journals, and collections of letters. I was encouraged to read through these much as I had read through the copies of *Punch* in the Moser Library.

The library did more than this. As I remember it, Gothic bookcases in golden oak projected from the walls, cutting the room into a series of bays. This was very different from the regular rows of desks and tables, facing a blackboard, that characterized the normal classroom. The chairs were capacious armchairs in which we could sit back, surrounded by well-bound volumes as in a gentleman's library. Indeed, the History Sixth room was not a classroom. It was a clubroom. And we were little clubmen. Better still, we were little parliamentarians. We would weigh the respective merits of the great politicians of the Victorian Age as if we were their contemporaries, judging them from the comfort of the London Athenaeum or the Reform Club.

GROWING UP

In the Duke's opinion, the time had come for us to think like grown-ups. And this is what the Duke did for me. I still have a long, stiff-backed notebook, in dark red, in which I wrote an essay for the Duke every week of the term, from October 1950 to early 1951. The essays ranged from "The Function of the Historian" to topics such as "The Effects of the French Revolution on English History."

Rereading these essays, I was greatly impressed by Duke Senior's comments on them. Each essay was marked up with marginal remarks written in a firm hand in bright-red ink. The Duke's comments were intended to provoke a dialogue between equals. They amounted to a crash course on how to think like a grown-up by being treated like one.

And what was it to be a "grown-up"? In the first place, to be grown-up was to avoid sweeping generalizations. Purple passages of high moral content flowed all too easily from me. I had to be restrained. I wrote of the Industrial Revolution that it had produced "a discontented, suppressed, wretched industrial class, women and children labouring in vast new gangling and smoking machine-ridden cities." If only Britain had not been diverted by the French Revolution and the Napoleonic Wars, this horror might have been avoided. Not so, wrote the Duke: "This is the biggest assumption you make. . . . I think it is overdone."

And what about seventeenth-century Ireland? Surely "Ireland was completely different from England in all respects." No, wrote the Duke (and this came as a revelation to me): "Much of the tragedy of Anglo-Irish relations arises from the <u>similarity</u> of the two islands."

And above all, the Duke was concrete. Discussing the "Tudor compromise in government" (the awkward balance of monarchy and Parliament maintained by Elizabeth and upset by Charles I), I had begun with a long, euphoric paragraph on the liberation of political thinking in the Renaissance. The Duke was unimpressed: "Too vague and vast. . . . The essay is about government and can be kept on a calmer level altogether."

On looking back, after reading these comments, I realize that, in listening to the Duke, I was listening to the voice of "grown-up" history throughout the British Isles in the 1940s and 1950s. It would follow me through school and into the university. Suspicious of generalizations; demanding facts and figures; and notably averse to "vast and vague" talk about ideas: the Duke's comments have always been for me the beginning of wisdom.

But they were only a beginning. To be challenged by being treated as a grown-up at the age of sixteen was a bracing experience. But to continue this intellectual pruning was calculated to cramp the spirit. Carried into later years, by college tutors in the universities, this insistence on doing history "like a grown-up" often tended to lead students and their mentors into a narrow emphasis on political and institutional history and a deeply philistine avoidance of grand topics such as religion and the history of ideas.

This cramping of the imagination was the product of a system designed to turn out members of a ruling class—politicians, colonial officials, and bureaucrats. Such persons were expected to be good at passing exams devoted mainly to political history and to the discussion of institutions. This prepared them well for careers as civil servants and administrators, dashing off memoranda and approaching problems with due caution in what was assumed to be a stable, commonsensical world—a world of solid structures such as I had not come across in Ireland.

And in the early 1950s, this limiting of the field of history was not an entirely innocent matter. The system had developed, in part, so as to rule an empire. And now that empire was failing. The educated classes in nations under British rule were demanding freedom; and they were being denied this freedom because it was said that they had not yet "grown up." Could one really trust the educated elites of Sudan (as of India and other countries) to handle the dangerous gift of independence? "Not yet" was the usual answer.

This answer was invariably couched in terms of a failure to achieve a level of intellectual grooming—of "grown-up" attitudes—such as we were receiving in Shrewsbury. If it was difficult enough for public school boys to grow up (so it was said), what could we hope of the half-baked *babus* of India or the *effendis* of Khartoum—the derogatory terms applied to the educated classes who increasingly challenged British rule? In the words of Sir Douglas Newbold (1894–1945), one of the last civil secretaries (the head of civilian government) in Sudan:

> The *effendia* are going to write and read and talk about "democracy", "self-government" and "nationalism". And . . . we cannot completely clear their minds wholly (any more than public schoolboys' immaturity can be purged at Oxford).[1]

---

1. K.D.D. Henderson, *The Making of the Modern Sudan* (London: Faber, 1951), 538.

But minds "purged at Oxford" in this manner could turn out to be very dull minds indeed. The Duke had truly fortified my mind. But he had not fed my imagination. This came in October 1951—after the Duke had left the school to take up a headmastership in Bury Grammar School, near Manchester. He was replaced by a young man of twenty-three, only seven years older than myself, and recently down from Oxford—Laurence LeQuesne.

INTO NEW WORLDS

LAURENCE LEQUESNE AND FRANK MCEACHRAN

Laurence Lequesne: Into a New World

"Larry" LeQuesne brought with him the air of a slightly different world. He came from the Channel Islands. He was not Lawrence LeQuesne, but Laurence—a distinctive French spelling current in the Channel Islands. He also brought a laugh that seemed to belong to another age—the slightly high-pitched chortle of an Edwardian gentleman confronted by some particularly delicious absurdity: a chortle that always seemed to say, "Why not?!" Laurence's laugh was proverbial in the school. A little later, he supported Richard Inglis—the future editor of *Private Eye*, no less!—in his first ventures in satirical writing for *The Salopian* (the school magazine), "with the loudest laugh you'd ever heard."[1]

What struck me at the time, however, was not only that laugh, but also a voice plainly accustomed to telling the truth. It was said that Laurence was a Quaker. In fact, his family were Baptists. But his voice was certainly a Quaker voice—a voice accustomed to absolute directness. When he first appeared in the History Sixth Form Library, Laurence faced (as we have seen) a clubroom rather than a classroom. Tweaks of various persuasions, from myself, a mere nerd, to the school captain of football (how grand can you get?!), lolled and shuffled ostentatiously, in a mood to show their "cool" in front of a new master.

---

1. Harry Thompson, *Lord of the Gnomes* (London: Heinemann, 1994), 42.

Laurence simply told them that he did not want so much noise. Carried on so clear a voice, LeQuesne's seriousness was as infectious as his laugh.

We settled down to study the history of England at the moment of a major crisis of identity, in the first part of the nineteenth century. It looked as if English ancien régime society might founder as dramatically as did that of France, in the French Revolution of 1789, under the double impact of the Industrial Revolution and the ideological storm of radicalism and the Romantic movement.

Laurence's heart was in those stormy decades. He later wrote a book about Thomas Carlyle (1795–1881), who reached the peak of his fame in the troubled 1840s. The book catches the molten core of Carlyle and his age:

> The immensely fruitful tension, between the moral and the practical, between marvel and horror at the achievements and monstrosities of industrialism . . . [and the] inconsistent but nevertheless profound humanity that enabled him to function as the voice and the conscience of the most open and socially sensitive generation of the nineteenth century.[2]

Laurence introduced us to this age of crisis from the inside. Duke Senior had already taken us through the history of nineteenth-century England and Ireland with majestic and well-balanced tread. Unlike Senior, Laurence took us into the minds and hearts of the protagonists. He encouraged us to read the original memoirs and tracts of the times. He conjured up the feelings of young men of the 1800s, as the storm winds of the Romantic movement shook down the dry leaves of the eighteenth century Enlightenment. He did not describe the Industrial Revolution itself. Instead he entered with marked pathos into the hopes and fears of both the radicals and the Romantics as they watched rural England change under the pressure of incomprehensible forces. Inspired by Laurence, I read all of the *Rural Rides* (1830) of William Cobbett (1763–1835) and many radical manifestos and plans for a better world.

For Laurence always had a soft spot for the losers—for their failed utopias and for their yearnings for an idealized, premodern past. In a word, he took us into a new world. While only a year previously my mind had been filled with thoughts of scientific utopias placed in the future or in the stars, I now explored the inner hopes and fears of real persons in a real past, set in the real landscapes—alternately beautiful and menacing—of nineteenth-century England.

2. A. L. LeQuesne, *Carlyle* (Oxford University Press, 1982), 94.

"The Free-est Man I've Ever Known":
Frank McEachran (1900–1975)

What we boys could never have guessed was that, at exactly the same time as he was inspiring us, Laurence himself was being brought into a new world by a fellow member of the staff—by Frank McEachran, a long-established teacher of French and German literature, with whom he shared bachelor lodgings on the edge of the school grounds. "Mac" or "Kek" (Laurence called him "Mac"; we boys called him "Kek") stuck out from the mass of his colleagues at Shrewsbury (as he would have stuck out anywhere) like an aerolite dropped from outer space.

Kek was the son of a construction engineer in Wolverhampton and a product of Manchester Grammar School. He had studied the German Romantic philosopher Johann Gottfried Herder (1744–1803) at Leipzig. He joined the staff at Shrewsbury in 1936. There was nothing public school about him. He regarded organized games and organized religion as the two great enemies of the human mind. He lived for the mind, in amiable indifference to convention and prejudice. With a halo of loose white hair, eyebrows raised in perpetual amazement behind horn-rimmed spectacles, he had the look of a vatic leprechaun. He had a voice with a distinctive twang, where words came out, through slightly clenched teeth, in all the languages of Europe. In ancient times, Kek would have been one of those Cynic philosophers whose magnetic serenity and pithy sayings both subverted and instructed the elites of the Greco-Roman world.

Altogether, Kek was the great awakener. He acted as "a goad, an inspirer, a kicker of young imaginations and sensibilities into life" (the phrase is Laurence's). He did this by introducing them to English and to European poetry of all ages and in many languages in an anthology of poetry that he called *A Cauldron of Spells*. In this anthology he extracted short and incantatory passages from any number of poems. They were not to be read in silence, or in solitude. They were to be memorized and then made to explode on the world by recitation.[3]

Each one of us would be called to stand on a chair ringed with a circle of chalk, to emphasize the magical quality of the recitation. Or we would chant in unison, filling the school building with a burst of massed sound, like the

---

3. F. McEachran, *A Cauldron of Spells* (Wells, Somerset: Greenbank Press, 1992).

ringing of hammers on an anvil. Kek always had a spell for me—as a signature tune—chosen from G. K. Chesterton's *The Battle of the White Horse*:

> For the great Gaels of Ireland
> Are the men that God made mad,
> For all their wars are merry,
> And all their songs are sad.[4]

He made sure that we knew what it was to be possessed by cunningly crafted verse. Sheathed in magic sound, I never stammered for a moment when I recited his spells.

A large number of the spells were taken from the works of T. S. Eliot (1888–1965), and especially from those of W. H. Auden (1907–1973). These poems were written before World War II. It was through them that I entered the nightmare world of interwar Europe. This was yet another new world for me. Until then, Europe had not figured greatly in my imagination. "Abroad" usually meant for me the territories of the British Empire in Africa and Asia. The poems collected by Kek introduced me, for the first time, to the tainted decade that had witnessed the defeat of civilized society all over Europe—the victory of Franco in Spain, the rise of Hitler in Germany, and the monstrous consolidation of the totalitarian state in Stalin's Russia. These were the spells that I still remember as if I were reciting them only yesterday. (Oh, would that they were not still relevant!) Take, for example, Auden's poem *Refugee Blues*:

> Dreamed I saw a building with a thousand floors,
> A thousand windows and a thousand doors;
> Not one of them was ours, my dear, not one of them was ours.
>
> Stood on a great plain in the falling snow;
> Ten thousand soldiers marched to and fro;
> Looking for you and me, my dear, looking for you and me.[5]

Kek introduced me, through his selection of poems, to the desperate mood of interwar Europe. This mood was summed up in the title of Auden's long poem *The Age of Anxiety*. It was this poem that my compatriot E. R. Dodds would later choose to invoke as part of the title of his book *Pagans and Christian in an Age of Anxiety*. For Dodds, the last centuries of the Roman Empire

---

4. McEachran, *Cauldron of Spells*, no. 458, p. 214.
5. McEachran, *Cauldron of Spells*, no. 170, p. 76.

seemed to be engulfed in a mood similar to that evoked by Auden in describing the Europe of his time. Whether the parallel between the two ages was correct was an issue that I would take up in dialogue with Dodds in the late 1960s. But it was through Kek's spells that Europe first gained a place in my imagination. They were an introduction to the continent whose ancient and medieval history I would later come to study.

SENSE OF THE PAST

A Sense of the Past

I still look back on 1952, my last year at Shrewsbury, as the true beginning of my life as a scholar. Not only did I win an exhibition at New College, Oxford, which eventually brought me from Ireland to England for the next twenty-six years of my life. But something also happened on a deeper level. I developed a historical sensibility that led me, through a series of encounters with the sheer beauty of the medieval buildings and stained glass of Oxford and Shrewsbury, to a wish to study distant periods of history—the Middle Ages, in the first place, and then the later Roman Empire.

Laurence LeQuesne played a crucial role in this evolution, by passing on to me an acute sense of the past. A turning to the past was not, in itself, unusual in postwar England. It was part of a mood similar to the disabused view of history current among Irish Protestants. I suspect that what drew Laurence to Kek was a shared feeling that they both lived at a ninety-degree angle to the modern world. At a happy drinking party of fellow teachers at the Lion Inn at Shrewsbury, in later years, Laurence was somewhat surprised to find that

> all four of us, at bottom, hate the present; is it typical of our age and class, or what? . . . what is it that makes [us] quarrel with the present?[1]

What made Laurence's quarrel with the present so distinctive was the intensity of his sense of the past. This was his most personal and decisive gift to me. It was not the same as reactionary conservatism; nor was it mere nostalgia. It involved a more acute and more tragic sense. The past was *there*, and it was not the present. It had once been as full of life, sound, and color, as much an

---

1. A. L. LeQuesne, *After Kilvert* (Oxford University Press, 1978), 119.

arena of creativity and of human dignity, as the present. Now, like a treasure ship seen at the bottom of clear waters, it lay there, irrevocably trapped in time. Laurence's hero, Thomas Carlyle, shared this feeling: "a quite exceptionally acute private awareness of the mysteriousness of time as the transparent medium in which all human activity is irretrievably stuck."[2]

After Kilvert

Given his obsession with the irrevocable past-ness of the past, it is not surprising that Laurence conceived a brilliant thought experiment. Some twenty years after he taught me, he took the diary of a Victorian clergyman—the Reverend Francis Kilvert (1840–1897) who had lived in Clyro, in the Wye Valley[3]—and compared every entry in it with the present, to show how patterns of behavior in Victorian England and the landscape itself had changed over the past hundred years. He even went to live in Kilvert's house for the year in order to do this. There he conducted an investigation of the difference, over a century, between past and present that was as meticulous as any anthropologist's fieldwork. In each section of the book, a diary entry by Kilvert for 1870 was paired with a diary entry by Laurence for 1970, usually on the same day and at the same place. Both were followed by a comment.

By this means, past and present were placed in constant dialogue. What was it like for Kilvert, in 1870, to look out on the same landscape as Laurence did in 1970? For instance, how did Kilvert experience basic things—things too big to be seen, which we take for granted—such as space and light, in an age where he traveled on foot to most places and might see only one candle burning in an entire village that was now illuminated all night by sodium lamps?

Laurence went for all those telltale differences that showed that the past had well and truly parted company with the present. Even the seemingly idyllic scene of a harvest festival in the shadow of an ancient church, where time appeared to stand still, was not timeless. Kilvert's mention of a Volunteer Band on this occasion was a reminder of how, with the radio and the record player, music itself had lost its moorings. It was no longer tied to a single source of sound—as when the Victorian band had thumped and trumpeted through the long afternoon. In all these little differences, time was at work: "all of them,

2. LeQuesne, *Carlyle*, 32.

3. *Kilvert's Diary, Chosen and Introduced by William Plomer*, 3 vols. (London: Jonathan Cape, 1960).

like fallen leaves on a seemingly motionless stream, show the direction of the current."[4] Laurence was fascinated by that silent chasm that opened, irrevocably, between the present and the past: "It's an addiction, this passion for the past."[5]

In later years, I would turn to other disciplines—notably to anthropology—to bridge the gap between myself and the seemingly exotic societies of the past. But a "passion for the past" is what Laurence passed on to me in 1952. History, for me, has always been something more than a discipline—more than a set of problems to be solved, a narrative to be put together from bits and pieces of evidence about the past. It is, rather, a perpetual awareness of living beside an immense, strange country whose customs must be treated by the traveler from the present with respect, as often very different from our own; and whose aspirations, fears, and certitudes, though they may seem alien to us and to have turned pale with the passing of time, must be treated as having once run in the veins of men and women in the past with all the energy of living flesh and blood. I learned from Laurence that the aim of the historian was not simply to argue about the past; it was to bring that past alive—to recover a lost world.

Oxford or TCD?

It was in this way that Laurence (and, with him, Kek) prepared me to take the Oxford scholarship examination. I would try my luck on March 18, 1952, by "sitting" (literally sitting at a long table in a college dining hall, answering in longhand a series of three-hour-long papers) the examination for an Open Scholarship or Exhibition—the latter a slightly less valuable but no less prestigious award—to New College, Oxford.

I was all ready for the exam. But then an unexpected problem emerged. Did I really want to go to Oxford? I had somehow taken it for granted that I would go to TCD—to Trinity College Dublin. Founded by Queen Elizabeth in 1592, Trinity College was the university of preference for the Protestants of Ireland. When I grew up, Catholics were still forbidden by the Catholic bishop of Dublin to attend it. Quite naturally, my father had assumed, with all the pride of an Irish Protestant in *his* university, that the Oxford scholarship examination was only a trial run, to see whether I was good enough for Trinity.

---

4. LeQuesne, *After Kilvert*, 153.
5. Le Quesne, *After Kilvert*, 224.

I still thought of myself as an Irish boy. I did not know what forbidding toffs—what "Anglo-English" (to use my mother's sardonic phrase) at their most arrogant—might await me in Oxford or Cambridge. As I wrote to my parents in October 1952:

> I really do not like the prospect of involving myself too much in England. Finn [Seamus Finn: my fellow history tweak and former guardian angel] . . . does say that a person like myself, or himself . . . would be quite able to pick his own friends at University without getting in with the expensive drinking crowd; but once in England [I added] there is a grave danger of being cut off from Ireland.

I told Willy Matthews, my housemaster, about my hesitation. Not surprisingly, my father soon received a somewhat frosty letter from him:

> Peter tells me that he wishes to try an Oxford Scholarship next March. It would give him something to work for and would enable him to measure himself as a historian against others of his age. He intends to turn the scholarship down if he gets the award. Now this latter course would be rather hard on the man who would have gained the scholarship if Peter had not competed. . . .
>
> It may be that New College would allow him to sit the Examination and give him a private report on his paper, but I have yet to find out whether they would be prepared to do this. I am inclined to doubt whether they would.
>
> In any case, I think it quite possible that Peter would get an award next March, and I am very much in favour of his accepting it and reading history at Oxford. It would give him more standing—at least in this country—than a degree at T.C.D. The History staff here share my view on the matter.
>
> Would you let me know what you think?

My father was not entirely convinced:

> As regards whether Peter should go to Oxford or [Trinity College] Dublin University, we wish only to do what is best for Peter himself in the long run within the bounds of our means. . . . But means apart, there are considerations of all sorts that make us, and Peter too, lean towards our native Dublin. We can be persuaded, perhaps, but the balance of real advantage to Peter must be clear.

I now realize that factors other than Irish patriotism weighed with my father. In the draft of his letter to Willy M., after the mention of "our means," my father crossed out a half sentence—"which unfortunately are such that. . . ." His means were, indeed, less than he would have wished. As we have seen, his pension had been greatly reduced through his having been forced by illness to leave Sudan before he had completed his full term of service. Further expenses in Oxford were likely to be considerably greater than those that I might incur in Dublin. Bluntly, could my father's finances stand the strain?

Matthews answered this letter in a reassuring manner. He told my father that, under the new arrangements, if I gained a New College scholarship, I would also be entitled to support from a State Scholarship, subject to a means test. This amounted to £276 a year. This was, in effect, the full cost of my tuition and lodging for the year in Oxford. My father was reassured:

> Thanks for your letter of 23rd October with all the information it contained. The maximum State aid seems to be on a most generous basis and would seem to put a very favourable appearance on the financial side of Peter's going up to Oxford if he can get an award, providing there is no difficulty likely to arise from his being Irish; and provided [my father could not resist adding, with a touch of humor] the authorities (in the means test) take the same rather dim view of my means as I do.

But, of course, he was wrong to be reassured. Matthews had totally over-looked the fact that my father was an Irish citizen and that Irish citizens were not entitled to State Scholarships. It is some indication of the insularity of Shrewsbury (or—to exonerate Matthews—of the ambiguous status of the young Republic: for, until 1951, Ireland had remained a member of the British Commonwealth) that he had not discovered this fact. I do not know when the penny dropped. By June of next year, I had scored sufficiently well in the School Certificate examination to be entitled to a State Scholarship. But I now knew that, as an Irish citizen, I could not be given one. As I wrote to my parents: "now isn't it a shame the Dept of Education and myself are on different sides of 60 miles of sea?"

It is typical of my father that he never breathed a word to me of the financial strain that this absence of support would place on him, any more than he let me know of his difficulties in sending me to Shrewsbury. On both occasions, my father had encouraged me to go ahead, whatever the cost might have been for him. So when I took the train south to Oxford in March 1952, to take the scholarship examination, I did not know that my very success might restrict my father's finances even more drastically than his original decision to send me to Shrewsbury had done, in 1948. More than I realized hung on this exam.

OXFORD 1952

The Scholarship Examination

On March 17, 1952, I arrived in Oxford to take the scholarship examination for New College. As far as I can remember, the exam took three to four days. On my return, I described the whole affair in a long letter to my parents. As can easily be imagined, I made a special effort to sound grown-up.

> Here is how things now stand. I went to the exam having done as much as I think I could be expected to do and I do think that I did as well as I could— maybe I was a bit heavy in my first paper, only the most experienced hands aren't and I was pressed for time in the history paper—but who isn't? I was never stuck and I never lost my head—but I'm not expected to.

This was not mere bravado. I had already taken enough examinations to know that they were not really tests of knowledge. They were tests of intellectual poise. They were rhetorical performances in being a "grown-up" historian. I rose with zest to such a challenge. I reviewed my notes carefully and hoped for the best.

As an Irish boy from a "northern" school such as Shrewsbury (unlike Winchester or Eton), I knew that I was not on the inside track. Arriving at New College, I observed the competition with care. I wrote to my parents:

> THE COMPETITION!?**! I dream about them! There were about thirty of them, and quite honestly, I shall consider it a miracle if I get an award against them. . . .

They were a forbidding lot. For instance, there were

> the aesthetic young gentlemen—3 of them, one, the archetype, walked with his head in the air, flipping his hands, and bouncing from side to side.

He had an infuriating habit of throwing back his head for inspiration during the exam and pranced out of it with an almost supercilious smile.

Then there were the natural insiders:

> Of course geniuses are eccentric, [but] much more dangerous than [they, are the] cold clear intellects. . . . there were about 5 of them, were very nice but obviously very sure. They were Etonians and Wykehamists [from Winchester], in fact, they knew as much about their subject as I hope to know in a year's time. They were getting on to 18. [I was 16 years 8 months at the time.] These are the real danger as they are the type the college wants.

(On a page in the letter, I drew a series of caricatures of these various types.)

Faced by such competition, I was like a jockey who had to pull out of the pack. Laurence LeQuesne had told me how to do it.

> In the English History One, at least, I followed Mr. LeQuesne's advice in being a bit daring, in keeping off the beaten track of 1066 and all that and solving problems rather than reciting events—of course, all history scholarship papers are problems, historical debating points to be cleared up. For instance, I tackled the difficult one about Wolsey as opposed to a very formal one about Elizabeth's foreign policy, and also made an opening on Tudor Social Policy which interests me immensely but which I really hadn't done much directly upon, and also the same applies to my answer on Methodism. This pays when dealing with the terribly beaten track of English history. . . . The only thing I had had against the English History paper was that it showed a most irreverent disregard of early 19th century Radicalism.

(This was one of Laurence's favorite topics: but no question on it turned up.)

I rose to the challenge of the essay. It was on one word: "Commonsense." I made full use of the three hours:

> [It] was up my street. I went off on a delightful tangent miles from the beaten track [that would have consisted] of a recitation of the solid, unprepossessing virtues of common sense.

I did it my way:

> Well, your eccentric little astronomer of a son, proved, with liberal quotations from Voltaire, Rousseau . . . Pascal and, coup de grâce, Einstein, that common sense was the greatest bar to the progress of scientific thought as it can lend itself to a stereotyped system which can only be broken by an

act of the imagination resembling the elements of the credo quia impossi-
bile of an Act of Faith. . . . I wasn't pressed for time and I wrote 8 sides
so I enjoyed it immensely whether the stolidly commonsensical dons agree
or not is a matter of no concern to me—more fool them if they don't.

Here, I think, a touch of the disabused approach of an Irishman to upbeat narratives of progress—a quarrel with the present, as Larry LeQuesne would have
put it—played a role.

I ended the letter cautiously hopeful:

I don't know how I compare [with the other candidates]. I am not hopelessly eccentric, certainly not a genius, my facts are far from mechanical,
and I enjoy my subject not only because its deadly serious but because
it can become exceedingly amusing. . . . the rest is in the lap of the gods.
I don't think I'll get my results for a few days.

In the end, Larry LeQuesne's chortle won out. On March 27 I received
news that I had been awarded an Open Exhibition (a minor scholarship) to
New College, accompanied by a warning that dates the entire operation to the
immediate postwar years:

We shall not be able to allow you to come into residence until you have
completed your National Service.

This notice led to a further, somewhat baffled, exchange of letters between my father and Willy Matthews. It was finally ascertained that, as an
Irish boy, I was *not* liable for compulsory National Service. If Her Majesty
was not prepared to pay for my education, I would, at least, not have to serve
in her army.

What was a triumph for me was a financial challenge for my parents. An
Open Exhibition was an undoubted honor, awarded to only a few strictly on
the basis of their academic performance in the scholarship examination. But
it was by no means an offer of free tuition. If I remember rightly, it amounted
to £80 a year. I was also given a Leaving Scholarship of £90 a year from Shrewsbury. My father paid the rest, which would have been at least £150 a year.

To go to Trinity College Dublin (where I would have lived at home) would
have been far cheaper for my father; but with his characteristic unspoken
ambition on my behalf, he settled down to the prospect of my going to Oxford.
His application to the governors of Shrewsbury School for a Leaving Scholarship to pay part of my way through Oxford was made at this time. I knew

nothing of the extent of the financial difficulties that caused him to apply for this help. And so I did not gauge the depth of his generosity.

Eventually, it was agreed that there was no point in my staying any longer at Shrewsbury. I was too young to go to Oxford in the Michaelmas—the winter—term of 1952. Instead, I would spend a gap year in Ireland, before arriving at New College in October 1953.

But how would I use this gap year? On what periods of history would I concentrate? Until then, I had done nothing but early modern or modern history. As was the case for most schoolchildren in the British Isles, I had been taught no history before 1485. "Tudors and Stuarts" were our common fare, and nothing earlier. But my visit to Oxford changed this. I was stunned by the sheer beauty of the place. From now onward, the Middle Ages, a period of which I knew nothing at the time, claimed me because of the enduring visual impact of the Gothic colleges of Oxford.

A Touch of Beauty

My somewhat brittle report to my parents on the examination itself gave only a hint of this moment of conversion. All I wrote was this:

> As for Oxford itself, I don't think any written letter can do justice to it. I was absolutely enchanted. . . . I feel that I'd been there months when I left and was quite sad to leave it. It's got to my system and I feel very odd without it.

What I encountered in Oxford, for the very first time, was a glimpse of a truly premodern world. It was a reminder of the tingling strangeness of the past, such as I had learned to appreciate from Larry LeQuesne. But, unlike the past contained in books, late Gothic Oxford filled my eyes directly. I was looking, face-to-face, at what fifteenth-century persons had looked at: What did those strange eyes see? What did they think in seeing it?

In those days, the colleges of Oxford were far more open to the public than they are now. In between examinations, I wandered through them in a daze. It was as if I had crossed a magic frontier between the present and the past. I walked through cloisters supported by buttresses crowned with fantastic beasts, in and out of chapels bathed in multicolored sunlight from ancient glass, and passed under arches roofed with lacelike stonework studded with heraldic shields. Last of all, I vividly remember walking into All Souls College. I looked up at the crenellations of the Hawksmoor Towers, in light-golden stone set against the pure blue of a springtime sky. I resolved, at that moment, that I would study the Middle Ages. I would enter into the minds of the architects and craftsmen who produced such masterpieces. Steeled by this resolve, I went out of my way, in the examination paper on English history, to answer the question on Cardinal Wolsey. It was the nearest I could get to that charmed age.

Only later did I learn that those All Souls towers were pseudomedieval towers—brilliantly designed "citations" of Perpendicular Gothic architecture, built in the early eighteenth century by the architect Nicholas Hawksmoor! But, at the time, the magic of so much beauty worked on me. Scholars have become medievalists for a variety of reasons—a nostalgia for a Catholic past lost at the Reformation, or a taste for courtly legends, or an interest in the distant beginnings of institutions that are still with us today. I became a medievalist through my eyes. This was, perhaps, the most enduring result of my taking the scholarship examination in Oxford in those bright spring days.

ENCOUNTERS WITH
THE PAST

ARCHIVES AND ABBEYS

"An Orgy of Benevolence":
The Shrewsbury Election of 1796

In the short run, my time machine was not pointed toward the Middle Ages. Laurence had devised for me the perfect remedy for "senioritis." He persuaded the county archivists to let me examine the papers connected with an uproarious local election that had taken place in 1796, when two members of the same family—John Hill of Hawkestone (1740–1824) and William Hill of Attingham (1772–1842)—had fought each other for election as the member of Parliament for Shrewsbury. I settled down to read the papers connected with the campaign of William Hill.

This would be the only time that I ever worked in an archive. But it left me with a lasting awareness of how different archive-based history was from the text-based history that was the norm for ancient historians; and with a wish, whenever possible, to reach something of the degree of richness, when describing the ancient or medieval world, that was possible to achieve through diving into any archive of more modern times. Opening the boxes that contained William Hill's papers, I experienced the sharp, almost ghostly, thrill of direct access to the eighteenth century. They were filled with the bills and receipt books of the agents of William Hill, carefully folded and bound with ribbons. These bills and little booklets had not been unfolded or opened since 1796. I would draw out the pins that secured the pink ribbons which tied them together. I even sent my parents one rusted pin. This was truly a moment of encounter with the past.

Working through the account books of the election agents, I discovered God's plenty. The agents recorded innumerable small payments, each connected with some aspect of the canvassing and the mobilization of voters. I discovered that considerable sums of money were paid for lodgings for voters born in Shrewsbury but now living elsewhere—so as to enable them to establish residence by staying in town for a few days. Some money went to tidying up the damage caused by overboisterous campaigning: £9 pounds were paid out on April 25 "for curing broken heads." Much went into banquets. But the most impressive item, for me, at least, was 1,524 gallons of free beer consumed in one inn alone. Last but not least, on election day itself, £1,500 were spent on flamboyant satin "favors" (rosettes) to be worn by the supporters of the candidate. Adding up the sums, I calculated that, in this battle of the dinosaurs, William Hill of Attingham had spent £15,414 4s. 9d. to win the election in Shrewsbury, "that free, ancient and independent borough in which Venality and Corruption have never dared to lift their heads."

At first, such outlays seemed shocking. But the drudgery of totting up the paperwork connected with the election demystified the event. Candidates were supposed to make a splash. But exactly how big a splash? Victorians, committed to the cause of parliamentary reform, claimed that the Shrewsbury 1796 election had cost £100,000. For them, the election was an example of boundless corruption. They were entirely wrong. I found the overall cost to have been a little over £15,000.[1]

Furthermore, a comparison of the language of the pamphlets produced at the time of the election (many of them were kept in the rare books section of Moser Library in Shrewsbury School) with the nitty-gritty of the archives led me to a hypothesis on the nature of aristocratic giving in eighteenth-century England. To spend money in this way was not to bribe. It was not a matter of the transfer of "hard, dirty, sordid guineas" for votes (as later, Victorian critics insisted).

As I explained in a letter to my parents, something more ancient was at stake: the duty of the rich to show their love for the community by seeming to scatter the good things of life—such as beer and satin ribbons—as widely

1. R. G. Thorne, *History of Parliament 1790–1820: Introductory Survey* (London: Secker and Warburg, 1986), 6.

as possible. The expenditure of William Hill was supposed to be "an orgy of benevolence, in which all flows like water into the mouths of the unenfranchised as much as the enfranchised . . . a display of wealth and bounty, consistent with the 18th century idea that wealth in acres was not only the pillar of the community, but [was] like a reservoir which watered all around it." It was my first, but by no means my last, encounter with a psychology of heavy spending by the upper classes that intrigued me when I came, in later years, to study attitudes to civic benefaction and to almsgiving among the elites of the later Roman Empire.

My final study was over twelve thousand words long. My statistics and much of my narrative were later used by Richard Thorne in his monumental *History of Parliament*.[2] I was even told by Laurence that Sir Lewis Namier (1888–1960), the doyen of the study of eighteenth-century politics, had read the paper with pleasure. For me, those weeks in the Shrewsbury archives were a direct encounter with the past at its most rambunctious and seemingly alien to modern ways.

"As Proud as Our Own and Yet So Different"

But, despite my researches in the eighteenth century, it was the Middle Ages that slowly but surely riveted my attention. I remember sitting uncomfortably on a pile of ammunition boxes, which served as seats in the transept of Saint Mary's Church, in Shrewsbury town, during the service connected with the school's Fourth Centenary Celebration on June 20. I found myself underneath a great window filled with late medieval glass that had been brought from Trier by a Victorian vicar. One panel showed the emperor Constantine (306–337), the first Christian emperor, as a saint, dressed like a Holy Roman emperor of the fifteenth century—with a golden crown and a bright white beard that seemed like a ray of silver light breaking through his heavy purple robes. I remember asking myself what it must have been like to live in a culture with no sense of anachronism—for whom the figures such as Constantine could be shown, without any sense of incongruity, in fifteenth-century dress. What sense of time did late medieval people have, to enable them to think of distant Romans as contemporaries?[3]

2. R. G. Thorne, *History of Parliament. The House of Commons 1790–1820, II: The Constituencies* (London: Secker and Warburg, 1986), 337–339.

3. Ivo Rauch, *Trierische Glasmalereien des Spätmittelalters in Shrewsbury* (Trier: Bischöfliches Dom-und Diözesanmuseum, 1999), Abh. 34, at pp. 49 and 80–81.

Laurence also led us out on bicycles into the countryside to see historical sites. On one occasion, we cycled ten miles to the south to the ruins of Acton Burnell, the castle founded in 1284 by a bureaucrat-bishop, who had been chancellor to Edward I. I loved these visits. As with the archives, they gave me direct, concrete contact with the past. I wrote to my parents:

> Unless you do frequent tours of this nature, Medieval History tends to become an absolute fairy tale. . . . Their conflicts are over, the issues which perplexed them are, if not solved, ignored. But in the ruins of Acton Burnell at last you are in touch with a prosperous ecclesiastic, not an image in stained glass, but the tangible proof of a contented, self-made man, who by dint of pen-pushing, good Latin . . . became Chancellor of England. Here is the hall where he ate, here is his closet, where he gazed contentedly at the surrounding countryside and checked his accounts with the bailiff— and so on.

My letters also show that I had plainly picked up Laurence's acute sense of the irrevocable past-ness of the past, as it applied most sharply to the Middle Ages. Here was a truly distant world, ruled by its own values and committed to its own sense of time and beauty. Whether we liked it or not, the modern world was flanked by a majestic presence that would not go away. I described our visit to the ruins of Haughmond Abbey, four miles outside Shrewsbury and once the richest shrine in Shropshire: "There again there is tangible proof of a civilization as proud as our own and yet so, so different."

Somewhat to my surprise, in the following month, this pressing sense of the strangeness of the medieval past would be reinforced for me, not in England or in Ireland, but in Switzerland.

SWITZERLAND AND THE
LATE MIDDLE AGES

SWITZERLAND

On July 29, 1952, I left Shrewsbury and took the train to the south with Laurence LeQuesne. He was off to the Channel Islands and I to London. Writing to my parents, I summed him up in the characteristically laconic manner of a teenager:

> Mr LeQuesne seems no more than an overgrown schoolboy, yet he is a very brilliant man. He is absolutely perfect as a form master as he can get on with absolutely everyone. . . . He was enterprising and completely mad and has given our standard work a tremendous boost. I would not I am sure have done so well with Mr. Senior [the Duke].

I went on to London to take advantage of an unexpected opportunity. The father of Julian Crispin, a friend from Shrewsbury, intended to drive to Italy on holiday with his wife, and offered to drop us off in central Switzerland so as to hitchhike in the region.

This was a totally new experience for me for many reasons. For my family in Ireland, and for most of their acquaintances, foreign travel had meant travel "abroad"—to Sudan and Egypt—and not to the Continent. Even if they had wanted to explore Europe, first the war and then their tightly scheduled leaves gave them little opportunity to wander on the way. An anxious dash across Paris (having arrived from the Channel steamer) to catch the train to Marseilles, where their boat would leave for Port Said, was about all of France that they could hope to experience. (My father remembered being so thoroughly flummoxed that he addressed the porters in unusually fluent Arabic rather than in French!)

But the most redoubtable obstacle of all was posed by the draconian currency restrictions imposed on Irish and English travelers in postwar Europe. The quantity of currency that could be taken abroad was severely limited. It amounted to a wallet of twenty-five pounds' worth of traveler's checks, each of which had to be solemnly cashed at a bank and the transaction recorded so as to be shown at customs on our return. I learned that, even for well-to-do families, an air of smuggling surrounded trips to the Continent—banknotes hidden in the upholstery of cars, special arrangements with foreign friends.

Fragments of the journal that I kept at this time show that Julian and I went through the predictable ups and downs of young hitchhikers in those much-traveled mountains. But we were by no means the happy Eurokids of today. We had to make that precious twenty-five pounds sterling last for two weeks. Julian and I went hungry more often than I admitted when writing to my parents.

Along with these constraints went a sharper note of insecurity. This was a truly *postwar* Europe. To travel was to meet former allies and former bitter enemies. We traveled from Zurich to Einsiedeln with Werner, a sunny, brisk young German from Munich, *Lederhosen* and all. Halfway through the trip, without a moment's hesitation, he informed us that Hitler had been "A Man of the People"—*aus dem Volk*—and that it was natural that the Germans should have loved him. After that, we did not quite know what to say to Werner.

Hence, also, a touchiness on our part about being recognized as foreigners. For Julian and myself part of the adventure of travel abroad was the attempt to "pass" as natives, as if we were spies in a foreign land. It never worked. We were invariably spotted as English. I, at least, could parry that I was not quite what they thought I was. I was *kein Engländer*. I was Irish—and, therefore, somewhat of an oddity to them.

Looking back, I think that this spy's wish to merge with our surroundings was not entirely a young man's affectation. It was a tribute to a very real sense that, in postwar Europe, before the development of a European Community, countries and cultures were assumed to be very different from each other. We could not act as if everyone spoke English. A very real language gap and a culture gap separating the countries had to be crossed.

A respect for differences, experienced sharply in foreign travel, was no bad start for a historian of distant regions and periods. And, in any case, when it came to making our way on a slender budget, there was nothing affected about the wish to speak the local language. It was often a matter of bed and board, and of making those few pounds sterling stretch for yet another day. It helped greatly that Julian had been taught by Kek to speak good German.

Entering the Middle Ages

As I look back, what did this journey mean to me? Above all, it was an entry into the Middle Ages. I had already begun in Oxford and in Shrewsbury, with my enthralled wanderings through the cloisters of Oxford, with my ruminations beneath the stained glass image of Constantine in Saint Mary's Church in Shrewsbury, and my visits to the medieval ruins of Shropshire. My visit to Switzerland marked the culmination of a series of unexpected visual encounters that made me eager to study the Middle Ages.

In the Historical Museum of Bern I sat for hours in front of the *Burgunderbeute*—the Burgundian Booty. It consisted partly of splendid Flemish tapestries that had been taken by the Swiss from the defeated Burgundian army of Charles the Bold (1433–1477) after the fatal Battle of Grandson in 1476. This was my first direct contact with the sheer strangeness of the later Middle Ages. In these tapestries were beautiful men and women whose beauty was not our own—figures marked out by exquisite, angular gestures, with long, pointing fingers and supple hands. They had refined pale faces, curly hair, and long thin legs prolonged by pointed shoes, so that they looked like opulent frogs. Most puzzling of all was their sense of the past. The Roman heroes of antiquity were shown as medieval knights in full plate armor. The emperor Trajan appeared on horseback as a feudal prince, with a great shield that bore the two-headed eagle of the Holy Roman Empire.

To enter such a world was to pass a frontier between the modern age and something hauntingly different—ideas of beauty and of time not our own. Next to the tapestries were a series of rooms, each carefully reconstructed from the fifteenth century through to the baroque. This was my first experience of "period" rooms put on display in this manner in a museum. To linger in the subdued light of the late medieval room was to step back into a period just before the glare of the modern age, which began (for us schoolboys) with Christopher Columbus, Martin Luther, and the Tudors. It was to cross an almost occult threshold backward in time, into an unknown, stranger Europe.

The Waning of the Middle Ages

I returned to Ireland with the feeling that I had found an entire new world to explore, as distant and as challenging, in its way, as the planets floating in the depths of space that had riveted my attention only two years previously. In the first weeks after my return from Switzerland, I went into Dublin every morning to read *The Waning of the Middle Ages* by Johan Huizinga (1872–1945) in the marble-encrusted reading room of the National Library of Ireland.

No book could have conveyed more vividly the thrill of making contact with an alien world. Huizinga had an extraordinary gift for presenting the glittering surface of life in late medieval France and Flanders as if this plethora of vivid details, in itself, revealed a deep otherness, a formidable, challenging distance between ourselves and the past. He implied that the hearts and minds of late medieval people were not like ours. They saw the world differently in more ways than we had ever realized.

> To the world when it was half a thousand years younger, the outlines of all things seemed more clearly marked than to us. . . . Honours and riches were relished with greater avidity and contrasted more vividly with surrounding misery. We, at the present day, can hardly understand the keenness with which a fur coat, a good fire on the hearth, a soft bed, a glass of wine, were formerly enjoyed.

Even the sounds that surrounded medieval people struck them with greater force, as if they were human voices—such as the hideous clanging of the big bell of the city of Valenciennes, in 1455, as two citizens hacked at each other in a judicial duel.[1]

Religion, Imagination, and the Middle Ages

The vividness and the sense of strangeness communicated by Huizinga in his grippingly beautiful descriptions thrilled me. Yet I was also aware that I myself lived in a society, Ireland, which shared in religious traditions that went back to before the Reformation.

I was a boy from a Protestant household. My own religious imagination was molded by traditions of personal piety that derived (if largely unknowingly) from the inward-looking, Christocentric devotion of the late Middle Ages. Every afternoon, I would solemnly read *The Imitation of Christ* of Thomas à

---

1. J. Huizinga, *The Waning of the Middle Ages: A Study of the Forms of Life, Thought, and Art in France and the Netherlands in the XIVth and XVth Centuries*, trans. F. Hopman (New York: Saint Martin's Press, 1924), 1–2: this is a translation of *Herfsttij der Middeleeuwen* (Haarlem, 1919). For a more recent translation, see Johan Huizinga, *The Autumn of the Middle Ages*, trans. R. J. Payton and U. Mammitzsch (Chicago: University of Chicago Press, 1996). See also W. E. Krul, *Historicus tegen de tijd. Opstellen over leven en werk van J. Huizinga* (Groningen: Historische Uitgeverij, 1990).

Kempis (a product of the piety of the Brethren of the Common Life in fifteenth-century Holland and Flanders) as the radio of our next-door neighbor played Chopin's *Berceuse* at the beginning of *Children's Hour*. In this moment of repose, I found myself reading the *Imitation* both as a text of late medieval literature and as a guide to my own religious life. I was left wondering what Christ had meant to those who had first read the *Imitation* and had filled their eyes and hearts with his lean, pale figure, as shown in innumerable fifteenth-century paintings. These months were very much the time of what I would call my "Flemish Mood."

Hence the profound impact on me of a brilliant historical novel—*The Man on a Donkey* by Hilda Prescott (1896–1972).[2] It was about the Pilgrimage of Grace of 1536–1537—the great uprising in England against the dissolution of the monasteries by Henry VIII. It evoked the turning of an age, between the Middle Ages and the Reformation.

What impressed me most about Hilda Prescott was that she was a fully paid-up historian. By the time she wrote *The Man on a Donkey*, she had already written a biography of Mary Tudor and would soon produce brilliant translations and studies of late medieval pilgrims to the Holy Land.[3] She could convey the feel of a period through tiny, iridescent details as vividly as could Huizinga. She had an uncanny sense not only of the brittle splendor of early Tudor England but also of its chilling streak of cruelty. *The Man on a Donkey* was an unparalleled evocation of the religious imagination of medieval England in its last days.

Above all, it was a book of great beauty. I have always remembered Hilda Prescott's description, at the end of the book, of Gib Dawe, the failed priest, leaving London a broken but still proud man, passing Saint Paul's on the road to the West:

> As they passed Paul's great church it stood up to the south, between them and the drab ending of the day. But the light that smudged the sunset sky so mournfully . . . blazed fire-red in the west window, as though some feast were prepared within, with lights in plenty and flame leaping from the hearth for the celebration of some high holy day; as if a great King held

---

2. H. Prescott, *The Man on a Donkey* (London: Eyre and Spottiswoode, 1952).

3. Hilda Prescott, *Jerusalem Journey* (London: Eyre and Spottiswoode, 1954) and *Once to Sinai* (London: Eyre and Spottiswoode, 1957).

carousal there, with all his joyful people around Him, with all His children brought home.[4]

I had seen such beauty. Reading this passage, I remembered the stained glass of the antechapel of New College, alight with bright greens, deep purple, blue, and gold, as the early morning light blazed through it, at the time when worshippers gathered before breakfast for Holy Communion.

4. Prescott, *The Man on a Donkey*, 2:694.

GERMAN AT HOME

ERNST SCHEYER

DR. ERNST SCHEYER (1890–1958)

As had been arranged, I left Shrewsbury one year early and returned home to Ireland to spend a gap year before I was old enough to go to Oxford in October 1953. The gap year between high school and college is a far more common experience nowadays, and it is easy to forget that it was a rare event at this time. (Far from enjoying a gap year, English boys were required to do two years of National Service between school and university, which made my own case even more unusual.) For me, it was a decisive year. It was the first and only year that I had ever passed in its entirety in Ireland since I went to Shrewsbury in 1948. It was the year in which I developed on my own, by constant, lonely reading, a deep interest in the Middle Ages, followed, at the end of the year, by a fascination with the end of the Roman Empire. But the most important gain of all in that year was an entry into Europe at its very best through learning German from Dr. Ernst Scheyer at Trinity College Dublin.

I had returned from Switzerland determined to learn German. In order to do so I had planned to make another tour in Europe and then to stay with a German family. This was not at all to my father's liking. He wanted me to learn my German in Dublin at Trinity College. Trinity was only a three-quarter-hour journey from Glenageary on the familiar number 8 bus. (This was the bus from whose top deck I had seen the swastika waving at half-mast above the German Embassy on the day of Hitler's death, only seven years previously.)

Dr. Scheyer took me on as a private pupil. He was a Jewish refugee from Germany. Trained as a lawyer in Silesia, he had earned the Iron Cross in World War I. After Kristallnacht (November 9, 1938), he was placed for a time in the

Sachsenhausen concentration camp. He arrived in Ireland in 1939, without even a passport, having been urged to do so by his son, who happened to be studying medicine at Trinity. He worked his way up as a teacher of German to become assistant in German at Trinity College. He gave me lessons in a vacant classroom.

An imposing figure, invariably formally dressed in a gray pinstripe, Scheyer not only taught me German. He also showed me what it was to be a cultivated European. His first assignment was to write an essay, in English: "The Meaning of Culture." Similar assignments followed—"Must the Artist Always Be at Odds with Society?" and "What Do We Owe to Ancient Greece?"

Soon I was writing similar essays in German: for instance, on the medieval and Renaissance elements in the life and painting of Albrecht Dürer. For Scheyer not only taught me to read German; he also taught me to think German. His favorite teaching text was Stefan Zweig's *Sternstunden der Menschen*, with its mixture of vivid historical portraits and ruminations of a very German kind on the nature of history. It was my first contact with an entire culture, and not just with a language.

I ended up with the privilege of sharing tea with him at Bewley's Café in Nassau Street. He presided at the table, lavishing compliments on all the waitresses in an innocuously old-world style. They called him "Dearie" and fed him with cream puffs. He plainly loved Ireland. He told me with especial pride that he had recently delivered eight talks on the principal broadcasting station of the American-occupied zone of Germany as "The Voice of Ireland." A few years later Scheyer taught my cousin, Anthony Tatlow, inspiring him with a love of German that later made him a leading interpreter of the works of Berthold Brecht.[1]

There was yet another academic contact that I could have made through Scheyer. My father was concerned that I should keep up my Latin before I arrived at Oxford. Scheyer immediately suggested a friend, who taught at University College Dublin—none other than Ludwig Bieler (1906–1981), the great Austrian scholar of early medieval Ireland who had fled to Ireland in 1938. But Bieler's fees were too high for my father and the bus journey to where he lived was too complicated. Little did I know that I had missed the opportunity

---

1. On Ernst Scheyer, see now Gisela Holfter, "Ernst Scheyer," in *German-Speaking Exiles in Ireland 1933–1945,* ed. Gisela Holfter (Amsterdam: Rodopi, 2006), 149–169, and Gisela Holfter, *An Irish Sanctuary: German-Speaking Refugees in Ireland 1933–1945* (Oldenbourg: De Gruyter, 2017).

to learn Latin from one of the greatest scholars of early medieval Ireland, whose edition of the *Confessio* of Saint Patrick I have worked through line-by-line on many occasions.

It was only when I came to Oxford that I realized how much I owed to Dr. Scheyer. At this time, Oxford medieval studies concentrated heavily on England and France. With German, a larger Europe was opened up to me—the entire area east of the Rhine as far as Poland and the Balkans, as well as a formidable tradition of German scholarship on the ancient world and on Byzantium. In effect, knowledge of German doubled the range of my knowledge of medieval Europe, and later proved essential for my work in ancient history. At the same time, it opened me up to very different ways of thinking about history (especially about the role of ideas in history) from what I could have gathered from the sober empiricism that was dominant in England. German took me across a frontier of the mind, into a very different historical culture from that to which I was accustomed.

Quiet Days

I was happy to be back in Ireland. It was the first and only time ever that I was at home with my parents for an entire, unbroken year. I was very much on my own. The fact that I had gone to Shrewsbury, rather than to a local Protestant public school, meant that I had few friends. Instead, I walked, and read, and dreamed, digesting my German lessons and devouring the books that I would bring home from the Royal Dublin Society Library.

Glad to be relieved of the financial burden of yet another year of school fees, my father spent the one hundred pounds that he received every year from an educational insurance scheme—very pointedly—on a new anthracite-burning stove for the kitchen. The stove was a demanding creature. It required the regular removal of the caked ashes every evening—a ritual that my father performed with characteristic care and pertinacity. He called it "the Moloch." But the Moloch was a crucial addition to a house with no central heating of any kind. It kept the kitchen warm and enabled me to read beside it in a comfortable wicker chair, with which I associate the absorption of so many books, both at this time and in my later years, at Oxford. I owe a lot to the Moloch.

Glenageary was a good place to be lonely. Over the hill, beyond Dalkey Castle, the Vale of Shanganach spread out toward the south in the direction of Bray. This spectacular view was rightly likened to the Bay of Naples. Not for nothing were roads beside it named the Vico Road and Sorrento Terrace. On a bright day, the view through twisted pines to the golden rocks of Dalkey Island could have been a scene from the ancient Mediterranean.

Down the hill from Glenageary lay the Forty Foot—the Gentleman's Bathing Place, where the honey-colored granite rocks dropped sheer into forty feet of icy water. Pink gentlemen braved the waves in all weathers, launching themselves from a rusty iron ladder. Once, as I was standing somewhat hesitantly on the ladder, facing a stormy sea, an elderly gentleman edged past me with the words: "Keep an eye on me, young man. It's the old 'ticker,' you know." Wherewith the gentleman with the delicate heart struck out over the swaying waves as if on his way to Wales.

My father was happy to be back from "abroad." He seems to have had no nostalgia for Sudan and rarely spoke about his days there. He took over the management of the family firm of Brown and Gilmer, which manufactured compound feeding stuffs. Brown and Gilmer was not exactly an industrial giant; but it made a sufficient profit, every year, to pay my father a salary and to support my aunt Mai. The work required the exact touch that my father, as an engineer, was only too glad to contribute. He would tell me (from his carefully drawn-up charts) all about the precise balance of chemicals required for the weaning of piglets and the growth of young hens.

His clients, alas, did not always appreciate his pains. They were slow to pay their bills. My first taste of whiskey was when my father and I were being entertained by one such client, a prosperous farmer in the Wicklow Mountains, whom my father had visited in order to settle an account. We got whiskey but no check. I noticed that the powder room of the house was hung with expensive drapes to imitate a medieval tent. The farmer could have spared my dad a few hundred pounds.

TYPING AND SHORTHAND

My own outreach to modern Ireland was different from that of my father. I decided to learn shorthand and typing at the Dún Laoghaire Technical College. This was a visit to yet another world. It revealed, with particular clarity, the ambiguities of Irish nationalism at this time. The Technical College was a state institution. And Irish—not English—of course, was the official language of the state. Everything we did was in English. But my final diploma was in florid Irish, written in an elaborate neo-Celtic script.

This nationalism extended to the typewriters themselves. Their keyboards used Irish, not English, characters. They had been designed for the bureaucracy of the new Ireland, where, indeed, a knowledge of Irish was mandatory—hence their use in a course designed to produce future government servants. This led to strange anomalies. We learned to type and to take shorthand notes entirely in English. But it was on these stoutly national machines that we typed. In the final examination for the diploma, I remember typing a passage from Galsworthy's *Forsyte Saga* in Celtic characters that went directly back to the early Christian Ireland of Saint Patrick.

But Dún Laoghaire Technical College meant more to me than a diploma. It was the very first time that I shared a common learning experience with girls of my own age—and with Catholic girls at that. Drawn from the neighborhood, they were good-natured, talkative, and shrewd. They were also very motherly, as many of them were the eldest sisters of large families. I never stammered for an instant in their presence. It was a necessary reminder—at a time when Ireland was seen, from the outside, as a bastion of intolerance—of the common bonds of civility that, fortunately, contradicted the impression of unremitting conflict given, all too willingly, by the bullies and the loudmouths.

Encouraged by the newly acquired skills of typing and shorthand, I settled down to read and to take notes on the rich haul of books that I would bring back, every fortnight, from the Library of the Royal Dublin Society.

END OF THE ANCIENT
WORLD

Toward the Ancient World

Around halfway through this gap year, what I would call my "High Flemish" enthusiasm for the late Middle Ages waned a little. The reasons for this were partly connected with my living in Ireland, where I was constantly made aware of my parents' past in Sudan. Even if they did not talk much of their experiences, the bookshelves in our drawing room made me aware of a wider world—the challenging presence of the "abroad" with which our family had been involved. A large, deluxe edition of T. E. Lawrence's *Seven Pillars of Wisdom* was in the privileged bookshelf beside the fire in our drawing room, flanked by a copy of *Sudanese Courtesy Customs*. Whenever I came home from Shrewsbury and, then, from Oxford, I would read *The Seven Pillars* from cover to cover.

But I was not especially attracted to the present-day Middle East. Far more important was the ancient Near East. This was largely due to my Protestant background. The Church of Ireland maintained an intensely biblical version of Protestantism. This did not mean that it was in any way fundamentalist. Rather, it valued knowledge of the Bible—both of the Greek New Testament and of the Hebrew Bible: the Old Testament. Jacob Weingreen (1908–1995), the author of *A Practical Grammar for Classical Hebrew* (from which I later learned Hebrew) was professor of Hebrew at Trinity College Dublin from 1939 onward. A much-beloved mentor of the Protestant divinity students at Trinity, he ensured that they knew—and understood—the Old Testament in its original language.

As a result of this respect for biblical culture, the ancient Near East, revealed in the narratives of the Hebrew Bible, was a constant imaginative presence. When out of ideas on what to preach—a frequent enough occasion for him— our local rector would read to us, in his sermons, long passages from Sir Leonard Woolley's accounts of his excavation of Ur of the Chaldees. He read out these descriptions of ancient Ur with such enthusiasm that I was often left wondering why Abraham should have abandoned such a well-appointed city!

It was the same with Greek. The Galilee and Judaea of the Gospels and the Aegean world revealed by the Acts of the Apostles—Middle Eastern and Mediterranean landscapes—were more real to me than were the great cathedrals of northern Europe or even the cloisters of Oxford. In this, I was very much the product of a Protestant Hellenism—shared by Anglicans, such as the Reverend Furnival in Shrewsbury, and by members of the Church of Ireland. Greek, not Latin, was the key to my faith. In this way, the gravitational pull of the world of the Bible made me increasingly interested in the ancient Near East and in the Roman Empire that had formed the background to the New Testament.

Saint Patrick and the End of Empire

There was a further interest that pulled me toward the last centuries of the Roman Empire. Across the sea, in Britain, the Romans had left a heavy imprint. Roman roads were still visible in parts. Roman towns and villas had been excavated. The ruins of Hadrian's Wall reached across the North of the island, like the sloughed-off skin of a vast stone snake, as a perpetual reminder of the awesome discipline of an empire that had once stretched from Arabia to Scotland. Englishmen still tended to identify themselves with the Roman Empire as a model for their own dominions.

But across the Irish Sea, there was none of this. Ireland had remained a barbarian island, never occupied by Rome. And yet Saint Patrick, the national saint, had been a Roman—a Romanized Briton called Patricius, who had first been brought to Ireland as a slave (perhaps in around the year 430). He was a piece of human flotsam swept across the sea to county Mayo as a result of an upsurge of slave raiding that followed the crash of the fall of Rome. I realized that, to understand the beginnings of the Golden Age of early Christian Ireland, I had to understand the Roman Empire in its dramatic last days.

Rather than bask in an identification with Rome at the height of its power, which came only too readily to many Englishmen, I found myself looking at that colossal structure in its decline, seen from the outside, from the barbarian side of the frontier. It was a form of double vision—of Rome and of the world beyond Rome—that would stand me in good stead in future years.

THE DECAY OF ANCIENT CIVILIZATION

It was with this interest in the Roman Empire in my mind that I scanned the ample shelves of the Library of the Royal Dublin Society for something to read. In the early summer of 1953, I found a book that would prove decisive for me: one of the greatest masterpieces of Roman history written in our times—*The Social and Economic History of the Roman Empire* of Mikhail Ivanovitch Rostovtzeff (1870–1952). I lighted on Rostovtzeff entirely by accident. A massive, olive-green volume, brilliantly illustrated with photographs of ancient scenes and objects (each explained in lengthy captions) and written in a firm and pellucid English, the book ended with a grand finale—a chapter entitled "The Oriental Despotism and the Problem of the Decay of Ancient Civilization." In this chapter, Rostovtzeff sketched out in lapidary prose (all the more chilling for not being rhetorical) his views on "the social revolution of the third century, which destroyed the foundations of the economic, social and intellectual life of the ancient world."[1]

I read this chapter with the thrill of a young man when faced with any account of some truly memorable disaster. It was a disaster that seemed to speak directly to me. It told the story of an empire created and expanded by an enlightened bourgeoisie that, in the course of one century, was ruined and replaced by a military caste drawn from a rebellious peasantry. Rostovtzeff argued that the notorious civil wars of the third century were not irresponsible coups d'etat. They amounted to a thinly veiled social revolution, by which the vast majority of the Roman world—a peasantry largely untouched by classical culture—took their revenge (as soldiers) on the cities that had, for centuries, exploited and marginalized them. The later empire of the fourth century was a ghost of itself—a brutalized society, ruled by violence and swayed by irrational, religious forces that had been held in check in earlier times.

Rostovtzeff had written his masterpiece in exile from revolutionary Russia. The sharpness of his analysis owed much to the fate of his own class at the hands of the Bolsheviks. Furthermore, when the book appeared, in 1926, there

---

1. M. I. Rostovtzeff, *The Social and Economic History of the Roman Empire* (Oxford: Clarendon Press, 1926), 477.

was no telling whether this collapse might not happen throughout Europe. *Pro nobis fabula narratur*—the end of Rome, as told by Rostovtzeff, was our story also.

In later years I came to disagree with the main theses of Rostovtzeff and his followers. But it was through Rostovtzeff that I gained entrance to the ancient world. He had described the crisis of the third century AD and its consequences on a grand scale, in a way that linked Roman Britain, the Mediterranean, and the Middle East in a single, fateful convulsion whose ramifications I followed intently as the last months of my gap year slipped by.

As a result of this year of quiet absorption, I came to Oxford with two historical interests: the later Middle Ages and the crisis of the ancient world in the third century. What the two interests had in common was the excitement of studying two great and ripe cultures about to undergo shattering transformations—the fall of Rome and the Protestant Reformation. Brilliant beginnings, bright Golden Ages did not thrill me. Whether at the end of the Roman Empire or at the waning of the Middle Ages, it was the lurch of change toward the unknown and the unthinkable that held my attention. Which one of those two interests I would follow at Oxford, and which would come to form the basis of my more lasting scholarly endeavors, was entirely open at this time.

To Become a Historian

But I had already taken one irrevocable step—I had "historicized" my imagination. The history of distant ages now claimed my mind. I maintained my interest in amateur astronomy. I continued to attempt to put together telescopes. I exchanged with a zealous fellow astronomer, Frank Mechan, notes on how best to take photographs of the moon though mounted binoculars. The correspondence with Frank—a boy from a working-class family in Belfast whom I had met at a Dublin meeting of the Irish Astronomical Society—was a heartening instance of the ability of science to cross the charged frontier between the Irish North and South. I contributed to the *Irish Astronomical Journal* and even engaged, in its pages, in a lively correspondence with the director of the Dunsink Observatory concerning the origins of the lunar rays (those bright, radiating scars that partly covered the dark surface of the Mare Cassium). The later lunar landing proved us both diametrically and equally wrong! But the stars were no longer where my mind was. I had become an unregenerate historian.

Maybe I had gone a bit too far. I remember how, at the time when my journey to Oxford approached, I fell into conversation with an elderly man at the

National Gallery of Ireland as we both walked through the Flemish and Dutch rooms. It was a characteristically courteous and unassuming encounter such as often happened in Dublin. I explained to him my fascination with the hyper-realism of the Flemish Primitives. I expatiated on their value as historical sources—how much they told us about the society of the fifteenth-century Netherlands.

He told me that he, also, had once felt the same about those paintings. But now he felt that he had moved on. He wanted beauty. He had come to love the wild seas and lowering skies of the Dutch masters of the seventeenth century. Dressed in a heavy tweed overcoat, he must have been as old as I am now. He told me, at the end, that he was about to enter hospital for an operation. "This is my chance to take a breath of sea air."

I never saw him again. But it was a warning—not all of literature and art can be dragooned to serve a historian's agenda: people need to "breathe" paintings as well as to use them as documents. It would take not years, but decades, for this warning to sink in. It has never done so entirely. But that is part of what it means to become, for good or ill, a historian.

PART II

OXFORD TO
ALL SOULS

IDYLLS

OXFORD 1953

OXFORD 1953

From 1953 to 1956 I was an undergraduate at New College, Oxford. (It had been "new" to the university when founded in 1379.) In many ways, it is deceptively easy to write about those years. Descriptions of "Oxford Days"—like many other descriptions of student life—are a well-known genre, whether tinged with bitterness or with nostalgia. What is harder to communicate is the close interdependence of inner journeys of the mind (launched by the sudden profusion of imaginative and intellectual challenges provided by Oxford) and the unwieldy structures through which this energy was channeled in the university system of that time.

The distinctive structures of Oxford University were always difficult to explain to outsiders (such as Americans and Europeans) and have become so different nowadays from what they were in the 1950s that they need to be explained even to persons in contemporary Britain.

Studying at Oxford was intended to be a short experience: three years only. It was also a narrow experience: I was allowed to study only history. These three years culminated in a drastic occasion. I was not subject to continuous grading, as in an American university. Rather, everything depended on a final examination (two papers a day for about a week). This examination resulted in a grading into classes. Those who were in the first class (restricted to around 6 percent of the candidates) and the top of the second class found the world at their feet—they were sure of an entrée into the professions, and would be accepted as researchers and teachers in Oxford and elsewhere. But those who did not make it to the first or upper second class could barely hope to continue as scholars.

Oxford University itself was an archipelago of autonomous colleges, each of them a little university in itself, committed to preparing students for their final examination in any subject. Almost all of the teaching was done by tutors—the famous dons of Oxford—in each of these colleges. It usually took the form of weekly (and sometimes biweekly) tutorials of one hour each that consisted, ideally, in a one-on-one discussion of an essay read out to the tutor. There were few lectures, and none of them were mandatory: there was nothing like the American system of university-wide lecture courses. In the absence of a common grading system such as tracks the progress of students in American universities, everything depended on the one and only throw of the final exam. It was the business of the college tutor, through the privileged medium of personal tutorials, to prepare the undergraduates for the one, supreme test of a single university-wide exam on which, in many cases, their future careers depended.

How to communicate a system of teaching based to such an extent on the face-to-face methods of the tutorial system, without the help of the lecture courses and seminars that consume the time of so many American and European students? How to measure academic progress in a system where everything depended on the wager of one final examination—a veritable trial by combat—with no system of cumulative grading with which to back it up? How to explain the fact that many of the great names of Oxford of this time, though well known as Oxford "figures" (one thinks of C. S. Lewis) were almost exclusively in contact with students of their own college alone, and were known to other undergraduates only as creatures of gossip and rumor? How even to begin to describe the glacis that separated men from women students at every level up until the 1970s? There have been times when, speaking to my own graduate students at Princeton, I have thought that it was easier to explain the Merovingians than the ins and outs of the Oxford in which I had once studied and taught.

Yet this explaining must be done. The distinctive structures of Oxford exercised a silent but decisive influence on what was taught and what was not taught. For instance, the tutorial system, based on weekly encounters with a don, might seem a very relaxed and open-ended affair. But when harnessed to the need to satisfy examiners in a single final examination, the system tended toward a narrowing of the topics taught. Historians studied only history; and this history itself tended to be reduced to a set of topics that were sure to "come up" in the final examination, and that could be handled briskly in the single hour of a tutorial.

Hence a fatal drift toward the lowest common denominator of political and institutional history—to "grown-up" history such as "Duke" Senior approved of. This happened at the expense of the wider field of the history of religion and ideas and the history of the world beyond Europe. The result was at once philistine and Eurocentric. The history of Asia, Africa, and the Americas was left to specialists and made little or no appearance in the regular curriculum for undergraduates. Altogether, history, as taught in Oxford, was still seen as a training ground for civil servants, colonial administrators, and lawyers. It amounted to the study of power by future wielders of power, largely limited to England alone.

Choices that have come to seem quite natural nowadays, such as the teaching of non-European history or the joining of ancient and modern history, were largely unheard-of. For such options to be considered, entire worldviews had to weaken, and changes in the syllabus, such as seem quite innocuous nowadays, had to be hammered out through a process of negotiation as slow and ponderous as the retreat of a glacier. This was the Oxford to which I came as a student in 1953, and which I did not leave until 1974. Let me attempt, in these coming chapters, to set the story of my own intellectual development against the distinctive rhythms of an educational system that now lies, like an intricate coral reef, almost seventy years in the past.

But that, of course (thank God!), was not all that there was to Oxford. It was also a place where a small number of privileged late adolescents (a tiny proportion of the overall population of Britain, and mainly males) were set free, in a state of remarkable comfort, to enjoy nothing short of the idyll traditionally associated with life at Oxford.

Idylls

When I first arrived at New College, on October 7, 1953, and the college porter showed me to my rooms, I was convinced that there had been a mistake. These rooms seemed far too grand for an undergraduate. My two rooms—a bedroom and a sitting room—were on the second floor of a "Gothic" building of the 1920s. A large oak door stood open, faced by a splendid bay window, with mullioned frames, set in a deep, wide alcove. A fireplace in beige marble was decorated with heraldic Tudor roses and framed by white-painted Gothic paneling. These, surely, must be the rooms of a don. But no, said the porter: they were mine.

Next morning, I had another surprise. I was disturbed by sounds in the living room. Then the door of the bedroom opened and a spritely woman with tight-curled hair and a tight slit hobble skirt, which showed bright-orange silk beneath, walked past my bed to pull the curtains, with a "Brr, it's cold, dearie." She had already turned on the gas fire to warm the living room. She asked whether I would like a cup of tea. This was Rosie Thorne, the wife of Harry Thorne. She would be my "scout" for the next two years. Rosie and her husband, Harry, were a college institution. When I returned on one occasion, half a century later, in 2004, and talked to a college servant as he polished the wood of the stalls of the college chapel in the dim light of a wintry afternoon, I mentioned where my rooms had been. Yes, indeed: those were Rosie's staircases. Of course, he remembered "Rosie and Old 'Arry."

I became one of Rosie's young men. She took me in hand. She made sure that my shoes were polished. She arranged for an academic gown for me. She looked out for a reliable bicycle. She passed on a selection of the books left behind by the former occupant of the rooms. She told me what college rules were "silly," and which ones I would be well advised to obey. Within a few weeks, I was using my typewriter (with pride in the new skill that I had acquired in Dún Laoghaire Technical College) to address envelopes for her for the British Legion, of which Rosie was an active member. I could reassure my parents:

> in rooms, service, meals and everything, we are treated like the young gentlemen we are supposed to be; . . . [this] came to me as quite as pleasant a surprise as the furniture of my rooms.
>
> The thing I noticed immediately, before everything else, was the charming manner of the Porters and servants; no offhandness, no sleekness, not a single scrap of wrong information.

Well-cosseted by Rosie Thorne; graciously received by my tutor only once a week; under no obligation whatsoever to attend any university lectures; with no other academic obligation than a few gentlemanly classes given in college in preparation for a preliminary examination that lay a good half year ahead: I was free to do what we were all supposed to do in Oxford—to enjoy an idyll. And that, in New College in the late autumn, was not difficult. I could sink into the beauty that had first surrounded me when I took the scholarship examination in 1952:

> The sun is setting in a red haze behind the medieval crochets and spires of the skyline; the Virginia creeper and the weeping willows against the Old

Wall are like pink clouds in the sunset; the New College choir is singing gorgeously in the Chapel, and for some reason all the bells are tolling, and the pidgeons are wheeling to and fro around the silhouetted Bell Tower and the black-edged trees of the Quadrangle.

Or, at least, this was how it was supposed to be. Instead, the very beauty of the place, combined with the virtually gravity-free existence of an Oxford undergraduate of the 1950s, brought on, at the headlong speed of which only young persons are capable, a series of religious and imaginative earthquakes.

THE THIRTIES IN THE FIFTIES

It takes some effort of the imagination to recapture the sharp tang of loneliness that accompanied the life of late adolescents in so privileged an environment. Waited on hand and foot in the college, we were truly on our own. To "show the oak," by closing the large wooden door into one's rooms, was the sign of a right to absolute privacy.

I had never enjoyed such privacy at Shrewsbury, nor even at home. I had no ready-made peer group to fit into. In New College, Wykehamists (former boys from Winchester public school—the school founded by William of Wykeham in the fourteenth century as the twin of New College) had the reputation of being clannish. But this clannishness was less obvious than I had expected: the two years of National Service tended to loosen the bonds between members of the same school.

Now we were all equally alone. We were like little drops of mercury on a tray. How would that tray tilt, in such a way as to cause those lonely drops to run together again—to "re-glob"—in new friendships, coteries, societies, or sports teams?

As I look back, one thing strikes me. Many of my friends wished to re-create the 1930s. The war still stood like a shell crater between them and the supreme ease, mingled with disquiet, of prewar Oxford. They wanted to have their thirties in the fifties. This was not difficult. Many of the public figures who were invited to speak in Oxford societies or clubs were only too happy to fight the battles of those years. I described to my parents the talk delivered by Stephen Spender (1909–1995) to the Poetry Society at St Hilda's College:

The room was packed to bursting point, with the effect that we festooned ourselves in galleries, on window sills, stood on tables, perched, even on ladders, and the edge of the low dais . . . like prolific baroque cupids.

Stephen Spender was a very powerful character indeed; a big, greying man, in a blue serge suit and light brown shoes, he had a strong face, with bright eyes and prominent veins behind his eyes. He read some of his own poems, and, most interesting, read the poems he had read with [W. H.] Auden in the Oxford of the Thirties. He warned us all . . . that they had made an effort to keep politics and social problems out of their work and poetry, but that the slump, and three million unemployed, did more to shake them out of that mood than the Spanish War, Fascism or Communism. This is very interesting, as he is sure there will be a slump . . . and unemployment will be near enough [to] home to even the most idyllic poet [and would] have very much the same . . . effect as [it had had] on Spender and Auden. Spender's poetry was good; and we all shoved out, without paying [a membership subscription!] at nine-thirty.

We had been, for an hour, in the 1930s.

ARGUMENT

Nowhere were the battles of the 1930s relived with such intensity as on the issue of religion. The old trench-works of the confrontation between belief and unbelief, Marxism and Catholicism, were as clearly visible in the early 1950s as in the prewar days. If anything, they had been sharpened by the perils of the war and by the advent of the Cold War.

Hence the fascination of Evelyn Waugh's *Brideshead Revisited*, which had appeared in 1945. Here was a tale of the manner in which sacred and profane, Catholicism and class, were deliciously mingled in an imagined Oxford of the 1930s. *Brideshead Revisited* became something of a cult book in my circle. The worldly-wise among us claimed that Waugh's sickly-sweet mixture of snobbery and religion was best savored over gin and orange. They usually declared that they were, of course, unbelievers; but that, of course, the only Christianity that was worthwhile *not* believing in was the opulent, prickly Catholicism of Evelyn Waugh.

For an Irish Protestant boy to find himself in such a heady atmosphere was to tempt providence. What had been a frontier between two tribal religions, where identity was as fixed as granite on both sides—Protestant and Catholic alike—suddenly collapsed. In the climate of Oxford, religious allegiance became as labile as mercury. There was no telling which way the droplets might flow.

I found that some of my best friends were Catholics. Richard Bolney Brown—Dick Brown—(1935–2010) came from a recusant Yorkshire family. A Catholic of the old style, Dick was not given to the subtle paradoxes of sacred and profane represented by Evelyn Waugh. He was a solid and intelligent believer, well able to stand up for his faith; but I noticed that jokes about religion did not amuse him.

We bonded immediately. I wrote about Dick to my parents, with a heavy-handed jocularity. I was plainly worried that they might object to my having Catholic friends.

> I met and spent the evening with, a boy of about my age; Richard Brown, a commoner in Zoology and, shadows of the Jesuits, a Roman Catholic. We had a long talk about Catholicism, history, the evils of dialectical materialism, training falcons and astronomy. He is very nice and very widely read, and there is no lack of common ground to talk about and argue on; in fact I have been with him most of the time.
>
> . . . though we talk theology much of the time, it is done without any vehemence.

Dick introduced me to the work of his teacher, the great Niko Tinbergen (1907–1988), on animal ethology. I learned from him what visual signals triggered aggression in the stickleback, and about the rapid breeding habits of the short-lived fruit fly, capable of producing any number of generations in a nano-second; and how this high-speed flickering of the generations made possible experiments in the transmission of genetic mutations on which the theory of evolution depended. Dick was also a keen ornithologist. I reciprocated his introduction to genetics and ethology by translating for him a German article on the migratory patterns of the Arctic tern.

This cat's cradle of newly formed friendships was crucial. Undergraduates in 1950s Oxford were assumed to pick up their general culture from their environment, not from their tutors. Their tutors were usually cultivated, and often widely traveled, persons. It was assumed that some of their sophistication would rub off on their charges. But they related to their students primarily as coaches. Their business was to prepare the young for the final examination. Our friends were our culture. Dons could be dull dogs. What we talked about among ourselves was what really stirred us.

And in this culture of perpetual argument, religion played a major role. As I described myself and my friends to my parents, we seem an egregious bunch, out to enjoy our Oxford idyll:

I have had innumerable opportunities of tilting, over glasses of port, at a confirmed agnostic; yesterday we argued till all hours; Patrick Goodbody [an Irish boy, who had gone to Shrewsbury], Richard Brown and myself versus two bespectacled unbelievers. We chased them from premise to premise, spun a fine web of contradictions around their arguments and generally had a wonderful time of it; an enormous amount of give and take, without acrimony and mellowed with port.

But what tectonic plates of feeling might come to shift, in oneself, as a result of those long evening hours?

VERY "OXFORD"

C. S. LEWIS

Very "Oxford"

The best-known contributor to the religious debates of the time was C. S. Lewis (1898–1963). As a fellow of Magdalen College, Lewis had been a presence in Oxford since 1925. He left Oxford for a professorship at Cambridge in my first year; and although he continued to live on the edge of Oxford, in Headington Quarry, he was less often seen in town. I saw him only twice, and I never spoke to him. But what little I saw made a deep impression on me.

Early in my first term, on October 15, 1953, I attended a meeting of the famous Socratic Club—a club dedicated to debate between Christians and unbelievers. It was very much a student initiative, founded in 1941, after an undergraduate, Monica Shorten—later an eminent authority on squirrels—complained that nobody seemed to discuss the questions posed by agnostics. The women's chaplain, Stella Aldwinckle (1907–1989), an evangelical with the Oxford Pastorate, got to work to found a club—the Socratic Club. She prevailed on Lewis to act as faculty sponsor and president. He regularly attended its meetings.[1]

Lewis was there that evening. Given his formidable reputation as a debater, I was surprised to see a subdued figure, sitting low and long in an armchair, by no means the center of attention. Indeed, he seemed ill at ease as he listened to the presentation of Peter Geach (1916–2013), a rising star of the analytical philosophy movement, who dismantled, one by one, the rational proofs for the existence of God. Not that Geach was an unbeliever. Far from it: he and

---

1. Stella Aldwinckle, "Memories of the Socratic Club," in *C. S. Lewis and His Circle*, ed. Roger White, Judith Wolfe, and Brendan N. Wolfe (Oxford University Press, 2015), 192–194.

his wife—the better-known philosopher Elizabeth Anscombe (1919–2001)—
were devout, even traditional, Catholics. But they were also disciples of Ludwig Wittgenstein (1889–1951) and resolute upholders of the new, assertive
trend in critical philosophy that was then very much in vogue among the clever
young. This was plainly not the way that Lewis wanted philosophy to go.

Yet I sensed from my glimpse of him at that meeting that Lewis was caught
in his own reputation. He had "a gladiatorial side" and was not immune to the
intellectual truculence expected of an Oxford figure.[2] A review of one of his
first books on religion—*Pilgrim's Regress* in 1933—praised it as a "very 'Oxford'
book." By "very 'Oxford,'" the reviewer meant Lewis's capacity to administer
crushing intellectual put-downs in an urbane and fluent manner. He was expected to be a "bonny fighter."[3]

In Oxford of the early 1950s, a directness of argument that bordered on
rudeness—even browbeating—was highly esteemed, particularly among
young men. Undergraduates (particularly those who studied philosophy)
were supposed to value such agonistic qualities, and to thrive on intellectual
conflicts.[4] Many of us came to the Socratic Club in order to hear sharp Oxford
minds make mincemeat of each other. Hence my surprise to see Lewis uncomfortable, when the brittle and esoteric atmosphere of analytical philosophy
threatened to engulf his Socratic Club.

A few weeks later, I attended one of Lewis's famous lectures on Milton. This
was a very different Lewis. The lecture was delivered in the spacious South
Room of the Examination Hall. What I heard was an orator at the height of
his powers. Lewis's resonant voice transformed the room. The heavy swags
of carving in the great wooden canopy beneath which he spoke seemed to
come alive, and to tumble down in a baroque exuberance that mirrored the
richness of Milton's own poetic genius.

Then, suddenly, in the midst of this high oratory, an ad hominem argument
would come down with the trenchancy of a butcher's chopper. Some critics
seemed puzzled that, in his poem *Lycidas*, Milton spoke more about himself

2. John Wain, "Brothers and Friends," in *C. S. Lewis and His Circle*, ed. Roger White, Judith
Wolfe, and Brendan N. Wolfe (Oxford University Press, 2015), 223–238, at 227.

3. Walter Hooper, "Oxford's Bonny Fighter," in *Remembering C. S. Lewis: The Recollections of
Those Who Knew Him*, ed. James T. Como (New York: Macmillan, 1979), 241–308, at 247.

4. Benjamin J. B. Lipscomb, *The Women Are up to Something: How Elizabeth Anscombe,
Philippa Foot, Mary Midgley, and Iris Murdoch Revolutionized Ethics* (Oxford University Press,
2022), catches this atmosphere very well.

than about the dead person whom he was supposed to mourn. Nonsense! Lewis answered: if an acquaintance of yours was run over by a bus on High Street, your thoughts at the funeral would not be about the fellow in the coffin, but about yourself. It was a touch of earthy common sense deliberately deployed to clinch an overpowering rhetorical performance.

Looking back, I think that I had seen two sides of Lewis, each of which bore the imprint of his long years at Oxford. The side that spoke more directly to me was not Lewis the "bonny fighter," but Lewis the exuberant expositor of Milton and of other classics in the great tradition of European religious literature. His gifts as an apologist for Christianity grew out of a supreme confidence in traditional values and beliefs, nourished by his teaching and by a lifestyle that included idyllic moments among like-minded friends:

> My happiest hours are spent with three or four old friends . . . sitting up till the small hours talking nonsense, poetry, theology, metaphysics over beer, tea and pipes. There's no sound I like better than adult male laughter.[5]

The Oxford countryside spoke to him of a similar ideal. Writing of the sound of bell ringing as he walked down Cumnor Hill toward Stanton Harcourt, he described "the sense of absolute peace and safety: the utter homeliness, the Englishness, the Christendom of it."[6]

This was the sort of idyllic moment for which we all yearned and were encouraged to yearn. For Lewis, to become a Christian was, somehow, to regain that peace. Conversion to Christianity meant a return to basics—to something more solid and more ancient than the fads and feverish ideologies of the modern age: to certainties that had "the homespun truth of folk-tales . . . and the freshness as of earth in the morning."[7]

He agreed entirely with Dr. Johnson: "Sir, he who embraces the Christian religion rejoins the main tide of human existence."[8] It was his mission to show,

5. C. S. Lewis, biographical preface to *Perelandra* (New York: Macmillan, 1944); see Roger Lancelyn Green and Walter Hooper, *C. S. Lewis: A Biography* (Hammersmith: HarperCollins, 1974, 2002), 170.

6. *The Letters of C. S. Lewis to Arthur Greeves (1914–1963)*, ed. Walter Hooper (New York: Collier/Macmillan, 1979, 1989), 321.

7. C. S. Lewis, *Pilgrim's Regress: An Allegorical Apology for Christianity, Reason and Romanticism* (London: Geoffrey Bles, 1933), 172.

8. *The Collected Letters of C. S. Lewis*, vol. 2, *Books, Broadcasts, and the War, 1931–1949*, ed. Walter Hooper (San Francisco: Harper, 2000), 304.

in a major center of learning, that Christianity, and not unbelief, could still hold the high ground of culture.

Translation and the Desire for God

But I knew Lewis from his writings before I came to Oxford. My own relation to him was more inward-looking, less concerned with his feats as an apologist for Christianity than with with his works of religious advice. In my gap year in Ireland, I had read *The Screwtape Letters*. With their fine-grained analysis of personal motivation (combined with a dash of waspish social satire directed against "worldly" snobs and groupies) they were a natural successor, in my readings, to *The Imitation of Christ* of Thomas à Kempis. Both books grew, ultimately, from the same deep root of Augustinian interiority that I would later come to know, though I had no inkling of it at that time. There was also a touch of dour, Low Church Ulster Protestantism in Lewis the moralist's impatience with highfalutin nonsense, and his insistence on calling a spade a spade, which I recognized and valued.

This sense of kinship was not surprising. After all, we shared the same island. Though Lewis was an Ulsterman, he had taken many holidays in the South. It was while cycling around Glendalough and the Vale of Avoca (only ten miles inland from Bray) in 1913, at the age of fifteen, that he had experienced his first "imaginative renaissance," provoked by the sheer beauty of the site.

Indeed, I can well understand how this could happen. At roughly the same age as Lewis, I almost disposed of my entire family for the same reason. I had only just learned to drive. Coming over the crest of the hill that wound down from the Wicklow Mountains through the Sally Gap, I was so struck by the beauty of the monastic settlement of Glendalough, nestling between two silvery lakes, that I wanted to stop to admire the scene. But I mistook the clutch for the brake. The car lurched forward, threatening for an awful moment to take myself, my parents, and a plenitude of aunts at top speed down the hill!

What I truly admired in Lewis was his ability to treat his readers with respect. He wrote for the average Christian. He deplored the tendency to assume that laypersons were uninterested in theology and in the rational basis of their faith. His animus against High Church, neo-orthodox gurus was famous. He blasted T. S. Eliot for "trying to make of Christianity itself one more, highbrow, Chelsea, bourgeois-baiting fad."[9] Caught between the emotional "revivalism"

---

9. Roger Lancelyn Green and Walter Hooper, *C. S. Lewis: A Biography* (Hammersmith: HarperCollins, 1974, 2002), 132.

of many Protestants and the hieratic snobbery of many High Church theologians, Lewis wrote that "my task was therefore simply that of a translator—one of turning Christian doctrine into the vernacular, into language that unscholarly people would attend to and understand."[10] I loved him for it.

But there was more to it than that. I was also touched by Lewis's robust notion of the innate desire for God:

> That un-nameable something, desire for which pierces us like a rapier at the smell of a bonfire, the sound of wild ducks flying overhead . . . the opening lines of *Kubla Khan*.[11]

> All the things that have deeply possessed your soul have been but hints of it—tantalizing glimpses. It is the secret signature of each soul, the incommunicable, unappeasable want, the thing we desired before we met our wives, or made our friends, or chose our work, and which we will still desire on our deathbed. . . . If we lose this, we lose all.[12]

CONVERSION AND IMAGINATION

These were high thoughts. But in the Oxford of 1953 it was not easy to live up to them. To whom could I turn? A Protestant boy from Ireland, I had no built-in prejudice against the Low Church, Evangelical religion associated with OICCU—the Oxford Inter-Collegiate Christian Union. OICCU was called by some "Oik's Union." Its members were assumed to be boorish, anti-intellectual, and, somehow, lower-class. I did not share that snobbish view. Many of the leading figures in OICCU had been to Shrewsbury, though I had not known them there. They had a thriving church. It was also a church that I could describe with a good conscience to my parents:

> I usually attend choral evensong in Chapel, which is very beautiful but a bit Popish. The people I admire are the Christian Union; they are very low church and evangelical, and, in a very intellectual atmosphere, riddled with High Anglicanism, Neo-Thomism and sheer unbelief, they are very down-to-earth indeed; with prayer meetings, Salvation, and a wonderful, hulking great preacher in a packed church each Sunday [The Reverend Keith De Berry of St. Aldate's]. That was a refreshing sight, last Sunday; a parish

---

10. Walter Hooper, *C. S.Lewis: A Companion and Guide* (San Francisco: Harper, 1996), 27.
11. Lewis, *Pilgrim's Regress*, 9.
12. C. S. Lewis, *The Problem of Pain* (London: Centenary Press, 1940), 150.

church so full that they had to have chairs up all the aisles, chairs in front of packed choir stalls, and the door wide open, though, I would imagine that the numbers will thin off a bit in the next few weeks.

So it was toward OICCU that I turned. They offered a strong and active group. Their anti-intellectualism did not worry me. I did not want apologetics. I wanted moral octane. I wanted a new life, and I wanted it no longer as a "tribal" Protestant, but by choice. It was not surprising that, in early spring of 1954, I went to Harringay Arena to hear Billy Graham (1918–2018) preach in his Crusade for Britain. My memory is of the crackling atmosphere of a vast, metallic space, brilliantly lit by banks of searchlights. The sheer size of the gathering seemed to proclaim that this was an occasion where great things might happen. It was also strangely moving to hear hymns that reached back to my own childhood, at church in Bray and Glenageary, sung by a choir of hundreds.

But Graham himself was no manipulator. A description of his impact, next year in 1955, on a large congregation in Cambridge, catches very faithfully the essence of Graham's charisma:

> His voice was attractive, his sincerity unchallenged, and his approach to religious problems so artless . . . as to make his impact on large congregations equally surprising and alarming.[13]

It was the utter simplicity of Graham's message that caught me. He preached on one theme only—the Repentance of King Manasseh. Manasseh was one of the last kings of Israel. Having murdered the prophets and reinstalled the worship of heathen gods, he had been led into exile by the king of Assyria.

> He took Manasseh with hooks and bound him in fetters of bronze and brought him to Babylon. And when he was in distress he entreated the favor of the Lord his God and humbled himself greatly before the God of his fathers. He prayed to Him and God received his entreaty and heard his supplication and brought him again to Jerusalem into his kingdom. Then Manasseh knew that the Lord was God. (2 Chronicles 33:11–13)

It was time for me to do the same. I joined the crowd of persons who walked up the aisle to the front of the stadium in order to receive the forgiveness of God.

Then a strange thing happened. To the best of my memory I had gone alone to Harringay. Though I was allotted a counselor after I had stepped forward

---

13. V.H.H. Green, *Religion at Oxford and Cambridge* (London: SCM Press, 1964), 357.

(as was the normal practice during a Billy Graham crusade), I did not have an OICCU minder at my side to interpret the experience to me in orthodox Evangelical terms. To my surprise, I felt carried on a wave of sheer pagan joy. Somehow, tectonic plates in the back of my mind had shifted to set my imagination free.

I took the train to Ireland the next day, with Lewis's *Pilgrim's Regress* and *The Great Divorce* in my luggage. When I read them in the next weeks, it was not Lewis the moralist who spoke to me from them. It was the ebullient Lewis, the expositor of the "wild Platonism" of late antiquity and of the School of Chartres—a Platonism where every joy in Heaven was echoed, somewhere, somehow, on earth. The great scenes of victory and transformation that gave an epic tone to those two books were what I fastened on. It seemed that my imagination—somehow jolted free by Billy Graham—needed richer fare than what OICCU could provide.

"A Living and Organic Thing": Catholicism

In Oxford there was, in effect, only one other group that claimed to provide such fare—the Catholic Chaplaincy. The entire tone of Oxford and of those around me favored this route. I had Catholic friends such as Dick Brown. But Dick, as a good son of an old Catholic family, was largely uninterested in efforts to send converts along "the road to Rome." My main support came from the atheists. For them, the only Christianity worth either fighting or adopting was Catholicism. Many were aesthetes and already well used to travel on the Continent. Every cathedral, every monastery, every great painting in the museums they visited spoke in favor of Catholicism as the true religion of Europe. The growing Cold War emphasis on the "Unity of Europe" favored such a view. Whether one believed in it or not, Catholicism seemed to offer a way to a wider, richer world than did the unprepossessing Protestantism of the British Isles.

What I sought in Catholicism at this time differed greatly from what I had absorbed from C. S. Lewis. Lewis had taught me a morality based on introspection and on the desire for God. My questions to the Catholic Church were driven, rather, by an urgent need to know whether this world and the next, the natural and the supernatural, truly touched each other at any point, in any Christian ritual, within any Christian organization, and in any perceptible manner in the long history of humankind. Put bluntly: Did the history of the Church show that a naked wire of supernatural power somehow snaked in and out of the human past? Was Christ truly present in the flow of history as he was believed to be present in any Catholic church, where the red light glowed in the dimness of a side altar before the shrine of the Blessed Sacrament—that pure white wafer, which contained the real presence of Christ in this world? Looking, as a Protestant, into the Catholic churches of Ireland, I had glimpsed those lights. Was it possible that these mere "chapels" (as Protestants called them) were the place in which to find, against all expectation, a world-wide religion sheathed—here and now and in all previous centuries—in the tingling carapace of truth?

The notion of the church, as presented by Catholic apologists, caught my imagination. I was challenged by the claim that the history of humankind had room for a vast invisible community—best seen, in almost biological terms, as an organism spreading through the centuries. This is what I read in *The Spirit of Catholicism* of Karl Adam (1876–1966), which had been recommended to me by Catholic friends.

What Adam emphasized, in his presentation of Catholicism, was that the church was not a static institution. It contained within itself an immense capacity for growth, for adjustment, for the further development of its original doctrines that made it seem as fertile as the teeming earth, and as irresistible as the surge of an evolutionary process: "a living and organic thing . . . [driven] by the vital power of living fellowship."[14] Read by a nineteen-year-old, with the triumphant, almost menacing tread of Tchaikovsky's Fifth Symphony—heard for the first time—echoing in his head, these were intoxicating words.

Byzantium

But it was there that I stopped. The history of the church as I had come to know it (for I had begun to study the history of high medieval Europe) was not like that. Karl Adam might appeal to the huge self-confidence of western Europeans that history—and, a fortiori, the history of the Catholic Church—was on their side. But it struck me that there was something parochial in his insistence that this majestic growth was limited to the Church of Rome alone. What of the Christianity of the East? In the last months of my gap year in Ireland, my interest in an "abroad" that stretched beyond medieval western Europe had already led me to Byzantium. It was then that I read the *History of the Crusades* by Steven Runciman (1903–2000), which viewed the intrusion

14. Karl Adam, *The Spirit of Catholicism* (New York: Macmillan, 1929), 135 and 137.

of the Catholic Crusaders of the West into the ancient Christian lands of Byzantium and the Middle East as an inexcusable disaster.

In 1954, Runciman delivered the Waynflete Lectures on the Eastern Schism (the division between the Orthodox and the Latin churches after 1054) in the great dining hall of Magdalen College. I listened to them spellbound. In the dark hall, with his face lit up from below by the light on his podium, Runciman looked like a saint from a Byzantine icon of the Palaeologan period. He told a miserable story of misunderstandings, of high-handed bullying, and, eventually, of the sack of the city of Constantinople in 1204 by the Latin Crusaders, carried out in the name of the Roman Catholic Church.[15]

Such a sequence of events assorted ill with the euphoric panorama sketched by Karl Adam. My historical imagination said: No—there was no unique golden thread woven into the rough cloth of history. There were only human protagonists. But each of them was as strange and as challenging to the imagination as any imagined triumphal narrative, across the centuries, of an infallible, organically evolving church. Slowly, the strangeness of history won out as the dominant preoccupation of my mind. My sense of mystery lay there.

In any case, it was time for a break. The summer vacation of 1954 had come, and I was planning, with three friends, to tour the Gothic cathedrals and the Romanesque churches and abbeys of France. Here, if anywhere, we would make direct acquaintance with the Middle Ages.

Insensibly, over the months, I had drifted away from the Christian present into the Christian past. My interest in this past was that of a historian and not of a believer. For the next twenty years I was attached to no church. When I resumed worship in the mid-1970s, it was in very different circumstances, and with very different preoccupations from those that had gripped me, at the age of nineteen, in the 1950s.

15. S. Runciman, *The Eastern Schism* (Oxford: Clarendon Press, 1955).

FRANCE 1954

ON THE ROAD

In the summer of 1954 I was able to soak my eyes in the medieval churches and cathedrals of France. This journey proved decisive for my future study of the Middle Ages. Ever since my first experience in Oxford, when I had drifted in a dream in and out of the colleges in the spring of 1952, I had known that the sight of monuments and works of art gave me entry into the past. Now, on my first experience of France, I realized, once again, the extent to which I was a visual historian: stained glass windows, capitals filled with strange beasts, grand porticos, and high apses gave reality to what I read in texts.

From June 22 to July 23 1954, I traveled from northern France to Provence and back with three friends from New College in a large and antiquated car. It was not an easy ride. There was always the struggle (as in Switzerland) to make our currency allowance last for an entire month. We camped out every night. Every evening we drank our wine by the glass only, when we would have loved to drink the entire bottle that was invariably brought to our table.

We complemented each other very well. I was the only one who had not been to France before. The others were old hands. John Sainty was very much the "European" of the party. He spoke good French and planned to stay on in France with a French family. He would eventually become a senior civil servant, Clerk of the Parliaments and Knight Commander of the Bath. Back then he sported bright red hair and a vivid beard, which made him look like Vincent van Gogh. Every evening, he would be our leader in the all-important matter of negotiating a camping site in the depths of the country. We would approach a farm:

> The talking drill is superb; we advance daintily, through puddles and hay, avoiding barking dogs: at a given signal, we all take off our straw hats, hold

them humbly in our hands, while John advances slowly and negotiates for a camping site and "eau potable", with much gesticulation and rolled "r"'s.

Sometimes the camping was idyllic:

> dark green trees, splashed with light; a limpid stream bubbling from under a moss covered bridge; a soft clearing sloping from the roadside and protected by a bank from the stream; lichenous masonry half covered with leaves; a patch of young trees to the right; and the treetops all green and gold, up in the evening sky.

Sometimes it was spooky, as when we made our way through thick, dank vegetation, like the heroes of Conan Doyle's *The Lost World*, to find a sleeping place in the caves of the quarries outside Avignon from which the stone of the Palace of the Popes had been taken. As we moved farther south, municipal camping grounds replaced the isolated farmhouses, and we made contact with the local youth culture:

> That night, of all nights, was a beano ball; we sat drinking sirops through straws under fairy lamps . . . the loudspeaker blared forth hot American numbers, the soldiers from the barracks danced quicksteps and sambas, and the majority of girls danced in pairs . . . under the most glorious stars— the Milky Way, great clouds of light, all Scorpio [above the horizon] and Mars glowing well above the foothills of the Alps

Often it rained, with summer cloudbursts that left us flooded out.

Here Andrew Martindale, the disciplinarian of the party, would remind us that we "Had What It Takes," as our primitive stove alternately spluttered and exploded in the attempt to make breakfast. Andrew, like John, knew what he wanted. He had traveled in France before. He was already determined to be an art historian. The problem of the individuality of the medieval artist attracted him even then—as his later work on Simone Martini, on the nature of art patronage in the late Middle Ages, and on the world of Mantegna would show. He went on from Oxford to the Courtauld Institute, and taught the history of late medieval and early Renaissance art at the University of East Anglia until his early death in 1995.

Kester George was the Wykehamist of the party—an alumnus of Winchester School. As the mechanic and driver of the car, he had much occasion to practice the renowned *sang froid* of a product of Winchester. The car lacked a working petrol gauge, leading to unpredictable halts in the middle of nowhere.

I was the navigator. I had planned the itinerary through intensive reading in the art history section of the Ashmolean Library. It was there that I discovered *L'art religieux du XIIe siècle en France* by Émile Mâle (1862–1954), which had only recently appeared.[1] Our itinerary was largely based upon it. Though now dated in many ways, Mâle could not have been a better guide: his works unlocked the iconography of Romanesque and Gothic carving, imparting a sense of having mastered the grammar of an exotic language. He enabled students to understand displays of religious sculpture that, at first sight, were as exuberant and as opaque to the uninitiated as the mythological sequences of a Hindu temple. Scenes from the Old and New Testaments, pious legends, and mythical beasts all came together as parts of a grandiose diorama of the history of mankind, as it was known to medieval persons, from the creation of Adam to the Last Judgment.

Furthermore, Mâle was a robust diffusionist. He was interested in the spread of skills and motifs from one region to the other. This meant that his book followed artistic currents along the pilgrimage routes that reached from northern Europe to the depths of Moorish Spain. Mâle also gave due weight to the old-world grandeur of Byzantium, which continued to influence the art of the West in the eleventh and twelfth centuries.

Hence the shape of our itinerary, as we followed the flow of artistic creativity across Romanesque and Gothic France. It was an attempt to combine the Gothic North of France with the more southern regions in which Romanesque art had developed.

THE LURE OF THE SOUTH

The journal that I wrote at this time showed that my heart was already in the South and in the Romanesque rather than in the spectacular Gothic cathedrals of the North. I was duly stunned by Chartres and Bourges. But I sensed, in the Romanesque shrines of Burgundy and of southern France, a society still bathed in the long, sad twilight of Rome, before the brilliant but all-too-dazzling supernova of the Gothic Age. I was not particularly interested in ancient Roman ruins, and I knew next to nothing about the art of late antiquity. But I did know that I wanted something older and more southerly than the France of the great cathedrals of the North.

---

1. Émile Mâle, *L'art religieux du XIIe siècle en France* (Paris: A. Colin, 1949).

Hence my joy when I reached the Loire. The exquisite little church at Saint Germigny-des-Prés took me back to a more ancient Christianity.

It is a small, warm coloured little building with a low tower and three apsidal chapels bulging out on either side, roofed with red tiles, and screened with hedges of tamarisk and roses. In the porch, covered with rambling roses, and housing a baptismal font of the 7th century, sat M. Totti, the curé. . . . He led us into a beautiful little garden, overlooked by the apse of the church; here the red tiled roof rose up framed by rose bushes and four pure white doves waddled—as they have waddled for over a thousand years—along the path to the little vicarage. It was a charming scene, perfect for the little church, which does not seem to have changed since the days of Charlemagne.

Inside, the apse was covered with a shimmering mosaic of blues, greens, and darkened gold that could have come from Ravenna. It was a fragment of Byzantium nestling in the water-meadows of the Loire.

Later that evening, sitting in a restaurant looking out at the porch of Saint-Bénoît-sur-Loire (the great abbey of Fleury, founded in the seventh century and rebuilt in the eleventh), I knew that this was what I wanted:

Every now and then a saintly looking old man in a monk's habit would come in and have his evening bowl of soup; outside, tonsured monks walked from the basilica in the golden light, groups which could well have belonged . . . to an age a thousand years ago, before the Middle Ages had really begun—when there were emperors in Byzantium, boy-popes in Rome, and when the Arabs controlled the seashore of Provence.

There was no doubt, when I returned from my exploration of France, and especially of the warm South where Rome had died slowly if at all, as to what sort of medievalist I wished to be. But how should I set about it? And who would help me?

AN OXFORD
MEDIEVALIST 1954

CHOICES

So what was it like to be an undergraduate interested in medieval history in the Oxford of 1954? This needs some explaining. The Oxford of sixty-five years ago was not the Oxford of today. The structures that determined the lives of undergraduates in the 1950s are no longer there or have greatly changed. But at the time they seemed immovable. They were the landmarks by which we steered our course as undergraduates. There was no getting round them. They summed up, and quietly imposed, an entire view of what history should be. When they changed (as they began to do, if ever so slowly, in the 1960s), history itself changed its content and horizons in Oxford and elsewhere.

First and foremost, it was a system entirely geared, after I had passed a preliminary examination in the spring of 1954, to a single final examination, which would take place in summer 1956. I was awarded a Distinction in the preliminary examination. When the postman brought the self-addressed postcard with this news to our home in Glenageary, my proud father hugged me, without a word. But then I was left to myself for two full years, with the knowledge that everything would now depend on the grand ordeal of the final examination—known in the argot of Oxford as "Schools" or "finals."

At the time, I had my eye on that one examination, and not on a career. As far as I can remember, I had no idea of becoming a university teacher, or, indeed, of becoming anything. I do not know what my father had planned for me. With characteristic generosity and quiet pride in what I had done so far, he never pushed me in any direction. But I was certain of one thing: whatever I might do later, I was in the business of getting a first class degree in history. I put to one side any thought of the difficulties that I might have to face after Oxford. It was assumed by everyone (my tutors included) that if I had a First, somehow doors would open for me. I was there to do the college proud, by gaining a top degree—as with any college sports team (or, indeed, as with a racehorse) what mattered was that I got that prize.

It would be a First in history and in history only. At the time, there was no possibility of joining history with any other subject. Classicists could mingle Greek and Roman history with philosophy and with classical literature, in a mixture called (with no false modesty) "Greats." Those of a more modern turn of mind could combine philosophy, politics, and economics—the famous "PPE," which enjoyed considerable prestige as a "Modern Greats." But a joint school of that sort was unthinkable for Oxford historians in the 1950s. History there was and history we got. But exactly what history and how much of this history were we free to choose for ourselves?

Everything depended on a choice of papers—each of three hours—that would be taken in the final examination. These papers were offered according to a fixed syllabus. It was a choice from a rich but restricted menu. Every history student had to take three papers in the continuous history of England from Julius Caesar's invasion of Britain to 1914.

Then the choices began. Those who wished to do more medieval English history could choose an optional Further Subject of Jurassic solidity, which was examined in a single paper. This was English constitutional history from the Anglo-Saxons to the death of Edward I in 1307. Known eponymously as "Stubbs," it was based on the *Select Charters and Other Illustrations of English Constitutional History from the Earliest Days to the Reign of Edward I* assembled fifty years before, by William Stubbs, bishop of Oxford (1888–1901).[1]

I remember first opening this venerable volume when at home in Ireland, seated beside the Moloch on a windy night. My eye fell on the first pages: Anglo-Saxon laws from the seventh century onward. These included provisions for the preparation of the red-hot iron for an ordeal, alongside rulings that shepherd dogs should be fitted with bells and that strangers approaching a village from the woods should be careful to announce their arrival with a blast of the horn lest they be taken for robbers. It was hard to get more medieval than that!

European history offered wider horizons. I was determined to do the history of the Middle Ages. But, once again, my choices were strictly limited. There was

---

1. William Stubbs, *Select Charters and Other Illustrations of English Constitutional History from the Earliest Days to the Reign of Edward I* (Oxford: Clarendon Press, 1904).

no grand sweep—no equivalent to a West. Civ. or a World History course. European history was divided up into manageable periods. Faced by a millennium, from the last days of the Roman Empire to the Renaissance, the Oxford syllabus cut medieval European history into slices of roughly three centuries each, examined by two papers, divided chronologically. I chose European History III—the High Middle Ages—from 919 to 1273. It was entirely Western history—basically, the history of Europe, with Byzantium on the margins, and the Middle East seen only as a backdrop to the Crusades. In theory, I could have opted for an earlier period, but the High Middle Ages was the period that my college tutor, Harry Bell, was accustomed to teach. It was taken for granted that I would be taught by him. So European III was what I was taught—and I never regretted it for a moment, especially as Harry let me have my head in presenting a few essays on Byzantium as well as routine essays on France and Germany.

Last but not least came a Special Subject, based on original documents devoted to a significant person or epoch, examined in two papers. This was the true Quest Perilous, the most prestigious paper of all. In the stately language of the Examination Statutes: "The examination in the School of Modern History shall always include . . . A special Historical subject, carefully studied with reference to original authorities." Medievalists could choose among Saint Augustine, Saint Bernard, the Age of Dante, and the Reign of Richard II. I chose Augustine, and this would prove to be a crucial step for me, back to the world of Rome in its last days. But I did not make that choice until the beginning of my last year—in the summer of 1955. What I faced immediately was the continuous history of England and a vivid, three-hundred-year slice of the history of high medieval Europe. As far as an undergraduate in the History School of Oxford was concerned, no other sort of history could be studied— no history of Africa, of Asia, or of America.

LECTURES

So how was I to learn my European history? Not through lecture courses. The Oxford system of the 1950s was marked by the almost total absence of any forms of teaching other than the tutorial system based in the individual colleges. In a system that was directed toward success in a single examination, virtually the only forms of teaching offered to prepare for this examination were the one-on-one tutorials taught by one's college tutor. Only in the case of the Special Subject, were we farmed out to a tutor in another college who had specialized knowledge of the subject. Tied to a tutorial system devoted solely to producing successful examinees, Oxford was, in fact, a glorified crammer.

This meant that lectures played a very minor role in the life of most history undergraduates. Of course, there were lectures. Some lectures, such as those of C. S. Lewis for the English School (which I heard in 1953) were legendary. But, compared with the weekly encounter with our tutors, lectures were "noises off," to which we could pay attention or not. They were entirely voluntary. To attend a lecture was not to commit ourselves, in the American manner, by signing in on a course for which we would receive grades at the end of term. Far from it: lectures happened like free lunch-hour concerts. We could attend them or not. Once at a lecture, we did not need to stay the course—we could drop in and out.

I attended lectures in Byzantine history. Their scanty attendance made only too clear the extent to which Byzantium was treated as a marginal field. Steven Runciman's Waynflete Lectures entitled "The Eastern Schism" had been a bonanza. They had filled the great hall of Magdalen College for a few weeks. But this was not the case when I went to hear Dimitri Obolensky (1918–2001). An émigré Russian aristocrat, a prince reputedly descended from Prince Rurik (though, as a good historian, he questioned this link to the legendary founder of the Russian monarchy), Obolensky had already begun his career as a leader in the field of Byzantine-Russian relations. His first book, *The Bogomils: A Study of Balkan Neo-Manichaeism*, bore a title likely to attract any young person interested in religion and Byzantium.[2]

Attending Obolensky's course of lectures, on Byzantine diplomacy, I realized the extent of the vacuum created, in Oxford, by the tutorial system. At the first lecture, I found that the audience consisted of only myself and a Chinese lady. We looked a very small group indeed in the large, long room in the Examination Schools where lectures were delivered. Obolensky entered in a full academic gown. Undeterred by his lack of an audience, he made a stiff bow to us both with characteristic, somewhat Russian formality. Then, with his back to the blackboard, leaning backward on the table in front of it, he delivered his lecture in exquisite Russian-inflected English, entirely impromptu, without a single note, for exactly fifty minutes. Then, he bowed again, wished us both good morning, and disappeared. Next time, the Chinese lady did not appear. I was left alone to hear, lecture by lecture, what would later become the chapters of Obolensky's classic book, *The Byzantine Commonwealth*.[3] I had no further contact with Obolensky until we became good friends in the late 1960s.

2. D. Obolensky, *The Bogomils: A Study of Balkan Neo-Manichaeism* (Cambridge University Press, 1948).

3. D. Obolensky, *The Byzantine Commonwealth* (London: Weidenfeld and Nicholson, 1971).

Only the delightful Gervase Mathew (1905–1976), a Dominican priest from Blackfriar's Hall—and a friend of C. S. Lewis—was able to establish a thin but precious presence for Byzantium. Father Gervase was always scruffily dressed, with his dog collar invariably riding up his neck at an odd angle. He looked like a flustered parson; but his voice was magic. He gathered a respectably large audience who hung on his words. He spoke of the Byzantine court as revealed in the tenth-century *Book of Ceremonies* of the emperor Constantine VII Porphyrogenitus (945–959). His voice rose and fell, spacing his words with hieratic slowness as he described the birthday greeting of the emperor by his courtiers: "Row on row ... [pause] carrying golden apples in their hands [pause] their beards [pause] ... glistening with sweet perfume."

Gervase was at his best when lecturing on the age of Richard II (1377–1399), which was another of his passions. He did this in the dining hall of Balliol College, in the high summer, as a mechanical mower moved relentlessly up and down the lawn outside, coming close to the open window and then moving away. Unflustered, Gervase used the intermittent roar of the approaching machine as a metronome. Describing the intellectual life of Oxford in the late fourteenth century, he concluded,

And then [vrrrummm] as all embracing as the sky [vrrmmm] but quite as distant [vrrummm] was the belief in God.

Of those of whom he approved (notably the future Byzantinist Anthony Bryer, founder of the Birmingham Byzantine Center), he would declare, "He has the holy fire." Gervase had that fire also. But, in the 1950s, it burned virtually alone.

THE MEDIEVAL TUTOR: HARRY BELL (1913–1964)

With little or no backup from university-wide lectures or seminars, we were totally dependent on our tutors. My tutor in medieval history was Henry Esmond Bell—Harry Bell. In a letter to my parents, I described my first encounter with him, when I arrived in Oxford, in October 1953:

So far I had met no ogres, so I was rather anxious to find out what this imposing personage was like. I tapped nervously, and went in. A big room, with a low bookshelf running round it. Mr. Bell rushed up to me, grasped me by the hand, shoved me into a chair, and started talking about how much he admired Dublin. He is a small little man with a very unimpressive, rather weak face. . . . Rather untidy, but distinguished looking dark hair, and a very definite stoop. He gave the impression of a very shy, kind little man; which indeed he is. The last of the ogres is dead.

Harry Bell taught all medieval history, although his own research had been on the Elizabethan Court of Wards and on the last flowering of heraldry and the discussion of feudal dues at that time.[4] I did not know—for Harry Bell was so unassuming—that he had been a Monuments Man in Italy during the war: he had played a part in saving historical archives as the Allies advanced up the peninsula. This may account for the zest with which he encouraged me to pursue themes in Italian medieval history, rather than concentrating on the more standard history of northern France.

He was a reassuring presence, squeezing ever deeper into his narrow armchair, as he chewed his pipe with pleasure while listening to a good essay. He always had his three points. He always had one revealing anecdote of the period to round off his comments (an anecdote to feed to the examiners in two years' time). He always told us carefully how the theme of the next essay grew out of the one that we had just completed. He was neither the port-soaked guru nor the brilliant young don of Oxford's dreams. He loved his subject and his pupils. That was enough. He was all that a don, a teacher in the Oxford tutorial tradition, could be.

Harry and his wife kept open house in their college lodgings at the end of Holywell. I described one such visit to my parents:

> They have a lovely house: an old rambling little place at the base of Longwall Street, which is well decorated and painted, lined with books. After a whole series of anecdotes about the dons and professors they had both known, we were interrupted by his two sweet dogs. They are <u>Schnautzers</u>—dogs resembling Kerry Blues—and they are called <u>Otto</u> and <u>Charlemagne</u>.
>
> I learned many things of the pets [of fellow medievalists]: Sir Maurice Powicke has a beautiful cat called "Henry Bolingbroke"; McFarlane, <u>the</u> McFarlane, has a cat of enormous dimensions and, like his master, uncertain temper.
>
> Bell wants a giant Schnautzer, and will call him <u>Barbarossa.</u>

(Significantly, perhaps, one of McFarlane's cats was called "Stubbs.")[5]

4. H. E. Bell, *An Introduction to the History and Records of the Court of Wards and Liveries* (Cambridge University Press, 1953).

5. *K. B. McFarlane: Letters to Friends, 1940–1960*, ed. Gerald Harris with a memoir by Karl Leyser (Oxford: Magdalen College, 1995), xxvi.

MEDIEVAL FIGURES: MAURICE POWICKE (1879–1963) AND BRUCE McFARLANE (1903–1966)

This was an unexpected view of the medievalist establishment in 1950s Oxford. But it was not surprising that leading medievalists, such as Powicke and McFarlane, should be seen as legendary figures rather than as active teachers. Outside the colleges in which they were tutors (or, in Powicke's case, outside his duties as Regius Professor of History) they were not well-known to undergraduates. As a result, they easily became semimythological figures, who moved on the edge of our horizon, in the exotic bestiary of Oxford medieval studies. In all my undergraduate years, I never exchanged a word with either of them. But they stood for two contrasting approaches to the study of the Middle Ages.

Sir Maurice Powicke, the former Regius Professor of History, was the Grand Old Man of medieval history. His vast and wide-reaching learning was held to derive from total immersion in the past, through the abundant archives of medieval Britain. In sleuthing in the archives, Powicke made the thirteenth century come alive.

> Sometimes, as I work at a series of patent and close rolls [the documents where Powicke so often made his discoveries], I have a queer sensation; the dead entries begin to be alive. It is rather like the experience of sitting down in one's chair and finding that one has sat on the cat.[6]

The cat may have been "Henry Bolingbroke" himself.

I remember seeing Powicke once, sitting at the back of Merton College Chapel—a little man, dwarfed by his great umbrella. He seemed to be communing with the world of the fourteenth-century grisaille windows that surrounded him. He stood for an almost mystical familiarity with the Middle Ages. It was a degree of familiarity that I myself was anxious to acquire.

Bruce McFarlane was by far the more feline figure. In the imagination of the young, he stood for the other, harsher side of a medievalist's long dialogue with the archives. His apparent total mastery of the complexities of fifteenth-century England, largely based on access to archives of all kinds, both awed and cramped younger scholars. He acted on the study of late medieval history in Oxford like a polar ice cap. A fierce perfectionist, who published little and

---

6. F. M. Powicke, *Ways of Medieval Life and Thought* (London: Odhams Press, 1949), 67.

criticized others with memorable *terribilità*, McFarlane was a persecutory superego to us all—to mature researchers quite as much as to students.

I remember a set of lectures that McFarlane delivered on the Flemish painter Hans Memling (1430–1495). Given my "High Flemish" mood of only a few years before, inspired by Huizinga's *Waning of the Middle Ages,* I attended these lectures with great interest. They had grown from a redating of some of Memling's works based on archival discoveries by McFarlane, concerning the career of one of Memling's English patrons. But they offered no new perspective on the culture and society of the later Middle Ages. McFarlane made clear that he had no wish to be a Huizinga. Instead, the lectures turned out to be a public execution of art historians (one of them none other than the great Erwin Panofsky) who had dared to trust to intuition—as judges of the changes in a painter's style—while truth, hard truth lay only in the Public Records Office. Later research, based on new techniques for the analysis of wood and paint, seems to have proved McFarlane right. But it did not matter. As far as I was concerned, he had killed the subject.[7]

7. K. B. McFarlane, *Hans Memling* (Oxford: Clarendon Press, 1971), with Dirk de Vos, *Hans Memling: Catalogue* (Bruges: Stedelijke Musea, 1994).

FRIENDS AND BOOKS

FRIENDS

It was a commonplace among undergraduates at Oxford that we learned more from each other than we ever learned from any lectures or, even, from our tutors. Looking back on my various friends, I realize that each one of them, each in a different way, contributed to the grooming process that turned us into Oxford-style historians. Together, we listened in to the vast rumor box of the Oxford History School. We knew its principal figures, if from a distance, and what sort of history each stood for, if only in caricature. We knew which currents of history were "in" and which were "out." We were sharp judges of our own tutors. We loved to share inside knowledge about the different periods of history that each of us studied. The result of our long conversations was something of great value—a historical culture considerably wider and more rich than the cramped options offered to us by the Examination Syllabus alone.

My friends came from a variety of worlds, all of them new to me. Each brought me something different and exciting. Take one instance only—Jan Safranek. The son of a Czech diplomat and of a famous French pianist, he lived in Paris. He was Europe personified—the sad, divided Europe of the Cold War. Having spent the evening listening to Jan as he spoke about Eastern Europe under Soviet rule, I would shiver a little as I made my way down the ill-lit, cold staircase of the Victorian part of the New Buildings: Was this what it was like to descend into the basement of the Lubyanka Prison in Moscow?

Jan was very much a young Parisian in his fierce methodological partisanship. He considered that his principal tutor in early modern history was hopelessly out of the loop. Jan may have been right: a fact that did not endear him to the tutor in question. It was Jan who introduced me to that masterpiece of modern historiography, Fernand Braudel's *La Méditerranée et le monde méditerranéen à l'époque de Philippe II*, which had appeared in 1949. This was an extended essay, in the majestic style of a French *grande thèse*, on the relation between history and geography that was as applicable to the ancient world as to the sixteenth century. Braudel was my first contact with a book that placed a distinctive landscape, with its unchanging, silent restraints and perennial rhythms, at the center of the historian's imagination, rather than the narrative of events among the higher-ups, which was the usual subject of history as taught in Oxford and elsewhere. I would constantly turn to him in future years.

I should add—to get the sense of "period" right—that all my friends were from New College only, and that all were men. New College did not admit women until 1979, when I was already far away, in Berkeley. In the 1950s, it was as much an all-male environment as Aravon and Shrewsbury had been. Only when I moved out of college into lodgings, in my last year, did my horizons open to include regular woman friends as part of a life lived at a little distance from the heavy gravitational field of Oxford proper.

For a medievalist there was one further, somewhat unexpected source of inspiration. That was the Scala Cinema in Walton Street. For these were the years in which a succession of great Japanese films brought to Western audiences a touch of the utter strangeness of another Middle Ages—that of the Japan of the samurai. The exotic dress, the mettlesome horses, the stylized gestures, and, above all, the sheer riot of color in the silken robes, the fluttering pennants, and the palace décors, seen for the very first time in unfamiliar Eastmancolor, came as a visual shock. Teinosake Kinugasa's *Gate of Hell* appeared in 1953. Maybe the court of Byzantium looked more like the world of Kinugasa's *daimyos* than anything that even Gervase Mathew could evoke. When *Gate of Hell* played at the Scala, I sat through three continuous showings. Here was yet another exotic world taken in by my eyes.

Reading: Toward the South and East

More than anything else, my life in these two years was the life of a reader of books. In the long run, the only way into the European Middle Ages was an old-fashioned one: reading—tenacious *Sitzfleisch*, sedentary study, in one's rooms, in the Radcliffe Camera undergraduate library, in the Upper and Lower Reading Rooms of the Bodleian Library, and—when in Ireland—in the armchair in the sitting room or beside the Moloch in the kitchen during the long, quiet vacations.

To my surprise, I recently discovered a set of three long, hardback bound notebooks in which I took notes at this time. The first two were notes on the books I read in 1954 to 1955. The third was mainly notes on the lectures that I attended in my last year.

My notes made plain my drift toward the south and to the east. In my readings on European history, I gave little attention to the traditional "hot spot" of Anglo-French history. Because they were focused on political issues, conventional histories of Europe (at least those in French and English) tended to give most attention to England and to France because they were the two most successful feudal kingdoms of their times. Here were two nation-states in the making. By comparison, Germany and Italy were disregarded as unmanageable regions that had somehow missed the bus of progress. They were treated as failed states, condemned to disunity until the nineteenth century. In any case, most history undergraduates were expected to know French, but not necessarily any other modern European language.

I did not take this option. Instead, the German that I had learned from Dr. Scheyer opened up an entire world for me. It enabled me to look east of the Rhine, to the history of the Holy Roman Empire in medieval Germany, reading my way through articles and reviews, and eventually tackling the monumental *Kirchengeschichte Deutschlands* of Albert Hauck (1845–1918).[1]

German also took me farther east: I read the definitive *Geschichte des byzantinischen Staates* by Georg Ostrogorsky (1902–1976) a few years before it was translated into English.[2] Along with Steven Runciman's *History of the Crusades* and his lectures on the Eastern Schism, which had impressed me so greatly when I heard them delivered in Magdalen College Hall, such reading drew me to the ideological and military confrontation between the Byzantine Empire and the Catholic nations of the West as one of the great tragedies of the Middle Ages.

The relations between Byzantium and the West also took me south, into southern Italy and Sicily, where the two cultures mingled. Somehow I came to read Italian. I taught myself through reading articles in Italian journals and Italian books on tenth-century Rome, on the Norman kingdom of Sicily, and on the fascinating figure of the emperor Frederick the Second (1194–1250). I approached these books on the happy-go-lucky principle that Italian was,

1. A. Hauck, *Kirchengeschichte Deutschlands* (Leipzig: Hinrichs, 1904–1920).

2. G. Ostrogorsky, *Geschichte des byzantinischen Staates* (Munich: Beck, 1952); trans. Joan Hussey: *History of the Byzantine Empire* (Oxford: Blackwell, 1956).

somehow, a mixture of the best in French and the worst in Latin. To read the orotund prose of Italian historians was like coming upon the firm lines of a Roman inscription in a late, late Latin that had gone to seed, warmed in Mediterranean sunlight. Thus encouraged, I stumbled my way through books such as the newly published work of Paolo Lamma (1915–1961) on Byzantine intervention in the politics of twelfth-century Italy.[3]

In this reading, I found myself concentrating on the parting of the ways between Byzantium and the West. Here were two different Christian societies, with differing views on the relation between church and state and between clergy and laity. I was ripe for the Investiture Contest and its consequences—that great clash of the sacred and profane, in the eleventh and twelfth centuries, which made the thrusting feudal society of the Latin West so very different from its more ancient and slow-moving eastern neighbor. It was time to buy and to absorb (beside the Moloch in the kitchen) a monumental treatment of this theme: *The Growth of Papal Government in the Middle Ages* by Walter Ullmann.[4]

The Power of an Idea: Walter Ullmann (1910–1983)

Walter Ullmann was a refugee from Nazi Austria. Though hunted as a Jew, he was a devout Catholic. He brought to British scholarship a sense of the power of ideas, and of how ideas had been transformed into law and abiding institutional structures in the medieval West. As I made my way through his work, I realized that Ullmann had shown how a religious idea could bite into society. *The Growth of Papal Government* was a study of religion turned into power. His work flouted the unspoken Oxford consensus that religious ideas were of little interest to the historian.

This was an issue that we undergraduates debated vigorously among ourselves. I was aware that the overall atmosphere of Oxford favored an anti-intellectual approach: politics, economics, and society were the stuff of "grown-up" history—not ideas. This bias toward the concrete was shown with particular clarity in an acrimonious debate that had exploded among historians of early modern England. Known as the "Gentry controversy," it was a

3. P. Lamma, *Comneni e Staufer. Ricerche sui rapporti tra Bisanzio e l'Occidente nel secolo xii* (Rome: Istituto di Storia Medievale, 1955).

4. Walter Ullmann, *The Growth of Papal Government in the Middle Ages* (London: Methuen, 1955).

cameo performance of donnish fisticuffs. It had pitted Hugh Trevor-Roper (1914–2003), a writer of noted acerbity, against several other equally pugnacious pundits, in an argument on the changing economic and social position of the English gentry in the seventeenth century, and its effect on the onset of the English Civil War (1642–1651). Was this crisis caused by a social change—"the rise of the gentry" at the expense of the aristocracy—or were there other explanations?

The Oxford rumor box resounded with the dispute. It was an academic slaughter-fest, which, for a time, pushed all other historical debates to one side. Somehow, to be up-to-date on the "Gentry controversy" became a sign of being fully "with it" as a historian. I even remember a scene at the final examination. As everyone else entered the examination room to answer the paper on early modern England, a group held back. They gathered like a football huddle to rehearse the pros and cons of the "Gentry controversy" before sitting down to the exam. They were convinced that a question on a topic that was so urgently debated among the dons of Oxford was certain to turn up. Alas, they were wrong. The examiner (doubtless a troglodyte, irremediably out of the loop) set a question not on the social role of the gentry but on the social role of lawyers in early seventeenth-century public life.

What struck me about the controversy was the agreement of all the participants that religious factors, such as the rise of Puritanism, played no role in the crisis that led to the Civil War. Social and economic developments, not religious thought, set the pace for those troubled times. It was better to count manors and to tot up mortgages than to read sermons.

I found myself unconvinced by this dismissive view. My experience in Ireland showed me that some religious ideas might, indeed, be ineffectual—but not all of them were. Once given heft through being linked to a church, to a state, or to a social movement, religious ideas had it in them to change the world. Ullmann's *Growth of Papal Government* seemed to me to show that this was so.

Ideology to Reality: From Ernst Kantorowicz (1895–1963) to Karl Leyser (1920–1992)

But how did ideology and reality converge? This question explains my great interest, as revealed in my notes, not only in the papal but also in the German side of the story of the clash between papacy and empire at the time of the Investiture Contest and later.

The propaganda of Frederick II (who was Holy Roman emperor from 1220 to 1250) emerged as a test case for the power of ideology. Frederick's imperial ideology was as ambitious as that of the papacy itself. But did it bite into society? How did it relate to contemporary realities? And so I found myself following, largely in German articles, the debate sparked by a provocative portrait of the talented and cosmopolitan emperor. This was Ernst Kantorowicz's *Frederick the Second*.[5]

Kantorowicz's overblown portrait of Frederick II made him the whipping boy of all prudent scholars, in Germany as elsewhere. For English medievalists, *Frederick II* was a dreadful warning. It showed the consequences of an excessive study of ideas without any attempt to root these ideas in a concrete context. I myself found the book unbearably pretentious. But it made me face a problem. Given the overwhelming scholarly interest (largely on the part of German scholars) in the ideological aspects of medieval German kingship, how could the dramatic clash of ideas associated with the Investiture Contest and the counterclaims of the German Holy Roman Empire be, as it were, "grounded"? The language of power, both papal and imperial, was beguiling in its clarity and symbolic force. But it seemed to me to be permanently up in the air. At that time, I would have heartily agreed with Beryl Smalley in her review of a later book by Kantorowicz—*The King's Two Bodies*:

> By the end of the book I felt as queasy as one would after a diet of jam without bread. Is it possible to study the history of ideas without relating them to their genesis in actual problems and conflicts?[6]

It was for this reason that I owed so much to the lectures of Karl Leyser, which I attended in the early spring of 1956. They resolved a dilemma for me. For the first time, Karl presented German medieval history to me in the round. A vivid cast of characters, who until then had seemed to be perched on the high stilts of ideology, were brought down to earth. Their ideas and their slogans were, at last, given a concrete context. Altogether, Karl's lectures gave me God's plenty. They were the only course of public lectures that I sat through from beginning to end in my last year at Oxford.

When I listened to Karl's lectures in early 1956, I had already begun to be engaged with a figure who was larger and more vivid than any medieval pope

---

5. E. Kantorowicz, *Frederick the Second* (New York: R. R. Smith, 1931).

6. B. Smalley, *Past and Present* 20 (1961): 32; see Robert E. Lerner, *Ernst Kantorowicz. A Life* (Princeton, NJ: Princeton University Press, 2017), 353.

or emperor, and whose ideas would echo throughout the Middle Ages in both papal and imperial circles. In the summer of 1955 I had taken the final step in the learning process of an undergraduate in the History School of Oxford. I began to prepare for the papers in the Special Subject. And the Special Subject that I chose was not on a theme from the High Middle Ages, but from over half a millennium earlier, from the last days of Rome and the early days of Christianity in Europe: I would study Saint Augustine and his age.

THE AGE OF AUGUSTINE

The Age of Augustine (354–430)

I spent June and July 1955 in Oxford, reading for the Special Subject on Augustine. The Special Subject represented the culmination of a history undergraduate's preparation for the final examination. It gave the student the opportunity to study an important moment of history through a selection of original texts, which were listed in the Examination Statutes. These texts were set in stone. Examiners, students, and tutors might come and go; the texts to be studied remained the same. But there was no standard bibliography of secondary literature for the subject. It was up to the tutors or to the enterprise of the individual students to make their way to the books and articles that would enable them to interpret the texts.

For that reason, the choice of texts determined the entire shape and tone of the Augustine Special Subject. And this choice had been made in a manner characteristic of Oxford—it was a compromise reached after a lively tussle among the differing interests of the tutors who normally taught the Special Subject. These tutors formed a consortium, and the consortium of teachers of the Saint Augustine Special Subject had many different interests.

The result of this pooling of interests was an array of texts of quite remarkable richness and variety. The Augustine Special Subject was not a study of Augustine alone. It was, rather, a study of nothing less than "the Age of Augustine." And what an age! Alongside the well-known works of Augustine, the *Confessions* and the *City of God*, the set texts illustrated the end of paganism, the workings of imperial government, the crisis of the cities, and the first fateful decades of the barbarian invasions. It was an exciting range of topics. My medieval readings had already led me to ponder the relation between religious

ideas and the nitty-gritty of politics and social life. The Augustine Special Subject presented me with similar problems, and in a peculiarly invigorating
mixture.

READINGS

My work for the Augustine Special Subject marked the beginning of my life as
a student of late antiquity. Unlike the other subjects that I studied at Oxford,
what I read for the Augustine Special Subject has become part of my work
from that time onward. Texts that I first met in 1955 are the ones that I still
study. Even the books that I read at this time are still there on the shelves of
my library. They have marginal notes in them in a handwriting that I barely
recognize as my own, so that I sometimes have the strange feeling of being in
the presence of someone other than myself, looking over my shoulder as I
read. Let me relive something of the excitement of this first moment of
encounter.

Like many decisive steps in life, the choice to take the Saint Augustine Special Subject did not seem to be preceded by any very clear intention. Doubtless, my religious preoccupations of the previous year made me want to go
back to the problem of the historical origins of the Catholic Church. But just
as important as the religious issue was my feeling that, as a medievalist, I had
to go back to the fall of Rome, a topic that had already fascinated me when I
read Rostovtzeff's magnificent *Social and Economic History of the Roman Empire* in my gap year in Ireland. This was because so much of medieval culture
and society seemed to have originated in that time of upheaval. While an ancient historian might have been interested only in the fall of the Roman Empire, as a medievalist I wanted to know what came next—how something new
came out of the ruins of the ancient world.

What I do remember was a happy time. I found that I could indulge in
moments of eccentricity. Determined to maintain the *sprezzatura* of an Oxford man, I took Henri-Irénée Marrou's *Saint Augustin et la fin de la culture
antique* with me on a punt from Magdalen Bridge. The first stage of my absorption of this masterpiece took place against the swish of willows and of
splashing water, moored on the bank of the Cherwell beside the Marston
Ferry. It was the only authentically Oxford idyll that I ever went out of my
way to enjoy.

André Piganiol (1883–1968): "Roman Civilization Did Not Die a Natural Death"

As far as I remember, Marrou's *Saint Augustin* came last in my reading. In order to get right the general background to Augustine and his age, I began with *L'empire chrétien* of André Piganiol.[1] This book gripped me. I read it through in a single night. What Piganiol communicated to me in memorably pithy sentences was totally new to me. Here was a Roman Empire of the fourth century that was no longer seen as living in the shadow of a death sentence. It was not a shell of its old self. It had not been entirely ruined by the crisis of the third century, as Mikhail Rostovtzeff had supposed; nor was it caught in the pall of some deep-seated process of decadence (as was the vogue in more popular circles). Far from it. Until brought to its knees by barbarian warlords (those very warlords whose sinister rise to power and sack of Rome I would trace in the course of the Augustine Special Subject), the empire—despite its ancient ills—was still a going concern. I went out of my way to mark heavily Piganiol's last sentence:

> La civilisation romaine n'est pas morte de sa belle mort. Elle a été assassinée.

> Roman civilization did not die a natural death. It was murdered.[2]

But I marked other passages as well. I noticed that Piganiol was no lover of the Fathers of the Church. His perspective was magnificently *laïc*. He tended to regard Christianity as a disruptive force. His judgments on the champions of Christian orthodoxy were severe in the extreme. He characterized Saint Athanasius of Alexandria as "cette personnalité orgueilleuse et brutale"—"that proud and brutal character."[3] To this, I added, with evident glee, "*pace* Newman!!"—a polite academic form of "Take that, Newman!"

This was a rebuke, on my part, to John Henry Newman (1801–1890), the nineteenth-century leader of the High Church movement and eventual convert to Rome. In his history of the Arian controversy, Newman had presented Athanasius as the heroic upholder of Christian truth in defiance of the conformism of worldly courtier-bishops (who bore an uncanny resemblance to

---

1. A. Piganiol, *L'empire chrétien*, Glotz, Histoire générale: Histoire romaine IV (Paris: Presses Universitaires de France, 1947), 2.

2. Piganiol, *L'empire chrétien*, 422.

3. Piganiol, *L'empire chrétien*, 44.

the Low Church prelates of his own time). Plainly, this was not how Piganiol saw him.

I was in a mood for Piganiol's resolute *laïcité*. My religious worries of the previous year had dissipated. I was not embittered by that crisis. I was disposed to sit back for a time, so as to enjoy Christianity as a historical phenomenon. Beliefs and institutions that would come to dominate medieval Europe—many of which survived up to this day in Roman Catholic and Anglo-Catholic churches— gained human warmth for me through being traced back to precise moments in a historical process. I was now learning where it all came from—from the travails of a grand empire long before the beginning of the European Middle Ages.

The Theodosian Code

Inspired by Piganiol, I fell upon the brand-new translation of the Theodosian Code by Clyde Pharr (1883–1972).[4] This collection of imperial edicts (made in 438) showed the late Roman state at work. I read it in the library of Pusey House, which was the only place in Oxford where a copy could be found. Pusey House was the center of the Oxford High Church movement—a movement committed to the notion of the unbroken continuity between Catholic Christianity (Anglican as well as Roman Catholic) and the age of the Fathers of the Church, Augustine being the most prominent Church Father of all.

But a reading of the Theodosian Code proved that many links in that golden chain were problematic. The code was a collection of imperial edicts from the time of the conversion of Constantine, in 312. It revealed the Roman state at work in a no-nonsense manner defining, patrolling, and advancing the Christian church almost as if it were a branch of government. The edicts made plain how much Christianity had owed, for its expansion and establishment, to an ambitious and robustly secular empire. The Theodosian Code contained sonorous imperial rulings on the Christian faith—laying down creeds and condemning pagans and heretics. Other texts chosen from the Theodosian Code documented the ins and outs of imperial privileges granted to the clergy. Many of these privileges—such as the establishment of the bishop's law court— would last throughout the Middle Ages. Yet, at the same time, these pious concessions were often accompanied by peremptory orders for the arrest of monks as troublemakers and draft-dodgers.

4. *The Theodosian Code*, trans. Clyde Pharr (Princeton, NJ: Princeton University Press, 1952).

Altogether, to read such resolutely worldly texts in a library filled with the scent of incense that percolated upward from the High Church chapel below was a strangely remissive experience. Two worlds met—that of contemporary Anglo-Catholic piety and the world of a distant empire where it had all begun. I felt, at last, that I had my feet in the warm, rich clay of an ancient world that had by no means grown gray.

WILLIAM FREND (1916–2005): TWO CHURCHES, TWO SOCIETIES

It was the same with my readings of Augustine. Far from being faced by an etherial religious author (as first impressions of the *Confessions* and the *City of God* might have led me to suppose), I found an active bishop deeply rooted— indeed, almost mired—in the distinctive earth of Roman Africa. There was one reason for this way of seeing Augustine: William Frend's masterpiece, *The Donatist Church: A Movement of Protest in Roman North Africa*, had only just appeared.[5]

This book advanced a hypothesis that (if accepted) totally altered our view of Augustine and of his North African environment. The Donatist Schism had caused the division of the African churches into two irreconcilable parties as a result of the Great Persecution of AD 303. It was usually dismissed by scholars as an unsavory and vaguely ridiculous sideshow to the main work of Augustine, who was bishop of Hippo (modern Annaba, a town on the coast of Algeria) from 397 to 430.

Bill Frend challenged this opinion. I immediately realized that Frend was an author with a gift for endowing the conflicts of the early church (usually presented as purely religious and intellectual affairs) with a magical concreteness. He presented the schism as a clash between two landscapes, even between two classes and two ethnic groups. The Catholicism of the Romanized cities of the Mediterranean was represented by Augustine as bishop of Hippo—a coastal city that looked across the sea to Rome. Farther inland, the version of Christianity upheld by Romanized Africans such as Augustine was challenged by the fierce resistance of the populous Berber villages of the Numidian plateau. As Frend presented them, these barely Romanized villages were the homeland of the Donatist Church.

5. W.H.C. Frend, *The Donatist Church: A Movement of Protest in Roman North Africa* (Oxford: Clarendon Press, 1952).

Instead of two Christian groups, divided by seemingly trivial issues, two societies faced each other, represented by two churches, each with a very different view of the relations of the church to the Roman social order—conservative Catholics (such as Augustine) being met by radical Christians associated with the Donatist Church. The bitter struggle of these two versions of Christianity formed the background to Augustine's life in Africa. His writings on the nature of the Catholic Church, on the Roman Empire, on the "Earthly City" and the "City of God," would dominate medieval views of the relation between church and society. Bill Frend's *Donatist Church* and the texts that I now had to read for the Special Subject showed that these views had emerged in a distinctive landscape. They had first been hammered out in a situation of face-to-face social and ethnic conflict in the little towns and villages of a divided Africa. I had found, in the distant Maghreb (in what are now Muslim countries: Tunisia, Algeria, and Morocco), the beginning of the Western Middle Ages.

Otto Seeck (1850–1921): "An Inner Illness"[6]

This was exciting enough. But equally exciting was the realization that old stereotypes of the decline of Rome had begun to be challenged. This fundamental change in the evaluation of the later Roman Empire was summed up in the contrast between two authors on whom I took careful notes—Otto Seeck and Santo Mazzarino.

I read Otto Seeck first. Seeck was the Grand Old Man of late Roman scholarship. He had edited the letters of one of the great "last pagans of Rome," Quintus Aurelius Symmachus; he had established the chronology of Symmachus's contemporary and peer in the Greek world, the Antiochene rhetor Libanius; he had compiled (largely from the Theodosian Code) a register of the dated edicts of the emperors and popes from 284 to 476. I was unaware of those achievements; but I took careful notes on the first volume of Seeck's six-volume *Geschichte des Untergangs der antiken Welt*, which I found by chance in New College Library.[7]

---

6. Stefan Rebenich, "Otto Seeck und die Geschichte des Untergangs der antiken Welt," in *The New Late Antiquity: A Gallery of Intellectual Portraits*, ed. Clifford Ando and Marco Formisano (Heidelberg: Winter, 2021), 451–470 (henceforth *New Late Antiquity*).

7. O. Seeck, *Geschichte des Untergangs der antiken Welt. Band 1* (1895; last edition, Stuttgart: Metzler, 1921–1922).

The second part of the first volume offered a uniformly pessimistic valuation of the later empire. It was entitled "Verfall der antiken Welt"—The Decay of the Ancient World. Seeck explained that the later empire was a doomed empire. It was rotten from within:

> Nicht die Germanen haben das Römerreich zu Falle gebracht, sondern innere Krankheit verzehrte es.

> It was not the Germans who brought the Roman Empire to its downfall; rather, an inner illness laid it waste.[8]

It was precisely this opinion that André Piganiol had rejected with such firmness in 1947, in the conclusion of *L'empire chrétien*. Having just read Piganiol, in one unforgettable night, I was in no mood for Seeck's pseudoscientific evocation of the overall decay of the ancient world.

Writing immediately after World War II, Piganiol was right to be a bitter critic of Seeck's notion of decadence. But Seeck had not been a racist of the Nazi kind. His was a more subtle, cosmopolitan, and confident intolerance, shared by many American, English, and European thinkers in the late nineteenth and early twentieth centuries. His view of the decline of Rome was derived from social Darwinism. He was obsessed with the idea of decadence caused by demographic change. In his view, the extinction of the leaders of Roman society in the civil wars and the early empire had led to the rise of the mediocre and of the cowardly.

For Seeck, "weeding out of the best" and "hereditary cowardice" were more than metaphors: he believed that late Roman persons really had bad genes. A good north German (he was born at Riga and had taught in Berlin), Seeck felt that he needed only to look south of the Alps to find confirmation of his views. He thought that the constant suppression, execution, and exile of heretics in Catholic Spain had brought about the same state of moral anemia as seemed to him to have afflicted the Roman world. He was confident that this development accounted for "the known fact that also the other Catholic countries stand almost without exception at a lower spiritual level than do the Protestant."[9]

I had read enough. Such odious pronouncements were not for me.

What Seeck did for me at this time was pose a crucial question. Were the leading figures of the later empire (the emperors, the generals, the aristocrats,

---

8. Seeck, *Geschichte des Untergangs* 1:191.
9. Seeck, *Geschichte des Untergangs* 1:551/52.

and the bishops—even Augustine) mere wraiths struggling in the ruins of a decadent civilization, doomed to fail? Or were they agents in their own right, as robust as any other Roman statesmen and authors of any other time?

SANTO MAZZARINO (1916–1982): EAST AND WEST

These questions were answered for me in a single book: *Stilicone. La crisi imperiale dopo Teodosio* of Santo Mazzarino.[10] The first page of Mazzarino's preface gave me the answer to Seeck:

> The history of the later empire is in some ways a relatively young field of inquiry: long thought of as a history of imperial "decadence" (the history of a "lower" empire) it appeared above all in a negative light in relation to the periods that had preceded it. . . . The effort to give this period a historical autonomy and a positive function is, one might say, a relatively new achievement.[11]

Brave words. And Mazzarino set out, in no uncertain manner, to prove his point: he showed that it was possible to write about the politics of the later empire without invoking the notion of inevitable decay. I was also impressed by the way in which he set about doing it. In his *Stilicone* (as in all his later work), Mazzarino showed a genius for seizing on a few ancient texts (often out of the way and hitherto neglected texts) and reinterpreting them in such a manner that they cast a new light on major issues of the history of Rome, indeed of the ancient world as a whole.

It was, above all, this width of vision in Mazzarino's work that has impressed me ever since. *Stilicone* addressed the career of the barbarian generalissimo Stilicho, and his relations with the Visigothic king Alaric, which led eventually to the disastrous sack of Rome in 410. Mazzarino placed these events against a wider social background. He showed how the seemingly pointless maneuverings of Roman armies and barbarian war bands back and forth across Italy and the Balkans were part of a wider crisis.

What was at stake was the opening of a chasm between two worlds, between the old Latin West and the new world of East Rome. On the one hand

---

10. Santo Mazzarino, *Stilicone. La crisi imperiale dopo Teodosio* (Rome: Signorelli, 1942; reprint, Milan: Rizzoli, 1990, with a most perceptive introduction by Andrea Giardina).

11. Mazzarino, *Stilicone*, v. I use the translation of my friend and colleague Noel Lenski: "Santo Mazzarino: Revolutions in Society and Economy in Late Antiquity," in *New Late Antiquity*, 273–295, at 277.

there was the confident empire of Constantinople, secure in its loyalty to an emperor who enjoyed the support of increasingly Christian populations—a Byzantium built to last. Compared with the Empire of the East, the Western Empire proved to be the more divided, vulnerable society. It was a society increasingly controlled by its great landowners. Hence the fall of the Empire in the West in the course of the fifth century. But the empire vanished in the West only. East Rome survived for many centuries. It was the division between two worlds that lay at the heart of the "imperial crisis" faced by Stilicho. Mazzarino made clear that, rather than an overall "decline and fall" of the Roman Empire as a whole, it was the contrast between East and West—between a buoyant Eastern Empire and a fragile West—that was the key to the end of Rome. This picture, first sketched for me in broad, masterly strokes by Mazzarino, has remained with me ever since.

But, at the time, Santo Mazzarino did more than this. Passing from Seeck to Mazzarino, I felt that I had passed out of the chill shade of an overblown notion of decadence into living history. The notion of decadence had enjoyed such sinister prominence in much of European thought in the late nineteenth and twentieth centuries that it was difficult to detach the Roman Empire from the gray and glutinous embrace of theories of decay. Mazzarino banished those half-educated imaginings. He made plain that the Roman Empire in its last centuries was full of mighty tensions—tensions between great landowners and the state, between Christians and pagans, between the Roman civilian elites and a partly "barbarian" military caste. But it was not a decadent, nor was it even, at the time, a necessarily doomed society. As I read Mazzarino, life and warmth flooded back into the fourth century.

And so my reading raised a further question. The overwhelming majority of studies of the later empire had treated this period as if it were no more than an anxious prelude to the imminent fall of Rome. But what I had found in Piganiol and Mazzarino suggested otherwise: there was a lot more life in the later empire than we had thought. Far from being an awkward hiatus between the ancient world and the Middle Ages, it seemed to be a period with a vitality of its own. But, in order to become a field of study in its own right, the period needed a name. This name was provided for me by yet another giant among European scholars—Henri-Irénée Marrou.

"DECADENCE" OR "LATE ANTIQUITY"?

HENRI-IRÉNÉE MARROU

DECADENCE RECONSIDERED

Toward the end of my weeks of reading for the Augustine Special Subject, I emerged from Thornton's Bookshop—an Aladdin's cave of foreign publications—with a big book in two volumes written by Henri-Irénée Marrou (1904–1977). The format itself was strange: the first volume had six hundred pages, while the second had only ninety. They had been published together in 1949. The first volume was Marrou's *grande thèse*, completed in 1937; the second volume was Marrou's afterthought about his own *grande thèse*, written twelve years later.[1]

The first volume's title made its argument perfectly clear: *Saint Augustin et la fin de la culture antique*—Saint Augustine and the *End* of Ancient Culture. It described a culture that appeared to Marrou to be in the last stages of decay. The second volume had a more open-ended title. It was called *Retractatio*—a Rereading. And Marrou's "rereading" effectively rebutted the main theme of his *grande thèse*—the notion that the culture of the age of Augustine had reached its end. In other words, the second volume (written in 1949) was a critique of the large first volume (completed in 1937).

Marrou's second volume—the *Retractatio*—touched the very heart of my own preoccupation with the nature of the end of the Roman Empire. Had the

---

1. H. I. Marrou, *Saint Augustin et la fin de la culture antique* with *Retractatio*, Bibliothèque des Écoles françaises d'Athènes et de Rome 145 bis (Paris: de Boccard, 1949).

Roman world fallen because it had been sickened by some deep-seated, all-embracing, and incurable decadence—as Otto Seeck had suggested? Or was it still a living organism, developing successfully in new directions, as it passed from crisis to crisis, until, at last, it was overwhelmed—but only in its weaker western regions—by a largely unforeseen surge of barbarian war-lordism, as Piganiol and Mazzarino had contended? In this debate, with which I had wrestled in the previous weeks, Marrou cast the deciding vote. And he did so in the most cogent manner possible—by explaining that he had changed his mind on the issue of "decadence."

What I read in these two volumes were two Marrous—a younger and an older man. *Saint Augustin et la fin* had been written in 1937, before the outbreak of war in Europe. In it, Marrou presented Augustine as a *lettré de la décadence*, trapped in an age-old educational system that had run to seed. On this, the young Marrou (he was thirty-three at the time) was firm: "I have hidden nothing of the impoverishment, of the senile sclerosis of that ancient tradition as Augustine encountered it. . . . There is indeed something in Augustine [his culture] that is dead."[2]

Twelve years later, having experienced at first hand the horrors of the Nazi occupation of France, Marrou declared in his *Retractatio* that he had changed his mind. No: Augustine's culture had not let him down. It was not a dead culture. It was a culture that had changed, subtly but irrevocably, from classical times, but (like the Roman Empire itself) it had retained much of its ancient vigor. He could no longer say that

> Saint Augustine and, with him, the culture of his times were, as it were, being swept away on a current hurtling towards a void. No. . . .
>
> The civilization of the later empire [the *Bas-Empire*], as it is reflected in the culture of Augustine, is a vigorous organism, still evolving.[3]

To this I added in the margin, in capital letters, "Hurrah! Hurrah!!"

What Marrou wrote carried conviction with me precisely because it was not dogmatic in tone. To use a musical metaphor, such as Marrou himself used when describing the style of Saint Augustine, to read the *Retractatio* was like listening to a great symphony, made up of many themes, each exquisitely introduced. Grand theories of culture, the literary analysis of major late Roman writings (such as Augustine's *City of God*), the work of art historians, and

2. Marrou, *Saint Augustin et la fin*, 543/44).
3. Marrou, *Retractatio*, 689.

considerations of social history were brought together in a grand finale, to reassess the culture of the later empire. Here was no dried corpse, but an ancient civilization on the edge of yet another splendid flowering until unexpectedly brought to its knees (but in the Western Empire only) by the barbarian invasions of the fifth century.

"Toward a Healthy Civilization"[4]

That was enough. It gave me the green light to approach Augustine and his contemporaries in a new, less doom-laden manner. This was my first and most lasting impression on reading *Saint Augustin et la fin de la culture antique* and its *Retractatio*.

I took no notes on the book. I felt that it was too big, too full of life to be gutted in that manner—as I had gutted Seeck and Santo Mazzarino. What I still have is my own copy, its paper spine now almost totally broken so that it is little more than a pile of loose pages filled with excited marginal comments.

First and foremost, I was aware that I was reading a book shot through with tensions. But, at the time, as I read Marrou as an undergraduate in a punt in an Oxford summer, I knew nothing of the fierce origins of these tensions in the culture of interwar France in the 1920s and 1930s.

Little did I know, as I read him, that when he was my age, Marrou was already a fervent and radical young Catholic, anxious to come to grips with what he considered to be the crisis of the culture of his own times. He thought that it was decadent and stood in urgent need of salvation. The jottings in his notebooks (which were published after his death, in 2006) make this plain. In 1927, he wrote: "Our culture is making us into Byzantines. What human value is there in it, other than the social game that goes by the name of 'culture'?"[5]

This outburst of a twenty-three-year-old shows that, already at that time, Marrou tended to treat the culture of the age of Augustine—in what he saw as its "Byzantine" sterility—as a distant mirror of the decadence that he also saw in the culture of modern France. In 1934 he published a pamphlet-like book, *Fondements d'une culture chrétienne*. He made plain that what modern times needed was a "une civilisation saine"—a civilization that had recovered its health. The monstrous

4. See now Philippe Blaudeau, "Henri Irénée Marrou (1904–1977): Antiquité tardive et Cité de Dieu," in *New Late Antiquity*, 7–26.

5. Henri-Irénée Marrou, *Carnets posthumes*, VIII. iii, ed. Françoise Marrou-Flamant (Paris: Le Cerf, 2006), 37.

expansion of specialized disciplines had negated the humanizing role of education, much as the backward-looking pedantry of the late Roman educational system had cramped the souls of Augustine's contemporaries.[6]

Hence a heavy charge of disapproval ran through the first, six-hundred-page, volume of *Saint Augustin et la fin de la culture antique*. It was, indeed, about *la fin*. It laid bare what Marrou considered to be the decay of a great culture. This decadence did not spare even the greatest minds. The drama of the book consisted in watching Augustine struggling (never entirely successfully) with the enervating climate of his age.

"The Relation of Personal Thought to Its Milieu"

I remember that I was not entirely convinced by Marrou's presentation of the supposed decadence of late Roman culture (in *La fin*) even before I read his *Retractatio*. What excited me more was the other side of Marrou—the master's hand with which he joined the inner life of individuals to the wider frame of their culture. On this he was uncompromising. That was his job and his high skill. As he made plain in an entry in his notebook for some time after 1943: "All my theory of culture aims to throw light on the relation of personal thought to its milieu, to its tradition, to the community."[7] Marrou had not given me the conventional account of "Augustine and His Age," nor even "Augustine in His Age." He had given me "The Age of Augustine *in* Augustine." No one had done this for me before, for any period of history. I was thrilled. I really did not care whether the age that was analyzed with this magical touch was decadent or not. Marrou had brought it alive.

I have read Marrou ever since. To read *Saint Augustin et la fin de la culture antique* and the *Retractatio* now—sixty-five years later, in a very different world from 1950s Oxford—is to realize, as I write this chapter, that I had been, and from then on would continue to be, in the company of a giant.

Spätantike—Late Antiquity

Last but not least, as I turned to the *Retractatio*, I realized that Marrou had given a name to the period as a whole. Although he had shown with such masterly skill that Augustine's culture was deeply, almost irremovably, linked

---

6. Henri-Irénée Marrou, *Fondements d'une culture chrétienne* (Paris: Bloud et Gay, 1934).

7. Marrou, *Carnets*, XI (3) 77, 355.

to the ancient world, there was still much in Augustine that seemed also to prefigure the Middle Ages. Was Augustine, therefore, an ancient *and* a medieval man? This view struck Marrou as too abrupt a way of putting it. The Middle Ages were too far away to allow Augustine to be treated as "medieval" without severe anachronism. No: "Historical reality demands a more rich keyboard [*un clavier plus riche*: Marrou had found a musical image dear to his heart] than that summary dichotomy."[8] The peculiar in-between-ness of Augustine and his age demanded a name. Marrou found it:

> German, which welcomes neologisms with ease, has developed the habit of speaking of *Spätantike* [late antiquity].[9]

This suggestion was crucial. From then onward, I had a name for the period that had begun to intrigue me: "late antiquity." In my case, the term came to me from Marrou—and from Marrou only.

In fact, the word *Spätantike* had been current in Germany for some time. Marrou himself seems to have taken *Spätantike* from German art historians who had begun to use it in the 1920s or earlier, in order to characterize the hauntingly in-between quality of works that had already ceased to be classical while not yet becoming recognizably medieval. In order to illustrate what he meant, Marrou took a well-known example of such a work of art, for which the Germans already had an appropriate adjective—*spätantik*, late antique. This was the great bronze head of a late Roman emperor preserved in the Palazzo dei Conservatori on the Capitol of Rome. When Marrou wrote, it was ascribed to the emperor Constantius II (337–361), though it has recently been allotted to his father, Constantine (306–337). He pointed out that it would be absurd to speak of it as if it were a failed attempt to create a naturalistic portrait in the classical manner. With its upraised eyes and masklike features, it represented a new departure: a new art for a new image of the emperor—a superhuman being, whose intense, upturned gaze made real the invisible world from which he drew his power. In a silent mutation, a recognizably Roman bust had taken on the stylized, abstract features of a Byzantine icon.

"Late antique" was the only word for it. It is still there, in the Capitoline Museum. Since 1981, it has been joined by the great equestrian statue of Marcus Aurelius (161–180) that had once stood in the open air on top of the Capitol Hill. Separated by only some fifteen yards, they stare at each other across

8. Marrou, *Retractatio*, 691.
9. Marrou, *Retractatio*, 694.

the floor of a special section of the museum. Whenever I go to Rome, I sit between the two figures—Marcus Aurelius and Constantine—musing on the nature and the causes of the distance between these two images of two very different Roman emperors: one so very "classical," one challengingly "late antique." It is a lesson in the distinctive nature of late antiquity and the mystery of its emergence, after classical times, as yet another, surprisingly creative phase in the history of the ancient world.

COWLEY ROAD

Cowley Road: "Boys on the Make"

My last year in Oxford (from October 1955 to July 1956) was the happiest year of all. I no longer lived in college, surrounded by endless talk. I lived in lodgings halfway up the Cowley Road—on the way to the Morris Motors factory—with a friend from New College, Barry Clarke. After the hectic sociability and nightlong conversations of life in college, I found myself largely alone, in the company of unpretentious people. It was another Ireland for me. I wrote to my aunt Freda (Teedah) with genuine enthusiasm:

> On one thing I feel very superior indeed. That is, my lodgings. No one liked them when I chose them, now everyone is envying me. . . . They have been an enormous help in this term as they are just far enough away to cut down that useless visiting which takes up so much of the time, pleasantly but pointlessly for the first two years, but which is rather out of place for the "boys on the make" in the last year.

My colodger could not have been better. Barry Clarke was a scientist, an electrical engineer. He was very much a representative of the Other (the scientific side) of the "Two Cultures"—science and humanities—whose division would soon be lamented by Lord Snow.[1] This division troubled Barry not in the slightest. He was a grammar school boy—that is, he came from a local state school, not a private public school. Science was his way to the top. He had no job worries. He was already as good as signed on to a major laboratory. He had

---

1. C. P. Snow, *The Two Cultures and the Scientific Revolution*, Rede Lecture (Oxford University Press, 1959).

a fiancée whom he married as soon as he left New College to take up the post that was waiting for him.

LECTURES

I notice from my notebooks that I began, in the spring of 1956, to attend lectures. The lectures that truly held my attention were those of Karl Leyser on the Ottonians and Salians, the tenth- and eleventh-century rulers of what would become Germany. They conveyed inside knowledge, the fruit of personal passion and research.

Karl stood on the platform of the high table in Magdalen College dining hall. He was a short, robust figure with a worn gown over a sporty brown tweed jacket, beige waistcoat, and cavalry twill trousers, and his flashing eyes looked out from under a shock of raven-black hair. His enunciation was perfect, with the slight touch of a guttural, German accent that made his voice sink to a growl at significant moments. Karl Leyser just stood there and *became* the refined, Byzantinized Otto III (980–1002) or the gruff Conrad the Salian (990–1039) under our eyes.

Karl's lectures were what I needed. Each lecture was both a moment of total immersion in an unfamiliar and complex world, and, at the same time, an introduction to the equally unfamiliar traditions of modern German scholarship. Karl was a Jewish refugee. His parents had miraculously escaped by hiding throughout the war in Holland, only to be liberated by Karl himself, who marched into the village that had sheltered them as the commander of a troop of Black Watch Highlanders.

Listening to Karl, I felt that I was present at the building of a unique bridge between the hard-nosed medievalism of England (represented at its most forbidding by Bruce McFarlane) and a great tradition of Continental scholarship. In Karl's lectures, ideology and the history of religious and political concepts (very much the specialty of the German tradition) were firmly welded to social realities—the arming of knights and the building of castles, the taming of forests, the endless journeys of a traveling court, and the constant push toward the Slavonic lands in the East. These lectures formed the basis from which Karl's own, powerful analyses of the political culture of medieval Germany would emerge in later years. Like a storage heater, Karl simply radiated knowledge of the world east of the Rhine.[2]

2. K. Leyser, *Rule and Conflict in an Early Medieval Society: Ottonian Saxony* (London: Edward Arnold, 1979) and *Communications and Power in Medieval Europe: The Carolingian and*

Tutors: Tom Parker (1906–1985)

As finals (the final examination) approached, my friends and I began, even, to take notice of our tutors. Previously we had been much too busy educating each other with urbane scholarly gossip. Now we needed our tutors, for reviewing and for advice. Each was different. Harry Bell was as dependable and solicitous as ever. But the great discovery of my last year was the Reverend Thomas Parker, the chaplain of University College.

Tom Parker taught me for the Augustine Special Subject from October 1955 to spring 1956. I approached his rooms in University College along a passageway that led past a life-size marble nude of a young man stretched on a beach: the memorial for the drowned poet Percy Bysshe Shelley (1792–1822), who had been an undergraduate at University College. Tom's room lay beyond this voluptuous late Victorian confection. To enter it was like entering a series of trenches of the First World War. This was Tom's library. Not only did his books cover every wall: they had expanded in a series of parallel bookcases that took up most of the floor.

Tom sat at the far end of this labyrinth. He was a Humpty Dumpty of a man. He sat in an armchair where the seat was so pressed down that he squatted, in effect, on the floor. I soon learned that, to gain time in tutorials, it was sufficient to mention a fact or a problem and he would heave himself up from his seat to rummage in his vast library, and would then flop down—having expended much tutorial time in the venture—with a large tome across his knees.

A convinced Anglo-Catholic (dog collar, black waistcoat, black, wide-brimmed hat, and all), Tom was a robust man—the son of a Londoner and a member of the Honorable Company of Butchers. Medieval political theory was his principal interest. He delivered the Bampton Lectures entitled "Christianity and the State in the Light of History" in 1955. These were delivered from the pulpit of Saint Mary's Church, the university church. He boasted that, when discussing sacral kingship, he was the first preacher ever to have used a Nilotic language in church!

Like many religious persons, Tom combined an acute sense of the sacred with a shrewd appraisal of the profane. He knew how Oxford worked. In his priestly capacity, he was father confessor to the nuns of the Anglican Community of Saint Mary the Virgin in Wantage. These were the "Some Ladies at

---

Ottonian Centuries and *Communications and Power: The Gregorian Revolution and Beyond*, ed. Timothy Reuter (London: Hambledon, 1994).

Wantage" to whom C. S. Lewis dedicated his theological science fiction novel *Perelandra*. To judge by Tom's account, they were a lively lot. On one occasion, the younger nuns, for a spree, painted bright red the statue of King Alfred the Great that stood in the center of Wantage looking toward the downs on whose crest he had defeated the invading Danes in 878. In the coming year, Tom would be much more to me than a tutor. With Harry Bell, he was my guide into academe. I would need such guidance. But first I would have to face the grand wager of "finals"—the final examination.

"A VERY SPECIAL DEGREE"

FINALS

FINALS

This chapter is about final examinations. But I hasten to reassure my readers that the "very special degree" was not, as they will see, my own. As for myself, I needed a top degree more than, perhaps, I was willing to admit. Being Irish, I could not count on state aid for continued study in Britain; and it was far from certain that my father would be able to support me. To make matters worse, I had made my way to topics that were far from the main line. Late antiquity and Byzantium were exotic subjects, and aroused interest in those I spoke with; but they were no passport to a teaching job, or even to a research fellowship. If I was to continue as a full-time historian, I would have to aim high in the one venture over which I had some control—my performance in "finals."

Finals began on May 31, 1956, and ended a week later. The day after this ordeal, I took to the river in a rented canoe with Bruce Hyatt, a friend of mine from St. John's, a gifted artist and future evangelical missionary, who still produces beautifully illustrated religious books. As I wrote to my parents:

> We made believe we were Vikings. We paddled up to Godstow. We stopped at a pub near Godstow which advised us to go on to the Trout Inn, near the nunnery where Henry II kept his poppet, Fair Rosamunde. Not being really experienced Vikings, we rushed to the river bank, pushed our long boat out into the fjord and jumped in. [It capsized.] After an hour [drying out] in the hot sun two damp sea-kings were able to set out on their adventures. . . .
>
> [Next] time the sea-kings got into their dragon-craft very gingerly.

But by then the weather had become deliciously Norse. Great bleak meadows ringed with vast trees. No sign of anything. Fringes of bulrush and a dark water, with little scales of dull light. It had not changed since the Danes had come up river after the sack of Oxford. There was a vast flash of lightning and the rain came sweeping down. There were even waves. We rode into the storm, zig-zagging from bank to bank, chanting weird ditties. . . . . against the bronze sky of a sunset before a terrific storm. It was extraordinary to think that in these savage conditions we could still almost see the towers of peaceful, domesticated Oxford.

As for the examination, I added (almost as a postscript to that grand adventure—as a sign of late adolescent "cool"):

I should give a guarded reply, in the manner of the Abbé Sièyes in 1798, when asked about the French Revolution: J'ai survécu [I survived]. On the whole, I cannot complain of my luck in the exam. Some people regard luck as enabling people to shine by handing them really good questions on their pet topics: as far as that was concerned I got a suitable number of questions on Byzantine social policy and on Daniel O'Connell. But, on the whole, the important thing is the run of solid questions which you felt you could answer directly without taking evasive action. . . . I was even able to work in the Shrewsbury Election without too obvious a subterfuge.

As was usual, my neighbors soon became a source of absorbing interest. . . . To my left was a man with an empty head; I distinctly saw a star of daylight shining through his ear. To my right was a clairvoyant; he put his writing paper over his exam paper, and seemed to write over half a sheet before he looked at the questions. Behind me was an amiable Rugger Blue; he just sat looking at the paper all the time, getting redder and redder. . . . I can safely say that we all have been through what is perhaps, and what we would like to believe [to be], the toughest examination in England (eleven papers is some chicken) without batting an eyelid.

Late Roman or Medieval?

The results of the final examination would not be known until mid-July. I spent a tense month preparing for a future that, for all I knew, would not happen. The first question concerned the proposed subject of my research. How, in the Oxford of the 1950s, would I deal with the splay of my own interests between the later empire and the Middle Ages? I consulted with Harry Bell and Tom Parker on this issue. I told my parents:

> The main problem seems to be at the moment that I am caught in an awkward position between my research interests and what would be most advantageous. In the long run, it would probably be more eminent to do a Continental topic—such as the Lower Roman Empire[1] or the Crusades or Byzantine history; Bell says that he would be very glad indeed if I could have my head to do exactly this sort of stuff. But the problem of getting a post arises; here the authorities would prefer someone with a straight knowledge of straight English medieval history to someone who has done a Continental line of research, especially something as esoteric as Byzantine. Hence, when I first see Jacob,[2] I am to manifest enthusiasm for the English church in the fifteenth century. This is the best type of English topic, because the English church, as Jacob is never tired of pointing out, was an international institution, and could, therefore, serve as a springboard for [study of] the Renaissance. However, at the moment, it is quite obvious from my own booklist that I am most widely and deeply read in European history; particularly Byzantine and Lower Empire.

My situation almost forced me to try to get in from the top—to go at once for a prestige research fellowship that would give me the time to follow my own interest in Byzantium and the later Roman Empire:

> The most pleasant manner of cutting the Gordian knot is to go straight ahead and grab a Fellowship at All Souls—which Bell advises me to try—but, of course, this has the nature of an academic wild goose chase. Anyway, the object of the exercise is to get a good degree in Schools, so I am not greatly concerned about these little têtes à têtes, but they are a rather challenging test of my sincerity! It is quite obvious that despite a great enthusiasm for history in general I have no patent hobby horse; personally I regard this as a healthy sign and a great advantage to anyone who is going to teach a wide syllabus, but authorities do have an awkward habit of asking for specific notions—to which I can hardly answer. . . . I am sure I will get many useful hints from Tom Parker tomorrow.

1. Note that the French *Bas-Empire, Lower* Empire—and not yet the *Later* Roman Empire—was still the dominant term for the period.

2. Ernest Jacob, the Chichele Professor of Medieval History (1893–1971), responsible for graduate studies in the medieval field.

The next evening, Tom Parker took me to dinner at the high table in University College. We decided that I should apply to the British School at Rome for a fellowship to work on a study tentatively entitled "The Social and Economic Position of the Roman Aristocracy in Italy in the Sixth Century A.D." This was my first, clear step in the direction of late Roman history.

The topic that I had chosen did not represent for me a complete break with my medievalist inclinations. To study the social and economic history of aristocracies was very much in fashion in Oxford. Bruce McFarlane and his students—such as George Holmes[3]—were doing for the aristocracies of late medieval England what Lewis Namier had done for the eighteenth century and what Ronald Syme had done, with infectious success, for the elites of the Roman Republic. I felt secure that, in choosing to work on the late Roman aristocracy, I was tapping into a theme that was part of the "common sense" of Oxford historians, ancient and medieval alike.

Furthermore, the sixth century AD was about as close to the Middle Ages as any historian of the ancient world might venture. I already knew that, in sixth-century Italy, developments that were crucial to the history of the medieval West were well under way—the settlement of the barbarians, the rise of the papacy, the origins of Benedictine monasticism, and the reception of the works of Augustine. Tom Parker and I agreed that evening that a study of the Italian aristocracy in its last century was a topic that could act as a bridge between my two interests.

Yet a late medieval option was far from unattractive. My "Flemish" phase was not too distant from me. Late Gothic Oxford was all around me. Quite apart from its academic prestige in the Oxford of the 1950s, and the availability of jobs in the field, late medieval history could well tug at my heart. It represented a way back to the richness and complexity of the past that the distant glimmers of the sixth century could not equal.

Leading medievalists radiated an almost occult familiarity with their subject, based on rich archival resources. I remember one evening a few years later sitting beside Ernest Jacob at dessert in All Souls College. In the glow of the candlelight, his face had the transparency of the face of a late medieval bishop on his alabaster tomb. "Brown," he said, "I have spent all day with Archbishop Chichele." This was said with such evident pleasure and conviction that it took

3. G. Holmes, *Estates of the Higher Nobility in Fourteenth-Century England* (Cambridge University Press, 1957).

me some time to remember that Archbishop Chichele (ca. 1364–1442: a contemporary of Henry V and the Battle of Agincourt) had been dead for over five hundred years. I had felt this thrill myself, when working in the archives at Shrewsbury. At the time, it was far from certain that I would abandon so intimate and absorbing a way of communing with the past for the study of the distant ancient world.

Applications

So the first step, in June and July, was to try my luck in applications for the few research fellowships that were offered by different colleges. This was not a matter of mere prestige. As I could not count on state support for my graduate studies, I needed the money that such a fellowship would give me. The Harmsworth Fellowship at Merton College was the most promising of these. A week after my canoeing escapade, I was being interviewed at Merton and dined as a guest at Merton high table. I wrote to my parents:

> I have had a very tough interview for the Harmsworth Scholarship at Merton on last Tuesday. It is not easy to say what impression I made. The competition is high and they always choose in an arbitrary way. But even to have got an interview is a good sign.
>
> I talked to them about Cardinal Morton in particular.

The career of Cardinal Morton (ca. 1420–1500) was a possible dissertation subject if my fortune or interests turned me toward the study of the late medieval English church and of the churchman-administrators who had served the early Tudors: Morton was known, ever since my schoolday textbooks, as the servant of Henry VII and the originator of a particularly odious form of taxation, known as "Morton's Fork." A hard-nosed clerical administrator, he was the sort of bishop that an Oxford medievalist was supposed to study. I reported the dinner to my parents:

> I also talked about Byzantine Studies in general; Astronomy; The Building of a Telescope (!!); The Red Spot on Jupiter—Tidal theories [concerning the Red Spot]; The Shrewsbury Election; Augustinian Philosophy. To do so, in a cross fire of questions, was difficult. I did not stammer at all; but I don't know if I shot my mouth off too much. This is the greatest temptation in these circumstances.

This was a temptation from which my stammer, humiliating though it was, frequently protected me, giving me a quite undeserved reputation as a deep and diplomatic young man—when I would have loved to be able to burst into speech. Then I added:

> This business of application is like waiting for a bus at the wrong bus stop. If they don't happen to like or <u>want</u> your line of research, it is no reflection on you that they turn you down.

My lack of state funding, as an Irish citizen, lay in the background of my anxieties. It was the reef that could have sunk all my plans. State scholarships, generously awarded to British graduates, were not for me. And if I could not continue in Oxford, what else could I do? My stammer seemed to debar me from some of the more obvious careers that involved public speaking—as a teacher, lawyer, or clergyman. Until then, I had given no thought to these issues. Now they settled on my head, in a hot and sticky summer when I felt deeply tired and empty after the effort of finals. It was really only then—and then only in passing—that I gave thought to the fact that I might not be able to remain a scholar.

On July 4, I wrote again to my parents. My application to the British School at Rome had failed: I was runner-up to a candidate who had already done two years of research.

> I am disappointed as I am very fond of the topic I had offered for research and also because it was <u>such</u> a close shave. However, it is probably best: Rome at this time might be a backwater. I prefer to stay in Oxford. But I do hope you see what the position is. I have tried for all the <u>big</u> grants possible—Bell has been very helpful in this. If I do not get the Harmsworth Scholarship—and I am pessimistic in principle—I shall have to stay on on a lesser Scholarship or even a renewal of my Exhibition. The most valuable scholarship is £150—the most likely ones are £120 and £100. I have asked, as tactfully as possible, whether Shrewsbury has any fund. I could pick things up during next year; but the prospect is not altogether bright. . . . This is at its most pessimistic: if I get the Harmsworth, things will be easier; but I cannot count on that, much less on All Souls. This is the condition on which I shall have to start an academic career. I cannot even count on a requisite degree.

I knew that the examination results would not be known until around mid-July, and that I still had to face the "viva"—the viva voce interview with the examiners that marked the end of the final examination.

> Not much seems to be happening. College is very lonely and I am trying, very much against the grain, to summon up the enthusiasm for the viva

voce. It <u>can</u> be an important step, if I am on the borderline of a Class. I hope I shall not let myself down.

"A Very Special Degree"

On July 10 I went to the Examination Schools to face the viva. The interview varied in length. It usually involved a discussion of the examinee's papers and determined the final grade. These grades were called classes—first class, second class . . . right down to a fourth. The interviews were scheduled in alphabetical order. The scheduled length of the interview (announced on the day) was held to be an indication of possible success: a long interview could mean that I might have a chance to sing for my supper—to talk myself into a higher grade. Short interviews were usually taken to be a sign of unambiguous mediocrity.

I was perturbed to learn, on arrival at the Examination Schools, that I had been allotted only a short, ten-minute slot. When I came in, I found the entire board silhouetted against the blazing morning sunlight of a wide, mock-Tudor window. Karl Leyser, who was the medieval examiner, questioned me with great courtesy about my answer to a question set in the general paper on the uses of archaeology. What did I think of the relationship between the Anglo-Saxon epic *Beowulf* and the Sutton Hoo burial ship? I answered as best I could. Then there was a short silence, a shuffling of chairs, and the silhouettes rose above the table. The chairman of the board reached out his hand to me. "Congratulations, Mr. Brown. I do not think that you need to have any worry as to your final Class." I had received the rarest of all accolades—a "congratulated first." (I learned later that it was the top first in History.)

My parents, as any reader can imagine, were immensely proud. But glory lives in the mouth of others. My mother received a letter from her friend Hilda Baron, whose son, Rupert, had just taken the Cambridge equivalent of finals. An athlete through and through with little zest for scholarship, Rupert had received, in the Cambridge Tripos, the lowest of all imaginable grades— gloriously lower even than an Oxford fourth. It was a pass *speciali gratia*— by special grace: that is, by the special mercy of the examiners, in the light of his services to the University Rugby XV. But the degree "by special grace" was soon transmogrified. Hilda told my mother that Rupert had emerged from Cambridge with a "Very Special Degree." What had Peter got to equal that? My mother was mortified. In her subsequent letters to Hilda Baron, she never referred again to my humble Oxford first.

PRACTICAL IMPLICATIONS

But what exactly were the practical implications of an "Oxford first" in 1956? First of all, far fewer of them were awarded in history at this time than in later decades. Only 18 firsts out of 302 (6 percent) were awarded that year. It was a rare distinction, and a congratulated first was even rarer.

So far, so good. But beyond that, a first did not commit me to any particular career path. It was a singularly open-ended distinction. To gain a first was to receive a passkey that was supposed to open doors at the top—especially in the Civil Service, in the Diplomatic Service, and in similar public careers. Historical research was only one of those many doors, and by no means the most important one. Here, the English preference for the talented all-rounder—the adaptable and gentlemanly member of a ruling class—made itself plain. Most holders of firsts did not expect to stay in Oxford or in other centers of research and teaching. They made their way to the wider world.

Nor was the final examination itself—and the undergraduate teaching that prepared for it—designed to foster any special skills in research. The essays that were written for tutors every week were usually read out to them at the beginning of the tutorial. They were twenty minutes to half an hour long and were expected to be successful rhetorical performances. They were trial runs for the answers that were expected in the final examination. One was encouraged to "think on one's feet"—to give quick (even entertaining) answers to complex questions, even if these answers bordered on the flip and the facile. These were the virtues of civil servants and journalists. They were not those needed on the coalface of the archives or for studying texts in difficult languages—that is, for real research.

At this time, Oxford offered no equivalent of an American graduate school training. Nor was there even an equivalent to the American honors thesis, which gave an undergraduate a sneak preview of research. Anyone who embarked on research in Oxford, first or no first, started from scratch with little or no guidance in the years to come.

But a first did designate what in Shrewsbury language one would call "a tweak"—an avatar of some epic qualities. In my case, these were qualities of mind. But Rupert Baron also, in his way, was a "tweak"—a Cambridge Rugger Blue so gloriously indifferent to scholarship, so devoted to The Game, as to receive a pass "by special mercy" only. He, like me, was something of a *monstre sacré*—a prodigy, a summation of the virtues of the athletic circles in which he moved. Hilda Baron was right. Rupert had received a Very Special Degree, suited to a Very Special Person. As for me, I would have to turn my first into a career in the coming months, through a series of further, yet more ambitious tests.

TO ALL SOULS

So what now? For me, a top first ensured that I could return to Oxford. Merton offered me a Harmsworth Scholarship that gave me an income and lodgings in college for three years. It was understood that I would be writing a dissertation on Cardinal Morton, or on some such late medieval English figure.

But would I also try my luck at All Souls? A prize fellowship at All Souls was regarded as the pinnacle of an undergraduate's career. It was awarded to no more than two candidates each year on the results of an examination reputed to be of Byzantine difficulty, followed by an interview and a notorious dinner, where each candidate was wined, dined, and carefully vetted by the fellows. The prize was seven years of total freedom in a singularly comfortable college, whose members were among the leading lights of Oxford (as professors, scholars, and authors) and, indeed, of Britain (as lawyers, publishers, politicians, and civil servants). Prize fellows could pursue their research undisturbed in the company of these luminaries: there was no obligation to enroll in a graduate program; no obligation to teach; no obligation, even, to remain in Oxford—many prize fellows stepped immediately into careers in the wider world. All Souls, as viewed by undergraduates, was the stuff of legends.

Not surprisingly, given this golden fog, I was so uncertain that I would have a chance in such a venture that I took the final decision to apply only in late September, when I was on holiday with my parents at the farthest end of Ireland, at the Butler Arms in Waterville, in county Kerry.

It was a happy time for me. I sat on a sofa in the lounge, driven indoors by the rain, gravely discussing Sophocles's *Antigone* with Catholic girls my own age from a convent school. We danced together in the evening, culminating in a conga to the tune of "I'll take the last chuff-chuff to Bally James Duff." It was at the Butler Arms that I made telephone calls to Harry Bell and to All Souls, to put down my name to take the notorious All Souls Fellowship Examination in October. The phone call, in itself, was not as easy as one might think. It involved crouching in a cramped position, with piles of coins available, over a telephone placed beneath the main staircase, as Irish and then English voices transferred me from the Atlantic edge of Europe to the porter's lodge of All Souls.

A week later, I was back in Oxford, in comfortable rooms as a Harmsworth fellow at Merton College—at the end of Merton Garden, next door to the University Botanical Garden. I received a courteous welcome from the dons. Roger Highfield (1922–2017), a pupil of McFarlane's, the historian of Merton Library and a great lover of late medieval Spain, was kindness itself. But I felt like a ghost. Readers unacquainted with the Oxford of this time may not realize the poignancy of the term "postgraduate" applied to what we would now call "graduate" students. A "postgraduate" was, in many ways, regarded as a has-been. He or she was past the only "graduation" that really mattered—finals. "Postgraduates" lingered on, with little or no provision for their education compared with the immense pains lavished on even the most callow of undergraduates. They settled down as gray shades—leftovers from the glory days of their undergraduate career.

I adjusted none too badly to being a late medievalist—indeed, an *English* late medievalist. In the Oxford of the time, it was an eminently intelligible occupation. When I paid my official call (as a new postgraduate) to the Regius Professor of History, Vivian Galbraith (1889–1976), he was smoking his pipe, bent over his fireplace, vigorously stirring the fire. In between puffs and pokes, he validated my choice of a dissertation topic. Bishop Morton—later Cardinal Morton—was an admirable choice. "Everybody," he said, very firmly, and entirely without irony, "needs a bishop!"

And so I threw myself into reading chronicles of the Wars of the Roses and working my way through the printed registers of fifteenth-century archbishops of Canterbury. It was only occasionally that I would stop and read distant reports in these chronicles of the sinister advance of the Turks in southeastern Europe that would culminate in the fall of Constantinople in 1453. I even thought of changing my subject to one closer to my interests—the nature of excommunication in late medieval England. This would have linked up with my interest in the relation between religion and society, which I had already developed in my medieval readings.

It was with excommunication in Yorkist England on my mind that I was sitting in the Upper Bodleian on Saturday morning, November 3. I was reading the commentaries of fifteenth-century English canon lawyers. I noticed, with a twinge of nostalgia for the fifth century, that large extracts from the works of Augustine appeared on almost every page. Looking down out of the window opposite the Radcliffe Camera, I could see into the Codrington Quadrangle of All Souls College and the dining hall where I knew that the fellows were assembled to elect new fellows on the basis of their performance in the All Souls Fellowship Examination. I did not rate my chances very high. I went back to my fifteenth-century lawyers.

I had taken the Fellowship Examination only a few weeks previously. Ever since, I had done my best to put it out of my mind. I felt that I had taken a beating. I had never met such difficult questions. There was a menacing naïveté about them: "How Roman was Byzantium?" "Why did anyone expect the Crusades to succeed?" "Did the Eighteenth Century understand Greek art?" After the exam, I lowered my eyes whenever I saw a known member of All Souls on the street. I knew that I had shamed myself in front of him and his colleagues.

Only the memory of my performance on the single-word essay—"Islands"—gave me some comfort. I had just returned from the islands of the West of Ireland, and I had also followed my friend Jan Safranek's urging: in August I had read Braudel's gigantic and nourishing book—*La Méditerranée et le monde méditerranéen*—from cover to cover. Braudel was brilliant on the role of islands in the historical geography of the Mediterranean. My essay was a combination of county Kerry and Braudel.

As for the famous dinner to which examination candidates were invited as part of their screening process, all I remember was discoursing in front of a studiously courteous but evidently skeptical Isaiah Berlin, about the manner in which Aran Island legends of the arrival of a silver knight from the Western Ocean echoed island memories of the shipwreck of the last remnants of the Spanish Armada in 1588.

But that had been weeks ago. Now, on November 3, Oxford was in chaos. War was in the air. The Hungarian revolt was in full swing. The Anglo-French invasion of Egypt had begun. On October 31, British and French planes had bombed Egyptian airfields as the opening stage of Operation Musketeer. Leaving the peace of Bodley, I linked up with a new friend from Merton—Conrad Russell, the son of the philosopher Bertrand Russell, and a future historian of early modern England. We strolled up to St. Giles to view the scene, being buffeted on the way by placards to a loud chant of "Peace! Peace!" As we returned toward Merton, Conrad suggested that we should look in to the lodge of All Souls College . . . just in case. The handwritten notice declared that Charles Taylor—the philosopher and later the author, among much else, of *Sources of the Self: The Making of Modern Identity*[1]—had been elected, and so had I.

I returned to Merton to receive a note from John Sparrow, the warden of All Souls, inviting me to dine in college on Sunday; and there, on that Sunday evening, I realized that I had passed through a looking glass. Silver-haired men in tuxedos chatted about politics as they gathered around the television set in the warden's lodgings—the only one in the college. They did not argue about Eden or Gaitskill. They talked about "Anthony" and "Hugh."

I returned late that evening to Merton to find the college shut. I scrambled up a part of the wall where the row of spikes on its top gave me a handhold. The spikes were held on an iron spit, parallel to the top of the wall, between two andirons. These andirons had become loose. As I reached the top of the wall, the row of spikes gave way in my hands. Lifting it up, I threw it down on to the cobblestones below. Having recently read Tolstoy's *War and Peace*, I thought that it was an action worthy of the sturdy and occasionally madcap Count Pierre Bezhukov. But Russian novels are not, perhaps, the best guides to conduct. It was not a very large length of spikes; but it fell with a great clang. At once, in the row of buildings that faced Merton College on the other side of Merton Lane, window after window lit up. It was like a hillside city in a Neapolitan crèche or a giant Advent calendar. I turned to my audience, bowed deeply, and dropped over the side onto the compost heap that was conveniently piled high against the college wall.

1. C. Taylor, *Sources of the Self: The Making of Modern Identity* (Cambridge, MA: Harvard University Press), 1989.

ALL SOULS

COURTESY AND IGNORANCE

Co-optation

My success in the All Souls Fellowship Examination sent a happy clang around the circle of my New College friends. Writing from Paris, Jan Safranek composed a celebratory poem in the manner of *Winnie the Pooh*:

Three cheers for Brown
(For who?)
For Brown!
(Why, what did he do?)
I thought you knew:
He saved himself from the Morton!
Oh Brown was a Bear of Byzantine Brain–
(Of Byzantine what?)
Well, he knew a lot;
So now let's give him three Soulful cheers
(so now let us give him three soulful whiches?)
Because he's reached wisdom and riches
And hope that he'll greet his friends
Who remain somewhat at loose ends,
With erudite talk, and scholarly dinners
(What's this about <u>sinners</u>?)
HOORAY FOR THE BEAR OF BYZANTINE POWER
AUTOKRATOR OF OXFORD, TSAR OF THE HOUR!

Jan knew what this fellowship meant for me. I had been heading toward a thesis in late medieval English history, on the administrator-bishop Cardinal Morton. My prize fellowship at All Souls set me free to study late Roman and Byzantine history.

The prize fellowship lasted for seven years, after which I could be reelected as a full research fellow. I received a generous stipend and was able to live in the college. To live in college was like being welcomed into an eccentric but tightly bonded family. I was instantly astonished by the rare courtesy with which the older fellows of All Souls co-opted young prize fellows.

By Oxford standards, All Souls was an unusually diverse body. Not all those who had gained prize fellowships remained in Oxford as researchers or tutors. Most, indeed, went out into the wider world as lawyers, civil servants, diplomats, politicians, and journalists, principally in London. Yet they retained their full rights in the college. They were known collectively as the "London fellows." They would regularly appear at the weekends, having "come up" from London to what amounted to their Oxford club.

For this reason, weekend dining (especially on Saturday night) played a crucial role in fostering contact between the young prize fellows and their somewhat awesome London colleagues. At those weekend dinners, dinner jackets were obligatory. I now realize the important role played by this old-fashioned dress code. With the diners sheathed in identical black suits, in the flickering light of candles, vast distances of age and profession could be treated as absent. As I looked down the high table in the great dining hall and, later in the evening, in the more intimate setting of the dessert room, what I saw were not the great of the land, but rows of softly lit, seemingly ageless faces set in black jackets and shiny white shirts. (I should add that, except on special occasions, this uniform array was of men only—and would be so until women were admitted as fellows in 1979.)

There is a lot to be said for dinner jackets and candlelight as equalizers. Far from being marks of antiquated privilege, dinner jackets had a leveling effect. I was reminded of this function in the late 1970s. Having moved to Berkeley, I decided that I would no longer need my dinner jacket—my tuxedo. It was not a very glorious piece of clothing. I had bought it at Oxfam for only five pounds. But I had used it regularly for weekend dining in All Souls. When I arrived in California, it seemed out of place in the more democratic atmosphere of the West Coast. I left it on a bench in People's Park, for some lucky vagrant to appropriate. But as I looked up at a powder-blue sky at the far end of the world, I was surprised to feel a twinge of regret. I realized that the dinner jacket had been both a symbol of collegiality and the means by which unaffected courtesy could be extended by the old to the young.

On My Own

I needed all the courtesy that I could get. My deepest memory of my first years as a prize fellow at All Souls was of aching ignorance. I had been an unusually successful undergraduate in mastering large tracts of history, and skilled in producing quick and well-turned essays. I was the product of a culture of examinations, which stretched back to my days at Aravon and Shrewsbury. Now I had to change roles: I had to become a researcher, and eventually a teacher and a writer. Those were significant changes.

Worse still, as a researcher of the later Roman Empire, I was an utter ignoramus. I had none of the background needed for such research. I had read history, not classics, and so I had to start learning Greek again, which I had last studied at the age of thirteen at Shrewsbury. I had chosen for my research a period of history (the sixth century) that was virtually unknown either to classicists or to medievalists. I was now left alone, to find out whether my intellectual ambition was justified.

I realize that I must have appeared to be a very pretentious young man. I use the word "pretentious" without negative connotations. I was in an academic system that worked (as much at the graduate level of research as at the undergraduate level) through fostering the pretentiousness of the young. It offered constant encouragement to think and to speak beyond one's capacity—to stand on tiptoes, as it were, so as to be one's own brilliant future self in the far from brilliant here and now.

At the graduate level, it offered little else. To stay on to do research at Oxford was to be shot, within a few months, from a situation of weekly supervision, as an undergraduate, into a total educational vacuum. It was a strange feeling. When I returned to the Bodleian Library in the fall of 1956, it appeared as if nothing had changed. It was as if its readers, all in their familiar seats at the long desks, were frozen in time. But, for me, everything had changed. The world was drained of the rich atmosphere built up by three years of tutorial teaching, with its constant nurture and feedback, aided by the lively conversations of friends, none of whom remained in Oxford. Now I was on my own. It was as if I had landed on the face of the moon.

Little did I know it at the time, but as I sat in the Bodleian as an *âme d'élite*— a lonely select soul—all over America and Europe persons of my age and ambitions would be gathering in groups, with their fellow graduates, to attend seminars or proseminars in which (if they were lucky) a great professor would slowly but surely initiate them, over a term or so, into the mysteries of research in their field: bibliography, methodology—all the tricks of the trade; and they would take other seminars directly related to a chosen topic of research, as would happen in any American graduate school. By contrast, I sat alone in one of the world's greatest libraries, surrounded by shelves of books, which seemed at once exhilarating and menacing. I had to sink or swim. It was simply assumed that a winning product of the Oxford educational system needed no further help. I had got my first. Now I would do research. I would embark on writing a dissertation with no formal preparation whatsoever: no two years of seminars in a graduate program; no general exam; only a somewhat tenuous relationship with a supervisor. The dissertation—and the dissertation alone—was the only goal in an otherwise empty landscape.

Looking back, I think that I failed to recognize the advantages of my loneliness. My choice of an eccentric topic of research and the splendid isolation granted to young fellows of All Souls protected me from becoming enmeshed in the various factions among the ancient historians and the medievalists of Oxford. I was nobody's client—not a follower of Ronald Syme in ancient history, nor of Bruce McFarlane or some other dominant figure in medieval history. But at the time, such thoughts would have given me little consolation. It was an anxious moment.

My success in the All Souls examination had at least removed one anxiety. I was, at last, financially independent. My parents would no longer have to support me, as they had done so uncomplainingly, ever since I went to Shrewsbury in 1948. They took my success for granted, without any sense that I could perceive of the risks that might accompany my rare good fortune. I was less sanguine. I still have a chill feeling about those early years in All Souls. It was a time of danger, where I could have been frozen by the combination of loneliness and high expectations that characterized the life of many young scholars in Oxford, and most especially young prize fellows at All Souls. I needed all the help I could get.

Supervision: Arnaldo Momigliano (1908–1987)

Hence my singular good fortune to have as my supervisor none other than Arnaldo Momigliano. It was Peter Fraser of All Souls (1918–2007), the historian of Hellenistic Alexandria, who put me in touch with him. As I remember, we first met in Fraser's rooms. Momigliano immediately gave me one of his most recent articles—a brilliant intellectual portrait of Mikhail Rostovtzeff.[1] He agreed to take me on. At that time, he was deeply engaged in work on Cassiodorus and the noble family of the Anicii in sixth-century Italy.[2] For that reason, he was the natural supervisor for someone who intended to write the dissertation I envisioned: "The Social and Economic Position of the Roman Aristocracy in Italy in the Sixth Century A.D."—the topic that I had chosen with Tom Parker, and to which I was now free to return.

But it would be highly misleading to call Momigliano my "teacher" at this moment. In Oxford, dissertation supervisors were not expected to teach their charges, only to monitor their lonely progress. Momigliano would never "teach" or "train" me in the formal sense. Indeed, to be taught by Momigliano would be akin to being taught by a supernova in full explosion. It did not happen. I was content to listen, awestruck, as he talked on whatever topic was on his mind.

In one important respect, however, Momigliano proved to be very English in the best possible way—that is, in his unaffected courtesy to the young, such as I had experienced also in All Souls. Despite my youth, I was immediately co-opted by him as an honorary colleague—a fellow adventurer in the all-absorbing, vaguely comical enterprise of ancient history. From the moment he agreed to be my supervisor, he sent me an offprint of everything that he wrote. To keep up with the flow of Momigliano's articles, which ranged from the origins of Rome to the settlement of the barbarians in the fifth century West, was an education in itself.

He also gave me an even more precious gift than a constant share in his erudition. He trusted me to stand on my own feet. He viewed with sovereign contempt scholars (even great scholars) who attempted to make clones of their students. He left me strictly alone to form my own opinions and to follow my own instincts.

It was only eventually that Momigliano became a mentor and a friend to me. At the time, he was something of a persecutory superego—as supervisors tend to be in the beginning stages of a graduate student's career. On one occasion, when I saw Momigliano enter the Lower Bodleian as I was reading there,

---

1. A. D. Momigliano, "M. I. Rostovtzeff," *Cambridge Journal* 7 (1954): 334–346, now in *Studies in Historiography* (London: Weidenfeld and Nicholson, 1966), 91–104.

2. A. D. Momigliano, "Cassiodorus and the Italian Culture of His Time," *Proceedings of the British Academy* 41 (1955): 207–245, now in *Studies in Historiography*, 181–210.

I dropped my pen and hid beneath the desk, pretending to look for it, until he had passed by.

What Momigliano did represent for me was a very different pole from that of Oxford. Though a frequent visitor to Oxford, he was professor of ancient history in University College London. On rare occasions I would go from Oxford to London to meet him at University College in Gower Street. In doing so, I entered another world. On the first occasion I was lost. Accustomed as I was, in Oxford, to ask directions at the porter's lodge of a college, I looked down a corridor and saw, to my relief, a gentleman in formal, old-fashioned dress sitting behind a glass pane, as Oxford college porters were accustomed to sit. On drawing near, I discovered that he was not a porter. He was the great utilitarian philosopher Jeremy Bentham (1748–1832) in person, mummified in a glass case in University College, in whose foundation he had played a major role.

When I reached Momigliano's office, I found the table piled high with books newly arrived from Russia. He was engaged in a hot debate with a colleague on the Greek and Hebrew terms for a city wall. He drew my attention with a wave of the hand to the pile of Russian books, implying that, of course, I must be acquainted with them. Then, without introducing me to the colleague, he asked me straight out what I thought on the recondite matter of city walls. A supervision that consisted of heroic encounters of that nature makes for vivid memories. But it was hardly a systematic introduction to the later empire, such as an American (and now even a British) graduate student might expect in his or her first year.

What I did not realize at the time was that my contact with Momigliano in London was the beginning of an opening of my horizons that would take part of me away from the inward-looking atmosphere of Oxford. London was always more to me than a city. It was the intellectual and imaginative counterweight to Oxford, and a bridge to the wider world of European scholarship.

In these years, however, Oxford was the world I knew. And it was in the Oxford manner—through a process of co-optation, and not through any formal teaching relationship—that I slowly found my way to making personal contact with leading scholars in the field. They welcomed me with quite outstanding courtesy.

My first contact of this kind was with A.H.M. Jones—Hugo Jones (1904–1970). He had not yet published his monumental work, *The Later Roman Empire*, which would appear in 1964.[3] I met him in unusual circumstances.

---

3. A.H.M. Jones, *The Later Roman Empire: A Social, Administrative and Economic Survey, 284–602*, 2 vols. (Oxford: Blackwell, 1964).

Jones had been a prize fellow of the college, and would return to All Souls on the gaudy night—All Souls Night, when a solemn and bibulous banquet took place in the evening after the meeting in which the prize fellows were elected. On that occasion, the more worldly fellows would disport themselves after the banquet in the manner of a Guy Fawkes night. They would bombard the dome of the Radcliffe Camera with rockets launched from the lawn of the Codrington Quadrangle. Lord Hailsham (Quintin Hogg) would rush around the college, waving sparklers. Great fun was had by all.

Not so Hugo Jones. As Hailsham and his playmates roared outside, Jones would sit on the edge of the great green sofa in the deserted smoking room, puffing his pipe and thinking aloud to me about the history of the later Roman Empire. His dry common sense was rendered incandescent by his passion for the subject. He showed me what could be got out of the most unlikely texts—lives of saints, sermons of the Fathers of the Church, letters of bishops: each of these great piles of chaff could be winnowed to produce solid grains of evidence about the workings of late Roman society. He was always grappling with some important but neglected aspect of the social history of the later empire. Did I know that Roman notions of divorce—which gave each party the right to divorce the other, as in the termination of any other form of contract—had lasted until the end of the sixth century? The thought that such freedom had survived for so long into Christian times evidently pleased him. Did I know that a good book had yet to be written on the Visigoths of Spain? Encounters such as these, followed up by patient reading of every one of Jones's articles on a late Roman topic—footnote by footnote to take the measure of the vast range of evidence on which they were based—showed me what it was to be a master of the ancient historian's trade.

The gathering of models of the historian's craft did not always take place against such a flamboyant background. But those who offered me help did so with an openness that needs to be remembered. Many of them were Marxists. This was particularly the case with a towering scholar of the ancient world: Geoffrey de Sainte Croix of New College (1910–2000). Geoffrey did not share the tendency of ancient historians of classical training to lose interest in Roman history the moment that Tacitus put down his pen. As a Marxist, he wanted to know about the stormy later centuries of Rome: to follow the ancient world to its final grand demise, with the collapse of the slave system and the rise of feudalism. His very hostility to Christianity made him take seriously its rise in the Roman world.

Above all, Geoffrey was quite prepared to look beyond the narrow canon of classical authors in order to seize the evolution of Roman society as a whole. It was Geoffrey who told me, with evident excitement, that the only source in the entire history of the ancient world that traced, month by month, the rise in the cost of foodstuffs in a time of famine was not any classical Greek or Latin text. It was a sixth-century Syriac chronicle of the city of Edessa— the *Chronicle of Joshua the Stylite*. This was my very first, deliciously unexpected, introduction to the largely unknown riches of Syriac literature in late Roman times.

Apart from these moments of personal contact, what kept me going in those uncertain years? Three things. I began to teach. I was commissioned to write. I was encouraged to spend time abroad, at the British School at Rome.

TEACHING, WRITING, AND ROME

SCARCITY AND RICHES

In many ways I was uniquely privileged: I had gained a top first and was a prize fellow of All Souls. This gave me financial security and an enviable freedom. It also gave me time: the prize fellowship lasted for a full seven years. I needed every moment of that time to educate myself in a field of which I was largely ignorant, having been taught mainly modern and medieval history as an undergraduate.

But I was given no guidance. I had no structures such as an American-style graduate school could provide, through its seminars and term papers, to direct my study and to initiate me into the field of ancient history. I had no ever-present *Doktorvater* to turn to: at that time, Arnaldo Momigliano (in London) was still a distant figure to me. Nor did I have an academic patron to whose school I could attach myself, as in Europe. My first and my fellowship were deemed to be enough to get me anywhere: I did not need to become a member of an *équipe*. This situation freed me; but it also left me isolated. Despite many friendships, I did not have a cohort of fellow students of my own age engaged in studying the same field as myself, and bonded by a shared experience of graduate training, or (as nowadays) through working as members of a team in a research project.

It was a dangerous moment. Lack of instruction is not necessarily the way to true originality. A graduate training often gives the students an ability to stand on their own feet that they would not have enjoyed if they had been left entirely to themselves. Without formal guidance, it was only too easy, in the Oxford of the 1950s, to turn to other ways of making oneself acceptable. I had already noticed that Oxford worked best on a system of co-optation. I was treated by the old, with great courtesy, as one of themselves, and was thereby encouraged to join them. For some this system of tacit recruitment proved disastrous. It turned them into perpetual wannabees, dangerously over-identified with the institutions or the mentors with whom they wished to be identified: weaker (or nastier) souls became more Oxford than Oxford, or the clones and attack dogs of their older protectors.

I remember being told by an immigrant from Germany, Richard Walzer (1900–1975), a wise head and a scholar of late Greek and Islamic philosophy to whom I came to owe much, that what he found most unnerving in Oxford was the way in which nobody was prepared to tell him what he should do in the college common room to which he had been admitted. He observed shrewdly that, as a result of the total absence of explicit guidance, he felt himself under constant pressure to overconform, to become more English than the English, lest he sin, in an unguarded moment, against the unspoken codes of his environment. I sympathized with his dilemma. I needed every bit of support that I could muster to avoid the situation that he described. As a result, I found myself taking advantage of certain distinctive features of the Oxford of that time which compensated for the almost complete absence of a formal training. I was a magpie; but I had rich pickings.

"Making the Period Interesting": Teaching

In the long run, it was the university and its college-based tutorial system that provided the keel for my life as a scholar. I became a tutor, and my teaching saw me through those anxious years. The personal, face-to-face nature of the tutorial was easier on my stammer than exposure to large classes would have been. It also involved a style of teaching that was easy to imitate. After three years of exposure to tutorials it was not difficult to become a tutor myself. Though perched on a lonely eminence in All Souls, I soon gained a reputation as a teacher whose pupils got firsts or top seconds in their final exams.

My position as a prize fellow at All Souls made me particularly open to demands to act as a tutor for undergraduates from other colleges. There was something paradoxical about that situation. It was a carefully maintained principle that All Souls was a college devoted to pure research, an Oxford equivalent of the Princeton Institute for Advanced Study. This, in fact, was pure myth. The prize fellows of All Souls were the supply teachers of the university. They were constantly being asked to take on pupils from all over

Oxford. Already in Michaelmas term of 1957, Tom Parker, my former tutor for Saint Augustine, unloaded on me at the last minute ten young persons who needed tutorials in a tract of history (English history from 1307 to 1660) that was over a thousand years, and well over a thousand miles, away from my proposed subject of research. These students took time. But they were worth it. At the end of term, I wrote to my parents, with a touch of pride:

> The only relief this week has been the farewells of pupils.... Some seemed really enthusiastic, and actually thanked me in a rather embarrassed and embarrassing way, for "making the period so interesting, Sir."...
>
> ... Life has been terribly circumscribed by writing reports on people [after the term's tutorials] ... and teaching them any subject from the Causes of the Fall of the Roman Empire to the Foreign Policy of James I.

I throve on this teaching. It steadied my nerves. At a time when I was well aware that I knew far less than I should about the late Roman Senate, I was not at a loss to tell the young three interesting things about the Wars of the Roses, with which to dazzle the examiners when they came to their final examination. Altogether, this teaching brought a touch of normality into what was otherwise an overprivileged and isolated existence.

An All Souls Job: *The Concise Encyclopedia of World History*

I was also given my first opportunity to write. This happened in a manner that reflected very well the workings of All Souls. All Souls was an unusual college in the way in which the world of London was joined to the more local, inward-looking world of Oxford. The fellows included London publishers and editors who were eager to seek out young writers for books or essays written for the general public, and not only for the academic world. They would often turn to All Souls for advice on potential young authors. One of these ventures was *The Concise Encyclopedia of World History*, edited by John Bowle (1905–1988). On the recommendation of A. L. Rowse (1903–1997), a senior fellow, who prided himself inordinately on being a literary man, a great author and not a stuffy don, Bowle turned to me to write a chapter: "Palestine and the Making of Christianity." This amounted to nothing less than a history of Judaism, of the mutation of paganism, and of the rise and triumph of Christianity in the ancient world— fifteen hundred years of ancient history, all in thirty pages! I jumped at it.

My enthusiasm was genuine. I was already determined that no history that I studied would be of any use unless it could be communicated in such a way as to reach a wide and cultivated public, such as I liked to imagine existed, beyond the walls of Oxford. When asked for whom I wrote, I would always say that I "wrote for my aunts." That is, I wrote for persons of sufficient education and cultural interests, but who had never been to university, such as my aunt Mai and my aunt Freda. Such persons, and not necessarily the dons of Oxford, would be my readers. In the words of W. B. Yeats (writing in 1891):

> To please the folk of few books is one's great aim. By being Irish I think one has a better chance of it—over here is so much to read and think about.[1]

Judaism, the rise of Christianity, and the fall of the Roman Empire were certainly topics for an average reader (and especially an Irish reader, with his or her religious preoccupations) "to read and think about."

But what mattered most for me was the opportunity to read myself into a totally new subject. I had not been an ancient historian. The biblical Near East, Judaism, Greco-Roman paganism and the earlier centuries of the Christian church were terra incognita to me. It was time to use the opportunity offered by *The Concise Encyclopedia* to complete my education.

The college provided me with the guides I needed. Peter Fraser lent me a brilliant little book by Norman Baynes, the great Byzantinist (1877–1961). Baynes's mission as a scholar had been "to make the Byzantine Empire interesting," which he did in a series of remarkable public lectures at London University and elsewhere. But this book was not about Byzantium. Entitled *Israel among the Nations*, it was a short history of Judaism in the time of the Old Testament. Baynes had written it mainly for members of his church: for he was also a Baptist preacher. Eloquent and accessible, it was everything that a book for a popular audience should be.[2] I wanted to write like Baynes. Alas, I was not always successful. Once, when trying out part of my chapter by reading it to my mother, I noticed that, by the time that I had advanced, in somewhat purple prose, from the conquests of Alexander the Great to the revolt of Judas Maccabaeus, she had fallen fast asleep.

---

1. R. F. Foster, *W. B. Yeats: A Life*, vol. 1, *The Apprentice Mage* (Oxford University Press, 1997), 110–111.

2. N. H. Baynes, *Israel among the Nations* (London: Student Christian Movement, 1928).

The Prof.: R. C. Zaehner (1913–1974)

Among the fellows of All Souls, some were more outgoing with their advice and encouragement than others. My principal guide at that time was Robin Zaehner—R. C. Zaehner, known since his youth as "the Prof." Zaehner was Spalding Professor of Religion and Ethics and a fellow of All Souls. He had been British consul in Tehran during and after the war. Rumors circulated about his activities at that time.

He never discussed his experiences in Iran with me. Rather, he became a mentor in out-of-the-way religious matters. The Prof. was the perfect denizen of All Souls. He lived to read. He looked forward to the summer vacation, when the college closed, and he was free to cook for himself. He would soften beefsteaks by beating them with the college croquet mallet and would settle down to marathons of reading. He read the entire Sanskrit epic of the *Mahab-haratha* in one such summer. Unfailingly kind to young persons, and gifted with a delicious sense of the absurd, Zaehner wore his learning lightly. He liked to recount (preferably with drink in hand and with Berlioz playing loudly in the background) Gnostic, Zoroastrian, and Ismaili myths. As he lived in college, as I did at this time, he was always available for long after-dinner conversations that were tutorials in themselves.

Zaehner introduced me to Zoroastrianism, to Gnosticism, and to Manichaeism. He also introduced me to the earliest publications on the Dead Sea Scrolls—the documents associated with a radical Jewish community at Qumran, near the Dead Sea, whose recent discovery had caused a sensation. This discovery had raised the hope that scholars had found, at last, a hitherto unknown, direct way, into the world of Jesus and John the Baptist.[3]

I owe to the Prof. my first interest in Iran and in many of the wilder aspects of Judaism and early Christianity. But Zaehner was also engaged in contemporary religious debates. His best-known book was *Mysticism Sacred and Profane*.[4] He once introduced me at lunch to a mystic of his acquaintance whom he studied: a sweet, old-fashioned English country gentleman, with large, dark eyes. He had recently injured his hand, for an ecstasy had come upon him while he was driving a lawn mower across his back meadow.

---

3. Millar Burrows, *New Light on the Dead Sea Scrolls* (London: Secker and Warburg, 1958).

4. R. C. Zaehner, *Mysticism Sacred and Profane: An Enquiry into Some Preter-Natural Experiences* (Oxford: Clarendon Press, 1957).

Altogether, Prof. Zaehner introduced me to God's plenty. I emerged from my readings with my imagination saturated with ideas, myths, and religious imagery taken from all over the Mediterranean and the Middle East. What I now needed to do was to ground these grand imaginings in a concrete social context, for without such a context they were insubstantial ghosts. It was time for me to travel to Rome, to take a closer look at things on the ground.

ROME AND THE CATACOMBS

For a month in the spring of 1957, and for another month in the spring of 1958, I was at the British School at Rome.

On my first visit, in 1957, I alternated between the well-stocked library of the school and the museums and churches of the city. In the library, I devoured Santo Mazzarino's recent book, *Aspetti sociali del quarto secolo*.[5] I was inspired by his brilliant proof that the population of Rome did not drop in the fourth century AD—that the city had not yet become a ghost of itself but had remained a booming megalopolis up to the time of its sack by the Goths in 410. It made the great buildings of the Forum seem even larger, even more solid as I moved around them. Santo Mazzarino made plain that fourth-century Rome, *my* Rome, had been no ghost town. This one book, read beside his earlier *Stilicone*, decisively influenced my overall view of the later empire from this time onward.

In the Museo delle Terme and in the Vatican Museum, I lingered for hours in front of the great sarcophagi of the third century AD. I would stare at those tranquil, still classical faces—those grave public servants; those solemn children guarded by austere philosophers; those wives posed book in hand, as Muses to their husbands. Could they have dreamed of the future that lay in store for them within only a few generations? Could they have dreamed of Constantine? Or were they already, beneath their classical robes, dreaming of new worlds, but in a manner that escapes us?

My letters to my parents reflected my enthusiasm at this time. The British School at Rome had opened a new world to me:

> The main item was the arrival of Professor Jocelyn Toynbee, who is the first woman Professor of Archaeology in Cambridge. She is a very sweet elderly

5. Santo Mazzarino, *Aspetti sociali del quarto secolo* (Rome: Bretschneider, 1951).

lady, who reminds me enormously of a large cat. [She herself, indeed, had a handsome white cat called "Mithras."] . . . She has the lovely habit of really purring, with strange swallowing noises, when she is interested in anything. She had a lot of purring to do. We were shown round by a host of very big names in the Italian, German and Dutch archaeology world. I was taken along as a sort of neophyte-cum-prize exhibit of Young England scholarship. You can imagine how very exciting it was. We saw catacombs which are as yet entirely closed to the public, and were shown round them by the greatest experts in the field. It was fascinating how they worked at their problems; and it was very heartening to see how much, if you gave your attention to it, you could notice [things] yourself. This meant that we all played a part in making suggestions in deciphering inscriptions and particularly in trying to understand the weird iconography which was a result of a real mixture of Pagan and Christian motifs. I have never had an opportunity to study early Christianity at such close quarters.

I should add that our leader on that occasion, Professor Josi, proudly carried a large bundle of keys labeled "Catacombe Gnostiche—Sincretistiche." It could not get better than that. Here, in the galleries of dark red tufa, was the rich mud of reality in which the mighty dreams of salvation, transformation, and ascent of which I had read so much back in All Souls had once been planted.

MUD ON THE BOOTS

I returned to Rome in 1958. On that occasion, I had received a De Rivoira Scholarship to participate in the Southern Etruria Survey conducted by the director of the school, John Ward-Perkins (1912–1981).[6] As my dissertation topic was on the social and economic position of the late Roman aristocracy, I was recruited to help in the fieldwork and to identify, from late Roman sources and early medieval documents (mainly from charters that described the boundaries of properties), possible sites of late Roman villas, roads, and churches for survey and excavation. I would work all morning in the Vatican Library, combing charter collections for place-names, mentions of basalt roads—for these were often cited as boundaries—and similar hints of

6. Not to be confused with his son, Bryan Ward-Perkins, the distinguished archaeologist of the late Roman and early Medieval West

settlement that dated back to the early Middle Ages or even before. Then, in the afternoon, I would whizz, on the back of a Lambretta, up the Via Cassia to explore the countryside around Nepi and Sutri.

This was an unusually happy time for me. As I wrote to my parents:

> To be an archaeologist is rather like being a fisherman: you have to know so much about so many things—geology, forestry, farming, architecture, chemistry and ceramics among the few. It is a wonderful experience in this way; to be a historian among archaeologists, and a medievalist among ancient historians—no longer as an outsider, but actually as a colleague. Archaeology is very strange to me as an historian. It is timeless: the bones of normal life. It is so normal: it is not concerned with popes and emperors who careened over this area . . . but with the bare bones of living—roads, wells, aqueducts, foundations. This is not digging; it is a topographical survey. . . . The country is volcanic; ridges with fingers, and perfectly blue lakes caught in craters; every now and then you come from tufa to clay—the mud of a volcanic explosion—and a flat plateau of hard lava, which dries slower and which shows rather like parts of Connemara. You then walk through fields literally strewn with Roman fragments of pottery. . . . Personally, this is a type of field work which I find intellectually much more exacting and exciting than mere digging; it really does require immense powers of memory and observation.
>
> . . . medievalists come into their own when it comes to dealing with the little churches with fragments of fresco which litter the countryside, and were remnants of settlements founded in the ruins of big Roman villas. There is a most exciting one two miles from Sutri, which is entirely unpublished and virtually unknown. We found it in a cave cut into the tufa rock, where there were many un-Roman looking grave berths in the same cliff face. Our entry was met by a habboob [Arabic: sandstorm] of white hens. And by standing on straw bales, I was able to wash it down, to reveal beneath the dirt the un-faded colors of a 12th–13th century fresco in the Byzantine provincial style which you can see in the cathedral: with an inscription of the priest who had made it, and Christ—with an archaic gesture—with SS. Peter and Paul, and a priest with a soldier martyr! I could meditate about such sort of archaeology for days and days.

A photo of this time shows me perched on a ladder held by Richard Duncan-Jones—no less! Richard was the future master of the Roman economy. This chapel was called by the strange name of San Giovanni a Pollo—Saint John at the Hen. The Hen was a misnomer—a peasant corruption of San Paolo–one of the two patron saints (SS. Giovanni e Paolo) of the little church carved out of the rock.[7]

The fieldwork led to many strange encounters. Outside Nepi,

> [I met] a family of fascist firework makers, who have a hut strewn with medieval glazed fragments and a full length portrait of Il Duce in evening dress. Between letting off a display of fireworks for my benefit (Personally, I think that their main activity is making small bombs for fish poaching) and telling how their great grandfather brought back the secrets of the art from Birmingham, they shake their heads at the picture and say [with evident regret] "è morto."

I remember that, on one occasion, I fell into the basement of a ruined castle, to be confronted, eye-to-eye, by a large toad seated on a vivid majolica dish of the fourteenth century. And so I returned to Oxford in June 1958. I was glad to be back, with the mud of Rome and its countryside on my boots.

John Ward-Perkins, the director of the school, did not approve of my subsequent report. I gave him a draft in my last days at the school. It was more cautious than he had wished. I carefully spelled out the reasons why so many of the medieval documents could *not* be used to reconstruct Roman conditions. I argued that the distribution of settlements had changed too drastically over the centuries that followed the fall of Rome. They reflected a different agrarian landscape, organized more around villages than around great estates. I now notice that the monumental study of Pierre Toubert, *Structures du Latium*, seems to support my novice's hunch.[8] But this was not what John wanted to hear. It was not a happy interview.

I did, however, suggest that archaeology could be brought to bear on the *domus cultae*—the planned estate-centers of the papacy in the eighth and ninth centuries, one of which, I told him, was located on the site of the church of Santa Cornelia, near Veii. John affected to be uninterested. He replied, "You must tell me, Brown, in words of one syllable . . . what *is* a *domus culta*?" Only three years later, in 1961–1964, archaeologists of the British School went to the exact spot that I had indicated: the *domus culta* of Capracorum, Santa

7. Peter Brown, "Sutri (Sutrium), 701785: Chapel of San Giovanni 'a Pollo,'" *Papers of the British School at Rome* 36 (1958): 127–129.

8. Pierre Toubert, *Structures du Latium médiéval*, Bibliothèque des Écoles françaises d'Athènes et de Rome 221 (Rome: Palais Farnèse, 1973).

Cornelia, which lay fifteen miles north of Rome between the Via Cassia and the Via Flaminia. Their results are now on display in the Museo dell'Alto Medio Evo in Rome. The excavation was hailed as one of the first ventures in medieval rural archaeology in Italy. *Si jeunesse savait . . .* Somewhere in the British School my large card index box, portentously stuffed with place-names, references to basalt roads as boundaries in medieval charters, and coordinates of possible villas, may still be gathering dust.[9]

9. Neil Christie, *Three South Etrurian Churches: Santa Cornelia, Santa Rufina, and San Liberato*, Archaeological Monographs of the British School at Rome 4 (Oxford: Oxbow, 1991), 6 and 201. It notes that the site of Santa Cornelia "was identified by John Ward-Perkins," 3.

LIBRARIES, LECTURES, AND TALKS

Gelehrtes Europa in the Bodleian

On my return from Rome in May 1958, I continued, in the absence of any formal supervision, to educate myself in the Bodleian Library.

There was no seminar on the later empire from which to gather bibliographies, no websites to surf. Just books and references to books in the seemingly endless number of journals that lined the walls of the Bodleian. There I scanned the itemized bibliographies of major European periodicals and worked my way along the new accessions shelves for books and periodicals. I did the same in the Library for Classical Studies, attached to the Ashmolean Museum. I would approach those shelves like a water-diviner, hoping against hope to touch some new, fresh spring in the daunting array of new publications. At times I was lucky. A single article might open up an entire new way of seeing things. Sometimes nothing more than a few pages—often painfully puzzled-out in a largely unfamiliar language—would give me the green light for budding thoughts. The books and articles, which now lie piled up in my footnotes as mere titles (many of them now more than a little out of date) were once charged objects for me. They were signs from the gods, that I had not entirely missed my way.

I did most of my reading in the Lower Bodleian—"Lower Bodley" on the second floor, where classics, ancient history, Byzantium, and theology succeeded one another in a great U, looking down over the Bodley Quadrangle. Lower Bodley was more than a library to me. It was my entry point into a *Gelehrtes Europa*—a learned Europe—that was wider in its interests than the cramped world of Oxford ancient history. I am not speaking here of individual

Oxford scholars—many of whom were learned and widely traveled. But the range of ancient history that was taught and thought to be worth studying at Oxford was exceedingly narrow. It was tied to the horizons of the major classical historians: students of Greek history studied Herodotus and Thucydides but did no Near Eastern or Hellenistic history. As for the Roman Empire, students were expected to stop with the reign of the emperor Trajan (AD 98–117), when Tacitus wrote, and to go no further. It was as if no future lay in store for Greeks and Romans in the long, last centuries of the ancient world.

Religion in general and Christianity in particular were treated as secondary concerns. I remember my friend Fergus Millar reporting to me, with disgust, that in a meeting of ancient historians, a leading classical scholar had declared that "the Acts of the Apostles are not history, they are footnotes to history." Politics and the problems of running the Roman Empire predominated. I used to call this bias, on the part of Roman historians, a "Pontius Pilate complex"—a legacy of the Victorian identification of the Roman Empire with the British Raj. It is good that such parochialism is no longer the case in Oxford; but it was widespread at the time.

What helped me to escape this imbalanced vision was to travel to Europe along the shelves of foreign journals on display in Lower Bodley. The definition of ancient history was often wider in European universities. It was assumed to extend beyond the early Roman Empire as far as the reign of the emperor Justinian I in the sixth century AD. In many European countries, issues that had come to the fore in the later empire were still more alive than in England. In the 1950s, in particular, discussions between German and French scholars on the role of the barbarians in the fall of the empire were still tinged with bitterness from the First and Second World Wars. In some parts of Europe, the end of paganism and the triumph of the Catholic Church stirred contemporary passions among lay and clerical scholars. Altogether, reading in Lower Bodley, I felt that I was listening to a grand debate of Europe on its own past.

In the Cold War years, this debate extended even farther to the east. There was a wish (not limited to Communists) to engage Russian Marxist scholarship on large issues such as slavery and the fall of Rome. In my excursions into Europe along the shelves of the Bodleian, I ventured across the Iron Curtain on occasions, pitting my rudimentary Russian against articles by Zenija Udal'cova on the conflict of social groups in sixth-century Italy and Aleksandr Diakonov on the circus factions of Byzantium. The dark-green volumes of the *Vizantiiskij Vremennik* were all there—in the Lower Bodleian, in a corner devoted to Eastern European periodicals beside the window that overlooked Hertford College and the Bridge of Sighs. To have a go at them was as exciting as passing through Checkpoint Charlie.

Lectures

But how was all this reading to be organized so as to find its way into articles and books? The first step for me was to commit myself to lecturing on the later empire to anyone who might be interested in the subject. As a young fellow of All Souls, I was encouraged to become what was known as a CUF lecturer. I would be paid from the Common University Fund to deliver one lecture a week over two terms—sixteen hours in all. The times, places, and titles of my lectures were advertised in the university *Gazette*. Anyone who wanted could attend.

As I have explained in an earlier chapter, these lectures were open to all comers, and with no obligation to continue in the course. All they offered was the chance to come, to listen, and to learn. But I remembered that some of those lectures, such as those delivered on medieval German history by Karl Leyser, had truly inspired me. Now was my chance to become a Karl Leyser for the later empire.

The CUF lectureship did not in any way affect my tutorial teaching. This continued as usual. The lectures did something entirely different. They encouraged me to shine on my own subject for fifty minutes every week. They were frankly rhetorical occasions. Above all, they helped me to develop a tone of voice in which to talk about crucial issues of late Roman religion and society.

I gave my first lectures in the winter of 1958. When I arrived, I was surprised to find the room filled with young persons, largely of the male persuasion. I soon realized why. Following the convention that still spoke of the later empire as *le Bas-Empire*—the *Lower* Empire—I had, in all innocence, entitled my lectures "Lower Roman Society." Alas, what I told these young gentlemen was not nearly as low as they had hoped, given the time-honored reputation of Roman society for the low life. All they got was a disquisition on the relation between social stratification and the circulation of gold coinage in the age of Constantine. It was not what they had come for. Next week we were down to a loyal core of six. But the six stayed the course. Two, at least, went on to become historians: John Dunbabin became a modern historian; his wife, Jean, became a medievalist. John's sister, Katherine Dunbabin, would write a book on the Roman mosaics of North Africa that is still the best introduction to the worldly culture that flourished so exuberantly there in the later empire.[1]

"Vers le Bas-Empire": State and Society in the Later Empire

I still have the handwritten text of these lectures. I reread them with some embarrassment. They were very much the work of a young don wanting to make a splash. But they do show clearly the historical problems that scholars of the later empire were facing at the time. The biggest of these problems was the role of the late Roman state in the formation of late Roman society. Let me explain why this was so.

The fall of Rome had always elicited anxious parallels to modern times. But these anxieties changed over time. Edward Gibbon's *Decline and Fall* had stressed the dangers of "immoderate greatness" joined to despotic rule. A century later, Otto Seeck had indulged his readers with sickly notions of decadence due to the emergence of genetically inferior populations. In the twentieth century, the fall of Rome seemed even more present, with the rise of totalitarian regimes and planned economies all over Europe. The fate of Rome came to be treated as a warning example for modern times of what could happen to an overgoverned society.

This sharp sense of danger dominated scholarship on the later empire in the 1920s and 1930s. Twentieth-century historiography on the end of the empire began in 1926 with Mikhail Rostovtzeff, a refugee from Bolshevik Russia, whose masterpiece, *The Social and Economic History of the Roman Empire*, was read by scholars who witnessed the rise of dictatorships in Germany, Italy, and Spain and the further, monstrous extension of the totalitarian state in Stalin's Russia. The story of the growth of the state in the later Roman Empire was their story.

In a moving passage, Rostovtzeff summed up the imperial system set in place by the emperors Diocletian (284–305) and Constantine (306–337) after the crisis of the third century:

> They took their duties seriously and they were animated by the sincere love of their country. Their aim was to save the Roman Empire, and they achieved it. To this end they used, with the best intentions, the means which were familiar to them, violence and compulsion. They never asked

---

1. K.M.D. Dunbabin, *The Mosaics of Roman North Africa: Studies in Iconography and Patronage* (Oxford: Clarendon Press, 1978).

whether it was worthwhile to save the Roman Empire in order to make it a vast prison for scores of millions of men.[2]

That the once-benign polity of Rome should end up like Soviet Russia was writing on the wall for all historians in what remained of liberal Europe. This was the opinion of the Romanian Byzantinist Georges Bratianu (1898–1953) in his essay of 1938, "Vers le Bas-Empire: Towards the Lower Empire":

> The men of our time can follow the way that once led a great empire to its end and ruined a whole civilization. That is why it is the duty of all men . . . to give the alarm when they see spreading over the world the baneful shadow of economic slavery and social tyranny—the centuries of servitude of a Lower Empire.[3]

Alas, Bratianu's warning came only too true. He died in prison in Romania under the Communist regime in 1953.

"A Decadent Leviathan"

In America, also, the opponents of the New Deal regarded the later empire as a fearsome example of the dangers of Big Government. The English translation of the Theodosian Code (to which I had owed so much when studying for the Saint Augustine Special Subject) was made, in part, as a warning. The plethora of edicts preserved in the Theodosian Code seemed to show that the Roman Empire had died of overgovernment. America might go the same way as a result of the New Deal: "we shall ignore the Code at our peril; for it can provide us with new insight into that period of classical civilization during which the organization of society most resembles that towards which we are moving." The Theodosian Code revealed the Roman Empire in its last days to have been be a "decadent Leviathan."[4]

The reputation of the later empire as a "decadent Leviathan" dies hard. Faced by a choice of economic policies, President Ronald Reagan once declared that price fixing has not worked since the days of the emperor Diocletian, and he mischievously added that he was one of the few people old enough to

---

2. M. I. Rostovtzeff, *The Social and Economic History of the Roman Empire*, 2nd ed., rev. by P. M. Frazer (Oxford: Clarendon Press, 1957), 532.

3. G. Bratianu, *Études byzantines d'Histoire Économique et Sociale* (Paris: Geuthner, 1938), 22.

4. C. Dickerman Williams, introduction to Clyde Pharr, *The Theodosian Code* (Princeton, NJ: Princeton University Press, 1952), xii and xxii.

remember that. The president's wisecrack was the last gust of a hurricane of disapproval of what was imagined to have been the rigid social system of the later empire. To dismantle such a view of the late Roman state, in the late 1950s, was to deliver oneself from the weight of a collective nightmare, projected by modern Americans and Europeans onto the Roman Empire of the fourth and fifth centuries.

An Age of Gold: Empire and Social Mobility

So what did I give my hearers to replace this sinister image of overblown state power? Apart from my reading in more recent literature (where a less exaggerated view of the later empire seemed to be emerging) I was galvanized by hearing one outstanding lecture—Hugo Jones's "The Social Background to the Struggle between Paganism and Christianity," which he delivered in the winter of 1958, as the first lecture in the series of Warburg Lectures subsequently published as *The Conflict between Paganism and Christianity in the Fourth Century*. Delivered in the dry, almost hesitant manner that was characteristic of Jones, the lecture was electrifying. Under a shock of light-ginger hair, his eyes glittered with inspired good sense.

Jones concluded with a suggestion (delivered in a tentative, almost offhand way that was characteristic of him) that the sudden rise of Christianity had been due to the unprecedented degree of upward social mobility that characterized Roman society at the time. Christianity was adopted by the new aristocracy— an aristocracy of service. This aristocracy of service was very different from the well-ensconced and naturally conservative grandees of the age of the Antonines (in the second century AD), and, for that reason, was more vulnerable to the influence of the Christian court of Constantine and his successors. If Roman society had ever been rigid and divided into stable castes, it had been in the Antonine Age, and not in the fourth century. Upward mobility and not regimentation had been the overall characteristic of the society set in order by Diocletian and Constantine, and would remain so for centuries to come, especially in the eastern parts of the empire. Fluidity, not rigidity, was the hallmark of the later empire. These few remarks of Jones, delivered with characteristic modesty, acted as a catalyst to my work in the coming years.[5]

5. A.H.M. Jones, "The Social Background to the Struggle between Paganism and Christianity," in *The Conflict between Paganism and Christianity in the Fourth Century*, ed. A. Momigliano (Oxford: Clarendon Press, 1963), 17–37.

Put briefly, Jones had unfrozen the image of the later empire. Following his lecture and the evidence that he adduced in the many articles which preceded his masterpiece, *The Later Roman Empire* (which appeared in 1964), I tried to show, in my lectures, that this was not a society rigidified, from the top down, by governmental regulation. The opposite was the case. The laws of the Theodosian Code, if interpreted correctly, showed that attempts to hold people in place failed to work. For the imperial administration itself had fostered a remarkable degree of social mobility. Far from freezing society into static castes, it sucked talent upward like a great vacuum cleaner.

Furthermore, I pointed out how this race to the top had been accentuated by Constantine's stabilization of the currency around the gold solidus, which had introduced an "Age of Gold." Those who had access to the new gold coinage, as soldiers and government servants, found themselves "in the enviable and invincible position of the dollar-paid agents of an international organization in a country such as Greece after the war." My analogy dates the course!

The role of the solidus in quickening the upward rush of Roman society was hot news at the time. I had derived this view from Santo Mazzarino's *Aspetti sociali del quarto secolo*, which I had read so intently in the British School at Rome in 1957. In this brilliant study, Mazzarino stressed the privileged role of gold coinage in heightening the gap between those with access to gold and those without, which characterized the reign of Constantine and his successors. This development, by which the solidus became the Mighty Dollar of the Roman world, was presented as the economic motor that drove the social fluidity to which Jones had drawn attention. My lectures, indeed, were largely based on the combination of those two great scholars.

A TONE OF VOICE

The views of Santo Mazzarino and of Jones have entered so deeply into the bloodstream of late Roman studies that we tend to forget their startling novelty at this time. As befitted a young lecturer in Oxford, it was up to me to pass on to the young (all six of them!), with almost mystagogic excitement, the challenging freshness of those breakthroughs.

The weekly rhetorical occasion of a CUF lecture turned my slowly accumulated knowledge, almost instantly, into a tone of voice. It was the tone of voice that often lingered with the audience. This was perfectly consistent with the Oxford system. Lectures were treated as a way of opening up vistas for the young, based on the most up-to-date research, which often (to their delight) contradicted the wisdom of their elders and the dominant stereotypes in the field. Furthermore, the Oxford lecture format proved invaluable as a way of organizing the material that I had been gathering from all over the place on the nature of late Roman society.

Most important of all, these lectures were a preparation for writing in a synthetic and persuasive manner. Looking back, I am struck by the extent to which my writing style in all later years would reflect the constant practice of oral delivery. At least half of my books and articles have grown out of rhetorical occasions—lecture series, contributions to conferences, talks. Whenever possible, I have tended to reproduce, in print, the rhythms of speech. Growing up in Ireland, a very verbal culture, had given me an appreciation of the well-turned phrase, spiced with wit.

Furthermore, because of my stammer, speech itself was always something of an achievement for me—a form of hang gliding, at once frightening and exhilarating. For good or ill, I am a rhetor. But then, in around 1960, I faced a different problem: How could I move from the voice—the perennial instrument of Oxford teaching: the tutorial and the lecture—into the harder realm of cold print?

The After-Dinner Talk

Along with lectures, another institution was equally characteristic of the Oxford of that time—the after-dinner talk. University-wide societies—such as the Stubbs Society for historians—would invite a speaker to offer a paper after having been dined and wined by members of the society (who were undergraduates) or by a college fellow at high table. The aim was to surround the reading of the paper with a relaxed, almost bibulous atmosphere.

The meeting usually took place in the college common room or in a similar comfortable space. There would, of course, be no podium. The speaker was expected to read his or her paper from the depths of a large armchair. The audience would lounge in similar comfortable furniture. This audience consisted mainly of undergraduates drawn from all colleges. But it would also include a significant number of senior persons. Standards were high. The after-dinner talk was often the venue in which original work was exposed to discussion for the first time. It was a strange mixture of comfort and the cutting edge.

There were times when the search for a relaxed tone went a little too far. I remember watching a distinguished medievalist being plied with port by Ernest Jacob before speaking to the Stubbs Society, which had gathered to hear him in the welcoming, low-lit depths of the Hovenden Room of All Souls.

Installed, after an all-too-good dinner, in a high, deep chair, the speaker addressed us in a silvery voice on the much-debated subject of the origin of the fief—a serious issue, as the fief had always been held to be the basic building block of feudal society. It was only when he began to throw in the occasional comment—"Oh dear! My typist has written baboons instead of barons!"— that the audience sensed that something was not quite right. Soon the silver thread of the voice seemed to vanish into the back of the chair. The speaker's head nodded forward in sleep, only to wake up with a start. Finally, he sat back, opened his arms with a beatific gesture, and said: "Here I am. I am your Saint Sebastian. Riddle me with your arrows!" Seeing that the audience contained many leading medievalists—Vivian Galbraith, Beryl Smalley (1905–1984), and Naomi Hurnard (1908–1986)—each of them with firm views on the fief, he may not have mistaken their intention.

THE STUBBS SOCIETY: THE ROMAN ARISTOCRACY— CONTINUITY AND CONFLICT

When I gave my talk entitled "The Christianization of the Roman Aristocracy" to the Stubbs Society in early 1960, I received nothing but courtesy. I was grateful for the gentlemanly atmosphere of the society. For the paper that I offered was a new departure for me. It was not based on my lectures, which dealt with Roman society as a whole. It grew out of my more local, "Roman" research on the Italian aristocracy in the sixth century and earlier. Put very briefly: I argued that, in the fourth and early fifth centuries, the Roman aristocracy had not been irreconcilably divided between pagans and Christians; nor was the process of the Christianization of the aristocracy hastened in a brutal manner by the Christian emperors: rather, I suggested that the swing to Christianity was best seen in terms of a long-term evolution, the result of intermarriage and of shared social and cultural values.

I wrote the talk entirely on my own. Though I was deeply influenced by Momigliano's recent work on the aristocratic family of the Anicii, I prepared the paper and my subsequent article without his guidance. He first read it when I presented it to the editors of the *Journal of Roman Studies*; and, to my great relief, he approved of it and urged its publication. Unlike many articles by young scholars, nowadays, it did not emerge from a seminar. Nor did I feel in any great hurry to publish it. Unlike a modern graduate student (American or British) I did not need to build up a résumé well stocked with articles based on my dissertation. As a young fellow of All Souls, I could take my time.

What I did experience, at the talk itself, was the system of co-optation at work. Senior persons mingled with the undergraduates in the audience. Even Ernst Gombrich (1909–2001), the director of the Warburg Institute, was present. In the discussion, he declared that he did not agree with my tendency to minimize the extent of the conflict between pagans and Christians in Rome. He followed this up with a charming letter, further explaining his reservations. But, in the same letter, he even suggested that I might apply for a post at the Warburg Institute, to teach seminars on ancient and medieval cosmologies.

I answered Gombrich carefully. I wrote that, given the melodramatic nature of most accounts of the end of paganism, I had "tried to trail my cloak in the other direction." It was a diplomatic reply, couched in terms of a criticism of the current historiography on the subject. But Gombrich had seen clearly what I had been getting at. I had, indeed, wished to demolish the notion of an out-and-out conflict between pagans and Christians in Rome. It seemed that the notion of conflict, when applied to a group as cohesive as the Roman aristocracy, was excessively dramatic. It assumed an abiding antithesis—even a hatred—between pagans and Christians that, in my opinion, did not exist at the time.

I argued that there had been no heroic "Last Pagans": no last stand of the old religion, through the Roman Senate, as this had usually been presented. What I proposed was a new way of seeing things, and one with which Gombrich took issue.

Indeed, only a year previously, in 1958, the last pagans of Rome (all linked to the Roman Senate) had been described, in a moving lecture by Herbert Bloch (1911–2006), as having led a heroic "Pagan Revival" that culminated in the invasion of Italy by the Christian emperor Theodosius in 394. Bloch's lecture was part of the series at the Warburg in London later published as *The Conflict between Paganism and Christianity in the Fourth Century*. This was the same series where I had been riveted by the lecture of Hugo Jones on the social background to the rise of Christianity in the fluid society of the later empire. My talk was an implicit criticism of the use of *Conflict* in the title of that collection.[6]

---

6. H. Bloch, "The Pagan Revival in the West at the End of the Fourth Century," in *The Conflict between Paganism and Christianity in the Fourth Century*, ed. Arnaldo Momigliano (Oxford: Clarendon Press, 1963), 193–218; see now P. Brown, "Back to the Future: Pagans and Christians at the Warburg Institute in 1958," in *Pagans and Christians in the Roman Empire (IVth–VIth Century A.D.): The Breaking of a Dialogue*, Proceedings of the International Conference at the Monastery of Bosé, October 2008, ed. P. Brown and R. Lizzi-Testa (Münster: Lit, 2010), 17–27.

Altogether, transformation, not conflict, was what interested me. Looking back, I realize that I was struggling to find a language that did justice to the balance of continuity and discontinuity in the religious and cultural life of the Roman aristocracy. For this reason, I avoided placing undue emphasis on the binary division of pagans and Christians. Rather than tell a story of conflict and of heroic pagan resistance, I wished to tell a less dramatic, but no less significant, tale of the resilience of an elite in a time of religious change.

CONTINUITY

A world without heroes was, nonetheless, a world with a future. Here the renegade medievalist in me spoke. It was not sufficient for me to end my story with the supposed last pagans of the late fourth and early fifth centuries—nor even with the sack of Rome by Alaric in 410. It was the continuity of the Roman aristocracy into the early Middle Ages that also needed to be explained. Without a slow, almost subterranean drift into a "respectable Christianity" through intermarriage and through shared cultural activity, the preservation of so much of the classical tradition and of the myth of Rome itself would not have occurred. An aristocracy fissured by religious differences (such as Bloch and others had imagined) would not have survived in such a way as to produce, in the sixth century, figures like Boethius, Cassiodorus, and Gregory the Great. And so I ended my paper to the Stubbs Society with a quotation from the Christian poet Prudentius, where Rome is made to speak:

Quae vivendo diu didici contemnere finem.
By living long, I have learned to scorn the end.
(PRUDENTIUS, CONTRA SYMMACHUM 2.660)

The paper was a success. It was delivered in the common room of Christ Church, in a room hung with the portraits of eighteenth-century grandees. My audience liked to hear that, once again, an aristocracy had pulled through in difficult times. This was, after all, the Oxford of Ronald Syme (1903–1989) and Bruce McFarlane, deeply influenced, also, by the researches of Sir Lewis Namier: the resilience of elites was in the air—whether in the last days of the Roman Republic, in the Wars of the Roses, or in the Whig ascendancy of the eighteenth century. To have added to their number the last pagans of Rome and their Christian peers was an altogether welcome contribution.

As I look back, it seems that I had attempted to alter the palette with which to paint the well-known scene of the end of paganism in Rome. I had opted for more muted shades. I had also opted for a longer time span: I had tried to bring together developments in Rome in the fourth century with the story of the further resilience of the Roman aristocracy in the fifth and sixth centuries. If I succeeded at all, I did so by painting with greater nuance and on a wider canvas than hitherto. In the next few years, I would try to do the same for an even larger, even more fiercely contested landscape—the North Africa of Saint Augustine.

RELIGIOUS DISSENT

THE CASE OF NORTH AFRICA

The Landscape of Dissent

For the next few years, I would be in constant dialogue with William Frend's masterpiece, *The Donatist Church*. Engagement with the work of Bill Frend in its many aspects was the equivalent, for me, of graduate school: it turned me into a late Roman historian. Eventually, this engagement would prove to be my way into a biography of Augustine of Hippo. In other words, my first approach to Augustine did not lie through the *Confessions* or the *City of God*, or through his theology of grace (as one might expect); but through the unforgiving confrontation of two Christian churches, on the ground, in the mean streets of the towns and villages of Roman Africa as these had been brought alive for us by Frend's *Donatist Church*.[1]

In 1960, Bill Frend was unavoidable. Though he himself was a fellow of Gonville and Caius College in Cambridge, his *Donatist Church* had entered the bloodstream of Oxford academic life through the teaching of the Saint Augustine Special Subject. His daring hypothesis on the relation between theological controversy and social protest presented Roman North Africa as a veritable sociological laboratory. It was in Augustine's Africa that one could trace most clearly the repercussions of the rise of the Christian church within the society of the later Roman Empire.

For Romans, "Africa" and "African" referred to the Mediterranean regions of Africa alone (now called the Maghreb in Arabic), and not to the great

1. W.H.C. Frend, *The Donatist Church: A Movement of Protest in Roman North Africa* (Oxford: Clarendon Press, 1952).

continent of Africa as we now know it. In the fourth century it was the most prosperous and intellectually vigorous region in the Roman Empire in the West. Furthermore, in the 1960s, interest in the social and ethnic tensions of late Roman Africa was nourished by events in modern Algeria, where a major War of Independence had only recently been fought out on the very doorstep of Europe.

As I have already explained, Bill Frend offered a view of the Christianity of fourth-century Africa that mapped what was known as the "Donatist controversy" onto a distinctive landscape. He claimed that the fault line between the two opposing Christian groups did not lie in any doctrinal disagreement. Rather, it lay along an ecological frontier: the eternal contrast between the Tell—the fertile landscapes of the Mediterranean, from Carthage and Hippo westward, where Roman cities were abundant and the Roman way of life was firmly implanted—and the austere High Plains of Numidia, a dusty landscape, swept by desert winds, alternately chill and scorching, with few towns, but covered with the villages of a robust and independent-minded peasantry.

As Frend saw it, Christianity had come to Numidia as a "Movement of Protest." Those who rallied to the charismatic leadership of Donatus of Carthage (from 311/12 to 355) adopted the confrontational ecclesiology of the martyr-bishop Cyprian of Carthage (248–258), with its powerful notion of a pure church, tensed against an evil world. They were proud to have resisted pagan Roman emperors. They refused, in the name of religion, to collaborate with the Roman state. They viewed the world from the deep South of Numidia; the cities of the Mediterranean were distant to them. The Roman Empire (even the supposedly Christian empire of Constantine and his successors), was regarded as an alien power whose shadow fell across their high, dry land like the chill shade of Antichrist.

Above all, Frend asserted that Donatism rested on a secure ethnic bedrock. The Numidians were Berbers, and that was what mattered: "Is Donatism part of a continuous native religious tradition, as fundamentally unchanging as the Berbers themselves in the routine of their daily life?"[2] He expected his readers to answer the question with a resounding yes.

Nowadays, it is easy to overlook the exhilarating novelty of Frend's approach. Hardly anyone had dared to treat a major Christian controversy in such a manner.[3] And yet it struck me that, somehow, this book was wrong.

2. Frend, *Donatist Church*, xvi.

3. E. Rebillard, "William Hugh Clifford Frend (1916–2005): The Legacy of *The Donatist Church*," Papers of the Sixteenth International Congress of Patristic Studies held in Oxford in

There was a heavy-handedness in Frend's grand certitudes. He seemed to be so intent on joining the religious and the social that he ended up ramming them together at the cost of confining Donatism to a single landscape and to a single niche in the complex society of Roman Africa. His unabashed insistence on the "native," Berber roots of Donatism seemed to me to block the way toward an appreciation of the role of religious dissent among Christians in the Roman Empire as a whole. I suggested that what was at stake in the Donatist Schism was something more than the grievances of a particular ethnic enclave. The schism was part of a far wider debate on the extent to which Christians could identify with the social order. It was this consideration that provoked my article in *History* for 1961, "Religious Dissent in the Later Roman Empire: The Case of North Africa."[4]

A FORUM: *HISTORY* 1961

I was encouraged to submit my article to *History* by Ralph Davis—R.H.C. Davis (1918–1991)—a medievalist and tutor at Merton College. This was a significant choice for me. *History* was the journal of the Historical Association. Its members included schoolteachers, clergymen, and persons of scholarly inclination quite as much as academics. Many considered *History* to be a "B-team" journal because of this commitment to a wider public. I admired it for that very reason.

The sense of a diverse audience provided by *History* enabled me to step back and take as wide a view as possible of Frend's *Donatist Church*. In my criticism of Frend, I wished to avoid a donnish Punch-and-Judy show. I disliked the academic controversies that raged in Oxford, much to the delight of the agonistic young—such as the "Gentry controversy" (on the social origins of the English Civil War), which had pitted Hugh Trevor-Roper against Lawrence Stone and others in the 1950s. This debate was driven by such an unusual degree of personal and ideological rancor that it irreparably divided the field of early modern English history. Instead, I wanted to do justice to a great if wrongheaded book—to draw out its implications to the full as well as to

---

2011, ed. M. Vinzent, *Studia Patristica* 53 (Louvain: Peeters, 2013), 55–71, provides a careful and admirably fair appreciation of Frend's work.

4. Peter Brown, "Religious Dissent in the Later Roman Empire: The Case of North Africa," *History* 46 (1961): 83–101, reprinted in *Religion and Society in the Age of Saint Augustine* (London: Faber, 1972), 237–259.

suggest my own, alternative views before a cultivated but not necessarily exclusively academic readership.

For this reason I wrote the article as a review essay. This was a genre of which I approved greatly. A review essay took a controverted topic and placed it against the widest possible historiographical background. It was with this wider picture in mind that I set about my critique of Bill Frend.

LOCAL AND UNIVERSAL IN THE MAGHREB: JACQUES BERQUE (1910–1995)

What finally galvanized me to write the article came from an unexpected source: from a French tradition of sociology and anthropology that had recently been reviewed by Jacques Berque in a trenchant article in *Annales*—a journal closely associated with the work of Fernand Braudel, devoted to the joining of history and the social sciences.

I found Berque's article almost by accident when flipping through recent periodicals in the Codrington Library. I picked it up in a rather flat mood, between an uneventful college meeting and the prospect of a heavy gaudy dinner in the evening. It was just what I needed. I still have my notes on Berque, tucked into my copy of Frend's *Donatist Church*. Here was the answer, from a master of the culture and religion of the modern Maghreb, to Frend's lopsided insistence on the Berber background to Donatism.[5]

In his review of French anthropology in the Maghreb, Berque singled out for criticism the tendency in French anthropology and in French colonial ideology to isolate the Berbers. Anthropologists tended to treat them as the underlying "reality" of the Maghreb, while they dismissed the religious and cultural activities of the Arabophone elites of the cities as a mere "façade."

As Berque presented it, this fascination with the Berbers was far from innocent. It was linked to the French colonial policy of "divide and rule." Among colonial admnistrators, the Berbers were presented as the "real" inhabitants of North Africa. In such circles, the intensely local nature of Berber culture was cried up in marked contrast to that of the educated elites. For these elites were distinguished by their access to the Arabic-speaking, Muslim world. It was this contact with the wider world of Islam that threatened to make the populations of the Maghreb (Berbers and non-Berbers alike) dangerous, because it had led

---

5. Jacques Berque, "Cent vingt-cinq ans de sociologie maghrébine," *Annales* 11 (1956): 296–324.

them to embrace pan-Arabism and its anticolonial ideology. Faced with such a challenge, the colonial power found it reassuring to privilege the Berbers and to dismiss the urban elites of the Maghreb as if they were rootless, squeaky voices that would soon fall silent.

Berque warned his French readers against this one-sided view. He pointed out that it was precisely the combination of local discontent with the universal message of Islam and pan-Arabism that had led to the explosion of the Algerian War of Independence.

> Le génie de l'Afrique du Nord réside dans un certain genre d'interaction entre le particulier et le général.

> The genius of North Africa lies in some kind of interaction between the. particular and the general.[6]

Bluntly, the notion of the "eternal Berber " was a construct. It had arisen as a result of French efforts to isolate the Maghreb from the wider and more dangerous currents of international Islam. By emphasizing the exclusively Berber roots of Donatism, Bill Frend had allowed himself to slip into a view of Roman Africa that reflected the politically motivated bias of a century of French colonial anthropology.

At the time, I knew little of the fierce debates among French scholars and politicians on this issue. All I knew, as I read Berque on that dull afternoon in All Souls, was that he had given me what I wanted—a cogent critique of any attempt to reduce North African religious movements to nothing but their imagined local roots. The real dynamite was compounded when the local and the universal came together. The Donatist Church was not simply a Berber church. It also claimed to be a true church. Its adherents shared a common, universal hope for an independent Christianity—a Christianity of protest, which joined urban intellectuals to the Numidian peasantry in ways that stretched across sociological and ecological boundaries. It surrounded even the humblest Donatist chapel with the dignity and subversive potential of a universal claim to truth.

"Pious Liberty": Church, Society, and the Martyrs

So what was the role of Christian dissent in the later empire? I suggested that its role was less dramatic than we had thought in the short run, but more far-reaching in the long run. To reduce all cases of religious dissent to pockets of

6. Berque, "Cent vingt-cinq ans de sociologie maghrébine," 320.

local ethnic discontent (as Frend had done for Africa) was to tie dissenting groups too tightly to specific trouble spots.

By contrast, I suggested that the problems posed by the rise of Christianity affected Roman society as a whole, in all regions of the empire and in remarkably various social situations. The new religion was a loose cannon. Memories of Christian resistance to the pagan authorities in times of persecution had opened a hairline crack in the religious structure of the ancient city, as this had been described by Fustel de Coulanges, where "the state and religion were so completely merged that it was impossible, not only to have the idea of a conflict between the two, but even to distinguish the one from the other."[7]

But once state and religion had drifted apart, if only so very little, every Christian bishop, in any part of the Roman Empire, was a potential Donatist, empowered to challenge the government in the name of religion. Constantine's conversion and his heavy-handed patronage of the Catholic Church failed to mend that fateful crack. He had tried to close the stable door when the horse had already bolted.

In the fourth century, the Christian catacombs in Rome and elsewhere were already filled with frescoes and with carved sarcophagi that depicted the heroic refusal of the Three Children of Israel to bow down to the idol erected by King Nebuchadnezzar (in Daniel 3). These three Jews were treated as paradigmatic Christian martyrs. Significantly, the idol that they refused to worship was often shown in the form of an imperial bust such as was displayed in every Roman courtroom. It was Augustine, not a Donatist writer, who pointed to the annual Christian festival of the Three Children of Israel, which was celebrated by a chanted reading of their story in the book of Daniel. He added that he hoped that Christian emperors would take to heart the *pia libertas*, the "pious liberty" of the martyrs. All over the empire, the fateful notion of a conflict between state and religion had become, at last, thinkable. And so I concluded:

> And in this revolution, which affected so deeply the North African provinces of the fourth and fifth centuries, the issues at stake were not merely the local grievances of a province; they were nothing less than the place of religion in society.[8]

These were my arguments against Bill Frend. The reader might wish to know how the author of *The Donatist Church* responded to what I, at least, had

7. F. de Coulanges, *La cité antique* (Paris: Hachette, 1885), 197, cited in "Religious Dissent," 258.
8. Brown, "Religious Dissent," 259.

intended to be a respectful but searching criticism. The answer: he did not respond at all. He always treated me with the utmost good nature and wrote with great generosity in support of my biography of Augustine when it was sent to him as a reader by the publisher. Young scholars like to think that their first article will be like the trumpet blast of Joshua—that it will bring down the walls of Jericho with a resounding crash. In Bill Frend's case, it appears, I blew my trumpet in vain.

I last saw Bill on November 24, 1993. I had come to Cambridge to deliver the Tanner Lectures that would become a short book: *Authority and the Sacred: Aspects of the Christianization of the Roman World.*[9] The lectures were followed, the next morning, by a roundtable discussion. A short way into the discussion, Bill Frend made his appearance, wrapped in a heavy tweed coat. He soon rose to speak. Reaching deep into the pocket of his coat, he pulled out a length of leaden piping. With a magnificent sweep of the arm, which caused the person in front him to duck (a fact that I noted with some concern, for that person was my wife), he brandished his archaeological trophy. "Do you know what this is?" he asked, turning to our table. "It is a length of pipe which I have excavated in my garden. It is a piece of Roman piping. It is the pipe of a vast imperial villa of the fourth century whose wide acres fed the armies of the Rhine. Imagine that!"

My colleagues and the younger souls among the discussants writhed with evident embarrassment. The old boy was at it again. I, by contrast (and my wife, for Bill Frend's books had done much to enliven the history of the early church for her) were spellbound. The round face, the glinting eyes, the orotund phrases (as if they dropped ready-made from the pages of one of his grand survey books) showed the old magician still at work. I had not heard this for thirty years. I basked in it. It was good to have known so boisterous a scholar.

9. Peter Brown, *Authority and the Sacred: Aspects of the Christianization of the Roman World* (Cambridge University Press 1995).

RELIGIOUS COERCION

MAPPING COERCION

In 1963, I wrote another article for *History* on the subject of religious coercion in the later empire. In both my article on religious dissent and that on religious coercion I was in dialogue with William Frend. It seemed to me that, despite my criticisms of *The Donatist Church*, Frend had contributed handsomely to the grand debate on the role of Christianity in the later Roman Empire. While Mazzarino and Jones had taught me how to view the later Roman Empire as a whole, Frend had set me a problem that would not go away: the relation between religion and society.[1]

The article on coercion addressed relatively straightforward issues. What was the nature of religious coercion in the later Roman Empire? How did it work? Who suffered most from it? Who benefited most from policies of repression? Last but not least: How did the constant striving for religious uniformity in what was now a Christian empire come to mold perceptions both of the Roman state and of the Christian church?

I found that things were not quite as they seemed. Despite the authoritarian nature of the late Roman state, religious coercion was a less brutal feature of late Roman society than one might have expected. With the exception of the exotic Manichees, no religious dissident was threatened with the death penalty for his or her beliefs (though some were lynched, as Jews and pagans became increasingly exposed to lethal attacks by Christian mobs). There was no burning of heretics, no Albigensian Crusade, no Saint Bartholomew's Day

---

1. Peter Brown, "Religious Coercion in the Later Roman Empire: The Case of North Africa," *History* 48 (1963): 283–305, in *Religion and Society in the Age of Saint Augustine* (London: Faber, 1972), 301–331.

Massacre, and no Revocation of the Edict of Nantes. In sheer religious beastliness, the later Roman Empire was quite outclassed by medieval and early modern Europe.

I also discovered that, when it came to the issue of intolerance, the classical Roman Empire had been no paradise: cults were strictly controlled; alleged sorcerers were hounded; Christians had been executed in large numbers, and their buildings destroyed. The religious legislation of the Christian empire had not brought to an end some age of innocence, where all beliefs had been tolerated.

Instead, a succession of laws, issued by Christian emperors from the time of Constantine (306–337) and Theodosius I (379–395) onward, slowly reduced "unorthodox" Christians, pagans, and Jews to the status of second-class citizens. These laws were coercive in the true sense: they did not aim to annihilate, but to convert—to edge dissenters, willy-nilly, into the Catholic churches.

Not all classes in the empire were equally vulnerable to such pressure. In a society marked by a rush to the top among the upper classes, and by a feverish scramble at all levels for privileges, exemptions, and other badges of status, heretics, Jews, and pagans were placed at a permanent disadvantage. As a result, the search for wealth and privilege associated with the "Age of Gold" instituted by Constantine did more to spread a conformist Christianity throughout the Roman world than did the sermons of any number of bishops.

But the impact of this system varied. Townsfolk and civic elites who depended on imperial privileges caved in easily to official pressure. But in wide stretches of the countryside and in mountainous regions beyond the reach of the Roman state, hardy groups of Christian dissidents of all kinds—and also Jews and pagans—held out undisturbed for centuries on end.

IMPERIAL LAW, LOCAL OPINION

Indeed, the more closely I examined the capacity of the Roman state to impose its will in religious matters, the more I found a colossus with feet of clay. The whole structure of the late Roman administration militated against the effectiveness of religious coercion. Provincial governors depended on locally recruited staffs to get things done. These local officials had no wish to push through measures that offended the religious sentiments of their region. The later Roman Empire was by no means a police state of the modern kind, as we had been encouraged by scholars of the 1920s and 1930s to imagine it to have been. If the constitution of the later Roman Empire (like that of tsarist Russia) could be described as "despotism tempered by assassination," so the religious policies of the Christian emperors could be called "theocracy tempered by inefficiency."

All this added up to a paradox. At the top, the late Roman state was committed to a proactive religious policy. But, at the bottom, at the local level, there was very little that the government could do to enforce its own laws. This meant that enforcement was left to militant grassroots organizations. Hence a sinister aspect of the period: the prevalence of spasmodic religious violence. In many places, the ineffectiveness of the state led to fear rather than to freedom: "The result of this weakness was a particularly venomous situation. The Emperors, in their public edicts, set a tone of lofty intolerance, while leaving local groups to carry it out in their own way."[2]

REFRACTION

I ended up by suggesting that this vacuum of power on ground level had enabled the Christian bishops to rise to prominence in the cities. It was they who had a vested interest in the application of the laws. It was they, in effect, who decided to whom the laws applied—who was a heretic; whose conversion was sincere. Above all, it was they who imposed their own meaning—we would now say their own "spin"—on the laws themselves, by presenting them as part of a providential order designed to further the interests of the church.

It was a case of the tail wagging the dog. The day-to-day symbiosis of imperial and ecclesiastical power, at the ground level—and not high theories on the relation between church and state—ensured that a subtle change of roles took place, by which the empire came to be seen as serving the church, because the church had come to serve the empire, as the only institution with a vested interest in making the imperial laws effective on a local level.

In this article, I felt that I had paid my dues as a historian of the later empire, by deriving a conclusion with wide implications from work on the nitty-gritty of late Roman society. Hence I was particularly pleased to receive a letter from Wolfgang Liebeschuetz, then at the University of Leicester. Liebeschuetz was a pupil of Jones, and already a model scholar of the later empire. In the coming years, I would draw with unfailing gratitude on his work on late Roman Antioch.

2. Brown, "Religious Coercion," 308.

Praise from him was the sort of praise that I had wished for, because it was for qualities that I valued:

> Dear Mr. Brown,
>
> Thank you for your letter and the off-print on Religious Coercion in the Later Roman Empire. Like your earlier papers it conveys the true "feel" of the Later Empire. This success is achieved—or so it seems to me—by a deliberate refusal to simplify complex situations by forcing them into predetermined schemes. I was particularly interested in the paragraphs dealing with the place of the bishop in municipal affairs and his key role in the enforcement of anti-heretical legislation. The foot-notes too have taught me a great deal!

The issue now was this: Where would this work on religious coercion lead me?

The Long Debate

An article on religious coercion and religious intolerance kept open a bridgehead into the Middle Ages, the Reformation, and the Counter-Reformation. No issue had been debated with such fury, in the Reformation and Counter-Reformation periods, as the choice between persecution and toleration in the Christian churches. Both sides looked back to the early church and the later empire to find precedents for their actions. As a result, the book of Joseph Lecler, *Histoire de la Tolérance à l'époque de la Réforme*, served me almost as a handbook throughout these years. There were very few late Roman texts on the issue of toleration and persecution that had not been cited by Reformers or by Catholics, and discussed by Lecler in his levelheaded and comprehensive book.[3]

The Problem of Authority

It was the same with medievalists. I was particularly struck, at this time, by the opening words of Sir Maurice Powicke's *The Christian Life in the Middle Ages*: "The legacy of medieval Christianity to later ages was the problem of authority."[4]

---

3. J. Lecler, *Histoire de la tolérance à l'époque de la Réforme* (Paris: Aubier, 1955); trans. T. L. Westow: *Toleration and Reformation* (New York: Association Press, 1960).

4. F. M. Powicke, "The Christian Life in the Middle Ages," in *The Christian Life in the Middle Ages and Other Essays* (Oxford: Clarendon Press, 1935), 1–30, at 1.

I agreed entirely with Sir Maurice. This, for me, was where the later empire had been heading. Already in the fourth century an intolerant church allied itself with an authoritarian regime to impose its beliefs, from the top down, on the mass of the population. Whether we liked it or not, this was the most immediate and decisive legacy of Rome to the Christianity of western Europe.

Powicke's essay was the voice of a doyen of medieval studies. Meditative and involuted, it was heavy with intellectual reservations and nuanced suggestions that lent a note of almost vatic authority to his writings. The essay was a deeply felt evocation of the manner in which a religion could come to dominate an entire society. But on the role of force in bringing about this dominance, I noticed that Powicke waffled: "Christians [he went on to say] have never been proud of it, for it has been for them a tiresome perplexity, an unmanageable side-issue in a labour vastly more important."[5]

I viewed such statements with distinctly cold eyes. They seemed to me to impose a benign amnesia on the rougher edges of the rise of Christianity. I detected in Powicke a touch of the Anglican romantic attachment to the Middle Ages that, as a Protestant from Ireland, I found both intriguing and, in the end, naive. In Ireland, religion was serious. It could be expected to have hard edges. In postwar Ireland religious issues were prominent as the new republic took on an increasingly Catholic face: divorce was not available; contraceptives could not be sold; censorship was imposed on books and films. All these issues were hotly debated in the correspondence columns of the *Irish Times* for me to read at home, or were sent to me as cuttings by my father. I was convinced that it was to those hard edges, where state power merged with religion, that thinking persons should direct their attention if they were to understand the history of Europe.

I notice that Bob Moore, an Ulsterman from Enniskillen in Northern Ireland, whom I had taught for the Augustine Special Subject in 1962, was driven by a similar dissatisfaction to write his pungent masterpiece, *The Formation of a Persecuting Society: Authority and Deviance in Western Europe, 950–1250*. "Tiresome" though this fact might be, Western Christendom, for all its spiritual achievements, had also been a "persecuting society"; and the roots of the attitudes that made it so reached back to the Africa of Saint Augustine.[6]

---

5. Powicke, The Christian Life in the Middle Ages," 1.

6. *The Formation of a Persecuting Society: Authority and Deviance in Western Europe, 950–1250* (Oxford: Blackwell, 1987).

The Grand Patriarch of Persecutors

It takes some effort to recapture the extent to which religious coercion of any kind was regarded as an obscene topic in the academia of the early 1960s. Reviewing the published version of the Warburg Lectures entitled *The Conflict between Paganism and Christianity in the Fourth Century*, in 1963, I spoke of it as "the cloven hoof of the religious history of the Later Empire."[7] Despite the relative leniency of late Roman coercive measures—compared with medieval and early modern examples of religious persecution—the very fact of putting pressure on the conscience of others made large areas of late Roman religious life seem toxic to many historians. These scholars maintained an upright, liberal view that set a clear boundary between free and forced religion, and that treated those who strayed across that boundary, by advocating any form of coercion in matters of belief, with particular repugnance.

Yet in Africa, in around 405, one of the subtlest minds of all antiquity deliberately crossed that boundary. Having originally claimed that he wished to deal with his Donatist rivals by free discussion alone, Augustine of Hippo changed his mind. He embraced and justified at length the imperial laws against the Donatist Church. Furthermore, this change was not simply a reaction to unusual circumstances. It settled into his mind as part of his vision of a Christian society: "His acceptance of [the] forced conversion [of Donatists], after 405, far from remaining a reluctant capitulation to necessity, pushed deep roots into the main body of his thought."[8]

In this, as in so much else, Augustine proved to be, for good or ill, a Maker of the Middle Ages. His justification of the coercion of the Donatists circulated for the next thirteen hundred years in Christian Europe. As late as the early eighteenth century, Jean Barbeyrac (1674–1744), the great Huguenot scholar, described Augustine as "le grand patriarche des persécuteurs."[9] To be known as "the Grand Patriarch of Persecutors" was hardly a savory reputation. But it was, in part, so as to get inside the mind and life of such a person who, among so much else in his boundless theological and pastoral activity, could think such dark thoughts and justify such practices, that I turned increasingly—and, after 1963, exclusively—to writing a biography of Augustine of Hippo.

---

7. Review of *The Conflict between Paganism and Christianity in the Fourth Century A.D.*, in *Oxford Magazine*, May 16, 1963, 300–301, in *Religion and Society*, 147–150, at 149.

8. Brown, "Religious Coercion," 323.

9. Jean Barbeyrac, *Traité de la Morale des Pères de l'Église* (Amsterdam: Herman Uytwerf, 1728), 304.

PART III

AUGUSTINE TO THE HOLY MAN

WRITING *AUGUSTINE* *OF HIPPO*

LEARNING TO LISTEN

In 1962 I began in earnest to write a biography of Saint Augustine of Hippo, which occupied me full-time until the spring of 1966. It was published by Faber and Faber in the summer of 1967.[1]

One would have thought that a biography of the great bishop of Hippo was a natural subject for any scholar interested in the history of the Roman Empire and of Latin Christianity in the fourth and fifth centuries. Here was a figure where history and autobiography intersected, and whose career summed up the stormy passage of an age. In 397 Augustine wrote the *Confessions*, a work generally acclaimed as the first autobiography in Western literature. In 413 he began the *City of God*, which was a deeply meditated comment on the nature of history, provoked by the Gothic sack of Rome in 410. As we have seen, his controversy with the Donatists determined all future thought on the relation between church and society in western Europe. In his old age, Augustine's opposition to the ideas of Pelagius, on grace and free will, left an indelible mark on Latin Christianity up to the time of the Reformation and beyond. What could be more challenging than to attempt to bring all these great moments together by writing a complete *Life* of this singular man?

Yet this had not been done. The rich and humane sketch of Augustine as a preacher and pastor by Frits Van der Meer (1904–1994) in his *Augustine the*

---

1. Peter Brown, *Augustine of Hippo: A Biography* (London: Faber and Faber; Berkeley: University of California Press, 1967); *Augustine of Hippo: A Biography*, new ed. with an epilogue (Berkeley: University of California Press, 2000)

Bishop dealt only with his activities as bishop of Hippo. The admirably learned and fair-minded book of my friend Gerald Bonner (1926–2013)—*Augustine of Hippo: Life and Controversies*—was only a study of the theological controversies in which Augustine had been engaged.[2] As far as I was concerned, here was a mountain still waiting to be climbed.

To move Augustine to center stage by writing his biography was a new sort of history writing for me. I would find myself in the company of a solitary giant—a religious genius, whose thoughts still ran, for good or ill, in the bloodstream of all western European Christians (Catholics and Protestants alike); the most prodigious author in the entire history of Latin literature; and—behind all this, it seemed to me as I came to know him in the course of those years—a person of magnetic charm and riveting originality, whose quality of mind was unmistakable even in his smallest turn of phrase and most routine writing.

I had to learn to listen to a single voice. I was no longer involved in an ongoing historical controversy, such as I had engaged in with Bill Frend. Nor was I out to prove a single point or push through a single agenda for the study of Augustine. I was there to listen. I had to learn to hear Augustine clearly as he spoke the unfamiliar language of an ancient Christian from a millennium and a half ago, and then to pass on what I heard to modern readers. In brief: I had to stretch my heart in order to read Augustine's heart. That was the greatest challenge, and the greatest joy, of those five years.

A Gentleman's Agreement

The first part of the business was easy. It involved the crucial link between All Souls and the wider world through its London fellows. As I have explained, the London fellows did not remain in Oxford as academics; but they retained their membership of the college and would often appear at weekends. Charles Monteith (1921–1995) was one such fellow. He was an editor in Faber and Faber in London. In December 1959 I discussed with him, over a drink before dinner, the possibility of a biography of Augustine. I then sent him a full proposal. As one fellow of All Souls to another, he agreed that Faber's would consider a biography of Augustine whenever I chose to hand in the manuscript. It was as simple as that. With his characteristic, wry view of the English

---

2. Frits Van der Meer, *Augustine the Bishop* (London: Sheed and Ward, 1961); Gerald Bonner, *Augustine of Hippo: Life and Controversies* (London: SCM Press, 1963).

academic scene, Arnaldo Momigliano was amused: "Does Monteith allot bits of ancient history to every fellow?"

At that time, I barely realized that I was enjoying an incomparable privilege. I did not have to look for a publisher. The gentleman's agreement with Charles Monteith set my mind at rest. I may have been wrong to be so confident: in reality, Faber's had their own system of screening manuscripts that was as discreet and prompt, and as exacting, as that of any university press. In the meantime, however, my constant contact with Monteith, through his weekend visits to All Souls, spared me much anxiety. I felt confident that I could write what I wished as long as it passed muster at the end of the day. So how did I set about it?

READING AUGUSTINE

First and foremost, these were years of deep reading. I would sit in a large armchair with a board across the arms and read my way through the folio volumes of the works of Augustine published by the Benedictine scholars of St. Maur between 1679 and 1700. I would work my way down those generous pages noting on a piece of paper the page, the letter on the margin of each vertical column, and the position, within each letter, of the passages that interested me (so that "11r D mbm" would be page 11, right-hand column, division D, middle-to-bottom-middle). Then, having read through the entire text, I would return to copy into my notes those passages that I had marked. This method of taking notes had a direct effect on the way in which I absorbed the works of Augustine. I hardly ever made a précis of what Augustine wrote. Instead, I went out of my way to copy by hand every passage in the original Latin. By doing this, I aimed to capture, through citations, not only what Augustine said, but, quite as much, how he said it. By taking notes in this way, I found myself catching his tone of voice.

What struck me most about Augustine was the care that he took to make his ideas intelligible to his readers. Here was someone who had grappled, throughout his life, to express himself—to drag his thoughts into the open, "through the narrow lanes of speech." Augustine once wrote in 399 (when he was at the height of his powers as an author) to console a deacon who was anxious about his catechism classes. The young man should not worry: "For my own way of expressing myself almost always disappoints me . . . I am saddened that my tongue cannot live up to my heart."[3] I found that, as a young

---

3. Augustine, *de catechizandis rudibus* 2.3, cited in *Augustine of Hippo* (2000), 253.

author, I could identify my own ache to communicate with Augustine's constant awareness of the hiatus between himself and the outside world. I knew instinctively that I myself would grow as a communicator (as well as in many other ways) by keeping close to such a person.

LEARNING ON THE JOB

It was lonely work. In many ways, I was the wrong person to be doing a biography of Augustine. I was not a clergyman—though, a little later, I was often amused to receive letters addressed (on the strength of my known acquaintance with Augustine) to "Monsieur l'Abbé." Nor was I a theologian or a classical scholar. These were the people most usually engaged with the study of the Fathers of the Church. I lacked the abstract cast of mind of the one, and the training in handling difficult texts of the other. I was an out-of-place medievalist, whose Latin (fortunately) was up to the job. The best I could do was sit and read.

OLD TOMES: THE MAURIST EDITION AND THE "INDEFATIGABLE TILLEMONT"

As far as reading went, I realize that I was doubly spoiled. I was able to carry the magnificent pages of the Maurist edition of the complete works of Augustine, one by one, out of the basement of the Codrington Library of All Souls where they had been stored. But I was also able to make my way up to the upper gallery of the Codrington, to mount a ladder so as to take from a high shelf, poised vertiginously a good twenty feet above the marble floor below, the thirteenth volume of the *Mémoires Écclésiastiques* of Louis Sébastien le Nain de Tillemont (1637–1698).

Tillemont was a Jansenist scholar, connected with Port-Royal, who continued his work on his family estate after Port-Royal had been destroyed by Louis XIV in 1679. The thirteenth volume of his *Mémoires* contained a complete *Life of Augustine* put together with unfailing accuracy, and in strict chronological order. It was published in 1702, a few years after Tillemont's death. I would not begin to write on any incident or embark on any chapter of my book until I had established its chronology and the place in his life through a careful reading of the relevant pages of that tenacious Jansenist scholar.

I realized, with something of a thrill, that in doing this I was following in the footsteps of Edward Gibbon. Gibbon would always refer, with gratitude, in his *Decline and Fall*, to "the indefatigable Tillemont": he was "the sure-footed mule" whose patient work on the chronology of the later empire as a whole (not only of the life of Augustine) enabled Gibbon to unroll, with majestic certainty, his narrative of the rise of Christianity and the fall of Rome.[4]

New Evidence

So I had all the books I needed—on my own doorstep, as it were—but how to write the *Life*? When it came to listening to Augustine, I could not have wished for a more readily accessible subject. Augustine wrote prodigiously on innumerable topics and in many different genres. From the time of his writing the *Confessions*, in 397, to his death in 430, he wrote over a million and a half words: I am glad that I did not know of this statistic when I began my reading! More important yet, we also know exactly when, and even why, he wrote almost everything that he wrote. This was because he went out of his way to complete what might be called, in modern terms, his own c.v. At the very end of his life, in 426–427, he put together his *Retractationes*—his "Rereading" of his own works. He placed all of his ninety-two formal works in chronological order—each with a small comment on why it was written. It is hard to exaggerate the importance of this fact, which we all too easily take for granted. Here was a figure who had already laid out the chronological framework of his life for future historians.

This huge advantage was well known to every scholar who studied Augustine. What I did not realize fully at the time was that there was an important part of Augustine's works that he had not put into chronological order in this way—his abundant letters and his sermons. As a result, many of these still pose serious problems of dating and context. They remain loose cannons. But they have also proved to be one of the growth points of modern Augustinian scholarship.

4. See now Daniel-Odin Hurel, "The Benedictines of the Congregation of St. Maur and the Church Fathers," in *The Reception of the Fathers in the West*, vol. 2, *From the Carolingians to the Maurists*, ed. Irena Backus (Leiden: Brill, 2001), 1009–1038. It is now possible to read Tillemont's *Life of Augustine* in an English translation: *Louis Sébastien, le Nain de Tillemont: Mémoire Écclésiastique*, vol. 13, *The Life of Augustine*, trans. Frederick Van Flateren (New York: Peter Lang, 2012). Tillemont himself has been well studied: see especially Bruno Neveu, *Un historien à l'école de Port-Royal. Sébastien le Nain de Tillemont (1637–1698)* (The Hague: M. Nijhoff, 1966); David P. Jordan, "Le Nain de Tillemont: Gibbon's 'Sure Footed Mule,'" *Church History* 39 (1970): 483–502; and Jean Laporte, "Le Nain Tillemont sur saint Augustin," in *Le Nain Tillemont et l'historiographie de l'Antiquité romaine* (Paris: Honoré Champion, 2002), 411–425.

Partly because of the great advances in computer digitalization in recent years, we have become more aware of the fact that letters and groups of sermons by Augustine may still linger, as yet unrecognized, in medieval collections, hidden beneath the cramped Gothic script of unprepossessing late medieval manuscripts. In the last few decades alone, entire groups of letters and sermons, of which we knew nothing in the 1960s, have surfaced. One of the joys of writing an epilogue to my *Augustine of Hippo* (which I did in 2000) was the opportunity to hail some of these discoveries. We now have twenty-nine further letters from Augustine's old age, which were discovered by Johannes Divjak and first published in 1981. Furthermore, a group of sermons, preached in the years when Augustine was writing the *Confessions* and beginning his career as a bishop, were discovered by François Dolbeau and published in 1996.

Although these new letters and sermons contain no spectacular revelations, they have brought Augustine, once again, into vivid focus as a preacher and as a conscientious bishop. We often see him from unexpected angles. This was not the ethereal figure that we imagine the author of the *Confessions* to have been. He is a bishop with mud on his boots, battling injustice in the harsh world of late Roman Africa. In one of the most remarkable of the letters discovered by Johannes Divjak, we find Augustine, at the age of seventy-three (only three years before his death), interviewing a terrified country girl who described how her farm had been raided by slave-traders. The poor child could not even speak Latin—only Punic. Her older brother translated for her. This was part of a dogged attempt by Augustine and his congregation to break a ring of slave-traders who operated (with the full protection of local bigwigs), out of the port of Hippo.

On a lighter note, in an unexpected aside in one of his newly discovered sermons, we hear Augustine (in 403) telling his congregation, with total *sans gêne*, how, as young students in Carthage, he and his friends would attempt to pick up girls at the heady festivals that took place at the tomb of Saint Cyprian. What could I have done with these nuggets in 1962![5]

It is precisely in this undergrowth of sermons and letters that we have been able to discover, against all expectations, further, vivid traits in our portrait of Augustine. In the moving image of François Dolbeau, we meet him again, in such sermons, "with the emotion that one feels when a tape-recording brings back the voice of a long-dead friend."[6] I must confess that, every time, in the

---

5. Brown, *Augustine of Hippo* (2000), 442–443 and 462–473.
6. Brown, *Augustine of Hippo* (2000), 440.

past fifty years, when a new sermon of Augustine is identified, when a new letter is discovered or an old one redated and set in a new context, I suffer a twinge of regret. I wish that it had been to hand in the 1960s, to add a touch of yet further life to a figure who slowly, as I read him, had begun to come alive.

At the same time, I have every reason to be grateful to the older traditions of Augustinian scholarship represented by the Maurists and by Tillemont. They had laid down for me solid tracks. Along those solid tracks I would now attempt to run the bullet train of a modern biography.

FROM *LIFE AND TIMES*
TO BIOGRAPHY

LIFE AND TIMES

What form would my biography take? For several years, this was by no means clear to me. Originally I had intended to write what might be called a *Life and Times* of Augustine. When I approached Charles Monteith with my first proposal, what I offered was a picture of Augustine and his age. I wrote that recent studies

> only make us realize all the more how necessary it is to treat S. Augustine 'in the round', and to try to conjure up the importance of his life as a whole. If this attempt is not made, the study of S. Augustine will soon be divided by specialists into almost watertight compartments—his personal evolution, his philosophy, the society and politics of his age—each of which will be developed with excellent results, but in complete independence of the others, and far above the range of the general reader.

We needed a book "which would treat the bishop in Africa as seriously as the convert in Milan, and with the aid of the most modern research."

In effect, what I proposed to Faber's was a *Life and Times* that would set the well-known Augustine, the convert and the bishop, against a backdrop of his times that would be newly painted, as it were, to do justice to the most up-to-date research on the later empire.

It was only a few years later, in the early summer of 1963, that I began to see things differently. In my reading, I moved suddenly (for some reason that I do not recall) from the writings of Augustine at the time of his conversion (the famous Cassiciacum *Dialogues* of 386) to the writings of his extreme old age.

In 426/27, Augustine was doggedly defending his doctrine of predestination against a younger generation of African and Provençal monks in what is known as the "Semi-Pelagian controversy."

It struck me, as I moved forty years in a week, from the Cassiciacum *Dialogues* to the sermons, letters, and writings of the last decades of Augustine's life, that this was a man who had done more than change his mind on many issues over the course of the years. He himself had changed deeply in himself. Even in small matters—such as the manner with which he would address a friend, confront an illness, or, even, look out over the iridescent sea—Augustine had come to look with different eyes on a different world. To follow those inner changes, and especially as they intersected with the changes of the times: that was what biography was all about. From then onward I would write not a *Life and Times* but a *Biography*.

INSIDE OUT

In order to do this, I found that I had to write a life of Augustine, as it were, from the inside out. He demanded such an approach. He was a man of the inner world, a master of introspection. I had taken from my reading of him a sense of vertigo. The gap between the opaque material world "outside" and the huge dimensions and seemingly limitless energies of the soul "inside" was a fixed component of his thought, which he had taken from the radical Neoplatonism of Plotinus (205–270). This hiatus meant, above all, that the links between inside and outside, between thought and expression, seemed fragile in the extreme. The sadness that accompanied the gap between heart and tongue that Augustine experienced as a preacher even on the most routine occasions—a gap to which he referred in his gentle words of encouragement to the young deacon—was for him an inseparable feature of the human condition.

My very first impression, when reading the *Confessions*, was of the perilous immensity of the inner world. It seemed to me that, for Augustine, the conscious self floated on the surface of unplumbed and troubled depths:

> Man is a great deep, Lord. You number his very hairs and they are not lost in Your sight: (*Matthew* 30:30; *Luke* 12:17) but the hairs of his head are easier to number than his affections and the movements of his heart.[1]

---

1. *Confessions* 4.14. 22, trans. F. J. Sheed (1942; reprint, Indianapolis, IN: Hackett, 2006), 67–68.

Great is the power of memory, a thing, O my God, to be in awe of, a profound and immeasurable multiplicity: and this thing is my mind, this thing am I. What then am I, O my God? What nature am I? A life powerfully various and manifold and immeasurable.[2]

Looking back, I think that I took into myself, at this time, something of Augustine's profound sense of the complexity of the self, and of the hiatus between the depths of the inner world and the brittle surface of things. It seemed to resonate with my own disquiets in the world of Oxford, where so much seemed so congealed by common sense, so opaque and hard to shift—like the heavily upholstered furniture of an Oxford common room.

Philistines: Augustine and Oxford History

How was a historian to do justice to this acute sense of the individual as containing unplumbed depths beneath the surface of ordinary life? I realized that what I was learning from Augustine was not only a challenging notion of the person. I had also begun to think that a different sort of history could be taught and written, which did better justice to the inner life as Augustine and many others after him had experienced it.

Put very briefly: I found that there was little or no room in the routine teaching and general outlook of the tutors and students in history for the study of aspects of the inner life, such as literary and artistic creativity, nor for the history of ideas and of religion. In deciding to write the biography of a religious genius and great thinker such as Augustine, I claimed a place for individual subjectivity, for ideas, for culture, and for religious experience as proper objects of historical study for young and old alike in a modern university. I wanted to throw down the gauntlet—to issue a challenge to the tweedy philistinism that (in my jaundiced eyes) appeared to dominate the Oxford History Schools.

Historical Intelligibility

As part of this campaign, I remember giving a talk in late November 1964 to a group of history students at St Anne's College, on the invitation of Marjorie Reeves (1905–2003). Marjorie was one of the distinguished women

2. *Confessions* 10.17.26, p. 203.

medievalists at Oxford at that time: I think of Beryl Smalley, Barbara Harvey, Naomi Hurnard, and the gifted nonacademic Hilda Prescott. For all of Oxford's gender imbalances and tendencies to exclude women at the undergraduate level (in the world of inward-looking, resolutely single-sex colleges), the top ranks of its ancient and medieval scholarship could boast of a cluster of truly remarkable women, of whom I found Marjorie Reeves to be the most open and enterprising.

Marjorie studied Joachim of Fiore (1135–1202)—the wild Calabrian abbot and author of millennial prophecies: a far from conventional figure. She also stood for the best kind of intellectual and social outreach from the universities to the British school system. The role of history in education concerned her greatly. She wrote and commissioned textbooks on all sorts of historical topics, designed for schoolchildren. What history was taught and how it was taught were issues close to her heart. Hence her invitation. As for me, the occasion marked the beginning of a collaboration, over the coming years, with a distinguished woman teacher and her pupils, that led me, for the first time, into the world of the women's colleges at Oxford.

My talk was entitled "Historical Intelligibility." It was a critique of the dominant fashion that wished to make history immediately intelligible in terms of single structures and causes. In criticizing this view, I used the image of a Henry Moore sculpture with a hole in the middle. The hole was to be the undetermined workings of individual agency and of individual imagination. It was a cri de coeur against reductionism. I argued that the drive to make all history intelligible as quickly as possible led to a flattening of the profile of individuals and a watering down of the idiosyncrasies of their worldviews and beliefs.

Only fragments of this talk have survived. It now reads like a young don's rant. It was not a model of intellectual coherence. It left the young flummoxed. Their reaction was that if historical developments were not intelligible, if there was always some "black box" of individual creativity to be accounted for and studied, then what happens to historical causation? What could they answer in Schools—at the final examination—when asked about the causes of events and the evolution of institutions?

The students were right to be leery. My paper was not an abstract discussion of historical methodology. It was an attack on the existing structure and syllabus of the final examination in history that they all had to face. Here I took sides. I criticized the exclusive study of political and administrative history.

This bias was most evident in the papers on medieval and early modern England—papers that, we should remember, were compulsory for all history students. I pooh-poohed the idea that concentration on such a narrow range of topics was sufficient in itself to open up the riches of the past.

> It is even claimed that this narrowing carries with it an increase in "quality" by direct contact with the original sources. One must ask whether this is so: I find it difficult to believe that an undergraduate who spends a week chasing the household account-books of Henry VII through the footnotes of three modern articles will, at the end, be any nearer to the "original sources" than one who has spent the same time studying early Humanism in England, and [who is] enabled to study this subject <u>direct</u> by reading well-commented editions of Sir Thomas More and of Erasmus.

> Alas it is my experience that it is possible, in Oxford, to perform the almost incredible feat of remaining a fully competent, highly sophisticated and, even, successful student of the history of modern England without having, at any time, to come to grips with—the Renaissance, the Counter Reformation, Shakespeare, the Cambridge Platonists, the Royal Society, the rise of Methodism, or the theory of evolution. Judged by what it excludes, our preoccupation with a thin line of fully intelligible political and social history seems very lean fare indeed.

These were fighting words. But Oxford remained Oxford. Tutorial teaching, often of the most routine kind, was still what really mattered. Marjorie Reeves's letter of thanks ended with practical business—the courteous horse-trading by which students were farmed out to external tutors such as myself: "[Could I] bear to have V. Smith back for 4 revision tutorials next term? . . . She would explode if I suggested anyone else." It was by these humble, day-to-day links, and not by the occasional intellectual fireworks (such as were only to be expected from up-and-coming young dons), that an academic community was formed in Oxford which might—just might—come one day to tip the balance toward more enterprising forms of history.

For the time being, I was firmly established in Oxford. Despite my somewhat peripheral position as a fellow of All Souls (nominally a research post only) I was part of the network of tutors to whom students from every college (men's and women's alike) could be farmed out for teaching. It gave me a secure base and wide contacts in the Oxford community as I settled down to write on Saint Augustine.

From Cassiciacum to the *Confessions*: A Lost Future

Meanwhile, I had to look outside Oxford for the intellectual sustenance that would help me to write the sort of biography which I had begun to think was possible. I found this sustenance in a lively debate, mainly among French scholars, on the nature of Augustine's conversion to Catholicism in Milan in the years 385 to 387.

Put very briefly: in the 1950s and early 1960s the study of Augustine had been revolutionized by new discoveries concerning the intellectual background to his conversion. They were due largely to the researches of the great French philologist Pierre Courcelle (1912–1980), summed up in a groundbreaking study, *Recherches sur les "Confessions" de Saint Augustin*.[3]

Courcelle identified in the writings of Augustine at the time of his conversion distinct traces of non-Christian, pagan philosophy, taken, principally, from the works of the great Neoplatonic sage of the third century, Plotinus. Furthermore, he went on to suggest that Augustine may have been introduced to pagan Neoplatonism by none other than Saint Ambrose. Seeing that Ambrose was usually known as a notoriously intransigent Catholic bishop, this discovery opened up unexpected vistas on the relation between pagan and Christian thinkers in late fourth-century Milan—they may have been closer to each other than we had thought.

As a result, Augustine's intellectual evolution between the time of his conversion, in 385, and his writing of the *Confessions*, in 397, gripped the attention of Augustinian scholars. This decade had begun, for Augustine, with leisurely philosophical dialogues at Cassiciacum, in the bucolic foothills of the Alps. But it ended on a very different note—with the intensely Christian tone of his *Confessions*. Why had this change happened?

The scholarly debate on the nature of Augustine's conversion and the subsequent evolution of his thought came as a challenge to write a biography. The more I studied the decade between Augustine's conversion and the writing of the *Confessions*, the more I realized that I was not simply studying an intellectual evolution. Augustine himself had changed over the years. He had begun with one view of himself and of his future in the Christian church.

---

3. P. Courcelle, *Recherches sur les "Confessions" de Saint Augustin* (Paris: de Boccard, 1950). The best summary in English remains James J. O'Donnell, *Augustine, Confessions II* (Oxford: Clarendon Press, 1992), 413–424.

Initially, he saw himself as a Christian sage who could expect to live a gentle life of continued spiritual progress. Ten years later, in his *Confessions*, he presented himself very differently—as a wanderer still far from his goal, still held back by sin. The loss of this sense of a sunny future and its replacement by a very different image of himself affected all aspects of Augustine's life and thought in a drastic manner that amounted to a change of character. Seated in the Bodleian Library, I made my way through the recent books and articles that threw light on that mighty change.

Then, in the late summer of 1963, this debate came to my doorstep: what appeared to me to be nothing less than the entire world of Patristic and Augustinian scholarship arrived in Oxford for the fourth international Oxford Patristics Conference.

PATRISTIC SUMMER 1963

AT THE PATRISTICS CONFERENCE

The fourth international Oxford Patristics Conference met in Oxford for a week, September 16–20, 1963. This conference had already met at four-year intervals—in 1951, 1955, and 1959. It was a triumph of foresight and tenacity on the part of its convener, F. L. Cross (1900–1968), the Lady Margaret Professor of Divinity. It had begun as an occasion for outreach to the churches of postwar Germany. It soon became a worldwide event, attended by scholars from every Christian denomination or from none, but its postwar origins were not forgotten. It met in an atmosphere still charged with hope for ecumenical dialogue. It also led to the mingling of hitherto separate scholarly traditions, linked to different churches and to different countries. For me, it was my first contact, in one place, with scholars from all over Europe and elsewhere. My horizons widened considerably in the course of the week as names known to me only through footnotes took on faces as colleagues and eventually as friends.

The conference itself was a truly daunting affair, made possible by the organizational genius of Elizabeth Livingstone. Six hundred participants converged on Oxford from all over the world. They had to be fitted into venerable structures. The "Miscellaneous Notices" printed at the end of the conference program warned participants who were lodged in colleges that college gates would shut from 11 p.m. to 6 a.m. "Any who wish to go out or come in [after 11 p.m.] should give previous notice to the College Porters, who are entitled to a small fee for opening gates."

There was a special message for the clergy addressed, appropriately, in Latin: "*Ad Clerum!* Clergy (Roman Catholic and Anglican) requiring the use of an altar during the period of the Conference should apply at the Chapter

House." Those who wished to attend the Anglican services in Christ Church Cathedral were reminded that "by ancient tradition the times of services in the Cathedral are reckoned by local time (kept by the Cathedral clock) which is five minutes later than British Standard Time (kept by the clock in Tom Tower)."

The meals were held in the great hall of Christ Church. Oxford college cuisine caused predictable consternation and merriment among the Europeans. We instantly bonded in shared horror, as scholars (some with great futures before them) quailed. I remember taking a seat at the long table beside Franco Bolgiani of Turin (1922–2012), who was soon to be director of the Biblioteca Erik Peterson. He was known to me at this time as the author of a study of Augustine's account of his conversion in book 8 of the *Confessions*.[1] I had read this book with care. But it was the college food that really brought us together. I found myself having to comfort Franco, who had just boasted that he had survived his first Oxford dinner, when a college servant unexpectedly placed before him the final touch of old-world British gentility—a glutinous mass of half-burned cheese, which I explained to him was a Welsh rarebit. We remained friends from that time on.

It was a time of spirited conversations at dining tables, in and out of college quadrangles and cloisters, and up and down the High Street as we moved from lecture to lecture. In the evenings, the conversations continued until late at night in pubs. They were not always academic. I remember meeting none other than Heinrich Bacht (1910–1986), the doyen of studies of Pachomius and Egyptian monasticism. He was a large man, dressed in the dark suit of a German professor—like a Mormon missionary. I explained to him, in my best German, how to rob a train.

There was a reason for this strange conversation. Only a month earlier, on August 8, and only thirty-five miles from Oxford, the Great Train Robbery had occurred. The Royal Mail Train had been stopped and relieved of 2.5 million pounds sterling at Bridego Railway Bridge, near Aylesbury. The foreign visitors to Oxford were on tenterhooks to learn more about this bold coup. As I had driven out to view the scene of the crime, I was much in demand. It was just as well that I could offer so much information on this daring crime, seeing that the other piece of major news from Britain, at that time, was the Profumo scandal and the erotic exploits of Christine Keeler. I deemed it better, with a monastic scholar such as Bacht, to dilate upon the Great Train Robbery.

---

1. F. Bolgiani, *La conversione di S. Agostino e l'viii° libro delle "Confessioni"*, Università di Torino, Pubblicazioni della Facoltà di lettere e filosofia 8:4 (Turin: Università di Torino, 1956).

I had other links to foreign visitors than those provided by local misdemeanors. The fact that I could introduce myself as a student of Arnaldo Momigliano opened many hearts among the Italian contingent. Michele Pellegrino (1903–1986), at that time the professor of early Christian literature at the University of Turin, and soon to be cardinal archbishop of Turin, had been admired by Arnaldo for his courage during the Fascist regime, and had been promoted to a professorship in Turin on Arnaldo's urging. I introduced myself to him on the strength of this connection, and we fell to talking with the greatest ease. He presided over the paper that I read, "Augustine's Attitude to Religious Coercion."[2]

These were exciting days for me. As far as I was concerned, the conference was an entirely new event. Until then, I had not been to a conference of any kind anywhere—neither in Oxford, nor elsewhere in England, nor on the Continent. In 1963, scholarship had by no means gone global. Unlike nowadays, attendance at conferences was not taken for granted as part of the normal career pattern of a young scholar. An international conference such as this one was a major and infrequent event. I did not go to another one like it for three more years. It was an opportunity that I grabbed with both hands.

For this was the first time that I could meet the scholarly elite of Europe gathered in one place. I was impressed by the diversity and learning of the Catholic clergy and by the members of the Catholic religious orders—monks and nuns alike. But the conference was far from being only a clerical occasion. I was particularly impressed by the contingent of French women scholars—all of them laypersons and professors in the French university system: Marguerite Harl (1919–2020)—on Origen—Thérèse d'Alverny (1903–1991)—on medieval philosophy—and Anne-Marie La Bonnardière (1906–1998)—on the chronology of the works, letters, and sermons of Augustine. Here were major scholars who were not tied (as was the case in Oxford) to women's colleges where their main duty was to teach other women. They were plainly treated as full peers of their male colleagues in the more open system of European universities and institutes.

I particularly remember the paper of Marguerite Harl on the "nudity of Adam." In discussing Patristic views on the nakedness of Adam and Eve in Paradise, she conjured up two enduring views on the true nature of humanity—the

2. Peter Brown, "Augustine's Attitude to Religious Coercion," *Journal of Roman Studies* 54 (1964): 107–116, in *Religion and Society in the Age of Saint Augustine* (London: Faber, 1972), 260–278.

contemplative and the practical. In the first tradition, Adam and Eve were presented as wrapped in contemplation, unconscious of their bodies until the rude awakening of the Fall. In such a view, human society and human efforts at self-improvement were always viewed as a sad comedown, as a distraction from the vision of God.

The second tradition stemmed from Origen and was later revived in the medieval Latin West. Medieval scholars claimed that Adam's awareness of his nudity acted as a positive stimulus to invention. A succession of devices designed to lessen human vulnerability after the Fall began with the making of trousers and continued, through the invention of agriculture and the building of cities, to culminate in the building of the great Gothic cathedrals of Europe. As Harl pointed out, this exegesis of the Fall, elaborated in the medieval universities, lay at the root of the modern notion of technological progress. Her paper (along with many others) made a lasting impression on me.[3]

A CLIMATE OF HOPE

It is easy to recapture those happy moments. But it is more difficult to conjure up the crackle of expectations within which the Oxford Patristics Conference took place. Many of the participants at the conference felt that they had come together at a turning point in the history of Christianity. The Second Vatican Council had met only a year before. The second session of the council was due to open immediately after the conference, on September 29, 1963. Many important Patristic scholars were involved directly in the council as leading ecclesiastics and as experts attached to various commissions.

Not only did the Catholic Church face a program of internal reforms; but the heady possibility of a reunion of the churches was also in the air. Cardinal Jean Daniélou (1905–1974), a leader of the ecumenical movement, closed the conference with a lecture chaired by the archbishop of Canterbury himself. The title of the lecture was "Les Pères et l'Unité chrétienne." It was a loving evocation of the way in which Basil of Caesarea had struggled, by every means possible, to keep the Christians of his time interested in the common good of the church. Daniélou described how Basil had instituted the exchange of little

---

3. Marguerite Harl, "La prise de conscience de la 'nudité' d'Adam: une interpretation de *Genèse* 3,7 chez les Pères Grecs," *Studia Patristica* VII, ed. F. L. Cross, *Texte und Untersuchungen* 92 (Berlin: Akademie Verlag, 1966), 486–495; see Peter Brown, *"Treasure in Heaven": The Holy Poor in Early Christianity* (Charlottesville: University of Virginia Press, 2016), 67.

terracotta tokens of solidarity between churches; how he had crisscrossed Asia Minor and Syria with messengers; how he had constantly appealed to the medical notion of *sympnoia*—of the mysterious power of the breath of life that coursed through the body, holding it together like a magnetic force. And all this to ensure that, come what may, Christians (though they might be temporarily divided) would continue to talk to each other. Would that the leaders of the churches were prepared to do the same today! It was a virtuoso display of erudition, mobilized by Daniélou in the service of a deeply held commitment:

> The example of the Fathers raises in us the hope that a stunned world may yet recognize, one day, the mark of a living God in the amazing spectacle of unity regained.[4]

From the Anglican side, also, Henry Chadwick (1920–2008) had begun to reach out to Catholics with a series of deeply learned studies. These would eventually feed into the balanced phrases of the final report of ARCIC—the Anglican Roman Catholic International Commission—*Salvation and the Church* (which appeared in 1976). Striding across the lawn of the cathedral, with its flowerbeds in full bloom, bending from his great height to lend a courteous ear to prelates in all degrees of finery, Henry *was* the Church of England. Local wits told stories of how Spanish, French, and Italian priests would peer through the shrubbery hoping to catch a glimpse of him: "the Anglican Church may not have a pope, but it does have Henry Chadwick."

RESSOURCEMENT

How did this climate of hope affect the historians among us? First and foremost, there was the excitement of discovering that the Patristic period—from AD 200 to 600—was not a period of decline. Far from it. It had witnessed an outburst of creativity that encouraged a climate of hope for our own times. Hence the importance of the word *ressourcement*—return to the sources—which was current among French liberal Catholics at this time. By "return to the sources" these scholars, lay and clerical alike, meant much more than a scholarly reexamination of the thought and institutions of the early church. *Ressourcement* conjured up the hope that our own age might yet see a reenactment of the drama of those distant centuries. They believed that, in the

---

4. J. Daniélou, "Les Pères de l'Église et l'Unité des Chrétiens," *Studia Patristica* VII, ed. F. L. Cross, *Texte und Untersuchungen* 92 (Berlin: Akademie Verlag, 1966), 23–32, at 32.

Patristic age, Christianity had risen from the status of a minority religion to occupy the intellectual high ground of an entire, mature civilization. And it had done so because Christians had been prepared to enter into open dialogue with Greco-Roman pagan culture. It was by reaching out beyond itself, and not by walling itself off, that Christianity had come to dominate the Roman world.

Looking Back

On Saturday September 21, the participants dispersed. Some would go straight from Oxford to Rome, to attend the Second Vatican Council. It was hoped that they would bring with them some of that crackle of expectations which had played around the conference. Now, over half a century later, the Oxford Patristics Conference, like the far bigger moment of the Vatican Council, seems very far away. Many of the hopes of those who went on from the Oxford Conference to the Vatican Council were not realized. They were thwarted and have now faded. So what were these hopes?

It struck me, even at the time, that the basic hope of the conference was a very scholarly one. Many of the contributions and lectures were motivated by a touching faith in the collective memory of Christianity. They believed that the writings of the age of the Fathers could be sifted by scholars in such a way as to bring healing to the present. Understanding the Patristic age was like a *remedium* (to use a late Roman Latin term). A *remedium* was a homeopathic poultice—like a modern medical patch—which was thought to work slowly, and with almost occult power, to heal: to redress deep-seated imbalances; to fortify good humors; to smooth away the cramps and to soften the hard constrictions that wracked the body. It was hoped that a *remedium* could be concocted, from our renewed and ever-deeper knowledge of Patristic Christianity, that could be pressed against the fevered body of the church in our own times. *Ressourcement* was the key word for this remedy. To remember the days of the Fathers of the Church was not an entirely academic matter: it was to relive the exhilarating moment when a minority religion had taken over an entire civilization because it had been open to the wider, non-Christian world.

The wish to look to the past so as to invigorate the present took many forms. When Cardinal Daniélou evoked the titanic efforts of Basil of Caesarea to make sure that divided Christians continued to listen to each other, he plainly meant to bring hope to the present-day ecumenical movements.

Above all, to get things right, through the careful study of Patristic texts, was to gain a new language with which to speak in a more flexible manner about issues that still divided Christians in modern times. To take only one example: Henry Chadwick's early article "Eucharist and Christology in the Nestorian Controversy" was a gem of scholarship that was much appreciated at the conference. But it was also part of Chadwick's effort to bring clarity and a room for maneuver to modern debates between Protestants and Catholics on the nature of the sacraments.[5]

It was sincerely hoped that a *remedium* compounded with such care would work on Christians in the modern world. But was the remedy strong enough to heal their discontents? The size of the issues faced in the modern world often left readers of the Fathers at a loss. The postwar churches were already grappling with the challenge of worldwide poverty, with the difficulties of reconciliation between the churches, and with the problems of outreach to nonbelievers. But even those heavy issues seemed to be not enough. Only a few years after 1963, the agendas of reform in every Christian church widened dramatically. A *remedium*, carefully culled by scholars working on a distant age, seemed to many to be inadequate—like a Band-Aid on an open wound. The cry for Justice, in the here and now—justice for women, justice for the poor, justice for the excluded, justice for the victims of tyranny exercised by fellow Catholics in the name of the church—pushed to one side the scholarly outreach to the Christian past that was so much in evidence in the conference.

Ressourcement was not enough. The collective memory of Christianity—even the collective memory of the vivid age of the Fathers—was deemed by many not sufficient to heal the Christianity of our times. Scholars were saddened by the consequent loss of faith in the past. In the words of Henry Chadwick, addressing the General Synod of the Church of England in 1988: "Nothing is sadder than someone who has lost his memory."

On the ground, in academe, however, the field of Patristics itself has widened beyond anything that we could have hoped in 1963. At that time I was fortunate to be working on Augustine. He stood at the very center of the Patristic world. Despite efforts to widen the range of the conference, the study of Augustine and of a few major Greek Fathers predominated. It was like a massive grove surrounded by a mere scattering of other trees. Now this is no longer so. If anything, Augustine is neglected, and texts from the Christian

---

5. H. E. Chadwick, "Eucharist and Christology in the Nestorian Controversy," *Journal of Theological Studies*, n.s., 2 (1951): 145–164, now in *History and Thought of the Early Church* (London: Variorum Reprints, 1982), no. XVI.

East (in Greek, Syriac, and Coptic, along with many other Eastern languages) fill the landscape as far as the eye can reach.

And these texts are now owned by everyone. No one church or variant of Christianity claims a monopoly of any authors. The comfortable, false familiarity of those who once claimed Augustine, Ambrose, or Basil of Caesarea for themselves alone has largely disappeared among scholars. Jews and Christians, Catholics and Evangelicals, mainline Protestants and Mormons find nothing strange in sinking their minds into Christians of the Middle East, such as Ephraim the Syrian, Jacob of Sarugh, or Philoxenos of Mabbug, as writers as much deserving of attention as the Greek and Latin Fathers whose works still dominated the conference in 1963.

As for myself, the conference ended the isolation that had made the first years of my work toward a biography of Augustine absorbing but unusually inward-looking. I made lasting friendships with scholars from all over Europe, but particularly in France. In the coming years I would visit the Augustinians of the Assumption (the Pères Augustiniens) whenever I came to Paris. Goulven Madec (1930–2008), Georges Folliet (1920–2011), and Albert de Veer (1910–2003) received me in their office, which at that time was in the rue François 1er in the eighth arrondissment, in the district of the Champs-Élysées. They would produce a white wine of the Touraine, praised by Rabelais. Albert de Veer had me pegged as an *esprit fort*—an amiable freethinker, who deserved the wine of Gargantua. We would talk all afternoon. It was in Paris and not in England that I found my way to a vivid peer group of Augustinian scholars connected in various ways with the *Études Augustiniennes*. Ease of access to Paris from England (by air or the cross-Channel steamer) gave my work a distinctly French tilt in those years. For anyone interested in Augustine, to go to Paris in the 1960s was to participate in the belle époque of French scholarship.

This contact was of crucial importance to me for one other reason. In an age without websites, the "Bulletin Augustinien"—the exhaustive, commented bibliography produced every year by the Augustinian fathers in their *Revue des études augustiniennes*—was as inestimable a boon to scholars of Augustine as were the Maurist editions of his works and the sure-footed narrative of the indefatigable Tillemont. Now the "Bulletin" became for me more than a guide to the most up-to-date research on any topic connected with Augustine. It was something of an academic facebook, where I would trace the writings of my many new friends. Among those contacts, two stand out as particularly important for me—my longtime hero, Henri-Irénée Marrou, and my English friend Robert Markus.

ENCOUNTERS

HENRI-IRÉNÉE MARROU AND ROBERT MARKUS

Late Antiquity and the Fathers of the Church

No one expressed the climate of hope that characterized the conference with greater zest and urgency than my hero since undergraduate days, Henri-Irénée Marrou (1904–1977). As we have seen, it was Marrou who had introduced me to the notion of "late antiquity" in his extraordinary *Retractatio*—his Rereading (in 1949)—of his *Saint Augustin et la fin de la culture antique*.[1] It was only later that I realized that the notion of late antiquity, as a distinctive and creative epoch in the history of the ancient world, had a very specific meaning for him. For Marrou, late antiquity was, above all, the age of the Fathers of the Church. The Christians who were his heroes—such as Clement of Alexandria, Gregory of Nyssa, and Augustine—had ensured, through their daring dialogue with ancient culture, that the period between 200 and 600 was a time of unusual creativity. In his opinion, ancient culture was "healed" by contact with a creative minority of Christians. Could the Christianity of postwar Europe do the same, through a similar open and vigorous dialogue with the modern world?

This hope had suffused Marrou's work from his early days as a student, in the 1930s, through the horrors of World War II, and into a postwar Europe now overshadowed by the Cold War. It was accompanied by an austere message. Marrou urged Christians to accept the fact that they were, once again, in a minority. They must forget the days of Christian dominance associated with

---

1. Chapter 31: "'Decadence' or 'Late Antiquity'? Henri-Irénée Marrou."

the Middle Ages. The notion of "Christendom"—of a monolithic Christian society, such as was believed to have existed in medieval Europe—must be abandoned as a dangerous mirage. On this issue, Marrou was very much a liberal Catholic. Bluntly: for him, the hope of Christians in the modern world was to creep out from under the grandiose shadow of the imagined Gothic "age of faith." Instead, they would find, in the ebullient, religiously diverse society of the Patristic age, a Christianity on which to model their own revival of the church.

Marrou had brought this message to all previous Patristics conferences. He opened the first conference, in 1951, with an inaugural lecture, "Patristique et Humanisme."[2] It was a flat denial of Christian exceptionalism. He insisted that, despite their new beliefs, the Fathers of the Church had remained ancient persons. They were rooted in a culture dedicated, for centuries, to bringing out the best in human beings. This Hellenistic and Greco-Roman culture had fostered an aesthetic sensibility, a love of music (Marrou himself was a passionate musician), and a sense of balance in human affairs. It had also provided a schooling in decorum and self-restraint. The Fathers had upheld these ancient virtues wholeheartedly. They did not borrow bits of ancient classical culture only in order to make themselves appear *salonfähig*—acceptable in polite company. They did so because they themselves *were* ancient persons. The rich blood of centuries flowed in their veins. If we recognized this, Marrou insisted, we ourselves would be that much more able to allow the blood of all that was good in the modern age to flow in *our* veins, and, maybe, with the same remarkable results.

Marrou's lectures at previous Patristics conferences had been largely devoted to Clement of Alexandria (ca. 150–ca. 215). At this time, he was editing the *Paidagogus* of Clement (in collaboration with Marguerite Harl) for the new series of French translations of early Christian literature, the indispensible *Sources chrétiennes*.[3] Clement provided him with God's plenty. Marrou conjured up the layers of Hellenistic and Greco-Roman culture on which Clement drew in order to formulate his notion of Christian decorum. With his characteristic sense of humor and openness to his environment, Marrou expatiated on Clement's image of the good Christian's soul: like a patch of grass—well cut, well watered, and springy. He did so, he said, "en hommage aux *lawns*

---

2. Now printed in *Patristique et Humanisme. Mélanges*, Patristica Sorbonensia 9 (Paris: Le Seuil, 1976), 25–34.

3. *Clément d'Alexandrie: Le Pédagogue. Livre I*, Sources chrétiennes, 70 (Paris: Le Cerf, 1960).

oxoniennes"—in homage to the [great college] lawns of Oxford." He urged Christian Patristic scholars to do what Clement had done—to adapt to Christian ends the resilient and diverse modern civilization in which they found themselves.[4] This was the man to whom I introduced myself, for the first time, on Tuesday afternoon, September 17, 1963.

ENCOUNTERING MARROU

I had first seen Marrou from a distance in late 1958, when he delivered a lecture at the Warburg Institute in London as part of the memorable series later published as *The Conflict between Paganism and Christianity in the Fourth Century*—the same series in which Hugo Jones had spoken on the social background to the conflict of paganism and Christianity. Marrou spoke about Synesius of Cyrene and Alexandrian Neoplatonism.[5] It was a topic after his own heart—the portrait of a Christian bishop who had by no means disowned his Hellenic culture. In the glow of the reading light on the podium, Marrou's long, white face was as translucent as the bust of a late antique philosopher. His arms and fine hands moved up and down, like the wings of a great bird in flight, as he evoked the contemplative ascent of the philosopher to God.

Now I saw him at the Oxford conference. On the Tuesday afternoon, he delivered a paper entitled "The Place of Jesus of Nazareth in the Valentinian Gnostic System." He sat upright in a high, plush-lined chair, in the Memorial Room of Queen's College, beside a window that looked out over the garden of St. Peter's-in-the-East in full bloom. Next evening, I saw him transfixed by the Orthodox vespers service that was performed for the conference—very much as part of its ecumenical mood—in the apse of Christ Church Cathedral. Energy sparked from him like an electric wire stripped of its insulation.

Summoning up my courage, I invited him to have dinner with me at All Souls. As it was in the depths of the vacation, we dined with a small group in the dessert room, looking out in the golden light across the Codrington Quadrangle to the dome of the Radcliffe Camera and the spire of Saint Mary's. He

4. H. I. Marrou, "Morale et spiritualité dans le Pédagogue de Clément d'Alexandrie," *Studia Patristica* II, ed. F. L. Cross, *Texte und Untersuchungen* 64 (Berlin: Akademie Verlag, 1957), 538–546, at 539 and 542.

5. H. I. Marrou, "Synesius of Cyrene and Alexandrian Neoplatonism," in *The Conflict between Paganism and Christianity*, ed. Arnaldo Momigliano (Oxford: Clarendon Press, 1963), 126–150.

explained to Ernest Jacob, who presided at the head of the table, the relation between the English country dance and the French *contredanse* of the age of Louis Quatorze. All this in exquisite French. Though Marrou was deeply read in English literature, he seldom spoke the language. I suspect that (as with so many Frenchmen of his generation) the ancient rhetor in him was too strong. He did not wish his flow of beautiful words to be blocked by an alien tongue. It worked. Listening to Marrou's French, we were spellbound.

From then onward Marrou and I had infrequent contacts; but each was memorable. In 1964, I visited the Marrous for supper in Châtenay, outside Paris. At the end of the meal, Marrou put on his beret and played Savoyard folk songs on the piano. He told me how the great Savoyard smugglers who crossed the Alps in the nineteenth century adopted the names of Homeric heroes as their noms de guerre—Achille, Hector, Agémemnon. It was a little fragment of folk classicism—a late, late touch of the ancient world—which he appreciated deeply.

I sent him a copy of *Augustine of Hippo* in August 1967. He thanked me with characteristic generosity and grace: "Cette plume heureuse qui fait de l'anglais manié par un Oxonien une si belle langue: on a plaisir de se trouver entre Européens"—"That gift of the pen which makes English in the hands of an Oxford scholar such a beautiful language: it is a pleasure to find oneself with a fellow European." Knowing what Marrou thought of the college lawns of Oxford, I could not have wished for a more touching tribute. His wife, Jeanne Marrou, undertook the translation of *Augustine* into French.[6]

Jeanne Marrou's questions regarding the translation brought us together by mail. We exchanged notes on points of erudition like late Roman gentlefolk enjoying *otium*—a scholarly retirement on their estates. Together, we tracked down a passage from Proust that I had used to convey Augustine's sense of the need for spiritual growth in order to read the scriptures: they were a closed book unless the reader had (in Proust's words) "allowed the equivalents to ripen slowly in his own heart."[7]

Writing from his summer holiday retreat at La Ferrière (Isère) in the mountains behind Grenoble, he wrote a disquisition on the art of early Christian sarcophagi after I had described to him the dramatic play of hands (hands blessing, hands pointing, hands stretching out to touch the flesh of Christ)

---

6. *Saint Augustin* (Paris: Le Seuil, 1971).

7. Brown, *Augustine of Hippo* (2000), 279; M. Proust, *In Search of Lost Time*, vol. 1, *Swann's Way*, trans. C. K. Scott Moncrieff (New York: Modern Library, 2003), 206.

that had struck me when I visited the late Roman sarcophagi in the shrine of Mary Magdalen at Saint-Maximin-la-Sainte-Baume near Marseilles. He placed these striking gestures in a long tradition of classical sculpture, and then went on to suggest all the other places in Provence where I might view early Christian sarcophagi.

Alas, this was not entirely a time of *otium* for Marrou. Apart from his holidays in mountain valleys once frequented by heroic smugglers, his time in Paris, in the early 1970s, was devoured by the university reforms that followed the student uprisings of 1968.

I last saw Marrou in Paris in 1975, two years before his death. Over supper, he and his long-term friend, André Mandouze (1916–2006), fell to reminiscing about a journey that they had taken in Algeria sometime in the 1950s. They had visited the caves outside Tebessa. A precious Manichaean codex had been discovered in those caves in 1918. They had hoped to find more fragments. "And there they were [added Madame Jeanne Marrou], André et Henri, sautillants comme des petits chèvres—jumping in and out of the caves like little goats." It reminded me of that deep love of the concrete—of the soil of Africa and Rome, as well as of his native Provence—that never left Marrou, despite his openness to the high thoughts of the Fathers and the austerity of his religious commitments.

Only two years later, Marrou died. His little book *Décadence romaine ou antiquité tardive?* was published posthumously.[8] It is a brilliant distillation of Marrou's "polyphonic," musical sense of the unfolding of history. It is also a tribute to his warm attention to the importance of humble things. His evocation of the significance of changes in dress between the classical and the postclassical age—of the change from the toga to trousers—is a little masterpiece. It reminds me always of that combination of warmth, zest for the concrete, and the stern, wide vision that set me on my own way to the study of late antiquity as I first read Marrou's *Saint Augustin et la fin de la culture antique* in the summer of 1955.

ROBERT MARKUS (1924–2010)

I met Robert Markus (then teaching at Liverpool and soon to be professor of medieval history at Nottingham) for the first time at the conference, but in a very different manner from the way I met Marrou. Robert and I escaped together from the Babel of the conference to the Copper Kettle (on the corner

---

8. H. I. Marrou, *Décadence romaine ou antiquité tardive? iiie–vi^e* (Paris: Le Seuil, 1977).

of High Street and Queen's Lane). Robert sat beside the front window, with a pipe in his hand. He leaned back with his head cocked to one side like an alert bird, emitting purr-like chuckles whenever he encountered a good idea. Though I had not known Robert previously, we realized, instantly, that our concerns converged to a remarkable degree.

First and foremost, Robert, like me, looked for changes in the thought of Augustine. His paper for the conference was a model study of how "to trace the course of Augustine's intellectual crystallization." It showed how Augustine's notion of estrangement from the world had gathered richness over the years.[9]

Furthermore, Robert had begun to direct his attention to aspects of the life and thought of Augustine that had always been important to me ever since my dialogue with Bill Frend on the nature of the Donatist movement. He chose to study the middle-aged Augustine—Augustine the bishop of Hippo, and not the young convert in Milan. His masterpiece, *Saeculum: History and Society in the Theology of St. Augustine*, which appeared three years after my *Augustine of Hippo*, showed how much we had in common.[10] Like me, Robert did not limit himself to debates on the Neoplatonic sources of Augustine's thought in the early days of his life as a Catholic convert. Rather, he lingered by preference on the changes in Augustine's attitudes to society and to history in his later years. He proved that Augustine showed no slackening of originality as he grew older. He traced the subtle changes of Augustine's mind with the precision of a master jeweler disassembling a complex watch.

DISENCHANTMENT

What drew us together was not just a similarity of temperaments and interests, but the fact that we had both been inspired by scholars better known in the English-speaking world than on the Continent. Both of us were deeply influenced by the *Amor Dei* of John Burnaby (1891–1978).[11] This remarkable book was very much not the work of a *grand Sorbonnard*—of a great professor in the

9. R. A. Markus, "*Alienatio*: Philosophy and Eschatology in the Development of an Augustinian Idea," *Studia Patristica* IX, ed. F. L. Cross, *Texte und Untersuchungen* 94 (Berlin: Akademie Verlag, 1966), 431–450, at 450.

10. R. A. Markus, *Saeculum: History and Society in the Theology of St. Augustine* (Cambridge University Press, 1970).

11. John Burnaby, *Amor Dei: A Study of the Religion of Saint Augustine* (Cambridge University Press 1938).

European tradition such as Marrou. It was the work of a reclusive don, buried in his rooms in Trinity College, Cambridge, wreathed in a dense cloud of tobacco smoke. Like Marrou, Burnaby had a profoundly serious side. His experiences as an officer in the Gallipoli campaign of 1916 had marked him for life. He would always attend the annual gathering in a London pub of what was left of his platoon.

Burnaby had an extraordinary ability to communicate the living religion of Augustine as this was revealed in his sermons as well as in his formal writings. His *Amor Dei* set the gold standard for Robert and myself. If there was ever a book that spoke directly to the changes in Augustine's life, it was this one. In a memorable page, Burnaby caught, as no one else had done before, the pathos of Augustine's gradual abandonment of his hope for a serene progress toward the vision of God, which had characterized his first days as a convert in Cassiciacum. We had both been moved by the quotation from Augustine that Burnaby had used in order to drive home his point:

> Whoever thinks that in this mortal life a man may so disperse the mists of bodily and carnal imaginings as to possess the unclouded light of changeless Truth, and cleave to it with unswerving constancy of a spirit wholly estranged from the common way of this life—he understands neither What he seeks nor what he is who seeks it.[12]

Burnaby was not the only creative outlier in the field of Augustine studies. Across the Atlantic, Edward Cranz (1914–1998), later a professor at Connecticut College, was a similar idiosyncratic and deeply learned exponent of the changes of Augustine's mind. In 1954, he published a seminal article, "The Development of Augustine's Ideas on Society before the Donatist Controversy." This article showed how Augustine had changed his mind in the years before he wrote the *Confessions*. He abandoned an optimistic view not only of his own capacity for progress but also of the course of human history. He no longer saw the human race as capable of rising gently from concern with earthly matters to an ever more spiritual state, as some Greek Christian writers had promised.[13] Such bold hopes for himself and for society came to be postponed until the end of time.

12. Burnaby, *Amor Dei*, 36, citing *De consensu evangelistarum* 4.20.

13. E. Cranz, "The Development of Augustine's Ideas on Society before the Donatist Controversy," *Harvard Theological Review* 47 (1954): 255–316, now in *Reorientations of Western Thought from Antiquity to the Renaissance*, ed. Nancy Struever (Aldershot, Hants.: Ashgate/Variorum, 2006).

Cranz pointed out that, for Augustine, to abandon this optimistic view of himself, as well as the hope of progress for humanity as a whole, was no small change: it amounted to a tectonic shift in his worldview that ran parallel to the great shift in Augustine's thought, when he abandoned the hope of becoming, in this life, a transcendent sage. As a result of this silent shift, Augustine's *Confessions* proclaimed a very different vision of himself from that of the young convert—a wanderer and a sinner, haunted by a desire for God that would never be fulfilled until the end of time.

Robert and I agreed that many of our ideas went back to Cranz's article. Yet this article was so little known to European scholars (to whom I would usually look for information) that I had found it only by accident when consulting the *Harvard Theological Review* on a totally different subject.

Talking to Robert, I noticed that we both welcomed disenchantment. Robert stressed Augustine's progressive demystification of the Roman Empire in his middle age. I stressed Augustine's growing sense of human frailty in the years that led up to the writing of the *Confessions*. It seemed to both of us that Augustine had changed profoundly since his first years as a convert in Milan. He had passed through a dangerous moment of euphoria and had emerged with a more gray but more solid view of himself and of the world. Robert would later sum up this view in his Saint Augustine Lecture at Villanova in 1989—"Conversion and Disenchantment in Augustine's Spiritual Career." Altogether, having discussed these and other matters, Robert and I emerged from the Copper Kettle with a clearer sense that, although we sailed different ships, we were sailing them on the same winds.

The week of the Oxford Patristics Conference had been a moment of blessing. I had gained an entire new range of academic friends, and had found that the principal lines of my work were confirmed. Now it was up to me, in the next three years, to get *Augustine of Hippo* into print.

ALL'S WELL THAT ENDS WELL 1966

New Peers

Compared with the excitement of the Oxford Patristics Conference in September 1963, the two and a half years before I submitted the manuscript of *Augustine of Hippo* to Faber's in the spring of 1966 seemed uneventful. What changed in those quiet years was Oxford itself. The study of the later empire had become conceivable at the graduate level. I found myself supervising the dissertations of students from the School of Litterae Humaniores (known, with no false modesty, as "Greats"). These students had been trained in classics and ancient history only.

To move forward into the later empire was no small change of scene for them. As I have explained, undergraduates who studied Greats were taught no history or literature beyond the reign of Trajan (98–117). The period from Trajan to the accession of Diocletian (in 284) was a total blank. The exciting centuries of the later empire proper (from 284 to around 600) were studied only by undergraduates (and very few of them) in the Modern History School. Thus students from Greats had to fill in a large gap in order to move from their undergraduate training to work on late Roman topics. It was a choice for the bold who, fortunately, were not lacking in the Oxford of the 1960s.

I suspect that this novel impetus was due to Sir Ronald Syme (1903–1989), whose vivid curiosity for all periods of Roman history extended into the later empire.[1] Syme encouraged graduate students in Greats to work on topics

---

1. R. Syme, *Ammianus and the Historia Augusta* (Oxford: Clarendon Press, 1968). See now Giusto Traina, "Ronald Syme," in *New Late Antiquity*, 630–641.

from the third century to the fifth. I was often asked to be their supervisor. This was a new development for me. Up to the mid-1960s, I had no graduate students from Greats. Now they came my way and often complemented my own interests—adding an earthy touch at a time when I was wrestling with the higher reaches of the thought of Augustine.

The first of these students was Roger Tomlin. He embarked on a study of the reign of the emperor Valentinian I, in which he rehabilitated the frontier policy of that formidable emperor, making full use of recent archaeology in Germany, Hungary, and what was then Yugoslavia.

When teaching for a year at Cornell (in 1968), Roger sent me the poster of a lecture that he had delivered: "Ammianus Marcellinus and the Fall of the Roman Empire." It showed a flock of sheep placidly climbing over the ruins of Hadrian's Wall. Roger saw it as an image of the Christians (the sheep) bringing about the ruin of the empire. I still have the poster. It was good to find someone with whom to share a joke about Ammianus Marcellinus. An archaeologist at heart, and a gifted interpreter of scratched messages on slates, bricks, and leaden tablets that brought alive the world of ordinary people in the farthermost province of the Roman Empire, Roger kept me in touch with the distant world of the northern frontiers of Rome.[2]

I also supervised John Matthews, who became the first-ever lecturer in late Roman history in 1969, being succeeded by Tomlin in 1975. John's study of the relations between the imperial court and the aristocracies of Spain, Italy, and Gaul would later appear in a groundbreaking book, *Western Aristocracies and Imperial Court*.[3]

But the late Roman field had also attracted the attention of young scholars all over Britain. At Bedford College, in the University of London, Alan Cameron (1938–2017) had begun to dismantle, in a succession of memorable articles in the *Journal of Roman Studies*, almost every stereotype concerning the relation of Christian and pagan culture at Rome at the turn of the fourth and fifth century.[4]

2. See Charlotte Higgins, "How to Decode an Ancient Roman's Handwriting," *New Yorker*, May 11, 2017.

3. J. F. Matthews, *Western Aristocracies and Imperial Court, A.D. 364–425* (Oxford: Clarendon Press, 1975).

4. Alan Cameron, "The Roman Friends of Ammianus Marcellinus," *Journal of Roman Studies* 54 (1964): 15–28, and "The Date and Identity of Macrobius," *Journal of Roman Studies* 56 (1966):25–38.

Equally important for me was Keith Hopkins (1934–2004). He was then a research fellow at King's College, Cambridge, and later became professor of sociology at Brunel University at Uxbridge, 1972. Keith provided daring sociological models for the effects of elite mobility on the political and family life of the later empire.[5]

This was also the time when I first came to know Averil Cameron. She had begun to work on the Greek historians of the age of Justinian and afterward, under the eventual supervision of Arnaldo Momigliano. Working very much on her own to begin with, she showed how these historians transformed the classical tradition of Greek historiography that reached back to Thucydides and Herodotus by adapting it for Christian readers. Her dissertation was on Agathias of Myrina (ca. 532–ca. 580), the last representative of the classical tradition of Greek historiography.

As Averil interpreted him, Agathias was a strangely transitional figure. His stilted classical phrases barely covered the presence of the early Byzantine Christian culture to which he already belonged. It was precisely this awkward attachment to classical models in an increasingly Christian age that Averil seized upon with rare insight.

> Agathias' *History* in fact provides a peculiarly interesting case of the fusion of opposites characteristic of a transitional period. Christian and pagan, classical and Byzantine.[6]

At the time, this was an exciting new way of seeing the classical tradition in its last days, rooted in the study of a single author and his circle, in which classicism and orthodox Christianity (usually thought of by scholars as opposing poles) mingled in a paradoxical manner.

Though I was engaged with the study of the late fourth century and she with the late sixth, Arnaldo Momigliano would always introduce us to others as Averil "the Classicist" and me as "the Medievalist." Augustine was over two centuries earlier than Agathias; but Arnaldo was right. Our two different

---

5. K. Hopkins, "Eunuchs and Politics in the Later Roman Empire," *Proceedings of the Cambridge Philological Society* 189 (1963): 62–80, and "Elite Mobility in the Roman Empire," *Past and Present* 32 (1965): 12–26.

6. Averil Cameron, *Agathias* (Oxford: Clarendon Press, 1970): vii; see Peter Brown, "To Make Byzantium Interesting: Our Debt to Averil Cameron," in *From Rome to Constantinople: Studies in Honour of Averil Cameron*, ed. Hagit Amirav and Bas ter Haar Romeny (Louvain: Peeters, 2007), 1–9.

backgrounds summed up the Janus-face nature of late antiquity: Averil drew on her great skill as a classicist in order to understand the very last flowering of the classical tradition in the histories of Procopius and Agathias; by contrast, I was engaged with Augustine, whose thought and ecclesiastical activities set the scene for the Western Middle Ages.

This was an abiding difference between two groups of scholars drawn from two different teaching traditions. Those trained as classical scholars tended to be drawn to the study of late antique and Patristic literature, and to the fascinating transformations of the classical heritage in the fourth, fifth, and sixth centuries. Others, such as myself, tended to look forward, to beyond the fall of Rome, to the legacy of late antiquity in future ages both in Europe and in the Middle East.

This move into the later empire by a brilliant group of young historians of the classical world marked the beginning of late antiquity as a distinctive field in Britain. Their work provided me with a vivid and up-to-date background to the age of Augustine, and helped to create the buoyant academic atmosphere in which I prepared my book for the publishers.

To the Publishers

I remember very little of the final stages of the writing of *Augustine of Hippo*. What I do remember, from 1965/66, are the mechanics of the final draft of the book. By present standards it was an archaic business. Photocopiers were rare and prohibitively expensive. I did not even compose on a typewriter: I was strictly a man of the pen.

Having drafted a chapter in longhand, I would read it aloud to make sure of its rhythm. I was determined that *Augustine of Hippo* would be a book of literary value: that the very rhythm of its sentences, when read aloud, should maintain a momentum that carried the reader from one end of Augustine's life to the other. It would be a very oral book—written to be heard as well as read.

Then I would sit down and write out a fair copy (endnotes and all) and take the finished chapter up the lane to Mrs. Clayton, a professional typist who worked out of her house while taking care of her child. Using a touch-type typewriter, with her baby beside her in a carry-cot, Mrs. Clayton turned these long sheets of paper (handwritten fair copies in clear, blue ink) into a typed top copy with two thin carbon copies. She did this for two years on end, with a promptness and intelligence for which no formal recognition is adequate.

By early spring of 1966, the job was done. A little later, I wrote to Keith Hopkins:

> My book on Augustine is now under press. . . . Having emended an M.S. of 160,000 words, 3000 footnotes and a bibliography of 400 titles, I am either (or alternately) full of admiration for the Late Roman senators for having preserved the classics by such laborious methods, <u>or</u> convinced that they must have done it all by slave labour.

A month or so later, I took the clean copy—that is, the only typed copy in existence, the rest being carbon copies (forgive this reminder of more ancient days!)—down to Faber's in a small brown attaché case. I remember that, in order to open the locks of the case, I placed the attaché case on the floor and knelt beside it. I have a vivid visual memory of two pairs of perfectly creased trousers breaking just as they should over two pairs of shiny winkle-picker shoes. The trousers and shoes belonged to two well-groomed members of the staff of Faber's. *Augustine of Hippo* had reached London, where I had always wished it to be.

To take the measure of a half century of change: when I handed in the manuscript of my book *Through the Eye of a Needle* at the Princeton University Press, in 2012, I brought the hard copy manuscript. It was as large as a car battery. But that was not what they wanted. They asked me for the USB. I handed it to an assistant, who left the room. A few minutes later, the assistant returned with the USB, and declared, "It is in the system." On that occasion, the lights had not even dimmed for a moment! Technology keeps one humble.

Unfortunately, August Frugé (1910–2004) of the University of California Press was not so lucky. He did not get a virginal typescript of *Augustine*. In a world without photocopiers or computers, copies of manuscripts were scarce. Frugé got only a worked-over carbon copy. He read this worked-over manuscript on the plane when he returned from London to the University of California Press at Berkeley. It was not an easy read.

> The pages were amended and added to and written over . . . but around and underneath the markings the reader could detect a subtle mind at work on another.[7]

Around the end of 1966, I received the galley proofs of the book. I gave one set to Arnaldo Momigliano. It was the first time that I had shown any part of

---

7. August Frugé, *A Skeptic among Scholars* (Berkeley: University of California Press, 1993), 95.

my book to him. I was understandably heartened by his response: "I have finished your book a few days ago. It is a masterpiece, and has introduced me to the mind of Augustine as no other book. We shall talk about some details." Then he added, with the extraordinary clairvoyance of which he was so often capable:

> My feeling is that there is a weak spot in the last chapters. I do not know whether I can put my finger on it. A provisional indication may be that you have accepted the isolation of Africa without probing it. Whereas Augustine was clearly implying that he was fighting an ecumenic [worldwide] battle, you see him lonely and "safe". The paradox has to be explained that Africa, while crumbling away from the Empire, dictated the fortunes of Western Christianity.

It is, indeed, a paradox with which I—and many others—have been wrestling ever since.

At about the same time, I received a letter from the Oxford Registry. In frosty terms, it informed "Dear Mr. Brown" that the Oxford History Board had received no indication that I had completed my dissertation, "The Social and Economic Position of the Italian Senatorial Aristocracy in the Sixth Century A.D." Nor had they received any report from my supervisor, Professor Momigliano. For this reason, I was no longer eligible to apply for a doctorate. In blunt, American terms: I had been kicked out of graduate school. This was not unusual. I did not even keep the letter. Failure to complete a dissertation and to gain a doctorate was not viewed as a handicap at this time. Indeed, it could appear almost as a sign of distinction—as if I did not need the extra certification of a doctorate: Alan Cameron, already a scholar of superb, almost nonchalant ability, had done the same.

But the absence of a doctorate meant that my reputation depended that much more on *Augustine of Hippo*. And *Augustine of Hippo* was a "London" book, published by Faber's, and not an "Oxford" book, published by the university press. It would be a metropolitan audience—or, rather, a diffuse educated audience outside Oxford—that would judge its merits.

Reviews

But what would "London" think of *Augustine of Hippo*? The first review appeared in the *Sunday Times* on July 30, 1967. It was by John Raymond and entitled "Happenings at Hippo." I read it in a room bathed in the light of a late summer's afternoon. It was all that I needed:

Peter Brown's re-presentation of St. Augustine and his age (354–430) is a brilliant achievement. Intended at once for the scholar and for the general reader, it should make an impact on both: its air of freshness and discovery, of viewing old things in a new light, produces something of the effect of seeing a great painting newly cleaned.

Longer reviews soon followed. They were like a chime of bells. They showed that, at the very least, I had not misjudged my readers. I remember particularly the review by Richard Southern in the *New Statesman* on September 2, 1967. Richard Southern (1912–2001) was the doyen of medieval history at Oxford and Chichele Professor at All Souls (in succession to Ernest Jacob). He represented a peculiarly tense form of medievalism. He once told me that he had been converted to Anglican Christianity by reading both the *Grammar of Assent* of John Henry Newman and all six volumes of the *Chapters in the Administrative History of Medieval England* of Thomas Frederick Tout—a work of unrelenting, no-nonsense research into the sinews of power in high medieval England.

The creative tensions that resulted from that unlikely joining marked Southern. He was fascinated by the charged relation between the sacred and the profane in medieval society. This mirrored a dichotomy within himself—a combination of acute sensitivity to high thought and a leery sense of brutal realities. To be taken seriously by Dick Southern was no small matter.

Southern made clear from the start that he understood the main thrust of my book. He opened the review with a citation from Henry James by his biographer, Leon Edel: "To live over other people's lives is nothing unless we live over their perceptions, live over the growth, the changes, the varying intensity of the same—since it was by these that they themselves lived." I could not have wished for a more generous or more perceptive endorsement. "I salute Mr. Brown's achievement in bringing Augustine out of the tomb of theological doctrine, and setting his mind and emotions working before our eyes."

The Editor's Table of the *Church Times*, "Sinner into Saint," was less easily impressed. I was too clearly a cloistered scholar, without strong views of my own on theological matters:

This is a donnish book: Augustine is admired, not idolized and [believe it or not!] a good word is put in for his opponents, especially for the Donatists and Julian of Eclanum (an unattractive young man).

My friend Gerald Bonner (1926–2013) consoled me for the pejorative appellation of "donnish." He had worked in the British Museum. On the strength of this connection, the reviewer of his *St. Augustine of Hippo: Life and Controversies* had written that there was "something of the flavour of the civil servant" about the book. "Perhaps [Gerald added] publishers shouldn't reveal their authors' professions."

The most unexpected accolade of all came from a friend from my Irish days, the novelist James Farrell (1935–1979). In the 1950s, we used to climb together in the quarry of Dalkey Hill, discussing—of all things!—the value for a budding writer of the prose of *The Book of Common Prayer*. I was with James when he was struck with polio as an undergraduate at Oxford, and helped him on to the flight back to Ireland after a long stay in the Wingfield Orthopedic Hospital. James's *Empire Trilogy* (1970–1978) explored, in three novels, the collapse of English rule in Ireland, India, and Singapore, respectively. Alas, the polio finally killed him. He was swept from a rock by a wave when fishing in Bantry Bay, in 1979, and he was unable to use his crippled arms to swim to safety. Ten years before, I had sent him a copy of *Augustine of Hippo* as a memento of our literary walks in Dalkey. Writing to Carol Drisko, in 1969, James added as a post script:

> I'm reading Peter Brown's biography of St. Augustine. I think it's marvelous. Anyone capable of interesting me in schisms in the Church in Late Roman times must be a genius.[8]

8. J. G. Farrell to Carol Drisko, November 24, 1969, in *J. G. Farrell: In His Own Words. Selected Letters and Diaries*, ed. Lavinia Greacan (Cork: Cork University Press, 2009), 185.

RESONANCES

Resonances

Looking back, from the distance of over half a century, to the appearance of *Augustine of Hippo* in 1967, I realize that those years had a shape of which I was largely unaware at the time. The reviewers of *Augustine of Hippo* and their readers belonged to what was, perhaps, the last generation in Britain and Europe where some form of familiarity with traditional Christianity could be taken for granted. In a highly secularized, progressive Britain, nonbelievers with no church attachments whatsoever (such as I was at that time) might not have admired him. But they felt that, even if they disliked Augustine, they could not avoid him. He was like a disreputable uncle. He was "family." He was there to stay.

No one made this more clear than did Frank Kermode (1919–2010) in his review, "Forecasts from Hippo," in *The Listener* on August 31, 1967:

> It is a fact, but not a fact to which all can attend equally, that Saint Augustine is one of the writers who require to be known by any who would understand the shape of our world. . . .
>
> Yet he was provincial, vain, enslaved to a fierce mother, born into the petty gentry. . . . After a bout of literary and philosophical society in Milan he went home and became a terribly argumentative clergyman. . . .
>
> Why should we care for this ancient, disagreeable man?

My book seems to have answered Kermode's question. I had tried to make Augustine human, even if I did not always portray him as humane. Though Augustine had been long remembered as inflexible, I showed how he developed and changed his mind on many issues. By conjuring up the world in which he lived and the problems that he faced, I tried to make his choices understandable, if not always pardonable. By rescuing his theological opponents from caricatures (often of Augustine's own making), I hoped to render Augustine himself more three-dimensional and the issues at stake in his controversies more worthy of attention.

I went further than that. By the deliberate use of analogies drawn from many aspects of the modern world, I hinted that Augustine was "family" in a deeper sense. I suggested that, somehow, the vehement debates in which Augustine was engaged—with the Manichees on the nature of evil and perfection, with the Platonists on the capacities of the soul, with the Donatists on the relations among individual, group, and society, and with Pelagius on the limits of human freedom—could be transposed into modern terms. They were not only fifteen hundred years away; but in some way they were also still with us.

I believed that, through the careful use of such analogies, it was possible to rethink Augustine's thoughts and to relive his passions, even if we shared little or nothing of Augustine's own, distinctive late Roman Christian faith. As a result, I tried not only to "explain" Augustine to my readers. I also felt that I could make my explanation resonate for them, because a half-sensed web of kinship—of shared "family memories," as it were—still bound them, however lightly, to the Christian past and to Augustine.

But it was not only intellectuals who were affected by my portrait of Augustine. What moved me most were two letters.

One was from a gardener whom I came to know at this time. Mr. Ferris belonged to an extreme Protestant sect. He told me that he never took a bath, lest it relax his physical and moral fiber. He attacked weed-filled flower beds with a hoe, uttering war cries like a samurai. I gave him a copy of *Augustine of Hippo*. Soon after, he sent me this letter:

> The evening after giving a talk at a Bible class . . . I was feeling a bit down-hearted . . . I took up your book and read "when a man's finished, that's when he's just started" [Ecclesiasticus 18:6], and click—that's just exactly how I felt over the paper I'd given at the class. . . .
>
> Later on in the book I could enjoy and appreciate Augustine's frustration at not being fully able to project his feelings and enthusiasms into his hearers. I often share this frustration, being so full of an idea, a pleasure, a problem, and being unable to share it with others; like, for instance, writing this letter to you.

The other was from Thomas Stewart in Glasgow:

> I have come across your Biography "Augustine of Hippo." I am not in the habit of writing fan letters, and don't think this is one . . .
>
> Thank God you had an education.

Thomas Stewart had been taught by a self-educated woman who had fostered his wife. He was now widowed and the single parent of children. When caring for them, he had read

> Thomas Paine . . . and Thomas à Kempis. À Kempis impressed me most. I have quoated and quoated him. Now reading your work, I would say that à Kempis must have read Augustine.
>   Thanks for a good book.

I also had read *The Imitation of Christ* of Thomas à Kempis, on my return from Switzerland in 1952, dreaming of the late Middle Ages. Maybe my reading of Thomas à Kempis as a boy in Ireland had prepared me to discover Augustine, much as it had prepared Thomas Stewart, a widower in Glasgow, to do the same. There is no telling where the resonances of a religious culture may penetrate, and when and in what diverse circumstances it may do so. It was good to think that a book written far away from Glasgow, in the calm provided by All Souls College, Oxford, could play a role in this mysterious process.

Toward Another Augustine

But what do I now think of *Augustine of Hippo*? I have already had an occasion to say this in 2000, when the book was reprinted with a sizeable epilogue on the progress of Augustinian studies. I made special mention of the new letters of Augustine discovered by Johannes Divjak, in 1979, and the new sermons discovered by François Dolbeau in 1996.[1]

But 2000 is twenty years ago. What would I say now?

If I were to start again, I would certainly write a different book. In the first place, the study of all aspects of Augustine and of his North African background has progressed by leaps and bounds. This has happened in two ways: through the continued work of those scholars whom I first met in the Oxford Patristics Conference of 1963, most notably Goulven Madec and his colleagues, at the Institut des Études Augustiniennes, on Augustine himself; and through a thorough revision of our views on late Roman Africa, associated with the work of Claude Lepelley (1934–2015) and, more recently, with the work of my colleague and friend Brent Shaw.[2] Above all, I have been challenged by a

---

1. Brown, *Augustine of Hippo* (2000), 441–520.

2. Claude Lepelley, *Les cités de l'Afrique romaine au Bas-Empire*, 2 vols. (Paris: Études Augustiniennes, 1979–1981); Brent D. Shaw, *Sacred Violence: African Christians and Sectarian Hatred in the Age of Augustine* (Cambridge University Press, 2011).

development that I did not anticipate in 1967—the discovery of letters and sermons of Augustine that are directly relevant to his life as bishop of Hippo. These discoveries, in particular, have made me change my mind on many topics.

I would now admit that Augustine's thought may not have been as conflict-ridden and as fissured by discontinuities as I had believed. The studies of Goulven Madec, followed more recently by those of Carol Harrison and Robin Lane Fox, have argued that there was more continuity between Augustine the convert in Milan and Augustine the mature bishop.[3] Very briefly: they suggest that the young man was less naively optimistic, and that the old man was by no means as glum as I, in the 1960s, had imagined him to have been.

There is no denying that, in his basic theology, Augustine remained all of one piece. He never abandoned the hope of the Vision of God. No matter how difficult it might be to attain to that vision, it remained the heart of his religion. The Neoplatonic notion of the soul's ascent to God still bore him up, on strong and ancient wings. Near the end of his life, in a sermon preached before the lamps dimmed at the end of a simple service in the church in Hippo and the congregation shuffled out, he assumed that those great wings would beat as powerfully as ever, in the hearts of his congregation, as they still did in himself:

> I sense that your feelings have been drawn upwards with me to heaven. But now I will put away the copy of the Gospel. You will go home, each your own way. . . . It was good for us to be bathed for a moment in that common Light. It was good that we rejoiced. It was good that we exulted together. But now, as we walk away from each other, as we go each to our own home, may we not walk away from our shared God.[4]

A Bishop against the World: The Divjak Letters

What had changed for Augustine was the sense of the density of the *saeculum*—of the sheer mass of worldly cares that stood between him and the enjoyment of the presence of God. But these cares did not harden him, as I had

---

3. G. Madec, *La Patrie et la Voie: le Christ dans la vie et la pensée de Saint Augustin* (Paris: Desclée de Brouwer, 1989), 18–19; Brown, *Augustine of Hippo*, epilogue (2000), 490 and 497–498; Carol Harrison, *Rethinking Augustine's Early Theology: An Argument for Continuity* (Oxford University Press, 2006), and Robin Lane Fox, *Augustine: Conversions to Confessions* (New York: Basic Books, 2015).

4. Augustine, *Tractatus in Johannem* 35.9.

implied at times when discussing Augustine's role as a bishop and a controversialist in his old age.

On that matter, as in so much else, Augustine himself has proved to be my best teacher. The discovery of the *Divjak Letters* and their publication in 1981 came as a revelation to me. Here were a set of twenty-nine letters by Augustine, mainly dating from his old age, which had not been copied into the standard collection of his letters, and which had lain unnoticed at the back of a fifteenth-century manuscript, until discovered by the young Austrian scholar Johannes Divjak in 1975. The unexpected sound of a voice from the past—the voice of Augustine himself—made me rethink my views on the old Augustine by showing where I had misjudged him.

In the 1960s, my first entry into the study of Augustine had been through his involvement in the Donatist Schism. I caught the hard tone of the theorist of religious coercion. This bitter contest left me with the impression that Augustine the bishop had become a "severe and aggressive figure of authority."[5] If I remember correctly, in the 1960s, an "aggressive figure of authority" was not at all a good thing to be. In other words, I tended to dismiss the old bishop in terms loaded with overtones of psychoanalytic disapproval.

I was wrong to do so. In the *Divjak Letters*, I heard a more gentle voice. I realized that it was precisely in the low-profile and often rebarbative business of being a bishop, day in and day out, that Augustine showed that "infinite capacity for taking pains" which has rightly been deemed to be the mark of genius.[6]

The *Divjak Letters* show how Augustine, far from being a fierce and withdrawn figure, opened himself up uncomplainingly to every duty to which his public status exposed him. We meet an old man in these letters—old by ancient standards, that is: in his midsixties and early seventies. In one such letter he spoke of his work schedule. In three months he had dictated six thousand lines of writing (roughly sixty thousand words). These included three works, and a series of *Sermons to the People on the Gospel of Saint John*, edited on the nights of Saturday and Sunday, that were to be sent to the Christian congregation in Carthage. He had wanted to return to writing the *City of God*. But no: the bishop of Mauretanian Caesarea (Cherchel: 350 miles to the west of Hippo) had forwarded to him a two-volume book on the nature of the soul,

5. Brown, *Augustine of Hippo* (2000), 197.

6. Arthur Conan Doyle, "A Study in Scarlet 5: The Lauriston Garden Mystery," in *The Complete Sherlock Holmes* (New York: Doubleday, 1988), 31.

written by a local intellectual, which required an answer. The *City of God* would have to wait.

> I am annoyed because of the demands that are thrust upon me to write, arriving unannounced, from here, there, and everywhere. They interrupt and hold up all the other things that we have so neatly lined up in order. They never seem to stop.[7]

But Augustine's literary life was only one part of his activity as bishop of Hippo. The *Divjak Letters* enable us to see, far more clearly than ever before, the underside of the rise to power of the Christian bishop in late Roman society, to which I devoted so much attention in the 1960s. This was no triumphal progress. It was a long-drawn-out battle on the ground that stretched Augustine thin in his old age.

To take one example, to which I have already referred: in 428, Augustine led his congregation in an attempt to break a ring of slave-traders whose victims, captured in the mountainous hinterland, "poured in herds like a river" through the port of Hippo. As we have seen, Augustine himself had interviewed a terrified girl and her brother, who described one of these nighttime raids on a distant farm.

Led by a pious Christian, the congregation of Hippo had boarded the ships and opened the holding prisons. They liberated about 120 captives. Now, however, the slave-traders had mobilized powerful patrons. They intended to sue the Church of Hippo for having stolen their property. Augustine would have to consult a lawyer, to see whether they had a case. This was not the letter of a prince-bishop of medieval times, but of a pastor who had to fight every inch of the way in an uphill battle with the powers of this world. I knew none of this until I read the newly published *Divjak Letters* for the first time, in 1982.[8]

Altogether, Augustine has emerged for me as a kinder, braver, and more patient man than I had thought. Looking back, in the light of this new evidence, I wonder, at times, whether those great tomes of the Maurists had not, in some way, misled me. It is not in his treatises and stirring controversies that Augustine comes closest to us. It is in the flatlands of his routine duties—in

---

7. *New Letter* 23A*. 4, ed. *Lettres* 1*–29* (Paris: Études Augustiniennes, 1987), 378, trans. R. Eno, *Saint Augustine: Letters VI (1*–29*)*, Fathers of the Church 81 (Washington DC: Catholic University of America Press, 1989), 168–169.

8. *New Letter* 10*. 5 and 7–8, pp. 174 and 178–180, Eno, pp. 79–80, and *New Letter* 24*, pp. 382–386, Eno, pp. 172–174.

the undergrowth of letters and stray sermons, where many surprises may yet lie in wait for us—that we (as biographers) can take the full measure of the man.

An Ending

But in 1967, it was time for me to move on from Augustine.

As I look back, it is more clear to me now than it was then that I had come as far as I could go in one direction. A period of my scholarly life had reached an ending. I would not write the biography of any other person. Only Augustine, with his prodigious output already set in chronological order, allowed me to write as I had done. If I made biographical sketches, I would from henceforth draw them as figures in a landscape. I would no longer spend years listening to a single, inimitable voice.

But I think there was more to it than that. I had come as far as I could go in a distinctive approach to the past. Put very briefly: up to this time I had tried to be a faithful listener and communicator. I had sought out themes that still tugged at the heart of modern persons as the result of a barely acknowledged but still tenacious sense of kinship with the Christian past. I had tried to bring Augustine and his times into the present by reminding my readers of what he had in common with them despite the strangeness of the age in which he had lived.

This emphasis on communicating the past to the present led to vivid descriptive history—to the constant painting and repainting of the grand fresco of the later empire and the life of Augustine within it. I had attempted to depict with care the working of the forces that had moved the late Roman world in Augustine's times—the spread of Christianity, the genesis of religious dissent, the growth of religious intolerance. But now I found that I wanted to go back into the past again: to try to understand it in other ways. I wished to take apart the mechanisms of those forces. I wanted to see what made them tick.

My questions became "Why?" questions. They were directed to different problems and to different parts of the world from those that I had encountered in my study of Augustine. My work no longer concentrated on Africa and Italy, but moved farther east, toward the Eastern Empire, Mesopotamia, and Iran. Above all, I confronted wider issues of religious history. For instance: sorcerers were widely feared in all regions of the later empire. We all knew that. But exactly why? In the provinces of the Eastern Empire, holy men came to enjoy a prestige out of all proportion to their social status and level of culture. Why, and with what results? Throughout the Mediterranean and the Middle East, the shrines of saints came to be seen as places where the dead could bring healing to the living. But why? In order to answer these broader questions of religious history, I would have to leave the great pages of the Maurist edition of Augustine. I would have to flounder for many years, and in more languages than Latin and Greek; and I would have to use different modern disciplines to guide me—no longer psychoanalysis, but social anthropology. I trust that the following chapters will explain a little of how this development in my own work happened.

TOWARD THE EAST

BOHEMIA, THE BALKANS, AND EAST ROME

Journeys of the Mind: 1966–1967

Augustine of Hippo appeared in late July 1967. When the Fifth International Conference on Patristic Studies met again in Oxford, in September 1967, I was surprised to learn that the book was already in demand. It was a happy time for me. With a panache suited to a young Oxonian, I would appear every morning to greet my friends at the conference with a newly cut rose in my buttonhole, to the surprise of those who expected the author of a book on Augustine to be a wizened cleric. But, even then, I knew that I was not what I appeared to be. Despite the success of the book, I would never settle down to be what the French call an *augustinisant*—a student of Augustine alone. Why was this so?

Ever since the early spring of 1966, when I had placed the little suitcase with its manuscript of *Augustine* on the floor in front of the immaculate shoes of the office staff of Faber and Faber in London, I had felt the need for further journeys of the mind. I had been held spellbound long enough by a single mighty author as I followed intently the inimitable flow of Augustine's Latin words. I felt, instinctively, that I had given him all that I had for the moment. Quite literally, I needed a change of scene—a new landscape on which to feed my historical imagination.

The next two years were a time of flux for me. From early 1966 onward, I allowed my mind to roam: my interests ranged widely from the Balkans to Czechoslovakia, before turning to the East Roman Empire and to the relations between East Rome and the Sasanian Empire of Iran. Having lingered for years in my imagination in Italy and Roman Africa, I now found myself studying the Middle East and learning Hebrew as a prelude to learning Syriac, in order to read the sources for the history of the Fertile Crescent over which the two great empires of the East had fought continuously. Only toward the end of 1967 did contact with two magnetic figures—Edward Evans-Pritchard and Mary Douglas—challenge me to engage in yet another all-absorbing venture: the application of the methods of the social anthropologist to the religion and culture of late antiquity.

Beyond the Iron Curtain

But where to find a new landscape? First, I thought of what was then Yugo-slavia, which I had visited in 1960. I settled down with a *Teach Yourself Serbo-Croat* and a plan to study the Byzantine Balkans. I wanted to set the Byzantine society and culture of the Balkans (with its complex interweave of Greek and Slav) against the mighty landscapes in which it developed. This was to be a history from the bottom up, in the manner of Fernand Braudel's masterly pa-norama of the Mediterranean in the age of Philip II.

The plan soon fizzled out, but not before leaving me with a lively interest in Eastern Europe as a whole. These were charged regions. It is important to remember the extent to which the Iron Curtain weighed on the consciousness of Europe in the late 1960s. This was particularly true for scholars of the later empire and of Byzantium. The Danubian frontier of Rome ran close to or through many of the countries under direct Soviet control. To study that fron-tier was to make contacts with scholars from another world—from the world behind the Iron Curtain. And to pass through that Curtain at any point or for any reason was a serious matter.

But even at a time when travel to Eastern Europe was difficult, Eastern Eu-rope occasionally came to Oxford. The International Byzantine Studies Con-gress met in Oxford in September 1966. Large delegations from Iron Curtain countries attended, as a major theme of the conference was the relation between Byzantium and its neighbors in the Slavonic world. It was at this conference that I met Elka Bakalova, later to become the doyenne of Byzantine art studies in Bulgaria. At that time, she was working on the Byzantine frescoes of the monas-tery of Bačkovo. Now she has done more than anyone to preserve the Byzantine monuments and to maintain high standards of art history in Bulgaria.

I took her with some colleagues on a tour of All Souls. Perched in the gal-lery of the Codrington Library, looking down on its grand marble floor and olive-green bookcases bathed in light, we discussed as best we could, in a courtly mixture of French and Russian, how the life of a teacher in Oxford compared with that of a scholar under Russian tutelage in Sofia.

The topic of Great Powers and their frontiers was a central theme of the congress. Alas, frontiers were contemporary history for young scholars in Soviet bloc countries such as Poland, Czechoslovakia, and Bulgaria. The fact that they could attend a conference in Oxford gave them some hope that these frontiers might yet open up. It was a hope that was postponed for all too many years.

Bohemia: František Šmahel

That was why the crushing of the "Prague Spring" two years later, through the Russian invasion of Czechoslovakia in August 16, 1968, came as an amputation. After years of hope, it appeared that the axe had fallen on future links with Eastern Europe. In Oxford in September 1968, I witnessed the immediate results of this brutal shutdown. I found myself helping to host a delegation of Eastern European scholars. By a grisly turn of fortune, a group of Czech scholars had come to Oxford to attend a conference of Anglo-Czech historians. This had been planned some time before, in the heady days of the Prague Spring. The new Communist authorities had allowed them to come. For a tense week, scholars over whom the sword of Damocles now hung were treated to high thinking and high living at All Souls College. In his recent autobiographical interview, the great historian of the Hussite Revolution in fifteenth-century Bohemia, František Šmahel, speaks lightly of this uncanny moment of reprieve:

> For a week I could use a professor's room with a valet [a College "scout"] for whom I had no work. Other memorable experiences were the college dinners with many courses, which can perhaps only be seen in English detective stories.[1]

It was after one such dinner that I met Šmahel in the common room of All Souls. Seated in a corner, he poured out his soul to me in Czech. In many ways, it was a painful moment. I was barely able to keep up with his Czech, yet I did

1. F. Šmahel in *Times of Upheaval: Four Medievalists in Twentieth-Century Central Europe*, ed. Pavlína Rychterová, Gábor Klaniczay, Pawel Kras, and Walter Pohl (Budapest: Central European University Press, 2019), 254–255.

not wish to stop him in midflow. I came away with a heavy sense of his anger and of the uncertainty of his future.

It was, above all, the anger of a scholar whose life's work was threatened by ignorant bureaucrats. The Russians were not mentioned. What mattered was the progress of scholarship, inevitably brought to a halt by the new regime in Prague. Šmahel's mastery of the archives had already opened up an entire world, which placed the intellectual origins of the Hussite Revolution against an international scene, in the debates held by scholars in universities all over Europe in the late fourteenth and early fifteenth centuries. This work was endangered less by Marxist ideology than by the shutting down of contacts with the wider world that followed the suppression of the Prague Spring. How would Czech scholars have a chance to learn about the flow of ideas between Prague and Oxford in the days of John Wycliffe (d. 1384)? How would they be able to discuss (without ignorant claptrap) the novelty of the idea of "nation" in Hussite Bohemia? It was the voice of a young scholar whose future had been taken from him.

The evening laid a weight on my conscience for having been able to offer so little effective comfort to his pain. But I remained in touch with Šmahel. I sent him offprints and a copy of my *Augustine*. He reciprocated with long Czech articles on Hussite ideology and with two small books on heroes of the Hussite Revolution. One was on Jerome of Prague (1379–1416), a fierce intellectual who, like Hus, was burned at the stake in Konstanz in 1416. The other was on Jan Žiška (1360–1424), the great leader of the Taborite armies. Žiška was already known to me as a proto-Protestant hero. As a child in my grandmother's home at no. 60 Lansdowne Road in Dublin, I had been fascinated by the letters—Z-I-S-K-A—that formed the divides of a silver toast rack. Little did I think that I would be reading the life of a hero, formerly known to me only as the name of a yacht commemorated on the breakfast table of a Dublin Protestant family, in a book sent to me by a Czech colleague surviving, in a state of suspended animation under Communist rule, behind the Iron Curtain.

After 1989, Šmahel returned to public life, now as a leading scholar—in a dominant position that he has maintained until today. I learned only recently, from his autobiographical interview with Pavlína Rychterová, how much he had suffered. Denied a salary at the Historical Institute, he worked as a tram driver in Prague from 1975 to 1979. Typically, all that he complained of in those years was the fact that his job as a driver forced him to sacrifice spare-time pleasures such as music and reading novels so as to concentrate entirely on his historical work. This work continued unabated. He poured his learning into a three-volume masterpiece, *Husitská Revoluce*, which I have read from cover to cover in German translation, grateful for the inspiration of a scholar of rare tenacity.[2]

Toward East Rome

Late medieval Prague was a thousand years and a thousand miles away from late Roman Constantinople. And I might have settled for Prague. In those years, my contact with František Šmahel ensured that the Hussite Revolution of the fifteenth century remained a challenge to me. It might have brought me back to where, in part of me, I still thought that I belonged: to the medieval West. My knowledge of Augustine would have been of great use to me in understanding the roots of Hussite views on church and society. Seldom had the issues first raised in Augustine's North Africa, between Catholics and Donatists, been fought out with such ferocity as in fifteenth-century Bohemia. A book could well have grown from this interest in Czechoslovakia.

But it did not. After 1968, travel to Eastern Europe became prohibitively difficult and would have tied me to an ideologically blinkered group of sponsors. So I soon settled down to study the East Roman Empire in the fifth, sixth, and early seventh centuries up to—and, if possible, beyond—the rise of Islam. I did not regret the choice. For I found, on turning eastward, what I had so far lacked—a cohort of friends working in the same field.

Writing about Augustine had been a lonely business. Apart from Robert Markus, in Nottingham, my contacts had been mainly with European scholars, and especially with the French. But in the years when I was finishing the writing of *Augustine of Hippo*, a heartening growth of interest in the later Roman Empire had taken place among British scholars, most of whom were trained classicists, and many of whom became good friends. They began to apply their mastery of Greek to the superabundant literature—in poetry, prose, and historical writing—of the East Roman Empire, the empire of Constantinople and its eastern provinces, in the last centuries of the ancient world. The emergence of this cohort tipped the balance for me, away from the West to the late Roman East.

For this cohort, 1964 had been an annus mirabilis: Hugo Jones published *The Later Roman Empire, 284–602: A Social, Economic and Administrative*

---

2. *Husitská Revoluce* (Prague: Univerzita Karlova, 1993), translated into German as *Die hussitische Revolution* (Hanover: Hahn, 2003).

Survey.[3] A three-volume masterpiece of patient analysis, it captured—in a manner all the more convincing for being understated—the sheer vigor and complexity of a huge imperial society that controlled the Balkans, Egypt, and the western part of the Middle East, much as the Ottoman Empire had done in the sixteenth century. I wrote a long review article on Jones's *Later Roman Empire* for the *Economic History Review*. It was an occasion for me to take the full measure of an empire that had refused to decline and fall at a time when Edward Gibbon (with his profound Western bias) had lamented the "awful revolution" of the disappearance of the Roman Empire in the fifth-century West, ignoring the fact that the Roman Empire of the East had survived intact.[4]

From this time onward, I was in regular contact with other scholars in the field in England who had much to teach me. At the University of Leicester, Jones's student, Wolfgang Liebeschuetz, had begun on a study of Antioch in the fourth and fifth centuries that would revise many of our views of the post-classical city and of social phenomena such as the working of patronage in the countryside of northern Syria.[5]

As a research scholar at Cambridge and, later, as professor of sociology at Brunel University in Uxbridge, Keith Hopkins had adopted an austerely sociological approach to the role of eunuchs in the court of Constantinople. He argued that, far from being the symptom of irreparable decadence, the power of eunuchs was part of an ingeniously balanced system, by which eunuchs were used as a counterpoise to the influence of the traditional educated elites.

This new approach enabled Hopkins to present the court eunuchs, who usually played a thoroughly negative role in florid modern fantasies of Byzantine life, as spearheads of professionalization and of upward social mobility. After all, this was in the 1960s, when it was widely agreed that a modern society could not have too much professionalization and social mobility. It was good to know that East Rome, also, had had its fair share of both. Altogether, our image of the East Roman Empire was changing for the better year by year.[6]

3. A.H.M. Jones, *The Later Roman Empire, 284–602: A Social, Economic and Administrative Survey* (Oxford, Blackwell, 1964).

4. P. Brown, review of *The Later Roman Empire, Economic History Review*, 2nd ser., 20 (1967): 327–43, now in *Religion and Society in the Age of Augustine* (London: Faber, 1972), 46–73.

5. J.W.H.G. Liebeschuetz, *Antioch: City and Imperial Administration in the Later Roman Empire* (Oxford University Press, 1972).

6. K. Hopkins, "Eunuchs and Politics in the Later Roman Empire," *Proceedings of the Cambridge Philological Society* 139 (1963): 62–80, now in *Conquerors and Slaves* (Cambridge University Press, 1978), 172–196.

This positive image of East Rome was not entirely new. Recent studies had merely added a crispness of analysis and a wealth of vivid detail to what was already a well-established view of the East Roman Empire that dated back to the 1930s. It was based on an awareness of the contrast between the separate destinies of the western and the eastern parts of the Roman Empire—a contrast that had already been highlighted by Santo Mazzarino in his *Stilicone*. While the West collapsed, the East survived. And we tended to think that, compared with the fossilized West—underurbanized and dominated, first, by its great landowners and, later, by its clergy—it deserved to survive. In the words of the great British Byzantinist Norman Baynes (1877–1961): the East Roman emperors of the fifth and sixth centuries and their strangely assorted servants did their job successfully. They ensured that "the civil service and the army together formed the steel framework which maintained the entire structure of [Byzantine] civilization." Up to the time of the Arab invasions of the 640s, this steel framework had held remarkably well.[7] Jones's *Later Empire* merely confirmed this view.

What attracted me most was another surprising aspect of East Rome. That was the "dualism" in East Roman culture to which Norman Baynes had referred in his many brilliant exposés of Byzantine civilization.[8] Here was a vibrant society in which seemingly incompatible traditions coexisted. Members of the governing elite of East Rome were still schooled in classical Greek, and were capable of patronizing works of art and of literature in the best classical tradition. Yet this elite was also deeply involved in a rising tide of popular Christian devotion. As a result, in East Rome, things were never quite what they seemed. Classicism and Christianity often came together in startlingly anomalous ways. A poet and top administrator—the last person you might expect—could write a skilled Greek epigram in praise of a wild Syrian holy man perched between Heaven and earth on a column overlooking the Bosphorus. A young lawyer could commission an icon of the archangel Michael, "stirred to the depths of the spirit . . . by fear, as if He were present"; and then go on to bring together a collection of distinctly risqué classical epigrams devoid of any hint of Christianity; Silenus was shown chasing a dancing maenad

7. N. H. Baynes, "The Decline of Roman Power in Western Europe: Some Modern Explanations," *Journal of Roman Studies* 33 (1943): 29–35, now in *Byzantine Studies and Other Essays* (London: The Athlone Press, 1960), 83–96, at 94. Jones, *Later Roman Empire*, 2:1025–1068, thought much the same.

8. Baynes, "The Thought-World of East Rome," in *Byzantine Studies*, 24–46, at 35.

across a silver dish made in the reign of Heraclius (610–641)—the emperor who would march at the head of a Christian crusade against the pagan Empire of Iran. How was I to understand such dualism?

Faced by this conundrum, I could not have found a better guide than Averil Cameron. As I have already made plain, her study of the historical work of Agathias of Myrina opened up a new way to understanding the strange balance of classical and nonclassical in East Rome. But I owed more to Averil than this. In early 1966, I was asked by Arnaldo Momigliano to act as examiner for her dissertation on Agathias. This dissertation included a translation and commentary on two parts of his *History* that were of particular interest to the historian. These were the two long excurses on the Franks and on the Sasanian Empire of Persia. Averil's study of Agathias's excursus on the Sasanian Empire proved decisive for me. Here was a view, across the frontier as it were, of the great Middle Eastern neighbor of East Rome.[9]

FRONTIERS

When I settled down, in the summer of 1966, to read Averil's commentary on the excursus of Agathias on the Sasanians, I already had frontiers on my mind. This was not only because of my growing preoccupation with countries beyond the Iron Curtain. It was also a direct outgrowth of my long-standing interest in the rise of religious intolerance in the later Roman Empire. My work on Augustine and my debate with Bill Frend and others on the ethnic basis of religious conflict in the later empire had made me aware of the active role of Christianity in sharpening social, political, and ethnic boundaries. Like manganese added to medium carbon steel, Christian notions of orthodoxy and Christian intolerance of heresy, paganism, and Judaism tended to make preexisting Roman prejudices against outsiders doubly hard.[10]

Averil's commentary on Agathias was a masterly confirmation of this view. She showed how, in the East Roman world, attitudes to Persia hardened significantly in the course of the sixth century. Agathias's predecessor, Procopius

9. Averil Cameron, "Agathias on the Early Merovingians," *Annali della Scuola Normale Superiore di Pisa*, ser. 2, 37 (1968): 95–140, and "Agathias on the Sassanians," *Dumbarton Oaks Papers* 23 (1969): 67–183.

10. Brown, "The Later Roman Empire," in *Religion and Society*, 54, and "Christianity and Local Culture in Late Roman Africa," *Journal of Roman Studies* 58 (1968): 85–95, now in *Religion and Society*, at 299.

of Caesarea (ca. 500–ca. 570), the great historian of the wars of Justinian, still viewed Persians with the eyes of a cultivated Greek. They were "barbarians" in the old sense. They were alien and menacing, but they were not beyond the pale of humanity. A generation later, Agathias was less tolerant. He regarded Persians as worse than barbarians. They were pagans—Zoroastrian worshippers of fire. By the beginning of the seventh century, this process of hardening was complete. East Rome was thought of as standing against Persia as a united Christian society—a new "People of God," like Israel, faced by a pagan nation.

A Religion without Frontiers: Manichaeism

Averil's study of attitudes to Persia opened a world for me. But, in one way, I was already prepared for it. Ever since I began to work on Augustine (who had been a Manichee as a young man), I had been fascinated by Manichaeism. This was a religious movement that had originated in the interstices between Rome and Persia. The prophet Mani (216–277) came from southern Mesopotamia (from what is now southern Iraq, below Baghdad). On the strength of his visions, he founded a truly universal religion. Known as Manichaeism (and its followers as Manichees), Mani's religion was eminently suited to his position at the crossroads of Asia, on the frontier between Persia and Byzantium. Manichees asserted that Christ had preached only "to the Romans in the West," while Zoroaster had preached only to the Persians, and "the Lord Buddha" had preached only to India and Central Asia. By contrast, Mani would preach to them all. His missionaries soon reached the western Mediterranean (where Augustine met them in Carthage and Rome) and would later cross the Iranian plateau to Central Asia and China. To study the spread of a new religion across Eurasia was calculated to widen the heart.

Surprisingly enough, my relation with the religion of Mani went back a long way, to my days as a young man in Ireland. For many of the most important Manichaean manuscripts in Coptic were housed in the Chester Beatty Collection in Dublin. At the time, these manuscripts were not in their present magnificent exhibition space in Dublin Castle. They lay where Chester Beatty (1875–1966), an eccentric millionaire, had left them, in a sheltered house at the end of Shrewsbury Road, a suburban avenue lined with imposing embassies. The exhibition rooms were barely lit. The precious codex of the *Kephalaia*—a major collection of Manichaean teachings, found in the sands of the Fayyum Oasis in Egypt—lay beneath glass panes that were covered with dust and dead flies. Staring at them in the dim, underwater light, I resolved that one day I would learn Coptic to read these mysterious treasures.

As I prepared a paper, "The Diffusion of Manichaeism in the Roman Empire," for Ronald Syme's seminar on Roman Syria in 1968, it dawned on me that the story of the diffusion of Manichaeism in the Mediterranean and the Middle East was part of the story of the hardening of the frontiers between Rome and Persia. A period of open opportunity in the third and fourth centuries, when Manichaean missionaries traveled easily between Persia and the Roman world, was followed, in the fifth and sixth centuries, by a sharpening of boundaries and a narrowing of horizons. In western Europe, commercial activity receded and the newly Christianized Roman aristocracy came to blend traditional anti-Persian feeling with a new Christian horror of heretics. Much the same happened in the East. In Persia, an equally conservative Iranian upper class rallied against religious novelties. In both Rome and Persia stability was gained at the price of a greater distrust of the foreigner, the heretic, and the barbarian. The spread of a religion that had begun in a time of wide horizons, opened up by the crisis of the third century, was brought to a halt by the emergence, in later centuries, of more stable but more intolerant and parochial societies.[11]

But this hardening of boundaries was not the whole story. There was one crucial area where the frontier between the two empires remained wide open. This was the Fertile Crescent. The Fertile Crescent stretched in a great arc of intensely cultivated land from southern Mesopotamia, along the foothills of the Zagros and of the Anatolian plateau, to reach the Mediterranean at Antioch. Along this great corridor, a common Syriac culture joined the two sides of the political frontier. This was the bridgehead across which ideas and personnel had moved from East to West, and from West to East, since the very beginnings of civilization in the Middle East.

I had found what I wanted: a zone of free movement and religious ferment in between two massive empires whose attitudes to each other had begun to harden. To do a history of that region would be to stand at the very center of western Asia, equidistant from the Mediterranean and the Iranian plateau. From that position, I could follow, from the third century to the seventh, what Edward Gibbon had called the "Revolution of the East" that culminated in the rise of Islam.

---

11. Peter Brown, "The Diffusion of Manichaeism in the Roman Empire," *Journal of Roman Studies* 59 (1969): 92–103, in *Religion and Society*, 94–118.

Of all the journeys of the mind that I have undertaken, this one appears in retrospect to have been the most decisive. It took me in little over a year from Augustine of Hippo to the frontier between East Rome and Iran, giving my work an Eastern tilt that it had not had before.

Eventually, my turn to the East became part of a general recentering of the field of late antiquity as a whole. From being a strictly Greco-Roman affair, limited to the Mediterranean and to western Europe, the field has now come to embrace large areas of Africa and the Middle East, and to include the origins of Islam. It has come to require a command of oriental languages—such as Syriac, Arabic, and Coptic—to supplement our traditional knowledge of Latin and Greek. If there is a "linguistic turn" truly worth celebrating in the study of late antiquity, it is this new willingness of young scholars to master the languages necessary for the study of the Christian East and of early Islam.

With this turn we have entered a world far wider, far more complex, and demanding of far greater methodological sophistication than I myself had dared to dream, over half a century ago, when I first envisioned the possibility of a journey of the mind that included the eastern provinces of Rome, the Fertile Crescent, and the Empire of Iran.

BYZANTIUM, PERSIA, AND THE RISE OF ISLAM

New Opportunities: Richard Southern and Syllabus Reform

From 1967 onward, a fortunate set of circumstances enabled me, for the very first time, to throw myself into teaching the history of late antique Byzantium and Persia in a series of lectures, along with tutorials. It was no longer treated as a marginal topic, but as a fully recognized subject in the Modern History School of Oxford. That so seemingly exotic a theme should become an optional subject in the otherwise unyielding structure of the Oxford history syllabus was a revolution in itself. This revolution was due largely to two remarkable scholars: to Richard Southern, the Chichele Professor of Medieval History in All Souls College, and to Samuel Stern, an Islamicist and a senior research fellow of All Souls.

As a result of this change in the syllabus, Sam Stern, Dimitri Obolensky, and I found ourselves working together to create a Further Subject (that is, an optional subject): "Byzantium and Its Eastern and Northern Neighbours, 500–700 A.D." This was no big change in itself. A Further Subject was not the equal of the Special Subject, which had required texts in the original language and was examined in two papers. It was based on translations and was examined in one paper only.

But it was, nonetheless, a significant change. Before the introduction of "Byzantium and Its Eastern and Northern Neighbors," the only Further Subject available to medievalists had been the constitutional history of medieval England based on documents selected well over half a century before, by Bishop William Stubbs. Given the rigidity of the previous system, the introduction of this new Further Subject in 1966 was the academic equivalent—to use the language of the 1960s—of a gap in the Berlin Wall. A growing number of gifted undergraduates could escape through it into the study of the late antique Middle East.

Readers not acquainted with the rigidities of the Oxford of the 1960s need to be reminded of the extent to which a seemingly simple administrative measure—which involved (after all) only one, three-hour paper in a final examination—was seen as such a breakthrough for us all. To be "on the syllabus" was to exist. It was to be deemed to be doing *real* history. For that reason, the creation of a Further Subject that included the *Persian Wars* of Procopius, the *Miracles of Saint Demetrius of Thessalonica*, the *Life of Muhammad* by Ibn Ishâq, parts of the *Golden Meadows* of Mas'ûdi, and the *Conquest of the Regions* of al-Balahdurî (to name only a few of the texts that were set for the new Further Subject) was to make these exotic persons real for the first time in Oxford.

It was Richard Southern who made possible this small but decisive *aggiornamento*—this opening of horizons in the Oxford History School. Canny, instinctively conservative, and inwardly detached, on a deep level, from loyalty to any one form of academic institution, Dick Southern was a revolutionary insider—not unlike the otherworldly but highly effective medieval bishops (such as Saint Anselm) whom he studied with such sympathy.

Southern became Chichele Professor in 1961. He delivered his inaugural lecture in November 1961. It was entitled "The Shape and Substance of Academic History." Those who attended the lecture knew that they were listening to a skillful challenge to the status quo. He historicized the History School. He described how, from the Victorian Age onward, it had provided "a system of education for practical men"—for civil servants, colonial administrators, lawyers, and politicians. He went on to say that this was no longer what history was about. The present-day History School was stranded: it represented "the remnants of a discipline which had lost its original purpose. . . . The greatest developments in historical thought have been on the periphery of the old syllabus: the centre has remained comparatively unchanged . . . it is quietly ceasing to be the centre." *Cherwell*, the undergraduate magazine, got the message: "Top History Don Talks Change."

Once he got going, Dick had a gift for making other people work. I was recently astonished to find, among my papers, five long pages on publications in East Roman and early Byzantine history, complete with comments on the state of the field, which I had prepared for Dick Southern at this time. Now he announced that the old Further Subject on medieval English constitutional history—the famous "Stubbs"—was no longer the only Further Subject available to medievalists. He indicated that interested parties could approach him in order to frame new Further Subjects. He then stood back and waited for the zealous to push forward. To the best of my memory, I was at the head of the line.

THE WORLD OF ISLAM: SAM STERN (1920–1969)

I would not have been so confident if I had not been encouraged and constantly informed by another remarkable figure, the Islamicist Sam Stern. Samuel Miklos Stern was a Hungarian Jew who had fled to Palestine in 1939. During the war, he worked as an interpreter and censor in the Middle East. For a while, he had even been stationed at Port Sudan, at a time when my father was active in the railways there. For all I know, they might have met. He was elected a senior research fellow at All Souls in 1957.

Sam was a scholar's scholar. To me, he seemed to hold the keys to the treasure-house of medieval Islam, in exactly those areas where this extraordinarily rich civilization touched the Western world. He discovered love lyrics in early Spanish disguised by transliteration into Arabic script, thereby reopening the hotly contested issue of the role of Muslim Spain in the origins of courtly love. His work on the Ismailis showed the continued influence in the Arab world of Greek Neoplatonic mysticism at its wildest. His studies of the Fatimid Egyptian archives relative to the Monastery of Mount Sinai in the eleventh and twelfth centuries threw a vivid light on the interrelations of monks, Christian pilgrims, and Italian merchants at the time of the Crusades.

Furthermore, as the translator from the German of the *Muslim Studies* of the great nineteenth-century Islamicist and fellow Hungarian Ignaz Goldziher (1850–1921), Sam introduced me to the very core of Islam and to its mighty tensions from the time of Muhammad onward. Unlike Sam, Goldziher had been an orthodox Jew, who knew what it was to live under a Divine Law. Compared with many flaccid English-language syntheses of Muslim belief, the chapters in Goldziher's *Muslim Studies* were the genuine article.

To talk to Sam about Islamic matters was an "open sesame" to a magic cave. And Sam loved to talk. Most fellows eschewed talking shop at dinnertime—contenting themselves with small talk, or simply sticking to their glass of port. But Sam, by contrast, opened up at dessert. I would sit beside him at the dessert table, spellbound by his learning. As a result, I remember Sam only in profile, his large mouth and heavy face half-covered with bright brass spectacles caught in the candlelight, like a benevolent magic frog in a fairy tale. This was what All Souls was for. Along with Prof. Zaehner's after-dinner ruminations, those talks with Sam over dessert were crucial to my development as a scholar.

Sam died, tragically early and brutally suddenly, of an attack of asthma in November 1969. I attended the funeral. Albert Hourani (1915–1993) spoke of the grave filled with bright flowers. Alas, all I saw was mud on an icy, rainy morning.

At the memorial service for him in All Souls Chapel, on November 22, 1969, the warden, John Sparrow (1906–1977), fastened on the maverick in Sam—on the unpredictable actions of a devoted scholar, like a Parsifal among the courtly knights. He recounted one telling incident. In the competition for the research fellowship, candidates were invited to dine at the college as part of the vetting process. Sparrow told how Sam had risen to the occasion.

> The surroundings were unfamiliar, and as for his companions at table, whether or not they were congenial to him, he modestly supposed that he was not likely to be congenial to them, and very soon abandoned the hope of being admitted to such an inbred, esoteric body. The talk turned upon a project to admit women, not indeed to the College—this was fifteen years ago—but, as readers, to the Codrington Library. Not much enthusiasm was evinced for the proposal. And someone, perhaps the Librarian, sought to dispose of it with the argument—if it can be called an argument— "What would Archbishop Chichele have thought of such an idea?" Impelled by the recklessness of despair, Stern could not help inquiring "What would Archbishop Chichele have thought of the election to his college of a Hungarian Jew?"[1]

I doubt very much that Sam spoke out of despair. I think that, as usual with him, he simply told the truth as he saw it.

Sam was a truly great scholar, a model research fellow of All Souls. He was not a teacher. But our friendship showed that pure research of this kind was never imprisoned in an ivory tower. In Oxford (and especially in All Souls, where teachers and researchers lived in close proximity) research such as Sam's had an immediate trickle-down effect. It helped to open the teaching of

---

1. *Memorial Addresses of All Souls College Oxford* (Leopard's Head Press for All Souls College, 1989), 71–72.

history undergraduates in the university as a whole to entirely new horizons. By helping to create the syllabus for the new Further Subject on Byzantium and its neighbors, Sam gave the late antique Middle East a place in the study of history in Oxford.

"Byzantium, Persia and the Rise of Islam"

It was agreed that I would introduce the new Further Subject through a term of eight lectures, entitled "Byzantium, Persia and the Rise of Islam, 500–700 A.D." Preparing these lectures turned out to be a *joyeuse chevauchée*—a brisk march with much plunder—through the available literature on Byzantine-Persian relations, on the structure and culture of the Sasanian Empire in Mesopotamia, Iran, and Central Asia, and on the continuity of Byzantine and, especially, Persian institutions and views of the world in the centuries after the Muslim conquest.

My reading now took me to parts of the Oxford library system that I had not visited before. In the Ashmolean Library of classical history and archaeology, where I had long been a regular reader and borrower, I now made my way to less frequented parts. I would go up to the very top floor, beyond Egyptology and papyrology, to a small and unfrequented room devoted to Coptic texts. It was entirely appropriate that a small corridor in the form of a glassed-in bridge should lead from there, over the narrow lane at the back of the Ashmolean, to the Oriental Institute, where I would walk down, floor by floor, passing shelves of texts in all the languages of the Islamic world and the rows of specialized journals in the history and culture of the Middle East in all periods, but especially in Islamic times. This journey to the unfrequented top of the Ashmolean, across a bridge, and then down again into the Oriental Institute summed up for me a new vision of the late antique world.

It was this vision that I tried to communicate in my lectures on Byzantium, Persia, and Islam. They were intended to be an introduction to the rhythms of history in the late antique Middle East that would bring together the worlds of East Rome and Iran and their role in the creation of the Islamic Middle East. Hence their title: "Byzantium, Persia and the Rise of Islam, from 500 to 700." I explained what this meant in my first lecture:

> What I want to make clear is an aspect of the End of the Ancient World and the Beginning of the Middle Ages as far as it affects the Near East in general and the Byzantine Empire in particular. . . .

In this there is a danger that the historian of Late Antiquity will give up with Islam. It is assumed that Islam came to a *tabula rasa*—that after terrible wars of the early 7th century, the two giants left a vacuum. That the Arabs filled this with something entirely new—and not our concern.

I pointed out that standard treatments of the later Roman Empire (such as Jones's monumental *Later Roman Empire*) ended abruptly in AD 602, and that histories of Islam began, in around 610, with the preaching of Muhammad, and offered only the most perfunctory introduction to previous history of the Middle East.

> In fact, the real chasm may have happened earlier in Sasanian Persia, for instance, in the terrible crisis of the late 5th century; in Byzantium, perhaps after the death of Justinian in 565. . . . All through the 6th century, the Near East, divided between Byzantium and Iran, is slowly taking on the contours that will determine the future shape of Islam until the 10th century at least.

And so I concluded:

> Justinian (527–565) and Khusro I Anoširwan (530–579) in the mid-6th century, Heraclius (610–641) and Khusro II Aparwez (591–628) in the early 7th, are just as much "Makers of the Middle Ages" as are Muhammad and Charlemagne.

The lectures had, for me, the excitement of a journey into a new country. It was a novel theme in the Oxford history syllabus; and it seemed to strike a chord with those in need of wider horizons. I have recently discovered the sign-up sheet for one of my earliest lectures in this series, in the Hilary (spring) term 1969. (This was nothing like "registration" for a course of lectures as in the American system: it was simply a courtesy, like leaving one's visiting card at an old-fashioned tea party.) I am now surprised at how many of the names were those of persons who went on, in later years, to study Byzantium, Persia, and the Islamic world. Some were already graduate students: Robert Hillenbrand, future professor of Islamic art in Edinburgh, repaid me with a kind letter and a complete bibliography on Sasanian elements in medieval Persian architecture; Ze᾽ev Rubin (1942–2009), who had come from Israel to Oxford to study the age of Septimius Severus, would later study the reforms of Khusro I Anoshirwan. Others were undergraduates: James Howard-Johnston, whose *Witnesses to a World Crisis* and now his *The Last Great War of Antiquity* have summed up a generation of study of the wars of Heraclius and Khusro II Aparwez;[2] and Michael Wood, the brilliant director of historical travelogues on television. In this way, my lectures brought me into contact with a far wider group of scholars, of different ages, from undergraduates to graduate students—some of them foreigners—than I could have met in my tutorial teaching alone. It was a good beginning. But now I had to learn the languages that were needed to turn a happy venture, largely related to undergraduate teaching, into real research.

2. James Howard-Johnston, *Witnesses to a World Crisis* (Oxford University Press, 2011) and *The Last Great War of Antiquity* (Oxford University Press, 2021).

HEBREW

BACK TO THE ANCIENT NEAR EAST

In making a start on the languages of the Fertile Crescent, I began with the Hebrew of the Old Testament (Classical Hebrew). This decision puzzled many of my friends. So far I had relied on Latin and Greek. To launch out on a Semitic language was very much a new departure. And if I needed a Semitic language with which to study the late antique Middle East, Syriac (the lingua franca of the Fertile Crescent) or Arabic (the vast repository of so many of the philosophical and historical traditions of late antiquity) seemed to be the more practical choice.

But there were good old-fashioned reasons for my choice. At that time, Classical Hebrew was still treated as the Latin of the Middle East. It was regarded as the Semitic language whose grammar, once mastered, served as an entry point to all others—as Latin grammar was traditionally held to be the basis for the study of classical Greek and of the Romance languages of Europe.

Furthermore, Hebrew was the language of the Bible. The strong Biblicism of the Protestant Church of Ireland had ensured that the figures and landscapes of the Old Testament (the Hebrew Bible) had always been an imaginative presence to me. At an early age we were supposed to know many vivid stories from the Bible. Indeed, at the age of nine, I won the Scripture Prize in Aravon with the winning answer—that Jehu was the name of the man "who drove furiously" (2 Kings 9:20). This triumph led my aunts to declare, with evident satisfaction, that I would become a bishop.

But there was more to it than that. The more I came to know the thought of Saint Augustine, the more I realized the extent to which it was penetrated by the language and ideas of the Hebrew Bible—the Old Testament. In a man of entirely Latin culture, with little knowledge of Greek and no knowledge whatsoever of Hebrew, this permeation of an author's thought by a language known only through translation struck me as remarkable. Here was a man who somehow had managed to "think Hebrew" without any direct knowledge of the language, but simply through total absorption, through preaching and through daily reading, of the Latin translation of the Hebrew Bible.

This pointed to a wider change. Constant Christian use of the Bible in writing, preaching, and liturgy caused central words in the religious and social vocabulary of the later empire to change their valences. The hitherto exotic language of the Old Testament came to mold late Roman culture not only in religious matters: the self-image of Roman society also changed under biblical influence. The Roman Empire took on the profile of an ancient Near Eastern polity, from an age before the classical city—a profile characterized by sharp assymetries between rich and poor, between God, ruler, and people. In studying Hebrew I hoped to gain some knowledge of the original literature that had provoked this mighty change.

Roberta Chesnut

I could not have found a teacher more inspiring and more appropriate to such a venture than Roberta Chesnut, now Roberta Bondi. She had come to Oxford from the Perkins School of Theology in the Southern Methodist University at Dallas, Texas. When I first met her, she was studying Semitic languages in the Theology School and had just begun a dissertation on the Syriac works of three major anti-Chalcedonian theologians of the late fifth century.[1]

We began our Hebrew lessons in late 1967. I had not had such a learning experience since the time when I was taught German by Ernst Scheyer in Dublin, in the gap year between Shrewsbury and Oxford. Like Scheyer, Roberta Chesnut taught me the language from scratch and, at the same time, introduced me to an entire culture. I have usually learned languages on my own, without the energizing help of such teachers. But in the case of German and Hebrew I was singularly fortunate. Each of my teachers opened my heart to new horizons.

We worked our way through Jacob Weingreen's *A Practical Grammar for Classical Hebrew*.[2] Even this was appropriate: for, as I have mentioned before,

1. R. Chesnut, *Three Monophysite Christologies: Severus of Antioch, Philoxenus of Mabbug and Jacob of Sarug* (Oxford University Press, 1976).

2. My copy was J. Weingreen, *A Practical Grammar for Classical Hebrew*, 2nd ed. (Oxford: Clarendon Press, 1959).

Weingreen (1908–1995) was professor of Hebrew at Trinity College Dublin. My aunt Freda's curate, a clergyman straight out of Trinity, would speak of him with awe. His love of Hebrew opened a new world for his Irish students. Roberta did the same. When we turned to the book of Genesis, to Ruth, and to the historical books—especially to 1 and 2 Samuel—she would draw up for me a list of grammatical notes for my daily readings. At times she would add splendidly drawn pictures of Hebrew notions of the universe. I was caught in the strong summer breeze of her love of the language.

It was thirty years later that I came to know where this enthusiasm came from. Roberta later became professor of church history at Emory University in Atlanta, Georgia, from 1978 to 2006, having previously taught for a time in the Theology Department at Notre Dame. She changed in those years. Her studies of Monophysite and Nestorian Christology were succeeded by works of spiritual guidance for modern readers based on her deep knowledge of the writings of the Desert Fathers and of the ascetic theologians of the Christian East. Turning to Roberta's spiritual autobiography, *Memories of God*, I learned what lay behind the zest with which she taught me Hebrew.[3]

Hebrew had come to her as a deliverance from the chill world of a conventional Protestant childhood in Kentucky. It had opened wider, warmer horizons. In the summer of 1963, she bought a copy of a Hebrew Bible and *Learning Hebrew by the Inductive Method*. It was a moment of revelation for her:

> I still recall the way the shape of the Hebrew letters and the look of the light falling across the creamy paper were mixed up with what I can only call a sense of cosmic goodness and joy in all created things I had never encountered before. . . . It was as though the page itself were alive and the jots and tittles on the letters little flames. For the first time I could recall, life seemed all of a piece.[4]

It was only four years later that Roberta began to teach me. At the time, I knew nothing of her personal religious evolution. But her zest for the majestic tread of the Hebrew language and for the massive imaginative patterns from which the opening chapters of the book of Genesis were constructed swept me up, a little, into that vision.

At Oxford, Roberta had originally intended to write a dissertation on an Old Testament subject. But her enthusiasm had been chilled by the manner

3. Roberta Bondi, *Memories of God* (Nashville, TN: Abingdon Press, 1996).
4. Bondi, *Memories of God*, 66.

in which a distinguished Hebrew teacher had cut her off when, toward the end of a course on the Hebrew of the book of Job, she plucked up the courage to ask the simple question:

> "Could we take just a few minutes to talk about the *meaning* of the *Book of Job*?"
>
> Embarassed, the students looked at the table top. . . .
>
> "My dear madam [the professor had replied] *that* is something to ask your tutor in the privacy of his own tutorial."[5]

Alas, I can imagine the incident only too well. Instead of Hebrew, Roberta went on to study the spiritual writers and theologians of the Syriac world of the fifth and sixth centuries. I did not realize at the time what an impression these writings made upon her. I would soon find my way to the same authors, but only as sources for the history of the Fertile Crescent. Roberta read them for spiritual comfort. Her dissertation involved the analysis of Monophysite thought on Christology. It was an exacting task to which her careful, sharp mind was supremely well suited. She had a rare gift for communicating the seriousness of the concerns of seemingly remote theologians. But theology alone was not enough for her. It was the ascetic writings of the Syriac authors that truly moved her.

> One day, in a dusty autumn morning I opened in the middle of a book with the unpromising title of *The Thirteen Ascetic Homilies of Philoxenos of Mabbug*. . . . It was during this time in the Bodleian Library that I first met the generous and gentle God of the early monks.[6]

What Roberta had found in the writings of Philoxenos (ca. 440–523) was shrewd advice, based on long experience and deep self-knowledge, as to how to love one's fellow monks despite the constant strains of a monastic environment. Such gentleness was not what she had expected from a forbidding theologian of the late fifth century.

As I look back, it is good to think that what, for me, was a historian's venture into the history of the late antique Middle East could be experienced, by

---

5. Bondi, *Memories of God*, 69.

6. Bondi, *Memories of God*, 30 and 133. Roberta would have known the old-fashioned translation of Wallace Budge; see now Robert A. Kitchen, *The Discourses of Philoxenos of Mabbug*, Cistercian Studies 235 (Trappist, KY: Cistercian Publications, 2013), with David Michelson, *The Practical Theology of Philoxenos of Mabbug* (Oxford University Press, 2014).

others, as a personal source of comfort and an opening of spiritual horizons. I was fortunate to begin my study of the Fertile Crescent through learning Hebrew from a scholar whose enthusiasm for this new world more than matched my own.

Roberta left Oxford in late July 1968. Just before her final departure to the United States, she visited Dublin and had tea with my parents. Among many other things, my mother talked about her passion for novels about the American South. Later, with typical kindness, Roberta sent her a copy of Faulkner's *Absalom, Absalom!* Roberta also made her way to the Chester Beatty Collection and found it as much a treasure house as I had done:

> I have never seen anything like it. In most museums you have to look at a hundred pieces which are at best interesting before you see one which is beautiful: in the Chester Beatty museum the proportions are exactly reversed. There is nothing there which is not exquisite.

Her last good deed in Oxford was characteristic: she arranged with the abbess of an Anglican convent in Burford to teach Hebrew by correspondence to one of the nuns.

Back in America, she wrote from Kentucky that she missed Oxford terribly.

> Oxford seems so much closer to me than the room I'm sitting in, and it doesn't seem possible that I can't go outside the window of my room in Park Town and watch the misty sun on the trees and buildings.

Despite the few snubs and a mounting dissatisfaction with the cerebral nature of the teaching she received in the Oxford Theology School, the anonymous life of an American postgraduate in Oxford had suited Roberta's reclusive and meditative temperament. She was happy with a liminal existence among a circle of friends who accepted her for who she was: "This is the reason we loved it so much, though we also loved it for its beauty, its stone and gardens. In Oxford, internal things are externalized." Roberta was lucky: she had experienced something of the timeless idyll of Oxford that still hovered, tantalizingly close, behind the careworn university of the late 1960s.

Unlocking Doors

Meanwhile, I settled down without Roberta to make my own way through the book of Samuel, as far as the gripping narrative of the death of Saul in the Battle of Gilboa and the lament of David for Saul and Jonathan (2 Samuel 1).

If ever there was an unvarnished account of a warrior society in action, caught in the lightning flashes of the occasional intervention of a holy man—the prophet Samuel—this was it. I began to understand why the book of Samuel was so important to history-writers in Dark Age Europe, such as the Venerable Bede. Ancient Israel, and not the well-organized empire of Rome, was a society like their own—characterized by the same raw juxtaposition of violence and sanctity.

Later I moved on to rabbinic Hebrew, reading, first, the *Pirqe Avoth* (the Talmudic tractate known as "The Sayings of the Fathers") and, then, the *Kether Malkût*—The Crown of the Kingdom—of Ibn Gabirol (1021–ca. 1070), the great Jewish poet of eleventh-century Spain. I did this with Nicholas de Lange who, at that time, had begun his groundbreaking work on Origen and the Jews.[7] A true Sephardi, nostalgic for the Spanish background in which Judaism had once flourished, Nicholas would go on riding holidays in Andalusia. I would exchange postcards with him in Hebrew praising the hospitality and deprecating the rash driving habits of the locals.

Last of all, I began to learn Syriac for my work on the history and hagiography of the Fertile Crescent. I did this with Father Richard Vaggione, a member of an Episcopalian religious order. Richard had grown up on the West Coast of America, where his grandmother used to tell him stories of a much wilder California than the present laid-back coast—stories of gunfights in and out of the lines of laundry hanging in the back gardens of Monterey. Richard was working on the radical theologian Eunomius (335–393)—a model study of the role of a Christian intellectual in high society at the time of the Arian controversy. Much of the evidence for Eunomius's views consisted of texts that had been translated, centuries later, from Greek into Syriac. Only the Syriac versions of these texts had survived, preserved in the monasteries of the Middle East—a lesson, in itself, in the mingling of cultures in late antique and medieval Syria.[8]

Languages are not learned in a day. My language learning continued for many years to one side of my research and bore more fruit for me in later years (from the 1980s onward) than it did at this precise moment. But I did learn enough to open doors to evidence in Hebrew and Syriac that would otherwise have remained closed to me: these doors were now, as it were, "left on the latch" for me, unlocked, to enter when I needed.

7. N. de Lange, *Origen and the Jews* (Cambridge University Press, 1976).

8. R. Vaggione, *Eunomius of Cyzicus and the Nicene Revolution* (Oxford University Press, 2000).

And with the languages came the cultures in which they were embedded. It was here that I had the sense of coming upon horizons far wider than I had expected. Hebrew gave me access to patterns of thought and to images of society that lay at the very roots of Greek and Latin Christianity. Going through my notebooks and bibliographies, I now notice that whenever I began work on any major theme in the history of late antique Christianity—such as wealth, poverty, and almsgiving—I sooner or later found myself back with the Psalms, the prophets, and the rabbis of the Talmud. These Hebrew sources added an entire extra dimension to a history of Christian attitudes to society that was usually limited to Greek and Latin alone.

With Syriac, I encountered the populations of a Middle East divided between Rome and Persia. Lives of saints, local chronicles, sermons, and hymns in Syriac gave me a view, from the ground up, as it were, of the two empires at work through sources that had been ignored by classical scholars. I remembered how, in my first years in All Souls, Geoffrey de Sainte Croix had pointed out to me how much could be learned about the social history of late fifth-century Edessa (modern Şanlıurfa in southeast Turkey, a city perched on the frontier between Rome and Persia) from a Syriac chronicle, that could not be learned from any Greek or Latin text. Often written to console the subject populations of war-torn frontier regions, Syriac historiography recorded a history of suffering unequaled in the ancient world for its compassion and concreteness.

This, in itself, was enough to keep me busy. But learning Syriac offered more than that. It gradually opened up for me the other side of the bilingual (Greek and Syriac) Christian culture of Syria whose unusual vigor made itself felt throughout the late antique world. It was my way into *la Syrie bilingue* of Paul Peeters (1870–1950), whose study of the "oriental subsoil" of Byzantine hagiography influenced me deeply at this time.[9] In this distinctive zone, set back from the Greco-Roman Mediterranean, a succession of hymn-writers and preachers created an imaginative world significantly different from that of Greek and Latin Christianity. This world would continue up to and beyond the rise of Islam, leaving a mark on the Qur'ân and on the later formation of Islam.

At the time, however, the opening up of this larger imaginative world was of less interest to me than were the remarkable figures who emerged from the bilingual world of Syria and its neighbors in East Rome and in Persian

9. P. Peeters, *Le tréfonds oriental de l'hagiographie byzantine* (Brussels: Société des Bollandistes, 1950).

Mesopotamia. These were the holy men whose dramatic impact on the society and on the religious imagination of the Eastern Empire had come to fascinate me. Side by side with the learning of Hebrew and Syriac, I would devote the next few years to intense reading in order to understand the rise and function of the holy man in late antiquity. But first I had to equip myself with a new methodology that did justice to this challenging phenomenon.

ANTHROPOLOGY AND
HISTORY

E. E. EVANS-PRITCHARD

"An Acquaintance with the Habits of Savages":
Anthropology at Oxford

My language learning was an oasis of steady, low-profile progress in the middle of an academic life that had become ever more challenging. These were the years, roughly between 1968 and 1971, when I was swept up into what was for me a new enterprise—an attempt to apply anthropological thought to the religious history of late antiquity.

This ensured that, while my teaching remained much the same, my research was on brand-new themes. In April 1968, I delivered a paper at the annual conference of the Association of Social Anthropologists: "Sorcery, Demons and the Rise of Christianity: From Late Antiquity into the Middle Ages." The following year, I began to prepare an article, "The Rise and Function of the Holy Man in Late Antiquity," that appeared in the *Journal of Roman Studies* for 1971. Between April 1968 and November 1969, I wrote a short book entitled *The World of Late Antiquity: From Marcus Aurelius to Muhammad*, which incorporated some of the perspectives that I had recently developed. It appeared in June 1971.[1]

---

1. Peter Brown, "Sorcery, Demons and the Rise of Christianity: From Late Antiquity into the Middle Ages," in *Witchcraft Confessions and Accusations*, Association of Social Anthropologists Monographs 9, ed. Mary Douglas (London: Tavistock Publications, 1970), 17–45, now in *Religion and Society in the Age of Saint Augustine* (London: Faber, 1972); 119–146; "The Rise and Function of the Holy Man in Late Antiquity," which appeared in the *Journal of Roman Studies*

Behind this burst of writing lay a turn to anthropology that marked a decisive moment in my intellectual evolution. With hindsight, this turn can easily
be presented as an uncomplicated matter—as the result of an interdisciplinary linkup, such as would occur easily enough in modern conditions on many
campuses, American and British. But this was not at all the case. My relationship to anthropology took the form of a series of gradual enrichments, spread
over time, and hastened by a few unexpected but decisive encounters.

These encounters need to be set in the context of the Oxford of the 1960s.
This means that it is the story of a distant time. In fifty years, Oxford has
changed profoundly. So has anthropology. Its methodologies and the manner
in which it represents itself are now very different from what they were. Much
that seemed new and exciting in the 1960s has either come to be taken for
granted, or has fallen by the wayside to make way for new approaches. After
so many changes, all I can do is try to recapture something of the excitement
generated by a joining of anthropology and history both in my own work and
in the work of some of my Oxford colleagues.

Anthropology as a discipline hardly existed in Oxford in the 1960s. Unlike
many American universities, Oxford had no thriving department of anthropology from which to effect exchanges with other disciplines through lectures,
joint seminars, and similar interdisciplinary ventures. A professorship of social
anthropology had, indeed, been created in 1937, attached to All Souls College.
But the professor remained little more than the head of a small, highly specialized institute, responsible only for a handful of graduate students. Anthropology
was not expected to make any impact on the solid mass of tutorial-based undergraduate teaching in the colleges. To many, it was positively unwelcome. When
the creation of a professorship of social anthropology was debated, Hugh Last
(1894–1957), the doyen of Roman history and the leader of opinion in the
prestige-full School of Litterae Humaniores (of the classics), had roundly declared that "an acquaintance with the habits of savages is not an education."

A TIME MACHINE

But this was not the end of the story. Paradoxically, its very marginality within
the university gave to anthropology the aura of a dynamic counterculture.
It offered new ways to think about human nature and society. To historians it

---

for 1971 (*Journal of Roman Studies* 61 [1971]: 80–101), now in *Society and the Holy in Late Antiquity*
(Berkeley: University of California Press, 1982), 103–152; *The World of Late Antiquity: From
Marcus Aurelius to Muhammad* (London: Thames and Hudson, 1971).

offered more than that. It gave them a time machine. Anthropologists seemed to be engaged in the study of societies which resembled those that had existed in earlier centuries in Europe. They found that to read a study of a warrior society in modern central Africa helped them to step into early medieval Europe as it really had been—lived day in and day out, under the eyes of a living observer who could ask questions and receive answers, as a historian could never hope to do when confronted with the silent debris of the past.

This was the secret of the charismatic appeal exercised outside his own discipline by the professor of social anthropology, Edward E. Evans-Pritchard (1902–1973). Known always as E.-P., Evans-Pritchard held the chair from 1946 to 1970. We were told that he had studied medieval history as a young man. In a famous lecture, "History and Anthropology," delivered in Manchester in 1961, he invited historians to complete their education by finding (in contemporary Africa and elsewhere) an early medieval Europe on their doorstep: "There is a big difference between reading about feudal institutions in capitularies and living in the midst of something similar." Young historians (and especially medievalists) found it very easy to make this step, entering the distant past through reading about "something similar" in the present.[2]

I had already begun to do this on occasions. In 1956, as a new prize fellow of All Souls, I had read *Custom and Conflict in Africa* by Max Gluckman (1911–1975).[3] I read it over lunch on a Saturday in the garden of the Turf, beneath the bell tower of New College. I remember that I treated it very much as "weekend reading." It was not part of my routine work as a teacher or a researcher. Indeed, it was not even a proper "university" book. It was based on a series of talks, delivered on the Third Programme of the BBC, that were designed to make specialist knowledge available to the general educated public. (Fred Hoyle's talks on the nature of the universe had been broadcast, in the same way, on Radio 4.)

Gluckman was a student of Evans-Pritchard and shared with him the wish to make anthropological insights available to historians. I found that *Custom and Conflict* gave me the time machine that I needed. His discussion of feuding in modern African societies transformed my view of the Anglo-Saxons. It gave them, as it were, the third dimension of real life.

Gluckman showed that feuds did not necessarily result in mindless spirals of violence—the so-called law of the jungle. Rather, his patient observation

---

2. E. E. Evans-Pritchard, *Anthropology and History* (Manchester: Manchester University Press, 1961), 12.

3. Max Gluckman, *Custom and Conflict in Africa* (Oxford: Blackwell, 1955).

of the actual working out of feuds in contemporary Africa showed the opposite: feuds were held in check by a complex system of mixed loyalties; moments of conflict could become occasions for elaborate ceremonies of reconciliation. Altogether, to use the challenging title of Gluckman's best-known chapter, there was "Peace in the Feud."[4]

No medieval historian had told me this. Gluckman's reassessment of the role of the feud dramatically altered my view of the working of "barbarian" society in Dark Age Europe. In coming years, I was not slow to pass on this news to my undergraduates during tutorials on early medieval England. Undergraduates (who delighted in such eccentricities) liked to believe that I had once told a staid medievalist that the best book on the Anglo-Saxons was . . . Gluckman's *Custom and Conflict in Africa*.

"That Morass of Ignorance and Superstition": E.-P. and the Primitive Mind

But these occasional borrowings from anthropology did not give me an idea of the full measure of E.-P.'s contribution to the human sciences until I came across his *Witchcraft, Oracles, and Magic among the Azande*.[5] I read it because of an unexpected invitation. The Association of Social Anthropologists in Britain held an annual conference, and it was decided that the theme for 1968 should be "Witchcraft Confessions and Accusations." The published papers were to be dedicated to Evans-Pritchard at the time of his retirement in 1970. In tribute to E.-P.'s wish to make anthropology better known among historians, nonanthropologists were invited to contribute. The most notable of these were Keith Thomas and Alan MacFarlane, both already zealous in their use of anthropological methods for the study of witchcraft in early modern England.

An obvious subtheme in any study of witchcraft was the problem of evil. After *Augustine of Hippo* appeared, in the summer of 1967, I somehow came to be marked out as an expert on evil. I was approached by Mary Douglas, the

---

4. See now especially Stephen D. White, "'The Peace in the Feud' Revisited," in *Making Early Medieval Societies: Conflict and Belonging in the Latin West, 300–1200*, ed. Kate Cooper and Conrad Leyser (Cambridge University Press, 2016), 220–243—a volume most appropriately dedicated to the memory of Mary Douglas.

5. E. E. Evans-Pritchard, *Witchcraft, Oracles and Magic among the Azande* (Oxford: Clarendon Press, 1937).

organizer of the conference, who at that time was teaching in London, to offer a contribution either on Augustine and the Manichees or on Augustine and original sin. At that time, Mary was a total stranger to me. She suggested that I should read *Witchcraft, Oracles and Magic*, just to get my eye in, as it were, for an anthropological occasion.

What emerged from my reading was, perhaps, not quite what she expected. For, on reading it carefully over a summer vacation, I found that *Witchcraft, Oracles and Magic* carried with it a charge of meaning for me that grew directly out of the Sudanese context of its writing. The Azande were a Nilotic tribe in the southern Sudan. Evans-Pritchard had done his fieldwork among them at the same time as my father was working far to the north, in Atbara. Indeed, *Witchcraft, Oracles and Magic* appeared in 1937—a year before I solemnly fed my Mickey Mouse handkerchief to a large hippopotamus in the Khartoum Zoo.

Witchcraft, Oracles, and Magic immediately struck a chord with me. For Evans-Pritchard had addressed a central issue in British attitudes to the native populations. The notion that there was something intrinsically inferior about the thought processes of the mass of their subjects was accepted as a given. Belief in a "primitive mentality" held the natives at a distance. It enabled the colonial powers to claim that they had come to liberate their subjects from the evils associated with the vagaries of subnormal minds—thereby justifying the indefinite continuance of colonial rule.

Most books about Sudan had no doubt on this matter. The naval *Handbook of the Anglo-Egyptian Sudan* of 1922 wrote of the Muslim populations of the northern Sudan: "In viewing these beliefs one must take into consideration the unstable nervous and mental condition of a great part of the population."[6] The southern Sudan was deemed to be even worse. In the words of one top administrator, "In that morass of ignorance and superstition we progress slowly."[7]

As we have seen, the "Bog Barons" (the governors and district commissioners of the swamplands of the southern Nile) had spun around the Nilotic tribes, such as the Nuer and the Azande, a web of paranoid fantasies.[8] Many of these Bog Barons were convinced that they were dealing with irrational

6. *A Handbook of the Anglo-Egyptian Sudan* (Naval Staff Intelligence Division, 1922), 199.

7. Harold MacMichael, May 15, 1929, to the Sudan Agent, in R. O. Collins, *Shadows in the Grass* (New Haven, CT: Yale University Press, 1983), 135.

8. Chapter 7: "Sudan: North and South."

savages, held in the bonds of terror by prophets and witch doctors. The bombing of Nuer villages, the destruction of a major religious monument, and a wave of random arrests were the price that the Nilotic tribes had to pay for the anthropological naïveté of their masters—most notably of "Chunky" Willis, who became governor of the Upper Nile in 1927.

Hence the importance of the arrival of the young Evans-Pritchard (at the age of twenty-four) in the southern Sudan. He spent four years among the Azande (from 1926 to 1930). The result—*Witchcraft, Oracles and Magic among the Azande*—was a masterpiece of detailed observation winnowed by unfailing common sense.

As I read it slowly, in the summer of 1967, I realized that Evans-Pritchard had knocked away one of the most solid props of modern (and not so modern) rule over subject populations—the notion of their mental inferiority. But it was more than that: by contradicting the notion of a "primitive mentality," anthropologists such as Evans-Pritchard had recognized the full humanity of the tribes of the southern Sudan—and, with them, of a large proportion of the human race.

Witchcraft Dedramatized

Above all, *Witchcraft, Oracles and Magic* was a masterpiece of dedramatization. Evans-Pritchard pointed out that, for any Zande (any member of the tribe of the Azande), witchcraft was a commonplace happening, as it was not for Europeans. It was not a spooky practice. It was a way of talking about misfortune that could be used to explain mishaps by linking these mishaps to the ill-intentions or envy of other persons. As a result, belief in witchcraft put a human face on misfortune; and it did so because of a firm belief that what humans can inflict, humans can remedy—in this case, by seeking out the person whose "hot" envy (consciously or unconsciously) was held to have caused this particular mishap. The belief that the cause of any misfortune could be identified, challenged, and, as a result, reversed or made good in some way, accounted for the unusually sunny mood of the average Zande. Witchcraft was normal because witchcraft was fixable. This mood was the exact opposite of what others, such as "Chunky" Willis, had expected of societies in which witchcraft beliefs appeared to be rife.

> Unless the reader appreciates that witchcraft is quite a normal factor in the life of the Azande . . . he will entirely misunderstand their behavior

towards it. To us witchcraft is something which haunted and disgusted our credulous ancestors.[9]

But witchcraft was not like this at all for the Azande.

Just as Gluckman had shown that the feuds of Dark Age Europe were not necessarily mindless slaughterfests, so Evans-Pritchard had integrated witchcraft into the daily life of the Azande in a manner that made it unremarkable because subject to precise and prosaic forms of human control. If there could be "peace in the feud," as Gluckman claimed, then there could also be room for the working of mute common sense in the deployment of witchcraft beliefs.

This was news to me. Confronted with seemingly irrational and "primitive" beliefs—such as belief in sorcery—that were current in late antiquity, I wondered whether they might lose the histrionic and sinister associations wished upon them by modern scholars if examined in the same precise and low-key manner. If the Nuer and the Azande could be made intelligible by anthropologists, so could the varied inhabitants of the Eastern Empire.

It was time to seek advice from wiser heads. But this advice did not come from Evans-Pritchard himself. Although, as professor of social anthropology, E.-P. was a member of All Souls, I was never as close to him as I was to Prof. Zaehner and Sam Stern. This was partly due to his magnificent idiosyncracy. E.-P. was an Insider's Outsider: the son of a Welsh-speaking Anglican clergyman and a well-known convert to Catholicism, he was also very much an Old Wykehamist (a product of Winchester College, the quintessential southern English public school). He had something of the country gentleman about him. He talked more readily about his dog than about scholarly matters.

But there was also a structural reason for this distance. E.-P. was a university professor. In All Souls, a significant, hairline crack separated professorial fellows from research fellows. The main interests of a professorial fellow were assumed to lie outside the college. They were seen as busy men, engaged in university matters, who were not expected to linger in their cups in the evening.

Professorial fellows tended to appear only at lunch, which they would eat along with the other fellows, squashed on benches, at three cramped tables in the buttery, beneath the elegant oval of a coffered ceiling—a smaller echo of the exquisite baroque vaulting of Bernini's San Carlino alle Quattro Fontane in Rome. They had little room to sit back and relax, even if they had wanted to.

9. Evans-Pritchard, *Witchcraft, Oracles, and Magic,* 64–65.

Nor was the clatter of eating (amplified by the oval above them) conducive to conversation. And Evans-Pritchard was going deaf. It was his face and not his conversation that I remember. If I knew him, it was as I knew so many of my colleagues in Oxford and elsewhere: through his books, not through his teaching—and still less through his table talk.

If I wanted advice, I had to go elsewhere. For this reason, I went down to London in late December 1967, to have tea with Mary Douglas at the Commonwealth Club—the tearoom of the Royal Commonwealth Society, a literary and scientific body, founded in 1868, and dedicated to the greater understanding of what had once been the British colonies.

MARY DOUGLAS

Anthropology and a Medievalist: Paul Hyams

In 1966, Mary Douglas published the first of her many scintillating studies—*Purity and Danger: An Analysis of the Concepts of Pollution and Taboo.*[1] I probably got hold of it just before I went down to London to meet her in December 1967. I certainly remember who urged me to read it: Paul Hyams, a student of the administration of justice in medieval England. Given the stolid reputation of English medieval history, it might seem strange that an expert in medieval English law should recommend a book based largely on fieldwork in what had been the Belgian Congo. But this was less surprising than it seems: Paul would soon emerge as an exceptionally alert student of conflict and its resolution in the face-to-face communities of villagers who formed the basis of medieval English society.[2]

He took anthropology seriously. This was not only because medieval village communities and African tribes were manageable human units—appropriate laboratories for the study of face-to-face relations. It was also because both groups could be studied with little or no reference to state power. It was here that anthropology had a decisive effect on medievalists such as Paul. It offered an alternative narrative for the development of medieval polities—a narrative that did not concentrate exclusively on the growing power of the state. For Evans-Pritchard had not only shown that the Azande could handle witchcraft beliefs without terror and hatred. He had also gone on to describe how the

1. M. Douglas, *Purity and Danger: An Analysis of the Concepts of Pollution and Taboo* (London: Routledge and Kegan Paul, 1966). I have used the reprint, London: Ark Paperbacks, 1984.

2. Paul Hyams, *Rancor and Reconciliation in Medieval England* (Ithaca, NY: Cornell University Press, 2003).

Nuer, the neighbors of the Azande, functioned without any central power whatsoever. They lived in a state of "ordered anarchy" that up to then had baffled observers. In another masterpiece of fieldwork, *The Nuer*, E.-P. had described the complex social mechanisms that enabled this to happen without the entire society lapsing into disorder.[3]

For a medievalist, this was a challenging discovery. The accepted master narrative of the English Middle Ages had been the story of the triumphant growth of law and order in the hands of a central power. E.-P. showed that there might be exceptions to this upbeat narrative. It was possible for medieval European communities to idle for centuries largely untouched by the brisk progress of the state, resolving conflicts in their own way, without resort to royal justice and to the royal gallows. In other words, they were like the Nuer and none the worse for that. Altogether, an anthropological approach offered a way to do history from the bottom up—from the primary needs of small communities. It offered an escape from the emphasis on the growth of the state and the consequent bias toward top-down political and institutional history, such as was studied with antediluvian rigor in Oxford and elsewhere.

Sorcery in the Later Empire

I was impressed by Paul's arguments in favor of anthropology; but I went to see Mary Douglas with different problems on my mind. In order to prepare my paper for the Association of Social Anthropologists' conference, "Witchcraft Confessions and Accusations," I had begun to read all that I could about sorcery in the ancient world. This made me realize that I needed some new way to think about the convergence of religion and social structure in the later empire. How did these apparently bizarre sorcery beliefs fit into the actual working of late Roman society? Could I do for the late Romans what Evans-Pritchard did for the Azande—take a seemingly irrational practice and show how it functioned on a day-to-day basis?

Tea with Mary Douglas in the Commonwealth Club proved to be an extraordinary encounter. I had never met anyone with so consequential a mind, with such delight in joining seemingly unrelated phenomena, and with such zest in urging others to do the same. She spoke in a high whisper. Her eyes

---

3. E. E. Evans-Pritchard, *The Nuer: A Description of the Modes of Livelihood and Political Institutions of a Nilotic People* (Oxford: Clarendon Press, 1940), 181.

were always slightly raised, as if she were reading, from a screen in front of her, the laser-fast succession of her own thoughts. She did not speak *to* me but, rather, seemed to invite me to read with her the thoughts that flashed across that screen. I emerged from the tea with a thick sheaf of references to anthropological studies from all regions of the world, from the East End of London to the Kalahari Desert, and with the assurance that, if I looked in the right direction, I would be able to spot the crucial places where the strains, the limits, and the opportunities of a given social structure were echoed in the structure of its religious beliefs and practices.

Other than that, my memory of the tea is blurred. In any truly significant conversation with a person or reading of a book, the intensity of the first dawning of ideas scours the memory like the ground zero of an explosion. What I remembered best was the mood that this encounter generated. It convinced me that I could do it. Instead of writing on ideas, such as the idea of evil or of sin in Saint Augustine, I could write about people in action in a given social system, and about the beliefs that clustered around their persons as a result of the stresses generated by that social system. What Mary had given me over tea was not an answer to my questions but a tone of voice with which to write about a phenomenon as seemingly alien to modern persons as sorcery in late antiquity and the early Middle Ages.

I decided to do this in two ways: First I would follow Evans-Pritchard's *Witchcraft, Oracles and Magic* in looking closely (and in as unmelodramatic a manner as possible) at the rationale of sorcery accusations in late antiquity. The court of the emperor Constantius II (337–361)—notorious for the sorcery trials described so vividly by the near-contemporary historian Ammianus Marcellinus (ca. 330–395)—would be my Zandeland. Why did these trials happen? What did they really mean? What clash of ambitions generated a language of occult power in that tense world?

But I felt encouraged to go beyond Evans-Pritchard's study of the Azande in a direction that Mary Douglas had pointed out to me: I would try to use sorcery beliefs and sorcery accusations like barium traces in an X-ray. Their varying intensity would enable me to chart the stresses and strains of a social system caught in a muffled war between fluidity and rigidity. I would trace the differing forms of power (both real and imagined) associated with each group. Mary Douglas predicted that those with more fluid social roles tended to be more closely associated with sorcery than those whose power rested on more firm hierarchies and more rigid social structures. If that was so, I could go on to ask what the apparent rise and fall of sorcery beliefs in late antiquity could tell us about the overall structure and evolution of late Roman society from late antiquity into the early Middle Ages.

When I sent Mary the draft of the paper that I had prepared for the conference, I received an instant, long reply. Written on February 12, 1968, it was as characteristic of Mary as was her conversation at tea. It was a lesson in anthropological thinking. She showered me with comparative material, and discreetly nudged me toward ever more consequential and all-embracing interpretations:

> Dear Mr. Brown,
>
> I have read your paper with great pleasure. When shall we meet to talk about it? . . . The dangerous *demi-monde* is a marvelous idea. . . . But when I read p.15 [on] the transfer of blame on to capricious malevolent spirits who may use or who may not use [human] agents, I would look for something else in the social structure. . . . I have some suggestions for the kinds of social system which might produce these cosmologies [that is, the demon-filled cosmology of late antiquity].

It was typical of Mary, a field-worker through and through, not to rely on letters but to prefer one-on-one conversations over a good cup of tea. Her criticisms would always be accompanied by a list of articles and examples. This time she pointed me to recent work on the spread of Islam in West Africa as a parallel to the snowball effect of conversions to Christianity at a time of loosening social bonds in the later empire; and she added, "I would also love to talk about that. . . . Would it be impertinent of me . . . to congratulate you on a superb handling of anthropological materials?"

Heartened and firmly guided by such a letter, I rewrote my paper and entitled it "Sorcery, Demons and the Rise of Christianity: From Late Antiquity into the Middle Ages." I presented it for discussion when the conference met in King's College, Cambridge, April 3–6, 1968.[4]

Mary wrote to me again on June 30, 1968—after I had handed in the final version of my paper—with an invitation to contribute a book to a series that she hoped to edit on the theme of "religious anthropology." It was the offer of a merger between the two disciplines:

---

4. P. Brown, "Sorcery, Demons and the Rise of Christianity: From Late Antiquity into the Middle Ages," in *Witchcraft Confessions and Accusations,* Association of Social Anthropologists Monographs 9, ed. Mary Douglas (London: Tavistock Publications, 1970), 17–45, now in *Religion and Society in the Age of Saint Augustine* (London: Faber, 1972), 119–146.

My role will be to try to inject as much anthropology into it as I can in the research and thinking stages. . . . There are not enough anthropologists trying to make it [anthropology] relevant to other disciplines, and for lack of them anthropology itself is dissipating its energies and losing inspiration. . . . This series is an alternative channel which will draw other work to the attention of my colleagues and vice versa.

I did not accept this offer; but I had already begun to appreciate the stature of Mary Douglas and the seriousness of her agenda.

NATURAL SYMBOLS: RITUAL AND THE BOG IRISH

A little after the Cambridge conference, Mary gave me a carbon copy of the complete manuscript of what became the signature masterpiece of this period in her life—*Natural Symbols*. (In a world without photocopiers, the gift of a carbon copy was, in itself, an act of rare generosity.) I realized at once that we shared with Evans-Pritchard a dislike of the tendency to treat religious practices in societies unlike our own in a *de haut en bas* manner—to dismiss them as "primitive" or "superstitious." But Mary did more than that: *Natural Symbols* offered an entire new way to look at the relations between religion and society. This was crucial for me.[5]

I later learned much more about Mary than I knew at that time. What I learned partly explained the intensity behind *Natural Symbols*. I learned, for instance, that Mary's mother was a Twomey of Cork: in other words, she was a member of an important Munster sept (clan). Her father, like mine, had found employment in the British Empire—in Mary's case, in India and Burma. But, unlike my parents, her family no longer had a home in Ireland. Her link to Ireland was through a shared traditional Catholicism. She had grown up as thoroughly British as she was Catholic.

In 1970 this meant that she was deeply committed to the idea of Britain as a decent and humane community—to the "One Nation" Toryism of the time. This seems to have made her more than usually alert to the dangers posed by the loss of shared symbols and rituals that held society together. She distrusted idealistic programs of reform. In her opinion, these programs tended to be

---

5. Mary Douglas, *Natural Symbols: Explorations in Cosmology* (London: Barrie and Rockcliff, 1970). I have used the edition of Routledge (London and New York, 1996), which has a new introduction.

generated by persons from social niches that somehow made them indifferent to the ritual aspects of social behavior that played such an important role in the cohesion of British society. Their well-meaning reform programs (of which there were many in London at that time, particularly in relation to public housing and other social amenities) seemed to her to have unwittingly sapped the complex system of checks and balances on which real social decency depended.

Hence Mary's peculiar disquiet concerning the zest with which leading theologians in the Second Vatican Council and other members of the Catholic clergy threatened to purge the Catholic Church of ritual practices—such as abstinence from meat on Friday. These clerical reformers dismissed such practices as "primitive" and unworthy of the more "spiritual" and "enlightened" Christianity of modern times. In *Natural Symbols*, Mary challenged this *de haut en bas* attitude of the reforming hierarchy of the Catholic Church to the practices of its own laity. She did this in a deeply moving chapter entitled "The Bog Irish."[6]

As Mary described them, the "Bog Irish" were tenaciously attached to the observation of fasts and Friday abstinence. Mary did not defend their practices because she was notably conservative or reactionary in liturgical matters (as were many of the opponents of the reforms of Vatican II). She did it for reasons that were continuous with her attitude to contemporary British society. She was convinced that to sweep away such rituals—as if they were external and trivial practices—belittled the humanity of those who remained attached to them: it showed a high-minded contempt for the efforts of vulnerable groups to maintain their human dignity. In her view, a society without rituals was an impoverished society, stripped of its defenses against the antisocial behavior of its less community-minded members—many of whom, alas!, were rich, powerful, well educated, and, often, lethally high-minded.

It was not the Irish of Ireland whom Mary had in mind when she wrote the chapter on the "Bog Irish," but the immigrant Irish laborers in London whose "sense of exile is softened by a sense of continuity, the Irish newspapers sold outside Church after Mass, the weekly dances in the parish hall." It was they who were likely "to see on the doors of lodging houses: 'No Irish, no colored.'" For people in that situation, Friday abstinence was "no empty symbol, it means allegiance to a humble home in Ireland and a glorious tradition in Rome. . . .

6. Douglas, *Natural Symbols*, 37–53.

Who would dare to despise the cult of Friday abstinence who has not himself endured the life of the Irish laborer in London?"[7]

For this reason, Mary attacked what appeared to her to be the antiritualism of many of the post–Vatican II clergy. Their antiritualist stance was a serious matter. For, in her opinion, high-minded attacks on ritual weakened the paradoxical and largely unperceived supports of a decent society. Whether in society at large or in the church, the rejection of ritual was not the way "to humanize the system."[8]

Nothing could equal the verve with which Mary then went on to trace the congruence between antiritualist worldviews and "loose" social structures. She observed that intellectuals in general, and academics in particular, tended to emerge from environments where thoughts and words formed the primary basis of cohesion. Such persons were insensitive to the solid structures upheld by ritual.

As Mary saw it, societies could be graded according to the respect given to ritual as a means of social bonding. Some groups failed miserably. The Dutch Catholic bishops had recently produced a catechism that rejected most rituals, such as Friday fasting, and paid little attention even to the Eucharist. To Mary their attitude betrayed a dangerous level of "impoverished symbolic perception." The good bishops were "ritually tone deaf" and incapable of understanding what their own church meant to the millions who still sought it out as an anchor in a rootless world. It was the bishops and not the "Bog Irish" who were the true "primitives."[9]

I did not share Mary's passionate concern for the fate of the Catholic Church. But having watched many representatives of this reforming movement at the Oxford Patristics Conferences of 1963 and 1967, I sat up and took notice of her critique of antiritualism. For her, it was the expression of a vocal but limited niche in modern society occupied by academics and clergymen— persons produced by an unceremonious and loose-knit social environment.

Many Patristic scholars had, indeed, wished to get rid of the "primitive" inheritance of contemporary traditional Catholicism. A strong current of antiritualism had accompanied many of the very best efforts at *ressourcement*. Those who studied Christian practice—such as liturgy, penance, the care of the dead, and the cult of the saints—seemed to wish to see the Christianity

7. Douglas, *Natural Symbols*, 37–38.
8. Douglas, *Natural Symbols*, 159.
9. Douglas, *Natural Symbols*, 49.

of late antiquity as somehow more "enlightened" because less ritualistic than that of the later centuries. Even among the best scholars, it was normal to speak of a decline of Christianity from the more "spiritual" practices of the early church into the "barbaric" ritualism of the early Middle Ages.[10]

I came across these attitudes in abundance when I turned to the religious history of late antiquity. Along with Evans-Pritchard, Mary Douglas had made me aware of a challenging situation. A large proportion of the modern scholarly literature on the religious history of the ancient world—pagan, Jewish, and Christian alike—took absolutely for granted a division between the "primitive," ritualistic mentality of the masses and the enlightened ideas of the few that was as rigid as any maintained by a colonial government in the swamps of the Sudan, or advanced, nowadays, by critics of the Bog Irish.

These scholars tended to present late antiquity in a peculiarly sinister light. The great Martin Nilsson (1874–1967) spoke of it as a period when classical Greek religion became swamped with "Lower Forms of Belief" such as magic and demonology. This was "the most momentous and saddening development of the time . . . a thousand year nightmare that came to rest on humankind."[11] Even Sir Ronald Syme, not the most excitable of historians, was convinced that superstitious terror reigned throughout the fourth century AD: "High and low, Christian or pagan, the whole age was dominated by fear of supernatural forces."[12]

Such sweeping judgments (uttered with complete confidence) would not have been acceptable to any modern anthropologist. What would it be like to attempt to rewrite the religious history of late antiquity in less melodramatic terms, using the insights of Evans-Pritchard and Mary Douglas?

10. See, for example, A. Angenandt, *Das Frühmittelalter* (Stuttgart: Kohlhammer, 1990), 155–158.

11. M. Nilsson, *Geschichte der griechischen Religion*, 3rd ed. (Munich: C. H. Beck, 1974), 2:520 and 543.

12. R. Syme, *Ammianus and the Historia Augusta* (Oxford: Clarendon Press, 1968), 31.

SOCIETY AND THE SUPERNATURAL

TEXT AND CONTEXT

I felt that it was now up to me to attempt to look at the religious history of late antiquity with fresh eyes, inspired by what I had learned from Evans-Pritchard and Mary Douglas. I tried this out in a way that I had often done in Oxford: I advertised a new course of eight lectures, "Society and the Supernatural: Social and Religious Change from Marcus Aurelius to Muhammad," which I gave for the first time at five o'clock every Wednesday in the Hilary (the early spring) term of 1970.

The lectures took place in the Hovenden Room of All Souls College—a long, low-ceilinged cave of a place, with Jacobean paneling and a lack of lighting that added a mystic touch to almost any occasion. Like all my other Oxford lectures, these were free-floating events, open to all without commitment to a specific course. For this reason they were the perfect place in which to try out a new look at the relation between religion and society in late antiquity.

The texts of the first two lectures have survived, as have the bibliographies for all the others. They catch me at work, grappling with a new language with which to talk of social and religious change. As I reread them, they strike me as a vivid time capsule unearthed by chance half a century later. They were written so as to be spoken, not to be read. They make claims far more ambitious than I would ever make nowadays. But they catch the excitement of that moment.

First and foremost, I emphasized the difference between the historian who worked with religious beliefs contained in texts and the anthropologist who had daily access to the full context of these beliefs:

> I have been led to join the two [Society and the Supernatural] very largely because of the encouragement of the Social Anthropologists. What they

have to teach the historian is summed up neatly by one of them: While history is TEXTUAL, the studies of the anthropologist are contextual.[1]

> The student of the religious ideas of Late Antiquity begins [the other way round] with a vast body of religious <u>texts</u>.

To make this point, I drew on my recent reading of the seemingly boundless modern literature on sorcery beliefs in the later empire.

> To take an extreme example of the dangers of studying a body of ideas in texts alone, without attention to what the Social Anthropologist would call the context—sorcery in the Late Roman World. We have a vast body of texts that illustrate minutely the <u>technology</u> of sorcery—amulets, leaden cursing tablets, books of spells. They lead us into a world of higgledy-piggledy demonic powers (among them, "Jesus, great god of the Hebrews"), bad Greek and worse intentions.

The last phrase got a laugh. But this was my point: historians of religion interested in sorcery faced a superabundance of *texts*. By contrast, anthropologists approached sorcery in a very different manner:

> Compare Professor Evans-Pritchard, *Witchcraft, Oracles and Magic among the Azande*, Oxford 1937. He goes to a living tribe. He perceives what few students of ancient magic have perceived—that magic beliefs are not just a regrettable, unswept corner of irrational practices based on anti-social feelings, but that (among the Azande at least) they can be a sort of <u>common language</u>. . . . This shift to the <u>CONTEXT</u> results in our seeing the Azande and their problems of explaining themselves to themselves with more sympathy and understanding.

Demons in Context

Second: I argued that an attention to context enabled the scholar to dedramatize many of the more disturbing phenomena referred to in late antique texts. For instance: nothing could seem stranger to the modern reader than the sudden irruption of the demonic into the religious literature of late antiquity:

> Take one of the most important characters in Late Antique religious history: <u>the demons</u>. They pop out at us, fully articulated, in the pages of the religious <u>texts</u> of this period. Usually, they scare the living daylights out of us scholars. It is a firmly held belief that there were more of them, and that

1. R. Redfield, *Peasant Society and Culture* (Chicago: Phoenix Books, 1960), 51.

they inspired more dread, in the period after Marcus Aurelius than ever before. To enter Late Antiquity is like entering one of those ancient maps, with the slogan: "here be more and more demons."

But what did this irruption really mean? What did the demons look like if studied by anthropologists, such as Evans-Pritchard, rather than by conventional historians of late antique religion?

Let us ask the question crudely: what did people <u>gain</u> by believing in demons? That is, what anxieties were <u>allayed</u> by such a belief? <u>What system of control</u> was implicit in such a belief? Thus, what anxious unmanageable experience of Late Roman men was summed up and reduced to order by the idea of "a demon"?

Like witchcraft among the Azande, the demons often appeared as somewhat banal figures—as jinxes rather than as objects of occult terror. I cited a sixth-century Egyptian papyrus in which a demon was invoked, in a thoroughly undramatic manner, in a contract of divorce, in which the couple stated:

We were in time past joined to one another in marriage and community of life with fair hopes . . . thinking to maintain a peaceful and seemly married life with one another for the whole time of our joint lives; but on the contrary we have suffered from a sinister and wicked demon which attacked us unexpectedly from we know not whence, with a view to our being separated from one another. "After which," writes Professor Jones, "they get down to business details."[2]

Not much terror there. Why was this so? What made a belief in demons less troubling to late antique persons than we might think? I suggested that it was because such a belief kept evil within bounds. Like witchcraft among the Azande, demons were invoked because demons were fixable.

THE JACK-IN-THE-BOX

I then offered a different approach to historical change in late antiquity. Most views assumed that the apparent rise in belief in magic and demons in late antiquity could only be the result of some catastrophe. To sum up this view, I used the image of the Jack-in-the-box:

[In the Jack-in-the-box,] the spring of the irrational is held down by the culture of the élite. <u>We</u> are fairly sure either that we have the lid of our

2. A.H.M. Jones, *The Later Roman Empire* (Oxford: Blackwell, 1964), 2:975.

Jack-in-the-box well shut or that there is not much spring in the Jack. On the whole, we agree that, among ancient men, the lid was more loosely fastened and that the Jack had a more powerful spring. But we think that, in a certain period and among a certain élite, the lid was largely shut.

I went on to stress how much this Jack-in-the-box approach to the religious history of late antiquity fed into current, crude notions of "decline and fall," and especially into a melodramatic view of the "crisis of the third century":

> The very best accounts of Late Roman religious experience are still dominated by a fascination with the popping-up of the Jack-in-the-Box in the period after Marcus Aurelius. The religious evolution of Late Antiquity is still thought of as going in one direction only, AWAY from a classical ideal of civilization towards the Middle Ages; and this DIRECTION . . . is DOWN.

Hence the tendency to dramatize the so-called crisis of the third century as the catastrophe that unleashed these irrational beliefs. In the words of E. R. Dodds, one could expect nothing better from "a world so impoverished intellectually, so insecure materially, so filled with fear and hatred as the world of third century."[3]

Beyond the Third Century: A New Social History

But was the third century in any way like this? Ever since my first lectures, in 1958, I had spent much of my time attempting to modify contemporary views on the famous "crisis of the third century." I made plain that this period, though it witnessed major changes in the political and social structure of the empire, could not be described simply as a time of "catastrophe."

Altogether, I wanted to tell a new story about the later empire. I stressed the fact that Roman society would have a long future after the crisis of the third century. A revolution was followed by centuries of further, stable growth:

> The classical historian forgets this; it is enough for him to get the religious revolution on its way, in the 3rd century, and to assume that, by 400 A.D. at least, the damage was done—and that the medievalist better take over. This ignores the fascination of the 5th and 6th centuries, especially in the eastern Mediterranean. For there we can witness the social, political and

---

3. E. R. Dodds, *Pagan and Christian in an Age of Anxiety* (Cambridge University Press, 1965), 100.

religious stabilization of the Late Roman revolution. We can study this process in great detail up to the preaching of Muhammad in the early 7th century. And in the last century or so of this period, we can follow the subtle reassertion in Christian form of just those stabilizing forces that had buttressed the religious <u>consensus</u> of the pagan empire in the age of the Antonines. In this way, I think we shall come closer than if we were to concentrate solely on a supposed crisis of the 3rd century to understanding the social and religious transformation between Antiquity and the Middle Ages.

The lectures were a success. I put a lot into them. The Hovenden Room was crowded every Wednesday afternoon. The lists of signatures that I collected from those who attended my lectures from 1970 to 1973 (as I had done for my "Byzantium and Persia" lectures), reveal a colorful crowd of undergraduates and graduate students, with even a few dons.

Reading the list, I am struck by how many of those names are still well known to me, as colleagues and fellow adventurers in the field of late antique, early medieval, and Byzantine studies. Any reader in touch with the field will recognize them. In 1970, they were the future of what has become the present. There were dons, ancient and medieval—Ewen Bowie, an expert on the Second Sophistic and Greek culture in the age of the Antonines; Peter Parsons, a papyrologist; the indefatigable Geoffrey de Sainte Croix, with a large notebook open to record (with characteristic intellectual openness) ever more evidence of the vagaries of religious belief in the last centuries of an empire whose tensions he understood so well from a Marxist perspective; and Billy Pantin (1902–1973), a medievalist best known for his book on the English church in the fourteenth century.[4]

There were also a number of of my future colleagues, many of them now long-term friends, heroes, and heroines: Roger Collins, John Drinkwater, Garth Fowden, David Ganz, Martin Henig, James Howard-Johnston, David Hunt, Edward James, Rowena Loverance, Paul Magdalino, Judith McClure, Rosemary Morris, Sister Charles Murray, Oliver Nicholson, Richard Price, Francesco del Punta (later at Pisa), David Rollason, Philip Rousseau, Clare Stancliffe, Richard Vaggione, Otto Wermelinger (later at Fribourg-en-Suisse), Chris Wickham, Ian Wood, Patrick Wormald; and Sally Purcell, a poet, who was often a source of rare information in Dark Age matters.

4. W. Pantin, *The English Church in the Fourteenth Century* (Cambridge University Press, 1955).

A few years ago, David Ganz, later a leading early medieval paleographer and then an undergraduate at Merton College, sent me a moving memoir of these occasions, as seen through the eyes of an observant and streetwise student, of which there were many in Oxford at that time:

> On Wednesday afternoons at 5 [they] trooped into the Hovenden Room, a long Jacobean parlor with central table. The elect or the overbold sat on the dozen or so chairs, [with] senior members of the university. . . . Other chairs might be found against the wall, the lithe ventured into window embrasures, or even sat on the ugly television set which sometimes enhanced the room. On one memorable occasion three students were sitting on a drop leaf table and suddenly one side dropped. "Well, that se . . . e . . . eems to be the end of that" he interjected, and resumed the lecture, without missing a beat. Mostly we lay on the floor, carpeting it with uncomfortable bodies, scribbling our notes, or folding those strange grey xeroxes with handwritten bibliographies.

One should note this detail: the introduction of the photocopier machine, which happened at this time, led to a flowering of bibliographies such as had not been dreamed of before. In these bibliographies, works of anthropology and medical sociology mingled with up-to-date articles on aspects of the later empire: they were statements in themselves of the interdisciplinary tone of the lectures.

> But it was not just the range that made these lectures incomparable. The stammer came into its own as a rhetorical tool, and he did the holy men in different voices. I still remember the desert father Pambo tempted by demons carrying feathers on a stick and crying out "Go, go". All of us laughed, only to be told how the holy man did not laugh, for to laugh is to dissolve, the holy man had to be hard as clay. "Are you human?" the lay man asked Symeon Stylites. The holy man, we found, was the self made man, another Julien Sorel. In defining the holy man and his temptations the lectures offered a way of defining oneself. We all struggled with the demon of fornication, but here we learned that men were perceived as sons of their mothers, and women were the sources of all that is stable and enveloping. We learned of the pressure to atomization and differentiation, instead of explorations of late Roman power we heard about solidarity and concord. Best of all, these holy men erected antitheses to their past. The new self made man, keeping his wits about him, was the hero. And the demons were

the extension of the self "Our wills, turned into demons, make war against us". They were sixties figures, the rebels we had come too late to join; the anchorite in flight from the tax-collector, "this meant bumming off", the tenant farmers attacking the patron, the saint intimate with the imaginary private being. And they explored those areas we wanted to dodge: watering the ground with their tears, opening their life to grief.

Beyond the magic, the sense of excited awe which left most of us silent as we left the Hovenden Room and looked up at the emerging stars.

OXFORD UNDER STRAIN

The Ominous Bulge

It was around this time that I remember standing with Dick Southern on the edge of the Codrington Quadrangle as Venus and Mars burned in the western sky, alongside the dome of the Radcliffe Camera. He asked me what it must have been like for a medieval person to look up at those planets. Thinking of Ibn Gabirol and his vision of a universe shot through with energies radiating from the planets, I suggested that it must have been strange to look up at those two points of light, and to imagine them to be mere pinholes in the opaque firmament that stood between earth and the intolerable blaze of the true heavens—miniature lenses through which streamed the disruptive influences of love and war: so much trouble on earth caused by such tiny orbs!

It was a very Oxford encounter. But Oxford itself was changing. My publications of this time (my article "The Rise and Function of the Holy Man" and *The World of Late Antiquity*) now appear in bibliographies and footnotes as if they were weight-free products, linked one to the other by purely intellectual agendas. But this, of course, was not how they happened. They emerged against a background of conflicts in an Oxford that was, in many ways, a tired and angry place.

Part of the reason for this sense of strain lay in the sheer weight of numbers pressing against a rigid teaching system. "The ominous demographic bulge pushing up through the primary and secondary schools" all over Europe, as a result of the baby boom of the postwar years, had come to affect even Oxford.[1] The student body grew by a fifth—to almost nine thousand.

1. Tony Judt, *Postwar: A History of Europe since 1945* (New York: Penguin, 2005), 393.

Compared with the explosion of university students in Europe and the three-fold growth of the student population in Britain as a whole, this was a mere touch. But it was felt as the touch of the finger of a giant. The ancient teaching system began to creak. Too many undergraduates were passing through the colleges. Too many by far seemed to be turning up at tutorials.

Almost for the first time, the Oxford tutorial system appeared to be at risk. The articles and correspondence for and against tutorials in the *Oxford Magazine* of that time give the impression of a university whose principal teaching medium was under question. Tony Quinton (1925–2010)—later Lord Quinton and the president of Trinity College—spoke for many of us: "How has this wasteful and exhausting practice come about?" He pointed out that dons were tied to fifteen hours a week of tutorials, in each of which the same, predictable set of problems would be thrashed out with each student. It was the life of a galley slave, not of a scholar. He wondered "whether we should not be more effectively propelled through the heavy waters of the bulge" by other teaching devices—undergraduate seminars and carefully coordinated lecture courses.[2]

The Tutorial under Strain

In 1966 the Franks Report appeared. It amounted to an inquiry as to whether Oxford was up to the job of preparing students for the modern world. In the report, the tutorial system received a reprieve. According to many, only the tutorial system provided the intimacy of a one-on-one relation with a teacher on which the Oxford system of education was based. The tutor

> has rooms in a college which is small enough to have something of the atmosphere of a family. His own pupils come to him as individuals. . . . He is aware of them not as blurred outlines of an audience [at lectures] but as sharply defined characters sitting by his fireplace.[3]

But was this cozy scene what really happened? By 1969, 61 percent of students in history were being sent—"farmed out" was the term used—to tutors outside their college, especially for teaching in the increased number of Further and Special Subjects.[4]

---

2. A. Quinton, *Oxford Magazine* 70 (May 19 and June 9, 1960): 284 and 324.

3. *Report of the Commission of Inquiry*, paragraph 208 (Oxford: Clarendon Press, 1966), 1:98.

4. Brian Harrison, *Oxford Magazine*, March 14, 1969.

This situation caused the rigidity of the history syllabus (and of other syllabuses) to stand out that much more clearly. As we have already seen, the anxieties aroused by a system geared to a single and irrevocable final examination had always encouraged tutors to concentrate only on topics that would be certain to "come up" in the final exam. The cost of this rigidity became ever more clear now that the study of different periods or different sorts of history became easier to envision. Even the proud school of Litterae Humaniores had begun to realize that there was more ancient history "out there" than the narrow tracts studied for the final examination.

> The influences of syllabuses on research, given the Oxford climate, is a frightening thing, and it would be a disaster in the long run if the concentration on the high classical periods for teaching discouraged the teachers from widening their horizons, and especially from venturing into post-classical literature, thought and history.[5]

But, all too often, the tutorial system was invoked to block any widening of horizons. One retired don had already declared:

> The demand for wider history American, Asian and African is objectionable. . . . It would burden the tutors. . . . [Indeed] it seems to be infected with the most pernicious of all educational heresies—that which would identify education with the acquisition of useful information.[6]

WOMEN

Such debates were not new. But in the late 1960s and early 1970s, my interstitial position as a research fellow at All Souls College, a little to one side of the teaching routines of the other colleges, made me that much more aware of the underlying tensions that these debates addressed. There was one important change that crept on me almost without my noticing it. I found myself teaching many more students from the women's colleges. As a research fellow of All Souls, I had always been called to teach students on topics not usually taught by college tutors: the Further Subject on Byzantium and its neighbors, the

---

5. D. A. Russell, "Litterae Humaniores 1968," *Oxford Magazine*, February 23, 1968, 208.

6. Reginald Lennard, "The Modern History School," *Oxford Magazine*, n.s., 2 (January 25, 1962): 143.

Augustine Special Subject, and the earlier periods of European history. These topics had become increasingly popular. By the late 1960s, I found that as many as half of the students who were farmed out to me for tutorials in these topics were women, although women were only one-fifth of the undergraduate population.

The reader may be surprised that this was so significant a turning point for me. That a not-so-young man of thirty-five should find increased contact with women as a teacher to be something of a novelty seems barely credible. But, as I have already pointed out, from 1942 to 1952 I had lived in all-male boarding schools, with contact with women and girls of my age only in the holidays. My last experience of coeducation had been at kindergarten at the age of six. Indeed, my parents could have thought of no other form of education for me. Even day schools (where the students lived at home) were for boys only or for girls only. If I had had a sister, she would have been fitted into the grooves of a single-sex education quite as much as I had been.

Oxford was no different. Colleges were resolutely single-sex until 1974. The system of women's colleges mirrored that of the men. The tutors of the women's colleges were entirely female, just as the tutors of the men's college were entirely male. Oxford was divided into colleges: of these, only five were for women, and all the rest were for men. As a result, in 1960s Oxford, men and women lived on different planets to a degree that is now barely imaginable.

There was one narrow bridge between the two worlds that widened at this time: that is, the practice of farming out female students to male tutors in subjects off the beaten track of the History School, such as my own. It was in this way that I came to know many woman tutors with whom I would not otherwise have had any institutional link. I had long known and admired many woman scholars, such as Marjorie Reeves; but as an undergraduate I had never had the opportunity to be taught by a woman. What relations I had with the women's colleges were purely personal. They amounted to links with individual tutors, through agreeing to take on students interested in my own field.

I have recently discovered among my papers a correspondence concerning one student from Lady Margaret Hall. It is a time capsule of a highly personalized teaching system at work—in a series of ad hoc arrangements, tutor to tutor, in what is now a very distant Oxford. Anne Whiteman (1918–2000), the principal tutor for medieval historians in Lady Margaret Hall, approached me in the summer of 1969 to arrange tutorials for a student in the coming academic year.

> Dear Peter,
>
> I am writing to ask you whether you could find time in the next academic year to take a pupil of mine for Period I [European History, 284–717]. . . . She is both very eccentric and intelligent and I think that you may find her rather <u>gauche</u>. . . .
>
> I am sure she has considered her choice of subject very carefully. . . .
>
> I very much hope that you will be able to fit her in. If you can do so, will you kindly let me know when you would like to see her about vacation reading?
>
> I know that I may seem to be anticipating things rather by writing to you now, but sad experience shows that under present competitive conditions it is essential to approach one's friends early in the season.

"A Quiet Domesticity, Inimical to Intellectual Ambitions"

Male prejudice throve on this division of the sexes. In donnish circles, women were only too often treated as bluestockings and what we would now call "overachievers." The female dons were deemed to be formidable—veritable dragons. The performances of their charges in the final examination was kept uniformly, depressingly, high: they seemed to fill the second class (in American parlance, the solid B++ range).

Occasionally, the *Oxford Magazine* addressed this theme with a streak of nasty irony that was, alas, only too revealing of widespread attitudes. In 1966, "A Tutorial Typography" appeared, as an "Unsolicited Supplement to the Franks Report." It presented a gallery of stereotypes, in which women emerged consistently as caricatures of the least acceptable type of male. There was the Energetic Examinee, to whom tutorials were a means to a career and who only considered writing essays on topics sure to "come up" in Schools. It adds: "Females wear glasses, cardigans, heavy shoes and stoop." Then there was

> the Phlegmatic Plodder: heavy jawed and grimly determined. Writes long, jejune outpourings weekly; accepts criticism, but never applies it. Drink: nothing stronger than cocoa. . . . Often female.

But their teacher, the Militant Martinet was worst of all:

> While less conscientious fellows are sunning themselves in summer deck chairs, militant martinets are eagerly scanning the examination results. Often female.[7]

Behind these toxic jibes one can sense the turning of an age. For over a century, Oxford had endeavored to produce imperial administrators and civil servants of the old style, brisk and adaptable: manly men with manly minds— argumentative, tough-minded, taught to think on their feet. Many believed that the inclusion of women would somehow weaken this tough-minded culture. One of the most revealing arguments produced against mixed-sex colleges at this time, when they were first mooted in the 1970s, was that life with women would eventually lead to "a quiet domesticity, inimical to high intellectual ambitions and the cut-and-thrust of academic argument."[8]

In such an atmosphere, certain forms of history became gendered. "Real history" (a distant but faithful echo of the "grown-up" history of Duke Senior) still consisted in the standard fare of political and institutional history as taught by tutors in history. What room would there be in Oxford for other, "softer" forms of history, such as the history of religion and ideas? But for me and for many of my students, these were among the most exciting aspects of the field of late antiquity: to opt for late antiquity was not only to opt for a little-known period; it was also to opt for a little-taught kind of history. What breathing space was there for such history in a university that was still locked, in so many ways, into ancient habits?

GRADUATES

As far as women were concerned, deep-rooted prejudices dissolved slowly. It was not until the year that I left Oxford, in 1974, that five male colleges agreed to accept women. But change had begun in yet another group of marginals— the graduate students.

At this time, I was brought into ever-closer contact with graduate students in late antique and medieval history. Many of these graduate students (the "postgraduates," to use the Oxford term) came from America. I had already

7. *Oxford Magazine*, Michaelmas 7, 1966, 121–124.

8. *Oxford Magazine*, November 20, 1970, 83.

been in contact with a few such students; but from January 1971 onward I became directly concerned with them as a group, through serving on the Board of the History Faculty as the representative of the medievalists. I was, in effect, a stand-in for the current Chichele Professor, Geoffrey Barraclough (1908–1984), who, with an insouciance worthy of a late medieval pluralist, seldom came to England (we were told, for complex reasons of tax avoidance) and rarely appeared in Oxford.

Through the Applications Committee, I would vet the applications for admission of potential medievalists. I would then meet them once they arrived. This was a pleasant occasion, when I got to know them personally and discussed their projected dissertations. As a result, the future leaders in many fields passed my way. For instance: one of the notes in my engagement diary was a somewhat incredulous entry: "Paul Magdalino, VLACHS??" Now a doyen of Byzantine studies, Paul had intrigued me by suggesting a study of the nomadic pastoralists of late Byzantine northern Greece.

With the American and other foreign graduates, I would attach to their name a list of Oxford medievalists (other than their official supervisor) whom they could contact for advice and, generally, to get themselves known in Oxford. I would then be on the phone to those colleagues, urging them to take an interest in this or that young person. Some responded handsomely. Paul Hyams, for instance, arranged evening "at homes." At such gatherings I would meet many Americans and Canadians, thereby entering into a world of different universities and scholars; and I would hear of non-British approaches to medieval history of which I had previously known little.

Yet, by and large, the situation was deplorable. Even Lord Franks admitted, "It must be confessed that the care of post-graduates has been the blurred panel in the triptych of academic activity in Oxford."[9] I was shocked but not surprised that this should be so. The grip of the college and of the tutorial system on undergraduates left most dons with little energy or interest left over for other categories of students: it was like expecting a person with a broken arm to lift yet another stone. So graduate students were left dangling. I had read Mary Douglas's *Purity and Danger* carefully enough to know that persons and animals who did not fit into the normal classifications of a society were usually treated as "loose," "impure" creatures—vaguely threatening objects for whom no right place could be found. In Oxford, graduate students in history were like that.

---

9. *Report of the Commission of Inquiry* , paragraph 60, p. 26.

Too "Late" to be Respectable

I would not have felt this so strongly if I had not shared with many of my friends the feeling that we, also, represented a field that did not as yet quite fit in. As an academic enterprise, the study of the later empire—at least, at the graduate level—had come to stay. But it resisted classification. It notably fell outside the firm definition of ancient history that was current in the one school to which the late Roman period should have belonged—the School of Litterae Humaniores: the school of classics, where Latin and Greek (up to a high standard) were part of the normal equipment of a young scholar.

All over Britain—and especially in Oxford, Cambridge, and London—there were young scholars who had, as it were, "gone late." But they continued to fear that this deviation from the conventional framework of ancient history and literature might stand in their way in the job market.

My correspondence with Averil Cameron shows how this situation weighed on her as on many others. After her fine dissertation on Agathias, Averil applied for a readership in classics in King's College London. As she wrote to me at the time, she was careful to make sure that the committee knew all about her publications on "straight" classical topics: "I don't need to explain myself to you I know, but I also know that there are those who think that you cannot be interested in both literature and history at the same time!—or in more than one period of history at once!" Her husband, Alan, was anxious on her behalf: "I suppose they may consider her (as people do me) too 'late' to be quite respectable—but she got alphas on every paper in Greats (as she did also for Mods, no mean achievement), and is very well informed about the early Principate." Rereading Alan's letter, I noticed the "but": success in Greats was still the ultimate, unchanged standard of judgment.

John Matthews, whose work on the Western aristocracies I have already mentioned, was another "unclassifiable" late Romanist. He was fortunate to be appointed to a lectureship in late Roman history (a post created at the urging of Ronald Syme) in 1969. But his relations with the majority of teachers in Litterae Humaniores were always tense. On one occasion, we were at a meeting together in an attempt to see how some periods of late Roman history might be taught to undergraduates in classes open to students from the History School as well as from Litterae Humaniores. The meeting did not go well. He wrote to me afterward: "Some of the opinions I found frankly unbelievable. . . . You were absolutely right on what undergraduates want. . . . Some of the prejudices which I heard last night seemed rather personal as well."

THE SEMINAR AND THE PHOTOCOPIER MACHINE

What is interesting about this outburst of frustration is that it centered, once again, on the issue of undergraduate teaching. John had suggested seminar classes on wide themes; but could any teaching count as proper teaching except that offered through tutorials? At the meeting, many doubted this. They considered late Roman topics to be too new and too complicated to be passed on to undergraduates through tutorials. Therefore, they argued, late Roman history could not be taught.

Hence a dichotomy in the outlook of the ancient historians in Oxford. On the level of undergraduate teaching, changes happened with glacial slowness. Yet one of the most heartening features of this time was the flourishing of advanced seminars attended largely by graduates and faculty members. Here many of the classics dons of Oxford showed themselves to be admirable colleagues. At these seminars, all dons were equal, and all were equally happy to pitch in and learn in an atmosphere closer to that of a learned society than a rigidly hierarchical seminar. Geoffrey de Sainte Croix, for instance, was a regular presence at such meetings, as well as many others. It was through these seminars, many of them organized by Fergus Millar and by John Matthews, that late antiquity got under way among ancient historians in Oxford.

And for this to happen, one unsung hero remains to be praised: the photocopier machine. It is impossible to overestimate its importance for the freeing-up of scholarship in the late 1960s and 1970s. It both multiplied and delocalized knowledge. To understand this, we must conjure up a world where huge accumulations of books went hand in hand with an acute shortage of available copies of any one book. No book could be taken out of the Bodleian Library, and even when the libraries were circulating—as in the case of the Ashmolean—there was usually only one copy of each book.

The photocopier machine suddenly made this knowledge accessible at any time and in any place. I could take with me photocopies of the lives of saints and the acts of church councils that until then had been available only in vast tomes stored in the far corner of Duke Humphrey Library, and read them anywhere.

Better still, the photocopier machine made the same texts available at the same time to any number of people who wished to study them. To take, for example, my very first experience of a photocopied text: the notorious *Carmen adversus paganos*—the Poem against the pagans—was a lampoon written by an anonymous Christian author against an unknown pagan leader of Roman society, sometime in the late fourth century. It was a dramatic text, crucial for our knowledge of the last days of Roman paganism. The great Theodor Mommsen had dated it to the year 394, to the time of the last great pagan, Nicomachus Flavianus, when momentary hopes for a pagan revival were raised at a time of a civil war.

But was Mommsen right? Edited in the Teubner edition of classical texts, the *Carmen adversus paganos* had stood for decades in Bodley (to be exact: in the Lower Reading Room, along with all the other Teubner editions, near the circulation desk). Now, through the photocopier, each of us could have our own copy of the poem to read anywhere at our leisure. John Matthews, Timothy Barnes, and I each took home a copy of the text—a sticky yellow photocopy—and read it at our leisure. Each of us came up with a different judgment as to the date, the author, and the person attacked.[10] This was a situation, brought about by a machine, from which magical seminars would grow in future years.

10. See, most recently, Alan Cameron, *The Last Pagans of Rome* (Oxford University Press, 2011), 273–319, with a translation on 806–808.

THE HOLY MAN

Concordance

By early 1970, I had completed "The Rise and Function of the Holy Man in Late Antiquity." In that article, I attempted to explain the rise to prominence of a group of unlikely figures: the holy men of Syria, whose most flamboyant representative had been Symeon Stylites (396–459)—so-called because he stood on top of a *stylé*—a sixty-foot pillar. I asked how it was that Symeon and those like him came to crystallize an entire imaginative world around their persons. Furthermore, I asked how the rise of the holy man in late antiquity cast light on the evolution of late Roman religion and society in general throughout the Mediterranean and the Middle East.

I chose to study figures such as Symeon Stylites partly for their known shock value. To Edward Gibbon (1737–1794), Symeon, as presented by his hagiographic biographer, Bishop Theodoret of Cyrrhus (393–ca. 458), represented the nadir of the long decline of civilization in a decaying Roman Empire:

> If it be possible to measure the interval between the philosophic writings of Cicero and the sacred legend of Theodoret, between the character of Cato and that of Simeon, we may appreciate the memorable revolution which was accomplished in the Roman empire within a period of five hundred years.[1]

If such a figure could be delivered from the scorn of Gibbon, then our view of an entire age might come to be revised.

1. Edward Gibbon, *The Decline and Fall of the Roman Empire*, ed. David Womersley (London: Allen Lane, Penguin Press, 1994), chapter 37, 2:429.

This article has been widely discussed; and I have offered my own thoughts about it in relation to the field of late antiquity as a whole.[2] In this chapter I will concentrate, rather, on the immediate circumstances of its writing—how I came to put it together and what new approaches and recent discoveries inspired me.

First and foremost, I approached the subject with the wind of Mary Douglas's *Natural Symbols* full in my sails. She and Evans-Pritchard had effectively demolished the notion of a "primitive mentality" with all the ugly freight of contempt that went with it. Given the tenacity of such prejudices in the field of ancient religious history, this was no small deliverance.

But Mary Douglas's *Natural Symbols* (which I had read in typescript a year before it appeared) took me one step further. In *Natural Symbols* Mary resolved a dualism that weighed heavily on the study of religion and society in the later empire. Everyone wrote as if, somehow, religion and society were two distinct things. It seemed as if the scholar's business was to measure the impingement of the one on the other. How much were religious movements "pushed" by social forces? How much did religious ideas "impinge" on society?

Mary Douglas offered an alternative to this dualism. She urged scholars to look at religion and society as if they were the two faces of the same social structure, which, as it were, spoke of its own stresses and strains through the language of religion—through myths and dogmas, through rituals, through narratives of miracles, and through accounts of the lives of holy persons. Somehow, the one mirrored the other. Mary put it very clearly, in a later introduction to *Natural Symbols*: in any given group there was always a "concordance between symbolic and social experience." In her opinion, this concordance was so intimate that "we should be able to say what kinds of universe are likely to be constructed when social relations take this or that form."[3]

2. Peter Brown, "The Rise and Function of the Holy Man in Late Antiquity," *Journal of Roman Studies* 61 (1971): 80–101, now in *Society and the Holy in Late Antiquity* (Berkeley: University of California Press, 1982), 103–152, at 103. For my own rethinking of many of the issues raised in this article, see Peter Brown, "The Rise and Function of the Holy Man in Late Antiquity, 1971–1997," *Journal of Early Christian Studies* 6 (1998): 353–376, and, most recently (on Syrian asceticism), *Treasure in Heaven: The Holy Poor in Early Christianity* (Charlottesville: University Virginia Press, 2016).

3. Mary Douglas, *Natural Symbols: Explorations in Cosmology*, new ed. (London: Routledge, 1996), xxxv and viii–ix.

This was no small claim. I doubt very much if I followed Mary's views as consequentially as she might have wished. I had no desire to reduce religious phenomena to mere expressions of the creaking of a social system. But the hint that social and religious phenomena should be studied together with an eye to their possible concordance inspired me. Rather than any particular information or sociological doctrine, Mary passed on to me a confidence that such work could be done. Her notion of "concordance" offered an entirely new way of viewing the relation between religion and society, as the one mirrored the other in a time of momentous change.

This approach also encouraged me to turn to whole new bodies of evidence in my research. I was no longer limited to a privileged body of texts. Like an anthropologist in the field, I could treat anything as a potential clue to the workings of late Roman society. Indeed, the more commonplace the evidence, the more likely it was to throw light on the intimate stresses and strains from which the religious imagination grew. The wording of stray inscriptions; lines from a magical papyrus; an iconographic detail on a mosaic; a dream book or a long-neglected collection of horoscopes—all were potential evidence for the structures of society and for their imaginative echo in religious belief and practice. This was a major change for me. Within less than four years I had abandoned the writings of Augustine and similar grand texts, to scramble through the undergrowth of evidence for the religious and social practices of an entire East Roman society.

As a result, I left the Bodleian Library for the Ashmolean Library of classical history and archaeology. Here was God's plenty. To take one example only: it was there that I found the magnificent two volumes, *Les villages antiques de la Syrie du Nord* by Georges Tchalenko (1905–1987), which laid out, for the first time, the archaeology of the villages of northern Syria in which Symeon Stylites had been active.[4]

HAGIOGRAPHY AND HISTORY: FROM NORMAN BAYNES (1877–1961) TO DERWAS CHITTY (1901–1971)

Faced by a world of archaeology, epigraphy, and papyrology that had suddenly opened up before me, I also turned to a tradition with which I was already well acquainted. There was in England a well-established scholarly and religious

4. G. Tchalenko, *Les villages antiques de la Syrie du Nord* (Paris: Institut français de Beyrouth, 1953).

interest in the monasticism and hagiography of the East Roman Empire. This field had an outstanding advocate in Norman Baynes.

Baynes summed up in his person the challenge of Byzantine studies to the educated public as a whole, at a time when Byzantium was little regarded. He came from a leading Baptist family. His uncle was editor of the *Encyclopaedia Britannica*, and his father was general secretary of the Baptist Missionary Society. He himself continued to preach on occasions: hence his masterly historical introduction to the history of ancient Judaism, *Israel among the Nations*, which I had read in my first years at All Souls. He practiced law for a time; and during World War II he produced for the government the authoritative translation of Hitler's speeches. A brilliant speaker himself, he knew the sinister power of words.

Baynes always thought of himself as a "cockney," devoted to London University, where he held a personal chair in Byzantine studies. I knew him best from a series of brilliant and passionately presented articles and lectures, in which he already drew attention to the importance of holy men of monastic background in what he called the "thought-world" of East Rome. In many ways, my essay on the holy man was an attempt to explain, in modern terms, a phenomenon that Norman Baynes already highlighted as central to the study of Byzantium.[5]

Baynes also pointed to the importance of Byzantine saints' lives for our knowledge of East Roman society. These lives often presented a bottom-up view of society that was almost entirely lacking in other, elite sources. In a brilliant little article, Baynes had shown how much we could learn about the religion of average Byzantines—their passions, their fears, their deep religious loves—from a single text such as the early seventh-century collection of pious tales, the *Spiritual Garden* of John Moschus (ca. 550–619). With Elizabeth Dawes, Baynes had also translated and commented on three major saints' lives, on which I depended at every turn.[6]

Baynes died soon after I was elected to All Souls. But his approach to Byzantine studies was represented magnificently in 1960s Oxford by the Reverend Derwas Chitty. I did not know Chitty personally, but he was an iconic figure

---

5. N. H. Baynes, "The Thought-World of East Rome," in *Byzantine Studies and Other Essays* (London: Athlone Press, 1960), 24–246, at 43–46. Brown, "Rise and Function of the Holy Man," 103–104.

6. N. H. Baynes, "The *Pratum Spirituale*" (1947), in *Byzantine Studies and Other Essays*, 261–270; and *Three Byzantine Saints* (Oxford: Blackwell, 1948).

for me. He was the very model of the learned Anglican clergyman. Since 1931, he had been vicar of Upton, near Didcot, in the Vale of the White Horse—a strangely deserted countryside that had been isolated for centuries by a change in the course of the river Thames. I saw him first at the garden party associated with the Oxford Patristics Conference of 1967. He was seated in a chair on the Deanery Lawn of Christ Church surrounded by friends and ceremonious Eastern monks and bishops—a large man with a game leg and a great white beard shining against a face tanned to the color of terracotta (the result, one felt, of many daring visits to the monasteries of the Judaean Desert).

He was a passionate man. Dimitri Obolensky once told me that, as a boy, he had been sent to live with Derwas to perfect his English. One day, Derwas spotted a rabbit which had invaded the vegetable garden that he maintained with monastic intensity. Enraged by this intrusion, he slammed his hand against the glass pane of the kitchen window so hard that it shattered with the blow.

Chitty's *The Desert a City* appeared in 1966.[7] It came as a revelation to me. It was my entry into the human—indeed, the humane—side of the early Christian monastic movement. First delivered as the Birkbeck Lectures in Cambridge in 1958/59, Chitty's account of the origins and spread of the monastic movement in Egypt, Palestine, and elsewhere in the Middle East was a masterpiece of condensed original research: with characteristic modesty he warned the reader that "not a little original research lies buried in the notes."[8] But he treated this tangled tale in a conversational tone of voice that made three hundred years of monastic experience (from Saint Anthony in the late third century to the Islamic conquests of the seventh) sound like an extended family saga, with its unforgettable characters, its high hopes, bitter disappointments, and tragic family feuds.

These were not the monks as they were usually presented. They were not masochists, driven by hatred of the body. The desert was not always an uncanny, hostile place for them: they often responded to its beauty and were content with the little nooks of water and greenery hidden among the dunes of Egypt and in the arid folds of the hills and wadis of Palestine.[9] Nor were they all fanatics. Chitty constantly reminded us of their gentler role as

---

7. Derwas Chitty, *The Desert a City: An Introduction to the Study of Egyptian and Palestinian Monasticism under the Christian Empire* (Oxford: Blackwell, 1966).

8. Chitty, *Desert a City*, x.

9. Chitty, *Desert a City*, 4 and 6.

mentors and men of peace. In the words of one of them, Dorotheus of Gaza (ca. 505–565),

> For I tell you, brethren, that there is not a pagan, or a Jew . . . who has genuine piety and gentleness, who is not loved and found acceptable with God.[10]

Eventually, Chitty bequeathed his library to the House of St. Gregory and St. Macrina, adjacent to the Orthodox church in Canterbury Road (near Summertown in North Oxford). His donation was a testimony to his lifelong commitment to a union of the Anglican and the Orthodox churches, in the hope that this union would allow something of that ancient sweetness and warmth to flow back into the more frigid Christianity of the West.[11]

"THE MOST SAVAGE PRIMITIVE": A.-J. FESTUGIÈRE (1898–1982)

Chitty's humane approach to the ascetics of Egypt and Palestine was unusual. A far more representative figure, in his attitude to monasticism in general and to the monks of Syria in particular, was the great Dominican scholar André-Jean Festugière. The works of the two men were very present to me in those years. They could not have been more different in their treatment of the monks.

Festugière was a magical exponent and translator of Greek thought and mysticism in the classical and postclassical age. His *Personal Religion among the Greeks* was a classic evocation of the ever more intense turning of religious persons toward flight from the world and the contemplation of God in Hellenistic times and later. The four volumes of his magisterial *La Révélation d'Hermès Trismégiste* traced what was, for him, the sinister mutation of Greek thought in the course of the second and third centuries AD in the direction of the occult and a reliance on revelation rather than on reason.[12]

Here was a man whose heart was firmly in the classical world. I remember, as a young prize fellow, attending a lecture that he gave on the Hellenism of Libanius of Antioch (314–393), the famous *rhetor* of the fourth century, and his relations with his students. Sprawling in his great black gown across a large

---

10. Chitty, *Desert a City*, 152.

11. See Kallistos Ware, "Derwas Chitty (1901–1971)," *Eastern Churches Review* 6 (1974): 1–6.

12. A.-J. Festugière, *Personal Religion among the Greeks* (Berkeley: University of California Press, 1960) and *La Révélation d'Hermès Trismégiste*, 4 vols. (Paris: Gabalda, 1950–1954).

chair in golden oak, he gave the sort of talk that gives graduate students the most precious gift of all—the gift of perseverance. After hearing Festugière, I was determined to continue the study of the later empire.

But when he turned to the monks of Antioch[13] and produced a series of remarkable translations of the lives of monastic saints in Egypt, Syria, and Palestine, Festugière treated his subjects with a contempt more toxic even than the scorn of Gibbon. He was utterly dismissive of their thought-world, and of the role of demons in it. On such topics, he spoke with the shrill voice of the nineteenth-century French "civilizing mission" in Africa and the Middle East.

> Let us go back to the demons. Let us try to imagine for ourselves the terrors of those persons of the past. Let us try to get into the skin of such people [the monks], whose modes of thought and feeling do not really rise above those of the most savage primitive lost in the forests of Equatorial Africa.[14]

Once, when asked by my friend Pierre Hadot what he thought of the monks of East Rome, Festugière answered, with a full load of colonial contempt: "*Fakirs!*" (a derogatory term used by the British in India for Hindu and Muslim holy men).[15]

It was this contempt, as much for modern Africans as for ancient monks, that I was determined to overcome. But how would I set about it? Prompted by Mary Douglas's notion of concordance, I would try to fit the holy men of Syria and elsewhere into the precise context of the society in which they were active, so as to explain their prominence: What was it about the stresses and strains of that society which caused it to turn to such apparently untoward figures for leadership and guidance?

Figures in a Landscape

In many ways, I had picked the right moment to do this. Knowledge of the social conditions of the East Roman Empire had begun to progress by leaps and bounds, in a way that challenged many of the stereotypes on which conventional outline histories of the late Roman Empire had been based.

---

13. A. J. Festugière, *Antioche païenne et chrétienne* (Paris: de Boccard, 1959), 245–310.

14. A. J. Festugière, *Les Moines d'Orient*, vol. 1, *Culture et Sainteté* (Paris: Le Cerf, 1961), 33.

15. P. Hadot *Annuaire de l'École pratique des Hautes Études* 92 (1983–1984): 31–35.

Archaeological surveys of the countryside outside Antioch—the Limestone Massif, still known after its hero as the Djebel Sem ʿan (Symeon's Mountain)— where Symeon had been active, contradicted the notion that the countryside was occupied by a uniformly impoverished and oppressed peasantry. Far from it: this was not a society of broken-backed serfs. It was a new society of upwardly mobile and intensely competitive villagers. It was up to me to try to find a place for the holy men of Syria as figures in this ebullient landscape.

The work of Tchalenko and others showed that the inhabitants of these villages were new men. I suggested that they also needed new leaders. They needed persons who could link their villages to the wider world, and who could act, like the "governor" of an engine, to calm the tensions that arose from the impact among them of new wealth and new opportunities. They needed patrons. But what was a patron like in the Eastern Empire?

"The Good Patron Writ Large"

The archaeological discovery of a new society in the villages of the Middle East went along with recent discoveries by scholars of late Roman legal texts and of Egyptian papyri. These documents showed that many of the institutions which bulked large in conventional accounts of the later empire were being used in new ways by an enterprising peasantry. This was particularly the case with the well-known phenomenon of the patronage of villages by powerful persons. Until then, scholars had assumed that the growth of such patronage had been an entirely negative development. It was thought to mark the rise of "proto-feudal" conditions in the countryside—an ominous prelude to the Middle Ages.

Now this negative image had begun to change. Papyrologists such as the supremely gifted Roger Rémondon (1923–1971) showed that Egyptian villagers were well capable of manipulating patronage networks to their own advantage—setting one patron against the other and expecting benefits from their patron on the ground, in the form of arbitration and protection from rival villages.[16] In the case of Syria, I found that the work of Wolfgang Liebeschuetz on the social history of Antioch and its hinterland in the fourth century was decisive. I had read the manuscript of his book before it was published, and found there exactly what I needed—the possibility that villagers could use

16. R. Rémondon, *La crise de l'empire romain* (Paris: Presses Universitaires de France, 1964), 302–308.

powerful patrons for their own ends. For them, there could be such a thing as "a good patron."[17]

In recovering agency for the villagers of the Middle East, I realized that I had found a place in village society for holy men such as Symeon. These seemingly bizarre figures slid with ease into a template of expectations carved for them by the activities of the good patron. Their actions mirrored faithfully those of rural men of power. Their curses and blessings enforced norms of village neighborliness and imposed peace on rival households. Their prayers of intercession frequently moved not only God in his distant Heaven but the great of the land in distant Antioch.

Gradually, I discovered that the holy men of Syria were not wild, spaced-out recluses. They did their job, day in and day out, as mediators and peace-keepers in a boisterous rural world that needed their services. Symeon Stylites was the most awesomely remote of such holy men. Yet even he intervened in the daily life of the villages so as to impose water rationing in times of drought. He wrote to the priest of one village laying down acceptable rates of interest. Perched sixty feet up on his column, but constantly visited by suppliants and little delegations from the churches of the rich lands at the foot of the Limestone Massif, Symeon was "the lion . . . before whose roar the oppressors trembled." Altogether, "Symeon, the model holy man of the early Byzantine world, was the 'good patron' writ large."[18]

It was for this reason that I always spoke of the holy *man*. This was not due to a failure to be inclusive. There were many holy women in the Syrian world. They played many roles. Some were remembered as legendary martyrs, others as leaders in large convents, and yet others as saintly lovers of the poor and as fearless protectors of dissident groups. Even when living a low-profile life, they were renowned for wielding the power of prayer. Their various roles have come to be ever more fully recognized in modern scholarship.[19] But it seemed to me that women were seldom, if ever, called upon to play the role of a Symeon Stylites—that is, to act in a fully public role as a surrogate patron and enforcer.

17. J.W.H.G. Liebeschuetz, *Antioch: City and Imperial Administration in the Later Roman Empire* (Oxford University Press, 1972), 192–208.

18. Brown, "Rise and Function of the Holy Man," 129.

19. *Holy Women of the Syrian Orient*, trans. S. Brock and S. Ashbrook Harvey (Berkeley: University of California Press, 1987).

POWER ON THE GROUND

I was naturally excited when this part of the puzzle of the holy man's role appeared to slide into place. It seemed to me as if a constellation of social expectations was at work, tacitly nudging the holy man toward a role that mirrored that of a rural patron. Here was a clear case of a major figure in the structure of late Roman society—the patron—reflected *in* religion. In this way, Mary Douglas's notion of the concordance between social experience and religious expectations helped to explain the authority wielded by such persons.

Patronage offered to the villagers power on the ground: the presence of strong men who could allay local feuds and represent the community in its relations with the outside world. But how was this power reflected in religious terms? Here I was struck by the accounts of exorcism that played an important role in the religious literature of the time. Every *Life* of a holy man seemed to include melodramatic accounts of demonic possession overcome through exorcism by the holy man. What did these incidents mean "on the ground"— that is, what did they mean to those who witnessed them and those who sought relief from possession by exorcism? As we have seen, Father Festugière would have told me with utter confidence that such scenes revealed the working of a mentality like that of the "most savage primitive lost in the forests of Equatorial Africa."

Festugière was doubly wrong—wrong about the Africans and about the monks. Analyzed in the unruffled manner of Evans-Pritchard, the melodrama of exorcism could be seen very differently. It was a carefully controlled and basically reassuring spectacle. It took the form of a duet between the holy man and the demon, in which the holy man asserted the stable power of God over the random violence of the demonic world. It marked out the holy man as a source of power and order in the locality.

Hence I was faced with a fascinating phenomenon. Here was power that grew from the ground up, with all the accompaniments of popular acclaim associated with the exercise of power in secular society in the later empire. The entry of holy men into cities and villages was accompanied by the same bursts of acclamation as practiced in the circus by fan clubs, and in the high ceremonies surrounding the appearances of emperors. Miracles of healing were greeted in the same way. Bursts of shouting declared them to be miracles—for it was believed that the same spirit which had effected the miracle also caused all those present to recognize it as a miracle, much as an emperor was deemed to have been chosen by God through the inspired acclaim of the army, Senate, and people.

Put bluntly, holy men were deemed to be holy because acclaimed as holy by others. Their position was not linked to any official institution. No holy man received an imperial mandate as did officials in the carefully graded hierarchy of the imperial government. Few were ordained by bishops—and if they were, they tended to keep a distance from the regular clergy. It seemed as if holy men wielded a different sort of power. They notably lacked what Mary Douglas, in *Purity and Danger*, had analyzed so acutely as "vested," "articulate" power—power that was based on solid institutions. Instead, the holy man seemed to be surrounded by a troubling aura of "inarticulate power"—power that lacked that institutional backing.[20] Where did this power come from?

"ARE YOU HUMAN?"

It seemed to me that the holy man was powerful because he was regarded as not quite human. A layman once climbed the ladder to Symeon and posed the direct question: "Are you human or are you an angelic being?" From the sociological point of view, the holy man was neither. He could not be an angel: no creature of human flesh could belong to that category of vibrant, ethereal beings. Yet he was not fully human. For he had reduced to a bare minimum those links with society that defined the humanity of ordinary persons. He had no wife; he ate as little food as humanly possible; he had broken with the settled world by flight to the desert or (in the case of Symeon) by occupying a dizzying position on a high pillar, poised between Heaven and earth. He had become the total stranger. He represented a vortex of complete noninvolvement in the middle of a crowded and restive world. Attached to no one, the holy man could impinge on local affairs as objectivity incarnate.

Paradoxically, after a brutal period of dissociation from society (which often involved the acting out of the sort of mortifications that repelled scholars such as Festugière), the holy man reentered society as the perfect arbitrator. Hence the impression given by East Rome of a society ringed with figures whose authority stemmed from the fact that they were thought to be totally unconnected with it.

20. Mary Douglas, *Purity and Danger: An Analysis of the Concepts of Pollution and Taboo* (London: Routledge and Kegan Paul, 1966; reprint, London: Ark Paperbacks, 1984), 94–113.

"The Leitmotiv of the Religious Revolution
of Late Antiquity"

This phenomenon challenged me to widen my horizons. In studying persons such as Symeon Stylites, I seemed to be looking at something like the working of a sociological and psychological mechanism that extended far beyond Syria, and was not limited to dramatic pillar-squatters such as Symeon. In many other areas in the Eastern Empire, late Roman people opted to depend on figures who could act as arbiters because they were ascetics, totally stripped of the normal attributes of social living that had made them human.

This had not happened to such an extent previously, in classical times. It did not happen in every region: the Catholic West struck me as notably unendowed with holy men compared with the Christian East; in the West, bishops ruled the roost. Nor did it happen in every period of Christian history. Even in East Rome the holy man was never entirely secure. At the time that I was working on my article on the holy man, I also became fascinated by the Iconoclast controversy of the eighth and ninth centuries, which seemed to have involved a backlash against monastic holy men as well as against icons. This backlash coincided in a significant manner with the drastic restructuring of Byzantine society in the wake of the Muslim invasions, which involved an assertion, by the Iconoclast emperors, of vested, articulate power at the expense of the inarticulate power of the monks as guardians of icons.[21] But between the fourth century and the seventh, the rise of the holy man was the hallmark of an age.

> The predominance of the holy man . . . marked out a distinct phase of religious history. The classical period conjures up the image of a great temple; the Middle Ages of a Gothic cathedral. In between, it is the portraits that strike the imagination, the icons of the holy men, the austere features of philosophers, the ranks of staring faces in frescoes and mosaics. For some centuries, the *locus* of the supernatural was thought of as resting on individual persons.[22]

21. Peter Brown, "A Dark Age Crisis: Aspects of the Iconoclastic Controversy," *English Historical Review* 88 (1973): 1–34, now in *Society and the Holy in Late Antiquity* (Berkeley: University of California Press, 1982), 251–301.

22. Brown, "The Rise and Function of the Holy Man," 151.

The way in which face and halo came together in this distinctive manner was one of the principal themes in the religious history of East Roman society in late antiquity on which I would come to work for many years. I had begun with an attempt to find a context for the strange figure of Symeon Stylites. I had ended by offering a viewing point from which to judge the quality of an entire epoch. Almost at the same time as I wrote the article on the holy man, I found myself challenged to produce a survey of that epoch, under the title *The World of Late Antiquity*.

PART IV

THE WORLD OF LATE ANTIQUITY TO IRAN

THE WORLD OF LATE ANTIQUITY

AN INVITATION AND A TITLE

An Invitation

In April 1968, I received a letter from Geoffrey Barraclough, who was then teaching at the University of California at San Diego. It was an invitation to write a short book on late antiquity for a series called the Library of European Civilization published by Thames and Hudson. The letter came out of the blue, as I was beginning to write my article on the holy man, and at that time I had no plans to write a work of synthesis. Yet, within three years, this is exactly what I did: *The World of Late Antiquity* duly appeared in 1971.[1]

I accepted Barraclough's invitation readily for three reasons.

First: the Thames and Hudson series gave me access to a wider, nonacademic public. At a time when I was deeply committed to publishing specialist articles, this would be "a book for my aunts"—an extended essay on late antiquity as a whole, meant for the average reader. I had always loved that kind of writing, and this was a challenge to write nothing less than the portrait of an age.

---

1. Peter Brown, *The World of Late Antiquity: From Marcus Aurelius to Muhammad* (London: Thames and Hudson, 1971; reprinted with expanded bibliography, New York: W. W. Norton, 1989); see also Peter Brown: "The World of Late Antiquity Revisited," *Symbolae Osloenses* 72 (1997): 5–90. For an acute evaluation of *The World of Late Antiquity*, see now Andrea Giardina, "'Tutto il vigore è negli occhi': Peter Brown e la nascita della New Late Antiquity," in *New Late Antiquity*, 183–235.

Second: I already knew Thames and Hudson as a publisher of art history books. The books in the Library of European Civilization series were lavishly illustrated. Late antiquity had attracted me first, as it had attracted many others, because of its works of art: its vivid mosaics, haunting faces, and majestic basilica churches. Abundant illustrations, combined with pertinent captions, would tell more than half the story that I wished to tell. But these would not be mere "illustrations." As they moved from the classical art of the Roman Empire at its height to the age of Justinian and beyond, readers would see an ancient world changing into something strangely different before their eyes.

A TITLE: *THE WORLD OF LATE ANTIQUITY*

The third reason was perhaps the most important: Barraclough had the same view of this period as I had myself. He wanted a book on *late* antiquity; and he wanted it for the same reasons as I did: that is, he wanted an account of the hitherto neglected period that lay between the two well-known epochs of classical antiquity and the Middle Ages. Barraclough wrote:

> The very tentative title that I have in mind was "The World of Late Antiquity". It has always seemed to me that there has been very little attempt in English to explore the differences between classical antiquity and late antiquity which nevertheless seems vastly important in so far as it is really late antiquity which is the foundation of the medieval world. . . .
>
>   . . . among other things I found the work of Max Dvorak and E[rnst] Kitzinger very stimulating.

This last remark acknowledged the origin of the notion of *Spätantike* in the great tradition of late nineteenth- and twentieth-century German art history, of which Ernst Kitzinger (1912–2003) was a distinguished modern representative.

Readers may remember how I had been introduced to the notion of "late antiquity," when still an undergraduate, by Henri-Irénée Marrou in the brilliant *Retractatio* of his study of Augustine and the end of ancient culture.[2] For Marrou—as for Barraclough and the German art historians to whom he referred—late antiquity meant a period in which the artistic, cultural, and religious forms inherited from the ancient, classical world underwent a series

---

2. Chapter 31: "'Decadence' or 'Late Antiquity'? Henri-Irénée Marrou."

of more or less drastic mutations without, however, being severed from their ancient roots.[3]

The term "late antiquity" had originated among art historians in order to describe those subtle mutations of style and sensibility that did not march to the brisk rhythm of war and politics. For this reason, it was best applied to the social and cultural developments that took place in this period, when the classical core of Greco-Roman civilization had held firm in some aspects and taken on surprising new forms in others. These long-term evolutions in religion, art, and culture, and not the usual brisk tale of emperors, civil wars, and barbarian invasions, were the central theme of the book.

Hence the importance, for me, of the title "late antiquity." In the first place, it was a challenge to the view that the last centuries of the Roman Empire could be seen only as a period of decline and fall—as Edward Gibbon and many others had seen them. In fact, the ancient world continued for many centuries; and these centuries were marked by unexpected creativity in religion, art, and literature. Second, this creativity was not limited to the Roman Empire alone. It was shared by a wider world, which included Mesopotamia, Arabia, and Iran.

Until this time, I had tended to use the term "late Roman" to describe developments that had happened within the frontiers of the Roman Empire. But "late antiquity" seemed to be the better way to describe those pulses of creativity that crossed these frontiers, and that circulated in the wider world in which the Roman Empire was only a part.

FROM DECLINE AND FALL TO CHANGE AND CONTINUITY

Given a free rein to write a book on "late antiquity," I finished the job quickly: Barraclough received the final draft in November 1969. From then onward, I collaborated with Stanley Baron (the deeply cultivated and accessible editor in the London branch of Thames and Hudson) and with Georgina Bruckner, a gifted Hungarian picture researcher. Working out of the Ashmolean Library, I identified over 95 percent of the illustrations and wrote the captions for

---

3. See now *Late Antiquity in Contemporary Debate*, ed. Rita Lizzi Testa (Cambridge: Scholars Publishing, 2017); P. Corby Finney, *The Eerdmans Encyclopedia of Early Christian Art and Archaeology*, s.v. "Late Antiquity" (Grand Rapids, MI: Eerdmans, 2017), 2:44–45; and Jás Elsner, "Alois Riegl: Art History and the Beginning of Late Antique Studies as a Discipline," in *New Late Antiquity*, 167–182.

them all. As a result, the illustrations in *The World of Late Antiquity* were a photo-essay in themselves on the visual aspects of the classical world's transformation—the changing styles of portraiture, the vivid mosaics in villas and churches, the emergence of provincial, subclassical traditions in art and clothing, the majestic new basilicas, and the touches of exotic styles brought from far beyond the frontiers of the Roman world.[4]

I recently discovered among my papers a handwritten draft of what must have been an extensive proposal for *The World of Late Antiquity*. It is tentative and overwritten, but it shows very clearly the sort of book that I wanted to write. I made clear that this would not be a book like Edward Gibbon's *Decline and Fall of the Roman Empire*: late antiquity marked not the end of a civilization but its transformation into new and adventurous forms, which would directly influence all subsequent centuries.

> To Gibbon, this theme had seemed the only one possible for our period. He regarded it as the "awful revolution" that turned the commodious edifice of the classical civilization of the Age of the Antonines into a devastated ruin. Gibbon, like his contemporaries, had a refined sense for classical ruins. In the 19th century, a more sinister theme appears—a sense of "decadence" replaces the sad contemplation of the august debris of the Roman past. The Late Antique world was treated not only as the story of a great Empire that fell: it was regarded as the tale of a civilization that was tainted, corrupted, atrophied by conservatism, in its surviving classical literature, and deeply undermined by the irrational in its basic attitudes to the world. The theme of the "Decline and Fall of the Roman Empire" gave way to "The Decay of the Ancient World". In both cases, however, this period was thought to have left no direct legacy: for Gibbon, darkness descended; for the 19th century, the sad corpse of a decadent Antiquity had to be dragged from the stage before the next act of the Middle Ages began.

Instead of this, I wished to emphasize the many direct legacies of late antiquity to the medieval and even to the modern world:

> It is in our sense of the existence of the immediate and lasting legacy of the Late Antique period that we differ from such views. Since the end of the

---

4. This aspect has been studied in a most illuminating article by Bryan Ward-Perkins, "The Making of the *World of Late Antiquity*," *Revista Diálogos Mediterrânicos* (Brazil) 21 (2021): 4–18.

last century, the roots of medieval society have been traced to their origins in the "restored" society of the Late Roman world. The 4th century aristocrat in his fortified estate has been hailed as a distant prototype of the medieval baron, just as the titles of medieval feudal courts—count, for instance, for <u>comes</u> "companion of the Emperor; "duke" from <u>dux</u> . . . first appear in the official hierarchy of Diocletian and Constantine. . . .

In a way less easy to define but more immediately striking to modern eyes, the art of the Late Antique period began a way of seeing man and the world that lasted up to the 13th century. We have only to look at the eyes of a Romanesque saint to see that he is closer, across seven centuries, to the portraits of a 3rd century philosopher, than this 3rd century philosopher was to the art of his grandparents in the age of Marcus Aurelius. It is the same with the thought of the age: up to the 17th century, it was to Plotinus, to Augustine, to the laws of Justinian that men turned as models. The "ancient" world of medieval and Renaissance men was, in fact, the Late Antique world: for the vigorous autumn growth of classical civilization— into new philosophy, new theology, new art and new law—quite overshadowed the preceding centuries. It is only recently that Europeans have come to place the "classical" age of Greece and Rome [that is, without its crucial Late Antique sequence] on a lonely, and precarious, pedestal.

For this reason, I made clear that the geographical focus of the book would not be on the Roman provinces of western Europe. Compared with most accounts of the period, this represented a major change of focus. As I pointed out in my draft:

> This book has tried to capture the quality of what struck the author as the most profound changes that occurred in the Late Antique period. This was not the transition from a Roman to a post-Roman world in Western Europe. Instead, this account has given more prominence to the southern societies that had been the heart of the classical world, and to the ancient cradles of civilization in the Near East. For the changes described in the book were all the more vertiginous for having taken place, on the whole, among sheltered and slow-moving populations. They were set against a physical environment that had not greatly changed for millennia, and played out in centers overshadowed by classical temples, for instance, which were older, by the 4th century AD, than many Gothic cathedrals in modern England.

Put briefly, *The World of Late Antiquity* would not be a study of decline and fall, followed by catastrophic barbarian invasion, as the last centuries of the ancient world had usually been presented. Rather, it would be a study of change and continuity in a deeply rooted and sophisticated society. Under the title of "late antiquity," it would offer the general public a view of the period between 200 and 800 as a distinctive and creative moment of history—a "world" of late antiquity. And this world would gravitate around a different center than before: no longer concentrated on Rome and western Europe, it would embrace the ancient cultures of North Africa, Egypt, and the Middle East.

FROM MARCUS AURELIUS . . .

E. R. Dodds (1893–1979)[1]

It was easy to agree with Barraclough that the title of the book should be *The World of Late Antiquity*. More than that: the reign of the emperor Marcus Aurelius (161–180) was the obvious place to begin. In his *Decline and Fall of the Roman Empire*, Edward Gibbon had chosen his reign and the reigns of his immediate predecessors as marking the apogee of the Roman Empire before the swift onset of its decline and fall. For Gibbon and his contemporaries, Marcus Aurelius was more than a ruler: he was the embodiment of a Golden Age.

> If a man were called to fix the period in the history of the world, during which the condition of the human race was most happy and prosperous, he would, without hesitation, name that which elapsed from the death of Domitian to the accession of Commodus [most particularly, the age of the Antonines: Antoninus Pius (138–161) and Marcus Aurelius (161–180)].[2]

But I had not met Marcus Aurelius in this capacity. Rather, I had met him in the brilliant but chilling pages of what was then a recent masterpiece by E. R. Dodds, *Pagans and Christians in an Age of Anxiety*, which had appeared in 1965. Dodds did not share the enthusiasm of Gibbon and his contemporaries for the age of the Antonines. Rather, he saw the educated classes of the Roman

---

1. For a generous appreciation of the work of Dodds in many fields, see now C. Stray, C.B.R. Pelling, and S. J. Harrison, *Rediscovering E.R. Dodds: Scholarship, Education, Poetry, and the Paranormal* (Oxford University Press, 2019).

2. Edward Gibbon, *The Decline and Fall of the Roman Empire*, ed. David Womersley (London: Allen Lane Penguin, 1994), chapter 3, 1:103.

Empire around the year 200 as on the edge of a collective nervous breakdown. He treated Marcus Aurelius as a psychological case, a man haunted by a sense of unreality and by "the desolation of not belonging."[3]

This somber diagnosis was based on a psychoanalytic reading of the *Meditations*—the philosophical thought experiments—of the great emperor. And there would be worse to come. From the time of Marcus Aurelius onward, it appeared that "contempt for the human condition and hatred of the body was a disease endemic in the entire culture of the period."[4]

Had the third century really been like this? On this issue, I found that I differed totally from Dodds. What we had come to know about the evolution of Roman society in the third century, and in the centuries that followed, made me suspicious of this view. The debate on the work of Mikhail Rostovtzeff, conducted by social historians such as Hugo Jones and Santo Mazzarino, had shown that this catastrophic view needed to be replaced. Dodds seemed to be using an out-of-date social history of the Roman Empire on which to base his characterization of the period. For this reason, the second section of *The World of Late Antiquity* was driven by a continuous dialogue—at times admiring, at times deeply opposed, but always appreciative—with Dodds's negative view of the spiritual crisis of the third century and of the civilization that emerged from it.[5]

Quite apart from our shared interests in late antique religion, there was much to draw us together. Dodds was very much an Irishman. His family had moved to Dublin from Bangor, a seaside town, the Ulster equivalent of Bray. He had thrown himself into the Irish nationalist movement in a way that no member of my family had ever done. Though he came from a Protestant background, he did not identify himself in any way as a Protestant. Indeed, when his autobiography, *Missing Persons*, appeared in 1977, I was struck by an anecdote that he told about his fiancée. Just after they had announced their engagement, she was approached late at night by her mother:

> "Darling", said an anxious small voice, "Father says, *Is he a Roman Catholic?*" "No," said Bet sleepily, "he's an atheist". "Oh, thank goodness! I must tell Father; we couldn't sleep for worrying".[6]

---

3. E. R. Dodds, *Pagans and Christians in an Age of Anxiety: Some Aspects of Religious Experience from Marcus Aurelius to Constantine*, The Wiles Lectures Given at the Queen's University Belfast, 1963 (Cambridge University Press, 1965), 9 and 21.

4. Dodds, *Pagans and Christians*, 35.

5. Brown, *World of Late Antiquity*, 49–112.

6. E. R. Dodds, *Missing Persons: An Autobiography* (Oxford: Clarendon Press, 1977), 84.

It was a quintessentially "Dublin" story. Alas, I wish that these prejudices had been such a joke in the case of my poor aunt, when she announced that her prospective fiancé was a Catholic.

Dublin was a small place. Dodds and his sisters settled in Shrewsbury Road in Donnybrook, where the Chester Beatty Library would come to be built. Shrewsbury Road fell within the radius of houses in which my aunt Mai would play bridge. If I remember correctly, the Misses Dodds were spoken of with approval by my aunts. I never met them; but they were on my map of Dublin.

The Irrational

Sometime in the early 1970s, I also came to know of a side of Dodds that was remembered in Dublin. I visited Monk Gibbon, the poet and cousin of W. B. Yeats, whom I had known in Aravon as "Gubb-Gubb"—the teacher who had notably failed to teach me Latin. He showed me an anthology that included a set of poems of an extreme Neoplatonic nature written by Dodds at the age of twenty-six for the London journal *Côterie*:

> We are the partly real ones
> Whose bodies are an accident,
> Whose phantasies were never meant
> To fix their insubstantial thrones
> Inside a house of blood and bones.
>
> . . . .
> O undefiled, O lucid Moon!
> Hear our attenuated cry!
> . . . .
> O Moon, shall our release be soon?[7]

I have recently learned, through Wikipedia, that this fin de siècle confection was read and translated into Spanish by a twenty-year-old Argentinian, Jorge Luis Borges.

Despite these youthful flights of fancy, Dodds always struck me as a sturdy representative of the Protestant Enlightenment. He took the irrational seriously, at least in others. Whether in modern Ireland or in ancient Greece, the irrational was always close to hand. It had to be watched carefully, lest it swamp the all-too-frail defenses of the rational mind. Dodds was always interested in

---

7. *Côterie*, no. 3 (December 1919): 10–11.

"the more exceptional and extreme forms of human experience." Unlike some of his contemporaries, in England and Ireland, he did not dabble in the occult; but he did eye it as a "scientific" phenomenon—half fascinated and half repelled.[8]

Whenever he came up against Spiritualist circles in early twentieth-century Dublin, Dodds invariably proved hardheaded. Writing to his wife in 1923, he described a discussion of mysticism with W. B. Yeats. He found Yeats and his circle terminally pretentious:

> I tried to persuade them not to converse wholly in capitals [as if always talking of grandiose, Gnostic entities, such as Great Mother, Ancestral Soul, and The Above] . . . Yeats advised me to read Plotinus and consult Mrs. Wreidt the trumpet-medium. I wish I was not so incurably rational.[9]

Though "incurably rational," Dodds remained drawn to what George Devereux (1908–1985), a psychoanalyst turned ancient historian and Dodds's adviser on psychological matters, called "a turbulent cluster of unexplained facts"—such as cases of telepathy, poltergeists, and possession.[10] He remained throughout his life an active member of the Society for Psychical Research.

These paranormal phenomena had a reality for Dodds that infused his scholarly work with a rare intensity. The mystical ecstasy of Plotinus was a state that could happen to modern persons, just as their rational selves could be swamped in a manic breakdown, as portrayed in the *Bacchae* of Euripides.

Dodds's magnificent Sather Lectures published as *The Greeks and the Irrational* presented a disturbing vision of the underside of what had once seemed to be the clear and rational world of the ancient Greeks.[11] His vision was all the more unnerving because of the frequent hints—in the form of references to up-to-date modern literature on personality disorders scattered throughout the immensely learned footnotes of *The Greeks and the Irrational*—that nothing, perhaps, had changed: all that was most primitive and horrendous in the blood-soaked tragedies of ancient Greece lay just beneath the surface in the modern age. What had happened once had, indeed, happened in our own times,

8. Dodds, *Missing Persons*, 55.

9. Dodds, *Missing Persons*, 59.

10. Dodds, *Missing Persons*, 98.

11. E. R. Dodds *The Greeks and the Irrational* (Berkeley: University of California Press, 1951).

and would happen again if reason failed—yet again—to ride the dark horse of the Unconscious.[12]

The Third Century: Breakdown or Creativity?

The title of Dodds's book, *Pagans and Christians in an Age of Anxiety*, made his approach plain. It was taken from the title of one of the more portentous poems of his friend W. H. Auden. The poem set the tone for the entire book. Dodds implied that the nightmares which haunted modern Europe had already gripped the Roman world in the century between Marcus Aurelius and Constantine, "when the material decline was steepest and the ferment of new religious feelings most intense."[13]

On that issue, I found myself disagreeing *toto caelo* with him. It seemed to me that Dodds accepted without question the histrionic characterization of the "crisis of the third century" against which I had set my face since my very first lectures in Oxford. He also applied an old-fashioned Freudian interpretation to the figures and the texts of the period. The result was a singularly bleak, clinical view of famous writings such as the *Meditations* of Marcus Aurelius, and of less well-known texts such as the Gnostic writings in the Nag Hammadi Codices (which had only recently come to light, in 1945). Dodds presented the protagonists of those views as lonely and estranged persons, burdened with guilt and filled with hatred of the body.[14]

But was this really what the texts said? Take, for instance, the dichotomy between self and body that had characterized so much of the philosophy of ancient Greece: in the words of Dodds, this was "the most far-reaching, and perhaps the most questionable of all her gifts to human culture."[15]

Dodds assumed that heightened belief in the dichotomy of body and soul could only be regarded as a symptom of the rise of a desperate mood. I did not agree: this emphasis on the divide between body and soul might sometimes mean something entirely different. For many, to discover the immensity of the soul was not to flee the world: it was to become that much more confident of the link between the individual and higher realms. Men and women could draw

---

12. Dodds, *The Greeks and the Irrational*, 254–255.
13. Dodds, *Pagans and Christians*, 3.
14. E.g., Dodds, *Pagans and Christians*, 8, 20, and 35.
15. Dodds, *Pagans and Christians*, 29.

on a heightened sense of the majesty of their own souls to gain the inspiration and courage needed to leave their mark on the real world. The dichotomy of body and soul was a doctrine for fighters quite as much as for recluses.

It always struck me that the crisis of the third century had released many such fighters on the Roman world. Far from being a symptom of desperation and of a retreat from reality, the stress on the possibility of ever-closer links between humans and the divine as a source of energy and inspiration was no bad thing. It was altogether congruent with a "sudden release of creativity such as often follows the shaking of an *ancien régime*."[16]

The Late Roman Revolution: Social Mobility

My answer to Dodds was that of a historian interested in the social basis for cultural and religious change. I suggested that the centuries after Marcus Aurelius were not characterized by a collective neurosis. Rather, the religious ferment of the times made greater sense when set against the background of a less dramatic view of the evolution of late Roman society that had begun to be current, as we have seen, among scholars such as Mazzarino, Jones, and other, more recent students of the later empire.

This ferment reflected a major shake-up of Roman society that left it changed but by no means entirely depleted. Hence I called the entire part 1 of the book, where I described that shake-up, "The Late Roman Revolution." In this choice of title, I was consciously adapting the title of Sir Ronald Syme's classic study of the end of the Republic and the emergence of a new order under the emperor Augustus—*The Roman Revolution*.

The chapters on late Roman society were an attempt to do justice to the tension between change and continuity that made late antiquity such a distinctive period. I tried, region by region and generation by generation, to conjure up the social basis on which this intriguing balance of the new and the old depended. It seemed to me that widespread social mobility explained the tension that lay at the root of East Roman upper-class society from the days of Constantine (306–337) to the reign of Justinian (527–565).

From AD 300 onward, the Roman bureaucracy and the court absorbed talent like a sponge. But this upward movement was not indiscriminate. It drew largely on the educated elites of the Greek world—a basically conservative scholar-gentry still rooted in the ancient cities and groomed by the ancient

16. Brown, *World of Late Antiquity*, 33.

paideia associated with a classical education. As a result, there was more mobility at the very top of imperial society (among the generals and the top administrators) than halfway down—in the more numerous ranks of the bureaucracy proper. Hence an enduring tension: "Like the opposed vaults of a single arch, the 'new' society of imperial servants came to rest against the more rooted and backward looking society of the educated upper classes."[17]

The members of this scholar-gentry were like the mandarins of imperial China. They supported the empire with their talent; but they also slowed down the workings of a fiercely active court. In this way, they created a new East Roman Empire in their own, Greek image—a remarkable phenomenon, now well described by my friend from those days Fergus (Sir Fergus) Millar as *A Greek Roman Empire.*[18]

I confess to having shown a soft spot for such persons. I could not resist a class that had produced Olympiodorus of Thebes, an amateur philosopher and diplomat who

> went on missions as far apart as Rome, Nubia and the Dnieper—accompanied by a parrot who spoke pure Attic Greek.[19]

Nor could I resist being impressed by the succession of gifted poets from Egypt described by Alan Cameron in "Wandering Poets,"[20] or by the remarkable balance of pagan and Christian attitudes in a later representative of this mandarin class—the great historian of the wars of Justinian, Procopius of Caesarea (509–565), whose religious views had recently been studied in a brilliant article by Averil Cameron.[21]

We now tend to take this aspect of East Roman society for granted. But in 1968 the tensions inherent in the culture of those Greek scholar-bureaucrats were a new discovery, largely due to the work of Alan and Averil Cameron, both at that time working in London University. Together, they made the Eastern Empire look a very different place from the image of a sclerotic and decadent society that had usually been conjured up by the name "Byzantium."

17. Brown, *World of Late Antiquity*, 29.

18. F.B.G. Millar, *A Greek Roman Empire*, Sather Classical Lectures 64 (Berkeley: University of California Press, 2006).

19. Brown, *World of Late Antiquity*, 140. (Alas, I was misled by my enthusiasm: the parrot spoke Greek, but Olympiodorus does not say whether it was "pure Attic" Greek.)

20. Alan Cameron, "Wandering Poets," *Historia* 14 (1965): 470–509.

21. Averil Cameron, "The 'Scepticism' of Procopius," *Historia* 15 (1966): 466–482.

The Ancient Wisdom

Yet, as I look back, it seems that the happiest chapter in this part of the book—chapter 6: "The Last Hellenes"—was devoted to a group that had stood to one side of the rat race of government service: the pagan philosophers.[22] Though they were members of the same class as the scholar-gentry of East Rome, they ostentatiously resisted the temptations of the upwardly mobile. They remained pagans at a time when the adoption of Christianity had increasingly become a "party card" necessary for a successful career. From Plotinus onward, these philosophers devoted their energies to the rediscovery of what they took to be the authentic teachings of Plato. They stood for an Ancient Wisdom, earlier than the shrill radicalism of their own age. They defended the numinous beauty of the material universe against the Gnostics, who devalued it, and against Christians, who denied the multiplicity of divine beings who hovered close to the earth, making nature itself a holy thing.[23]

Such men saved the Greek sense of the majesty of the universe. I valued them as a reminder that it was often from moments of stability and revival, and not only of headlong change, that later ages received the legacy of the ancient world, passed on to them in the late antique period. In fifth- and sixth-century Athens and Alexandria, a remarkable succession of teachers, thinkers, and commentators strove fiercely to retain a continuity with the classical past. They upheld the ancient sense of the beauty and intelligibility of the cosmos—the star-filled heavens above the earth. Their stand for the cosmos ensured that it would be an ancient, Greek sky (a sky still, to pagans, inhabited by glowing gods) which would soar above the heads of Christians of the Middle Ages, and that Greek wisdom (made available in Syriac and then in Arabic translation) would continue to inspire Muslim and Jewish intellectuals throughout the Islamic world.

The Democratization of Culture

I also paid special attention to another aspect of the social and cultural evolution of late antiquity, which had been brought to the attention of scholars by that giant in the study of the ancient world, Santo Mazzarino. In the International Congress of Historical Studies, which was held in Stockholm in 1960,

22. Brown, *World of Late Antiquity*, 70–80
23. Brown, *World of Late Antiquity*, 21.

in the presence of a large Russian delegation, Mazzarino had proposed that there had, indeed, been a "revolution" at the end of the ancient world. But it had not been such a revolution as Marxists might expect. Rather, it had been a revolution brought about by a *democratizzazione della cultura*—a "democratization of culture"—from above.

As a result of this process of democratization, the values of the classical world came to be transmogrified by being taken out of their narrow elite context and extended to the provincials of the empire as a whole. At the same time, the later empire witnessed a reemergence, in the provinces, of cultural and religious traditions that had been suppressed or ignored in classical times. The issue was whether these provincial traditions would prove hostile to the empire or whether the provincials would be enabled to participate more fully in the empire, at the cost of lowering the high wall of an upper-class culture that had once guaranteed the superiority of the elites of the Greco-Roman world.[24]

The very title of Mazzarino's pungent intervention at the congress gave a signal that was taken up in different ways by many different scholars. It seemed that what made the culture of late antiquity so distinctive was not only the balance between change and continuity within the elites who maintained the classical tradition. There was also a more profound revolution, by which the classical culture of the time opened itself up to a hitherto unprecedented degree of cultural fluidity: "inner barriers collapsed. Another side of the Roman world, often long prepared in obscurity, came to the top, like different-colored loam turned by the plough."[25]

The lowering of ancient cultural boundaries and the extension of the franchise of Greco-Roman culture into hitherto peripheral areas was particularly marked in the evolution of the Christianities of the Roman East—in Armenia, Mesopotamia, Syria, and Egypt. It was in the Middle East, and not in the less ebullient and more rigid West, that the effects of the democratization of culture were most clearly visible.

---

24. Santo Mazzarino, "La democratizzazione della cultura nel 'Basso Impero,'" *XIᵉ Congrès international des sciences historiques (Stockholm 21–28 aôut 1960). Rapports, 2: Antiquité* (Göteborg, 1960), 35–54 = *Antico, tardoantico ed èra costantiniana* (Rome: Dedalo Libri, 1974), 74–98. See now J.-M. Carrié, "La 'démocratisation de la culture' dans l'Antiquité tardive," *Antiquité Tardive* 9 (2001): 27–46, and Noel Lenski, "Santo Mazzarino, " in *New Late Antiquity*, 280–282.

25. Brown, *World of Late Antiquity*, 9.

As a result of this democratization, the Christian churches in the eastern provinces could no longer be treated as peripheral, and still less as intrinsically hostile to the empire. I wrote *The World of Late Antiquity* when I had begun my work on the holy men of Syria and Egypt, and was in the process of learning Hebrew and Syriac. As a result, I struggled throughout the book to do justice to the role of two exuberant provinces within the new Greek Roman Empire of the East. One was Syria, a bilingual region, whose rich imaginative subsoil, in Greek and Syriac, would feed the piety of Byzantium and fill its churches with unforgettable chants. The other was Egypt, the home of the monks, where Coptic and Greek coexisted to spread throughout the Middle East, the Mediterranean, the monasteries of southern Gaul, and even, eventually, of Ireland, a distinctive body of Christian teaching—the *Apophthegmata Patrum* (*The Sayings of the Desert Fathers*) that was the last great flowering of the Wisdom Literature of the ancient Near East.

But there were yet further participants in the late Roman revolution, from yet more distant regions. I must explain what led me to include, in my account, societies of the wider Middle East—the Iranian empire of the Sasanians and the early empire of Islam—as participants, in their own way, in the social and religious ferment of the Greco-Roman world in its last centuries.

TO MUHAMMAD

LATE ANTIQUITY IN
A WIDER WORLD

"The Two Eyes of the Earth": Byzantium and Iran

Two sections toward the end of *The World of Late Antiquity*—"The Empires of the East" and "The New Participants"—were the result of my recent interest in the Middle East.[1] From 1966 onward I had become increasingly fascinated by the Fertile Crescent and by the Syriac culture that stretched across the political frontier between the East Roman and the Persian (Sasanian) empires. This unbroken corridor of prosperous towns and villages, which ran from Mesopotamia to the Mediterranean—from Ctesiphon to Antioch—was a region of unusual cultural and religious ferment. Far from dividing Byzantium from Persia, as if they were two, totally separate worlds, the Fertile Crescent drew them together in unrelenting conflict for supremacy in the Middle East.

As I saw it at the time, the Persia of the emperor Justinian's contemporary, Khusro I Anoshirwan (531–579), was a menace to East Rome not because it was a totally alien, "barbarian" power, but because it was not alien enough. It shared with East Rome many features of a late antique society—a state-established religion (Zoroastrianism), a reformed tax system, an increasingly powerful bureaucracy, and a renewed courtly culture. The Sasanian Empire also contained a strong Christian presence, whose dominant language was Syriac. Syriac-speaking communities stretched from Mesopotamia to Antioch, joining one side of the frontier to the other. Furthermore, an "Eastern

1. Brown, *World of Late Antiquity*, 160–171 and 189–203.

Hellenism," based on the translation of Greek works, or their Syriac versions, into Pahlavi, also flourished at the court of Khusro Anoshirwan to such an extent that the last pagan philosophers of Athens considered relocating to the Persian Empire to avoid the intolerance of Justinian after the Platonic Academy was closed in 532. The two empires were close enough to speak of themselves, in diplomatic exchanges, as "The Two Eyes of the Earth."

At the time, my views on Persia were based on relatively slender evidence—on scattered articles and on one major synthesis, *L'Iran sous les sassanides* of Arthur Christensen (1875–1945).[2] Christensen may have exaggerated the "westernizing," "Byzantinizing" aspect of the political reforms of Khusro I. But the more we have come to know in recent years about the nature of Sasanian culture as a whole, the more it appears that Persia was indeed a participant in a Middle Eastern late antiquity—a late antiquity based on Mesopotamia rather than on the Mediterranean. One of the most heartening breakthroughs in more recent late antique studies has been the discovery of further evidence for a strong presence of late antique Syriac and Greek culture in Sasanian Mesopotamia and, even, in Iran itself.[3]

It seemed to me that the long wars between East Rome and Persia in the sixth and early seventh centuries were not (as East Roman writers presented them) between two incommensurable cultures—Greeks and barbarians, Christians and Zoroastrian pagans. Instead, they were a family feud for the undivided mastery of the Fertile Crescent.[4]

But why did I choose Muhammad (570–626), rather than, say, Justinian or even Khusro I Anoshirwan, as the second figure in my title—as an appropriate bookend to the period of late antiquity? And why did I then continue for a further chapter beyond the death of the Prophet, to the age of Harun al-Rashid (788–809) and Charlemagne (768–814)?

2. A. Christensen, *L'Iran sous les sassanides* (Copenhagen: E. Munksgaard, 1944).

3. See now Kevin Van Bladel, *The Arabic Hermes: From Pagan Sage to Prophet of Science* (Oxford University Press, 2009); Richard Payne, *A State of Mixture: Christians, Zoroastrians, and Iranian Political Culture in Late Antiquity* (Berkeley: University of California Press, 2015); and Joel Walker, "The Limits of Antiquity: Philosophy between Rome and Iran," *Ancient World* 33 (2002): 45–69.

4. See Matthew Canepa, *The Two Eyes of the Earth: Art and Ritual Kingship between Rome and Sasanian Iran* (Berkeley: University of California Press, 2009) and *The Iranian Expanse: Transforming Royal Identity through Architecture, Landscape, and the Built Environment, 550 BCE–642 CE* (Berkeley: University of California Press, 2018), 251–374.

THE MESSAGE OF MUHAMMAD:
IGNAZ GOLDZIHER (1850–1921)

My work on Syria and the Middle East increasingly indicated that I should not isolate the Arabian Peninsula from the politics, economy, and culture of the East Roman and Sasanian empires, as if the preaching of Muhammad and the formation of Islam had occurred on another planet. Compared with the magnificent recent studies of Arabia and the origins of Islam by Glen Bower-sock and Christian Robin, which have appeared in the last decade, I had little to go on when I explored this theme.[5] But I did have my friend and colleague at All Souls, Samuel Stern, who introduced me to the works of Ignaz Goldzi-her, which he was in the process of translating.

Goldziher's essays on the conflict between Arab aristocratic, warrior values and the message of the Qurʾân gripped me. I was deeply impressed by the manner in which he evoked the contrast between the ethics of the aristocratic shame culture of the Arabs, which guided the life of individuals in a tight-knit tribal world, and the very different message of Muhammad, which insisted on the relentless stripping down of individual believers to their bare selves, as sinners or saved—like single grains of dust before God. It was a call to a proud elite to govern their lives, no longer by braggadocio and the opinion of their peers, but by the hope of Heaven and the chill fear of the Last Judgment.

This was an ascetic message that could have come from any contemporary Syrian monastery, where monks lived their lives under the same constant awareness of the Last Judgment, the same fear of Hell, and the same hope of Paradise as that conjured up by Muhammad to guide the conduct of pious Muslims. In this sense, the preaching of Muhammad was the last, and the most challenging, echo of the religious revolution that I had studied since its begin-nings in the age of Marcus Aurelius.[6]

Reading Goldziher, I realized that the message of the Qurʾân carried clear echoes of the Syria of the holy men whom I had just come to know: the same vivid imagery of Paradise, the same call to repentance, the same fear of Hell, and even—as in the case of the "commandments" of Symeon Stylites—the

---

5. G. W. Bowersock, *Empires in Collision in Late Antiquity* (Waltham, MA: Brandeis Univer-sity Press, 2012) and *The Crucible of Islam* (Cambridge, MA: Harvard University Press, 2017), and C. Robin, "Arabia and Ethiopia," in *The Oxford Handbook of Late Antiquity*, ed. Scott Fitzger-ald Johnson (Oxford University Press, 2012), 247–332.

6. I. Goldziher, *Muslim Studies*, vol. 1 (London: George Allen and Unwin, 1968).

same attempt to bring the Law of God into daily life so as to master the tensions of a fractious society, as Muhammad did in Mecca and Medina. The Syriac background to the religious imagination of early Islam held my attention. The book of Tor Andrae (1885–1947), *Mohammed: The Man and His Faith*, had revealed parallels between the hymns of Ephraim the Syrian (ca. 306–373) and the religious imagery of the Qur'ân.[7] This was only a beginning, but it was enough to inspire me.

Altogether, recent work on the origins of Islam had challenged the historian of late antiquity to sit up and take notice. I realized that Muhammad had to be included as one of the most impressive "new participants" in the religious turmoil of the late antique Middle East. This did not mean that I considered Muhammad to be derivative. Far from it. Rather, he summed up in a new language and with a new claim to authority, all that was most distinctive in the Christian and Jewish piety of his time.

THE FATE OF THE MEDITERRANEAN: HENRI PIRENNE (1862–1935)

There was also a more humdrum, Oxford reason for the last chapter. The *Mohammed and Charlemagne* of Henri Pirenne, which appeared in English in 1939, was a "must" for every undergraduate who studied the early medieval West. The "Pirenne thesis" was regularly debated in tutorials and in the lectures on historical geography for the preliminary examination in the History School (an examination that undergraduates who had opted for history took in their first year). A brilliant little book, *Mohammed and Charlemagne* was one of the first attempts to measure the impact of the rise of Islam on the economy of the early medieval West.[8]

Henri Pirenne was an outstanding historian of the cities of medieval Europe. In *Mohammed and Charlemagne* he moved backward in time. He told medievalists exactly when the ancient world ended and the Middle Ages began, and exactly why. It was the fault of the Arabs. He argued that the

---

7. Tor Andrae, *Mohammed: The Man and His Faith* (London: George Allen and Unwin, 1936).

8. Henri Pirenne, *Mohammed and Charlemagne*, trans. B. Miall (London: George Allen and Unwin, 1939); see Peter Brown, "*Mohammed and Charlemagne* by Henri Pirenne," *Daedalus* 103 (1974): 25–33, now in *Society and the Holy in Late Antiquity* (Berkeley: University of California Press, 1982), 66–79.

barbarian invasions of the fifth century had not fundamentally altered the basis of Western society. This society had continued to be based on the Mediterranean. A somewhat broken-down "Romanity" survived for as long as the Mediterranean remained open to the commerce of the East.

But with the Arab invasions from the 640s onward the Mediterranean became a Muslim lake: it fell into the hands of a hostile power. In Pirenne's opinion, the Muslim blockade of the Mediterranean brought the ancient world to an end. As a direct result of this blockade, the under-Romanized, Germanic North took over from the societies of the Mediterranean South whose commerce had been strangled. The empire of Charlemagne was based on Aachen, over six hundred miles to the north of Marseilles, in territory that had never been part of the Roman Empire. Cut off from its Mediterranean roots, it was the first truly post-Roman society to emerge in western Europe. Hence Pirenne's famous remark: "It is therefore strictly correct to say that without Mohammed, Charlemagne would have been inconceivable."[9] Seldom has a short book conjured up with such conviction a supposed turning point in the history of the West.

THE MISSING LINK: LATE ANTIQUITY IN ISLAM. UGO MONNERET DE VILLARD (1881–1954)

But was Pirenne right? Paradoxically, it was discussion of this frail but arresting hypothesis (proposed by one of the greatest Western medievalists of his time) that first introduced me to the problem of the survival of late antique forms of art, culture, religion, and administration in the Middle East in the centuries after the Muslim conquests. This was because the debate sparked by the Pirenne thesis had involved a two-pronged criticism.

The first criticism addressed Pirenne's views as an economic historian of the medieval West. He seemed to have overestimated the degree to which Western society had once depended on its commercial links with the eastern Mediterranean: only if these links had been crucial would a Muslim blockade of the Mediterranean have had such drastic effects. But many economic historians of the late antique and early medieval West thought that this was not the case—trans-Mediterranean trade had already run down considerably before the Muslims reached the sea. Throughout western Europe, many of the changes

---

9. Pirenne, *Mohammed and Charlemagne*, 234; see now Bonnie Effros, "The Enduring Attraction of the Pirenne Thesis," *Speculum* 92 (2017): 184–208.

that Pirenne ascribed to the Muslim invasions were already well under way by the end of the sixth century.

The Pirenne thesis posed a different problem for Islamicists. They were less concerned with the impact of the Muslim conquests on western Europe than with the effect of these conquests on the Middle East and on North Africa as a whole. How rapidly did the Muslims change the face of western Asia and the southern Mediterranean? Pirenne had assumed, on the basis of the scholarship available to him, that the Arab invasions had brought about a sudden and drastic change—that a new and alien society, very different from that of the ancient world, had formed rapidly along the eastern and southern shores of the Mediterranean and throughout the Middle East.

But was this the case? Everything that I had learned about the Islamic world in its first centuries spoke against this view. This was particularly so with recent studies of the art and architecture of the postconquest Middle East. They seemed to show that the Muslims ruled a society that changed far less rapidly than had been imagined by previous scholars. Palaces, country villas, bath-houses, and marketplaces, even mosques, continued to be built according to late antique traditions of art and architecture that endured for centuries, changing only slowly into their classical "Islamic" form.

Here I was fortunate to receive from Sam Stern a rare copy of an Italian masterpiece (for most copies of the book had been lost in the disastrous flooding of the Arno in Florence in 1966, which had swept away the warehouse in which they were stored). This was the *Introduzione allo studio dell'archeologia Islamica* of Ugo Monneret de Villard, the great Italian pioneer of the study of Islamic art.[10]

Reading the *Introduzione* was like discovering the missing link. Monneret de Villard showed how buildings and ornamental forms that had been thought to be quintessentially new and authentically Islamic were by no means new creations. They had developed naturally out of the provincial art of Syria in the long centuries of late antiquity. The splendid, mosaic-laden mosques and audience halls of the Ummayad caliphs of Damascus were not the fairy-tale products of some alien, Arab culture. They were late antique products, still unfolding with unbroken exuberance for centuries after the Muslim conquest of the Middle East.

In the same way, the non-Muslim populations of the seventh- and eighth-century Middle East have come to be studied in detail as active agents in the

---

10. Ugo Monneret de Villard, *Introduzione allo studio dell'archeologia Islamica* (Venice: Fondazione Giorgio Cini, 1966).

formation of Islam itself, to a degree that I could not have dared to imagine when I wrote *The World of Late Antiquity*. Just as Islamic architecture grew from deep roots in the preexisting traditions of Syria, so Islam developed in constant dialogue with Christians and Jews all over the territories of the new Islamic empire.

Nowadays, scholars such as Jack Tannous and the late Tom Sizgorich (1970–2011) have revolutionized our knowledge of this last and most tantalizing phase of late antiquity in the Middle East. They have shown how persons reared in a world still bathed in the long late afternoon sun of late antiquity brought the skills, the learning, and the questionings that would root the new religion in the rich subsoil of a very ancient world. In 1968, I had only the most fragile hope, supported by a few outstanding friends and a few really good books, that such a story might be told, and with such an ending.[11]

"Overlooking the Core of Classical Civilization"

The World of Late Antiquity appeared in May 1971. In June I received a warm letter from Ralph Davis, the medievalist who had encouraged me to publish my first articles in *History* (the journal of the Historical Association, whose outreach I had always admired), and who was now professor of medieval history at Birmingham.

> Dear Peter,
>
> Just a line to say how very much I enjoyed reading <u>The World of Late Antiquity</u>. . . . Who would have thought that the best qualities of Powicke and Jones could be so gloriously married in one book. I don't know if you like it to be labeled, but I'm sure it will start a New School. Ancients and Medievalists alike are thrilled because we've got something to <u>think</u> about. Not many books do that, and prompt so much self-recognition.

Ralph was referring to Sir Maurice Powicke's capacity for immersion in the past and Hugo Jones's understanding of the workings of late Roman society. It could not have been a more welcome compliment.

---

11. T. Sizgorich, *Violence and Belief in Late Antiquity: Militant Devotion in Christianity and Islam* (Philadelphia: University of Pennsylvania Press, 2009); and J. Tannous, *The Making of the Medieval Middle East: Religion, Society and Simple Believers* (Princeton, NJ: Princeton University Press, 2019).

Moses Finley (1912–1986), who had recently succeeded Jones as professor of ancient history at Cambridge, was less thrilled. He was a sturdy brawler for the classical world. *The World of Late Antiquity* confirmed his worst suspicions of those who wandered too far beyond its limits. His review appeared in *The Times* for May 1971:

> The historian of the later Roman Empire leads a hard life nowadays. The words "decline and fall" have become taboo in the most fashionable circles. So has "progress". Social anthropologists have indoctrinated us with a relativism about social systems in which value-judgments are not allowed. Artists and collectors have discovered modernity in Byzantine icons, Benin bronzes, Aztec pottery and carved boomerangs. Peter Brown agrees enthusiastically and adds Plotinus, the mystical neo-Platonist to the catalogue of "late Antique" moderns.
>
> That the historian can no longer rest content with war, politics and institutions but must also be an art historian, a sociologist, a theologian, a philosopher and moralist, and a psychologist is no bad thing. But universality has its risks. Mr. Brown's paean to neo-Platonism in particular, and to Byzantinism in general (embracing the civilization of Persia too) manages to overlook the core of classical civilization.[12]

Coming from Finley, this was an excommunication rather than an argument. Other newspaper reviewers were more charitable. Philip Toynbee (1916–1981) entitled his review (with a pointed dig at the title of Gibbon's masterpiece) "Decline and Fallacy":

> It is obvious from the first pages that Mr Brown *likes* this highly-coloured, disputatious, confused but courageous world. . . . His intention is to make us look at this old material with a new and kinder eye.

Among the academics, the review by Averil Cameron was the most perceptive. I still have the typescript of that review, which she sent me in advance. In the review, she raised the same problem as she had already done in a long letter to me on the draft of my article on the holy man—the problem of generalization. Given how little we know about the ancient world, she questioned how much our glimpses of individual people in the past could bear the weight of generalization that we place upon them. How much can a person be a type?

---

12. Moses Finley, "Overlooking the Core of Classical Civilisation," *The Times*, May 1971.

The fact is that by and large our knowledge of the ancient, even of the late antique world, is still largely a knowledge of individuals. The mass of information which the modern historian takes for granted is simply not there. This is less of a handicap for Peter Brown . . . for his forte is precisely in the sensitive handling of isolated scraps of evidence often relating to individuals, whether obscure or famous. His history . . . is very much a history of people. Names like Plotinus or Athanasius recur from page to page until they acquire an evocative aura of their own, and the book is full of such curiosities as the pagan gentlemen of Harran [south of Edessa] who worshipped Socrates, Plato and Aristotle as late as the tenth century. It makes for absorbing reading, but a warning bell would sometimes be welcome when such aberrations are treated as types. . . . The method, then, is seductive but risky, especially when used in conjunction with a literary style of such gloss. . . . There is even danger in the bountiful illustrations and their interesting captions.[13]

My answer to Averil, both in correspondence and in conversation, was that, as a medievalist, I was used to dealing with periods of rich evidence. This meant that I was more confident than she was that one example—if well chosen—would be corroborated by many others. It was a matter of choosing the right example out of a large pool of available evidence. I had two outstanding models for this anecdotal use of evidence—Marc Bloch's *Feudal Society* and Richard Southern's *The Making of the Middle Ages*. Both made extensive use of incidents and details culled from a rich hoard of charters, annals, and chansons de geste that made the Middle Ages come alive.[14] I had hoped to do the same for late antiquity.

13. Averil Cameron, *English Historical Review* 88 (1973): 116–117.

14. Marc Bloch, *Feudal Society*, trans. L. A. Manyon (London: Routledge and Kegan Paul, 1961); and Richard Southern, *The Making of the Middle Ages* (New Haven, CT: Yale University Press, 1953).

MEDIEVAL CHANGE

TEACHING THE MIDDLE AGES

There is a danger, when describing any academic trajectory, of concentrating on the high points—on the decisive articles and the well-known books. But, in many ways, these are only the tips of icebergs. Beneath them lies a whole world of teaching and administrative duties, relations with colleagues, friendships, and secondary interests.

This was certainly the case with me in the Oxford of the early 1970s. My work on the holy man and *The World of Late Antiquity* showed that I had thrown myself into the study of late antiquity, and particularly into the study of its Middle Eastern regions. This was where what I would call my active interests—my principal objects of research—lay.

Yet I remained deeply attached to the Western Middle Ages as a whole. On a personal level, I was surrounded by friends who were medievalists. Furthermore, beginning in 1972, I held a lectureship in medieval history at Merton College. Despite the title, the lectureship involved no lecturing. Rather, I was expected to give tutorials to all history undergraduates in Merton on the compulsory paper in English history from the Roman Conquest to 1307.

This was no small undertaking. It meant that I would spend at least seven hours each week for one term each year trying to persuade intelligent young persons, many of whose hearts lay in the modern field, that the Norman Conquest and the legal reforms of Henry II (which they were condemned by the Oxford history syllabus to study whether they liked it or not) were of any interest whatsoever.

Quite apart from those institutional links, there was one further fiber of the heart that held me to the Middle Ages; and that was my love of the English countryside. At this time, landscape meant far more to me than a pretty background. The fields, villages, and ancient churches of Oxfordshire offered a direct way into the past, as it had done for me when I first cycled around Shropshire with Laurence LeQuesne. They kept me in touch with the continuous history of England from the last days of Roman Britain onward, as I made my way around an ancient landscape, whose roots reached back—layer after layer—to the later empire.

To take only a few examples: an eighteen-mile drive along the A40 from Oxford to Swinbrook and a short walk beside the river Windrush would lead, across fields, to the little medieval chapel dedicated to Saint Oswald (635–642)—a Saxon king and warrior-saint, known to the Venerable Bede. In a hole in the floor, covered by a glass pane, visitors could look down and see the mosaic of the Roman villa in whose ruins an early Saxon church had been founded. The Saxon church had been rebuilt in the later Middle Ages. Its walls were covered with frescoes of the fourteenth century, showing the quintessentially late medieval, macabre scene of the encounter between the Three Living and the Three Dead: a thousand years of history in one small country church.

A further fifteen miles west, along the A40, lay Chedworth, a lordly Roman villa of the fourth century AD; and, close to Chedworth, in the valley of the Coln, there was the village of Withington, which had only recently been shown to have been the center of a Roman estate whose boundaries remained intact and productive, despite the collapse of Roman rule in Britain, from the age of Constantine to the age of King Alfred (848/49–899).[1]

To return from the Frogmill Inn at Withington to Oxford in the evening, as I once did, past gentle downs walled with golden stone, as the sun sank in the west and a great moon rose in the east, was to have bonded with the early medieval past through the earth of Oxfordshire. Whenever possible, when teaching, I would use my journeys into the countryside to illustrate themes in the history of medieval England—a Roman villa here, a Saxon church there, the ruins of a castle or a monastery gave reality to the history that I taught to my students from Merton. In this way, afternoon drives through the Oxford countryside, combined with tutorial teaching, kept me in touch with the Western Middle Ages at a time when my mind had traveled far to the East.

1. H.P.R. Finberg, *Lucerna: Some Problems in the Early History of England* (London: Macmillan, 1964).

Daedalus in Rome

On one occasion, I wrote an article on a medieval topic. I had been invited to take part in a workshop organized by Arnaldo Momigliano in collaboration with the American Academy of Arts and Sciences. It took place in Rome in September 1972 and continued in Venice in September 1973. It was an exciting occasion for me, as I had not been in Rome since my stay at the British School at Rome in 1958. The workshop was ostensibly devoted to a discussion of the notion of an "Axial Age" propounded by Karl Jaspers (1883–1969). But Jaspers's grandiose ideas were soon left behind. Instead, we focused on the more manageable topic of how decisive intellectual changes happen in traditional, premodern societies.

I offered to represent the Middle Ages, by addressing a problem from a field that had always attracted me—the relation between society and the supernatural. I proposed to reinterpret a significant shift in the role allotted to the supernatural in human society by studying the abandonment of the ordeal in twelfth-century Europe. I thought that if I could use the social anthropology of Evans-Pritchard and Mary Douglas to make sense of the role of sorcery in the later empire, I could also make sense of the seemingly barbaric ritual of the ordeal in the early medieval West.[2]

The Medieval Renaissance

The end of the ordeal in the twelfth century called for a reexamination of this kind. It had usually been presented as a decisive step in the grand narrative of European progress toward ever-greater rationality in law and government—a "birth of reason" in western Europe that signaled the end of the Dark Ages.

Medievalists were proud of that birth of reason. They had long pointed out that medieval Europe had been the very opposite of a static society. In particular, the eleventh and twelfth centuries had witnessed a massive reordering of society through the growth of a knightly class, through the establishment of an ever-sharper division between clergy and laity, and through an intensive fostering of intellectual life connected with the birth of the universities. In this view, the changes of the twelfth century were presented as the dawn of a new

---

2. P. Brown, "Society and the Supernatural: A Medieval Change," *Daedalus* 104 (1975): 133–151, now in *Society and the Holy in Late Antiquity* (Berkeley: University of California Press, 1982), 320–332.

age, a Renaissance before the Renaissance, to invoke the challenging title of the great Harvard medievalist Charles Homer Haskins (1870–1937), *The Renaissance of the Twelfth Century*.[3]

"THE PRIMITIVE AGE"?

But was this really how it happened? I had no quarrel with the achievements of the twelfth century. What I did not accept was the tendency to present these changes as if they had emerged from a profoundly archaic, prerational society. In his brilliant little book *Western Society and the Church in the Middle Ages*, even Dick Southern succumbed to this prejudice. His chapter on the early Middle Ages was entitled "The Primitive Age c700–c1050."[4] In line with this view, the withering of the ordeal in the twelfth century was acclaimed as a triumph of reason, a sign that Europe had emerged from the long tunnel of its barbaric past.

I challenged the view that early medieval Europe could be treated as no more than the "primitive" predecessor of an increasingly rational High Middle Ages. Such a view seemed dangerously close to that of the proponents of the idea of a "primitive mentality," entirely different from that of modern Europeans. But was the ordeal as primitive a mechanism as scholars made it out to be? Was its abandonment a sign that medieval society had become notably more rational? By working through the rituals of the ordeal and the social circumstances of its abandonment, I intended to chip away at one link, at least, in what struck me as a self-satisfied master narrative.

THE ORDEAL IN ACTION: RITUAL AND CONSENSUS

How did I do it; and why did I choose this topic of all the changes that had occurred in the twelfth century? First and foremost, I wanted to show what an anthropological approach to a complex ritual could do. Once again, I owed much to Paul Hyams, the historian of medieval law who had introduced me to the work of Mary Douglas and who was also working on the ordeal.[5] Paul

3. Charles Homer Haskins, *The Renaissance of the Twelfth Century* (New York: Meridian Books, 1957).

4. R. W. Southern, *Western Society and the Church in the Middle Ages* (Harmondsworth, Middlesex: Penguin Books, 1970), 27–33.

5. See now P. Hyams, "Trial by Ordeal: the Key to Proof in Early Common Law," in *On the Laws and Customs of England*, ed. M. S. Arnold (Chapel Hill: University of North Carolina Press, 1981), 90–126.

provided me with a crucial lead: he directed me to a register of cases that had been settled by ordeal in the early thirteenth century, at Varad in Hungary.

I worked my way through the descriptions of ordeals in the Register of Varad much as Evans-Pritchard had worked his way through the dancing sessions of Azande witch doctors. It seemed to me that these rituals functioned in ways that had a reason of their own. They were far from being the result of mere "barbaric" credulity. They were ways of dealing with a specific distribution of power in society that changed—and not necessarily for the better—in the course of the twelfth century.

I suggested that the ordeal was a carefully orchestrated device for the resolution of conflict in societies where no power could act as a tiebreaker, other than the power ascribed to the supernatural. Those who resorted to the ordeal were usually communities of equals or near equals, where neither side would give way except to God.

Furthermore, I pointed out that the ordeal was by no means a cut-and-dried affair—a sudden miracle that would be accepted by all out of sheer credulity. On the contrary: it depended on signs that were inherently ambiguous. Each form of ordeal had its built-in uncertainties. Had the champion cheated in trial by battle? Had the festering wound caused by holding the hot iron truly healed, to show the innocence of the contestant? In the ordeal by water, had the person truly floated? I spent much time in a municipal swimming pool, testing whether I was able to sink unambiguously or to remain buoyant. I invariably ended up floundering in a manner from which no clear conclusion could be drawn.

Hence the final result of the ordeal was never really left to God alone. It was worked out in the face-to-face group gathered to witness the ordeal. One side had to agree, eventually, that the signs of God's intervention (highly ambiguous though they often were) spoke in favor of their opponents. But in giving way, they gave way to God, and not to their opponents. Thus belief in the intervention of God was a face-saver. Even more important, it was a decelerator. The solemn rituals of the ordeal were spread out over time. They slowed down potentially violent confrontations and gave both parties time to negotiate. Far from being "irrational," the ordeal was a tried-and-true device for the achievement of consensus in societies without strong local leadership. Its solemn ceremonies were a tribute to "the vast bedrock of cunning with which medieval man actually faced and manipulated the supernatural in their affairs."[6]

6. Brown, "A Medieval Change," in *Society and the Holy in Late Antiquity*, 325.

So why had it ended? Was it really because twelfth-century persons became more rational? No. It was because the state grew stronger. The growth of state power in many areas of Europe undermined the communities of roughly balanced persons who had made use of the ordeal. These communities had consisted of villagers at the bottom, and warrior-elites at the top. Persons in each group had the support of families or dependents behind them; they needed much persuading before they would back down. As a result, law and order were treated as consensual matters—they had to be negotiated, not imposed. In the same way, the ordeal helped to create consensus in a group that, without it, could have been permanently disrupted. Closure could be reached only through consensus; and consensus could be reached only by an appeal to a force outside the human community—to the supernatural.

In the course of the twelfth century, this situation changed. The notion of a consensus formed around the ordeal lost out to more forceful ways of bringing disputes to an end. Royal agents no longer needed to massage consensus among villagers by solemn and time-consuming rituals before coming to a judgment: "The gallows could speak for itself, without mystification."[7] In this way, the hangman brought the ordeal to an end far more effectively than did any rational argument proposed by the schoolmen. Far from being a triumph of reason, the end of the ordeal registered a triumph of state power at its most abrasive.

"Society and the Supernatural: A Medieval Change" was my last article written in Oxford. It showed the drift of my thought. It was something of a manifesto against the European exceptionalism that was implicit in many narratives of the Western Middle Ages. This view seemed to imply that Europe had a monopoly of rationality and progress; and that its more ancient neighbors in Byzantium and the Islamic world had somehow missed out, because they had not passed through the changes that occurred in the privileged West.

But this, of course, raised a further question. If such rituals—and others like it, such as the cult of saints, which flourished at the same time—were not to be dismissed as part of a "Primitive Age," then what had the early Middle Ages in the West really been like? It seemed to me that the quality of an entire epoch was at stake. This was a theme worthy of extended research. It was time to leave the living holy men of the East and to return to the Latin West—to examine more closely the role ascribed, in Western society, to the "presence" of the long-dead saints in their splendid tombs, as sources of healing, justice, and dignity among the living.

7. Brown, "A Medieval Change," in *Society and the Holy in Late Antiquity*, 323.

PRESENCES

The Aesthetics of the Holy

The *Daedalus* group met again in Venice in late September 1973 to continue its discussion of the Axial Age. But the discussions meant less to me than the fact that I was back in northern Italy. I had not traveled there for some time. I found myself deeply moved by what I saw.

This was not the first time that this had happened to me. Ever since I first wandered spellbound through the colleges of Oxford at the time that I took the scholarship examination, and had been converted by the experience to the study of the Middle Ages, I found myself challenged to take in entire periods of history through my eyes. To look at works of art, and to ask myself what it had been like to see them for the first time, had been an integral part of my evolution as a historian.

Now, on coming to Venice on the occasion of the *Daedalus* workshop, I felt as if I had grown new eyes to carry a load of beauty that spoke directly to me. I wandered around in the great golden honeycomb of San Marco, and then I drove down to Ravenna, to view the iridescent mosaics of San Vitale. At Sant'Apollinare in Classe, I was struck by the great sarcophagi that lay in the side chapels. They were in Parian marble, so smooth as to seem almost transparent—so transparent, indeed, that local legend could have it that, in such sarcophagi, it was possible to see the body of the dead person, as if trapped in milk-white glass.[1]

The churches of Ravenna were filled with the shimmering greens of Paradise. Ingeniously arranged apses sheathed in gold mosaic and lit by candles

---

1. Agnellus of Ravenna, *The Book of Pontiffs of the Church of Ravenna*, trans. D. M. Deliyannis (Washington, DC: Catholic University of America Press, 2004), John I, 138.

seemed to trap the light of day in the midst of darkness. In these moments of nonverbal, visual encounter with the past, I received a lesson in the aesthetics of the holy in the late antique and early medieval West.

I had always admired late antique and Byzantine art; but this was something different. What I sensed was an immense effort to make the special dead present in the here and now through the beauty that surrounded their graves. I realized that I would have to learn what that sense of the presence of the glorious dead, evoked by such beauty, had meant to early medieval persons. Most studies of early medieval art told me what ideological message was conveyed by the images on the mosaics or by the architectural décor of the shrine. But they did not tell me what it felt like to worship at such a shrine. To understand this, I would have to learn to look at the art with early medieval eyes, and to read the texts with an early medieval sensibility in mind.

In Italy, my thoughts were triggered, almost subliminally, by the shimmer of mosaics and by the transparent, flesh-like white of marble tombs. What reassured me, when I returned to England, was that the link between beauty and the holy which I had experienced visually in Venice and Ravenna was congruent with what I read in the pages of a well-known author writing in early medieval Gaul—Gregory of Tours (538–594).

I had embarked on a reading of all the works of Gregory—not only his well-known *Histories*, but also his little-read *Books of Miracles*. I did not know what to expect. Somewhat to my surprise, I found the same aesthetic sensibility in his accounts of the miracles of the saints in the shrines of Gaul as I had found in the mosaics and sarcophagi of sixth-century Ravenna. The miracles he recorded were beauty in action. He conjured up a world filled with tombs in shining Parian marble, with hints of unearthly perfumes, and with stories of church pavements covered in red roses that bloomed miraculously in midwinter. When they appeared in dreams, the saints had lily-white skins and vivid red cheeks. As Gregory described them, they could have stepped straight out of the mosaics of their time.

I had not associated Gregory with such a sense of grace and beauty. As bishop of Tours (from 573 to 594), Gregory was best known to historians for his *Histories*. These were consistently misnamed as a *History of the Franks*, as if to place them firmly in the barbarian world. His Latin was judged to be as barbarous as the events that he described. His credulity was held to be unbounded. As I said in a paper that I wrote at this time, "a tradition of interpretation . . . is inclined to join, as in a maximum and minimum thermometer, the low ebb of Gregory's Latinity with the high tide of his credulity."

And yet, as I read him, it seemed to me that Gregory, usually presented as the mirror of a brutish age, shared with his contemporaries in Gaul and the Latin West a distinctive and refined aesthetic of the holy, of which the mosaics of Ravenna were only one example among many. It struck me that this visual beauty was not simply there to be enjoyed by viewers. Beauty was a sign of power—of power over death. As Gregory described them, the miracles at the shrines of the saints represented strange inversions of the grim decay of nature. Withered limbs "flowered" like the green trees of Paradise; the stench of the grave was replaced by wafts of heavenly perfume; trees blossomed with leaves like a flock of white doves to show that those buried beneath them flourished in the other world. Reading such accounts, I realized that Gregory, and others like him, had performed the remarkable emotional feat of turning the *summum malum* of physical death into something that condensed all that was most beautiful and refined in the life of their age.

The saints themselves were represented as graciousness itself, models of late classical poise. A paralyzed woman dumped by her relatives so as to live from begging alms at the shrine of Saint Julian at Brioude was approached by the saint in a dream:

> He was tall, he was spotlessly dressed, suave, he had a lit-up face, blond hair graying slightly, brisk in his movements, smooth-spoken and charming to talk to; his complexion was brighter than a lily, so that out of all the thousands of men she had ever seen, she had never seen the likes of him.

He gave her his arm, and led her to the tomb—and she woke up cured.[2]

FROM FUNCTION TO PRESENCE

These stories came as a challenge to me. They led me to reconsider aspects of my own work on holy men and women. In my article "The Rise and Function of the Holy Man" I had stressed the role of the holy man as an uncommitted arbiter in the midst of a conflict-ridden society. I had claimed that, by adopting the role of a total stranger, the holy man became "objectivity personified."[3] His magnificent opacity to the world around him seemed to make him an

---

2. Gregory of Tours, *De virtutibus sancti Iuliani*, 9, ed. B. Krusch, *Gregorii Turonensis Miracula* Scriptores rerum merovingicarum 1:2 (Hanover: Hahn, 1885), 118–119, now in R. Van Dam, *Saints and Their Miracles in Late Antique Gaul* (Princeton, NJ: Princeton University Press, 1993), 170.

3. Brown, "Rise and Function of the Holy Man," in *Society and the Holy in Late Antiquity*, 132.

object rather than a person: one Syrian holy man, for instance, was transported from one village to another, cell and all, without noticing it. He had already become an icon. In this way, the line between a holy person and a holy object was deliberately blurred.

I wondered whether something analogous could have happened with the great closed tombs of the saints in Gregory's Gaul, wrapped as they were in mysterious opacity. Silent blocks of marble, they could be saturated with the hopes and fears of the group gathered around them while themselves remaining faceless. The holy dead could have become, in effect, not persons, but holy things.

Gregory of Tours: *Praesentia*

Yet this was not what happened. The saints were not faceless to Gregory. His literary artistry was devoted to conjuring up the vivid men and women who lay in those seemingly impenetrable sarcophagi. They were living presences to him, more vivid and more active, now that their souls were in Heaven, than they had ever been on earth.

Praesentia, praesens—"presence," "present"—were crucial words for Gregory. They summed up an entire view of the relation between Heaven and earth. Saints were present in their tombs because their souls were fully alive in Paradise: it was as if the energy of Paradise flowed back into their dead bodies, so that their tombs "blazed" like crackling lightning with miracles of healing and similar deeds of power.

This meant, among other things, that Gregory's relations to the saints were not governed by anything as unreflecting as mere "credulity"—as all too many scholars claimed. They were governed by a punctilious code of etiquette toward imagined invisible persons. This etiquette was summed up by Gregory in the word *reverentia*. *Reverentia* had a heavily freighted opposite—*rusticitas*. By this, Gregory did not mean surviving remnants of rural paganism. Such paganism caused him little worry. What mattered for him was slobbishness—a lack of attention on the part of Christians of any class and region to the exacting codes that were supposed to govern their relations with the invisible presences who stood in their midst.

And these codes were surprisingly courtly. The heavy, proto-feudal relation of patron to client was a part of these codes: Gregory knew what it was like to approach a saint in fear and trembling, as if the saint were an angry lord. But the more I read, the more I realized that this was not all there was to it.

Gregory's relations with the saints also seemed to be suffused with a late classical courtesy. *Amicitia*—friendship—was included, as was imagery taken from the heady loyalties of members of the late Roman elites for their teachers and mentors. These people had been approached as objects of gratitude and love. In the same way, the saints, as Gregory imagined them, were not merely faceless wielders of power: they were beloved persons, dear to the heart.

The Invisible Companion

My interest in the hagiographical work of Gregory of Tours was not only guided by my visual experiences. I had also read extensively in general studies of ancient religion. What struck me most in this reading was a very old and widespread theme—the belief in an intimate bonding (amounting almost to the merging) of the higher reaches of the self with an Invisible Companion. This bonding was rooted in the nature of the universe. Person and invisible protector were seen as linked together in the great chain of being that united the rustling, many-layered cosmos of late antique thought.

A millennium of Mediterranean piety lay behind this search for invisible friends and guiding spirits who joined Heaven and earth: the *daimôn*—the guiding genius—of Socrates; the divine *Comes*—the personal protecting god—of the emperors; and the more homely figure of the guardian angel in Judaism and Christianity.

As I read Gregory, I was impressed to see how much of this ancient theme lay in the background of his treatment of the relations between the saints and their human protégés. It marked him out as a man whose thought-world still belonged to late antiquity. Far from being a grim harbinger of the Middle Ages, Gregory had gathered into his works the rich harvest of the Christian imagination of late antique Gaul.[4]

Altogether, I was made aware, by my work on Gregory's deep roots in the late antique religious world, that new problems had crept up on me. I realized that a place had to be found for a wider range of relations between holy figures and the society they lived in than the one I had offered in the late 1960s.

When I first wrote on the holy man, it had seemed sufficient to stress his role as an objective figure who functioned as an impersonal arbiter in a

---

4. For my most recent thoughts on Gregory, see Peter Brown, *The Ransom of the Soul: Afterlife and Wealth in Early Western Christianity* (Cambridge, MA: Harvard University Press, 2015), 149–182.

tension-ridden society. But holy men and women were also persons. Living or dead, they had to be approached not only in terms of their social function. The scholar also had to make due allowance, when studying the expectations of those who turned to them for guidance and healing, for the heavy tug on the heart of worship and for the need for a sense of closeness to benign and beautiful beings with much-loved human faces.

One scene summed up the change for me. As I wandered around San Marco, I remember being struck by an exquisite Byzantine image of the Virgin and Child. It was placed at eye level on one of the corner piers of the central dome, on the way to the Treasury. It was not a painted icon but was sculpted in low relief in pure white marble. Caught in the dancing light of many tapers and worn down by innumerable kisses, the marble seemed as luminous and as transparent as a waxen candle. It was known as the Madonna of the Kiss. Returning to Oxford, I found the verses of W. B. Yeats that summed up, for me, the discovery of "presence"—of Gregory's sense that certain things or persons could be picked out, in a dark world, as uniquely charged with love and beauty:

> Both nuns and mothers worship images,
> But those the candles light are not as those
> That animate a mother's reveries,
> But keep a marble or a bronze repose,
> And yet they too break hearts—O Presences
> That passion, piety or affection knows,
> And that all heavenly glory symbolize.[5]

In late antiquity and in the early Middle Ages, "Presences" had it in them to "break hearts." They touched my heart also. The cult of the saints in early medieval western Europe became one of the themes that I would study most actively in the coming years. My reading of Gregory of Tours proved to be the beginning of a new research agenda that I would pursue, for many years and in many different environments, until the publication of my book *The Cult of the Saints: Its Rise and Function in Latin Christianity* in 1981.[6]

5. W. B. Yeats, "Among Schoolchildren," in *The Tower* (1928).

6. Peter Brown, *The Cult of the Saints: Its Rise and Function in Latin Christianity* (Chicago: University of Chicago Press, 1981). The enlarged edition of 2015 contains a long introduction, which surveys the progress of the field and includes my second thoughts on many of the themes touched on in the book.

FROM THE
MEDITERRANEAN . . .

Landscape and History: Fernand Braudel (1902–1985)

Meanwhile, in 1973, my teaching of historical geography for the preliminary examination (for which I had volunteered to give lectures) added a whole other dimension to my study of the world of late antiquity around the Mediterranean, in the Middle East, and, yet further to the east, in the immense and largely unknown world of Sasanian Iran. This widening and deepening of my historical horizon was due largely to the availability, for the first time in English, of a single, remarkable book.

In 1972, Siân Reynolds published her English translation of Fernand Braudel's masterpiece, *La Méditerranée et le Monde Méditerranéen à l'Époque de Philippe II.* I had first read *La Méditerranée* in 1956, on the urging of my New College friend Jan Safranek. It had lingered in the back of my mind. But now I returned to it, in Reynolds's translation, and found that it opened up new horizons for me. It encouraged me to place the drama of the last centuries of the ancient world and the beginning of the Middle Ages against the background of the varied landscapes of the Mediterranean and the Middle East.[1]

The translation of Braudel's panorama of the sixteenth-century Mediterranean acted like an intravenous drip in English academic circles. It altered our historical imagination. Though devoted to the reign of Philip II (1555–1598), its magisterial evocation of the enduring features of Mediterranean history—the rhythm of

---

1. F. Braudel, *La Méditerranée et le Monde Méditerranéen à l'Époque de Philippe II* (Paris: Armand Colin, 1949; rev. ed. 1966); *The Mediterranean and the Mediterranean World in the Age of Philip II,* trans. Siân Reynolds (Collins: London, 1972), 2 vols.

the seasons, the unceasing dialogue between plain and mountain, settled land and desert, and the unique ecology shared by all its coasts—made it a book for all periods.

Braudel was never as dominant in Britain as he was in France. I suspect that most of us read his *Mediteranean* as a masterpiece of historical writing, not as the source of a brand-new methodology. I certainly did. But what this book conveyed, with great power, was belief in the possibility of a wider history than hitherto, linked to the rhythms of extensive landscapes. Compared with those enduring structures, the politics and battles that were the stuff of conventional, event-based history (of *histoire événementielle*) were mere "surface disturbances, crests of foam that the tides of history carry on their strong backs."[2]

Braudel's masterpiece has come to be frequently debated, especially in recent times, when the relation between history and ecology has become a major field of study. These debates have made us realize that Braudel painted with a large brush. His account of the Mediterranean emphasized enduring antitheses: busy plains and bulging cities overshadowed by immense gray mountains where time seemed to have stood still; and, to the east and south, the seemingly limitless sands of Arabia and the Sahara that dwarfed the Mediterranean, making its intensely fertile lands seem small—like a thin green ribbon sewn onto the hem of a sackcloth robe. To come upon Braudel's evocation of these vast spaces, after generations of purely political and administrative history, was to regain a sense of scale. Here were human societies whose vociferous hopes and fears were silently molded by constant adjustment to the slow, enduring rhythms of the seasons and the land.[3]

THE MEDITERRANEAN AND ITS NEIGHBORS

Now made accessible by Siân Reynolds's lively translation, Braudel's perspective brought a new dimension to the teaching of late antiquity and the early Middle Ages in Oxford. This was because there was already a perfect slot into which to insert his perspective. The preliminary examination in history had a mandatory paper on historical geography. Medievalists could choose to study

2. Braudel, *Mediterranean*, 21.

3. See now Peregrine Horden and Nicholas Purcell, *The Corrupting Sea: A Study of Mediterranean History* (Oxford: Blackwell, 2000), and W. V. Harris, ed., *Rethinking the Mediterranean* (Oxford University Press, 2006).

the historical geography of the period between 300 and 1000 for a paper that bore the grandiose title "The Formation of Europe."

Up until 1973, that paper had been dominated by magnificently old-world notions. Students were expected to put the barbarian invasions on the map, and then to study the origins of the nation-states of modern Europe which were thought to have grown out of the barbarian settlements that had resulted from those invasions. When I took the historical geography paper in the preliminary examination in the spring of 1954, a friend told me that it was easy: "All you need tell the examiners is that the Huns put butter on their hair, and that they ate their grandmothers; but don't forget to tell them that the Theiss, the Danube, the Sava and the Drava lie in between."

In 1973, I gave the lectures on historical geography under a new title: "The Mediterranean and Its Neighbors, 300–1000 A.D." I began by suggesting that a new perspective could put old themes in a new light. It would give a sense of proportion to current historical narratives of the end of the Roman Empire. For instance, we all knew the conventional dates for the barbarian invasions: 378, the defeat of the Roman armies by the Goths at the Battle of Adrianople; 410, the sack of Rome; 476, the end of the Western empire. But what about 364?—now that was a *real* date: for it marked the first massed appearance of camel nomads on the southern frontier of Roman Africa. This was the beginning of a truly decisive development. For these camels were the harbingers of a fundamental shift away from the Roman civilization of the Mediterranean coastline toward a civilization based on the great inland routes of the Sahara—a vast and silent change that began in the fourth century AD and would be rendered irrevocable by the rise of Islam.

I should add that, as far as the history of the camel was concerned, this somewhat melodramatic view would soon be muted by the work of my friend Brent Shaw. He showed that the camel nomads had appeared in North Africa much earlier, and that they had been absorbed with little disruption into the economy of the settled land.[4] But, at the time, it served a good purpose. It gave the young a sense of proportion. I pointed out that not every date in the conventional narrative of the decline and fall of the Roman Empire was of equal importance, because not every development in this period was equally

4. See especially "The Camel in Roman North Africa and the Sahara: History, Biology, and Human Economy," *Bulletin de l'Institut Fondamental d'Afrique Noire* (Dakar) 41 (1979): 663–721, now in *Environment and Society in Roman North Africa* (Aldershot, UK: Variorum, 1995), no. IV.

profound. Some were mere flecks of foam. Others (such as the rise of nomad-
ism along the fringes of the southern Mediterranean and the Middle East)
were carried on rollers of incalculable power.

To see the nomads in this way, I had to go beyond Braudel. At the time, I
remember being particularly impressed by the work of Xavier de Planhol
(1926–2016), *Les fondements géographiques de l'histoire de l'Islam.*[5] This book
showed how the nomads of the Middle East and North Africa were not a peripheral group, known only as raiders. They had always played a vital role in
the life of the settled populations. After the Arab invasions of the early seventh
century, the nomads came into their own—but not as destroyers of urban life.
Far from it. In the early centuries of Islam, nomads and townsmen cooperated
to create an immense commercial network. As a result, the Mediterranean
came to be overshadowed by the vast hinterlands that lay behind its southern
and eastern shores.

In these lectures, I put together two different traditions of scholarship—
Braudel's study of the societies of the Mediterranean and the emergent study
of the relations between the nomads and the settled world in the hinterland of
the Mediterranean and in the Middle East. I joined them so as to create a narrative by which the one—the world of the nomads, the masters of distance
over dry land—took over from the other, earlier, and more inward-looking
world—the ancient world of the inland sea.

From Core to Periphery

I argued that there had been two phases in the history of the period between
300 and 1000. In late antiquity proper, up to around 600, the Mediterranean was
still at the center. This solid core had been little shaken by the barbarian invasions of non-Mediterranean Europe. Before 600, also, the nomadic societies
of the Sahara and the Middle East still seemed "as fragile as a handful of human
dust blowing in the wind."[6]

Then things changed. I devoted the second part of term to the eastern and
southern neighbors of the Mediterranean. I conjured up the unexpected
resources of the nomadic world that Mediterranean observers of the time
had failed to appreciate—as had modern scholars with their exclusively

5. Xavier de Planhol, *Les fondements géographiques de l'histoire de l'Islam* (Paris: Flammarion, 1968).

6. Braudel, *Mediterranean*, 176.

Mediterranean focus. Hence I moved to the Hijaz, in Arabia, in order to explain the career of Muhammad (ca. 570–632) and the subsequent Arab conquests.

Ultimately, because of its command of distances based on the camel and the caravan, the Islamic empire of the eighth, ninth, and tenth centuries was able to create a whole new world based on a network of great inland cities. These commercial hubs were set back from the Mediterranean, along lines of communication that stretched from Timbuktu in the southern Sahara, along the inner plateau of the Maghreb to Kairouan (inland to the south of Carthage), to Egypt, where Fustat/Cairo (over a hundred miles up the Nile) replaced Alexandria, and across the Middle East and Iran, to join the cold deserts of Central Asia.

The huge sweep of the Islamic empire did not bring ruin to the Mediterranean, as Pirenne had suggested in his *Mohammed and Charlemagne*. It simply passed it by. From 800 onward, the Islamic empire was placed at the crossroads of western Asia, Africa, and Europe. It would dominate the world as Rome had once done. But it did so far from the sea. The immensity of a Eurasian empire dwarfed the vivid but narrow world of the Mediterranean that had been brought alive for me by the work of Fernand Braudel.

The Camel and the Bath

The lectures entitled "The Mediterranean and Its Neighbors" were the last that I ever gave in Oxford. When I visited Berkeley a little later, in early 1975, as a visiting professor, they formed the basis of my outline lecture course on late antique and early medieval history. The Berkeley students immediately grasped where my enthusiasm lay—in the balance between two worlds: on the one hand, the compact world of the Mediterranean that had supported an age-old urban civilization, with its grand forums, theaters, and busy public baths; and, on the other, the wide open spaces, crossed slowly but surely by the camel and the caravan, which finally came to dwarf the Mediterranean, in a land-based empire that stretched, through oceans of sand, gravel, and dead earth, from the Atlantic to the borders of China. They rightly called the course "The Camel and the Bath."

TO IRAN

AN EMPIRE IN A LANDSCAPE

My lectures on the Mediterranean and its neighbors, in late 1973, attempted to do justice to the magnificent perspectives opened up by Fernand Braudel. But, following Braudel's example, they did not attempt to cover the whole of the Middle East. For Braudel himself was well aware that yet another, very different world lay far to the east of the Mediterranean. This was Persia (Iran), whose sheer immensity caught his imagination:

> The Venetian Giacomo Soranzo describing Persia in his report of 1576, suggests in one sentence its vast emptiness: "one can travel through this land for four months without leaving it."[1]

For Braudel, Persia remained the great unknown. But for a historian of late antiquity, and especially one concerned with the Middle East, Persia was not a distant region. It was the immediate, ever-present neighbor and rival of East Rome. The Sasanian Empire of Iran (which lasted from 224 to 651) came to be locked in conflict with East Rome along a front that stretched from the Caucasus to Yemen.

Inspired by Braudel, I was eager to go back to the East once again; but this time I wanted to follow the conflict between the East Roman and the Sasanian empires in a different way. The conflict was not simply a military and diplomatic matter. It was a conflict between a Mediterranean empire and its vast, non-Mediterranean counterweight in the Middle East. Two different styles of empire faced each other, each linked to a different geography.

1. Braudel, *Mediterranean*, 173.

With this in mind, I rewrote the "Byzantium, Persia and the Rise of Islam" lectures, which I had first given in 1969, and delivered the new version of them in early 1973. To give such lectures was a further, resolute step toward the East. I intended that they should be the basis for a possible book on the relations between Byzantium and Iran, up to and beyond the Muslim conquest of the Middle East. In the lectures, I attempted to compare the two empires. I wanted to explain how those features of the Sasanian Empire that had struck East Romans (and which also had struck most modern scholars) as alien and "barbaric" might have functioned in terms of the adjustment of politics—always the art of the possible—to the mute constraints of an immense landscape.

Hence I began my lectures with a sense of the tyranny of distance in an empire based on the Iranian plateau. Although the Sasanian Empire was firmly established in southern Mesopotamia, in the royal city complex of Ctesiphon (just south of modern Baghdad), in the heart of one of the most ancient and fertile landscapes in the Western Hemisphere, it also stretched northward and eastward, like the tail of a great dragon, over the Zagros Mountains toward the Caucasus, and across the bare Iranian plateau as far as what are now Afghanistan and Turkmenistan. Whenever this huge bulk unfolded to lurch toward the west, it was a time of deadly danger for the Eastern Empire.

By contrast, the East Roman Empire was a compact polity. It was a creature of the Mediterranean, held together by rapid sea transport. It looked inward on itself from shore to shore. Few major cities were more than fifteen days' sailing from each other. In the words of Mu'awiya (661–680), the first Arab caliph to launch a Muslim fleet in the Mediterranean, "The song of a bird on the coast of Syria can be clearly heard in all the cities of Rûm." By contrast, the Sasanian Empire was an empire of the open road. It sprawled ever outward, across the "vast emptiness" that had so struck Braudel.

HEGEMONY AND WORLD-EMPIRE

The difference between the geographical settings of the two empires showed in many ways. Both made claims to universal rule. But the way in which this claim to rule was expressed was different in each case. In Iran, the notion of the hegemony of the Iranian empire in a world of many kingdoms was a core belief among the governing classes. The recent brilliant work of Richard Payne and of Matt Canepa has shown, at length, how this ideal worked out in practice in the foreign policy and in the monuments of the Sasanian Empire. I only wish that these two books had been available when I spoke in 1973.[2]

I did what I could with the literature available to me. Reading the *Letter of Tansar*, which had recently been translated by Mary Boyce (1920–2006),[3] and other Persian sources, I found that the sheer size of the Sasanian Empire and its geographical location at the crossroads of western Asia fostered a distinctive outlook. As I said in my lecture:

> An historian who comes from the study of the East Roman empire to that of Iran is immediately struck by the beauty and by the appositeness of the imagery by which the Sasanian governing class articulated their sense of standing at the cross roads of Asia. While the compact East Roman world that crowded around the Mediterranean thought of itself as a pool of light, surrounded by the faceless shadows of a barbarian world, the Sasanian empire took up its position at the centre of a world of clearly defined regions, whose characteristics and distinctive contributions to the arts of living were respected. The theory of the seven Keshvars, of the seven climates, which linked the individuality of Iran's neighbours to the influence of the planets . . . validated this view.

I pointed out that, in this worldview, the ruler of the Sasanian Empire was truly a "king of kings"—a *shahanshah*. He did not present himself as ruling an empire encircled by uncivilized "barbarians," as the East Roman emperors claimed to do. Rather, he claimed to stand at the head of a pyramid of fully civilized, stable kingdoms of which he was the rightful overlord:

> The idea of the world divided between four great monarchies [according to the points of the compass]—Rome (Rûm) in the West, Persia in the middle, the empires of Central Asia and China to the North and East and, far to the South the kingdom of Axum (modern Ethiopia)—grew up in Sasanian Mesopotamia. The throne room of Khusro Anoshirwan was supposed to hold three vacant thrones—one for the Emperor of China, one for the King of the Khazars (that is for the ruler of nomad confederacies of Central Asia) one for the Emperor of Rûm, in case any of these distant vassals of the Shahanshah [the king of kings] chose to take up their seats at his court.

2. Richard Payne, *A State of Mixture* (Berkeley: University of California Press, 2015), and Matthew Canepa, *The Iranian Expanse* (Berkeley: University of California Press, 2018).

3. *The Letter of Tansar*, trans. Mary Boyce (Rome: Istituto italiano per il medio ed estremo Oriente, 1968), 16–22.

HEGEMONY AND TOLERANCE

This ideal of a relaxed hegemony spilled over into the treatment of religious diversity within the Sasanian Empire itself. The king of kings was committed to upholding the Zoroastrian faith. It was an ancient religion, dating from the preaching of Zoroaster in the first millennium BC. It was centered on fire temples dedicated to the one god, Ahura Mazda, who was perpetually engaged in holding at bay the assaults of Ahriman, an eternal and independent principle of evil, not unlike the Christian Devil. Iranians spoke of their religion as "the Good Religion," and were fiercely loyal to it in their homelands on the Iranian plateau and in Central Asia.

Zoroastrianism was the official religion of the empire. But it was not the only religion. The attitude of the king of kings to the other religions of his empire was very different from that of the Christian emperors of East Rome. While the empire of Justinian (527–565) was committed to a claustrophobic maintenance of Christian orthodoxy at the expense of all other faiths (persecuting heretics and pagans and imposing cramped conditions on Jews), the Sasanians made room for any number of different religions in the different regions of their empire—Christians of all varieties, Jews, and Buddhists.

I stressed this contrast. Altogether, I was struck by the vigor of the inter-confessional encounters that took place all over the Sasanian territories:

> Religious disputations between Christians and Jews, Zoroastrians, Hindus and Buddhists; these were part of the culture of the Sasanian empire. [The king of kings] Bahram Gur (421–439) would spend time in the royal archives: "He studied and compared all the religions of his empire with the Magian (Zoroastrian) religion . . . and brought Christianity into this comparison, and said in his anger (with the obdurate Armenian Christians) 'Examine. Ask questions. Observe. Let us choose the one which is best.'"
>
> Orthodox Zoroastrian though he was, Bahram viewed the other religions of his empire with a certain cold tolerance: even they had a right to exist as so many cubes in the shimmering mosaic of a culture drawn from the seven climates of the world.[4]

Given the reputation, among East Romans, of the Sasanians as cruel persecutors of Christians, the discovery that martyrdoms were the exception rather

---

4. See now Payne, *A State of Mixture*, 23–58, and Katharina Heyden, *Die "Erzählung des Aphroditian"* (Tübingen: Mohr Siebeck, 2009), 116–143.

than the rule came as a surprise to me. I found that the Christian churches usually enjoyed a remarkable degree of tolerance. Even pagan philosophers persecuted by Justinian fled for a time to the court of Khusro I Anoshirwan in order to find a more open environment. Altogether, the basic structures of Sasanian rule favored diversity. A polity pitted against "Distance, the First Enemy" of all extended empires was held together by a tacit consensus that it took all sorts to make a world.[5]

SPLENDOR AND CONSENSUS

It was this element of tacit consensus that Mediterranean observers failed (or refused) to see in the workings of the Sasanian Empire. Yet everything that seemed to East Roman observers to be most grandiose, top-heavy, and, at times, frivolous in the actions of the king of kings rested, in fact, on the effort to create a consensus of the governing classes around the person of the ruler.

In my lectures, I examined the towering position of the king of kings. The Sasanian ruler claimed to be a kinsman of the gods. Though such a claim seemed outright blasphemy to East Roman Christians, it rested on a widespread consensus on the part of the Persian nobility. Highly competitive among themselves, they agreed to treat the king of kings as axiomatically superior to everybody else. They did this for a good reason. By treating the king of kings as somehow suprahuman, they ensured that they would not have to bow to any of their human peers. I cited a legendary incident in the *Letter of Tansar*. It was said that, before leaving Iran for India and China, Alexander the Great had wished to massacre the Persian nobility. He regarded such independent persons (grouped in great families and in control of entire regions) as a potential danger to his rule. The wise Aristotle dissuaded him from doing so. Instead, he should honor the nobles, so that they would prefer to honor him rather than have to honor any of their equals:

> The best course is to divide the realm of Iran among these princes, to bestow a throne and a crown on whomsoever you appoint to any province. . . . For the title of king is a great pride, and none wearing a crown is ready to pay tribute to another, or to humble himself for any man. There will appear among them so much disunity and variance from presumption and haughtiness, so much bragging and vaunting of wealth, so much contention over degree, and so much wrangling over retainers, that were you at the very

5. Braudel, *Mediterranean*, 355.

farthest bounds of the earth each would menace his fellow with your dread, invoking your power and support.[6]

I concluded that, in such a situation, if the *shahanshah* had not existed, he would have had to be invented. Indeed, much of the ceremonial life of the Sasanian Empire consisted in "inventing" the king of kings as superior to everyone else. Historical accounts of the Sasanian Empire were full of memorable court scenes, where the king of kings appeared ablaze with jewels. He wore a crown so heavy that it had to be held above him by a chain from the dome beneath which he stood lest its weight break his neck. East Roman observers tended to dismiss these gestures as signs of megalomania. But they were not used to express the vanity of the ruler. Seen in a Persian context, this splendor was a sign of the agreement of the Persian nobility to invest their ruler (and no one else) with such unearthly majesty.

A Style of Life

Most significant of all, this consensus was made real, on a day-to-day basis, by the lifestyle of the king of kings. Nothing could be more different from that of the rulers of East Rome. The king of kings reciprocated the consensus of the nobility by sharing with them the joyful, generous habits of a nobleman. Hence I pointed to a marked contrast between the rulers of the two empires:

> Compared with the Shahanshah the Emperor of Byzantium was a remote and over-worked man: he sat at his desk crushed by the load of paperwork that suited the head of a bureaucracy—Justinian was proud to be known as 'the sleepless one'. The Shahanshah, being the symbol of the stability of the Persian aristocracy, was a Persian aristocrat writ large. Solemn banquets, drinking, hunting and love: though these were indulged in spontaneously, they were as much part of the ceremony of rule as any more formalized governmental actions.

An International Style

As I read what was available on the subject—mostly by art historians, such as Oleg Grabar (1929–2011) and Prudence Harper—I was struck by the way in which the court culture of the Sasanians, with its frank enjoyment of life, paved the way toward the creation of a cultural empire that rivaled that of East Rome.

6. *Letter of Tansar*, 27.

I cited Oleg Grabar, whose work on Sasanian and early Islamic art I had begun to know. His remarks made sense of the haunting beauty of the images of the king of kings as the great hunter and lord of the banquet. As Grabar wrote:

> Religious attitudes and meanings attached to hunting around the 3rd century created a visual typology of hunting which the Sasanians transform into a theme illustrating primarily princely power. . . . Most of them [the Zoroastrian themes] became meaningless outside of their original context, but eroticism, dancing and feasting could be and were translated into a permanent secular language.[7]

The "permanent secular language" created by the Sasanian style of rule proved to be as tenacious, in the Islamic world, as were the Arthurian legends and the refinements of courtly love in medieval Europe. This language of mingled power and pleasure had originated in the court culture of fifth- and sixth-century Iran. Its wide diffusion in the Middle East and in Central Asia was the most sure symptom of all of the silent turning of the tide of civilization that would soon—with the Arab conquests of the seventh century and the establishment of the Islamic empire—race away from the Mediterranean toward Mesopotamia and the Iranian plateau. It was time for me to look for myself at that distant land. I would visit Iran.

7. Oleg Grabar, *Sasanian Silver* (Ann Arbor: University of Michigan Museum of Art, 1967), 55 and 67; see also Prudence Harper, *The Royal Hunter: Art of the Sasanian Empire* (New York: Metropolitan Museum, 1978).

THE ROYAL ROAD

TEHRAN TO KERMANSHAH

An Innocent Abroad

From April 12 to May 6, 1974, I traveled in Iran. At the age of thirty-nine, I was still very much an innocent abroad. But I knew what I wanted. I wanted to see Iran with my own eyes so as to place the history of the Sasanian Empire against a living landscape.

With instant generosity, friends in the British Institute of Persian Studies arranged with the British Council that I would deliver a lecture entitled "The Sasanian Empire in the Near East" in their various centers in Iran, and that the council's local representatives would look after me as I traveled. The lecture was an attempt to understand the Sasanian Empire (from 224 to 651) on its own terms, from the inside, instead of judging it by Western standards—and usually finding it wanting.

I soon realized that I had to tread carefully on that issue. Most people outside Iran had heard of the Achaemenid Empire of Cyrus, Darius, and Xerxes, in the sixth and fifth centuries BC. They could visit the stupendous ruins of the Achaemenid palace at Persepolis. In October 1971, Reza Shah had celebrated the twenty-five-hundred-year anniversary of empire in Iran with a grandiose historical parade in front of the ruins.

But the Sasanian Empire of the fifth and sixth centuries AD was another matter. It was an uncomfortable presence. I sensed that Iranians tended to regard it with acute ambivalence. This empire was part of the glorious past of Iran. Its passing had been mourned, throughout the Middle Ages, by a succession of Persian poets. But it was also remembered as the corrupt and arrogant empire that had been swept away by the victorious armies of Islam. The palace of Persepolis belonged safely to the dreamtime of Iran. But the Sasanians were still the subject of bitter contemporary debates as to how much or how little modern Iran owed to its pre-Muslim past. I would have to walk a tight-rope. But I would at least get to see the country.

Throughout my visit to Iran, I was entertained and guided by people of rare generosity, whose love for Iran was infectious and all-embracing. But it was a cocooned existence on my part. I met only a self-selected company of Iranians, connected with the cultural activities of the British Council. And this was in 1974. Most of us did not have a glimmer of the Iranian Revolution that would happen only five years later. We were like travelers making our way through a pearly fog. Soon a more savage landscape would be revealed, as the fog burned off in the blaze of the Iranian Revolution. Only then did we have time to be wise after the event.

Accessibility and Majesty: The *Iwân*

I came to see Sasanian monuments on the ground. Not surprisingly, I saw a lot more than that. I also saw religions on the ground. This was the first time ever (apart from my childhood in Sudan) that I had been in a Muslim country. But I was soon confronted with the immense reach of the Islamic world as viewed from the plateau of Iran. The day after my arrival, an enthusiastic architect drove me to Varamin, forty miles southeast of Tehran, where the ruins of a Sasanian fire temple lay close to an exquisite mosque complex made up of four *iwâns* (great arched apses) founded in the late thirteenth century by a Mongol khan. It was a reminder of the Central Asian dimension of late medieval Iran of which I knew little.

The architect had just returned from Beijing, where he had designed the embassy of Iran in the form of a vast *iwân* arch. He told me that the *iwân* was a distinctive building, with a mystique of its own: in his opinion, it unfolded like the rays of the rising sun. A high-arched gateway backed by a rectangular space, the *iwân* presented to the world a great opening behind which lay a majestic or divine presence.

What I already knew from my reading was that the *iwân* was one of the most ancient architectural features of the Middle East. It was in the form of the gate of a palace or a city. From the time of the great Gate of Balawat in the British Museum to the Sublime Porte (the Exalted Gate) of the Ottoman Empire, the *iwân* had been the symbol par excellence of royal power—of an awesome combination of accessibility and majesty that was characteristic of the Sasanian style of rule.

Looking at the *iwâns* of Varamin, I realized that I was now on the other side of the world from East Rome. In Byzantium, the immense domed church of the Hagia Sophia in Constantinople became the characteristic form of a Christian church. The Ottoman Turks followed the model of the Hagia Sophia for their mosques. The distinctive domed mosques with which Europeans were most familiar were Ottoman echoes of the Hagia Sophia that spread, in all sizes, from Sarajevo to Damascus. By contrast, from the Iranian plateau eastward to the Taj Mahal in India and far beyond, the *iwân*—and not the dome—reigned alone as the preferred architectural form for a mosque. I realized that I had come a long way from the Mediterranean.

And how did we orientate ourselves in Iran, to find north and south, east and west? To do this was a reminder of belonging to the world of Islam, where all roads led to Mecca. As I wrote in a letter:

> Arriving at the ruins of the fire-temple, the first thing that we did was to ask a local boy for the *qebla*, the *qibla* [the direction of prayer to Mecca]. Instantly, the boy stopped, faced the plain where cyclists pedaled between cotton fields, joined his hands in the direction of a row of blue hills caught in the sinking light—there, far, far to the south was Mecca, as distant as the late light itself, over how many plains, how many ranges of blue hills.

For almost half a century, I have retained this image of the boy standing on a hillock, turned, with a sure sense of direction, to face a plateau bathed in a seemingly endless sunset light.

On the Royal Road: Tehran to Hamadan

Next day, I took the measure of the spaces of Iran on a bus that went southwest from Tehran to Hamadan, ancient Ecbatana, along the Royal Road that led to Kermanshah, and then, down from the Zagros Mountains, to Qasr-e Shirin, close to the frontier of Iraq. This was the road that snaked across the Iranian plateau, joining Mesopotamia to Central Asia.

We set out in the early afternoon crossing a vast plain ringed by mountains. For double safety, the bus carried both Muslim invocations in curling, calligraphic letters and an icon of the Virgin Mary. I talked to a passenger who had been quietly singing a *masnavi*—a poem of Jalal ad-Dîn Rûmi, (1207–1273), the great Persian mystical poet—just behind me. He was a post office official from Hamadan and had a brother in Bournemouth. He carefully wrote down my English address: "All Sins Kolidj" . . .

I knew Hamadan as Ecbatana, one of the great royal cities of the Achaemenid Empire, standing on the edge of the Iranian plateau before the Royal Road wound its way down the Zagros Mountains to Mesopotamia. Esther, the supposed wife of Xerxes (486–465 BC)—known as Ahasuerus in the Bible—was buried there. Her mausoleum is still a place of Jewish pilgrimage.

What I did not know, at this time, was that Hamadan was also famous in the Islamic world as the burial place of a philosopher and scientist who founded an empire of the mind that once reached farther than the empire of Xerxes—from Samarkand to Oxford. This was Ibn Sina (980–1037), known to the West as Avicenna. Ibn Sina's daring synthesis of philosophy and medicine, of Platonic mysticism and Aristotelian logic, dominated medieval thought in both the Islamic and the Christian worlds. Here was a man, now buried behind the Zagros, whose commentaries, when translated into Latin in the twelfth and thirteenth centuries, had set the universities of Europe afire. The entrance ticket to the Mausoleum of Ibn Sina was justly proud:

> The number of his publications is said to be between 195 and 243, most of which, such as the Ghanoon [the Qanûn], the Shafa and the Esharaat are still used by scholars.

Avicenna had died in 1037.

Strolling around Hamadan, I found myself at my ease among the mullahs in the courtyard of a mosque. I stood there as a group of middle-aged men, squatting on a carpet, sang the Qurʾân to each other. I wrote "sang": "recited" the Qurʾân would be more correct; although to my unaccustomed ear it sounded like Russian or Greek Orthodox chant. They smoked cigarettes, joked, settled down in turn to recite, taking the book, kissing it first, and laying it on their brow along their nose. A man of great fineness of face, in a black cloak like an Oxford gown, stood all the time, propped against the doorway of the mosque. He may have been the imam. Outside, the mullahs squatted and gossiped in gentle tones. I have always carried the memory of this moment as my first contact with living Islam.

MOUNTAINS, WATER, AND MONUMENTS: BISOTUN AND TAQ-E BOSTAN

The most significant part of the Royal Road lay beyond Hamadan. The rock carvings at Bisotun that towered above the road are well known to ancient historians. They carry the great inscription of King Darius (552–486 BC), which described his triumph over usurpers and listed the twenty-three countries in his possession—truly a king of many kings. This inscription is so well known, carved onto a high cliff, that I was surprised to find that the mountain of Bisotun itself was a site of eerie grandeur. It was the mountain, rising straight from the plain, that was spectacular, not the inscription. As I wrote in my letter:

> What matters is the superb amphitheater at its foot, with the water rushing into the pool among cypresses and the distant view of a river and of fields with hillocks as far as the eye can see. Nothing grandiose about the inscription. It is a signet stamp carefully impressed on the irreducible mass of rock.

I had learned something. Close-up photographs of Achaemenid and Sasanian rock carvings encourage us to treat them as if they were freestanding monuments. I now saw that they were really only the markers of sites—of privileged ecological niches in a harsh land, where the Zoroastrian goddess Anahita showed her presence in the permanent miracle of water and green trees.

I had come up against something that I had not considered before. I had traveled to Iran to see landscapes in the manner of Braudel—the great stretches of plain, desert, and mountain that formed the background to history. But what I had just seen was something different: it was a sacred landscape saturated in the beliefs of those who lived in it—where mountains, plains, and water were revered as joining points between the human and the divine.

I would have the same experience when we reached Taq-e Bostan, outside Kermanshah. The rock carvings of Taq-e Bostan were to be found in a row of carved grottoes standing at the foot of a bare cliff. The largest of these has always been linked in legend with Khusro II Aparwez "the Victorious" (AD 591–628)—the most grand and romantic of all the Sasanian kings. The sides of this grotto are covered with dramatic representations of the royal hunt—a huge affair, like an army in motion. The protecting angel of the king of kings is shown at the bottom of the cave as a mounted horseman in full armor, with a high helmet, raising a massive lance above his armored horse—for all the world like a medieval knight: a specimen of the new skills in cavalry warfare learned on the plains of Central Asia.

This was exciting enough. I knew it well from the superb photographic record made by the Japanese Institute of Iranian Studies.[1] But I also wanted

1. Shinji Fukai and Kiyoharu Horiuchi, *Taq-i Bostan* (Tokyo, 1969).

to see what the site itself would have meant to a sixth-century Iranian. On arriving in the bus, I knew at once that I was in the presence of a miracle of water.

> There is a crescendo of Aye sabz! Oh, the greenery! [from the passengers on the bus]. . . . Close to the rock face and the carved caves, the river bubbles in and out of poplar groves. A still lake stands in front of the rock face, and—nearer to the carvings—a still, perfectly circular pool, with a mulberry tree pruned for Persian heads (I hit mine every time I passed). . . . Pleasure boats row in the lake. Good restaurants. It is a place bi-sifâ—"with purity": a place of relaxed pleasure. Kurdish girls wash their silver bowls in the stream beside the pool and the first cave.

FROM THE WORLD OF THE GODS TO A HUMAN COURT

I spent my time in Taq-e Bostan trying to figure out how the rock carvings of the grottoes related to this idyllic scene and the cliff into which the grottoes had been carved. Scrambling up the side of the cliff (a somewhat perilous undertaking in the high wind), I saw how the rich carvings had been gradually added to the original raw surface of the grottoes. Originally, these had been caves, natural indentations of the rock face, in the depths of which the king of kings had been shown face-to-face with the High God, Ahura Mazda, to receive the wreath that was the symbol of empire.

By the time of Khusro II, the largest grotto had become no longer a meeting place with the gods, but a palace in its own right, with a Roman-style archway flanked by plump, Roman figures of winged victories and ornamented inside with a spectacular representation of the royal hunt. This was the human world, a world of human power and human pleasures, where previously there had been raw rock, from whose feet water flowed in miraculous abundance.

Altogether, the great grotto attributed to Khusro II Aparwez was a vivid sign of the "secularization" of royal ideology. It showed how the iconography of kingship could be set loose from its original Zoroastrian roots to become an idiom of power and the good life throughout Central Asia and the Middle East, irrespective of religion. It was his triumphal arch, flanked by Roman victories, and the frank worldly glory of the royal hunt that made Khusro II victorious—and not initiation by a god, as was usual in Sasanian rock carvings. My climb up the rock face to feel the layering of the carved stone on the side of the great arch had been a bracing exercise in putting scenes well known to me in photographs against their dramatic physical background.[2]

Down to the "Heart of the Empire": Qasr-e Shirin

Next day I was driven down to Qasr-e Shirin, to within a few miles of the Iraqi border. This was a visit to a very different part of the Sasanian world—to the lush Mesopotamian plain that lies at the foot of the Zagros. Qasr-e Shirin was the site of a major Zoroastrian fire temple—designed to resemble a royal audience hall, where the fire "reigned" perpetually even when the king of kings was absent at the far end of his empire. Shirin was the name of the Christian wife of Khusro II, and the subject of endless legends as poignant as any in the Arthurian cycle in the West. All that remained of the great fire temple was a low mound of tumbled, uncut stones. But all around it was a world of little gardens and rustling trees, noisy with birds and frogs. After the gray, winter-stunned mountains, it was a Mesopotamian paradise. Little wonder that the Sasanians called Mesopotamia (effectively modern Iraq) *dil-i Eranshahr*—the Heart of the Empire of Iran. Its hot, immensely fertile lands were the very opposite to their own, austere plateau.

I left early next morning for Tehran.

2. See now Matthew Canepa, *The Iranian Expanse* (Berkeley: University of California Press, 2018), 360–365; and James Howard-Johnston, *The Last Great War of Antiquity* (Oxford University Press, 2021), 184–186.

PALACES AND ROCK CARVINGS

FIRUZABAD AND NAQSH-E ROSTAM

A Landscape on the Move: The Qashqai

I lectured for the first time on April 17 at the British Institute of Persian Studies in Tehran. It was a vivid occasion. But my heart was in the landscapes of Iran. I wanted to be out in the country again. The principal monuments of the early Sasanians were to be found outside Shiraz, which was 420 miles by air south of Tehran. The ruined palace of Ardashir (224–241)—the founder of the Sasanian Empire—was at Firuzabad, 70 miles south of Shiraz. It was not only the palace that I wished to visit, but also the surrounding region, to see how its monuments hung together in a single system. While Bisotun and Taq-e Bostan were sacred landscapes, this would be a royal landscape—an interlocking web of roads, palaces, and monuments connected with the movements of the king of kings and his court.

It was from the region around Shiraz that Ardashir had risen from the status of a provincial magnate (a mere subking) to becoming king of kings of a new empire named "Sasanian" after his ancestor Sasan. Ardashir's son, Shapur I (AD 240–272) consolidated this empire, most notably through his defeat and capture of the Roman emperor, Valerian, in AD 260, in a campaign that took place near Edessa (modern Şanlıurfa, in Turkey), in the very middle of the Fertile Crescent. Shapur's victories were celebrated in rock carvings at Naqsh-e Rostam (near Persepolis) 35 miles northwest of Shiraz, and at Bishapur, 58 miles west of Shiraz. In visiting these sites, I would be at the ground zero of the explosion of energy by which the Sasanian Empire came to dominate half of the Middle East throughout late antiquity.

I was prepared to study the way an ancient monarchy had traveled between its palaces and monuments. What I had not expected to see was the population of an entire landscape on the move. But this was exactly what I saw on the journey from Shiraz to Firuzabad.

I was picked up at my hotel in Shiraz by Henry Speck, who taught English at Shiraz University. He had come to take me by Land Rover to the third-century Sasanian palace at Firuzabad. What excited him were not only the Sasanians but also the news that the annual migration, the famous *kuch*, of the Qashqai nomads was under way. The Qashqai were Turkmen tribes, who spoke Turkish rather than Persian. They were believed to have gained access to the mountains of Iran as a result of the Mongol invasions of the thirteenth century. To most Iranians—townsfolk and sedentary peasants alike—the Qashqai were a disturbing reminder of the presence of Central Asia in the midst of Iran. The homelands of the Qashqai were the mountains, as they moved up and down the mountain slopes throughout the year from altitude to altitude in search of grazing land. Now that the pastures of the south were drying up with the approach of summer, they were headed north and into the highlands of the southern Zagros where they had been told that rainfall had been abundant. This is what Henry told me. As I wrote in a letter:

> The *kuch* (the annual migration of the Kashgai) was an occasion of pride— like a royal court on the move. In earlier times, they would move straight through Shiraz—hence the houses ringed with fortress-like walls and look out towers. Now they were more cabined and confined, and were viewed with suspicion by the Iranian authorities.

On the way to Firuzabad, we passed the Qashqai. A girl wrapped in a pure gold lamé shawl was spurring a white horse up the mountainside across an emerald-green field. A caravan of camels passed, with woolly foals. I was struck by the meticulous packing of the camels: the loads were tightly bound with wooden pegs and knots. Girls covered the entire haunches of their horses with their billowing crinolines of pink, blue, green, and gold. These were the clothes they wore to add to the splendor of the *kuch*, the migration, while, in the evening when encamped, they wore drab clothes.

The Road and the Water Goddess:
Anahita and the Tang-e Ab

Soon we arrived at the great ravine of the Tang-e Ab River, some ten miles from Firuzabad. Where the river became dark blue in two deep pools, sure enough, above it, on a little flattened surface of rock, there was a carving of Anahita, the Zoroastrian goddess of water. It being Friday, the pools were full of happy bathers.

This was our first clue to the placing of the Sasanian rock carvings of the region: they invariably appeared where the double blessing of water and the Royal Road converged. Looking up from the pools, from the bottom of the ravine, we could see Qaleh Dokhtar (The Castle of the Daughter of the King of Kings) above us on a high spur of rock. It was an enormous structure (somewhat like a Romanesque church) with a great dome, a circular apse decorated on the outside with pillars, and an impressive *iwân* as an entrance. The resemblance to a church came from the fact that this huge building, though now called a castle, had been a royal palace, complete with a solemn audience hall, with an *iwân* entrance, a vaulted nave, and a dome over the circular apse beneath which the king of kings stood, like a holy thing, in sacred majesty.

Qaleh Dokhtar had been a summer palace. Perched above a ravine on the edge of a wide plateau, it would have caught the breezes, as it floated above the sizzling plain. The king of kings and his entourage would have ridden out to it in a procession quite as colorful, and as tied to the rhythm of the seasons, as the *kuch* of the Qashqai that we had just seen. These were our thoughts as we looked upward. But we decided to explore the roads to Firuzabad before we made our way up to Qaleh Dokhtar. Here are my notes:

The rock carvings in the ravine below Qale-i Dukhtar are not monuments. They are quite invisible from the modern road that runs on a higher contour. [Instead, one should] ride along the road that leads from the palace of Firuzabad to the bridge over the Tang-i Ab to Qale-i Dukhtar. We found traces of this road as we walked along. It is there that you would meet the rock carvings. What you would then see, as you pass on horseback, is a series of scenes, like miniatures from a Shahnameh [an illustrated copy of the Book of Kings by Firdausi (940–1025)—the medieval Persian verse epic of the kings of Iran] clustered along a wall of rock. Shapur I holds his enemy in a chain-mail clad grip—this is added to the end of the series, nearest to Firuzabad. The fairy-tale violence of a skewered enemy, dangling at the end of a lance—it could be from Firdausi. Is this history, or is it not, rather, a kaleidoscope of heroic deeds, performed interchangeably? It is closer to epic than to the narrative carving of the ancient Near East. It is the flying tails of the horses that one remembers.

The carvings belong only to the world of the road beside the water. The road itself is dwarfed by a great hood of mountain that rests above it. It is pressed up to the rock, in such a way that the carvings are always viewed one after the other and always in close-up.

We arrived at the palace of Firuzabad . . . Henry meets friends. How odd, they say, to find you in this out of the way place. But we are in the capital of the third century Sasanian empire: where else would one find people?

Again: what is a palace? It is the marker of a favored site.

The Center of the World

Firuzabad stood at the center of an amphitheater of mountains. As often in Iran, mountains never seem to shut in a plain. Rather, they act as amplifiers to a sense of spaciousness. They hint at the limitless stretch, toward all corners of the world, that lies just beyond their peaks. It is not surprising that the Sasanian city of Firuzabad, placed in the plain at some distance from the palace, should be round, and that its gates should open to the four points of the compass. The city and the palace of Firuzabad were there to impress. They were a challenge to the land, claiming to reach beyond the amphitheater of mountains to the limitless spaces that the king of kings might yet come to rule. The building of such a palace and its neighboring city would have been Ardashir's first step on the road to power.

By Horse to Cool Air: Qaleh Dokhtar

Then we returned to the ravine of the Tang-e Ab. The ascent to the great ruin of Qaleh Dokhtar was not as difficult as we thought it would be. The moral: This was horse country. While our heavy Land Rover was tied to the modern road, riders on horseback could make their way to the top along an easy diagonal pathway up the side of the ravine. As with the rock carvings along the river, the Sasanian world opened easily to the rider. This was the landscape over which the Qashqai swarmed without difficulty, using the same tracks as the king of kings and his mounted entourage had once used. The view of the river was superb. We had reached a palace suited to a crucial stage in the annual rhythm of the Sasanian court—perched on the edge of the high plateau to catch the breezes in the summer season, and complete with deep underground galleries in which ice would have been stored.

The Epic of the Kings: Naqsh-e Rostam

Next day, I went to Persepolis to view the remains of the gigantic Achaemenid palace, whose ruins dominated the plains like a great stage. The Sasanian carvings lay a few miles farther north, at Naqsh-e Rostam—the Picture of Rostam, a legendary hero of Sasanian times. Here were the rock carvings that celebrated the victories of Ardashir and Shapur I, and especially the triumph of Shapur I over the Roman emperor Valerian in AD 260. Valerian, an old-fashioned Roman gentleman, had been no match for the warrior king of kings. Tricked and encircled, he was the only Roman emperor ever to be taken alive by a "barbarian" enemy. He died in captivity, but not before he had been paraded through Iran as a proof of the reach of the Long Right Hand of the king of kings.

The carvings at Naqsh-e Rostam turned this triumph into stone. They were carved into the rock a little above head level. Each victory showed the king of kings defeating his enemy in person. This was single combat, epic warfare. I knew these carvings well from photographs—especially the classic image of the Roman emperor Valerian crouching in homage to the victorious Shapur. But the site of the carvings at Naqsh-e Rostam came as a surprise. Two pasts—over seven hundred years apart—met on the rock face: the Achaemenids and the Sasanians. This is how I described it:

> First you see the Achaemenid tombs, static and square. Forms that express a royal power as solid as four-square architecture. . . . Then suddenly, [below them] where the Sasanian rock carvings are, you are in a world of dramatic movement. There is an explosion of fighting, of victory over falling enemies and warriors riding at full tilt at each other. On the first carving, the left hand grips the bridle, the left shoulder is hunched over the lance, the fallen enemy is a truly fallen enemy: he is truly trampled on, not simply subjected to a ritual gesture of dominance—the hooves are descending on him as a second enemy braces for the charge; one down and one to go. In the top panel, the shock of the charge is shown with a vigor that has survived all erosion of the rock face.

The explosion of energy shown in the rock carvings set me thinking about the rhythms of Sasanian history: their empire seemed to have a "boom-or-bust" quality. The problem of writing the history of such an empire was that it saw itself in terms of high moments of energy, associated with great conquering kings. But these high moments were often followed by long periods of quiescence, which have left little or no trace in our sources. It was like studying the astrophysics that led up to the explosion of a supernova. As historians, we have to account for those irregular pulses of light in what has remained for us a faraway galaxy, large parts of which were already opaque to East Romans and were only gradually being understood in the 1970s, by historians of ancient and medieval Iran. I returned to Shiraz with a whole new set of rhythms of history in my head.

THREE CITIES

ESFAHAN, TABRIZ, AND MASHHAD

ESFAHAN: THE SOUND OF ISLAM

Next day I was in Esfahan. Nothing Sasanian there. My first reaction was depression at the absence of space. Dust from the developing city swept in clouds over the Maydan—the great rectangle flanked by Safavid mosques and palaces of the time of Shah Abbas (1571–1626) and his successors—and I had to visit the mosques in a dim light more suited to English cathedrals. While the palaces and monuments of ancient Iran were usually lost in the countryside, placed near the roads and the holy places of a society with few towns, the heart of medieval and modern Iran lay in its great cities; and in the heart of these cities lay a living Islam riven by tensions whose explosive power, though known to some scholars and observers, largely escaped the notice of Western travelers at this time.

It was in Esfahan that I encountered, once again, as I had in Hamadan, the unexpected sound of Islam. I found my way to the Chahar Bagh—the avenue of the Four Gardens—made up of a succession of exquisite courtyards, beside a sixteenth-century madrasa—a theological school and place of meditation.

I found myself in a reception room that overlooked a garden of roses. It was explained to me that a young man had died after four years in a coma as the result of a car accident. A memorial recitation was being held. Coffee was brought to every guest. We all sat quietly as the sound of the Qur'ân and of Persian mystic poetry brushed over us softly. I now understood this description by the Muslim biographer of the Prophet Muhammad of the impact of the recitation of the Qur'ân on an outsider: "When I heard the Qur'ân my heart was softened and I wept, and Islam entered into me."[1] For, in the Qur'ân, it is God, not the worshipper, who is the sweet singer.

JULFA: THE SOUND OF THE MARTYRS

Next day, I wandered around the Armenian quarter of Esfahan—the famous Julfa, named after the Armenian community transported there in the late sixteenth century by Shah Abbas to Isfahan from the town of Julfa, in the far northwest corner of Iran. There, equally unexpectedly, I experienced a further touch on the heart of the songs of yet another religious community. Coming to the great Armenian cathedral, I approached a splendidly dressed cleric to ask him about the times of services. But the cleric spoke no Persian. He was Mesrob Ashjian, the new bishop, who had come straight from the Armenian community in Beirut. He spoke perfect English. And who was I? A teacher from Oxford, Mr. Brown. Not Peter Brown? The bishop had just returned from Princeton Theological Seminary and had read my *Augustine of Hippo*. He invited me to return next day for the celebration of the Memory of the Martyrs of 1915. I described this in a long letter:

> The chant was made by a women's choir dressed in blue robes. They stood on a raised platform to one side of the great curtain that veiled the raised stage of the sanctuary. Such curtains had once veiled the King of Kings on his raised throne. I could not follow the Armenian of the liturgy. But the movements around the high altar struck me as a combination of the ceremonial of a royal court and worship on the High Places. At moments, the priest was left all alone, standing in the raised sanctuary, with his head lifted to heaven as on a mountain top. The chalice was a holy thing, a burning bush like that which Moses had seen on Mount Horeb. Bells jingled on the altar fans.

But this was also the worship of a throne. It was explained to me that the curtain was lifted as the King showed himself to the people: Christ seated on the throne of the Eucharist. Then there was a moment of piercing drama when the curtain came down again, to hide that glimpse of majesty.

Above all, there was the drama of memory. We sat and meditated as the priest read an endless list of names to be remembered on this day. These names were not only the names of modern martyrs—the victims of the massacres of

---

1. Ibn-Ishaq, *Life of Muhammad*, 228, trans. A. Guillaume (Oxford University Press, 1955), 158.

1915 to 1917. They reached back to the very beginnings of late antiquity. And this was an Eastern late antiquity—the memory of a church beyond the frontiers of the Roman Empire, whose past was significantly different from that of the Greek and Latin churches. The bearers of these names belonged to a Christianity of the East that thought of itself as older than that of the West. Abgar the Black, the king of Edessa (who died ca. AD 40) was connected in legend with Jesus Christ himself. Trdat (Tiridates), king of Armenia (250–330), may have been a Christian a whole generation before Constantine. These were the names I noticed. But for Armenians—and especially for those in Lebanon, such as Bishop Mesrup—it was the generation of their own grandfathers that was also being remembered.

In this great Eastern liturgy, God did not sing, as he had sung in the recitation of the Qur'ân. Rather, he was serenaded by a women's choir, in voices as pure and light as their blue silk robes. The constant refrain was "Jerusalem, Jerusalem." As the poets declaimed, as the chant rose, and the black-edged banners waved in front of the great curtain, one sensed a seismic shaking of the whole church at the coming of God in the Eucharist: it was what I had always been told in books on the theory of religion, but never seen—the liturgical creation of a community. This moved me as deeply as had the Qur'ân recitals in the Chahar Bagh. In two days, from two religions, I had learned something of what it was to worship God.

Outside the cathedral, the high-mounted machine guns, the water cannons, and the wireless aerials of the armored personnel vehicles of the Persian security forces surrounded the church, looking down on us from the other side of the wall, throwing their shadows into the rose-filled courtyard.

TABRIZ: WHOSE HISTORY?

Next I went to Tabriz. This was a very different landscape, far to the northwest, some three hundred miles by air from Tehran. I was only fifty miles from the frontiers of Turkey and Russia, in the border province of Azerbaijan. In the early spring, the countryside was covered with unpruned cherry trees in exquisite, full blossom, with branches twisting like flames, like those of the Timurid manuscripts of the fifteenth century that seemed to bring a breath of China all the way to northern Iran.

It was only in Tabriz that I received a direct impression of the tensions of modern Iranian society. I learned that my lecture was to be given, not at the British Council, but at the University of Tabriz. The university had a dangerous reputation. The police had occupied it for two years. These were Shirazi police, I was told—hard men, not locals. In the previous year, some twenty-five students were said to have been killed, mostly from being beaten up.

I gave my lecture on the Sasanian Empire in a long room, filled with intense young men with short beards. I was surrounded by a posse of anxious professors. Halfway through, something like barracking set up from the back. I lifted my pointer, stopped dead, and said, in Persian, "I cannot be heard." Dead silence ensued. But the professors were visibly flustered. As soon as I sat down, the professor who had introduced me barked out: "Questions. No questions? Then go!" Deliberately not understanding, I stood up and said that I would be delighted to discuss the lecture, as I had much to learn about Iran. Discuss they did, with all the intensity that I had often encountered in young men in Iran.

The students and I were on a collision course. My lecture had been devoted to furthering what I thought was a worthy cause—to rescue the history of Iran from Eurocentric value judgments. I wanted to present the functioning of the Sasanian Empire in terms of its own, distinctive political culture, so as to avoid the usual negative value judgments, based on Western ideas of what an empire should be like, that had been applied to the Sasanian political system by Western scholars. My aim was to vindicate the Sasanians in the face of this orientalist prejudice, by showing how the system worked in its own terms.

But this was not at all the way that my audience heard it. To them, my attempt to defend the Sasanian Empire from Western prejudice sounded like an attempt to whitewash the present-day imperial regime of Shah Reza. Seen by the radical young of Tabriz, the Sasanian Empire (corrupt, caste-ridden, and doomed to fall) was a mirror of their own times: to attempt to view it in any other light was to surrender to the shah.

The questions came thick and fast. Why was my lecture so superficial? Why had I not told them about the social weaknesses that had led to the fall of the Sasanian Empire, and to its replacement by a triumphant, more democratic Islam? Why did I not tell them about the revolution of Mazdak? Mazdak (died 524 or 528) had been a notable figure from the last centuries of the Sasanian Empire. He was a Zoroastrian preacher of equality, whose movement had shaken the basis of noble power throughout the Iranian plateau in the late fifth century.

I answered them directly in halting Persian. I told them, as best I could, that historians were not social scientists. I had to say what my evidence told me. I admitted that there were serious weaknesses in the social structure of the Sasanian Empire, and that they should be studied. But the evidence could not tell me everything. I had to try to understand what was most prominent in the sources; and that was the structure of the Sasanian Empire and how it functioned. Would they agree that there was a difference between a historian (who had to make a society intelligible to modern persons on its own terms, and to shield it from modern prejudices) and a social scientist or a reformer who had the right to judge a society from a modern viewpoint?

They thanked me politely for my explanations. But I went away having learned a sharp lesson. To understand a regime on its own terms—an effort that was dear to my heart as I studied the Sasanian Empire, the great counterweight to the East Roman Mediterranean—could all too easily seem to others to come dangerously close to appearing to legitimize it.

With these thoughts in my mind, I returned to Tehran once again to fly (some 450 miles by plane) to the northeastern corner of Iran, where the great Shiʾa shrine of the Imam Reza at Mashhad stood on the borders of Afghanistan and Central Asia.

Mashhad: The Glory of Islam

Mashhad means "The Place of Martyrdom." It is the holiest city in the Shiʾa world—that is, in Iran and in many regions outside Iran. It is said to be visited by millions of pilgrims every year. In order to understand the intensity of the expectations surrounding the shrine, I had to put myself—as best I could as a non-Muslim—into the frame of mind of a Shiʾa pilgrim. For such persons, the shrine was a perpetual memorial to the clash between legitimate and illegitimate power, and a reminder of a huge sadness.

For the Shiʾa, the history of Islam should have gone differently. The descendants of Ali, the son-in-law of the Prophet Muhammad, should have ruled as caliphs. If that had happened, Islam would have remained pure—a Utopia of just rule on earth. Instead, they were pushed aside by ruthless politicians who usurped the title of caliph. The concluding act of this sinister takeover was the poisoning (in 818) of the last descendant of Ali—the Imam Reza. This was done so as to forestall the pious Reza's claim to the caliphate, which (it was said) had been recognized even by the son of the grandiose Harun al-Rashid (788–809).

Harun al-Rashid is known to us as a flamboyant figure in the *Arabian Nights*. But to the followers of Ali, he was the epitome of corrupt, illegitimate rule in the name of a false Islam. This fierce loyalty to Ali and his descendants as the true caliphs—as the great might-have-beens of Islamic history—cut the mainly Persian Shiʾa off from the great majority of Muslims, especially in Arabic-speaking lands, who are known as the *sunni*—the followers of the *sunna*, which was a broadly defined, less radical tradition.

The followers of Ali were known as the Shiʾa—the "party" of the followers of Ali. In a world governed by gross power, they yearned for the return of a just ruler. They believed that the Imam Reza, now lying in his martyr's tomb at Mashhad, had been the last, living hope of a true Islam on earth. Now his tomb was the focus of the hopes of millions—if not for justice, at least for healing and the forgiveness of sins. Mashhad was St. Peter's in Rome and Lourdes rolled into one—at one and the same time a center of pilgrimage for a distinctive version of Islam and a place of healing. The vast shrine was the heart of the city to which I had come. It had a noise of its own. This was not the mechanical noise of the bazaar and the city streets. It was the sound of a great sea of human voices raised in worship and prayer: not pious mumbling, but shouts of adoration mingled with cries for help.

I arrived in Mashhad on April 29 to deliver my lecture for the British Council. The visit to the shrine and its adjacent buildings was an overwhelming experience. Here are my impressions, as I described them in a letter:

> Meshed [I wrote, using a different spelling] is the door to Central Asia. I am now standing among people who seem to stretch as far as China . . . Mullahs who look like Lamas. Carpet sellers who bow like Mandarins. This is Khorasan. And they know it. The cherries of Meshed, says the chauffeur, are as big as apples. There is a sense of ease and of sweetness in the air. It is a strip of green between two deserts. The poplars, in silver bud in Tabriz, are out here . . . Meshed has entered into its long, easeful spring.

First, as a visitor to the British Council, I was shown round the treasures of the shrine on display in the museum.

> The Museum of the shrine was wonderful. It was the Glory of Islam on the edge of Central Asia. The walls were lined with great rugs and carpets; stately, flowered red robes of Shah Abbas; silk brocades of 1804 with patterns based on Chinese seals. A turquoise the size of an ostrich egg, that made the eyes of the Turcoman visitors glitter with delight.

Shrine and museum seemed to merge in the minds of the pilgrims:

> In the Museum, visitors kiss the foot of the great standard [dedicated to the shrine by a victorious shah] and fasten padlocks to it as tokens of their

devotion. A man pushes a piece of paper into a shrine that is on exhibit, and then bends down to watch intently where it comes to rest in the sediment of offerings. The huge noise of pious acclamations comes in great gusts through the windows that overlook the shrine.

The library was a depository that did full justice to the immense horizons of the Islamic world. Asia and the Mediterranean were joined here, on the borders of Central Asia, halfway to China.

A copy of the Directory of the Lands of Yaqut al-Hamawi (1179–1229) shows the world as a great wheel: on top, the Zandj (Equatorial Africa) and, at the bottom, Frozen Deserts with China at one end and al-Andalus (southern Spain) on the other. [There was also a copy of] Theodosius the Greek On World Globes, bound by Hajji Nasir of Tus, the vizir of Hulagu Khan (died 1265), the Mongol conqueror of much of the Middle East.

What really caught my eye was a copy of the *Herbal* of Dioscorides (a Greek doctor of the first century AD) translated into Arabic by the Syrian Christian Hunayn ibn Ishaq (809–873), a copy of which had been presented to Shah Abbas. "The only Dioscorides in the world," the librarian affirmed. But, in Vienna, I had seen a copy of the *Herbal* in the original Greek. It had been prepared in around AD 500 for Juliana Anicia, a descendent of one of the last Roman emperors of the West and a great patron of the arts. Descended also from the famous Roman family of the Anicii, Juliana was a figure from the old nobility, who linked Constantinople (where she resided) to Old Rome. She had greatly preoccupied Arnaldo Momigliano and myself in the 1950s.

Knowing what I knew, the librarian's assertion made my head spin. I had entered another galaxy. Seen from Mashhad, the Greek volume owned by the famous Juliana Anicia had sunk below the horizon in the distant West. But, in Arabic translation, the message of this Greek book had spread all over Asia. I was looking at a remarkable example of the survival of the classical tradition in the Islamic world.

THE GATE OF THE IMAM

The shrine of the Imam Reza was a shrine such as I had come to know through my work on Gregory of Tours and the cult of saints in the early Middle Ages. Non-Muslims were not allowed into the core of the shrine—the burial place of the Imam Reza. But from what I heard, it was like entering the Basilica of

Saint Martin at Tours in the sixth century. The inner shrine around the tomb was full of mirrors. It was a shimmering place. The crowds trooped through it rapidly, bathed in a sea of happy noise.

Outside the tomb chamber, however, the individual pilgrims were frozen in their tracks with reverence. They would press themselves for hours against the gate of the shrine, touching and rubbing the silver bars with their faces. It was there, I was told, that the pilgrim was truly in contact with the saint, pleading with the imam to be admitted to his presence. Only when they felt confident that the imam had heard their prayers and forgiven their sins would the pilgrims pass through the gate to join the euphoric surge around the tomb.

Hence it was at the gate, and not at the tomb, that the real drama of asking for healing and forgiveness was played out. Young men would hang weeping to the bars of the gate for hours on end, folded into them with all their strength, their shoulders heaving with sobs. Less melodramatic pilgrims would rub their picnic baskets against the grille (along with their swaddled babies) to secure the blessing of the imam on their long journey home. Later in the evening, I was told, one could see men asleep, with strings around their necks, to bind them to the imam at whose gate they lay. I hoped that the imam would bring them comfort in their dreams.

YAZD

When I first arrived at Mashhad, I had lunch with the McCaffertys, who headed the British Council there. Their enthusiasm for eastern Iran inspired me so much that I decided not to go back to Tehran, to linger in that brash, chaotic city until I had to return to England. Instead, I would strike out by myself across the desert from Mashhad to Yazd, the last major holdout of Zoroastrianism in Iran. So, on May 2, 1974, I was at the bus station at 4:30 a.m. The hour of assembly, of course, was not the hour of departure. But I was in no hurry. I had the rising feeling of a traveler who has nothing to do but travel all day. Incense sellers entered the bus, to give their smoke in blessing. A hajji recited a prayer, and then we were off on the Asia Highway. High mountains rose above the morning mist.

The desert was in the full wonder of spring. The rocks were covered with the pillar-box red of poppies. We passed through villages where the houses were palaces in mud—each of them was exquisite, no matter what size, with a fretwork of crenellations in silhouette, and domes like little Byzantine churches framed by the towers of the *bâdgîrs*, the high chimneys that catch the desert wind and lead it down, through a reversed fireplace, into the shade of the house. In the public gardens of the few desert towns through which we passed, there were rows of heavily scented roses already dried on their stems. They had stood untouched as the Iranians, great connoisseurs of perfumes, bent over ever so delicately toward them, careful not to disturb the dried-out petals. Eventually, I reached Yazd.

THE ZOROASTRIANS OF YAZD

While Mashhad had been at the extreme eastern corner of Iran, Yazd was at the very center of the plateau. I was made welcome in Yazd as a result of a happy serendipity, such as often happens in expatriate communities connected with institutions like the British Council. After my lecture in Tehran, I had met a businessman, Anthony Wynn. Among his many activities, he was studying Persian poetry with a dervish in Hamadan. It was from him that I got the address of Mr. X. (I shall call him)—a *mobed* (a religious leader) in the Zoroastrian community in Yazd. It was partly in the hope of meeting Mr. X. that I had headed for Yazd, rather than returning directly from Mashhad to Tehran. Here were the survivors of the religion that had bolstered the self-confidence of the Iranian governing class at the time of the Sasanian Empire, and had inspired the villagers of the Iranian plateau in their ceaseless battle with an unforgiving natural environment.

To the Christians of the East Roman Empire and to the Christians within the Sasanian Empire itself, the Zoroastrians had been the only "pagans" that mattered. The gods of Greece and Rome were less of a challenge to them than was this ancient faith. Zoroastrianism—largely derived from the teachings of Zoroaster (Zardusht): a legendary figure of the first millennium BC—was already a deeply rooted religion by the time of the Sasanian Empire.

Zoroastrians (Zardushtis) were known to Christians as the "worshippers of fire." Their perpetually burning fires stood for the triumph of the good in a dark, polluted world. They survived the Muslim invasion and the spread of Islam, though their numbers diminished sharply. Many emigrated to India, where they are still known as Parsis—"Persians." But, through all these drastic changes, they had retained a direct relationship with their last days of glory under the Sasanians. To meet a Zoroastrian in 1974 was like meeting a person from the world of late antiquity still alive and well, and adjusting to a difficult world with still-unshaken hope.

A FIGHTING FAITH

Zoroastrianism had always been a fighting faith. Zoroastrians believed that human beings had been created by the High God—Ahura Mazda—to be his helpers, not his servants. They were placed in the world to fight evil. And this was evil of all kinds. It was the spiritual evil in the human heart. But it was also the evil of a material world, which was seen as being constantly under attack from invisible demonic powers. Ahriman, the personification of the forces of evil, was independent of Ahura Mazda and was his perpetual enemy. Human beings were called upon to hold Ahriman at bay on all fronts—both the spiritual and the material. They were responsible for spreading "the good things of Ahura Mazda" over a landscape that was thought of as constantly under threat from the dry, chill malevolence of a negative power.

As a result, Zoroastrian belief had always involved a strong sense of social responsibility. Zoroastrians valued upright and generous behavior, which held together the villages of the Iranian plateau—from the village headman down to the smallest farmer. They felt themselves to be committed to unremitting work on the land, which ensured that water, greenery, and livestock throve in the face of visible and invisible forces of destruction.

Those precious oases of water and rustling trees where the Sasanians had placed their monuments (which I had recently visited in Bisotun, Taq-e Bostan, and Firuzabad) were the signs of a world where the good had held out and would, one day, triumph over the forces of aridity and disorder. They were seen to be the product of a successful collaboration between human beings and the hosts of benevolent invisible beings (angel-like figures—minor gods called "Benevolent Immortals") who guarded the landscape.

The double work of ritual and hard labor—tending the holy fire to keep invisible enemies at bay, and nurturing the ox to plow the visible earth—kept the world alive. By means of the fire and the plow human beings strove to maintain the "good things of Ahura Mazda" on earth until the end of time. Then Ahura Mazda would finally triumph; and a new world, rock-solid in its perfection, would replace the tattered, conflict-ridden age in which human beings now lived.

The Justice of God

I have included this short explanation simply so as to orientate the reader. At the time, there was much that I did not know about modern, living Zoroastrianism. The studies of Mary Boyce on the contemporary Zoroastrian communities of Yazd had not yet appeared.[1] What I did know was that the Zoroastrians were a tiny minority in modern Iran—twenty-five thousand in

1. Mary Boyce, *A History of Zoroastrianism*, Handbuch der Orientalistik (Leiden: Brill, 1975); *A Persian Stronghold of Zoroastrianism* (Oxford University Press, 1977); and *Zoroastrians: Their Religious Beliefs and Practices* (London: Routledge and Kegan Paul, 1977).

all. Most had emigrated to Tehran. This left the six thousand Zoroastrians of Yazd as the only true surviving community—the last outpost of a religion whose fire temples had once stretched, under the shadow of the king of kings, from Cappadocia to Afghanistan.

It would be wrong to say that I met an entire "community." I simply met the remarkable Mr. X. I met him as he came in from the fields, which were a green promontory reaching, with evident effort, out into a waterless plain that was as flat and hard as an airstrip. Almost his first words were "Mr. Brown, you who are a teacher of religion. You who know such things. What do you think of the justice of God?" I am ashamed to admit that my first instinct was to say, "Not much." Instead, I mumbled vague platitudes. That was not good enough for Mr. X.

> What do you think, Mr. Brown? Does God see with an equal eye? He sees all things fairly, does he not? If so, why is there evil? It cannot be from God. It must come from an other than God. Do you not agree?

I suddenly realized that I did not agree. So we sat for two hours on the bank of an irrigation canal, arguing about the justice of Ahura Mazda and the power of his enemy Ahriman. When I hear colleagues say that ordinary people could not be expected to have understood the theological issues that were debated so fiercely in late antiquity, I think of Mr. X. He would have been astonished by such a view.

FOOD AND THE GODS

We returned from the fields to Mr. X.'s family. They came as a surprise to me. I had grown accustomed, when traveling outside the cities of Iran, to a world where women and children were virtually invisible. I had not seen a single woman in all the desert towns through which I had passed on my way from Mashhad to Yazd. Now I found myself surrounded by unveiled women with handsome leonine faces, dressed like fairy godmothers in greens and purples, as they squatted on the sides of the immaculately clean lanes of the Zoroastrian quarter.

It was a strange experience. The Zoroastrians looked more picturesquely "oriental" in their old-fashioned clothes than did the Muslims, where the men, at least, were largely Europeanized in their dress. But in Mr. X.'s household it was as if I was back in Europe, surrounded by visible and vocal women and children. When a brother telephoned, the women pushed the men aside and took control of the telephone. The patriarch swatted flies as the younger children jumped up and down in front of him on the bed. The houses were spotless, surrounded by pure mud walls.

I noticed that the households in the quarter were linked, as if by an invisible chain, through the giving of food. The mother-in-law took me to the fire temple. If I remember correctly, it was a low room with the entrance screened in such a way that the fire was invisible until one entered the chamber proper. This was to ensure that impure eyes did not fall on such a holy thing. Under the cypresses of the temple's courtyard, a boy prayed and burned incense. We ate nuts and raisins "for the gods." Charity took the form of a constant process of distribution from a center of the holy. This distribution ranged from the great stewpots that produced "pure" food for the community after every funeral, down to small gifts of chickpeas, which Mr. X.'s mother-in-law gave to all comers on her return from the holy fire.

GOD'S WELL

While the fire was the center of a symbolic distribution of good things, the heart of the Zoroastrian quarter of Yazd was its irrigation system. And the heart of the irrigation system was the great Leyland engine with which Mr. X. pumped up water from the artesian well to irrigate the entire neighborhood. "This is not my well," he said. "It is God's well." But Muslim farmers paid him one hundred rials for an hour of water. For them, Mr. X. employed a Muslim fore-man and rent-collector. "He must be a very tough man," I opined. "No, sir, he must be a very *mild* man. If I have a tough man, the farmers get together and they hammer him good." Mr. X. then pointed to the blooming trees. If his Leyland failed, all this would be straw. "This land has strength. The water is a lasting charity."

Next day, I continued my dialogue with Mr. X. This posed no linguistic problems, as he spoke perfect English, having served for fourteen years as a soldier in the British army in India and elsewhere. We discussed the nature of religious intolerance. In Mr. X.'s opinion it was all over the place, as was shown by his experience in India. Hindus say, "Good health" (to Parsis) in public, but, in private, they feel polluted by them: "they drink their tea over there." In Yazd, he told me, Zardushti ideas of ritual purity were a constant irritant to the local Muslims. What was most annoying to Mr. X. was Muslim rejoicing over con-verts made through mixed marriages. One such marriage had happened six months earlier, "and they rejoiced as if they had conquered Europe."

THE GOOD PATRON AND THE GUARDIAN ANGEL

Mr. X. saw himself as a local patron. He seemed always aware of the fragility of the land and of the social relations that could make the land prosper or turn to dust. We rode brakeless bicycles along the edges of the fields as Mr. X. arbitrated between the farmers on water distribution. They waved formidable, long-handled spades as part of the drama of the settlement.

In the afternoon, a dust storm from the Dasht-i Lut Desert hit Yazd. The sky was covered. The air tasted like salt, and the great silver-burnished cauldrons piled up in the cooking area spun around the yard in the fierce wind. Everything was caught in a strange luminous glow, and the birds hid at the very bottom of the trees.

Then, as we were about to settle down, a rainstorm suddenly broke over the mountains. Mr. X. jumped up. "It is worth a dollar a drop!" he cried, and we raced on our bicycles to the engine shed to stop the engine, so that we could clean the filters. When we were leaving the engine house, having cleaned the filters, I noticed that Mr. X. had left a light on. I reminded him of that. Oh no: every night he leaves that light on above the engine:

"It is for the angel there."

MAZDAK IN YAZD

Talk of the protecting angel brought us back yet again to the justice of God. As I wrote in my journal, Mr. X. could see no way out but belief in an independent power of evil:

> God sees all things and sees them all with one [equal] eye. Yet Mirah, his workman, is only forty and looks sixty; he has a bad chest and his land has been stolen from him by city lawyers. He is working so as to build a single hut in among the little allotment plots that have grown up in the newly-irrigated land. "And yet I eat fish every day". Another worker, ill for eleven years, can only say: "I no longer think that there is Death. You are fooling me. I want Death to come and he does not". How can God see all this "with one eye"? There must be an independent Evil One who alone is responsible for such suffering.

Faced by these arguments, I remembered that there had been other, more radical solutions to this dilemma in earlier ages of Zoroastrianism. One such solution had been offered by the Mazdakite movement of the late fifth and early sixth centuries. Mazdak, a radical interpreter of the Zoroastrian scriptures, was said to have blamed the rich for the sufferings of the poor. He claimed that it was not the blind malevolence of Ahriman, the Evil One, which caused famines. It was the avarice of the rich. In the late fifth century this preaching by Mazdak had unleashed a leveling movement. He was said to have preached that men and women were equal because their souls were equal. He also declared that all Iranians were free, and that the lower classes were not tied at birth to positions in an unshakable hierarchy, on whose solidity the peace of society depended—as was the traditional Zoroastrian view. Mazdak was said to have opened up the storehouses of the rich at a time of famine. He was also supposed to have broken down the caste system through which the nobility protected its vast fortunes by means of close-cousin marriages. This was the Mazdakite movement that the radical young Muslims in the University of Tabriz had admired.

The Mazdakites were remembered in the Zoroastrian tradition. While we serviced the Leyland engine together late at night, discussing how Mr. X. had sold shirts to Italian POWs outside Benghazi during the war, Mr. X. told me all about Mazdak. Of course he knew about Mazdak. There are, he said, Mazdakis (Mazdakites) in Yazd. Yes: they were followers of Mehr Baba (an Indian theosophist) who held that, as all souls were equal, so all men and women should be equal. They kept silence "to rest their souls." They served tea with great dignity. I should meet them, Mr. X. said, when I returned to Yazd.

Shah Vahram and the Kingdom of Peace

Back at home, Mr. X. expatiated. We talked about the great kings of old. It was sad talk about the might-have-beens of Iranian history. Shapur I had savagely suppressed the Arabs. That was what a good king of kings should do. Khusro II Aparwez (the shah connected with Taq-e Bostan) was the subject of much courtly romance in medieval Muslim literature. But to Mr. X. he was a bad king and a womanizer, who had weakened the empire. He had tried to exterminate the Arabs because an astrologer had told him that the Arabs would conquer Iran. But he failed. Evidently, Mr. X. wished that he had succeeded.

Then the conversation took a serious turn. Mr. X. moved closer to me. Did I know about the Shah Vahram? The Shah Vahram was the legendary Iranian ruler who would appear at the end of the Evil Age to set things right again—to renew the Zoroastrian religion all over Iran after centuries of humiliation, and to usher in a Kingdom of Peace.

Who, Mr. Brown, do you think is the Shah Vahram? The Shah who will come to end the evil epoch? It is the present Shah, he whispers to me. For here I am, I sit with my door open without fear of the Muslims, my children are well, my engine pumps water, there is electricity. Surely the Kingdom of Peace has come.

Thirty-six hours later I was back in England. On Monday, I was attending a meeting of the Research Committee in the Hovenden Room at All Souls. Trinity term was already under way.

I had returned from another world. My journey to Iran had been no lighthearted holiday trip. I had truly traveled. I had been infected by the huge spaces of Iran. From then onward, spacious regions outside Europe became part of my imaginative world. Following the inspiration of Braudel, I had seen many of the landscapes on which the Sasanians had based themselves when they challenged the East Roman Empire in late antiquity. But I had also added a sense for other kinds of landscapes: sacred and royal landscapes, saturated with human notions of the sacred and linked to the majesty of empire.

Without knowing it, I had passed through a country only a few years before it was to change profoundly, with the onset of the Iranian Revolution. This accounts for the somewhat travelogue-like tone of these last chapters: they are glimpses of a world that (as far as I can gather) is now in the past.

It was also a journey of the mind. By traveling to the landscapes and monuments of the Sasanian Empire, I added a whole new dimension to my knowledge of the late antique world. Hitherto, for all my curiosity, I had known about the Sasanians only through books: now Iran existed for me as a series of unforgettable images. Scrambling around monuments and traveling over the long roads of the Iranian plateau, I somehow got the "feel" of another world, far from the Mediterranean shores of East Rome.

More important yet for the religious historian, it was a journey of the heart. For the first time, I made contact with Islam as a living religion not only through the drama of a shrine such as Mashhad, but also through the sweetness of recitations of the Qur'ân overheard in passing in mosques, in the recessed corners of madrasas, or in snatches on long bus rides. From then onward, the presence of Islam, in all its different forms, in past and present alike, has always claimed my attention as a weight on the heart as well as a challenge to the historian.

I was also touched by the chanting of the Armenian church at Julfa and by the metaphysical wrangling of Mr. X., the Zoroastrian elder from Yazd. I came to feel that there was nothing strange about the desire to worship God. On my return, after a lapse of twenty years, I resumed regular attendance at a Christian church.

PART V

BERKELEY 1975
TO CAIRO

BERKELEY 1975

"It Might Be Mars"

In 1974 wider horizons began to open up to me at an unaccustomed pace. The year began with my springtime journey to Iran. By the summer, I had decided to leave Oxford. I accepted the offer of a professorship at Royal Holloway College in the University of London.

Quite frankly, I needed a change of scene. I was aware that I lived a highly privileged and productive life as a senior fellow of All Souls College. But it was an interstitial position, to one side of the workings of the university. Such a position would have been ideal for a fully committed researcher—such as Sam Stern and many of my other colleagues at All Souls. But I was also a teacher, committed to finding a place for the new field of late antiquity in a university system that changed slowly, if at all.

At the age of forty, I felt in danger of becoming a sacred cow—a well-known scholar, but somehow shielded by a studied sense of reverence from having any real impact on the world around me. Royal Holloway offered me a new field of action as permanent head of the History Department. I would prove to myself and to others that I could hold down a major job in a university whose teaching methods and structures were very different from those of Oxford.

So I thought in the summer of 1974. The following chapters will show how this worked out in practice. Meanwhile, I found that I had a few months to fill before I took up my new job at Royal Holloway in early summer 1975. I spent some of those months opening up to yet another distant horizon: from January 3 to March 31, 1975, I was a visiting professor in the History Department in the University of California at Berkeley. It was my first long-term stay in America.

I came to Berkeley as a short-term replacement for Paul Alexander (1910–1977), the Byzantinist, who was on sabbatical leave. At the time, I had no idea that I might come to Berkeley on a more permanent basis. Instead, I came to explore a distant world, much as I had explored Iran, but also to accustom myself to the workings of a university very different from Oxford and more similar, in its structures and ethos, to the University of London. I spent much time learning what I could about administration and teaching in an American university, hoping that it might be helpful to me in Royal Holloway College. At Berkeley, I had no obligations other than to teach one graduate seminar and one undergraduate lecture course in the History Department. I was entirely on my own with the prospect before me of a stretch of solitary reading at the far end of the world.

Two years previously, Beryl Smalley (1905–1984), the Oxford medievalist, had been at Berkeley. She wrote to me:

> A little Sicilian here is planning to write a thesis in aid of Women's Lib. on changes in attitudes to Women in the Middle Ages. . . .
>
> That's a sample of what one can be confronted with here. My first applicant to register for my course was a young man majoring in psychology who belonged to a "Society for Creative Anachronisms"; they stage revels and tournaments. One of the next put down "computer science" as his major, but it turned out that the computer had got him wrong and couldn't be altered; he is really studying languages. Dogs come to classes. . . . In fact, it might be Mars.

This was the astringent humor of an Oxford college tutor, accustomed to grooming a small, selected group of students for a single final examination, when faced by the daunting openness of the American elective course system.

The Athens of the West

The Berkeley of the protest riots of 1968 was still very much present and talked about with pride by many. Long-term graduate students would speak to me, with a touch of shame, of the day when they lapsed from the counterculture— shaved, put on a suit, and went to their first job interview. Yet, rather than this recent epic, what struck me about Berkeley was that large areas of campus (both architecturally and culturally) had a strangely old-fashioned air. And, indeed, my research during the three months that I spent in Berkeley took a decidedly old-fashioned turn. I went back to the classical world—to authors such as Plutarch (ca. 50–ca. 120) and Galen (129–199/216), and to figures from the early church, such as Cyprian, bishop of Carthage (ca. 200–258), Origen (184–254), and Eusebius of Caesarea (ca. 260–339). In other words, I went back to the world before Constantine. Having only recently reached out to the Sasanian Empire in the Middle East on the eve of the rise of Islam, and to the cult of relics in sixth-century Gaul, this was no small step backward in time. Yet there was something about Berkeley campus that encouraged it.

Berkeley was the formidable flagship of an entire fleet of campuses of the University of California, which had been established so as to bring the best of American education to the Golden State. Though first founded in 1868 as a mining college, Berkeley soon came to present itself as the Athens of the West—an outpost of Western Civilization (very much in uppercase) brought to the shores of the Pacific. It looked the part. In 1904, a Greek Theater, modeled on the famous theater of Epidauros, was built up against the hill at the top of the campus, creating the sense of an environment where time had stood still for two millennia.

Beneath a timeless Mediterranean sky, the overripe Beaux-Arts classicism of Dow Library could have been built, if not by Pericles, at least by the emperor Hadrian. It was the right place in which to begin a stint of reading on the Antonine Age (138–180)—the Gilded Age of the Roman Empire—in preparation for the Jackson Lectures that I had agreed to give at Harvard in 1976: "The Making of Late Antiquity." These were published in 1978.[1]

Antonine Bodies

In Dow Library, the Classics Seminar Room was beautifully maintained. It was an oasis of order and comfort in the somewhat ramshackle bulk of the library proper. Flooded with evening light as the sun sank behind the Golden Gate Bridge, it contained all that I needed to read of the authors of the Antonine Age and other texts from the late classical period.

The work that I did there was, in many ways, a follow-up to my debate with E. R. Dodds on the nature of the crisis of the third century. The usual view was that this crisis was an outright catastrophe that had marked the end of the ancient world. I had come to feel that this was not so. The third century was a

---

1. Peter Brown, *The Making of Late Antiquity* (Cambridge, MA: Harvard University Press, 1978).

time of transformation rather than of disaster, in which many of the long-term tensions of the Roman Empire—the relations between empire and cities, between Romans and provincials, between rich and poor—came to the fore with new intensity and were resolved in new ways.

I had already written on this period in *The World of Late Antiquity*. But that had been a work of synthesis which covered the entire period of late antiquity, written for the general public. I planned *The Making* as a very different book. It would be an essay in change: a detailed study (heavy with footnotes!) of the social and religious developments in the two centuries between the reign of Marcus Aurelius and that of Constantine—between around 138 and 337.

My notes show that I read deeply in the *Moralia* of Plutarch and the medical works of Galen along with other recondite works on physiognomics, astrology, and alchemy. I turned to these texts because I needed to understand how the codes of behavior current in the Antonine Age (which included political behavior) were rooted in images of the body in such a way that the stresses and strains of Roman upper-class society could be seen as somehow mirrored in its medical concerns.

It seemed that the search for social stability was reflected in the balance of the body itself. Galen's anxious preoccupation with the balance of "heat" in the body, though inherited from Hippocrates, also bore the mark of its age: it betrayed a sharp concern for the dangers of aggression in a highly competitive society, where physical violence lay close to the seemingly cool and polished surface of the elites. Sheathed in a network of distinctive meanings, Antonine bodies were not like our own.

SOCIETY AND THE COSMOS

And did these persons walk beneath the same stars as we do? The answer was very definitely: no. In my reading I was brought up against the richness of the late classical view of the *kosmos*, the physical universe. It was a murmurous world filled with invisible beings—an entire hidden society of gods, demons, and angels, in which human beings and human society were embedded. This representation of the *kosmos* served as a diagram of society and its ills: the pure order of the heavens above the moon stood as the antithesis to the disorderly interplay of random powers below it. Those who won out in the great social and imaginative convulsion of Roman society of the third century were those who claimed to have brought the order of the serene heavens down to earth. I realized that I had to think more about those vibrant heavens.

Here I detect the influence of the *genius loci* from the very first night of my arrival at Berkeley, when Tom Bisson and Bob Brentano (1926–2002) drove me to the Faculty Club. As we passed the open vents of heating systems belching steam like a series of volcanic geysers beneath towering clumps of eucalyptus, I looked down toward the East Bay at the most dramatic sunset that I had ever seen. A recent, minor eruption of Popocatépetl in Mexico (they told me) had filled the air with shimmering dust. It stretched across the horizon in an opalescent necklace of purple and gold. It continued for many evenings. Walking up to the Rose Garden on the north side of campus, I would see people standing, alone or in little groups, looking out to sea as if riveted by some awesome sight—a great ship sinking, perhaps, or Godzilla devouring the Golden Gate Bridge. No. It was only the sunset.

Whether in Berkeley or along the Pacific coast of Marin County, nature was not beautiful. It was stunning and, somehow, profoundly prehuman. It drew one out of society, as if human settlement were a thin film that could be stripped away to reveal an older world unmarked by human structures and without human names. It was calculated to set one thinking about the late antique sense of the imperturbable majesty of the *kosmos*. In the awed words of Plotinus, "*Pas de ho khôros hieros*: All the place is holy"—as Oedipus had exclaimed on reaching Colonus.[2] To a pagan such as Plotinus, humans were the "late born" in this universe—latecomers to a landscape that was not their own.

To sit on a beach in Marin County and to watch flocks of pelicans—timeless, antediluvian birds like pterodactyls—fly in perfect order in the troughs of giant waves, passing in front of a distant view of the plate-glass skyscrapers of San Francisco downtown glittering on the horizon, was to feel something of the smallness of humanity. It caused late antique debates on the relative importance of human beings and of human society in a divine universe to take on a new weight for me.

HOLY HILL: ANGELS, DEMONS, AND THE COSMOS

But what about the early Christians, whose strong notions of power derived from Heaven would finally produce the "holy men" of fourth- and fifth-century Syria and Egypt? To understand these early Christians, I would have to study the New Testament and the early church from the days of Saint Paul to the age of Constantine to a degree that I had never done before. I found the perfect

2. Plotinus, *Enneads* 1.8.14, trans. A. H. Armstrong, Loeb Classical Library 1, p. 312, with n. 3.

place to do this in the Graduate Theological Union Library, in a complex known as "Holy Hill," perched at the top of a steep avenue of palm trees that ended with a spectacular view of the East Bay. I had never before encountered an interdenominational library devoted to all aspects of Christianity and its environment from Old Testament times up to the present. I quickly set up a carrel and got to work.

I began in Holy Hill by reading what I could about Christian attitudes to the demonic and angelic beings who were believed to share the *kosmos* with the human race. While most modern accounts of the period tended to present the demons as omnipresent and all-threatening, late antique writers, in fact, confined the demons to a clearly delimited niche in the world beneath the moon. A sense of the immensity of the universe enabled late antique persons, as it were, to corral in the demons. Their power was bounded and capable of being overcome by those who wielded more secure, more "heavenly" power.

Furthermore, the pyramidal nature of the *kosmos*, with its hierarchy of ascending powers, gave to special individuals a strong sense of agency. They could feel that they shared a universe filled with caring spirits—with the hosts of angels to whom they could draw close for protection and for inspiration. Far from living scared in a demon-ridden world, they thought of themselves as possessing reserves of energy that were both within them and, at the same time, above them—in the form of protecting gods or guardian angels who hovered so close to their charges that they could be thought of almost as upward extensions of the self.

It seemed to me that this warm sense of closeness to powerful, invisible presences braced believers to perform feats of courage, of creativity, and even (in the case of Constantine) of daring statesmanship that broke with the caution of an older, more conservative age. Whether it was a bishop leading a large congregation, such as Cyprian (bishop of Carthage from 248 to 258); the founder of a world religion, such as Mani (216–277); or a crowned revolutionary, such as Constantine (306–337): a tenacious belief in the presence of divine protectors produced a remarkable succession of persons prepared to challenge and to change the world.

THE MASTER

A few weeks later, I encountered a surprising modern representative of this view. I was given a lift to see a friend in Sonora. The driver, Bruce, was a much-traveled and well-informed man. He told me that he had been a ship's purser all over the Pacific. Now he was a teacher of the Urantia cult, on his way to instruct a congregation of fellow believers. He carried with him a holy book—*The Urantia Book*—a story of the earth that had been delivered by angels in Chicago sometime in the 1920s.

Bruce described a world ruled by infinite ranks of guardian angels, clustering one on top of the other above each believer, to protect and inspire them. I hazarded a guess. "I am sure, Bruce, that you have many more than one guardian angel." "Gee, Peter, how did you know *that*!" In fact, he explained, as a master in the teachings of Urantia, he had as many as ten. I felt that my readings on Holy Hill had not been wasted.

There was a sequel to this moment of self-revelation. My Sonora friend taught a course at Columbia Junior College in Sonora. During my friend's lecture, the young sprawled in their chairs, sucked at their drinks, adjusted their earphones in magnificently insouciant gestures of adolescent "cool," in a largely empty room. On the way back, we looked into the seminar room where Bruce was teaching his charges. His long silver beard sparkled in the upward light of a desk lamp. He held *The Urantia Book* before him. Around a crowded table, his disciples all sat bolt upright, all leaning forward over their own copy of the holy text. None of them stirred. They were riveted in the presence of a teacher and his ten angels. For a moment, I had glimpsed a scene straight from the third century AD.

On Campus: Graduate Students

A little after that meeting, in mid-February, I fell ill with a virulent and tenacious form of Bay Area flu. I would spend days on end grounded—watching talk shows and flamboyant quiz games on the television. Even the local cinema gave no relief. It was sufficiently close to the intellectual pretensions of campus, alas, to offer nothing other than a season of the more depressing of Ingmar Bergman's movies.

I suffered from a dramatic loss of energy. I now knew what it was like for Plotinus to look up into the blue sky with sadness that his own body was so fragile, so very distant from the radiant vigor of the body of the sun. I became only too well aware that, in winter, the blue sky of California was not necessarily a warm sky: a thin breeze as sharp as an icicle often blew underneath it, a breeze that seemed to come straight from Antarctica. A little later, even the weather collapsed, as monsoon-like rain blew in from the Pacific, making the clean-cut stones of the campus sweat with clammy heat.

It was in this low season that I began to really make friends. Most important of all, at that time, were the group of graduate students who attended my seminars and lectures. It was through them that I became accustomed to the ways of a university so very different from Oxford.

I learned these differences early and in unexpected ways. For instance, following my Oxford habit, I had scheduled my seminar for the late afternoon—after tea, as it were. I had also hoped, by such scheduling, to have an open space of free time afterward, where I might repair with whichever students were in the mood, to a pizza and beer garden—many of which I had observed on the north side of campus, at the bottom of Euclid Avenue.

I soon realized that this was not an entirely good choice of time. For when darkness fell, the great campus could be a place of danger, especially for women. Furthermore, many graduates had driven into campus from a long way out of town and wanted to start back home before it got too late. There was a whiff of dangers and of family responsibilities which told me that these students were not young persons, late teenagers, like the sheltered undergraduates (and even the graduates) of Oxford.

They were would-be professionals. I learned this in the very first meeting of my seminar on the age of Augustine. I began by passing out bibliographies for the topics that we would discuss in the coming weeks. I then asked for volunteers to offer a short presentation on the topic of the week as a way of getting the discussion going. Some were keen enough, and well-informed enough, to put in bids for well-known topics, such as Augustine's Neoplatonism or the *City of God*. But, apart from them, what was notably absent was the cheery amateurism of my Oxford class. Though far more reticent than Americans, the English undergraduates had been prepared to try their hand at anything. To learn to be a jack of all trades and master of none was part of a gentlemanly education. They could wing it.

Not so for graduate students in Berkeley. When it came to allotting a speaker to introduce the very first topic—Augustine and the Manichees—I was met by an anxious silence. Surely the Manichees, with their strange writings in Coptic, Soghdian, and Chinese, could not be approached by mere amateurs from the History Department? Somewhere, perched in an office at the top of Dwinelle Hall (among the many experts in recondite oriental languages), there must be a professional or a future professional to fill that slot. To attempt to wing a presentation on the Manichees, when such persons were available, would be the height of unprofessional behavior. And then the door opened, and in came Martin Schwartz, the professor of Iranian languages, altogether looking the part, with a raven-black Babylonian beard, accompanied by a large man in a green checked suit—his student, engaged in a dissertation on Manichaean Soghdian—whom we knew only as "Mr. Flaherty." The day was saved. The correct professionals had arrived.

What I had not realized, with my cheery approach, was that these graduates were serious grown-ups as well as students. Many were married. Many had returned to graduate school having tried other careers. The ancient notion of a late "conversion to wisdom" (whose intense sense of commitment had been explored by Henri-Irénée Marrou in the case of Augustine) was alive and well in the Berkeley of the 1970s. Many spoke of "going back to school" as just such a conversion. Hence a seriousness that many of my Oxford friends (confronted by visiting American graduates) had tended to dismiss as a sign of a pedantry. But they were not pedants. For many of them, to go to graduate school was an existential choice. They felt that they could never be professional enough in following it through.

It was a frankly vocational training. They studied with professors so as to become professors. In early 1970s Oxford (and especially in All Souls), there was still a sense that, having shown one's brilliance by gaining a first or a prize fellowship, one might then go on to higher things in London—the law, the foreign service, banking. This was not so among these graduate students. One of my greatest gaffes, in my first month in Berkeley, was to ask an exceptionally gifted student what he would do "after graduate school." The poor man thought that I had put a jinx on him. He knew what he wanted to be: a professor, like myself.

Gradually, a group of friends formed around me, gathered in pizza parlors or as visitors to my office in Dwinelle Hall. They illustrated the impressive range of interests available among the graduate students of Berkeley. At Berkeley, ancient and medieval history joined without so much as a murmur. (I looked back to those long hours spent in Oxford, attempting to negotiate even one shared paper between History and Litterae Humaniores.)

Pericles Georges was engaged with Greek attitudes to Persia in the fifth century BC.[3] A man given to much worldly wisdom, he had already taken me in hand, after the end of my very first seminar and on the way to a pizza parlor, with advice as to the remarkable substances—tranquilizers and ingredients for hair rinse—that were to be found in American bottled beers.

---

3. P. Georges, *Barbarian Asia and the Greek Experience* (Baltimore: Johns Hopkins University Press, 1994).

Art Eckstein was a devoted student of Eric Gruen. Already a gnarled figure, only recently (or barely) detached from the Los Angeles counterculture, he had made very much his own the cantankerous warlords of the Roman Republic at the height of their feeding frenzy.[4] His sweet friend Jeannie Rutenberg (1950–2009) introduced me, as a connoisseur of holy men, to the *Lives of Saint Francis*.

Michael Maas was already well launched into the study of sixth-century Byzantium, under the guidance of Paul Alexander, whom he revered and whose widow, Eleanor, he would always go out of his way to visit after Paul's death in 1977. A few years later, he completed his dissertation and published a prizewinning book on the erudite and alienated figure of the Byzantine bureaucrat John Lydus (ca. 490–ca. 565).[5] These friends represented only a sample of the remarkable range of interests and talents, seriously engaged with scholarship, that gathered with such apparent ease in the light air of campus.

Topsy-Turvy

During my stay in Berkeley, I visited other American campuses. On March 6, I flew to Chicago to lecture at the Divinity School. I had arranged to give myself the adventure of returning from Chicago to San Francisco by rail. It was in the middle of lunch, after the last discussion group, that I learned that South Bend was no more than two and a half hours by train from Chicago, and that my friend and Hebrew teacher, Roberta Chesnut, was now teaching at the Catholic University of Notre Dame, beside South Bend.[6]

I was soon on a train to South Bend. The train passed Gary, where the wind was blowing the snow parallel to the water across Lake Michigan, and stopped at stations where it seemed that nobody spoke anything but Polish. I racked my memory for suitable phrases in biblical Hebrew with which to greet Roberta.

Apart from the joy of seeing Glen and Roberta again, securely settled in South Bend—a town, Roberta told me, "so quiet that they roll up and stow

---

4. Arthur M. Eckstein, *Mediterranean Anarchy, Interstate War, and the Rise of Rome* (Berkeley: University of California Press, 2006).

5. Michael Maas, *John Lydus and the Roman Past: Antiquarianism and Politics in the Reign of Justinian* (London: Routledge, 1992).

6. See chapter 48: "Hebrew."

away the sidewalks every evening"—I found myself observing what to me, as a traditional Irish Protestant, was an utterly unimaginable situation: a great Catholic university turned topsy-turvy.

I had been accustomed to think of a Catholic university as an institution like Maynooth, a proud bastion of traditional Catholic learning. Notre Dame was not like that at all. Confessional barriers appeared to have vanished. The Theology Department was filled with non-Catholics, Roberta among them. A Catholic charismatic movement was in full swing. Above all, the women's liberation movement (as it was then called) was prominent on campus and was forcing its way with gathering strength through the narrow channels of the local churches, Catholic and Protestant alike.

What struck me forcibly was the way in which the various churches had thrown their weight into the radical movements of the time. As Roberta explained it to me, the churches had always been, in some ways, cultural theocracies. Often, it was the clergy, and not secular institutions, who had mediated high thinking and progressive ideals to their congregations. And now this high thinking had taken a radical turn.

Unlike the protest culture of the West Coast, in which so many of my graduate students at Berkeley had been involved, this was a grassroots movement that worked through religious channels—through prayer groups, vestry meetings, church teach-ins, and sermons. This would not have come as news to an American who had witnessed the civil rights movement in the South; but to a person from the British Isles, this peculiar blend of religion, culture, and political activism gave much food for thought.

I felt the same when I met Roberta's students. Many came from conservative or even sectarian religious backgrounds—Protestant, Catholic, Eastern Orthodox, and Mennonite. Unlike so many of my Californian students, many of these midwesterners had deeply rooted family religions in their immediate background, to defend or to rebel against. They were much more like the Protestants of Dublin than the English, whose polite disregard for religion had always puzzled me as a young man.

For such persons, religion and intellect were not opposed. Religion was often the one way through which students grew to intellectual and imaginative maturity. To learn how to face the Bible and the history of the early church as scholars, as Roberta insisted that they should do, was to turn childhood beliefs into reasoned objects of belief or criticism. It involved crossing a real threshold. Roberta, with her combination of fierce scholarship and religious seriousness, could not have been a better teacher for them, nor could they have been more rewarding students for her.

Altogether, I returned from America to England, not as if from Mars, but from a large and serious place, to take up a job in a large, public university that was more like Berkeley than like Oxford—the University of London, where I would be head of the History Department at Royal Holloway College.

ROYAL HOLLOWAY
COLLEGE

MYTHS, ANCIENT AND MODERN

From May 1975 to March 1978, I was professor and head of the History Department at Royal Holloway College—a part of the confederation of colleges that made up the University of London. Academically, it was a more than usually productive period for me: *The Making of Late Antiquity* and *The Cult of the Saints* were written there. But what mattered most, in those years, was a sudden widening of my horizons. As head of the History Department (the equivalent of permanent chairperson in America) I was brought into direct contact with entire new fields of history and with new, more flexible approaches to teaching. In these years I also traveled more widely—once again to Iran and frequently to America.

Royal Holloway College was in Egham, Surrey (close to Windsor Castle), perched on a hill that dominated the water-meadows of the Thames valley, some forty minutes by rail to Waterloo Station and central London. Among the many colleges that made up the federated University of London, Royal Holloway was something of an outlier. It was not as well known as other London colleges. Yet its distinctive position and ethos influenced me immediately and profoundly.

I took instantly to the interesting balance of past and present around Egham. The Thames valley was almost a theme park of British history. Runnymede, where Magna Carta was signed in 1215, lay in the valley at the bottom of Egham Hill. When I drove from Oxford, along the M4, I would turn off at Windsor, where I would pass the fifteenth-century chapel of Eton College, rising in the morning mist like a Victorian watercolor above flatlands still grazed by picturesque cows. Then would come Windsor Castle, glimpsed from the road at the head of a ceremonious avenue of trees, followed by the woods and open walkways of Windsor Park.

At the same time, a vibrant symbol of the modern age lay only a quarter of an hour's drive from the college. That was Heathrow Airport. Every morning and evening the great jumbo jets from America and Asia would level off above the college for their final descent. Those planes spoke to me of large and spacious lands—of Iran and, increasingly, of America. It was the age of the Concorde supersonic jet. I remember one morning, in 1977, sitting in a British Airways plane to Washington, passing the Concorde as we taxied out over the tarmac. It looked surprisingly small and lonely. I thought differently when I arrived at Washington. For here was the same Concorde, standing cool and aloof, as if it had always been there. It had beaten us to America by six hours.

In 2003, I watched the Concorde coming in over Paris, to land for the last time. As it glided through the clouds above Les Invalides, a most unmodern scene was taking place in the great square. The Knights of Malta and their wives emerged from the chapel of Les Invalides, having attended a funerary mass for one of their fellows. Beautifully dressed elderly ladies in mantillas, with exquisite handbags, hobbled across the cobblestones with extended arms to embrace silvery gentlemen in full dress uniform: "Ah, mon général . . . !!" The ancien régime had outlived the symbol of the bright new age. It was a scene calculated to remind the historian of how little we can know the future. In 1975, Concorde seemed fixed forever in the busy sky above Heathrow.

"Because They Are the Greatest Sufferers"

In its own time (in the late nineteenth century) Royal Holloway had been a potent symbol of modernity. Its founder, Thomas Holloway (1800–1883), was a Victorian millionaire turned philanthropist. He made a fortune through selling patent pills by means of relentless, worldwide advertising—"Holloway's Pink Pills for Pale Persons." He then decided to spend his wealth on works of benevolence. Having built a sanatorium for the mentally disturbed at Virginia Water, near Egham, in 1873, he went on to plan nothing less than an entire university for women, "because they are the greatest sufferers." He was said to have done so on the advice of his wife, Jane.[1]

---

1. Caroline Bingham, *The History of Royal Holloway College* (London: Constable, 1978), 36.

This may be no more than an edifying legend. What is certain is that Holloway looked to America for his model—to Matthew Vassar's new foundation for women, Vassar College in Poughkeepsie. What Vassar had created beside the Hudson River, Holloway wished to place on top of Egham Hill, close to the queen at Windsor and at a respectable distance from the unruly sights and stimuli of London. He pushed through a grand plan: "I hope we shall be able to beat Vassar into fits. It shall not be my fault if we don't."[2]

Holloway succeeded. His architect, William Crossland (1835–1909), brought back to England exact measurements of the Renaissance Château de Chambord on the Loire. From these he created a building twice the size of Chambord, arranged around two immense rectangular quadrangles. I was often told, "Chambord was not the model; it was only the module." Flaming red brick, interlaced with bright white Portland stone, "fairly scorched the eye."

It was said that nine hundred stonemasons worked on the carvings alone. The entire mythology of progressive England was there. The keystones of the outer arches of the chapel showed Muhammad, Confucius, Savonarola, and—most surprising of all—Pope Julius II, placed there because he was regarded as the archetypical Renaissance patron of the arts.[3]

Holloway himself wished to be known as a patron of the arts like Julius II. He put together an impressive collection of eminently Victorian paintings to cover the walls of a grand art gallery in one corner of the college. Among these was a huge canvas by Sir Edwin Landseer that showed the grisly end of Sir John Franklin's expedition to the Arctic in search of the Northwest Passage in 1845, with large polar bears tearing the last shreds of the sails of Franklin's ship, crushed in a sea of ice. Painted in 1864, it bore the inauspicious title *Man Proposes, God Disposes*. On the days when the gallery was filled with chairs and desks for students taking the final examination, the picture would be veiled with a large Union Jack, lest it disturb those seated beside it.

Holloway had intended this huge pile to be a complete, autonomous university, awarding its own degrees, as an American women's university would do. This plan was not realized. Instead, London University offered to provide certification by including Royal Holloway in its federation of colleges. Admirably progressive on this as on so many other issues, London University had awarded degrees to women as early as 1878: Oxford and Cambridge granted full degrees to women (as opposed to mere certificates of attendance at

2. Bingham, *Royal Holloway College*, 46.
3. Bingham, *Royal Holloway College*, 56 and 59.

lectures) only as late as 1920 and 1948, respectively. Thomas Holloway, a very modern man for his times, had placed on top of Egham Hill a fragment of the future.

In 1975, much of this future had come true, despite continued ambivalences and many changes. "Holl Coll," as it called itself, remained somewhat peripheral to the London University system. Its splendid isolation in Egham constantly tempted the college residents to settle down to the cozy ethos of a boarding school. Male students had been accepted since 1965. But women still predominated in the student body (715 to 576 in 1973/74). In many ways, the overall ethos of the college was that of a women's campus. To the best of my knowledge, I was the first male head of the History Department, though it had long had its fair share of male teachers. Lionel Butler (1923–1981), who had played a major part in my appointment, was the first male principal. He had come only recently, in 1973, having been a charismatic professor of medieval history in St. Andrews.

In the evenings of May and June 1975, I would sit up late in my office in the corner of the block to which the History Department had recently moved, away from the splendors of Founder's Building—the original, gigantic college. Silhouetted in india-ink black against the twilight, the elaborate domes and chimneys of Founder's Building were almost swallowed up by the magnificent trees and high shrubbery of the gardens that surrounded them. It could have been a view of some great Indian temple or of Angkor Wat. All it lacked, I wrote to a friend, were tribes of sacred monkeys.

GENIUS LOCI

POLITICAL THOUGHT, WORLD HISTORY, AND ISLAM

COLLEAGUES AND COUNSELORS

What I found, to my delight, on arriving at Royal Holloway, was a History Department ready for change and extremely congenial. As the new head of department I was expected to encourage a more modern profile than that favored by my predecessor, Joan Hussey (1907–2006), a strict Byzantinist. Here I had the greatest good fortune. My coprofessor (the holder of a personal chair) was Neville Sanderson (1919–2001). "Sandy" was a robust Yorkshireman. He had little patience with what he called "the Southern Counties blancmange" whose genteel and undemanding spirit, in his view, constantly threatened to infect the college. He was a rock of good sense and fairness, as deeply versed in the ways of the central government of London University as of the college. Any administrative skill that I showed in my three years at Royal Holloway, I owed largely to him.

I quickly realized that I shared a world with Sandy. He was an old Sudan hand. He had been head of the History Department in Khartoum University from 1953 to 1965 and would still travel there regularly to represent the University of London, whose famous external examination system granted degrees throughout the former territories of the British Empire.

With his wife, Lillian, Sandy later wrote a study of education in the southern Sudan. This was an unflinchingly honest book that told the story of the murderous working out of the "baleful mirage" that had encouraged, first, the British, and then—after Sudanese independence—the Muslims of the northern

Sudan, to impose a rigid control on the vast territories of the South: an attempt that had led to the slaughter of the civil wars of 1955 to 1972.[1]

My other rock of certainty was Rita Townsend, the departmental secretary. Quiet as a wise mouse, she knew everyone and everything. We all consulted Rita. She combined roles usually kept far apart in American universities. She was mother and school matron all in one to the undergraduates. At the same time, she was at the top of her class as an administrator. Above all, she was a fount of humanity. At the time, I was unused to the professorial grandeur of having a secretary to take letters and memoranda from dictation. When I did this, I would always watch Rita's face as I dictated. On any delicate issue—and especially on any issue that involved the problems of individual undergraduates—I could tell at once from her expression whether I was doing the right thing.

As far as the younger members of the department were concerned, I came at a significant moment. Structurally, the Royal Holloway History Department had suffered from being seen as a stepping-stone to better posts, in Oxbridge or elsewhere. With the freezing of jobs in history throughout Britain, however, gifted young scholars knew that they could no longer count on passing rapidly through the college to higher things. They had to face the fact that they might be at Royal Holloway for the long haul. As head of department, it was up to me to try to ensure that their life there would be intellectually and personally rewarding.

This effort also affected the students. As a residential college, perched at a distance from metropolitan London, Royal Holloway was always in danger of turning in on itself. Young and old alike needed to feel that interesting things could happen even in the wilds of Egham. Hence the importance of the newly reinvigorated History Society. Each term we would invite distinguished historians to deliver a paper and to dine at leisure with us.

For me, the most moving of those visits was from Kathleen Hughes (1926–1977), the scholar of early medieval Ireland, whose book *The Church in Early Irish Society* had been my most sure—indeed, at the time, my only—guide to the Christianity of Dark Age Ireland.[2]

For Kathleen, the invitation to Royal Holloway had meant a return to a not altogether happy past. Like many leading women scholars, she had taught at Royal Holloway at the beginning of her career under the ferule of my

---

1. Lillian Passmore Sanderson and Neville Sanderson, *Education, Religion and Politics in the Southern Sudan, 1899–1965* (London: Ithaca Press; Khartoum: University of Khartoum Press, 1981), 246.

2. Kathleen Hughes, *The Church in Early Irish Society* (London: Methuen, 1966).

predecessor, Joan Hussey. They had been grim years. Now it seemed that the lively occasion laid on by the History Society had removed a burden for her:

> In fact the visit laid a bogey for me: I met JMH [Joan Hussey] in the UL [the Cambridge University Library] yesterday, and actually <u>spoke</u> to her, told her I had been to RHC. She said "I suppose it was awful" (typically), and I said "Quite the reverse. I enjoyed it very much". She just looked a rather pathetic pale splodge, not a horror any more.

Kathleen had spoken on the relation between sanctity and pilgrimage among the holy men and women of early medieval Ireland. It was an inspiring talk—a glimpse of another world, seldom explored by British medievalists. Barely over a month later, on April 20, 1977, she died unexpectedly of a heart attack. Walking through the garden beneath the Founder's Building to absorb the news, I came upon a heavy patch of daffodils in full flower. It was as if a little bit of Paradise had broken through the earth.

POLITICAL THOUGHT

As professor in medieval history and head of department, I could have invoked my privilege and limited myself to teaching medieval history only. But that would have left me somewhat isolated in a department that was tilted toward the modern age, and would have limited my contacts with students. By contrast, political thought was an obligatory part of the syllabus for every history student. To have a hand in teaching it would give me the width of contact that I needed. Here I was fortunate. In London University I found a vigorous tradition of the study of the history of social and political thought through the ages, from ancient Greece to modern times. The history of political thought had always interested me. Now was a time to get to know more about it.

At Royal Holloway College, the teaching of the history of political thought had been somewhat piecemeal. I was determined that it should have a higher profile, as a star subject, and that I should take part in it. In the general reshuffle of seminars and lectures that took place soon after my arrival in the summer of 1975, I offered to deliver a series of lectures for Royal Holloway students: "Theories of History and Society from the Enlightenment to Karl Marx."

Lectures on such modern themes might appear somewhat quixotic in a professor of medieval history. But they served a good purpose. Writing the lectures helped me to put together what I already knew about the intellectual predecessors of the social anthropologists and the sociologists to whom I had owed so much in recent years. Furthermore, my new commitment to the history of social and political thought introduced me to the works of the Scottish Enlightenment—especially to David Hume (1711–1776)—which helped me greatly when I wrote about Edward Gibbon's views on culture and society.[3]

Apart from this immediate payoff for my own study of late antiquity, I felt that I had joined a London tradition which I had long admired. Ever since my first contacts with Arnaldo Momigliano, I had been intrigued (as he was, also) by the metropolitan, radical aspect of London University that dated from the days of Jeremy Bentham (1748–1832), the great utilitarian philosopher. (The reader may remember that I had already met Bentham, to my surprise, in 1957, as an embalmed figure in a corridor of University College.) This liberal tradition spoke to Arnaldo from his very first days in England as a refugee from Fascist Italy. It was said that, when Italy entered the war and all Italians in Britain were interned for a spell as "enemy aliens," Arnaldo reported at the local police station with a copy of John Stuart Mill's *On Liberty* in his coat pocket.

In a metropolitan university, with a radical background, the history of political and social thought was treated as a serious matter. Though it was only one paper among others, the paper on political thought was given special weight in the final examination. It somehow summed up the Victorian ideal of an urban university where people of all classes and both sexes were expected to think hard and to argue hard about politics and society. It was part of the *genius loci* of London University.

In July 1977, I acted as examiner for the political thought paper in the university-wide final examination. My colleague was Michael Wilks (1930–1998), an expert on late medieval political theory. Michael taught at Birkbeck College, which had been founded as a college for workers. As a result, its lectures always happened in the evenings. It was the Victorian ideal of the workers' evening class now made part of the flexible structure of the university.

One candidate wrote a quite outstanding paper. When his name was finally revealed (for, in the sober London tradition, the paper had borne a number up to the time of the giving of the final grade, so as to ensure total anonymity and total fairness), it turned out that Wilks knew him well as a student at Birkbeck. He explained to me that this candidate was the man who played the guitar sitting on the floor of the entrance to Tottenham Court Road Underground

---

3. Peter Brown, "Gibbon's Views on Culture and Society in the Fifth and Sixth Centuries," *Daedalus* 105 (Summer 1976): 73–88, now in *Society and the Holy in Late Antiquity* (Berkeley: University of California Press, 1982), 22–48.

station. I had frequently passed him and often dropped a coin into his glass. In an essay that began, "Kephalas [the conservative old Athenian in the opening dialogue of Plato's *Republic*] is the clue . . . ," he had produced the most searching critique of Plato's attitude to myth and society that either of us had ever read. Our Tube-station musician was a progressive hope come true.

WORLD HISTORY

At Royal Holloway I also found myself engaged with a lively group of young scholars in modern British history, and in the history of South and Southeast Asia. They had already set about creating a course in modern world history that was unique in Britain at the time. It covered Asia and Africa since 1900, with special attention to comparisons between the regions, such as comparative studies of the peasantry. It also examined the fate of transnational movements in politics and ideas as these impinged on differing societies—Communism, anticolonialism, secularism, Islamic and Hindu revivalism. We had every reason to be proud of this course. It gave a distinctive flavor to the teaching of history at Royal Holloway that it had lacked before.

The efforts of the world history group influenced my own work deeply at this time. So far, my readings in anthropology and in the comparative history of traditional societies—Iran, India, and East Asia—had a bookish quality. But scholars such as Neville Sanderson (for Egypt and Sudan), Francis Robinson (for India and Pakistan), and Anthony Stockwell (for Malaysia) studied living societies that they would visit regularly, through those long flights from Heathrow, and whose recent history and present-day dilemmas they could observe at close quarters. My own recent experience in Iran (the first non-European country that I had ever visited) made me doubly appreciative of their skills.

This was particularly the case with the study of modern Islam, in which the University of London excelled. Outside Royal Holloway, I gained immensely, at this time, through contact with Michael Gilsenan, at University College London—whom I knew best through his *Saint and Sufi in Modern Egypt*—and with Ernst Gellner (1925–1995), at the London School of Economics, author of *Saints of the High Atlas*, whose unstinting generosity helped me greatly in my work on the Christian cult of the saints in late antique and early medieval Europe.[4]

---

4. M. Gilsenan, *Saint and Sufi in Modern Egypt* (Oxford: Clarendon Press, 1973); Ernst Gellner, *Saints of the High Atlas* (London: Weidenfeld, 1969).

ISLAMIC REVIVAL

As a result of the work of my colleagues at Royal Holloway, Islam, which had always fascinated me, took on the weight of living flesh and blood, much as it had done in my short visit to Iran. It was not an altogether comfortable realization. It showed me that what we had thought was a sleeping giant was, in reality, fully, dangerously awake: it was modern Europeans who had failed, through ignorance and prejudice, to understand the rhythms of its breathing. It was more than a little scary to think that we—well-schooled scholars that we were—could have been so very wrong in dismissing Islam as a moribund religion.

I owed most to my colleague Francis Robinson for this enrichment of my approach to the Islamic world. Francis was a new arrival in the department. He had come to Royal Holloway in 1973. His *Separatism among Indian Muslims: The Politics of the United Provinces Muslims, 1860–1923* appeared the next year.[5] It described how the scattered and somewhat faceless Muslim community of a crucial Indian region emerged, in the course of the late nineteenth and early twentieth centuries, as a highly self-conscious and militant political group. This rallying of Muslim opinion eventually led to the creation of the separate Muslim state of Pakistan. The book was acclaimed as a model study of the relation between political mobilization and the rise of nationalist feeling in a major Third World country.

When I first met him, in 1975, Francis was facing a dilemma for which I had the greatest sympathy. Despite the success of his book, he felt that he had not entered deeply enough into the living texture of the world that he was studying. *Separatism among Muslims* had been a highly successful performance within a clear-cut tradition of British scholarship on India. It studied the jostling of elites. It concentrated on the manner in which the Muslim leadership in northern India had mobilized Islamic beliefs in competition with Hindu rivals for a share in the patronage of the British government; later, for a share in the government of an independent India; and, eventually, for the formation of the separate state of Pakistan.

But something was still lacking: in the preface to a later edition, Francis pointed out that this insistence on the maneuvering of elites for a place in the sun had caused him to overlook the religious ideas and traditions that gave weight and urgency to those maneuvers. As he admitted, "Ideas were not

---

5. Francis Robinson, *Separatism among Indian Muslims: The Politics of the United Provinces Muslims, 1860–1923* (Cambridge University Press, 1974; reprinted with an introduction, 1993).

thought to have a significant power to move men."[6] Above all, Francis thought that he had overlooked the Muslims' own view of the place of Islam in the modern world. As a result, he turned away from the politics of the Muslim elites in India alone to the considerably wider theme of the Islamic revival of the nineteenth and twentieth centuries. In his articles, he showed how the Islamic revival had sent a "surge of energy" throughout Africa and Asia. A major, silent shift in Islamic priorities took place, from the otherworldly Islam of the Sufis to a this-worldly emphasis on the need to reform society in the here and now.

Though barely visible to outsiders, this was a shift as massive as any experienced in the history of Christian Europe—as decisive as the Protestant Reformation and Catholic Counter-Reformation of the sixteenth century. Beginning in the nineteenth century, this movement had spread throughout the Islamic world. Francis knew of it especially from his Indian researches, in the form of the movement for the establishment of Islamic schools based on the Deoband Darul Uloom, which was founded in 1866, and on the networks of scholars connected with the Farangî Mahall, a center of learning based on Lucknow.[7]

All this was news to me. From the British Sudan to Dutch Indonesia, Islam had been dismissed by European observers as on its deathbed. Francis showed that it was an awakening giant. He took on himself the task of following this immense awakening across the entire stretch of the Islamic world. His work at this time was summed up in a masterly *Atlas of the Islamic World since 1500*.[8]

Alas, one has to put a date on this generous moment of realization on the part of European scholars of Islam: 1976 is not 2020. Islamic revivalism has taken many different forms between 1976 and today. A few of them rightly appall us. But, at least, there was a moment, in the 1970s, when scholars began to treat Islam as a living religion, fully engaged with the modern world, and not as some grandiose ghost from the Middle Ages. For me, a nonexpert, this was an important discovery.

Saints of Learning

Francis's work did more than provide me with a challenging panorama of the renewal of a world religion in the modern age. His research nourished and challenged my own work on the late antique holy man.

6. Robinson, *Separatism among Indian Muslims*, introduction to the 1993 reprint, xv.

7. Francis Robinson, "Other-Worldly and This-Worldly Islam and the Islamic Revival," in *Islam, South Asia and the West* (Oxford University Press, 2007), 171–188.

8. Francis Robinson, *Atlas of the Islamic World since 1500* (Oxford: Equinox, 1982).

In late antique Syria and Egypt, holy men had tended to stand alone (or to be presented as standing alone) as embattled, charismatic figures, straight from the desert. Francis opened up a world filled with less dramatic figures— with learned, this-worldly saints who maintained, with rare grace, a balance between Sufi mysticism and active involvement in the affairs of this world, as husbands, merchants, teachers, and politicians. As Francis described them, these modern saints of learning reminded me of the Greek philosophers and their pupils in the time of Plotinus and the last days of the Platonic Academy of Athens: mystics, but also men of vast learning and often pillars of their community. I realized that, in my study of late antiquity, I would have to pay more attention to similar figures—to philosophers, bishops, and rabbis—and not only to "my" rugged holy men.

ON THE EAST COAST

ART AND RELIGION

In the spring of 1976 my horizons opened yet further. I spent the entire month of April on the East Coast of America, making contact with an academic world hitherto largely unknown to me, and feasting my eyes on splendid late antique and Byzantine artifacts in museums all the way from Boston down to Washington, DC, and the Byzantine Research Center at Dumbarton Oaks. My visit fell into two parts, representing two very different intellectual agendas. The first—a lecture at the Pierpont Morgan Library—came from my interest in the meaning and function of late antique and Byzantine art. The second—in the Carl Newell Jackson Lectures at Harvard, "The Making of Late Antiquity"—stemmed from my interest in the origins of late antiquity in the crisis of the third century.

On April 13 I went to New York, to give a lecture at the Pierpont Morgan Library entitled "Art and Religion in Byzantium and the Early Medieval West." The lecture was based on two reviews that I had recently written for the *New York Review of Books* in 1974 and 1975. In them I had tried to recapture the strangeness of the works of early Christian and Byzantine art that we had come to take for granted through constant viewing in art books and in museums. I attempted to give readers a tingle of vertigo, as they looked down a drop of almost two millennia into a world that shared little or nothing of our own, modern notions of art and religion. I also wanted to take objects, such as icons, Gospel books, or precious relic cases, out of the hygienic exhibition cases of museums and place them back into the noise and movement of their original context.[1]

---

1. P. Brown, "The View from the Precipice," *New York Review of Books* 21 (1974): 3–5, and "Artifices of Eternity" (with Sabine MacCormack), *New York Review of Books* 22 (1975): 19–22,

I tried to conjure up the Christian crowds that had once swarmed around the shrines of early medieval saints, much as I had seen the crowds pressing against the silver gates of the shrine of the Imam Reza in Mashhad. I encouraged my audience to take a second look at the Byzantine icons that they were accustomed to viewing in the cool of air-conditioned galleries; and to imagine them swaying at the head of boisterous processions that wound their way through Mediterranean cities of the late antique and Byzantine periods.

In this I sought to do justice to a heartening recent development in late Roman and Byzantine studies that stressed the role of ceremonial, drama, and movement in the life of the cities. The work of recent scholars had reversed many earlier negative judgments on the later empire. They showed that the ceremonies of the imperial court were not mounted only as overbearing shows of power, as Gibbon and many others had thought. They also had a popular element. Those who engaged in them were held to have given their assent to power by their rhythmic acclamations, by their waving palm leaves and scented lamps, and by the stately order in which every segment of society turned out to greet their ruler. Through such ceremonies, they allowed themselves to be swept into a grand theater, whose elements—the chants, the waving banners and placards, the heavy clouds of incense, the scattered flowers and sweet-smelling herbs—grew from the streets up, with folkloric vigor. They were not cowed spectators (like many who witnessed the parades of modern dictators), but an urban populace seeped in centuries of festival. It was not the emperors who made the ceremonies. It was the ceremonies that made the emperors.

I pointed out that this was also the case with the liturgies of the Christian churches. These were not the stilled and reverent occasions that we might imagine. Loud acclamations, solemn candlelit processions, carpets of roses and scented herbs strewn across the brightly colored marble pavements of the churches were all part of a single great tide of celebration that swirled backward and forward from the depths of the churches into the noisy courtyards and the ancient streets. Late antique and Byzantine churches were not the silent, empty buildings that they have become. They were seen, at the time, as the grand stage on which the Christian community played out, through ceremony, the high drama of the worship of God.[2]

---

now in *Society and the Holy in Late Antiquity* (Berkeley: University of California Press, 1982), 196–221.

2. Thomas F. Mathews, *The Early Churches of Constantinople: Architecture and Liturgy* (University Park: Pennsylvania State University Press, 1972); and S. G. MacCormack, *Art and*

Paradise

I also wished to do justice to the intuitions of Father Gervase Mathew (1905–1976), a wise and free spirit to whom I had grown close in these years. News of his death (on April 4, 1976) had come to me when I was attending the Orthodox liturgy in South Bend only a few days before my lecture in New York. Gervase's lectures on Byzantium had once thrilled me as an undergraduate. His *Byzantine Aesthetics* had posed the question of the sheer, sharp beauty of so many Byzantine and early medieval works of art.[3] These were something more than mere carriers of Christian ideology. Still less were they simply teaching devices, whose message had to be decoded by learned iconographers. Instead, their strange, unfamiliar beauty in itself spoke of the beauty of an Other World. But of what sort of Other World did they speak?

Here I pointed out that this was not the Other World of the modern Christian imagination, an ethereal Heaven crowded with serried ranks of human faces. It was Paradise—a more ancient place of rest and of primordial delight. The notion of Paradise as a royal garden was one of the greatest legacies of the ancient Near East, through Persia, to the imagination of the Jewish, Christian, and Muslim worlds.[4]

The idea of Paradise as an ancient garden of delights came into its own in the unexpected drama and sensuous thrill of early Christian and Byzantine liturgies—with their shimmering lights, heavy scents, and scattered flowers. Paradise, and not some abstruse theological propositions, was what was hinted at in the exuberant, bright-green vegetation that reached up to the dome in the sixth-century church of San Vitale in Ravenna; and in the figures of the martyrs in Paradise in the ninth-century chapel of Santa Prassede, in Rome, shown as they "tread on poppies as red as they still grow every spring in the Roman Campagna."[5]

Ceremony in Late Antiquity (Berkeley: University of California Press, 1981). See now John Weisweiler, "Paideia in the Andes: Sabine MacCormack on the History of Imperial Culture in Late Antiquity," in *New Late Antiquity*, 643–657, at 647–649.

3. G. Mathew, *Byzantine Aesthetics* (London: J. Murray,1963).

4. Annemarie Schimmel, "The Celestial Garden in Islam," in *The Islamic Garden*, ed. E. B. MacDougall and R. Ettinghausen (Washington DC: Dumbarton Oaks, 1976), 11–39.

5. Brown, "The View from the Precipice," in *Society and the Holy in Late Antiquity*, 205.

Bob Silvers (1929–2017)

After the lecture at the Pierpont Morgan Library, I met for the first time the man who had prompted me to write about such themes—Bob Silvers, the already-legendary editor of the *New York Review of Books*. What I remember from that evening was Bob sitting deep in a large, black padded chair in a club bar, surrounded by happy and talkative friends, like cherubs around a sunburst. Then he was gone. At the time, I did not know about the extraordinary self-discipline with which he would retire, every night, to work until early morning on the *Review*.

I had come to know Bob through his brief and invariably encouraging notes, and through the piles of books that would come in the mail, seemingly overnight, from New York to Royal Holloway College. From 1976 onward, Bob was installed in my mind as a polestar in the literary world that I had recently come to know in London and America. He was a benign superego. Every invitation to write a review was preceded—as by a heavy artillery barrage—by innumerable packets of books of varying qualities on any number of subjects. Bob left it up to me to sort them out into a plausible theme for a review, as if I were playing a game of Consequences. At a time when I was far from certain that the pressure of work as head of department in Royal Holloway College would leave me any time at all to write, his requests for reviews came like breathing holes punched through thickening ice. They gave me the opportunity to write in a relaxed style on topics that were close to my heart, without the heavy metal and gladiatorial stances of reviews in academic journals.

Looking back, I now realize that, in some ways, the *New York Review of Books* replaced Faber and Faber in London in my imaginary map of the publishers through whom I wished to address a wide reading public. I still liked to think of myself as writing "for my aunts"—for average people interested in history and religion. But now I began increasingly to think also of the sophisticated, well-educated, but not necessarily academic readers of the *New York Review of Books*, scattered throughout America and elsewhere. When I imagined such an audience, from now onward I would say, "I write for Bob Silvers."

Glen Bowersock

Next day I took the train to New Haven, to join up with Glen Bowersock. We had agreed to meet at a lecture that he gave at Yale, and then to proceed together to Harvard. His host at Yale introduced the lecture by praising Glen's recent books, vividly and accurately, as like those high-gravity stars that burn with incandescent energy. This referred, in particular, to his masterly *Greek Sophists in the Roman Empire*.[6] This book had given me the courage to enter the Antonine Age—the age of Aelius Aristrides, Marcus Aurelius, and Galen. I had also been impressed by his use of an Arabic text—the Arabic translation of the *Physiognomica* of Polemo (ca. 88–144)—that described a failed assassination attempt on the emperor Hadrian. Glen's careful use of Arabic was an augury for his move ever farther east, which has taken him, in an exemplary scholarly odyssey, from the second-century Aegean, through Roman Arabia, to Axum, Yemen, and the Hijaz on the eve of the rise of Islam.[7]

In subsequent years, our friendship deepened as my admiration for Glen grew. Not only did he show the way to ever-wider worlds, by moving from the Mediterranean to the Middle East. He also conjured up the sheer thrill of the late antique period as a whole by exploring the many ways in which the classical world opened itself up to new possibilities, both delightful and disturbing—to new forms of fiction,[8] but also to new forms of horror, in the blood-soaked drama of Christian martyrdoms acted out on the bright stage of the theaters, main squares, and town halls of the Greek cities.[9] He showed how Hellenism itself—Greek culture and Greek art—did not recede in late antiquity, but, rather, that it reached out to embrace local cults and immemorial traditions, providing them with "a new and more eloquent way of giving voice" to their rich particularity.[10]

Throughout this meteor shower of brilliant studies, Glen has caught the wonder of it all. Writing on the abundance of shimmering mosaics that covered the floors of churches, synagogues, and grand villas alike with scenes of cities and the pantomime, as well as with symbols of Jewish and Christian worship, he concluded,

> The late-antique Near East was a kind of miracle, and its like has never been seen in that region again.[11]

6. G. W. Bowersock, *Greek Sophists in the Roman Empire* (Oxford: Clarendon Press, 1969).

7. G. W. Bowersock, *Empires in Collision in Late Antiquity* (Waltham, MA: Brandeis University Press, 2012); *The Throne of Adulis: Red Sea Wars on the Eve of Islam* (Oxford University Press, 2013); *The Crucible of Islam* (Cambridge, MA: Harvard University Press, 2017).

8. G. W. Bowersock, *Fiction as History: Nero to Julian* (Berkeley: University of California Press, 1994).

9. G. W. Bowersock, *Martyrdom and Rome* (Cambridge University Press, 1995).

10. G. W. Bowersock, *Hellenism in Late Antiquity* (Ann Arbor: University of Michigan Press, 1990), 7.

11. G. W. Bowersock, *Mosaics in History: The Near East from Late Antiquity to Islam* (Cambridge, MA: Belknap Press of Harvard University Press, 2006), 122.

After Glen's talk at Yale, we took the train together to Boston. Next day we strolled round Boston in a miniature heat wave and were politely refused entry to a restaurant as we were without tie and jacket. We later went together to the *Saint Matthew Passion* in Symphony Hall. I still remember the end of the very last chorus:

Wir setzen uns mit Tränen nieder.

We sit down with tears.

The last flakes of sound seemed to float down from the curved ceiling, leaving a total, stunned silence.

AMONG THE ELEPHANTS: HARVARD

I gave the Jackson Lectures at Harvard, "The Making of Late Antiquity," from April 19 through 23. They went well. As a *captatio benevolentiae* I offered a passage from the mid-second-century *Dream Book* of Artemidorus of Daldis. He wrote that it was good for a man to dream of elephants, for that meant that he would go to Italy and mingle with the greatest of the land. At Harvard, I had, indeed, found myself among a mighty herd of elephants—scholars of all ages and interests. Many lasting friendships were formed at this time—not least with Caroline Bynum, then teaching in the Harvard Divinity School and finishing her dissertation, *Docere Verbo et Exemplo*, a marvelously nuanced study of the various styles of leadership and instruction in the monasteries of the twelfth century.[12]

Later in the lectures, I likened the circle of upper-class mystical Platonists who gathered around the philosopher Proclus in Athens (411–485), in the late fifth century AD, to the society of Boston, described in a rhyme of 1910:

> This is to good old Boston,
> The home of the bean and the cod,
> Where Lowells speak only to Cabots,
> And Cabots speak only to God.

There was a burst of laughter. Being a foreigner, I may have got the families reversed. A few years later, I had to enter into a prolonged correspondence

---

12. C. W. Bynum, *Docere Verbo et Exemplo*, Harvard Theological Studies 31 (Missoula, MT: Scholar's Press, 1979).

with my French translator, who was totally flummoxed by this touch of local humor.

Even the weather did well by me. As a Boston sea storm darkened the room, my description of the pagans' fear that the rise of Christianity might incur the wrath of the gods was echoed by a heavy roll of thunder.

The Jackson Lectures were published in 1978 as *The Making of Late Antiquity*.[13] As I look back, it strikes me as my most adventurous book. It was a reappraisal of the well-known "crisis" of the third century and its later repercussions.

I fastened on what seemed to be a paradox in the history of that tumultuous century: a time of rapid change in the structure of Greco-Roman society coincided, outside the world of the elites, with religious movements led by leaders whose role in the imagination of their followers mirrored, to a remarkable degree, the increasingly vertical ordering of upper-class Roman society.

The Rise of the "Friends of God"

It was this verticality both in society and in the religious imagination that held my attention. In the course of the third century, the emperor came to be increasingly seen as the chosen of the gods. Those who served the emperor also emerged ever more sharply at the expense of their peers. Their new prominence, due to their links to the court, disrupted the little oligarchies of town counselors and local landowners, who had long maintained the traditional life of the cities.

A paradox of the third century was that the emperor was not alone in claiming to enjoy a divine mandate. The emergence of the "pyramidal" society of the later empire was accompanied by an outburst of religious creativity among classes and in regions that lay outside the horizons of the Roman governing class. Individual religious leaders emerged who claimed to have been chosen by God or the gods to accomplish great things—to teach, to spread their faith, to face down opponents, even to court death as martyrs.

These persons were regarded by their devotees as "Friends of God." In the religious sphere, they were thought to have risen above their peers as sharply as the friends of the emperor rose above all others in contemporary upper-class society. The dominant role of these religious leaders was highlighted in

---

13. P. Brown, *The Making of Late Antiquity* (Cambridge, MA: Harvard University Press, 1978), 1.

language heavy with reverence, often using imagery and forms of ceremonial behavior borrowed directly from the secular exaltation of the emperor and his servants.

A Crisis in Human Relations

Why had this happened? Put briefly, I suggested that, in many regions, the lower reaches of Roman society had changed as much as had the elites. An entire new class of "middling" persons had emerged, to whom the new, more vertical styles of religious leadership appealed.

This was particularly the case with the monastic movement in late third- and fourth-century Egypt. Ever since Edward Gibbon, scholars had been puzzled by the rush to the desert that seemed to have taken place at that time. Most explanations have treated it as a movement of protest and despair. I disagreed. Appealing to the studies of modern anthropologists working in the villages of Egypt and the Middle East, I argued that the ascetic movement did not arise from the misery of the peasantry. Far from it: the ascetic movement emerged, on the village level, from a crisis of human relations brought about by new prosperity and by new possibilities for social mobility.

In Egypt, a newly formed class of comfortable farmers and of small-town notables provided the leaders of the monastic movement. Saint Anthony (ca. 270–356), the hero of the monks of Egypt, had been a substantial landowner. At a time when the average holding of some villages was forty-four *arourae*, the family of Saint Anthony owned some three hundred (almost two hundred acres), "very fertile and beautiful to see."[14] These were the sort of people whose rising expectations and sharpened spiritual ambitions fed the monasteries and the Christian churches with a ready supply of talent for new, experimental forms of communal living.

And so I concluded: many aspects of late antiquity repel us modern persons—the sense of hierarchy, the strident militancy, the ever-sharper boundaries that emerged after the delicate equipoise of the Antonine Age; but precisely those features, through the fierce sense of agency that they unleashed, had to be accepted by historians as the dark earth from which so many of the achievements of late antiquity sprouted.

14. Brown, *Making of Late Antiquity*, 82.

TO THE TOP OF THE WORLD

TAKHT-E SOLEYMAN

DREAMTIME

From July 16 to August 29, 1976, I traveled in Iran and Afghanistan. Apart from a few days, I was on my own. I wrote no journal and no letters, and I took no camera. I had decided not to shield myself from my environment—even through the very slightest imposition of a framework such as writing a diary, or fixing a view through a camera lens. As a result, this journey comes back to me almost as a series of vivid dream images.

There was a purpose in this openness. In my previous visit to Iran, I had wanted to view the principal monuments of the Sasanians, so as to place each of them in its distinctive landscape. Now it was not so much the monuments as the landscapes themselves that I wished to view. I traveled some five thousand miles, through Iran and Afghanistan, as far as Bamiyan and Kabul. All these places had been part of the immense Sasanian Empire. I wanted to do justice to the sheer size of this empire that, at its height, had extended from Mesopotamia (modern Iraq) as far as Central Asia and northern India. By viewing this vast expanse, I hoped to sketch, as it were, the second, Eastern panel of the diptych whose Western side was the Mediterranean empire of East Rome.

Looking back, I cannot resist a certain sadness. I had intended this journey to be the first of many journeys. No one I talked to at that time—even those with a reputation for being old Persia hands—foresaw the Iranian Revolution of 1979, which would slam down an iron shutter between Iran and the West. Of all the academic ventures that I have embarked upon, my outreach to the history of Iran (though it greatly enriched my historical imagination) was the one that has left least trace in my published work.

When I arrived in Tehran in July 1976, I knew nothing of what would happen in the coming years. Yet I soon developed a sense of foreboding. The more I traveled in Iran, with many kinds of companions and in many different environments, the more I had the feeling of an entire society slipping out of the grasp of the official image that the shah's regime had created for itself and projected to outsiders—the image of a rapidly westernizing country in which religion was doomed to play an ever-diminishing role. A sense of dread—of having come close to something very large about to slide—is what I brought home from Iran at that time.

Bobby Warren and the Peacock Throne

There was one thing of which I was totally ignorant: I had a real live cousin at the court of the shah. In 1965, my cousin Bobby Warren, from a branch of the Warrens of county Meath, which had emigrated to Argentina, became the *maître de ballet* of Shah Reza (1919–1980). I had heard of this vaguely, but had assumed that so exotic a figure must have belonged to an earlier generation of more swashbuckling Warrens. Far from it. He was only a few years older than myself. In 2009 he published an autobiography, appropriately entitled *Destiny's Waltz: In Step with Giants*. In it, he described his years at the court of the shah.

Often the ballet troupe performed in private, in front of the shah and the diplomatic corps. On one such occasion they danced in praise of the shah's westernizing reforms, in a ballet that showed the liberation of the peasantry and the finding of oil. I can only imagine what it must have been like. As Bobby described it, the performance was a tense affair, like a court masque under Queen Elizabeth I:

> Our job was now completed. We held our breath awaiting the reaction of our very exclusive audience.
>
> All eyes turned to the Shah and *Shahbanou*. Their reaction would set the tone for the reception we would receive. The Shah seemed pleased and applauded with dignified restraint, immediately followed by his courtiers. The Diplomatic Corps set its own pace and applauded with more intensity, their expressions relieved. The courtiers observed their reaction and added

more fervor to their applause as the Shah stood and continued his applause. After that it was thunderous.

I had been petrified but began to breathe more normally.[1]

Bobby and I could have met in Tehran—but not in July 1976. For, at that time, Bobby was leading the Iranian Ballet on a tour of the United States. It was not an unqualified success. When Bobby's troupe performed Iranian dances at Bovary Hall on the campus of UCLA, anti-shah protesters stormed the stage. Bobby received a blow on the face, as a large banner declaring "Death to the Shah!" was unfurled from the balcony. Savak, the Iranian secret police, covered up the awkward incident. They reported back to their master that Bobby had received his injuries through being mugged somewhere in Los Angeles. Soon after that incident, Bobby left Iran.[2]

A Local Call to Hell

I had returned to Iran with more Persian than I had possessed in 1974. I soon had occasion to use it to pick up vibes. Making my way through Tehran, I found myself in an old mosque. Against a background of shining tiles, the guardian lectured me (as far as I could follow him) on the reality of angels. The orientation toward Mecca of the whole complex (graves and all) was a silent rebuke to the chaos of new buildings, whose girders pointed every which way around the little island of order represented by the mosque. The same day I picked up a joke that went the rounds at this time. The present shah, feeling insecure, resolved to ring up his father, the old Reza Khan, in the other world. He had the call put through. Father and son talked for hours on end about the problems of modern Iran. But when he was finished, the shah was surprised to find that there was no telephone charge. Why? The old shah was in Hell; and in Tehran, Hell is a local call! Looking at the impacted traffic in central Tehran, I saw the point of the joke.

A View from the Mountains

I stayed at the British School of Persian Studies, at a distance from the chaos of downtown. For members of the school, to leave Tehran for the countryside was a moment of escape. Being an archaeologist meant being out in the open,

1. Robert de Warren, *Destiny's Waltz: In Step with Giants* (New York: Eloquent Books, 2009), 234.

2. De Warren, *Destiny's Waltz*, 258 and 265.

away from the tensions that were building up in the big cities. Nobody led expeditions to the wide open spaces of Iran with more piratical zest than did David Stronach (1931–2020), the director of the British School. Packed into a Land Rover with David and his team, I found myself heading northwest, three hundred miles from Tehran in the direction of Tabriz, to visit the great Sasanian palace and fire temple at Tahkt-e Soleyman, perched on a high plateau of the Zagros Mountains overlooking Mesopotamia and the rising hills of northern Iraq.

Little visited by tourists, the spectacular ruins of Takht-e Soleyman marked the site of one of the four great fire temples of Iran. It also served as one of the rallying points for the northern thrust of the Sasanian Empire toward the Caucasus and Anatolia (Armenia, Georgia, and modern eastern Turkey). This flanking move from the far north—a maneuver favored by Khusro I (530–579) and Khusro II (591–628)—was particularly threatening to the East Romans. The region around Takht-e Soleyman was an ideal assembly point for the Sasanian armies. High above the hot and arid plains of Mesopotamia and Syria, the Iranian cavalry, as heavily armed as medieval knights, could graze their horses on the rich upper meadows of the Zagros before they pushed westward into what is now eastern Turkey or descended with devastating impact onto the plains of the Fertile Crescent.

We made the journey in stages. First we stopped at Ziwiyeh, the center of the civilization of Urartu (a mountain polity, often claimed as the original nucleus of Armenia), where a spectacular hoard of golden ornaments dating from around 700 BC had been discovered in 1947. In the golden light of the late afternoon we went out with David simply to taste the joy of being "in the field" and away from Tehran. We viewed the great conical hillocks that dotted the slopes. Any one of them might prove to be the *tel* piled up above an ancient city. David pointed out the foxholes on the sides of the *tels*. The low sun shone on them like a floodlight. It was by noticing fragments of ceramic lying in such a foxhole (pushed to the surface from deep beneath the earth by the persistent burrowing of foxes and rodents) that David had discovered the great Median site of Tepe Nush-e Jân near Kermanshah in 1967—a palace-city that included the earliest fire temple yet to be discovered in Iran.

It was a time to celebrate. At the end of our tour of the hillocks around Ziwiyeh we stopped the jeep to admire the sunset. The mountain amphitheater turned purple. We looked down toward the ridges beyond which lay Iraq. Once in the 1950s, David told us, he had been with Sir Max Mallowan (1904–1978) while excavating the great Assyrian capital of the eighth century

BC at Nimrud in northern Iraq—the site from which the enormous winged
bulls with human faces had been taken to the British Museum in the nineteenth century. Pointing upward to the mountains of Iran, David had said to
Mallowan: "You know, Max. We should have a British School up there, in Iran."
"Oh, I don't know, David," Max replied, "Rather unstable country at the moment." "And here we are," David added, with some pride. It is as well that we
do not know the future.

THE TOP OF THE WORLD: TAKHT-E SOLEYMAN

The next day we moved farther northwest to yet wilder, Kurdish country,
toward Takht-e Soleyman (the Throne of Solomon). Takht-e Soleyman was
on the high plateau, rich in summer grazing, from which first Khusro II, in the
early seventh century, and, half a millennium later, the Ilkhanid Mongol khans
of the thirteenth century had overshadowed the entire Middle East. It was like
a vast Swiss *Alm*, where watercourses ran across bright-green fields. The calci-
fication of the water had pushed the watercourses ever higher above the
ground so that they looked like a system of miniature aqueducts—a hydraulic
model railway of great complexity.

Beside the quiet, circular lake that marked the center of the caldera of an
extinct volcano lay the ruins of Takht-e Soleyman. All Eurasia came together
in those ruins. A Sasanian palace arch of the time of Khusro II abutted the
slender columns of a Mongol pavilion erected by Hulagu Khan (1218–1266),
the grandson of Genghis Khan. Nearby, a Buddhist *stupa*, possibly brought by
the Mongols from Tibet, had been excavated. Just beside it, the German excavation team had recently pulled from the earth an exquisitely carved Gothic
capital, probably made by a European craftsman on the spot—perhaps to
decorate the chapel of the wife of Hulagu Khan, who was a "Nestorian"
Christian.

I rode a horse called Iskender—after Alexander the Great—up to the
nearby hill of Takht-e Bilqis—the Throne of Bilqis. This was the name in Muslim legend of the queen of Sheba, who had visited Solomon in his glory. In the
Muslim tradition (heavily influenced by Iranian ideas of kingship) Solomon
was far more than a wise king in Jerusalem. He was seen as a magical world
ruler. The view from his throne and that of his wife was worthy of him. I
looked down over the hills toward Lake Urmia, where Christians of the so-
called Nestorian Church of the East still survived. Beyond Lake Urmia lay
a series of plateaux that descended, in giant steps, into the lowlands of Iraq

and Syria. At Takht-e Bilqis I felt I was king of the castle. Those distant, flat lands lay at my feet. It was a place to think big—to plan a history of the relations between Byzantium and Iran in terms of a conflict between the Mediterranean and its great, Asian antithesis for control of the Middle East.

But most moving of all were the remains of the great Zoroastrian fire temple that had once housed the Royal Warrior Fire (the Adur Gushnasp)—one of the three great fires of the Sasanian Empire. As I remember it, it was a nondescript ruin, except for one striking detail: a low stone wall set at the entrance ensured that, from whatever angle one looked, one's eyes would not fall upon the holy fire (much as I had seen it in Yazd two years previously). Here was a trace of a deeply holy thing, surrounded by expectations and shielded by taboos that were totally different from those of Christian shrines. I realized that I had passed an invisible frontier between the Christendom of East Rome and its great rival—the confidently non-Christian world of Sasanian Iran. To view the palace and the adjacent Zoroastrian holy of holies of Takht-e Soleyman, and to take in the landscape that lay around them, made me feel that I was as distant from the Mediterranean as if I were on the face of the moon.[3]

I was left at Sanandaj (in the middle of Iranian Kurdistan) to make my own way back by bus to Tehran. Sanandaj was a bustling town, filled with Kurdish followers of the Ahl-e Haq—the People of the Truth—devotees of a Gnostic sect that had held out since late antique times in the inaccessible folds of the Zagros. The Kurdish young men carried rifles. They sported gold lamé cummerbunds and great drooping moustaches, grown long (so I was told) so that their hairs would dangle in their drink, in studied defiance of Islamic notions of purity.

---

3. See Matthew Canepa, *The Iranian Expanse* (Berkeley: University of California Press, 2018), 283–290; and James Howard-Johnston, *The Last Great War of Antiquity* (Oxford University Press, 2021), 226–227.

"GUARDIANS OF THE SACRED FLAME"

DAVID FROST

AT FIRUZABAD WITH DAVID FROST (1939–2013)

Only a few days later, I was in somewhat different company. I was with David Frost and a team of filmmakers, seated in the front of a large Iranian Air Force helicopter as we swerved perilously out to sea, over the bright-blue waters of the Persian Gulf, as the pilot (no archaeologist) attempted, unsuccessfully at first, to find the palace of King Ardashir at Firuzabad.

This change of scene requires some explanation. In January 11, 1976, I was approached to act as academic adviser for one part of an eight-part TV series (of one hour each) on the history of Iran. It was called *Crossroads of Civilization*, and was a coproduction of the National Film Centre of Iran with the Parradine TV Production Company, owned by David Frost. I was asked to be academic adviser for the episode devoted to the rise and fall of the Sasanian Empire, entitled "Guardians of the Sacred Flame."

I jumped at it. It was a chance to revisit the landscapes that I had explored in 1974. More than that: it was a chance to have a hand in producing a visual history of Sasanian Iran, set against the majestic and little-known landscapes of the Iranian plateau.

The venture was launched with much razzmatazz; but the job itself was fascinating. It brought me into contact with a whole world of intelligent and enterprising young people during the shooting itself. The camera team were masters of a high craft. There was no bullshit among the grippers, lighting experts, sound editors, and wielders of exquisitely calibrated movie cameras.

It was with the camera team that I landed with David Frost outside the great palace of Ardashir at Firuzabad, which I had already visited in 1974. Standing against the great pool of water in front of the ruins, David asked me for my views on the reasons for the fall of the Sasanian Empire. I was suitably sonorous. Then came a reminder that we lived in a world of craftsmen, where reality itself was a skilled construction. The moment I finished, the camera team shouted, in unison: "Hold it, David! Noddies!" And sure enough, Frost turned from me to the camera and did his "noddies." He solemnly nodded ten times, to express reverent agreement with the words of the professor. Carefully spliced into my monologue, David Frost and I were shown chatting amiably (himself nodding in a knowing manner) in a suitably exotic environment about the fate of an empire from long ago.

A Landscape from Above

Then David and I were taken by helicopter up over the cliffs above the narrow valley of the Tang-e Ab and deposited on the roof of the Sasanian palace of Qaleh Dokhtar—the Castle of the Daughter (of the King of Kings). Qaleh Dokhtar was perched like a medieval castle on a spur of rock with great drops on every side. David was filmed arriving in the helicopter, hovering above a winding ravine before descending from the sky into a golden cloud of chaff. Here, on the roof, the interviewing continued.

The real star of the filming operation was the Alouette helicopter flown by a pair of French pilots. It took me wherever I wanted to go, so as to explore the whole region from the air. We bounced across the hills beyond Firuzabad, Qaleh Dokhtar, and the valley of the Tang-e Ab. This flight over the uplands around Firuzabad taught me something. I saw that the entire mountain area was by no means inaccessible. Horse trails led up easily from the valley below along sloping paths formed from great layers of upended sandstone. Once one was on the plateau, all that was needed was to follow the trails of the Qashqai on their *kuch*—their yearly migration to summer pastures.

This capillary system of horse trails, now used by the Qashqai, explained the immense mobility of the Sasanian kings. A court the size of an army could traverse the great distances of the Iranian plateau, linking palace to palace and fire temple to fire temple with the ease of a hunting party. Here (in what were now the deserted homelands of the nomads) I was able to look down on a web of trails, walls, and castles that held together the Sasanian realm. Unlike the emperor of East Rome, who resided permanently in the Great Palace at

Constantinople, the Sasanian king of kings was perpetually on the move. He could always show himself to be a *dirâz-dâst*—a man of the Long Hand who could strike anywhere at the head of a mobile entourage.

IMAGE AND REALITY

Afterward, at the bar of the hotel, I spoke with the camera team. They were persons of skill recruited from all parts of the world (British, Canadians, Australians, and one Jordanian). They were prepared to go anywhere. They were positively angry that, in Iran, their work on the series had brought them up against a culture of great richness about which nobody had told them anything. Their schools had taught them nothing about Iran. "To think that they spent their whole time stuffing us with Queen Elizabeth and Sir Francis Drake—and all *this* was there to know about!" The evenings developed into small tutorials. The conversations reassured me that the making of this film might be of some use to a wider world.

It was only on the upper edges of the group—on its cultural façade—that the enterprise took on a more sinister tone. The Iranian Ministry of Culture stayed well hidden in the background. But this apparently hands-off policy was abandoned the moment it came to depicting the role of Islam in the history of Iran. When planning the episode on the coming of Islam, we were firmly presented with the government expert—a creamy-faced professor with shiny black hair and bell-bottomed trousers in heliotrope pink. He gave us the approved, rose-tinted version of metaphysical Sufism that was popular at court. I wondered what it would have been like to have interviewed, or even to have taken film footage of, the grizzled imam at the little mosque just off the main road outside Shiraz. From our hotel, I could see a single lightbulb burning all night in front of the little saint's shrine adjacent to the mosque, where truck drivers stopped to pray at all hours. Having had my interview with David Frost, I was free to go to see more of Iran—if from a less privileged, at least from a less constrained viewing point.

FROM THE ZAGROS
TO AFGHANISTAN

Between East and West: Qaleh Yazdegerd

Having said good-bye to David Frost and his team, I made my way by bus to Esfahan and then to Kermanshah and down, through the Zagros Mountains toward Qasr-e Shirin and Iraq, to visit a newly discovered Sasanian palace at Qaleh Yazdegerd (or Qal'eh-i Yazdigird). It was perched on a ledge of the Zagros, above the road to Qasr-e Shirin, overlooking the hot lowlands of Mesopotamia, as if in the hidden valley of some adventure story. Its ruins were associated (in local memory, though not necessarily in reality) with the Sasanian shah Yazdegerd II (438–457), around whom flamboyant legends had developed. Hence its name, Qaleh Yazdegerd—"the Castle of Yazdegerd." The palace was mysterious enough. But it lay below the even more mysterious village of an exotic community—the Gnostic Kurds, known as the Ahl-e Haq: "the People of the Truth," some of whom I had already met, farther north along the spine of the Zagros, in Sanandaj, in Iranian Kurdistan. I had come to know of the excavations at the "Castle of Yazdegerd" from the work of the expedition of the Royal Ontario Museum led by Ed Keall, whom I had met in Toronto (on my way to Harvard) earlier in the year.[1]

I found Ed Keall's team engaged in lifting fragments of third-century stucco from the ruined palace out of the damp ground. These fragments were intact but had been rendered as soft as white cheese. They were placed gingerly on boards so as to dry out in the sun. What Ed had discovered were fragments of

---

1. E. J. Keall, "Qal'eh-i Yazdigird: A Sasanian Palace Stronghold in Persian Kurdistan," *Iran* 6 (1967): 99–121, and "Qal'eh-i Yazdigird: The Question of Its Date," *Iran* 15 (1977): 1–9.

the inner glory of a Sasanian palace. Sasanian buildings were usually made of rough stone bound by cement, like clumsy beehives. When deserted, they tended to collapse into unprepossessing mounds.

These delicate fragments were a reminder that the interior walls of these palaces had once been covered from ceiling to floor with deep-cut, painted stucco work. We should imagine their occupants moving against a background made of intricate patterns, like the weave of great tapestries, and studded with emblems that radiated power, good fortune, and worldly delight. They spoke of a world with deep roots in the ancient Near East and in the mythologies of Iran and Central Asia. Some also reflected an Eastern Hellenism, where classical figures had become themes of folk art. Plump Venuses, cupids, and even a satyr were joined by creatures from the steppes of Central Asia and even from China—fabulous *simurgh* birds, griffins, and dragons with intertwined necks. Qaleh Yazdegerd, with the diverse strands of its art, summed up for me the fascination of the Sasanian Empire. Here was a world still poised, with haunting indecision, between East and West.

"Like Wolves to Each Other": The Ahl-e Haq

Farther up the road, on the very edge of the plateau, the village of the Ahl-e Haq was shaded with trees and watered by running streams. It was a prosperous place. The shrine of a revered leader of the sect was plainly thriving. A newly laid tarmac road brought pilgrims all the way from Tehran, where large numbers of immigrant Kurds of the sect of the Ahl-e Haq had prospered. Little city cars bumped merrily up and down it. At the time, this road was hailed as a triumphant sign of progress. I only hope that it was not used later to enable the jeeps of the Islamic Revolutionary Guard, and, then, of the invading Iraqis, to zoom up to the previously inaccessible upper valleys of the Zagros, to bring to a brutal end the ancient diversity of the mountain dwellers.

The present leader of the sect was visiting the village. He was known as the *Bâb*—the Gateway: the Gateway to all knowledge. And he looked the part: with a wide, placid face, he moved slowly in the midst of a large entourage. I was told that he was a man with seven guardian angels—powerful cosmic forces gathered to protect and guide him—while the average person had only one. I thought of Bruce, the ten-angel teacher of the Urantia cult, whom I had met in California.

Most touching of all was the behavior of the male members of the Ahl-e Haq. I was told that the families of the village were bound together by intimate links of spiritual parenthood. Grown-up men were the godfathers of small children. This meant that there was nothing strange in seeing a large, mustachioed man, armed with a shepherd's crook—or even a rifle—cuddling a baby in his arms.

It was with such a circle of mothering shepherds that I sat on the edge of a cliff looking out toward Iraq. As befitted such occasions, the conversation quickly turned to higher things. To exchange mere details of our lives was trivial stuff. What mattered were the wide open spaces of the mind. What did I think of God? Had Iran passed successfully from feudalism to modernity? Or was one step still missing? In any case, what was the nature and purpose of the state? On that they all agreed. Without government, they said, men would be "like wolves—*gorgsan*—to each other." Looking back over my shoulder, across the flat plateau, I saw gray shapes slinking between the boulders and the fields, edging closer to the flocks. Real wolves. I got the point.

To the Caspian: Gonbad-e Qabus

On August 9 I was back in Tehran, totally grounded. I had run into a situation that was common in the hectic last days of the shah's Iran. Everyone was traveling. The bus lines and the airways were all booked up. No reservations could be made. In a country where, in the provinces, one could travel everywhere with miraculous ease, Tehran had ground to a halt.

So, early next morning, I took a cab to the junction with the great trunk roads where I was told that it would be possible to hitch a lift from the oil trucks on their way to the East. Had I known more about modern Iran, the cab ride could have taught me something very important. The poorer suburbs of Tehran seemed to go on forever. Endless rows of faceless, low-lying buildings passed by. But I noticed that each neighborhood bristled with the outlines of small mosques. Many of them were flanked by what seemed to be storefront offices with green signs. They were Islamic credit unions. Without realizing it at the time, I had seen one of the secrets of the grass roots of popular Islam. It was based on the collaboration, in every poor neighborhood, of the mosque and the Islamic bank—the source of desperately needed, interest-free loans.

I found my truck heading where I wanted—that is, not directly east to Mashhad and the Afghan frontier, but northeast, so as to drop from the Iranian plateau down to the Caspian Sea and to the Central Asian frontier with the Soviet Union—what was then the Turkmen Socialist Republic. I wanted to visit the region of the Duwar-e Iskender—the ancient ruins of the "Wall of

Alexander" that marked the legendary frontier between Sasanian Iran and Turan—the vast plains occupied by the nomads of Central Asia, lumped together, in the Iranian worldview, as the dangerous lands of the Turks.

My hosts were well equipped to oblige me. In the course of the conversation, they revealed themselves to be grain smugglers. They were bringing the early harvest of the Iranian plateau down to Soviet Central Asia, where mismanagement more horrendous even than that of the shah's Iran enabled them to make a killing by rushing in the grain of Tehran and Rayy to remedy perpetual shortages in Turkmenistan.

To drop from the dry desert of Iran to the Caspian (where the moist air of the sea was held back on the mountain slopes) was like finding oneself back in Ireland or on the green Atlantic side of the Pyrenees. Sinuously twisted trees with large green leaves and heavy blossoms lined the road and followed the course of flowing streams.

After the disconcerting exuberance of the mountain slopes above the Caspian, it was almost a relief to turn east toward the flat, tawny landscape near the Soviet frontier, and to view the succession of great mounds that had once been the Sasanian wall, the Hadrian's Wall of Central Asia, known as the "Wall of Alexander." At Gonbad-e Qabus, in the late afternoon light, the biscuit-colored brick of the *Gonbad*—the exquisitely domed funerary tower—stood out against a powder-blue sky. This was the world-famous tomb of Prince Qabus (at one and the same time a savage warrior and a scholar and patron of scholars), which had been built in AD 1006.

To Afghanistan

Next day I returned to the plateau by taking the bus up to Shahroud, and from there to Nishapur, where I found myself in a tidy hotel, with an inner garden lined with bright white tiles. It was a hotel for businessmen or for families up from the country to settle legal issues in the provincial capital. Their talk was disturbing. Marked by frustration and anger, it was more serious than the usual rhetorical complaints that keep a Persian conversation rolling. Above all, I picked up—as a constant refrain in the background of every protracted narrative of failure, double-dealing, or injustice—the word "Islam": Islamic order was somehow seen as the only answer to a world out of joint.

Historians are often bad prophets. Their business is diagnosis. They can sometimes pick up with considerable alertness hints of strain and of unappeased anger. But they seldom commit themselves to a prognosis. They do not know the future course of the malfunctions and ancient grievances that they may have spotted. In Iran, in 1976, it was easy enough (even for a foreign traveler) to pick up strong undertones of discontent. It was also easy to link them, in some way, to Islam. In the provinces and on the road, appeals to Islam seemed to be ever present. But the speed with which a charismatic leader would emerge, in the person of the Ayatollah Khomeini (of whom I knew nothing at the time), and the sheer mayhem of what then happened took observers of Iran by surprise. In 1976, everyone expected a shake-up. They had not expected a revolution in their time.

I moved quickly through Mashhad. I did not linger, as I had done in 1974. Things had changed. The shrine was now surrounded by a glacis. The old bazaar that had grown up for centuries around the courtyard of the shrine, like an intricate wasp's nest, had been flattened. Instead, the way to the shrine passed across a raw new park, studded with menacing police posts. Shah Reza had taken Mashhad firmly in hand.

And so, on August 12, I entered Afghanistan at the checkpoint of Islam-Qaleh—the Fortress of Islam. I said goodbye to the row of glitzy buses, festooned with merrily blinking fairy lights, that were lined up on the Iranian side, to enter what seemed to be another, more picturesque and less tidy world. The famous "wind of a hundred and twenty days" was at its height. This was a prevailing wind that spread a film of dust across the Iranian plateau in the summer months, turning the sky an anemic powder blue. Old Testament figures, with long beards and flowing robes, chased blown-off turbans of green silk along the sides of a great open courtyard. At the far end of the courtyard, looking as merry as a circus, was a row of brightly painted trucks—the famous "lorries" (the Afghan loanword was taken from the British English current in India) that were the pride of the Afghan roads. In the middle of the courtyard, where the dust swirled most thickly, a group of gentlemen in well-coiled, pastel headgear, firmly in place, danced to the music of the Beatles emerging at full blast from a bulky record player. They were Sikh doctors returning home overland from Liverpool to India. They had brought with them the Liverpool Sound—the music of their adopted country.

AFGHANISTAN

From Herat to Mazar-e Sharif

To enter Afghanistan was to pass through a marked threshold. Eating was much cruder. The delicious, dry, light herbs and garden vegetables (a touch of the refined cuisine of great oasis cities) that made even the most meager Iranian dish memorable, gave way to true nomad food—great, greasy hunks of mutton buried in piles of rice.

Squatting in a restaurant set up to resemble a great tent, I was instantly aware that this was also a world entirely without women. Not only were women absent. They were replaced. The qualities of elegance, poise, and soft-spokenness that were usually delegated to women in Europe (and even in Iran) passed directly and in full to young men, with their beautifully wrapped turbans, long, pure white robes, and exquisite hand gestures.

The great tiled minarets of Herat, seen in the driving dust, had a ghostly look. More dramatic was a visit to the shrine of a local saint. As in the Gaul of Gregory of Tours, a great tree, heavy with incandescent blossoms, grew vigorously out of the tomb where the holy man was buried. Beside the tomb, two parties sat on the ground listening to a bearded elder. Weapons were piled outside the precinct of the tomb. The old man was the present-day representative of the saint. He was negotiating between the two groups on a matter that my driver explained (somewhat chastely, I suspect) as having to do with "an issue of insurance." It may have been blood money. Early next morning I went out to explore the fortress whose ruins dominated the town. The moment I set foot on the slope beneath the fortress, the heads of hundreds of feral dogs appeared at the top of the wall. It was time to go.

My journey from Herat to Mazar-e Sharif, a distance of 450 miles along the Afghan-Russian frontier, took place not in a colorful lorry, but in a gray, battered Russian bus. I was urged to keep a low profile. Foreigners, I was told, would be shot if they approached the frontier. And rightly so. For had they reached the frontier, they would have seen immediately that there was no frontier. At that time, northwestern Afghanistan virtually formed a single unit with its Soviet neighbors in the Turkmen Republic. Turkic-speakers moved easily from side to side. Unveiled women, dressed in Soviet style, were common. Russian, and no longer English, was the language with which to address foreigners. When, next day, our bus broke down, a Turkmen on horseback rode up to us. Looking down on us as we sat stoically in a ditch, he spotted me and said, with great emphasis, in Russian, "*Khorosho njet*"—"Not good!"; and then rode off, proud to own a more dependable mode of transport.

We passed through true desert that was the home of the nomadic Turkmen. Far from being treated as suspect outsiders (as were the Qashqai in Iran) the Turkmen nomads appeared to dominate the local economy. They controlled the transport of the region. Grain harvests extracted from widely scattered plots were brought together in the large side pouches of their camels and sold in the neighboring cities for hard cash. I had learned a further lesson about the relation of nomads to the settled world: their rare mobility provided the oxygen without which the cities could not breathe.

I was traveling with a party of young men who were returning to their homes having made the pilgrimage to the shrine of the Imam Reza in Mashhad. For them, to go to Mashhad was a substitute for the Haj to Mecca. But it was more than that: it was a *rite de passage*, which showed that these young men were fully grown up and could become chiefs. Sons of the gentry and future local powerbrokers, they returned home with the blessing of the imam and with large numbers of knockoff Swiss watches that they proudly showed to me.

After the endless dunes of kaolin clay that stretched to each side of the Soviet-Afghan frontier, Mazar-e Sharif was a dream city. A medieval creation of the Silk Road, it was full of color. Roses bloomed outside the Great Mosque with heart-piercing vividness. There was also beer—the best Czech pilsner beer imported to the main hotel for the delight of Russian crews working on the pipelines of natural gas.

From Mazar-e Sharif I visited Balkh, an ancient city, the supposed birthplace of Zoroaster and the center of the Bactrian kingdom—the easternmost outpost of Hellenism after the days of Alexander the Great—with huge, bulging walls of hardened clay. I also found, near Balkh, the ruins of the Masjid-e Haji Piyada (the mosque of the walking pilgrim), known as the No Gombad—the Nine Domed Mosque. This was a ninth-century mosque. With its stocky columns, sheathed in deep-cut stucco, it was the very earliest example of post-Sasanian, Islamic art in the region. The stucco work was recognizably continuous with what I had seen in Qaleh Yazdegerd. It was a challenge to the historical imagination (accustomed as we are to an Islamic art that developed in the Arabic-speaking Middle East, and later in the Ottoman Empire) to be confronted with an Eastern Islam, where the majesty of the new religion was expressed in an artistic idiom that reached back directly to the stucco-laden palaces of Sasanian Iran.

On Top of the Buddha: Bamiyan

I left Mazar-i Sharif next day at 4 a.m. hoping to ride up into the Hindu Kush and then to branch off, before Kabul, to the mountain valley of Bamiyan, the site of the stupendous carved Buddhas, one of which would be notoriously blown up by the Taliban in 2001. It was a journey of some 265 miles.

The assembly time for the bus was fixed by the position of Orion. It was time to go when the width of one fist held at arm's length separated the belt of Orion from the horizon. It was also time to face an unexpected obstacle. On leaving the hotel for the bus station, I ran into a traffic jam of camels. Herds of camels were stealing a march on the day by traversing the city in a single, compact mass. It was a ghostly affair. The feet of the camels made no noise. Only the occasional loud groan came from the packed beasts. Here was a major traffic snarl-up without the roar of engines or the honking of horns. Under the belt of Orion, the great sea of lurching beasts was like a movie where the sound track had been switched off.

My principal memory of that day was leaving the desert and grinding upward into the Hindu Kush. The road never flattened, and never seemed to stop. At the top we halted at the turnoff for Bamiyan. It was agreed that I would stay the night at the turnoff, before taking a lorry down to the valley. Next morning, at early dawn, I found myself standing at the back of a lorry filled with stoop laborers bound for the fields. It was icy cold as we trickled down the side of great red mountains. At last we passed Shahr-e Gholghola—the "City of Screams," whose inhabitants (I was told by my fellow travelers) had been massacred by Genghis Khan. Standing on the promontory of a mountain, it looked as exquisite and compact as a Tuscan hill city in the background of a quattrocento painting. Arriving at Bamiyan, I realized why the lorry was crowded with harvesters: we had entered the garden of Eden—a valley of lush greens, trellised fruits, and bubbling streams.

I went to see the great Buddha—the one that would be destroyed by the Taliban. To reach the top of the great statue, I climbed an inner staircase carved into the rock of the great niche. At the end of the staircase there was nothing but a narrow walkway to the round top of the head of the Buddha across a drop of 150 feet. I have no head for heights. Having made it across the chasm, I squatted cross-legged on the crown of the Buddha's head, frozen with vertigo. Very cautiously I began to turn, like the turret of a tank, to take in, slowly, the full extent of a bucolic landscape of shining greens, streams, and shimmering poplars.

Only gradually did I dare to look upward. I realized that I was surrounded by frescoes, painted on the sides of the arch above the head of the great statue. These frescoes were full of echoes of Sasanian royal iconography, adopted by Buddhist artists to express the majesty of the Buddha, as the true king of kings, and of his court of celestial beings. Indeed, so precise were these echoes of Sasanian royal iconography that Professor Katsumi Tanabe has been able to date the frescoes exactly to the last days of the Sasanian Empire, by comparing a distinctive crown worn in one image of the Buddha with that of the various shahs on Sasanian coins. Such was the imaginative reach of the Sasanian Empire in the valleys of the Hindu Kush.[1]

Kabul

Next day, my bus raced to Kabul. Literally—raced. Two rival bus lines ran vans out of Bamiyan. Both started at the same time. Urged by the young men in each bus, one would roar triumphantly past the other, as the buses hurtled down the rock-slope roads.

Kabul in 1976 was, in many ways, what a Persian provincial town of the nineteenth century would have been like. It consisted largely of houses set in groves and gardens, surrounded by high walls, around which the irrigation channels served also as moats. The British Institute of Afghan Studies was one such oasis. I settled into an empty house and caught up with my reading, in a library well stocked with up-to-date archaeological reports stacked on home-made wooden shelves.

The Russian reports on the excavated temples of Dilberjin interested me particularly.[2] Here there seemed to have been a blending of Greek and native

---

1. K. Tanabe, "Foundations for Dating Anew the 38 Meter Buddha Image at Bâmiyân," *Silk Road Art and Archaeology* 10 (2004): 177–223, at 193–204.

2. I. T. Krugilkova, ed., *Dilberdzhin: Raskopki 1970–1972* (Moscow, 1974).

divinities that followed the establishment of the Hellenistic kingdom of Bactria. Shiva, Parvati, and the Dioscuri merged into each other. But in other parts of the Hellenistic world the two cultures seemed to have coexisted side by side, without leading to a creative joining of Greek and Indian gods.

I saw the same compartmentation of cultures in the archaeological museum. I still have my entrance ticket to it, and a folder guide in Persian, heavily annotated in my own handwriting. Here Greek, Bactrian, and Indian cultures were displayed in separate rooms, the one untouched by the other. The recent finds of an unnamed Greek city at the site of Aï Khanum ("Moon-Lady" in Uzbek: in northeast Afghanistan, near the frontier of Tajikistan—and beyond that, of China) were hauntingly, purely Greek. By contrast, the Begram ivories, in the adjacent room, were exuberantly Indian. Each was encased in its own culture. No interesting hybrids seemed to have emerged.

What I also saw were the great terracotta statues that came from the tombs of the Buddhist princes of seventh-century Fondukistan. Duly beheaded by the Muslim peasants who first uncovered them, they still reclined with courtly ease in a side gallery, enjoying a long twilight of Sasanian imperial elegance, painted as if dressed in lavish textiles in whose design Byzantium, Iran, and China had mingled. I had come to the outer bounds of the Sasanian Empire, the melting pot of western Asia.[3]

KABUL TO MASHHAD

Next day I took the afternoon bus from Kabul back to Herat—a journey of some five hundred miles. We stopped north of Kandahar just before sunset. In the long evening light, I watched a caravan plod due south to Kandahar and, beyond Kandahar, to India. My heart went with them. Later, I slept under the bus, looking out to see an eerily silent herd of camels pass by. Their great feet slip-slopped past me as if they were wearing giant carpet slippers. Eventually we reached Herat and the Iranian border. It was a joy to see those proudly garish Iranian buses, with their chrome plate, fairy lights, and bright neon signs invoking the name of ʿAli.

By this time I was sick. I reached Mashhad light-headed with Imodium to find that the shrine had been transformed. One of the great annual pilgrimages

3. For the significance of the many new discoveries in Afghanistan and Central Asia, see Khodadad Rezakhani, *ReOrienting the Sasanians: East Iran in Late Antiquity* (Edinburgh: Edinburgh University Press, 2017).

was in full swing. Above the courtyard, a band with trumpets and heavy drums appeared on a balcony at regular intervals. The park, so forbidding when empty, was now filled with families. They squatted in groups, often with a large framed photograph of a loved one before them. In the neighboring streets groups of young men threw themselves into laments for the martyrdom of ʿAli, accompanied by a thunderous beating of their own chests. I had never known that weeping could be quite as infectious as laughter. Nor did I know that it was possible, when in a crowd, to join in its movements with such unconscious force. When I returned to my hotel, I was astonished to find that my entire chest was bruised. Two nights later I was back in England.

TWILIGHT OF EMPIRE

THE PAST IN THE PRESENT

Parradine Productions were not finished with me yet. On October 25, 1976, I was taken by limousine to Heathrow from the Senate House of London University, where I had lectured on Ostrogothic Italy and the imperial reconquest of Justinian. Next day I was in a hotel outside Shiraz, close to Persepolis, for the shooting of the scene of the triumph of the Sasanian king of kings, Shapur I, over the Roman emperor Valerian in the summer of 260. Parradine Productions and the National Film Center of Iran were collaborating to create a historical reenactment of the victorious return to Persia of Shapur's army, with Shapur himself leading the defeated Roman emperor on a rope beside him. My presence was required as academic adviser.

The reenactment took place in the Tang-e Bolaghi—a wide water-meadow behind the ridge that bore the real thing—the great stone carvings on the rock face of Naqsh-e Rostam, which included a scene of the triumph of Shapur I over Valerian.

Every morning we would be driven from the hotel past a series of rock faces honeycombed with little square holes. These were the ossuary niches in which the ancient Zoroastrians had placed the bones of their dead. Their sheer number had only recently come to the attention of archaeologists. In 1973, I had been riveted by a talk on these ossuaries given in Oxford by Paul Gotch, a former head of the British Council in Iran, based on the slides that he had taken when traveling in the region. Like the distinctive architecture of the fire temples that I had seen at Takht-e Soleyman, they were silent reminders of a distinctive belief system very different from that of Christian East Rome. They impressed me deeply as little-known traces of the deep Zoroastrian past of Iran.

When it came to the reenactment of Shapur's triumph, it proved difficult to re-create his army. For extras, we had been loaned the use of a paratroop regiment stationed at Shiraz. But this was a unit in a thoroughly westernized force. How could we turn them, within a few days, into triumphant Sasanians? The trouble began with beards. Proper ancient Persians had sported magnificent beards. But that was exactly the problem. The paratroop regiment was close shaven. I was told that the commander of the regiment would not allow his men to grow beards for the shooting. He was blunt. He pointed out that the regiment consisted not only of Iranians, but also of Azeri Turks from the far north—from around Tabriz. To encourage Azeris to grow beards was deemed dangerous. The uniformity of shaven faces was a matter of military security. The commander explained why: "These Azeri boys, when they grow a beard, they think they are men. When they think they are men, they wish to stick it to us Persian boys."

The Triumph of the King

A cargo of false beards was rushed from Harrods. This, in itself, caused problems on the ground. I had chosen from the ranks of the paratroopers a perfect emperor Valerian. Heavy-jowled, with an echo of Mediterranean features, this Valerian looked remarkably like Mussolini. Or, rather, he looked like the emperor Valerian as he was shown on the rock carvings of Naqsh-e Rostam and Bishapur: a Mediterranean face rendered by Persian sculptors. But I lost him for a whole morning: an overzealous dresser had plastered a great mock beard on him, thereby rendering my clean-shaven Roman emperor unrecognizable. We found him just before he was to make his appearance as the captive of the king of kings.

The emperor Valerian had been chosen from the ranks. But the role of Shapur I as king of kings was reserved for the commander of the regiment. Mounted on a white horse, with full beard and fluttering ribbons, he was a splendid sight. I remember a Polaroid photo that showed Shapur with the emperor Valerian standing at his stirrups. The king of kings was reaching down with an elegant lighter to light the cigarette of the abject Roman emperor.

The principal problem, however, was how to push the army itself back to ancient times. The Ministry of Culture had provided "period" uniforms that had been designed for the historical march-past, in the plain beside Persepolis, in 1971, on the grandiose occasion of the Twenty-five-hundredth-year anniversary of the foundation of the Iranian monarchy. It was not that these uniforms were anachronistic. It was rather that those who wore them were proud to be soldiers in a state-of-the-art modern army. Even when dressed in exotic uniforms, the paratroopers insisted on marching, as in a military tattoo, in rigid ranks. How could they be transformed into a riotous mass of the army of the king of kings?

My solution was to wear them down. First, they were told to roll, in their uniforms, in the sandy earth of the plain of the Tangi-e Bolaghi. Then they marched in a long, narrow ellipse from one end of the floodplain to the other, fording a shallow river both ways until they were thoroughly damp and dusty. But they still kept up their modern pride. Every time they passed the cameras, the ranks would straighten up, the chests would be thrown forward, and all eyes would turn, to stare proudly into the camera lens.

My strategy worked only when, at last, I shouted *"Tamam"*: "It's all over!" Only then did the ranks break. Swords were thrown in the air. Soldiers leaped up and down. A drum appeared and wild dancing began. Then the cameras rolled. Shooting against the sun into a tunnel of dust and splashing water, framed by ancient poplars, we got superb footage of a bedraggled ancient army on the move.

"Dynasties That Last So Short a Time"

On the last evening, before I took the night flight back to Tehran, I visited the ruins of Persepolis. There I met an Indian doctor. He had been visiting his brother who had been severely injured in the docks of Bandar Abbas, on the Persian Gulf. Standing on the great platform of the Achaemenid palace, and looking into a deep red sky, he meditated on the meaning of history. "Why is it, professor, that there is progress in some countries . . . so many dynasties, so great, so strong, so long-lasting. . . . Why is it that in other countries, dynasties are few, are weak, dynasties that last so short a time?"

I last saw him with his injured brother, as they brought him on a stretcher into the plane to Tehran. Coming back to the Institute of Persian Studies through downtown Tehran, I found a darkened world, with police cordons much in evidence, as the streets filled up with restless crowds.

From Iran to the Mediterranean

Next morning, on October 31, however, the troubling scenes of the evening before were no longer in my mind. I was given a dream journey across the Middle East on Iran Air. In perfect weather, the entire arena of my projected study of the conflict between the Mediterranean and the non-Mediterranean worlds passed beneath me as the plane flew at high altitude from Tehran to its first stop in Athens. The Zagros Mountains, where I had visited Takht-e Soley-man and Qaleh Yazdegerd in the summer, were now snowbound. Immediately below the snow, the river Tigris suddenly appeared as a vast, winding flood of bloodred water held in a thin fringe of green. Then the desert began. Lunch was served. Lunch was taken away. I dozed. Still the desert continued beneath me. Then, very suddenly, without preparation, we saw a streak of deep green—Lebanon—and beyond it a band of pure blue, the sea, succeeded by another patch of green, which was the island of Cyprus. After hours over empty desert and steppe land, we had passed over the Mediterranean coastline in only a few minutes. The lifeline of the Greco-Roman world was that thin.

When I resumed my Senate House lectures next day, it was appropriate that they were about the coming of the Great Plague of 543. In the opinion of many scholars, this plague had emptied the cities and finally burned out the heart of the classical Mediterranean. I then told how this disaster was followed by the loss, by East Rome, of control of the Middle East to non-Mediterranean powers—first to the Sasanian Empire of Khusro II (who, for a dramatic moment, overran Syria, Egypt, and much of Asia Minor) and then—this time for good—to Islam. I had seen the entire landscape over which this revolution had taken place only the day before.

The End of a Dynasty

Another sort of revolution overtook *Crossroads of Civilization*. On May 5, 1977, I went to a final showing—the only one that I attended—in a studio in Grape Street, Soho. I was saddened—but not surprised—to find that the historical material which the experts provided had been transmogrified and trivialized. Most of the hard history had dropped out of the production. Apart from the triumph of Shapur over Valerian, there were no wars. There was not even decadence. The end of the Sasanians was reduced to a hurried view of garishly dressed Kurdish folk dancers bouncing up and down in the firelight beneath the vault of the great rock carving of the royal hunt in Taq-e Bostan.

But images of Iran were there, often caught with remarkable skill. A Jordanian photographer had made a little masterpiece out of the solemn celebration of Zoroastrian rituals in a family home and in a temple in Yazd. We saw the entourage of the Sasanian king of kings in motion, as I had suggested, through a series of remarkable shots of the Qashqai nomads as they made their way up the mountains toward their summer grazing grounds. Shot against a background of dramatic mountains, the cavalcade of Khusro II slowly disappeared behind a sharp ridge under an immense Iranian sky. We all agreed that the landscape of Iran, at least, had not let us down.

There was an American buyer in the audience. We were later told that he was reluctant to invest in the series. He explained to us—what we had not known before—that the entire last part of the series was to take the form of an interview between David Frost and the shah himself—to be shot with the ruins of Persepolis in the background. This came as an unpleasant surprise. We had not been told that the National Film Center of Iran had intended to use the program to showcase Reza Shah.

The American then added that the shah looked as if he would not last long enough to have his triumphal interview with Frost. In the words of the pensive Indian whom I had met at Persepolis in the twilight of late October, Reza Shah was about to go the way of the "short, weak dynasties." David Frost finally got his interview with the shah in 1980: but by that time the shah was an exile in Panama; he never got to appear as a monarch at Persepolis. With the fall of the shah, the raison d'être of the production vanished. A very different Iran would soon be at the center of world attention.

Such an ending makes for an ironic story. It seems easy, in retrospect, to dismiss the entire enterprise—David Frost and all—as a bogus venture, conjured up in support of a bogus regime. But at the time it was a sad ending. Many historians—not least, two good friends: Robin Lane Fox, who was adviser for the section on Alexander the Great, and David Morgan (1945–2019), who was adviser on the Mongols—had joined in the enterprise with genuine enthusiasm. We never met on the job. But we shared a feeling with many members of the production staff (keen and widely traveled young persons) that we had been given a rare chance to view, and to attempt to interpret for a wider world, the history of a vast and little-known land. We were proved wrong. None of us had gauged the sheer weight and momentum of the boulder that was about to roll.

As for me, the Iranian Revolution soon brought my projected study of the conflict of Byzantium and Iran to an end. I had wanted this study to be based on travel; and that was no longer possible for me. At the time, it felt like an amputation. I had lost an entire horizon. Yet, brutally though it may have ended, it was an experience that had changed me. Those great spaces had widened my heart and had given me a sense of what it was like to live among them. More important still, that glimpse of the vivid slash of green as the plane from

Teheran approached Lebanon and Cyprus, on my journey home across western Iran and Iraq, reminded me how the Mediterranean (that vivid center of the classical world) bordered on the vast expanse of Asia. It confirmed my view that the study of late antiquity should embrace both worlds.

This was not the only lesson that I had learned. Travel through Iran opened the Islamic world to me in a manner that I had not anticipated when I first arrived there. It ensured that a sense of the challenge of Islam has remained with me ever since.

I went back to Ireland, after my summer travels in Iran, tired and sick. In Ireland I visited my father's doctor. A survivor of a Japanese prison camp, who had correctly diagnosed my father's tropical disease in 1945, he knew the illnesses of the Third World. He found that I was suffering from pneumonia contracted from desert dust. A little bit of the kaolin clay desert of northwestern Afghanistan was lodged beneath my ribs.

I also came to suffer from a low-intensity virus that drained me for many months to come. It was the first time that I had ever had to think about whether I had the physical energy to carry through the work, as professor and permanent head of department, into which I had thrown myself with zest at Royal Holloway College. I remember at the end of the year, in December 1976, leaning against the gray stone of the bridge above the lake in the park of Blenheim Palace, looking over the cold waters and thinking (really, for the first time ever) that I had never expected that the light of life could burn so very low.

INVISIBLE FRIENDS IN VISIBLE PLACES

"Invisible Friends in Visible Places"

My travels in Iran, in the summer of 1976, had been a deeply moving experience for me. But it was time to go west again. I returned to work that I had begun in my last year in Oxford, on the meaning of the "presence" of the saints in early medieval society in the West.[1] In October 1976, I delivered the Stenton Lecture at the University of Reading on relics and social status in the world of Gregory of Tours.[2] After that, I widened my view to include the original rise of the cult of the saints in the Latin world of the fourth and fifth centuries. Gregory of Tours would be joined by even better-known figures—Ambrose, Jerome, and Augustine, and by the poets of the saints, Prudentius (348–405+) and Paulinus of Nola (353–431).

The theme grew on me in easy stages, marked by times of contact with American and Canadian students and scholars. These transatlantic visits were new to me. Apart from my visit to Berkeley in 1975, I had not taught any seminars in America—I had only given public lectures. But from March 24 to April 20, 1977, I gave a seminar under the title of "Invisible Friends in Visible Places" for the newly founded Center for Early Christian Humanism, directed by Liz Kennan, at the Catholic University of America in Washington. Later in the year, in September 1977, I gave the same seminar at the University of Toronto, in the Department of Comparative Religion, headed by William Oxtoby.

1. Chapter 58: "Presences."
2. Peter Brown, "Relics and Social Status in the Age of Gregory of Tours" (University of Reading, 1977), in *Society and the Holy in Late Antiquity*, 222–250.

In Toronto, largely through the kindness of my friend Ann Hutchison, I was introduced to a particularly ebullient group of graduate students. Their spirits unbroken by the rigors of the Pontifical Institute of Medieval Studies and other forbidding landmarks of their graduate program, they quickly turned the seminar into an occasion for fun. A travel brochure entitled "St. Martin Tours" soon appeared. It promised to

HIT THE HAGIOGRAPHIC HIGHLIGHTS on the trail of our invisible friends, the portable people. . . .
ON THIS TOUR . . . you will

- reenact the temptations of St. Anthony in the Desert . . .
- try your luck at the exclusive tables of Monte Cassino . . .
- count the olive presses in North Africa . . .

But best of all was the recently discovered "Gothic Phrasebook":

AT THE BORDER

Your papyri, please.
Are you entering the Empire for the purpose of immigration or just invasion?
What is the purpose of your invasion?
How do you intend to support yourself while in the Empire?
Is there anyone here who speaks Old Low Ostrogothic with traces of Lombard influence?
If you and your tribe would be so kind as to wait just inside the next province . . .
Sorry, but we have to have a cognomen.

Finally, I delivered the Haskell Lectures on Comparative Religions at the University of Chicago, again entitled "Invisible Friends in Visible Places," in April 1978. These lectures became my book *The Cult of the Saints*.[3]

---

3. P. Brown, *The Cult of the Saints: Its Rise and Function in Latin Christianity* (Chicago: University of Chicago Press, 1981), reprinted with a substantial preface as *The Cult of the Saints . . . Enlarged Edition* (Chicago: University of Chicago Press, 2014). Those interested in the cult of the saints in Europe in late antiquity and the Middle Ages can now enjoy the comprehensive study of Robert Bartlett, *Why Can the Dead Do Such Great Things? Saints and Worshippers from the Martyrs to the Reformation* (Princeton, NJ: Princeton University Press, 2013).

The Breaking of Boundaries

In order to study the cult of the saints, I set aside my Sasanian interests. But I by no means abandoned the world of Islam. The cult of saints in Islam provided me with a constant basis of comparison with the cult of the Christian saints in late antiquity and the early Middle Ages. I owed this new dimension of my work to Ernst Gellner of the London School of Economics. His study of the Muslim *marabouts* of contemporary North Africa—*Saints of the High Atlas*—had introduced me to a new world.[4] When I mentioned my interest in the cult of saints to him, a large cardboard box appeared at Royal Holloway, filled with recent books on holy men and holy shrines throughout Islamic Africa. I could not have got off to a better start. So what was it that attracted me to such a theme?

First and foremost, I had been drawn to the subject by a problem in the religious imagination of late antique persons. The late antique and early medieval Christian attitude to the cult of the saints had a surreal quality about it. Here were dead bodies endowed with qualities that belonged elsewhere. It was as if a piece of the shining heavens had descended from its proper place to lie buried in the dull earth where normal human bodies stank and rotted before they turned to dust. With the bodies of the saints, and even with mere fragments of these bodies—known as relics—the axiomatic boundary between earth and Heaven was breached. The shrines of the dead saints "filled with great candelabra, their dense clusters of light mirrored in shimmering mosaic, and caught in the golden roof . . . brought the still light of the Milky Way to within a few feet of the grave."[5] They were little bits of Paradise on earth.

More than that, not only did the Christian cult of the saints seem to break the primal, cosmic boundary between the high, pure heavens and the earth. It also threatened to erode ancient civic boundaries. It moved the center of gravity of public worship from the city to the graveyard, where the tombs of the saints lay amid the tumbled monuments of the ordinary dead. In the course of time, in the early Middle Ages, entire Roman cities were pulled out of shape as if by the gravitational force of the saints' graves. The old civic centers—the forum with its temples—were deserted as urban settlement came to huddle increasingly around the great basilicas that lay in the cemetery area, in the

4. Ernst Gellner, *Saints of the High Atlas* (London: Weidenfeld, 1969).
5. Brown, *Cult of the Saints*, 4.

city of the dead, outside the ancient city walls, where the saints were buried in splendor.

Within a few centuries, between 300 and 600, an entire new structure of imagined human relations with the other world was created by Christian preachers, Christian poets, and Christian artists. It filled the imagination of believers with clearly delineated human faces, the faces of the holy dead. These were the invisible friends whose presence tugged at the hearts of so many Christians in late antiquity and the early Middle Ages.

This peopling of the invisible world with new holy figures, settled in places where such holiness had not been found before, was a challenge to the historian of religion in late antiquity. Why had this change happened, and why did it spread with such apparent vigor in the last centuries of Roman rule in the West and in the postimperial societies of early medieval Europe? This was the question that I attempted to address in my work on the cult of the saints.

By the spring of 1977, I was able to take advantage of the peculiarly congenial occasion of my inaugural lecture at Royal Holloway, on May 26, 1977, to sketch out my approach to this problem. The lecture was entitled "Learning and Imagination," and I took changing attitudes to the study of the cult of the saints as an example of the need to combine the two—learning *and* imagination—in order to understand this major shift in the imaginative world of late antique and early medieval Europe.[6]

"The Vulgar, That Is, All Mankind, a Few Excepted"

In this lecture, I presented the modern study of the cult of the saints as a challenge to do justice to a significant turning point in the religious history of late antiquity. I felt that this turning point had not received the attention that it deserved. It was not so much ignored as taken for granted. It was treated as a somewhat embarrassing fact of life that needed no explanation. It was assumed that the cult was no more than a passive survival of pagan habits that had imperceptibly made their way into Christian worship, as the price that Christianity had to pay for having become the established religion in a world still rooted in an aboriginal polytheism.

I soon discovered that this dismissive view had a distinguished ancestry. My work on the Enlightenment background to Edward Gibbon's views on

6. Peter Brown, "Learning and Imagination," in *Society and the Holy in Late Antiquity* (Berkeley: University of California Press, 1982), 3–21.

society and culture in his *Decline and Fall* had led me to the *Natural History of Religion* of David Hume. Published in 1757, Hume's essay was written in an urbane style that made it appear to be a statement of the obvious.

Hume claimed that polytheism, not monotheism, was the natural religion of mankind. And this was because of the mental limitations of the average person. For "the vulgar, that is, all mankind, a few excepted," were incapable of true monotheism. They always tended to believe in a multiplicity of divine powers, embedded in the physical world. By contrast, monotheism was based on a capacity for abstract thought that could only be the product of education and reflection. Like any other achievement of the Enlightenment, belief in one God, uncluttered by imaginary intermediary powers, was thought to require careful social and intellectual grooming, such as could not be found outside the small circle of the elite. Hence a perpetual tension between the beliefs of the many and those of the enlightened few. In the words of Hume: "It is remarkable that the principles of religion have had a flux and reflux in the human mind, and that men have a natural tendency to rise from idolatry to theism and to sink again from theism to idolatry."[7]

Edward Gibbon immediately picked up on Hume. For him, Hume's essay showed that the rise of the cult of saints in fourth- and fifth-century Christianity needed no other explanation. In a footnote at the end of the chapter on the suppression of pagan worship in the Roman Empire under the emperor Theodosius I (379–395), he pointed out that "Mr. Hume . . . observes, like a philosopher, the natural flux and reflux of polytheism and theism." He then went on to write, with superb certainty, about the cult of the saints: "The sublime and simple theology of the primitive Christians was gradually corrupted; and the MONARCHY of heaven . . . was degraded by the introduction of a popular mythology which tended to restore the reign of polytheism."[8]

THE TWO-TIER MODEL

After such a peremptory judgment, it seemed as if there was nothing more that needed to be said. Scholars were content to believe that, with the establishment of the cult of saints, the Roman world simply settled back into the natural

---

7. David Hume, *Natural History of Religion* VIII, in *Essays, Moral, Political and Literary* (London: Longman's, 1875), 2:334; Brown, "Learning and Imagination," 9.

8. *The Decline and Fall of the Roman Empire*, ed. D. Womersley (London: Penguin, 1994), chapter 28, 2:95–96 and n. 85 on p. 96.

inertia of a polytheistic popular religion, largely untouched by the elevated beliefs of the elite.

From the time of Hume and Gibbon onward, what I called a "two-tier" model of religious belief and practice became part of the common sense of learned persons in Europe, shared alike by believers and unbelievers, Protestants and Catholics: the "true" beliefs and practices of the few seemed to be invariably pitted against the degraded beliefs and practices of the many. This haughty attitude to "popular religion" often appeared where one would least expect it. "A people's religion is ever a corrupt religion." David Hume? No: John Henry, Cardinal Newman.[9]

Such frankly elitist notions were widespread among modern scholars and churchmen. But what if they were wrong? What if the cult of the saints had emerged for different reasons? It was time for this intellectual block to go, in order to do justice to the richness of the new forms of Christian devotion associated with the cult, and to attempt to understand their function in late Roman and post-Roman society.

POPULAR RELIGION

In the 1970s, the cult of the saints was still a charged issue in many circles. My previous criticism of the notion of a "primitive mentality"—a prelogical mentality similar to that which Hume had ascribed to "the vulgar"—had drawn on the work of anthropologists, such as Evans-Pritchard, whose ideas had been developed in a distant corner of the British Empire—among the tribes of the southern Sudan. But Hume discussed something far closer to home for many scholars. The "vulgar" were the majority of Christians in all ages. The debate on whether the cult of the saints was a mere recrudescence of paganism was a debate about the past of Christian Europe.

This debate was by no means purely academic. A controversy over the nature of "popular religion" had flared up all over Europe in the 1970s. In the Catholic world after Vatican II, fierce debates on popular religion appear to have swung both ways. The drive to "democratize" the church, by allowing a greater degree of lay participation, led to an interest in forms of popular Catholicism. But this was often a "popular" Catholicism that existed largely in the heads of intellectuals. The actual, traditional Catholicism of Europe (the

---

9. J. H. Newman, *Difficulties of Anglicans* (London: Burns and Oates, 1876), 80–81; Brown, "Learning and Imagination," 11.

cult of saints included) was frequently attacked by members of the liberal clergy as unworthy of a new, more progressive age of Christian worship.

Outside the churches, the search for an authentic "popular" culture—a potentially subversive culture, opposed to the culture of the elites—was enthusiastically pursued in neo-Marxist circles. In France, the Annales school encouraged studies of European Christianity, in all periods, as exercises in "historical anthropology." These field trips to the past were now conducted, not in colonial Africa, but in the vast unknown of Alteuropa—of a peasant Europe whose surprisingly archaic features (up to the nineteenth century) were revealed ever more clearly in the abundant archival evidence of the early modern period.

"Oh no . . . Only Hindus Do That . . .": A Visit to Chartres

It was this interest in popular culture that led me, at this time, to the work of Natalie Zemon Davis. I had already heard of her articles through American visiting fellows at All Souls. Her collected essays appeared in 1975, as *Society and Culture in Early Modern France*.[10] They addressed issues very similar to my own concerns—the interplay of elite and popular culture in a great pre-industrial city: sixteenth-century Lyons. Natalie approached this interplay with new methods, applied to an enviable abundance of evidence.

On one occasion in these years we met in France. We visited Chartres Cathedral, where Natalie, characteristically, had made contact with an *abbé* who delighted in taking visitors into every nook and cranny of the great shrine. We raced up a series of spiral staircases that led up from the nave into the clerestory, to come out within arm's distance of the topmost stained glass windows. Reaching out, *monsieur l'abbé* tapped the great, glowing pane. It yielded to his hand: the complex joining of glass and lead had made it as flexible as a spider's web. The thought that such a seemingly stable part of the cathedral could wobble in this way gave me a moment of vertigo. As my experience on top of the Buddha of Bamyan showed, I do not have a good head for heights.

But there was worse—or, for the zealous *abbé*, even better—to come. He took us into the loft, beneath the roof, where the high vaulting of the nave (which seemed so delicate from below) came together in great piles of

---

10. N. Z. Davis, *Society and Culture in Early Modern France* (Stanford, CA: Stanford University Press, 1975).

cemented stone like beehive huts or igloos. A wooden floor stood beneath the west towers of the cathedral, with a spiral staircase that led up to the belfry. This, for the *abbé*, was the final treat, the last mystery of the cathedral revealed. I edged up the wooden spiral staircase to fifty feet above the floor. Half of the steps had rotted through. The other half seemed to be occupied by nests defended by irate pigeon chicks. It was a memorable climb.

On the way down, we talked about the pilgrims who would sleep in these upper quarters. I asked whether they practiced incubation—sleeping overnight in the cathedral in the hope of receiving a healing dream, as was frequently the case in late antique Christian shrines. "Oh no, *mon professeur*, they were good Christians. Only Hindus do that."

Next day we had lunch with Jacques Le Goff (1924–2014), and discussed his recent work on what appeared to him to be a split between a folkloristic and a learned culture in Merovingian Gaul.[11] It was an inspiring encounter from which I learned a lot. But it still struck me that, for the *abbé* and the professor alike, popular religion was something "out there." Popular practices could be said to have nothing to do with "true" Christianity (as with the *abbé*), or they could be valued as offering a fascinating glimpse, beneath the thin veneer of the culture of the clerical elite, of another, older world, from the dreamtime of Europe (as Le Goff and others tended to do).

The Impresarios

In 1977, the current interest in popular culture in medieval and early modern Europe, led by scholars such as Le Goff, attracted me greatly. But these new studies did not seem to me to account for one important aspect of the rise of the cult of the saints in late antiquity—that is, the active and seemingly wholehearted engagement of a vivid group of upper-class Christians in promoting the cult, in framing the tombs or relics of the saints with splendid architecture and other visual manifestations of reverence, and, above all, in creating from their own social experience a language of devotion that would come to mold expectations of the holy dead for centuries to come. It was this burst of activity in elite Christian circles that needed to be understood.

The evidence for persistent upper-class agency in the formation of the cult of saints contradicted the impression, generated by the two-tier model, that

---

11. J. Le Goff, "Culture cléricale et tradition folklorique dans la civilisation mérovingienne," *Annales* 26 (1971): 587–603.

the cult of the saints lay somehow outside history—that it was no more than a passive residue of age-old beliefs. Rather, it struck me that it was the stuff of history, linked to the creation of a new imaginative universe adapted to the needs of late Roman society at a time when the empire had begun to lose its magic and would soon vanish forever from the West.

This was what I wished to communicate most forcibly: we knew so much about the cult of the saints in Latin Christianity largely because, far from leaving its promotion and articulation to "the vulgar," a succession of outstanding Latin Christians had gone out of their way to render it visible.

I called these people *impresarios*. This term brought upon me the severe criticism of Charles Pietri (1932–1991), the master of the history of Christian Rome: *Oh! Ce vilain mot!* Oh that nasty word![12] To Pietri, the word "impresario" seems to have conveyed a negative meaning, as if those who advanced the cult of the saints were mere "managers" of the cult. The word "impresarios" appeared to imply that the cult of the saints was tarnished by association with money-grubbing show business.

But this was not in any way my intention. I had chosen the word "impresario" in its wider, English sense of an active promoter and advocate who makes available some precious cultural resource. In doing so, I had in mind a figure such as Sir Thomas Beecham (1879–1961), the conductor of the London and the Royal Philharmonic orchestras, who was always spoken of not only as a conductor of the orchestra, but also as an impresario, for having introduced to England the work of European musicians such as Berlioz, Delius, and Richard Strauss. This was what I had in mind. Those who promoted the cult of saints did not merely "manage" it. They put their lifeblood into it, and made it available to an ever-wider circle of believers, much as Sir Thomas had brought new music to postwar Britain.

And to what effect? My conclusion was that those who promoted the cult of saints humanized the other world. They placed a recognizable human face upon what might have remained, in Christian circles, no more than a flickering awareness of the ancient dead, with little or no sense of their imaginative presence among the living. It was a frankly senatorial face. This has often been held against the upper-class promoters of the cult by modern scholars. But those who promoted it believed that only the strong imaginative presence of a powerful and beloved person, endowed with a human face, could rally those

---

12. C. Pietri, "Les origines du culte des martyrs (d'après un livre récent)," *Rivista di archeologia cristiana* 60 (1984): 293–319, at 304.

forces in society through which justice, amnesty, and concord might be achieved.

The shrines of the saints were visible places to which Christian worshippers turned to find invisible friends, to give them justice as well as healing. It was in front of their great sarcophagi that perjury was detected, that captives broke their chains, and slaves were set free. In the hard world that emerged after the fall of Rome, such places were needed in the Latin West.[13]

13. Brown, "Learning and Imagination," 17–19, and *The Cult of the Saints*, 106–126. On the theme of justice in the works of Gregory of Tours, see now Peter Brown, *The Ransom of the Soul: Afterlife and Wealth in Early Western Christianity* (Cambridge, MA: Harvard University Press, 2015), 167–174.

MAYNOOTH TO CALIFORNIA

At the beginning of 1977, I was approached by friends in Berkeley to see whether I would be interested in a joint professorship in the Departments of Classics and History. This was an unforeseen turn in my life. Though I had recently become accustomed to traveling in America, I had given no thought to so drastic a move.

Berkeley was looking for a replacement for Paul Alexander, who had fallen ill with cancer from which he eventually died in December 1977. Paul was a Byzantinist, a great and patient scholar, deeply loved by his students. I knew, and greatly admired, his work on the Iconoclast controversy and on Byzantine apocalyptic writings.

It was taken for granted that I would go to the History Department. But it was my fellow Irishman John Dillon, as chairman of classics, who made the daring and decisive move to create a joint appointment for me in classics and history. For the first time in my life, I would be a fully paid-up member of a Classics Department. This undoubtedly helped to make Berkeley attractive to me. But I had to think carefully over the offer. It seemed to present a great opportunity—but it was at the far end of the world.

I had no quarrel with my job at Royal Holloway. It had opened up for me intellectual horizons of which I had been unaware in Oxford—political thought and modern Islamic history being among them. I was more than happy with my colleagues and had greatly enjoyed my teaching there, as well as trying, as head of department, to create an interesting life both for members of the faculty and for the students.

But there was one factor that weighed more heavily with me than most of my friends knew: my health. I was dragged down by periods of tiredness connected with the unknown virus that I had brought back from Iran and Afghanistan in 1976. Bluntly: I needed energy for my present job, and it seemed that this energy might not be available for much longer. In going through my mother's diary and letters, I find that I was still having tests and blood counts throughout 1977. My doctors were worried. For a time, it looked as if I had to slow my pace or (if the virus proved more debilitating) to look for another, less demanding post. I had thrown myself into the role of a permanent head of department at Royal Holloway with enthusiasm: now I was not sure that I had the stamina to maintain this level of activity. At Berkeley, I would be only a scholar and a teacher, without the heavy administrative responsibilities that went with being a permanent head of department in the London system.

Looking back, I now realize that I had been worrying about the wrong thing. My health would improve in the 1980s. What declined dramatically and unexpectedly was the state of the British universities. At the time, I did not know—indeed, few of us could have known—that we would have to face the blizzard unleashed by the crisis in university funding brought about by the policies of Mrs. Thatcher. But I was in Berkeley by that time. My coming to America had nothing to do with that crisis, nor even with any premonition of it. As I saw it at the time, I was not abandoning a sinking ship. I was moving from one first-rate university to another.

An Irish Interlude: Maynooth

It took me some time to make up my mind. I first pondered this choice in what was, for me, an unexpected environment. In January 1977 (just after I had been approached by Berkeley), I found myself acting as external examiner in medieval history at what is now Saint Patrick's College in the National University of Ireland at Maynooth. In 1977, Maynooth was very different from what it is now. It saw itself as very much a university of its own—the place of training for generations of the Catholic clergy of Ireland. It had been open to lay students only since 1968. For me, from a Protestant family, to go to Maynooth was to enter the other Ireland.

I was lodged in the Bishop's Bedroom. Every morning a cleaning lady would come in to stir new warmth from the turf fire in the Gothic fireplace. Before leaving, she would turn the Breviary of daily prayers that lay on the prie-dieu (the desk-like kneeling bench) beside my bed to the right page— just in case!

I was immediately made aware that I had entered a world with wide horizons. At the end of the marking of the examination papers, if I remember
rightly, there was a discussion as to how my marks were to be translated into
"Vatican grades." In the cloisters of the striking neo-Gothic chapel designed
by Augustus Pugin in the 1840s, immense portraits of the Irish bishops of great
American cities (New York, Boston, and Chicago) of the nineteenth and twentieth centuries lined the walls, painted in eye-catching reds and greens. Here
was an "abroad" of which I had, until then, known nothing—the Irish diaspora
of America, guided by bishops out of Maynooth: a spiritual empire quite as
far-flung and as proud as the British Raj.

I was immensely impressed by the priests who formed the core of the teaching staff. One priest was a professor of sociology, deeply engaged with the
social problems of modern Ireland. These were real problems, at a time when
the activities of the Provisional IRA—the Provos—were on the rise, and when
Ireland was still a sadly poor country. As the son of a farmer and, for many
years, a conscientious priest and trainer of priests, he knew every farm lane on
both sides of the border between the Republic and Northern Ireland. But he
had only ever been in England to make the connection, at Heathrow, with the
planes that would take him to Catholic communities all over the English-
speaking world—to Canada, America, and Australia. His combination of a
modern sense of global horizons with concern for the hard life of a small country impressed me greatly. There was no danger that people such as he would lose
their identity in a strange land—so why should I be afraid that I would lose
mine, even if I moved to the other end of the world?

A Change of Systems

So what was it that tipped the balance toward my decision to go to Berkeley?
I did not see it as being as big a move as it might have been for me a few years
earlier. In many ways, the truly decisive change in my academic life had already
taken place, when I went from the Oxford of the colleges to the citywide
confederation of London University. By contrast, if I went from London to
Berkeley, I would be going to a comparable institution. Here was a great state
university, with a sense of mission to the wider public of California as a whole.
Its student body consisted largely of the products of good public schools
(good high schools, in the American meaning of the word) and not from
private schools (the "public schools" of England). London University was
similar—in its size, in its sense of mission, and in the wide social range of its
student body. To move to Berkeley was to move to another London.

But what really clinched the matter was my growing respect for the professionalism of American scholarship and for the university systems that supported it. This may need some explaining. Put very briefly, I was very aware that I had grown up in a system that consistently, silently favored the ideal of the gentleman scholar. No matter how learned the dons of Oxford might be, in their own field, the routines of their teaching encouraged each of them to be, for much of their time, a "jack of all trades and master of none." They were made responsible for teaching undergraduates (mainly through tutorials) large periods of history that had little or nothing to do with their own specialty.

Frankly, I had thriven on this system. There was a certain thrill of pleasure—a bit like a "Look, no hands!" cyclist—at finding myself keeping up with the modern literature on Magna Carta of 1215, for teaching purposes, at the same time as I was engaged with the religious crisis of the third century AD. It had given me great freedom. I could not have imagined my intellectual journey toward the East (which had culminated in my travels in Iran) without the carte blanche extended to energetic young teachers to develop an interest in fields more exotic than their own immediate objects of research, if only for the purpose of undergraduate teaching. I had been able to do this in Oxford when developing the Further Subject on Byzantium, Persia, and the rise of Islam, and had benefited enormously from it.

The offer from Berkeley came as a direct challenge to this way of seeing the relationship between my activity as a scholar and my duties as a teacher. It was a challenge to nail my colors to the mast as an expert in late antiquity, and in late antiquity only. More important still, one of my main duties at Berkeley would be to teach graduate students in formal seminars. I had already learned in Berkeley, when I visited it in 1975, that to teach graduate students was a demanding job: I would not just be supervising them in a somewhat detached manner, to one side of a predominantly undergraduate-oriented teaching system, as I had done in Oxford; I would be forming my future peers, many of them already my equals in intelligence and zeal.

This point was made to me very forcibly by Caroline Bynum, in January 1977, when I was first mulling over the Berkeley offer:

And of course you should be training the next generation. It is a great deal of work with good grad students (... you have already written a great book and more of your energy should go to the new generation). It won't leave you as much time for writing as you have now—but I wonder whether (this is a very subjective hunch from seeing your work recently) you may not need to pull back a little here, work a little more on method with some first rate students and then write a lot again in five years. I suspect that, under the stimulus of undergrad teaching, your beautiful prose begins to propel your ideas—with grad students the reverse would happen. Yes, yes, yes, you should take it!

This proved to be a most perceptive, even prophetic, insight. It tipped the balance.

I remember the morning, in July 1977, when the telegram of Berkeley's formal offer to me arrived at the History Department. It spelled out my teaching duties. They amounted to only six hours a week, all of them devoted to aspects of my own specialty. I compared this offer with what I was doing that day in Royal Holloway. At nine o'clock, I had, indeed, explained the sack of Rome of 410. This was "my" lecture—the Professorial Lecture—to a medium-sized group of those students in the college who had opted to do medieval European history. But then, in the next hour, I held a seminar–discussion group on Karl Marx and the *Communist Manifesto*; and the hour after that a similar seminar on the *Social Contract* of Jean-Jacques Rousseau. I faced an afternoon that consisted of a succession of three hour-long tutorials, each with two students— this week being devoted to King Alfred and the Viking invasions. We would be fortified throughout by cups of tea discreetly brought in, at regular intervals for me and the two students, by Rita Townsend. No graduate student had darkened my door for months. For the first time, perhaps ever, I felt acutely that this was all a bit too much. I had a responsibility to my own field. The Berkeley offer gave me the opportunity to take on this responsibility—full-time, as it were—along with the challenge to make good use of it.

But, given this freedom to concentrate entirely on the field of late antiquity, what would I choose? How much of my previous work—on Saint Augustine, on the rise and function of the holy man in East Rome, and, most recently, on the rise of the cult of saints in Latin Christianity—would I bring with me to America? Or would I use the opportunity given to me by Berkeley to branch out yet further, by including the origins of the Islamic world, as a direct continuation of the story of the rivalry of Byzantium and Persia? At the time, I was far from certain as to which it would be.

Hence I came to Berkeley, as it were, carrying two suitcases. One suitcase was well packed: it contained my previous work on various aspects of Christianity in the late antique and early medieval periods. Another suitcase was more hastily packed: it carried the weight of a relatively new preoccupation with the origins and consequences of the rise of Islam. How had this doubling of my luggage come about?

THE WEIGHT OF ISLAM

The World of Islam

In 1976, the World of Islam Festival took place in London. It was a grand affair, funded by several Middle Eastern governments, and opened by the queen. It was accompanied by exhibitions in museums all over London, by lectures, and by a conference in the Albert Hall that attracted some twenty thousand would-be participants, in a building with a capacity for only five thousand.

Bob Silvers of the *New York Review of Books* asked me to do a review of books on Islam, many of which had been published for the occasion of the festival. Package by package, the books arrived—eleven titles in all. This led to the most intensive "read-in" on Islam that I had ever done. It is not that I had been ignorant of Islam. In my *World of Late Antiquity*, I had already insisted on including Muhammad, the origins of Islam, and the early centuries of the Islamic empire as an integral part of late antiquity. But this was a closer look. I felt that the time had come to do justice to my long-term interest in the Islamic world.

This read-in was very necessary. I had gone to Iran, in 1974 and 1976, as a scholar of Byzantium and its great Eastern neighbor in pre-Islamic times. I had little interest in studying Islam itself. But while I was in Iran, I was brought into contact with living Islam. I had been deeply impressed by my experiences at the shrine of Imam Reza at Mashhad, in 1974; by my contacts with ordinary Iranians as I traveled; and by my visits to mosques both great and small.

I returned with a heavy sense of the unacknowledged importance of Islam in contemporary Iranian society. It was an awareness tinged with foreboding. Something must be wrong, I thought, for so evident a force to be so strenuously denied by the regime. I realized that I had been in the presence of a great, living religion, of which I still knew little. Now was the time to learn.

I did much of my reading during the break from work occasioned by the celebrations of the Silver Jubilee of Queen Elizabeth II in early June 1977. As the country rejoiced, and bonfires were lit from one end of England to the other, I enjoyed a short week of pure, undisturbed research. I remember writing to a friend, after the jubilee break, that I was like a lion who had escaped from the zoo. I would have to be shot. For I had tasted blood—the blood of a week of pure, unhurried scholarship. The hope that I might come to enjoy more of such leisure if I moved to America cheered me up greatly, as I began to consider what my life might be like in Berkeley.

Later, in an early August stay in Ireland, I read the remainder of the books on Islam that Bob Silvers had sent me. I composed the review in my head, in the warm sun of an unexpected heat wave on the granite rocks of the Forty Foot—the men's bathing establishment, beneath James Joyce's Martello tower—close to my parents' house. As I meditated on Islam, my father and two other elderly gentlemen of his acquaintance stripped down after a swim with their hearing aids removed, talking happily, and entirely at cross-purposes, to each other.

Back in my parents' house, I continued to read. It seemed to me to be altogether appropriate to read about Islam in a sitting room crowded with mementoes of Sudan and of the Middle East, beside a bookshelf where a luxury edition of T. E. Lawrence's *Seven Pillars of Wisdom* stood next to my father's copy of *Sudanese Courtesy Customs*.

Bob Silvers did not like the review that I first submitted to him. He found it heavy-handed. It was not until I had established myself in Berkeley, a year later, in August 1978, that I returned to my draft and rewrote it. The final version of my review appeared as "Understanding Islam" in the *New York Review of Books*.[1] The most thoughtful and well-informed response to it came from a Black Muslim named Naseer Shabazz. His letter was addressed to me from a correctional facility, and he praised me for my respect for Islamic learning, wishing that such an exacting and enlightened system were in place in the USA.

By the time that my review appeared, in early 1979, the role of Islam in the Middle East looked very different from how it had looked only two years before. The shah of Iran had fled, and the Ayatollah Khomeini had returned in triumph to Tehran. A major revolution had taken place, wholly unexpectedly, in the name of religion: in Europe and America, the public was confronted

---

1. Peter Brown, "Understanding Islam," *New York Review of Books* 26 (February 22, 1979): 30–33.

with images of Islam in action very different from the cheery stereotypes produced by the London World of Islam Festival in 1976.

The Weight of Islam

I recently found the earlier draft of my review—the one that Silvers rejected. It catches me in a conflicted mood. I was making up my mind on the *weight* of Islam. How much attention should I devote to Islam as a scholar of late antiquity and the early Middle Ages? How much effort should I expend to persuade the average, educated readers of the *New York Review of Books* (British and American alike) to pay attention to the colossus that had lain for centuries on the doorstep of Europe?

What troubled me most were Western stereotypes of Islam. As a historian of religion in late antiquity—that is, of the period which immediately preceded and coincided with the rise of Islam—I felt that many of the prejudices which rested on my own period rested, also, on Islam. I felt that it was my duty to challenge these misleading interpretations, so as to ensure that Islam would be heard. I wanted to encourage the readers of my review to stretch their hearts, so as to understand a distant faith that had emerged from the same religious turmoil, in late antiquity, as had Christianity and rabbinic Judaism.

I was happy to do this. After all, it seemed to me that I had spent many years lifting a veil of prejudice that had obscured our vision of late antiquity. I had gone out of my way to call attention to those phenomena that were often dismissed by outsiders as primitive, superstitious, and unworthy of consideration—sorcery, holy men, the cult of saints: indeed, late antiquity itself, as a period long held in scorn as a time of decadence. I considered it my duty as a historian to do justice to hitherto despised peoples and cultures, by removing the stereotypes that had piled up like guano dust against them.

Furthermore, the vital presence of Islam was not only a challenge to historians and observers of the modern Middle East. It also forced scholars and the educated public in general to reassess their views on the importance of religion in human affairs. In the 1970s, historians had only just begun to write religion back into their accounts of the past and of the contemporary world. To recover the weight of Islam meant working against the grain of a confident and well-entrenched tradition of historical scholarship and of sociological investigation that denied weight to religious issues in any society. Yet it struck me that religion would not go away. It had a weight of its own that we had to learn to appreciate.

Looking back, I realize that I was writing at a moment of calm before the storm. It was not that Westerners were entirely deaf to the message of Islam. It was, rather, that they refused to see the contemporary Middle East in religious terms. The local regimes colluded in this misperception. Most countries in the Middle East were ruled by dictators who wanted to disassociate themselves from the religious leadership of their own societies. These dictators wished to be seen as the leaders of secular nation-states on a European model—as Arabs or as Iranians first and as Muslims second.

As a result, most outside observers thought of the Middle East in secular terms. Either they viewed it in terms of the Cold War: treating it as a Third World region, caught between Russia and the West. Or they thought in terms of the anticolonial movements that had brought many Muslim nation-states into being—the movie *The Battle of Algiers* (1966) being one of the most vivid representations of such movements. In their opinion, anticolonialism, economic development, and the growth of nation-statehood were what mattered—and not the disquieting background noise of an impending religious revival.

This stereotype needed to be dismantled. For political reasons, the London World of Islam Festival had avoided the hot issue of Islam as a living faith. As a result, the publications connected with the festival struck me as having a tin ear on religious matters. Gothic Europe might have had its age of faith. Medieval Islam was presented, only, as a colorful age of affluence. I jibbed at this. In such accounts, I wrote (in the draft of my review for the *New York Review of Books*), "the deep religious anger of Muhammad, as it has echoed down the centuries among Muslims, is stilled." I felt that I had not recently been in Iran for nothing. Islam as a living faith could no longer be ignored. Whether this concern for Islam would ever become a research agenda for me remained to be seen. But there is no doubt that, at this time, it was a major interest.

HAGARISM

Hence, in my review, I drew attention to one book that seemed to fall like a hurricane on the grandiose yet cozy image of Islam projected by the festival: *Hagarism* by Patricia Crone (1945–2015) and Michael Cook.[2] Compared with the bland overviews of Islam elicited by the festival, it stood out as disturbingly

---

2. Patricia Crone and Michael Cook, *Hagarism: The Making of the Islamic World* (Cambridge University Press, 1977).

original. I organized around it both the draft and the final version of my review "Understanding Islam."

Hagarism was a book calculated to make scholars sit up and take notice. Put very briefly: the authors suggested, with rare verve, that we should not take for granted that Islam had emerged already fully formed from an Arabian setting. In their opinion, the early Arab Muslims had received from Muhammad only "a sort of elementary religious literacy."[3] They received the rest of their religion from contact with Jews and Christians in Syria and Iraq after the time of the conquests, in the seventh and eighth centuries. Far from bringing with them a monolithic and alien faith fully formed in the desert, the first Muslims stumbled into a religious melting pot on the boil. In its first centuries, Islam grew out of this melting pot, through continuous dialogue among Arab Muslims, Jews, and Christians that took place all over a largely Christian Middle East. Crone and Cook argued that, in its earliest phases, Islam was a religion in the making. It took shape as it encountered the ideas of the populations that the Arab armies had conquered.

Hagarism has gained such notoriety in academic circles that it is difficult to recapture what it first meant. Both Patricia Crone and Michael Cook later came to distance themselves from its more provocative statements. At the time, I remember that it grated on me. "Infuriatingly cerebral and non-historical," "flimsy and precipitate" were the kindest adjectives that I could muster to describe the tone of the book.[4] Filled with sociological jargon and arcane parallels, it read as if the protagonists had "stepped straight out of a brilliantly witty seminar."[5] The book seemed to be marred by the intellectual one-upmanship and in talk that I had come to greatly dislike in parts of English academe.

Yet, like a small charge of dynamite detonated in exactly the right place, this truculent little book did more than any other single publication to bring down the high dam that had previously separated "classical" Islamic studies from the study of late antiquity. It claimed to abolish the disciplinary divide that had isolated the study of Arabic from the study of the languages and cultures of the pre-Islamic Middle East—Syriac, Aramaic, and Hebrew among them. It brought scholarship on Islam into intimate contact with research into other religions—Judaism, Christianity, and Zoroastrianism. Last but not least, it saw

---

3. Crone and Cook, *Hagarism*, 15.
4. Brown, "Understanding Islam," 32.
5. Brown, "Understanding Islam," 33.

the Arabs themselves in terms of their relations with the populations of the settled lands with whom they had long had dealings. They had not been men from Mars.

Nonetheless, *Hagarism* struck me as a great opportunity missed. The book could have formed the basis for an entirely new study of the process of Islamization. It introduced an element of choice and negotiation into that process which had been lacking in most modern accounts. Most scholars simply assumed that conversion to Islam had been largely involuntary—a passive capitulation, over the years, to a conquering power. But was this always the case? What if some conversions, at least, had been voluntary—if they had resulted from the intense dialogues between Muslims, Jews, and Christians that Crone and Cook posited as lying at the very roots of the formation of Islam?

This meant that we would have to think again about the innumerable, different ways in which Islam spread throughout the southern Mediterranean, the Middle East, and Iran, much as Christianity had spread in the later Roman Empire. These ways, of course, included the ever-present pressure of state patronage. In a fluid society, conformity to the religion of the new Muslim rulers was as decisive a factor in the adoption of Islam, in the seventh, eighth, and ninth centuries, as the adoption of Christianity had been, when fostered by imperial authorities in the post-Constantinian Roman world of the fourth and fifth centuries. But this was a slow and piecemeal process. In many regions and sectors of society, Islam may also have talked itself, slowly but surely, into dominance through innumerable encounters, debates, and questionings from which Islam itself emerged enriched and changed.

In 1977, this was a challenging assertion, hinted at though not followed through by Crone and Cook. Nowadays there is no doubt that constant debates between Muslims and non-Muslims did take place. To take one example: the brilliant book of the late Tom Sizgorich, *Violence and Belief in Late Antiquity: Militant Devotion in Christianity and Islam*, has shown that Muslims and Christians did, indeed, argue about the relative merits of the monastic ideal of self-mortification and Muslim notions of self-sacrifice in holy war—the notion of *jihad*.[6] In these debates we can overhear a new religion arguing itself into shape, in constant dialogue with its religious neighbors.

Patient modern scholarship has also shown how many distinctive features of Islamic civilization emerged slowly, through a process of negotiation among

---

6. T. Sizgorich, *Violence and Belief in Late Antiquity: Militant Devotion in Christianity and Islam* (Philadelphia: University of Pennsylvania Press, 2009).

Muslims, Jews, and Christians. In a recent masterpiece, Jack Tannous has made plain that the first Muslim Arabs entered the Middle East as a small, if powerful, minority, surrounded by religious controversies as vocal as the roar of cicadas in the high season. It is not surprising that Islam emerged from such a background as a religion enriched by innumerable contacts, debates, and now long-forgotten conversations between Muslims and non-Muslims.[7]

Altogether, we have come a long way from the narrow image of Islam that was current in academe in the 1970s, and which Cook and Crone had attempted to challenge in their own way. Recent scholars have revealed a Middle East that was religiously more ebullient, more open to dialogue and to religious *bricolage*—to the mix-and-match adoption of religious practices and moral precepts by "simple believers" (that is, not only by theologians)—than we had dared to think forty years ago.

Forty years is a long time. None of these studies were available in 1977. But, at least, as I prepared the first draft of my review, I realized that I had much to learn about Islam if I were to meet the challenge posed by *Hagarism* and the horizons that Crone and Cook had, almost unwittingly, opened up to scholars of late antiquity. To do this I would travel once again to the Middle East, but no longer to the thrilling landscapes of Iran. There, in Iran, I had discovered Islam almost by accident. Now I would seek it out, by learning Arabic and by rooting myself in the heart of the greatest city in the Muslim Middle East. I would go to Cairo.

7. Jack Tannous, *The Making of the Medieval Middle East: Religion, Society, and Simple Believers* (Princeton, NJ: Princeton University Press, 2018).

CAIRO

Planning a Visit

It seemed easy enough to go to Cairo. The way had been prepared by a previous short visit. At the very end of 1977, I had joined my colleague Professor "Sandy" Sanderson on a visit to Cairo, to establish a link between the History Department of Royal Holloway College and ʿAin Shams University in Cairo. Sandy was long acquainted with Egypt and Sudan, having taught at the University of Khartoum. It was an official occasion that turned out to be delightful.

We did the usual things. We saw son et lumière at the pyramids, on the night when the voice-over was in Arabic. We were driven down to Saqqara in the dawn light, passing peasants carrying great bundles of reeds on their shoulders, which bent in the same perfect curve as did the doorway arches of the courtyard in front of the Step Pyramid. This was a reminder that, for all its colossal size, ancient Egyptian architecture never lost touch with a grace firmly based on the shapes of humble objects in the natural world.

We met the English Department of ʿAin Shams, dominated by a group of formidable Coptic ladies who had obtained their doctorates at Trinity College Dublin for dissertations on Anglo-Irish literature. I chatted with them about my distant cousin John Synge, author of *The Playboy of the Western World* and *Deirdre of the Sorrows*.

In the happy mood induced by the Camp David Accords, we spent New Year's Eve playing bingo in the apartment of a general who had fought in Sinai during the Yom Kippur War.

Most revealing of all, perhaps, was a visit to the theater to witness an avant garde Egyptian play. It was a retelling of the story of the *Oedipus Rex* of Sophocles. As it was explained to me, the message of the play was pointedly upbeat.

Oedipus's relation to his mother had nothing to do with incest. What mattered was that, with a mother's encouragement, he shed his Western, Freudian hang-ups and devoted himself, as a king, to the progress of the people of Thebes—as Gamal Abdel Nasser (1918–1970) had devoted himself to the people of Egypt.

I resolved to return for a longer stay. I set off for Cairo on May 13, 1978, and stayed there until July 18. Apart from learning Arabic, I had no academic role when in Cairo. I was simply there as a visitor. I was very much on my own. I was not integrated into some university-based Arabic course, where my experiences would have been laid on for me. Nor was I on a formal academic visit. As a result, my experience of Cairo was fragmented, and in many ways frustrating. I think that I underestimated the need for money and for prear-ranged contacts to make life easy in a country like Egypt. I tried to do it my way and, as a result, suffered much frustration. I kept no diary, nor did I write many letters. For this reason, my memories have a somewhat kaleidoscopic character. I remember a vivid succession of places and persons, from each of which I learned something that would remain with me for many years to come.

The Collège de la Sainte Famille

At first I stayed at a Coptic guesthouse in Zamalek; then I moved across the river to the Jesuit-run Collège de la Sainte Famille in Fagallah. This was in the area of Ramses Square and the main railway station to the south. In what seems to be an entire lifetime previously (but actually was only thirty years be-fore), my mother and father had been accustomed to arrive at that railway station on their way from Sudan to Port Said, so as to catch the boat to England.[1]

The world of the Collège de la Sainte Famille absorbed me with utter lack of surprise. French was the dominant language. But whether French or Italian, Spanish or German, they all seemed to me mere dialects of a common tongue, barely distinguishable one from the other compared with the intractable mass of the Arabic that I had set out to learn.

This was to be no time of easy travel over bracing distances, as in Iran. It was the hottest summer in memory, and I soon fell sick with a virus that left me, at times, as weak as a kitten. As a result, I saw none of the well-known monuments of Egypt outside Cairo. I even had to forgo, with a heavy heart, a proposed visit to Alexandria in the company of the football team of the collège.

1. Chapter 8: "Atbara: Life Abroad."

What I remember of Cairo is strangely dim. No bright colors. Rather, meetings by lamplight in the cool of the night. In the soft dawn, I would drag myself to the great flat roof of the collège, to look down over the winding lanes and courtyards of Fagallah. On the flat roofs a little below the high balcony of the collège, gentlemen in nightshirts were chasing their chickens. Farther down, at the end of lanes and in courtyards, the "invisible economy" throve. Stolen cars were carefully repainted or meticulously cannibalized.

I knew all this because the Spanish Jesuit who taught science pointed it out to me; he would usually buy the mechanical parts needed for his laboratory from this quarter. He loved Egyptian Muslims. He was convinced that God had given them an easier religion because of the intrinsic goodness of their hearts. But the best time of all was the evening, when the desert wind blew in, and, all over Cairo, from the narrowest, poorest lanes, kites would be carried upward in the floating breeze.

POVERTY

Very soon I realized that I would not only bring home from Cairo a sense of the weight of Islam. I would also bring a sense of the weight of poverty in a great Middle Eastern city. The poverty of Cairo engulfed me. I had, perhaps, less protection from it than the average European tourist. I had brought little money (if I remember right, some savings and a small Leverhulme grant from the British Academy) and was largely dependent, for getting around, on public transport or on walking the long hot streets, full of deep holes and hummocks as if they had been shaken up by an earthquake. I was by no means down and out in Cairo. I was well lodged and fed at the collège. But the moment I walked out the collège gate, I found myself close enough to the poverty in the surrounding streets to take notice.

This poverty affected me in different ways. The vast crowds, seemingly forever on the move at all times of day and night, did not worry me. For I was amazed by the gentleness and respect for the space of others that characterized this massed humanity, as it drifted down the avenues and went round and round the wide traffic circle of Tahrir Square. I bobbed around in this great Irish stew of people without ever being hustled or elbowed. It would be usual for me to board the crowded bus to the Coptic Patriarchate in ʿAbbasiyya through the open windows. Kind hands would always reach out to settle me in a seat.

What did distress me was the sheer permanency of this urban poverty. The Collège de la Sainte Famille did not lie in a privileged area. It towered over

Fagallah, a long street choked by small shops, from which led narrow lanes—
the lane of the circumcisers among them. The packed slum of Bulaq lay close
by. On many evenings, I would sit in a mosque in the middle of Bulaq, reviewing my Arabic through reading a collection of *hadiths*—Sayings of the Prophet
or stories concerning the Prophet.

The worst poverty was marked by a rhythm of frenzy and lassitude. Gangs
of diggers, laying drainage pipes outside the collège, would chew cheap aspi-
rins to relieve the pain in their joints. They were flat out by midday. I was once
driven by friends out to the oasis of Fayyûm (a major find spot for administrative papyri and for Manichaean texts buried in the ever-encroaching sands that
surrounded the oasis). The courtyards of the mosques were filled with sleeping beggars, and the boatman who took us across Lake Qaroun to the temple
of the Crocodile God was evidently so weak from malnutrition that we had to
take the oars and pull the boat ourselves.

But more distressing still was Shubra. This was a great stretch of dusty gray
buildings seemingly inhabited (at that time: things may have changed) by a
perpetually impoverished lower middle class. It was painful to see these enterprising people constantly ground down by shortages and discomfort, and
never quite able to gain a sure footing economically, compared with the rich
bourgeoisie of Cairo, whose sons (the grandchildren of Gamal Abdel Nasser
among them) were sent to receive a European culture at the collège.

In the middle of Shubra was the Catholic shrine of Saint Thérèse of Lisieux,
which was filled by Muslims, Copts, and Catholics alike. There seemed to be
some strange fascination in the figure of a pale, European girl, worn thin by
illness, surrounded by walls covered with desperate notes, begging for health,
for safety, and for success in examinations. I carried back from Cairo visual
memories of systemic poverty in a great city that prompted me, in all future
years, to pay more attention than I had done before to issues of wealth and
poverty in the later Roman Empire.

LISTENING

Though grounded by fever, I was by no means out of touch with the wider
world. The collège was a listening post of remarkable sensitivity. The newspapers carried regular reports of growing anger in Iran. Fellow Jesuits and other
clergymen arrived frequently from Lebanon. They would be asked to speak
after the Sunday lunch. They told tales that revealed a deeply divided Christianity. On one occasion, a heavy and overbearing Maronite cleric gave us an

upbeat sermon on the Falangist destiny of Lebanon. Next week, a small and soft-spoken Franciscan simply narrated, step by step, the descent into violence that began (in almost medieval fashion) with a brawl at a tollgate and which ended in the recent, sickening murder, in his country villa, of Tony Frangieh and his family. It was in this way that I heard about the beginning of the end of the regime of the shah of Iran, and about the further, fateful stages of the civil war in Lebanon.

The collège was also a remarkable gathering of persons. The Jesuit staff was drawn from all over Europe and from the Christians of the Middle East. My favorite was Father Zamalek. A large man, descended from Albanians who had been settled by the Ottomans as a garrison in southern Egypt, he would solemnly greet me every morning, teaching me the correct way to inquire, in Arabic, whether one's neighbor at the table had had auspicious dreams that night.

There were also numerous visitors, many of them with long experience of Egypt and the Muslim world. I gained as much from long conversations with them, seated on the roof of the collège in the cool of the night, as I did from my own forays into the city. I came to know Patrick Gaffney, a priest-anthropologist now at Notre Dame. This huge, redheaded man would sit for hours, with his long legs tucked beneath him, taking notes on sermons in a mosque in Minya, a sprawling agro-town in the Nile delta. From the dull sediment of popular preaching Patrick distilled a remarkable study of the role of Islam in a major Egyptian provincial city. The imam with whom he dealt was no bigot. He was a believing Muslim, he said: "But I do not wear my beard on my sleeve."[2]

It was through Patrick that I learned about the omnipresence of the Muslim Brotherhood. They had even approached him to warn him off his work in the mosques. In the long hot nights, I read what I could about them in books borrowed from the library of the collège, as my small portable wireless played Qur'ânic recitations and, occasionally, picked up classical music broadcast from Bucharest.

From another frequent visitor, Tom Michel, I learned about the vast Muslim populations of Indonesia. Tom had studied Indonesian Islam, and had come to be deeply committed to individual Muslims through his human rights work on behalf of Communists of Muslim background who had been imprisoned under Sukarno. He wrote to me later about Java as an island paradise stained with blood where, paradoxically, Islam and radical secularism were joined (so he hoped at that time) by a shared desire for a just society.

A Worldwide Islam

This sense of the size and continued expansive power of Islam was not restricted only to what I had picked up in the collège. It was in the air in Cairo. For liberal Egyptian Muslims, Islam stood out as the one religion that had retained its universal vision in the days of European colonialism. Cairo claimed to be the cultural capital not only of the Arab world but of all Africa—as witnessed by the flow of African students to its universities to avail themselves of English courses of high quality, such as those offered by the English Department at ʿAin Shams. Muslim intellectuals fervently believed that the measured Sunni Islam of Egypt (a faith that had stood up to colonialism and to racial prejudice) could make a bid to become the dominant religion of the Third World.

They thought big. I remember overhearing a conversation in the salon of one such liberal professor. He was speaking about how to bring a correct Sunni Islam to a distant extremist group. It was only later that I realized that he had been speaking of the Black Muslims of Philadelphia. There was a pride and an optimism about such people that takes some effort of the imagination to recall.

Altogether, it was instructive to spend some time looking at the West from the outside. Not only was the Muslim world turning its back on Europe. Europe also seemed, morally and culturally, to be doing the same to Egypt. I noticed that when French literature was being taught at the collège, the students responded instantly to the great realistic novels of the nineteenth century, to Balzac and Zola. Sons of the Cairo bourgeoisie, they knew that sex and money were what life was all about. The chill lucubrations of Sartre and Camus left them cold. It was as if a common human language, which had once been shared by the bourgeoisie on both sides of the Mediterranean, had shriveled on its northern, French shores.

Though I had been largely immobilized by illness, I returned to England having heard a lot and thought a lot. I had gained a sense of the size and sense of purpose of modern Islam. I visited Royal Holloway for a few days to attend a conference of the Historical Association. One session was on the Crusades. I was able to tell my audience that, in Cairo, it was still possible to buy little sugar statues of Saladin (1137–1193), the Muslim leader who had conquered Jerusalem from the Crusaders in 1187.

GOOD-BYE FROM IRELAND

Driving with a friend for a last time in the Oxfordshire countryside, I felt an acute sense of loss. I wished that the view of the Windrush River, as it flowed through the fields outside Swinbrook, would last forever. It was that intimate landscape, soaked in the past, which I was going to exchange for the wild sea-coast of Northern California.

Then I went to Ireland. It was reassuring to be in a country that took emigration to America for granted. When, in Oxford, I would announce that I was going to Berkeley, the answer was—"For a term, I suppose?" My "No: for good" was followed by a disapproving "OOooh!" Such a response was not intended to encourage me. Not so in Ireland. In Glasthule Post Office, I was presented with a whole list of the postmistress's relatives in San Francisco and Redwood City. My aunt Norah volunteered that an elderly gentleman in her nursing home—at the age of ninety-five a notorious Lothario—was rumored to have once been mayor of San Francisco.

On August 8, my parents took me to Dublin Airport to board the TWA flight to Boston. From Boston I flew a few days later to San Francisco. On the day I left, my mother entered in her diary, almost—I suspect—by way of consolation:

Peds looked well and happy—he had got the job he had always wanted.

It was a sad entry. But it was certainly what I had communicated to my parents, in order to justify my long journey from them. Only the next years would tell what use I could make of my new circumstances in a distant land.

PART VI

BERKELEY TO PRINCETON

BERKELEY 1978

THE PHILOSOPHER AND SOCIETY

Culture Shock

I arrived in Berkeley on August 11, 1978, braced for culture shock. But I found
that, if I suffered from culture shock at all, it was not from leaving Britain and
Ireland: it was the memory of Cairo, where I had been only three weeks before,
that made Berkeley seem so very strange. In Cairo, I had been struck by its
poverty and pent-up energy. In the Bay Area, by contrast, I was gently dazed
by a rare combination of impersonality and supreme ease.

In the first days after my arrival, I would stand in the clear, pure sunlight,
bemused that it did not bite into me like the sun of Cairo. I occasionally
paused, even more bemused, at a traffic light. Large cars silently came to a halt
at the red. More amazing still, when the light turned to green (and only then),
they slid forward without making a sound. It was as if a mighty vacuum cleaner
had sucked up into the blue sky the roar of a great, Middle Eastern city to
which I was accustomed.

Even shopping seemed to be preternaturally smooth compared with the
stores and bazaars of Cairo. I found that I missed the haggling. At the Safeway
on Shattuck Avenue and Cedar, I would fill my grocery cart in silence, would
wheel it in silence to the cash register, and with craven self-surrender (by
Egyptian standards) would pay not only the full price, but also the added state
tax, all without a word.

When the time came to collect my library and furniture from the docks of
Oakland, I expected, on the basis of anyone's experience of getting things done
in Cairo, to put a personal touch on the transaction. No such thing happened.
I rang the appropriate number. Over the phone, I heard the clicking of a

keyboard. Then: "It's OK. Have a good day"—and, after a short pause (as the agent scanned the screen of his computer for my Christian name) . . . "Peter."

Inevitably, there were times when I felt uprooted at the other end of the world. I would speak of myself to my friends as a *pomodoro pelato*—a peeled tomato. The image was humorous: the experience itself was no fun. And so I found myself taking a very Californian (and also, for me, a very Irish) way out: I made for the sea. I regularly drove out to Point Reyes beach in Marin County, an hour away from Berkeley. Armed with a beer, I sat in the sand dunes until the sun sank so low, in the late afternoon, that it shone into the wave tops, turning them into light-filled palaces where one could almost hear the mermaids sing. It also helped that the waves came in from the right direction—from the west—as they had done in the days of my holidays on the west coast of Ireland. The deeply prehuman (*prehuman*, not *inhuman*) beauty of the Californian coast, which I had already experienced in 1975, saw me through.

The Weight of Freedom

By the time that I began to teach, in late August 1978, I had moved into an apartment and had acquired (in a secondhand office supply shop in Oakland) an electric, golf-ball typewriter. This was a total novelty for me: until then I had been content to hammer at the keys of an Olivetti portable. With its smooth, automatic return and neat correction tape, this new typewriter was, for me, an emblem of the almost disquieting new ease that I had found in the Bay Area. Perching the machine on a packing case—for I had not yet acquired a desk—I used it to rewrite my review, "Understanding Islam," for Bob Silvers at the *New York Review of Books*.

Soon after, I set to work preparing a paper for a colloquy at the Center for Hermeneutical Studies in the Graduate Theological Union: "The Philosopher and Society in Late Antiquity."[1] This was the first of a series of papers (none of which were published) that signaled a change of direction in my work, toward a greater interest in the problems of power and moral authority in the later Roman Empire. My interest in this theme led eventually, fourteen years later, to a book: *Power and Persuasion in Late Antiquity*.[2]

1. Peter Brown, "The Philosopher and Society in Late Antiquity," in *The Center for Hermeneutical Studies in Hellenistic and Modern Culture*, Colloquy, no. 34, December 3, 1978 (Berkeley: Center for Hermeneutical Studies, 1980), 1–17.

2. Peter Brown, *Power and Persuasion in Late Antiquity: Towards a Christian Empire* (Madison: University of Wisconsin Press, 1992).

Looking back, I cannot resist the impression that, by settling down to work on such a topic, I already felt the tug of the *genius loci*. When I visited Berkeley in 1975, I had been forcibly struck, as an outsider, by the extent to which men and women enjoyed a degree of personal freedom unequaled in the modern world. Hence, among some at least, a streak of deep seriousness that was the obverse of California's reputation as the home of cranks and faddists. I was impressed by friends and colleagues who plainly gave much thought to the way they lived their lives. Their freedom weighed upon them. If so much of life was a matter of choice, then these choices had to be made; and they had to be right.

But there was more to it than that. Paradoxically, my experience of Iran (and to a lesser extent of Cairo) sharpened this interest in the forming power of distinctive codes of behavior. Iran and Northern California might seem worlds apart in the codes to which they rallied, as the course of the Iranian Revolution soon made only too clear. But they were both rapidly evolving societies searching for new rules of life. Both California and Iran seemed equally distant from Europe and the British Isles, which seemed somnolent places in comparison, where so much of life appeared to be lived, as it were, on automatic pilot. A sense of the seriousness of the search for a rule for life in both societies gave human weight and urgency to what, until then, had struck me as the rarefied lucubrations of the ancient ethicists. From now on, I would see these well-known figures of the late classical world as engaged in the serious business of the formation of souls. They were not only predecessors of the Christian monks but also harbingers of the learned and pious mentors of the Islamic world. What fascinated me, at this time, as a historian, was what these traditions of spiritual guidance (the classical and the Islamic) had in common and where they differed from each other in significant ways.

I gave more thought than previously as to how persons of the privileged classes in the ancient world chose to set their lives in order. I found myself turning with new eyes to the late classical philosophers in their role as moralists and spiritual guides—to Seneca, Plutarch, Epictetus, and Marcus Aurelius. Back in England, these Old Masters had left me cold. They seemed to be trading in uplift—Victorians of the ancient world. But, now, they looked very different. In addressing the elites of the Roman world, they addressed persons who felt themselves to be free, to a dangerous extent, to do anything or nothing with their lives. The ancient philosophers offered guidance on the best use of this vertiginous freedom. As a result, I wanted to provide a social and cultural context for the pagan philosophers of late antiquity that explained their role, not just as abstract thinkers, but as mentors, spiritual guides, and public figures.

The Philosopher in Society

In order to do this, I would have to dispel many misconceptions. The first of these was the conviction that, in late antiquity, philosophers had no social role whatsoever: that they were, all of them, world-fleeing mystics.

In my paper, I argued strongly against this view. I pointed out that even the most metaphysical philosophers, such as Plotinus (205–270), Porphyry (232–303), and Iamblichus (260–330), in the third and early fourth centuries, and Proclus (411–485), in the fifth century, had not been recluses. They had continued to play an active role in the social life of their cities.

I also added that there were many more examples of philosophers engaged in public life in the fourth and fifth centuries than we had thought. Scholars of the later empire had been so convinced that the philosopher played no role in society that they had paid little attention to the cumulative evidence for the presence of philosophers in municipal politics all over the empire and even as advisers at the imperial court.

I had noticed that historians of art and museum curators colluded with the stereotype of the otherworldly philosopher. In the exhibition galleries of major museums, the busts of late antique philosophers (or figures said to be philosophers) were usually presented beneath dramatic, vertical lights that emphasized their heavenward gaze. But was this how they looked in antiquity? In November 1977, I had visited the great exhibition, *Age of Spirituality*, organized by Kurt Weitzmann at the Metropolitan Museum of Art in New York. I earned a rebuke from the guard because I lifted my museum map to block the strong vertical light that shone down on the face of the well-known Bust of Eutropius, a fifth-century AD head taken from a statue erected in Ephesus. But I was satisfied with the experiment. Without the vertical light that seemed to draw his eyes upward, as if in rapt contemplation of the other world, the bust changed expression. Seen in normal daylight (as it would have been seen in fifth-century Ephesus), the face no longer looked "spacey." Instead, the eyes had the penetrating look of an intelligent man, very much at home in this world.[3]

3. *Age of Spirituality. Late Antique and Early Christian Art, Third to Seventh Century*, ed. Kurt Weitzmann (New York, Metropolitan Museum of Art, 1979), no. 55, p. 58, with Peter Brown, "Art and Society in Late Antiquity," in *Age of Spirituality: A Symposium*, ed. K. Weitzmann (New York: Metropolitan Museum of Art, 1980), 17–27.

A Saint of *Paideia*

So what did contemporaries see in the philosopher that gave him such moral authority in the upper-class circles in which he moved? Here I suggested that the philosopher was revered because he was held to have summed up in his person the ideals of an entire culture. This was the "civilization of *paideia*" to whose values and tenacity Henri-Irénée Marrou had drawn attention in so many eloquent studies—most notably in his youthful study of the manner in which educated persons were shown on their sarcophagi.[4]

Previously, I had tended to dismiss this classical education (known as *paideia*) as a superficial matter—as a mere badge of status that separated a mandarin class of civic notables and public servants from the mass of their uneducated inferiors. Now I realized that, in many cases, the acquisition of *paideia* was far from being a superficial process. The values implied in it were supposed to bite deep into the person. It involved more than a purely literary education. The emphasis on poise, on self-control, and on gracious behavior that characterized the "civilization of *paideia*" was thought to be echoed in the harmonious style of the ancient authors, and to be reinforced by the treasure-house of examples of correct behavior stored up in classical literature. To be educated in the classics was not just to learn a language and to read a literature. It was to undergo a moral grooming. It was to learn how to conduct oneself as something of a human classic—as a ceremonious and balanced person. Philosophers were believed to have internalized these values more successfully than any other people. Far from being "remote and ineffectual dons," they were "saints of *paideia*"—the superego of an entire class.

"Awe-Inspiring Centrality"

At the time, I still found it difficult to explain the chemistry of moral authority that enabled one figure (and a figure committed to such an arcane discipline as philosophy) to condense in his or her person the values of an entire culture. I wondered whether the image of the great scientist in modern society might be analogous to the aura that surrounded the philosopher in late antiquity.[5]

4. H.-I. Marrou, *Mousikos Anér: Études sur les scènes de la vie intellectuelle figurants sur les monuments funéraires romains* (Grenoble: Didier et Richard, 1938).

5. I used the recent article of Dorinda Outram, "The Language of Natural Power: The 'Éloges' of Georges Cuvier and the Public Language of Nineteenth Century Science," *History*

It is a sign of my recent arrival in America that, in this paper, I had not taken on board the penetrating work of Edward Shils (1910–1995), of which I had known nothing when in England. A little later, as I absorbed his *Center and Periphery: Essays in Macrosociology*, Shils helped me to see how a learned tradition and the persons who embodied it could be invested with a charisma quite as potent, in its quiet way, as the more flamboyant charisma associated with persons such as the holy men of Syria.

In Shils's words, such persons radiated a sense of "awe-inspiring centrality" as representing an entire culture at its best. It was in this way that more low-key, less melodramatic figures, from non-Christian traditions, came to interest me. Shils's subdued notion of charisma enabled me to understand better than previously figures such as the pagan philosophers, the Jewish rabbis, and, later, the learned and holy scholars—the ʿulema ʾ of the Islamic world—to whom I had already been introduced by Francis Robinson at Royal Holloway College, through his study of the learned and saintly Muslim scholars connected with the teaching network of the Farangî Mahall of Lucknow.[6] These were the people I wanted to understand.

"The Philosopher and Society" marked a shift in my thinking that had begun, a year or so earlier, in England. The work of Evans-Pritchard and Mary Douglas had helped me to explain the role of holy persons in terms of their function. They were useful as mediators, objective arbiters, and wielders of local power.[7] But this was not enough to explain their attraction as "presences"—as beloved figures and objects of personal loyalty. Now I had to catch up by exploring the nature of sanctity in widely different environments and in very different religious traditions. What was it that made certain persons loved and respected because they were thought to incorporate the highest expectations of their society?

It was a change of which I was aware at the time. In early February 1979, I received a letter from Franco Bolgiani, the head of the Istituto Erik Peterson in Turin. Franco had been my friend from my first days at the Oxford Patristics Conference of 1963. We had shared our horror at the opaque mass of a Welsh rarebit served to us in the dining hall of Christ Church College.

---

of Science 16 (1978): 153–178. I later used A. J. Friedman and C. C. Douley, *Einstein as Myth and Muse* (Cambridge University Press, 1984).

6. E. Shils, "Charisma, Order, and Status," *American Sociological Review* 30 (1965): 199 ff., now in *Center and Periphery: Essays in Macrosociology* (Chicago: University of Chicago Press, 1975), 256–275.

7. Chapter 58: "Presences."

He now wrote to ask me to explain some aspects of my intellectual itinerary. I wrote back at length on February 27, 1979. Having told him about my relationship with other scholars, such as Marrou, Arnaldo Momigliano, Evans-Pritchard, and Mary Douglas, I ventured to describe—somewhat clumsily, but as best I could—the more recent changes in my own viewpoint.

> For me at least, the 1960s and early 1970s were the age of analysis—of the almost occultist drive to seize, by modern methods, the inner springs and logic of societies and periods that had, previously, seemed impenetrable to us, or [I deliberately added in pen] had been endowed with a false familiarity. Now I think that, for a religious and social historian, the battle on behalf of the *rationale* of the irrational has been won (for the moment at least); and beliefs and actions which we had tried to render transparent with a new intelligibility can take back some of the mass and coloring of real flesh, [so that] we, who had spent so long peering at them through the X-ray machines of modern interdisciplinary interpretations, have [now] to allow them also the opacity of real flesh.

What I wished to communicate to Franco was that I had changed from wishing to know what holiness *meant*—to observe how it functioned—to seize a little of what holiness *was*: how expectations of holiness were built up, internalized, and set to work in a given society.

As a result of this shift of emphasis, two vivid human types—the philosopher and the monk—held my attention. Each seemed to be surrounded by a distinctive "aura" of holiness. The one—the philosopher—seemed to carry in his (and her) person the quintessence of the values of an ancient, classical society that struggled to survive in the changed social and political conditions of the later empire. The other—the Christian monk (and the Christian virgin)—summed up the opposite. They were the harbingers of a new order. Their renunciation of marriage and of wealth were more than individual acts of rebellion. Rather, these renunciations relativized and eventually undermined the ancient bond between the individual and the city, at a time when the city itself had begun to lose its classical profile.

From this time onward, my interests oscillated between the world of the philosophers and the world of the monks and virgins. The next few years would decide as to which of those two worlds I would give most attention. As it turned out, *Body and Society*, on sexual renunciation (which appeared in 1988), came first, and *Power and Persuasion*, where the role of the philosopher and the crisis of the ancient city held center stage, appeared four years later. But both themes were on my mind throughout my early days in America.

Meanwhile I had another debt to pay. This was my debt to a sense of the weight of Islam, which I had carried with me direct from Cairo to Berkeley. The need to come to grips with Islam was made even more pressing by the rapid progress of the Iranian Revolution. This revolution suddenly revealed that, far away in Tehran, forms of religious authority that we had tended to discount entirely in the modern world could suddenly emerge, filling our television screens in real time with figures whose charisma seemed to belong to another age.

THE RETURN OF RELIGION

FROM REVOLUTION TO *ADAB*

My Parents' Visit

The year 1979 was a very happy one for me. My parents visited me at the beginning of the spring term, from April 24 to May 15. They stayed at the Women's Faculty Club, a sumptuous Julia Morgan building. My mother recorded in her diary the lavish American breakfasts where all the guests sat together around the table:

> every nationality—man called Kevin O'Reilly . . . Told him about Peter!
>
> Mad on salads—Avocado Salads, [but] no egg cup . . .
>
> All so friendly, Joe's [Special] San Francisco Fry . . .
>
> Coca Cola, 7 UP..

All these were exotic details, stored up to relate to her sister Freda (my aunt Teedah). She noted many other strange things, such as "jogging" and a yet more unfamiliar notice: "Smoking Prohibited by Law."

In the middle of their stay, we drove out to Jackson, in the Gold Country. This was a half-Italian and half-Irish settlement, where, in the cemetery, four-square classical mausoleums bearing only the family name—such as Sanguinetti—lay beside graves marked by florid shamrocks and Celtic crosses with elaborate Victorian epitaphs. Outside the town hall, the Irish tricolor flew beside the bear flag of California. We stayed in the local hotel, where the bartender was well aware of the habits of the Old Country. No ice-chilled beer for us: "Pardon me, Sir, . . . would you like your Guinness . . . brought up to room temperature?"

My parents even sat in on one of the lectures in my "Byzantium, Persia and the Rise of Islam" course. My mother noted the occasion: "Lecture to about 40 students [about] Zoroastrian Religion. Easy to understand—about 1¼ hours—Irish accent. Bellows of laughter."

They passed through Sproul Plaza on many occasions during the high flood of the noonday break, where the air was slightly golden from tree pollen and the smoke of the falafel stands and charged with the background rhythms of the bongo drums. My parents—my father natty as always in his Donegal tweed jacket—made their way through crowds of young persons in various degrees of drastic undress. A young woman had installed herself, lying upside down, in one of the great stone flowerpots that flanked Sather Gate. Nothing could be seen of her but two long legs, sheathed in bright green tights, swaying to some inner music. Passing this scene, my mother fixed me with the same twinkle in her eye with which she used to fix me, in church, when some particular misdemeanor of King David or the patriarchs was read out in the Old Testament lesson. It was an eye that dared me not to giggle. They loved every minute of their visit and hoped to return the next year.

The Return of Religion

At the time of my parents' visit, the sense of the weight of Islam, which I had carried with me from Cairo to Berkeley, was still with me. It was made that much heavier by events in Iran. Just as I arrived in Berkeley, the landslide of which I had had a vague premonition when traveling in Iran in 1976 gathered momentum. On January 16, 1979, Shah Reza fled the country. On February 1, the Ayatollah Khomeini (1902–1989) returned from exile. Far, far away, across the Sierras, the One Big One—not the earthquake but the Iranian Revolution— was happening.

I was bruised by these events. During my visits to Iran I had noticed widespread discontent with the regime. I had also been struck by the vitality of traditional Islam. But I had never put two and two together. I had never guessed how quickly a political Islam could seize on this discontent and turn it into a revolutionary force.

My colleagues were equally puzzled. Many scholars of the 1960s and 1970s had been fascinated by the phenomenon of revolution. There were any number of theoretical models of different sorts of revolutions. But none of them were motivated by religion. Revolutions—in the modern world, at least— were assumed to be secular phenomena, driven by secular ideologies. The return of religion as a revolutionary force was like the return of a ghost.

The Islamic Revolution effectively debarred me from travel to Iran in the foreseeable future. My scheme for a book on the confrontation of Byzantium and Iran in the manner of Braudel had to be dropped. Yet, like my earlier project for a study of the Byzantine Balkans, the venture had greatly enriched my historical imagination and continued to influence my teaching.

At the same time, the memory of my contact with Islamic countries, in Iran and Egypt, lingered with me as a constant challenge. I felt that I still needed to understand societies whose social conditions and codes of behavior (notably but by no means exclusively on the issue of sex and the position of women) seemed so very different from those of modern America and Europe. I would now have to explore these issues not by travel but through books, by stints of careful reading of classical and early Christian texts in the Classics Seminar Room of Dow Library and in the library of the Graduate Theological Union. I had to return to the ancient world, to late antiquity, and to the early church; but I would do so with a sense of the seriousness of these issues that drew on my own experience of the Islamic world.

QUR'ÂNIC READINGS: HAMID ALGAR

For this reason, I persevered with learning Arabic. I signed up to attend a graduate seminar on Qur'ânic Arabic, which ran in the fall and winter terms of 1978/79. The course consisted of working our way through assigned parts of the *Tafsîr al-Jalâlayn—The Commentary of the Two Jalâls*. The *Tafsîr* was a massive commentary on the Qur'ân by two scholars of the fifteenth century—Jalâl al-Din al-Mahalli, and his pupil, Jalâl al-Din al-Suyuti. It remained a standard work in the Islamic world up to modern times. Indeed, it was so well known that I had already bought a copy in Cairo.

Little did I know when I signed up that, by so doing, I would find myself in a ringside seat for the unfolding of the revolution in Iran. The seminar was given by Hamid Algar, a convert to Islam and a staunch supporter of the ayatollah. He was one of the few Western scholars to draw attention to the ayatollah and to challenge the bland consensus that had encouraged experts on Iran to write off the religious opposition to the shah as a thing of the past. Now it looked as if his dark horse was about to win.[1]

---

1. Hamid Algar, "The Oppositional Role of the Ulama in Twentieth-Century Iran," in *Scholars, Saints, and Sufis: Muslim Religious Institutions the Middle East since 1500*, ed. Nikki R. Keddie (Berkeley: University of California Press, 1972), 231–255.

The Arabic class that met in Algar's office took place very much in the shadow of the ayatollah. A large photograph of Khomenei (the first I had ever seen) dominated the room. I even had a dream about the ayatollah, in December 1978, just before his return from Paris to Tehran. He was sitting, Iranian-style, on the floor in a corner of his apartment in Neauphle-le-Château, outside Paris. Speaking in French, he assured me that, by the end of the quarter, I would have read the entire Surat al-Baqara—among the longest chapters of the Qur'ân. He was right. I did complete the sura. On opening my copy of the *Tafsîr* just now, I see that I had carefully marked in red ink the numbers of the verses of the sura, so as to distinguish them from the learned commentary in which they were embedded.

Paideia and Adab: The Well-Constructed Life

Though I abandoned my projected study of Sasanian Iran, I was greatly attracted by the prospect of studying the Islamic world in harness with the world of late antiquity. I realized that I could do this on a topic directly related to my current work on the role of the late antique philosopher in the elite culture of his times. The nature and function of the rigorous education in the classics, known as *paideia*, had been central to my view of the role of the philosopher in society. The medieval and modern Islamic world seemed to offer a comparable phenomenon, known as *adab*. Like *paideia*, *adab* was about the intimate relationship between a tradition of teaching and a process of moral grooming. Here there was a real chance of making meaningful comparisons between two traditional educational systems and the types of human excellence that they fostered.

Adab carried a weight in the Islamic world similar to that of *paideia* in the Greco-Roman world. It represented a peak of human achievement, and insisted that this peak could be reached by the privileged few—through education and through following exacting codes of deportment modeled on the behavior of exemplary persons. In the words of my Berkeley colleague Barbara Metcalf, *adab* was based on "the concept of the well-constructed life."[2]

The notion of the "well-constructed life" had come to hold a particular fascination for me when I dealt with the moralists of the Roman Empire and their elite readers. These moralists challenged members of the elites to put their lives in order by self-discipline and by recourse to trusted mentors. I wondered

---

2. Barbara Metcalf, preface to *Moral Conduct and Authority: The Place of Adab in South Asian Islam*, ed. Barbara Daly Metcalf (Berkeley: University of California Press, 1984), vii.

how a similar system of moral grooming worked in another major civilization, that of Islam.

Hence my enthusiasm when Barbara Metcalf asked me to contribute to a conference that she had organized: "Moral Conduct and Authority. The Place of *Adab* in South Asian Islam." The conference took place in June 1979. I contributed a paper entitled "Late Antiquity and Islam: Parallels and Contrasts." I compared the "civilization of *paideia*" with its Islamic analogue, in order to show how our understanding of the one might enrich our understanding of the other.[3]

THE CIVILIZATION OF *PAIDEIA*

Islam, like late antiquity, had long been buried by Western historians under a pile of prejudices. The civilization of *paideia* in Hellenistic and Roman times had frequently been dismissed as decadent because of the extreme conservatism of the classical education on which it was based. Medieval and even modern Islam were dismissed in the same way. Islamic learning was presented as irremediably "traditionalist" and backward-looking. Compared with post-Renaissance Europe, Islam was deemed to have missed the bus of progress. It seemed to be frozen by its reverence for the past, as if history had stopped with the Golden Age of the Caliphate of Baghdad, in the ninth century, and as if all the rest was a decline.

But was this the case? Such a negative presentation of the culture of Islam challenged me, once again, to unpick the narrative of Western progress that cast a shadow over entire periods (such as late antiquity) and over major non-European civilizations (such as medieval and modern Islam).

So what had this "traditionalism" really meant: was it necessarily a sign of decay? I knew the answer for the Greco-Roman world. It had been given by Henri-Irénée Marrou in his magisterial *History of Education in Antiquity*. This book contained a magnificent evocation of the aims and significance of traditional education in the Greco-Roman world, as it had persisted along the shores of the Mediterranean for over eight hundred years:

> It is a mistake to say, as is often said by its detractors, that it was "born with its head back to front," looking back to the past. It is not autumnal, tormented with nostalgic regrets for a vanished spring. On the contrary, it looks upon itself as firmly established in an unchanging present, in the full

3. Peter Brown, "Late Antiquity and Islam: Parallels and Contrasts," in *Moral Conduct and Authority*, 23–37.

blaze of a hot summer sun. It knows what mighty reserves it possesses, what past masters it has had. The fact that these appeared at certain moments of time, under the influence of certain historical forces, is unimportant; what matters is that they exist and can be rediscovered in the same way, again and again, by each successive generation.[4]

Scholars interested in Islamic *adab* found that the same, unexpected resources existed in the seemingly unchanging traditionalism of the Muslim schools. At the conference, Francis Robinson described the present-day attitudes of the learned families connected with the Farangî Mahall of Lucknow in very similar terms to those used by Marrou for the products of *paideia* in the long centuries of the Hellenistic and Roman worlds. Guided by "a vision of a perfect and well-formed life, they live with their ancestors." Francis went on to show how, far from cramping their activities, this adherence to codes of *adab* rooted in the past gave them a rare independence of mind and action with which to face the political storms that accompanied the emergence of modern India and Pakistan.[5]

PAIDEIA, ADAB, AND THE FEAR OF GOD

But Islamic *adab* and late antique *paideia* differed from each other in one crucial respect. *Paideia* had been created by humans for humans. It was the creation of the Greek city and of the intense peer culture of the civic elites. Its sanctions were purely human—shame and loss of authority among one's fellows. Unlike Christianity and Islam, it had no room for supernatural rewards and punishments.

On this issue, an entire world separated Greek *paideia* from the fear of Hell that was supposed to motivate both the good Muslim and the good Christian. In the blunt words of John Chrysostom, deportment alone was not enough. There was only so much that the grooming of *paideia* could do: "How shall we tie down this wild beast [adolescent sexual urges]? How shall we place a bridle upon it? I know none, save only the restraint of hell-fire."[6]

---

4. H. I. Marrou, *A History of Education in Antiquity*, trans. G. Lamb (New York: Sheed and Ward, 1956), 161, cited in Brown, "Late Antiquity and Islam," in *Moral Conduct and Authority*, 24.

5. F. Robinson, "The ʿUlamâ ʾ of Farangî Mahall and Their *Adab*," in *Moral Conduct and Authority*, 152–183, at 161.

6. John Chrysostom, *On Vainglory*, trans. M.L.W. Laistner, in *Christianity and Classical Culture* (Ithaca, NY: Cornell University Press, 1961), 117.

That fear was supposed to rest on every Muslim. The Muslim philosopher al-Ghazali (1059–1111) described how the eighth-century Muslim mystic al-Hasan al-Basrî let his glass fall at the thought of how the damned in Hell cried to the souls in Paradise for one drop of water. When it came to the nature of human motivation, John, an Antiochene Christian of the fourth century, stood closer to a Muslim of the early Middle Ages, such as al-Hasan al-Basrî, than he did to his own teacher, the pagan exponent of *paideia*—Libanius of Antioch (314–393).

With the fear of Hell, something very new had entered the world of *paideia*, and its future lay not only in Christianity but in the long centuries of Islam. How had this drastic change in the imagination of the classical world come about? Furthermore: How did the moral codes that emerged from this revolution come to differ from each other in significant ways?

By way of conclusion, I suggested that these differences should be studied more intently. Why, for instance, was it the case that, in late antiquity and the Middle Ages, Christian codes of excellence came to place so great an emphasis on issues of sexual continence? Muslim *adab*, by contrast, seemed to privilege less icy virtues: it was a distinctly this-worldly, even world-affirming, code. Muslims seemed to regard marital sex (and even sex with slave concubines) as unproblematic. They reached out to catch almost any human activity, sacred or profane—from intercourse to war—under a fine net of Islamic propriety: each and all of these activities were performed beneath the eye of God, who bestowed a measured blessing on them all. I suggested that the time had come for an attempt to understand the parting of the ways in the sexual codes of Christians, Jews, and Muslims—a problem calculated to engage scholars of late antiquity, Islam, and the Western Middle Ages in a common venture.

Life Is Ceremony

In Barbara Metcalf's conference, many of these questions were hammered out by Islamicists and experts on southern Asia. The conference was something of a high-water mark. As in many successful conferences on Islam at this time, it was marked by "a sense of something like wonder" at the discovery of so much richness and resilience in a great civilization that we had neglected for so long.[7] The participants rallied to appreciate a world so very different from our own. They approved of *adab*, much as I approved of *paideia*. In the words

7. Metcalf, preface to *Moral Conduct and Authority*, viii.

of Ira Lapidus, in an enthusiastic overview of the notion of the human person implied in the cultivation of *adab*, we were attracted to the idea that "life itself is a work of art. . . . [that] Life is ceremony."[8]

OUTER ACT AND INWARD SELF

Looking back, I am struck by the extent to which the conference highlighted the positive role of ceremonious codes of behavior practiced by the elites of ancient empires, and stressed the manner in which many of these codes had survived into modern times in the Islamic world.

Many contributions to the conference set out to recover the warmth and the weight of the interpersonal bonds of friendship and discipleship on which Islamic education depended. Above all, in appreciating *adab*, they validated a psychology which assumed that the human person was open to a grooming of the self through external rituals that reached deep into the person. As Barbara Metcalf pointed out: the proponents of *adab* assumed "a subtle relationship between the outer act and the inward self," which led them to stress the role of "habit or *malaka* through which outer action transforms and colors the soul."[9] Such a view placed a "high valuation on the employment of will."[10] For someone like myself, who had spent many years grappling with the dark sayings of Saint Augustine on the weakness of the will and the unpredictability of the movements of the inner life, the Islam of *adab* seemed, quite frankly, refreshingly, deliciously Pelagian.

It was here that the study of the forms of leadership exercised by teachers and mystics in the Islamic world converged directly on my study of the "saints of *paideia*" in late antiquity. I was led to qualify the volcanic notion of charisma associated with the thought of Max Weber. I found that I was dealing with the bearers of a quiet charisma—with poised persons, whose very absence of dramatic stances enabled them to guide an entire society. They did not do this by being spectacular "outsiders"—as my Syrian holy men had been—but by the unruffled confidence with which they summed up, in their own persons, the central values of the society that they helped to direct. Philosophers in late

---

8. Ira Lapidus, "Knowledge, Virtue and Action: The Classical Muslim Concept of *Adab* and the Nature of Religious Fulfillment in Islam," in *Moral Conduct and Authority*, 38–61, at 57.

9. Metcalf, introduction to *Moral Conduct and Authority*, 10.

10. Metcalf, introduction to *Moral Conduct and Authority*, 3.

antiquity, pious men of learning in Islam: both represented human types worthy of admiration and of careful study.

As for me, personally, it was a relaxed moment. I linked up with English friends who had been invited to the conference. Francis Robinson came, fresh from the excitement of beginning his work on the private archives of the Farangî Mahall. Along with Simon Digby (1932–2010), with his long wisps of pure-white beard that floated in the air like those of a peculiarly raffish Sufi, we sat sipping gin on a hummock of chamomile flowers studded with bright yellow buttons, as in a Mughal miniature, at the top of Tilden Park. As Simon and I talked about what it was like to have grown up for part of the time "abroad"—he in India, I in Sudan—we looked out, eastward, away from the bay and toward the inner valley, to Mount Diablo and a light-gold landscape as exquisitely shaped as the Tuscan background to a painting by Piero della Francesca.

POVERTY AND POWER

ÉVELYNE PATLAGEAN AND
PAUL VEYNE

Under New Skies

It is an amiable myth that a move to a new academic environment in a new country must inevitably be accompanied by a great leap forward into some entirely new academic enterprise. This is not always the case. Old themes often take on a new interest when looked at under new skies. Comfortably surrounded by so many familiar books and journals in the Classics Seminar Room in Dow Library, I found myself going back to old topics with delight, as I discovered different aspects of them as a result of exposure to the new intellectual environment of Berkeley campus. In my reading and in my preparation for teaching, l lingered on themes that I had known almost since my undergraduate days in Oxford—on the end of paganism, on the city of Rome, on the nature of the late Roman state.

There was one topic to which I now returned with particular urgency owing to my recent experiences in Iran and in Egypt: that was the issue of poverty and its relation to the exercise of power in the later Roman Empire. I had brought from Cairo a sense of the weight of Islam and also a sense of the weight of poverty. The poverty of Cairo had left me bruised.

I could not rid myself of the thought of the Lazarus (the poor beggar at the rich man's gate) who seemed to lie at the door of the privileged West. For this reason I turned increasingly to the topic of poverty and the care of the poor in the later empire. My first years at Berkeley coincided with a period of intensive reading, on my part, of two great French scholars whose work on the charged themes of poverty and power has influenced me from that time up to the present: Évelyne Patlagean (1932–2008) and Paul Veyne (1930–2022). Many years before, when I wrote my biography of Augustine, I had turned to France; and now I turned to France again. There I found a tradition of social and cultural history of the ancient and late antique world that I found nowhere else.

ÉVELYNE PATLAGEAN: THE FACE OF POVERTY

I had known Évelyne since 1970. We had been brought together by Arnaldo Momigliano, who admired her greatly for her deep knowledge of Italy, where, he told me, she had once traveled through the Mezzogiorno along with a group of puppeteers. He also appreciated her work on early Byzantine Judaism. She belonged to a Russian Jewish family from the Black Sea area that had settled in Istanbul and had eventually made their way to France. Her surname—Patlagean—was striking. *Patlıcan* meant aubergine/eggplant in Turkish. Arnaldo and her other Italian friends would always speak of her as Signora Melanzana.

At the time, I found that Évelyne's academic stance was peculiarly reassuring. She was, in many ways, a rogue Byzantinist. Though her dissertation was on the life of the poor in the Eastern Empire, she pursued it by taking the seminars of Western medievalists—Jacques Le Goff, and the famous seminar on medieval poverty directed by Michel Mollat (1911–1996). At a time when Byzantine scholarship had tended to turn in on itself, her intellectual trajectory showed that Byzantium and the West could be joined creatively in the work of a single scholar.

On the prompting of Arnaldo, she first wrote to me on October 4, 1970, enclosing two very different articles: "Ancienne hagiographie byzantine et histoire sociale" and "Sur la limitation de la fécondité dans la haute époque byzantine." These two articles had established her reputation as a gifted interpreter of the social imagination of the Eastern Empire. She also drew attention to the grim realities of increasing poverty caused by the sheer mass of population pressing against the rigid structures of the ancient economy. In Évelyne's opinion, it was this grinding demographic pressure that brought about deep changes in the social structure and in the self-image of late Roman society.[1]

---

1. Évelyne Patlagean, "Ancienne hagiographie byzantine et histoire sociale," *Annales* (1968): 106–126, translated as "Ancient Byzantine Hagiography and Social History," in *Saints and Their Cults: Studies in Religious Sociology, Folklore and History*, ed. Stephen Williams (Cambridge

Évelyne came to London in 1971, and John Matthews and I invited her to talk at a seminar in Oxford. She spoke in a flawless English of the 1940s. She had derived this, she told us, from an English nanny of the old school, who had looked after her while she and her parents were in hiding from the Nazis in Antibes during the war. Her sheer presence as a scholar and a person impressed us all. She was the first person to whom I gave a publisher's advance copy of *The World of Late Antiquity*. Deeply generous and formidably well organized, she would lavish suggestions and bibliographies on me—both for myself and for my students—often suggesting lines of research that have only just now begun to be explored.

THE BODY IMAGE OF AN EMPIRE

These articles led up to a masterpiece that appeared in 1977: *Pauvreté économique et pauvreté sociale à Byzance: 4ᵉ–7ᵉ siècles*. This book offered nothing less than a new vision of the society of the East Roman Empire in late antiquity.[2]

In the past decade or so, much progress had been made in the study of late Roman society. The masterwork of A.H.M. Jones, *The Later Roman Empire: A Social, Economic and Administrative Survey*, had rested on the shelves of scholars for over ten years. In this monument of inspired common sense, the great dinosaur of the later empire had been pieced together, bone by bone, in a comprehensive survey. But the skeleton of the dinosaur of late Roman society had lacked one dimension. How did the dinosaur view itself: what was its body image; how did it categorize the constituent groups of which it was composed?

It was Évelyne who first drew attention to the way in which the body image of Roman society underwent a drastic change in the course of the fourth and

---

University Press, 1983), 101—121; and "Sur la limitation de la fécondité dans la haute époque byzantine," *Annales* (1969): 1353–1396.

On the work of Évelyne Patlagean, see now É. Patlagean, "Sorting Out Late Antique Poverty in Paris in the 60s," in *The Past before Us: The Challenge of Historiographies in Late Antiquity*, ed. C. Straw and R. Lim, Bibliothèque de l'Antiquité Tardive: Monographies 6 (Turnhout: Brepols, 2004), 79–87; and B. Flusin, "Récit de sainteté, famille et société: Évelyne Patlagean et l'hagiographie," in *Les réseaux familiaux. Antiquité tardive et moyen âge. In memoriam A. Laiou et É. Patlagean*, ed. B. Caseau, Centre de recherche d'histoire et civilisation de Byzance: Monographies 37 (Paris: Centre d'histoire et civilization de Byzance, 2012), 113–124.

2. É. Patlagean, *Pauvreté économique et pauvreté sociale à Byzance: 4ᵉ–7ᵉ siècles*, École des Hautes Études en sciences sociales: Civilisations et Sociétés 48 (Paris/Le Haye: Mouton, 1977).

fifth centuries. Put very briefly: in classical times, the more privileged inhabitants of the empire (those who provided most of the evidence for the modern social historian) thought of themselves as living in a commonwealth of cities. For them, the truly important divisions in their society were civic ones. Free citizens were sharply distinguished from foreigners and slaves. The inhabitants of the countryside (the vast majority of the population) were kept at a distance from the citizen body that was considered to be the core of the city. In classical times, these civic distinctions had been defended on behalf of a strictly delimited number of the overall population—the citizens in the cities—with the same tenacity as citizen entitlements to medical care and other benefits are defended today on the strength of the possession of a passport or a green card.

Then, according to Évelyne, this system broke down in the course of the fourth and fifth centuries, leaving the inhabitants of the Mediterranean to look at the world around them with disabused eyes. They ceased to think of themselves as living in a world made up of groups of persons divided one from the other by civic categories—citizen/noncitizen, free/slave. They put on, as it were, new spectacles—spectacles that enabled them to see Roman society as a whole in its gray immensity, as brutally divided in frankly economic terms— in town and countryside alike—between the rich and the poor. In a fundamental, silent revolution, late Roman society's image of itself changed: the classical Greco-Roman world of cities and of citizen entitlement awoke to the massive presence of the poor.

To See the Poor

How this fundamental change in the social imagination of the ancient world took place, and what were its consequences, constituted the subject of Évelyne's remarkable book. In her opinion, it had happened under the pressure of an explosion of population in the countryside and a consequent, massive immigration into the cities: "Everything happened as if the ancient frameworks of social organization had slowly burst open . . . and poverty appeared in its nakedness . . . stripped of the civic veil with which Rome had been able to cover it."[3] This great change in perception (coinciding as it did with headlong political and social developments) brought the ancient world to an end in the eastern Mediterranean, and ushered in the Christian society of the Byzantine Middle Ages.

3. Patlagean, *Pauvreté*, 429.

Patlagean's *Pauvreté* was a triumph of the historian's art. It dealt with East Roman society as a whole, on every level, in the manner of the *histoire totale* advocated by Fernand Braudel. I have always regretted that it was never translated into English as Siân Reynolds had translated Braudel's *Méditerranée*. In the manner of Braudel, this work offered a comprehensive vision of the life of the East Roman poor, drawing on evidence of every kind, interpreted with the greatest skill. Had it been translated, it would have entered the bloodstream of English-language scholarship on the society of the later empire.

"The Strange and Brief Moment"

What struck me most, as I made my way through this great book, was Évelyne's compassion. Behind her austere insistence on the economic and demographic aspects of late Roman poverty, it always seemed to me that she was unusually open to the pathos of the poor and to the "faceless ones" who haunted the pages of the early Byzantine lives of the saints and filled the courtyards of the great urban basilicas with moaning crowds. She knew what it was for Byzantines to weep.[4] She understood the paradox by which Byzantine civilization, though distrustful of the body, nonetheless showed an "obsessive compassion for the suffering bodies of others."[5]

Above all, Évelyne could catch the thrill of a world where the old structures had begun to "burst" and new human possibilities were glimpsed, if only for a moment, at the turning of an age. It is not surprising that she should also have studied, at this time, radical themes in early Byzantine hagiography. Her article "The Woman Disguised as a Monk" was one of the earliest and the most perceptive studies of what was then a daring topic.[6] She conjured up with electrifying vividness a world turned upside down by subversive forms of renunciation—by women who shaved off their hair, adopted male dress, joined male monasteries, or wandered through the countryside in the company of holy men. Far from being aberrant, these gestures "bear witness to the strange and brief moment of liberty that the fourth century experienced, in the interval between two civilizations."[7]

4. É. Patlagean, "Pleurer à Byzance," in *Cahiers de Varsovie* (Warsaw: Warsaw University Press, 1988), 251–261.

5. Patlagean, *Pauvreté*, 429.

6. É. Patlagean, "L'histoire de la femme déguisée en moine et l'évolution de la sainteté féminine à Byzance," *Studi medievali*, ser. 3, 17 (1976): 597–623.

7. Patlagean, *Pauvreté*, 130.

It was this acute sense of the changing of an age, due to the weakening of the ancient city's imaginative grip, that drew me to Évelyne's work at this time. It gave me the concrete background against which to place the holy persons of late antiquity. It cast into high relief the role of the pagan philosopher as a "saint of *paideia*." Philosophers stood for an ancient civic order, for the world of well-groomed urban notables, which was buckling under the pressure of the immigrant poor.

By contrast, in a society now perceived as divided, in town and country alike, by the primal economic binary of rich and poor, radical Christians gained the upper hand, as Christian holy men, Christian monks, and Christian bishops rose to prominence through charitable activities and through a symbolic identification with the downtrodden and the oppressed. Outreach to the poor was their way to the top of a civic world that had previously turned to philosophers for guidance. It was in this way that the Eastern Empire became Christian.

I look back to my first reading of Évelyne's *Pauvreté* as a decisive branching of the ways in my own work, away from the exclusive study of holy men and other kinds of late antique holy figures, toward continued involvement with the wider issues of wealth and poverty. But to understand what I first made of my reading of *Pauvreté*, I would have to add the work of another great French scholar, a master of intellectual surprises: Paul Veyne, whose *Le pain et le cirque*—Bread and Circuses—I read alongside Évelyne's masterpiece.

Paul Veyne: The Unfamiliarity of the Past

In contrast to my decadelong friendship with Évelyne Patlagean, I had known nothing of the work of Paul Veyne until my arrival at Berkeley. I first encountered him through his massive book *Le pain et le cirque*, which had appeared in 1976. I devoured *Le pain et le cirque* for days on end in the Classics Seminar Room in Dow Library, piling onto my table the texts and studies to which Veyne referred in a never-failing torrent of erudition enriched by daring comparative studies.[8]

Veyne's work overlapped with that of Évelyne Patlagean on many topics— on Roman perceptions of poverty, for instance, and on the difference between

---

8. P. Veyne, *Le pain et le cirque. Sociologie historique d'un pluralisme politique* (Paris: Le Seuil, 1976). Abridged English translation by Brian Pearce with introduction by Oswyn Murray, *Bread and Circuses: Historical Sociology and Political Pluralism* (London: Allen Lane, Penguin, 1990). I will use the English translations from this volume.

classical forms of civic benefaction (summed up in the title, *Bread and Circuses*) and the Jewish and Christian notion of charity. But this was not the only reason that I read *Le pain et le cirque*. It was also because I had found in Veyne a fellow militant for the unfamiliarity of the past.

Veyne went out of his way to drive home, at every point, the strangeness of the classical world. He insisted that Romans were not versions of ourselves, dressed up in togas: they were irreducibly exotic. Institutions and emotions that seem continuous with our own sensibilities, such as marriage and love, were profoundly different from what they are nowadays. "Roman" marriage and "Roman" love (even Roman love poetry) were as distant from us as were marriage and love in the aristocratic Japan of Lady Murasaki.

In *Comment on écrit l'histoire* (a short book that preceded *Le pain et le cirque*) Veyne had·nailed his colors to the mast.[9] He insisted that the duty of the historian was to seize the irreducible singularity of the past. Why, for instance, did the Romans not speak, as we do, of a "blue" sky, but of a *caelum serenum*—a "serene" sky, with all the overtones of an atmosphere troubled or made peaceful by the presence of the gods?[10] A worldview entirely different from our own was implied in that single adjective, *serenum*. As for the Romans themselves: "If the Romans are somewhat boring to the public, it is because we make them into a people identified with the highest values [un peuple-valeur] instead of seeing how exotic they were."[11]

PAIDEIA AND POWER

It was in this fighting mood that Veyne turned, in his *Le pain et le cirque*, to one of the most distinctive aspects of the classical city—the tradition of lavish giving by the rich to their own cities, which he called "civic euergetism." Civic euergetism had accompanied the growth of Greek-style cities in every part of the Mediterranean and the Middle East. Veyne brought to the study of this well-known institution his fierce talent for seizing the oddity of the ancient world—a talent displayed over 730 pages, with 60 pages of endnotes!

But it was not the grand phenomenon of Greek and Roman euergetism that impressed me most when I was reading Veyne. It was his remarks on the

9. P. Veyne, *Comment on écrit l'histoire* (Paris: Gallimard, 1971); translated as *Writing History: An Essay in Epistemology* (Middletown, CT: Wesleyan University Press, 1984), from which I will cite.

10. Veyne, *Writing History*, 15.

11. Veyne, *Writing History*, 44.

exercise of power in Roman society. Discussing the leaders of the Greco-Roman cities and the role of the emperor in his own city (the city of Rome), Veyne led the reader through a prolonged debate on the nature of the authority that the great—be they civic notables or crowned rulers—exercised over their subjects or dependents. I followed this debate intently. For what Veyne was proposing was a richer view of the exercise of power in the ancient world than that provided by the largely institutional accounts which had been current among ancient historians.

In that sense, Veyne's *Le pain et le cirque* was very much a book of the 1970s. His discussion of the exercise of power in the Roman world echoed the studies of ritual and society (largely in early modern Europe) which had shown that the levers of power in a society were not necessarily to be found only in its institutional structures, but in the "soft power" of its rituals as well. Veyne showed that this was also the case with Roman emperors. His insights (lavishly scattered throughout the pages and exuberant footnotes of *Le pain et le cirque*) provided me with a new grammar of politics in the ancient world.

Above all, Veyne's emphasis on the highly personalized nature of the exercise of power helped me to understand the role of *paideia* in the politics of the later empire. It explained the way in which the elites of the empire hoped to tame their emperors. Far from being mere ropes of silk, the restraints placed on upper-class behavior by education, and by the codes of decorum generated by the "civilization of *paideia*," were expected to hold even emperors.

Paideia acted as an "unwritten constitution." In the chilling absence of legal restraints on the exercise of power in the Roman world, moral pressure and a sense of decorum were all that remained. Hence the constant vetting of the personal character of each emperor in histories of the period. These accounts were not passing on idle tittle-tattle. They reflected the fear of the elites as they scanned their rulers with anxious eyes, looking for telltale signs of graciousness or savagery.

In this way, my reading of Veyne helped me to understand the enduring role allotted to the philosopher in the public imagination of the later empire. For in this highly personalized system, the philosopher could intervene as a mentor and a giver of good advice. As Veyne pointed out: "The notion of 'counsel', sometimes forgotten by the moderns, enjoyed for a thousand years an importance equal to that of representative democracy nowadays."[12] And it was the philosopher, with his reputation for moral courage and commitment

---

12. Veyne, *Bread and Circuses*, 404.

to speaking the truth, who could be treated as the bearer of the most precious political elixir of all—"good counsel" in high places.

To read Paul Veyne was to drink strong wine at midday. If ever there was a book that offered me an abundance of new insights into some of the old themes of Roman history, it was his *Bread and Circuses*. Our scholarly interchange would prove important for me in the next few years. Along with Évelyne Patlagean's *Pauvreté*, Veyne's *Bread and Circuses* gave me the impetus to continue work on philosophers and monks, and then on bishops and the poor, that would last me until the writing of *Power and Persuasion* (in 1992) and *Poverty and Leadership in the Later Roman Empire* (in 2002).[13]

So much for the readings that influenced me decisively in my first years at Berkeley. But what about the largely novel American teaching system that I encountered on campus?

---

13. Peter Brown, *Power and Persuasion in Late Antiquity: Towards a Christian Empire* (Madison: University of Wisconsin Press, 1992) and *Poverty and Leadership in the Later Roman Empire* (Hanover, NH: University Press of New England, 2002). For a brilliant summary of the issues, see now Brent Shaw, "Charity and the Poor in Roman Imperial Society," *Religion in the Roman Empire* 6 (2020): 229–267.

TEACHING

THE ELECTIVE COURSE SYSTEM

My return to older themes was greatly helped by my teaching. At that time, teaching in the American system was, for me, a venture into almost totally unknown territory. In Oxford (and also, if to a lesser degree, in Royal Holloway College) I was used to teaching undergraduates only, who were preparing to take a final examination in one subject (or at most a double subject) only. I would do this mainly in face-to-face tutorials. It was a narrow one-way street, taken by one kind of student only. Graduates were outside that system. Although a few seminars were provided for them (which became increasingly important in the 1970s), I met them mainly as if I were their private tutor.

By contrast, Berkeley offered me a spread of students and of teaching situations as generous, but often as baffling in its variety, as the many-laned freeways of the West Coast to which I had only begun to become accustomed. By English standards, the undergraduates seemed to enjoy a limitless freedom. They could switch lanes every term, trying out courses on any number of subjects in the humanities and the sciences, until they finally decided on their "major"; and even this decision did not limit them to one subject alone.

This was the elective course system, which came as a total novelty to me. Unlike the timorous concentration on a single subject, to which I had been accustomed in Oxford and London, the elective course system was a tribute to the robust Scottish Enlightenment belief in a "democracy of the intellect" where anybody could, in theory, study anything, combining science and the humanities in such a way as to produce the well-rounded, modern person. Enterprising undergraduates zoomed in and out of lanes, mixing courses from all over campus—history and languages, physics and classics, and so on.

These bold knights of the road were taught in lecture courses, in classes, and (at the senior level) in seminars at which attendance was mandatory, and in which their performance was graded every term. Despite the close links that some undergraduates could establish with their professors and teaching assistants, a tutorial system was out of the question.

Unlike the undergraduates, the graduate students had a highly privileged lane of their own. I would meet them every week, face-to-face, in the sort of intensive, highly professional seminars that had impressed me greatly when I first came to Berkeley in 1975. Hence the juxtaposition of two different kinds of teaching, each of which I was free to develop to its fullness: large lectures and classes on big subjects; small, intense gatherings (mainly of graduate students) around single problems and single bodies of texts.

For all its complexity, this system set me free. No longer constrained by the need to prepare students for the grand finale of a single, final examination, whose contents were set down by a rigid syllabus, I was the complete master of my own courses. I could teach what I liked in the way that I liked. I set the tests and the final examinations, and graded the end-of-term papers, assigning a grade for the course as a whole (though often with the help of a TA—a teaching assistant, who was usually a graduate student). In three quarters, it was possible to teach up to six entire courses, each on a different subject. Compared with these bold ventures in teaching wide themes, my principal graduate course was long and slow: a truly serious matter, it took two quarters—a full twenty weeks, which enabled a high degree of specialization and gave time for learning the languages necessary for research.

THE MILLRACE

Compared with England, my teaching load was remarkably light; but the pace of teaching itself was hectic. Berkeley functioned on the quarter system. Classes were held and lectures were delivered in three separate blocks of ten weeks each—fall, winter, and spring. In those three, relatively short periods, the elective course system flowed at the speed of a millrace—indeed, with the force of turbines turned by a mighty dam. Despite the relaxed atmosphere of a campus dotted with eucalyptus groves, crisscrossed by floating skateboarders, with music always playing in its public squares, the massive buildings themselves hummed with awe-inspiring educational resolve. Courses were chosen and registered through the omnipresent IBM cards—mysterious tokens of a commitment to a particular course at a particular time and place, chosen from a mind-stretching range of available choices.

Teaching rooms were allotted according to intricate schedules that varied from department to department. There was an element of stock-car racing in this process. Clashes were frequent. As a professor in two departments, I was doubly at risk. Once I received a cheery note from the organizing secretary of the Classics Department, written in an elegant calligraphic script:

> Classics 155 can fit into 102 Wheeler Tuesday-Thursday 3.30–5.
>
> However, Tuesday 3.30–5 has been set aside by Mr Murgia for faculty meetings . . . I will let you confront him with that.
>
> It will also conflict with Latin 150, Sallust, but I doubt that creates any problems.
>
> Good luck.

I needed it. The course itself could be taught in any building on campus. If I remember correctly, I once taught "Byzantium, Persia and the Rise of Islam" in the Chemistry Building, surrounded by gigantic models of atomic particles.

Course Offerings

Faced with this new freedom, I splurged. I taught lecture courses and seminars on topics that interested me. I would often teach the same subject on two levels. Thus the undergraduate lecture course "Byzantium, Persia and the Rise of Islam" (which my mother had attended) doubled with a graduate seminar: "The World of Procopius" (the major historian of Byzantine-Persian relations in the age of Justinian).

Looking back, I note that it was here, in my teaching, that I allowed myself to feel the tug of my English past in the direction of reassuringly old-fashioned topics: Society and the Supernatural, Julian the Apostate, From Pagan to Christian in Rome, Augustine and His Age. In these courses, it was a joy to communicate with a new freshness, to American students on the West Coast, themes that I had already developed over the years in Oxford and Royal Holloway. In this way, my course offerings were a lifeline to my past at a time when I was venturing into many new territories in my research.

This worked very well for my duties in the History Department. But I was also a member of the Classics Department. And classics meant the teaching of texts—and, at the graduate level, this involved the careful reading and stylistic analysis of the Old Masters in Latin and Greek. As a professor in classics as well as in history, I was expected to offer a course on a major Latin text. Not surprisingly, I chose the *Confessions* of Augustine.

Teaching the *Confessions* turned out to be a major test of nerves. Confronted with a class of keen graduate students, mainly in classics and comparative literature, I suddenly realized that I knew the *Confessions* inside out—but I did so only as a historian, instinctively looking at it for evidence of Augustine's life and times. I had never expounded it as a masterpiece of Latin prose. I had been like a window cleaner, wiping a pane of glass until I could see through it into the fourth century. Now I was expected to be a chemist, and to analyze the texture of the glass itself. I had to know how to parse each sentence in correct grammatical terms.

To make matters worse, many of the graduate students had just taken the Latin language summer course for which Berkeley was famous. This was an awesomely intensive course in Latin grammar—a veritable boot camp in which, so it was rumored, marriages were shattered and breakdowns occurred under the pressure to take on board the entire Latin language in ten weeks flat.

For successful survivors, grammar was the Queen of the Sciences, much as it had been in the early Middle Ages. And rightly so. They had worked for it. It stuck out in their minds like a rib cage. By contrast, I realized that I had read Augustine's entrancing Latin for so long that I took it for granted. I had to rummage in my memory for the grammatical terms with which to analyze it.

This happened in the winter term, when Berkeley was swept by warm gusts of monsoon-like rain. The class took place half underground, in a clammy basement room, with a half-submerged window to the outside. A student had brought his dog to class—a large, long hunting dog. The dog was left outside. But devoted to its master (or—who knows?—maybe it was devoted to the Latin language: we agreed that one could never tell with a Berkeley dog), it pushed its head beneath the window into the room. As a result, the torrential rain splashed down on its tail, ran along its spine and over its head, so as to drip relentlessly from its nose into the room. Altogether, this was a low moment in the history of the passing on of the classical tradition.

The Call of the North

I soon came to teach the lecture course—History 4B—that offered an outline of the history of the first millennium AD from Augustus to the age of the Vikings. This was attended by around three hundred undergraduates and a few interested graduate students. This grand survey made me aware of how much I had always depended (both for teaching and for research) on a sense of landscape. How was I to bring home, to a West Coast audience, a Europe and a British Isles at the other end of the world? What memories of home would this teaching arouse? In California, I had little difficulty in imagining myself back in the Mediterranean. Iran also seemed close—especially when I flew across the deserts of the American Southwest. But apart from the fogs, the wild seas, and the twisted pines among giant boulders on the coast of Marin County, there was little to remind me of the Dark Ages.

When in Oxford, I had always felt bound to Dark Age Britain through the land itself. It was the same in Ireland, as I passed high crosses and fields studded with stones inscribed in mysterious ogham characters when driving through the countryside toward the west. There was nothing like this for me in California. I needed a lifeline to that deep northern past.

At this time, the lifeline was provided by two of my very best friends—Ian Wood, the early medievalist, in Leeds, and Denis Bethell, the medievalist, in University College Dublin. They kept me in touch with scholarship on the early medieval West. Ian and Denis were more than colleagues to me: they were a link to my own past and to my continued interest in a period that all three of us found fascinating: late Roman Britain, Saint Patrick (died 461), Saint Columba (521–597), and the Venerable Bede (672–735). On the few occasions when we met in Ireland or England, to listen to them talking about Anglo-Saxon England and about the Celtic world was like watching a great rainbow form across a wide, northern sea. At a time when my own work had taken me from the Mediterranean to the borders of Afghanistan, they kept me straight on Dark Age northern Europe.

I showed my homesickness for the Dark Age North (and, by implication, for early medieval western Europe in general) by the shape of the History 4B outline lecture course, which gave due prominence to the history of northwestern Europe—and especially to the history of Britain and Ireland—from the end of the Roman Empire to the time of Charlemagne and the Vikings. As a result, teaching History 4B brought me back, every year, from the late antique Mediterranean and the Middle East to western Europe.

This aspect of my teaching marked the beginning of a tension of which I became increasingly aware in my new life in America. Two landscapes— the early medieval North (the world of Saint Patrick and of *Beowulf*) and the late antique Mediterranean and Middle East—tugged at my heart with equal force.

While many scholars have been content to explore only one major region, I was determined to explore both East and West. I was convinced that a wide canvas gave me the opportunity to compare regions that had usually been studied in isolation. The world of late antiquity looked even more interesting if viewed from its peripheries—both from Ireland and from Iran.

THE SOURCEBOOK

When designing the History 4B course, I was greatly helped by what was for me one crucial novelty: the photocopier machine. As I have described it, the photocopier machine had already made an appearance in Oxford. But, in Oxford, the use of photocopies was still confined to the circulation of reading lists and material for small seminars. In Berkeley, Kinko's Copy Center, just off campus, offered to turn out an entire sourcebook for only nine dollars.

With that sourcebook, I could make the Dark Ages speak. Using up-to-date English translations, I cut and pasted an anthology of texts written by contemporaries that stretched from Suetonius's portrait of the emperor Augustus, through visits to the camp of Attila, Saint Patrick, *Beowulf*, and the Venerable Bede, to the account, in the *Greenland Saga*, of the first contact between Vikings and the Inuit on the coast of the New World around the year 1000.

The sourcebook made the course. Many student evaluations, usually somewhat blasé, gave it top marks. "15! [10 was the maximum] loved it, loved it, loved it! Have made copies for my in-laws and parents. . . . At night I'd read some excerpts to my husband." Of course, not everyone was impressed. A major in business administration failed to see the point of the geography tests: "Its stupid to have to memorize dates and places in the maps that are not there any more."

My inclusion of the European Dark Ages in my main undergraduate lecture course was a sign of my continued love of the landscapes of Britain and of Ireland and a pledge—almost a rain check—that I would, at some time, return to the problems first raised by my reading of Gregory of Tours and of other representatives of the religious culture of the early medieval West. It was some time before my research on this period caught up with my teaching and spilled over into print; but it eventually did so: *The Rise of Western Christendom*, written almost twenty years after my arrival in Berkeley, began with those sharp moments of nostalgia for an old and long-familiar world that I had left behind to come to California.[1]

---

1. Peter Brown, *The Rise of Western Christendom: Triumph and Diversity, A.D. 200–1000* (Oxford: Blackwell, 1996; rev. eds. 2003 and 2013).

THE TRANFORMATION OF
THE CLASSICAL HERITAGE

The Past in the Present

Sometime in the summer of 1979, I attended a Renaissance Fair in the woods of Marin County. It had been organized by the Society for Creative Anachronism—that society of which Beryl Smalley had written to me with such amusement. I was enchanted by it. I wondered why this was so. Passing through Wantage (south of Oxford) a few years earlier, I had seen similar groups gathered for a re-creation of the Battle of Newbury (1643) in the English Civil War. They had assembled in front of a genuine brick inn dating from the seventeenth century. The juxtaposition of the group—with their plastic beer mugs, shiny cars, and bright new clothing—with a real relic of the past instantly destroyed their credibility. The old inn was real. They were not.

In Marin County, by contrast, where the arrival of Sir Francis Drake in 1579 was celebrated (for this remarkable Elizabethan had indeed touched land in California in his journey around the world), there were no ancient pubs to weigh in upon the present. Under the eucalyptus trees, Sir Francis met Queen Elizabeth in a cloud of golden dust, to the music of madrigals performed by a professional group. For a moment, time did indeed take a loop, and there was no heavy relic of the past to call its bluff.

That bucolic meeting between Sir Francis Drake and Queen Elizabeth in Marin County was congruent with a question that I had begun to formulate. How did late antique persons view their own past? How present was it to them? Did they think that an irreversible chasm had come to stand between them and the fullness of classical times? Or did they think that time could be, as it were, turned around, so that figures and values from earlier ages might become active once again in the present?

It seemed to me that the more I studied the role of *paideia* in late antiquity and of *adab* in the Islamic world, the more it seemed to me that, in these cultures, the past was thought of as immediately available in the present to a degree that was alien to a modern sense of the ineluctable passing of time. This was certainly the message of Henri-Irénée Marrou. He pointed out that the "civilization of *paideia*" had no sense that the passing of time had rendered its past masters obsolescent:

> The fact that these appeared at certain moments of time, under the influence of certain historical forces, is unimportant; what matters is that they exist and can be rediscovered in the same way, again and again, by each successive generation.[1]

In such a culture, the wall between past and present could seem paper thin: avatars from ancient days could be thought to step through that wall with ease, as if in a beneficent time warp, to inspire and direct the present.

A modern sense of time tends to be driven by an acute sense of irreversible, unidirectional historical change: the Roman Empire declined; paganism died; Christianity rose. There was no going back on those mighty, one-way historical processes that placed an ever-widening chasm between the present and the past. But was this the only way to think about the past?

Here I was helped by the appearance of a book by Clifford Geertz (1926–2006)—*Negara*. Bali, as Geertz described it, was a culture where time seemed to be pushed by a motor less overpoweringly unidirectional than our own. The weakening of the Balinese empire was acknowledged. But it "was not felt to be an inevitable deterioration, a predestined decline from a golden age.... For most Balinese the decline was the way history had happened to happen, not the way it had had to happen."[2] It seemed to me that, for late antique persons as for the Balinese, ordinary time did not pulse with great urgency. It passed. But it did not pass in a hurry toward some overriding goal, leaving the past irrevocably past and different from the present.

1. H. I. Marrou, *A History of Education in Antiquity*, trans. G. Lamb (New York: Sheed and Ward, 1956), 161.

2. Clifford Geertz, *Negara: The Theatre State in Nineteenth-Century Bali* (Princeton, NJ: Princeton University Press, 1980), 18.

I was tempted to think that late antique persons were not altogether self-deluded to see the world in this way. It was the juxtaposition of the shiny modern cars with the old brick of the inn that truly undercut the bravado of the latter-day Cavaliers and Roundheads whom I had observed in Wantage. But the gap between past and present would not have seemed so extreme if the material underpinning of life in Wantage had changed little since the seventeenth century: if we were still in a preindustrial world of horses and candles. Then the dissonance between past and present would not have seemed so strident.

After all, the ancient world experienced no industrial revolution. Times of travel by sea had not changed greatly since the days of Homer. A gentleman farmer in Pontus (Black Sea Turkey) could be praised, in the second century AD, for living "in the manner of Hesiod"—the Greek poet of around 700 BC. Given the limitations of the possible in an agrarian society, there was no reason why he should not have thought of himself as the Hesiod of his times. Even clothing had not yet changed drastically. When, in the second century AD, the Greek rhetors of the Second Sophistic claimed to be living and speaking like ancient Athenians, they actually still looked like ancient Athenians. They wore clothes that differed little from those of classical Greece. As Paul Zanker has pointed out, "At least in the matter of clothing the past really did live on in the present."[3]

These were random ruminations on which I drew for occasional papers and for teaching. But they addressed a real problem. What was at stake was the notion of *late* antiquity. Here was a civilization that had maintained, to a far greater degree than previous scholars had expected, innumerable links with the classical world that had preceded it. Yet, at the same time, it had opened itself up to face new dangers and new experiences. It eventually witnessed the transfer of much of its cultural and religious riches into new worlds—into the Christian church, into Judaism, ultimately into the world of medieval Islam and its neighbors, Byzantium and the Catholic medieval West. The founders of classical civilization, in ancient Greece and Rome, could not have dreamed of such great changes. Yet they had happened. How were we to do justice to the tension between past and present, continuity and discontinuity, inherent in the notion of the transformation of the classical heritage?

3. Paul Zanker, *The Mask of Socrates: The Image of the Intellectual in Antiquity* (Berkeley: University of California Press, 1995), 250.

CLASSICS AT BERKELEY: JOHN DILLON

I could not have found a better environment for such ruminations than Berkeley. I was now a member of a large Classics Department. And classics, in Berkeley, had a very special flavor. In 1980, the department was still somewhat old-fashioned in its self-presentation and in its teaching methods. Like the grand Beaux-Arts classicism of Dow Library, it stood out, among the humanities, as having brought a fragment of ancient Greece and Rome into the modern present.

At the time, John Dillon was chairman of the department. John was a true compatriot, a fellow Irishman, but far more deeply rooted in the culture and politics of Ireland than I was. He was the son of Myles Dillon (1900–1972), the renowned scholar of Irish folklore, and the grandson of *the* John Dillon (1851–1927), the great nationalist politician of the end of the nineteenth century and the beginning of the twentieth.

John had played a decisive role in securing a joint appointment for me in classics as well as in history. We would meet in his house on Euclid Street to discuss the cosmos of later Platonism. It was an all-embracing system that emanated, with benign inevitability, from the Wholly One—the *pantelôs hen*. (John's wife, Jean, would always refer irreverently to this Supreme Being, who plainly occupied a large space in the minds of John and his philosophical friends, as "the Pantyhose Hen.") I particularly remember one late afternoon, when we sat over drinks beneath a clear blue sky, discussing the magical unity of heaven and earth in the theurgic systems of Jamblichus and Proclus, as "the Blimp"—a great Zeppelin—hung above us in the sweet air, hovering over the University of California football field.

These conversations were a delight to me. In the first place, John's Irish background and early education—like my own, but in a Catholic version—made him acutely aware of the abiding appeal of the classics in Ireland. In an article on the classical tradition in Ireland, which he wrote for the *Crane Bag* (an Irish journal) in 1979, John showed how, throughout much of Irish history, the Irish had played the role of the witty Greeks to the cumbersome Romans of the British Empire. Old Irish was as rich and complex as Greek. Its epics were as vivid as Homer. Classical themes took on a strange new beauty in Irish translations of the Middle Ages: Where else in Europe would one read of Helen of Troy as "the Lime-White Lady, She of the Conflict"?[4]

---

4. J. Dillon, "Some Reflections on the Irish Classical Tradition," *The Crane Bag* 3, no. 2 (1979): 28–32, at 29.

John's commitment to late antique philosophy was a constant inspiration to me. We not only discussed the Pantyhose Hen—the *pantelôs hen*, the Wholly One, of the more rarefied reaches of Plotinus's metaphysics. We also shared an interest in the social position of the philosopher and the nature of his school. John showed that the Academy of Athens had not been an institution, like a modern university or a research center. It was a teaching tradition passed on from generation to generation by word of mouth alone (usually in the form of verbal commentaries on the works of the Masters), through intense master-disciple relations that were close to the way in which learning was passed down in the medieval and modern Islamic world.[5]

Altogether, John had a rare sense of the way in which the tradition of classical philosophy changed over time without losing touch with its past. His first masterpiece, *The Middle Platonists*, had just appeared, in 1977. *The Middle Platonists* showed how a seemingly dormant period in the history of the Platonic tradition had moved forward according to its own rhythms: as he put it so well, "like those humble sea-creatures whose concerted action slowly builds a coral reef." This slow process, seldom appreciated by modern scholars, eventually led to the formation of the mighty Neoplatonic synthesis, "perhaps the greatest philosophical edifice of all time," which would dominate the thought of Europe and the Islamic world for the next millennium.[6]

The Transformation of the Classical Heritage

In late January 1979, John Dillon and I had lunch with Doris Kretschmer, who was the acquisitions editor for classics at the University of California Press. On January 25, we sent her the full proposal that John and I had worked on together in the previous months, and which we had discussed over the lunch. We proposed a series: The Transformation of the Classical Heritage. We stressed the great interest of the period:

> This was a period when traditions that we associate with the classical world proper did not decline or waste away, but, rather, were transformed and re-interpreted to meet new needs. . . . More than the carefully arranged

5. J. Dillon, "Self-Definition in Later Platonism," in *Jewish and Christian Self-Definition*, ed. E. P. Sanders (Philadelphia: Fortress Press, 1982), 60–75, at 66–67.

6. J. Dillon, *The Middle Platonists, 80 B.C. to A.D. 220* (Ithaca, NY: Cornell University Press, 1977), 415.

debris of a great civilization [of classical Greece and Rome]; it was a great civilization in itself . . . seriously "built to last".

For this reason, we told Doris that we were particularly interested in what John and I called the "living classical tradition" that emerged directly from the late antique restructuring of the classical world—the "perennial Hellenism" of Byzantium; the classical tradition of learning in the postimperial West and farther east; the revival of philosophy in the Islamic world; and even the religious Platonism of modern times, from Milton to the American transcendentalist movement. This was the classical tradition in its late antique forms (Augustine and Boethius in the Latin West, Plotinus and Proclus in the East), which flowed almost imperceptibly in the veins of medieval and early modern western Europe, Byzantium, and Islam, and also in the mystical and philosophical traditions of Judaism.

At this time, August Frugé was withdrawing from the position of director of the press to his house in Twenty Nine Palms in Southern California. But he plainly put his weight behind the venture. Devoted to building up the classics, and with strong ties over the years to the Classics Department in Berkeley, he evidently approved of the idea of a series that extended this interest in the classical heritage into late antiquity and beyond.

And no one could have been a more enthusiastic and shrewd acquisitions editor for the series than Doris Kretschmer. Those of her letters to me that survive show her beating the bounds of the California university system for potential authors. She wrote of one "who turned out to be a very personable gentleman heading for Sacramento to hunt wild turkeys in a denim jacket festooned with revolutionary slogans."

Removing a Bottleneck

Doris's journeys and my correspondence showed that there was no lack of interest in a late antique series in America. Many departments of classics, religious studies, Jewish studies, and medieval studies taught courses relevant to late antiquity. But the field lacked books. In academe at large, late antiquity was still considered to be a marginal field. Thesis advisers tended to direct their charges to safer fields where employment and publication were more certain. Publishers were ready to accept manuscripts on conventional classical subjects; but manuscripts on late antique topics lingered in publishers' offices, partly because readers of such manuscripts were often hard to find. Altogether, there was a bottleneck.

What the series tried to do was to relieve this bottleneck. In the first place, John Dillon and I went over the list of readers used by the University of California Press, adding many with lively late antique interests and a reputation for speed and fairness. Among these readers, the older and more established scholars were often the most generous. They knew what the series needed. Hilary Armstrong (1909–1997), the great scholar of Plotinus, was one of those. In a somewhat raw dissertation manuscript he detected "an attractive warmth and animation" that pulled the author through. It was the same with Sidney Griffith, whose judgment was essential to me in making sure that works on Syriac Christianity would be part of the profile of the series. On one occasion he wrote:

> I did not expect to like this manuscript as much as I have done. . . . My preference is for smaller studies of closer focus. . . . But I have come to the conclusion that this book might just be what Syriac studies in the USA really needs . . . [it] shows the excitement and the relevance of it all.

Within the California system itself, Hal Drake at Santa Barbara was also an unfailingly helpful reader and advocate for the series.

The Shape of a Series

As a result of being able to offer quick and fair decisions, followed, if possible, by a contract (no small thing for scholars caught in the exacting American tenure process), we were able to build up a list remarkably quickly. Already by 1982, three books had appeared: on the interrelationship of imperial ceremony, art, and society (Sabine MacCormack, *Art and Ceremony*); on the role of women in imperial politics in East Rome (Kenneth Holum, *Theodosian Empresses*); and on a maverick philosopher-bishop in a coastal town in modern Libya (Jay Bregman, *Synesius*).

Many books would follow. Up to the present, over fifty titles have appeared in the series. Like a long river, the series has washed as many banks as there have been changes in the methods and interests of scholars. It began with publications that were largely limited to the Greco-Roman world; but, as ever-new horizons opened up to scholars, especially in the direction of the Middle East, it has come to include the Syriac-speaking world east of Antioch, Iran, and the late antique roots of Islam. In this way, a project first broached over lunch with John Dillon and Doris Kretschmer in January 1979 has come to give the much-needed weight of print to late antiquity as a field of its own.

SEXUALITY

MICHEL FOUCAULT

VIRGINITY AND SOCIETY

By the summer of 1980, I had begun to change gear. I had spent my first two years in Berkeley studying codes of excellence and their exemplars: Muslim men of learning; Christian holy men and women; pagan philosophers. Now I wanted to dig yet deeper into the differing notions of the self and of the relation between the individual and society that were current in late antiquity. I would try to offer a historical account of the emergence of markedly differing attitudes to sex in pagan, Jewish, and Christian circles in late antiquity and beyond.

In many ways, it is not surprising that I moved in this direction in the California of the 1970s. Sexual emancipation of all kinds was in the air. Though generally welcomed in the circles in which I moved, this emancipation raised sharp questions for the historian that many of us addressed, each in our different ways. My own approach was based on habits of mind derived from my previous work on late antiquity. I went for the phenomenon that offered the greatest challenge to the historical imagination of modern persons. That is: I did not claim to write about every aspect of sex, marriage, and the relations of men and women in this period. Instead I concentrated on a radical group—on those who had renounced sex entirely. It was these figures—men and women who seemed to live at one extreme of the human condition—who drew my attention. The problem that I had to explain was why they came to enjoy so much prestige in early Christian circles.

This approach suited me well. Ever since the late 1960s, I had chosen to concentrate on persons and on practices calculated to cause disquiet to modern persons—sorcery, holy men, the cult of relics, the ordeal. By doing this,

I wanted to challenge my readers to think and feel their way into societies and value systems very different from their own. How and why did these seemingly strange things happen, and with what consequences for society? I would now try to do the same for virginity.

My application for sabbatical leave in 1981 provided the occasion to lay out this change in the direction of my work. When I wrote to Dean Keppel in the summer of 1980, I titled my proposed study "Virginity and Society: Men, Women and Renunciation in Late Antiquity." I also applied for funding to the American Council of Learned Societies; and, a little later, I agreed with Joe Kitagawa, my former host in Chicago for the Haskell Lectures on the cult of saints, to give a series of ACLS lectures under the same title on various campuses in 1982/83. Renunciation of sex—not its celebration in modern times nor the evils of its supposed repression in the past: but, simply, what such renunciation meant for men and women in the last centuries of the ancient world—would hold my attention for the next seven years.

It was while preparing this application that I turned, for the first time, to the works of Michel Foucault (1926–1984). It is not that I had not heard of him before. He was the rage in Berkeley. Foucault's learned and brilliantly ironic demolitions of modern accounts of the progress of medicine and of the emergence of the modern obsession with sexuality had only recently become available in English translation. His books swept the campus like a brush fire. They became a must for graduate students and their teachers.

Academic conversations were liberally studded with references to Foucault—"Foucault this," "Foucault that." I remember one occasion when I was hanging out with my friend Tom Laqueur at Peet's Coffee in Walnut Square (as we regularly did): a lively old lady, who looked as if she had walked all the way into town from the crests of Tilden Park, approached us. "What is that Fu-Ko you are always talking about? Is it a form of martial arts?" From then onward Tom and I referred to the philosopher as "the Martial Artist." This happened in the summer of 1980. A few months later, I would meet Michel Foucault in Berkeley, in what proved to be a memorable encounter. But what had attracted me in his work in the first place, before that time?

"To Render Fragile . . ."

Looking back, I think that what struck me most about Foucault's work was his fierce sense that all that seemed most solid and unquestionable, all that was usually taken for granted in human affairs, had been made by people and so could be unmade by them. *Fragiliser*—to render fragile all that seemed most certain in the world; to show it to be less solid than we had thought—this was the duty of the thinking person.

And in order to do this, the philosopher had to become a historian—and a tenaciously observant historian at that. Foucault believed that only when we go back to the past, to see, precisely and without hindsight, how our own institutions and beliefs came about; when we strip them of the patina of the obvious: then we can do something about them—we can reform prisons, criticize medical systems, and altogether come to breathe a more free air.

This was very much the message that Foucault brought to Berkeley campus in October 1980. As he stated in an interview: "making things fragile" was his business, "through this type of historical analysis . . . showing at once why and how those things could be constituted in this way . . . constituted through a precise history. . . . And if it is historically constructed, it can be politically destroyed." (Here Foucault made plain that he used the word "politically" in the widest sense, to mean creative critical activity on all levels.)[1]

This, as far as I can reconstruct it, was the "Foucault Sound" as it was known in the early 1980s, through his publications and through his statements in the course of an increasing number of prestigious visits to American campuses.

Inevitably, not everybody liked that sound. Foucault irritated many, who dismissed him as an out-and-out relativist, a denier of the possibility of truth; as a determinist, who made all thought dependent on its epoch; as a disabused critic of the genuine humanitarian advances of recent times; as a vatic mandarin, who used terms of art, such as "discourse," that were as opaque as Sumerian logograms. For or against, Foucault's reputation had already ballooned. He had become a mythical figure to many different groups of scholars and admirers.

Because of this aura, it is easy to forget how little of Foucault's work was actually known at this time: many of his most important lectures—notably those that he gave at the Collège de France on the nature of government—-were not published (let alone translated) until very recently. The full implications of his work were unknown, or known only to a select few. What I picked

---

1. Interview with André Berten cited in Michel Foucault, *About the Beginnings of the Hermeneutic of the Self: Lectures at Dartmouth in 1980*, ed. H.-P. Fruchard and Daniele Lorenzini (Chicago: University of Chicago Press, 2016), 91. This invaluable volume contains, effectively, the lectures that Foucault gave at Berkeley—as they were the same (with a few variants) as those given at Dartmouth—and adds much material from his visits to Berkeley and New York in 1980.

up at this time was one aspect only of Foucault, but an important one: Foucault the historian of science at the point of becoming a historian of sex.

So what did this mean? In both the case of the history of science and that of the history of sexuality, Foucault's approach resolutely emphasized the differences between different periods of history. Each period had its own, distinctive worldview that had little or nothing to do with present-day certitudes. Nowhere was a sense of the discontinuity between the ages more challenging to the historical imagination than in attitudes to sex. Each age was caught—like a goldfish in a bowl—in a series of presuppositions about sex that were alien to any other age: a glass screen, transparent but impassable, had come down between past and present. To read Foucault at this time was to down a stiff tonic—a remedy for what had always been, for historians, the one unforgivable sin—anachronism: the invasion of the past by the present.

ANCIENT SEX AND MODERN REVOLUTION

The moment that I committed myself to a study of sexual renunciation, I realized that I would need Foucault. His criticism of upbeat narratives of progress toward ever-greater sexual emancipation was essential. For it helped to remove a solid barrier of modern misconceptions that rested heavily on the study of sexuality in the ancient world. These misconceptions were largely based on a sense of false familiarity with the past.

This was particularly the case when it came to the contrast between early Christian and modern attitudes to sex. I was well aware that my decision to study sexual renunciation in early Christianity took place at a peculiarly fraught time, owing to the sexual revolution in America and elsewhere. This revolution was unusually turbulent across the bay, in San Francisco. Harvey Milk, the gay supervisor of the city of San Francisco, had been murdered in November 1978, only three months after my arrival in Berkeley. In turning toward this theme in 1980, I had no doubt that, unlike many other topics that had preoccupied me up to then, this was a charged theme: a high wind of present-day concern would fill my sails.

This revolution had roughly two phases. The first, mainly in the 1960s, was a fight against what was considered sexual repression. It validated sexual activity and sexual choice in virtually any form. It saw itself primarily as a fight for freedom. The second phase, beginning with the seventies, was more a fight for women's rights and for gay rights. It saw itself primarily as a fight for equality. Both movements looked to the ancient world and to the early Christian past to find precedents for their own struggle, or, failing that, to find, in those distant times, the origins of their present discontent.

For this reason, both phases of the sexual revolution had implications for scholarship on the early church. To take one example: my projected work on sexual renunciation touched on a problem that was acutely relevant to contemporary debate on clerical celibacy in the Catholic Church. As a non-Catholic, I felt that I should not try to intervene directly in this debate, one way or another, as many of my Catholic friends were doing. Instead, I would try to understand and explain the origins of this tradition, which had evidently become so problematic in modern times.

I was impressed, both as a professional historian and as a new arrival in America, by the extent to which debate on sexual issues was driven by the churches. I had already experienced this when I visited Notre Dame University in 1975. Scholarly and religious concerns seemed to come together to flood the Christian churches and much of the scholarship in the early Christian field with issues raised both by the women's movement and by the sexual revolution. This took many forms—from the demand for a new role for women in the churches to a criticism of the foundational documents of Christianity and Judaism for what was considered their repressive and male-oriented language and ideology.

Many scholars and many committed religious persons thought that too much toxic waste, in the form of negative attitudes to sex and women, had accumulated in the headwaters of Christianity and in the long centuries that linked the Christian past to the present. It seemed as if Christianity itself was due for a process of detoxification; and that the job of the historian was to contribute to this detoxification. As a result, I found myself turning to the past to study the origins of what had become burning issues in the present. Not only that: I had chosen to study one aspect of early Christianity that was in direct contrast to the present—the mysterious force of the drive toward sexual renunciation that appeared to have gripped both men and women in that distant time.

Sex as a Constant: Repression or Emancipation?

One feature struck me in these debates, whether they happened in academe or in the churches. Almost everyone I read or listened to—from the most conservative scholars to the most radical feminists—seemed to assume that the sexual nature of men and women was a constant. Furthermore, it was taken for granted by most writers that this constant sexual nature had been unremittingly repressed throughout the ages, and that the goal of the present age was the removal of the millennial structures of repression that were held to weigh upon us.

This assumption—that sex had always been the same, and that sex had always been repressed—encouraged certain church historians and theologians to judge past ages in a peremptory manner, according to the degree to which the benign energy of sex had been accepted or constrained. The result was a highly ideological view of history. It involved a rating of the past. Grades were allotted to each group and period according to their conformity with modern norms of liberated sex. Pagans scored top marks: sex did not seem to trouble them greatly. Jews also scored high marks for accepting sex and marriage as instituted by God. And, somehow, Jesus and his earliest followers could not be thought of as other than exemplary (an interesting survival, this, of the Protestant belief in the purity of the primitive church).

But then, these theologians declared, the clouds rolled in. Paul, in the grip of an obsessive notion of fornication, scored badly. It was thought that later Christians did little better: under the influence of the world-denying trends of Greek philosophy, many of the most articulate among them seem to have recoiled in horror from the body and from sex. As for Augustine, at the end of the story of the early church, he flunked: he transmitted to later ages a view that saw in sexuality itself a dark symptom of the Fall of humanity. From Augustine onward, the history of Europe was said to have consisted of a thousand years of sexual repression, followed, in modern times, by a slow and painful process of emancipation from the incubus of a sexuality denied, constrained, and warped by the power of the Christian religion.

I trust that readers will forgive this highly simplified narrative. But it was precisely in these blunt terms that the issue of sexual renunciation in early Christianity was often posed. Sex (it was largely agreed) was good. Sexuality was a constant in human nature. All that remained to be seen—and judged—by the historian was the manner in which Christians, in various times and places, accepted or suppressed the primal, unchanging fact of their own sexuality. It was with this stereotypical image of the history of sex in Christian times uppermost in my mind that I turned to Foucault's *La volonté de savoir*, which had appeared in English in 1978, as the first volume of his projected *History of Sexuality*.[2]

2. M. Foucault, *La volonté de savoir* (Paris: Gallimard, 1976), translated as *History of Sexuality. Volume 1: An Introduction* (New York: Vintage Books, 1978).

"A Garrulous Sexuality"

Foucault's *History of Sexuality. Volume 1* was a book designed to shock. It turned on its head the current confident narrative that made our own notion of sexuality appear to be valid for all ages. It also dismantled the narratives that celebrated the modern person's emancipation from sexual repression. For Foucault, to say yes to sex was not necessarily the way to liberty. In fact, it led to yet further, more subtle forms of social control.

Foucault proposed that modern times were characterized by a crying up of sexuality—by an overproduction of knowledge about sex and the sexual determinants of human personality. In his opinion, this development was quite peculiar to Europe and America. He went on to show that what we thought was enduring in human nature was no such thing. The granting of primacy to sex was a passing phase. The way in which sex was approached and talked about as if it were the key to the human condition; the predominant role ascribed to sex in our experience of ourselves, in our expectations of normal behavior, and in our definition of mental health: all this was a mirage—a series of vastly exaggerated arabesques spun out of the reticent physical facts of pleasure and reproduction. Other ages and cultures might view the same facts with relative indifference. But we modern Westerners were caught—if only for a moment in time: from the eighteenth century onward—in a "garrulous sexuality."[3] Sexuality had become "the noisiest of our preoccupations. People will wonder what could have made us so presumptuous."[4]

Altogether, as Foucault saw it, sexuality, as modern persons experienced it and talked about it, was by no means a timeless constant. It was a time-bound creation. It was the result of a crisis of knowingness. And, for Foucault, this knowingness was far from innocent. In the name of medical expertise, it reached ever deeper into the human person, slyly insisting that we answer a scientific questionnaire on our own sexuality that placed our very identity in the hands of others.

Sexuality was declared to be basic to ourselves. But, paradoxically, only doctors, as the self-appointed experts on sexuality, along with bureaucrats and lawyers informed by doctors, could decide for us who we were: to which categories we would be allotted on the basis of our sexuality. Were we "normal" or "abnormal," "heterosexual" or "homosexual," "repressed" or "liberated"? These

3. Foucault, *History of Sexuality*, 127.
4. Foucault, *History of Sexuality*, 158.

were questions that involved the extensive, covert exercise of power over others—they might determine lawsuits, the allocation of housing, admission to institutions, evaluations by employers, judgments on colleagues.

Foucault's message was clear. The notion that modern persons were enjoying (and should strive to enjoy even more) a period of emancipation from a long age of sexual repression was wrong. In modern times, he insisted, sexuality had not been repressed. Far from it: it had been "incited"—moved to center stage and played up in a melodramatic manner as part of the ideology of modern times.

At the time, this was a hard saying. Faced by reports of Foucault's impending *Volonté de savoir* (*The History of Sexuality. Volume One*), French intellectuals debated his views on television and in other media. His proposition that sex had not been constantly repressed, and his insistence that, in modern times, it had been actively incited—played up and given undue prominence— left them speechless. In one such exchange of views, the presenter's "only response was a spluttered '*Fichtre*'" (Gosh!).[5]

There was a lot to say "Gosh" about in Foucault's *History of Sexuality*. For me, it came as a liberation. If the notion that sexuality was a constant through the ages—always present to be embraced or repressed—could be dismissed as no more than a modern creation (and a somewhat sinister one at that), then there was no need to project our modern, time-bound views of sexuality into the early centuries of the Christian church. At a stroke, we were freed from a cloying sense of false familiarity with the past.

By a certain irony, the work of Michel Foucault, often celebrated as the spokesman of radical modernity, had set historians free to do what they had always done: to study the past on its own terms. We were free to look over the edge of the chasm of two millennia and to wonder, with a tingle of vertigo, what strange bodies, what strange notions of sexuality lay at the bottom of that abyss, in the times of Jesus and Saint Paul. In a field dominated by anachronistic notions, mobilized in present-day polemics, we could become historians again.

5. David Macey, *The Lives of Michel Foucault* (New York: Vintage, 1993), 353.

AT THE BEAR'S LAIR

ENCOUNTERS WITH FOUCAULT

"One of Those Small Origins": Foucault, John Cassian, and Confession

Foucault came to Berkeley to deliver "Truth and Subjectivity" under the aegis of the Howison Lectures on October 20 and 21, 1980. The lectures were an event. Eight hundred listeners crowded into Wheeler Hall. A further seven hundred would-be listeners demonstrated outside, demanding to be let in. The police appeared on campus for the first time since the 1960s to drive away the disappointed admirers of the great man. I only managed to attend the second lecture, on October 21.

I did not know what to expect from Foucault. I was pleasantly surprised when I found that he would be lecturing on Christianity and confession. And not only that: what he talked about at great length, with fervor and a remarkable command of the text, were the views of the Desert Fathers on sexual temptation and the need for confession. These views had been passed on to the Latin world in the *Conferences*—the monastic talk-ins—of John Cassian (360–435), a contemporary and discreet critic of Saint Augustine. Based in Marseilles, he wrote to monks who had turned the rugged *calanques* and offshore islands between Marseilles and the French Riviera (a former lurking ground of Ligurian pirates) into the equivalent of the desert of Egypt. I myself had only just finished a spell of intensive reading of the *Conferences* of Cassian.

I was gripped. What struck me in particular was Foucault's style of delivery. This was a different Foucault from the somewhat vatic polemist I had known from his printed works. It was Foucault the master of an art that I had always associated with French classical scholarship at its best—the art of the *explication du texte*: the ability to draw out from a single text an entire world, through patient and perceptive commentary. André-Jean Festugière had the same magical touch to a high degree when conjuring up the world of the Hermetic treatises—a single passage (well-known or newly discovered, it did not matter) could be made to speak as if for the very first time. It was a style of exposition in which Foucault excelled. He used it in all the subsequent volumes of his *History of Sexuality*, endowing them with a classical lucidity that had been absent in his earlier writings.

As Foucault presented him, Cassian's addresses to monks were not what we expected. His thought on sexuality was not driven by an increasing need to repress it. Sexual acts (of the sort that medieval confessionals would catalog with minute care) were of no interest to him. Foucault pointed out that Cassian wished to probe deeper. The monk had to consider not only his actions but the course of his own thoughts. He had to give attention to the endless flow of images (many of them sexual) that flickered in the back of his mind. These thoughts were pointers to his deepest self.

And what a self! As Cassian presented it, this was not necessarily a self that was in the grip of sexual fantasy (a libidinous creature sweating it out in the desert, as modern readers liked to imagine) but a self for whom the ebb and flow of sexual thoughts was no more than an epiphenomenon—a surface manifestation of currents hidden in the depths of the self. And what lay at the bottom of that self? An antiself, an alien being—the Devil and his demons—Hidden Persuaders whose icy presence was betrayed by the course of the monk's own thought stream. As a result, the monk could not even trust his own thoughts. He always had to ask of his own mind, "Am I deceived?"—am I deceived by the Devil?

This last turn in Cassian's thought was eerie and exotic. Foucault did not linger on Cassian's demonology. It was his presentation of Cassian's attitude to the monk's own thoughts (whether demonically inspired or not) that made the audience draw breath. Foucault pointed out that here, for the first time in the long centuries of the ancient world, was an image of a person made up entirely by his or her thoughts alone. And, more frightening still, these thoughts could not be trusted. What was the monk to do? There was only one answer: tell all. Only by being prepared to turn at every instant to a wiser head—to an Old Man of the Desert: an elder monk, well versed in the ups and downs of the soul—could the monk resolve this fundamental uncertainty.

And so Foucault concluded: here, in the writings of a fifth-century monk, little known to scholars of modernity (though dear to my own heart), we could see the turning of an age. For Cassian's insistence on the need for a permanent guide—in fact, for a father confessor—lay at the roots of "the millennial yoke of confession" that had distinguished the Catholic Middle Ages in Europe.[1] This yoke, he pointed out, was not based on a fear of sex. It was based on a fear of the self. In Foucault's view, the abiding sense of a "fragment of darkness" lodged in the self had been passed on to the Middle Ages through the confessional practices of the Catholic Church.[2] It had subtly but surely prepared the enlightened classes of Europe to place a similar yoke upon themselves, in modern times, by turning to similar, priest-like figures—to scientists, doctors, psychoanalysts—to tell them who they really were.

Foucault ended the lecture with ill-disguised zest. Who would have expected such views, with so long a life before them, to come out of a Christian monastery hidden in the hills around Marseilles in the last century of the Roman Empire? In his opinion, the eventual spread throughout medieval Europe of the views of Cassian on the necessity for confession, based on a startlingly new model of the human person, was a delicious example of "one of those small origins that Nietzsche liked to discover at the beginning of great things."[3]

At the Bear's Lair

After the lecture, I was entrusted with Foucault by his Berkeley hosts—Paul Rabinow, Harold Dreyfus, and Leo Bersani. It has been said that he had read my *Augustine of Hippo* and knew it "almost by heart."[4] In fact, we hardly touched on Augustine in our conversation. A highly purposive man, who knew

---

1. Foucault, *History of Sexuality. Volume 1: An Introduction* (New York: Vintage Books, 1978), 61.

2. Foucault, *History of Sexuality*, 69.

3. Foucault, *Beginning of the Hermeneutics of the Self*, 74; this lecture had been accessible in a slightly different form as "Le combat de la chasteté," in *Communications 35: Sexualités occidentales*, ed. P. Ariès and A. Béjin (Paris: Le Seuil, 1984), 15–25, now in *Dits et Écrits* # 512, 2:1114–1127, trans. Carrette, pp. 188–197. On Cassian, see now Foucault's recently published manuscript of volume 4 of the *History of Sexuality*: *Les aveux de la chair* (Paris: Gallimard, 2018), 116–145 and 216–245, translated in *The Confessions of the Flesh* (New York: Pantheon, 2021), 87–110 and 166–189. For a criticism of Foucault's reading of Cassian, see Niki K. Clements, *Sites of the Ascetic Self* (Notre Dame, IN: University of Notre Dame Press, 2020).

4. D. Eribon, *Michel Foucault*, trans. Betsy Wing (Cambridge, MA: Harvard University Press 1991), 313–314.

what he wanted to know and to whom to turn for advice, Foucault did not want to discuss generalities. He wanted my immediate feedback on his lecture on Cassian.

We made our way to the Bear's Lair—the student pub on campus, at the edge of Sproul Plaza. As we sat down to our beer, there was an unnerving moment. The forceful lecturer suddenly became a pupil. It was like seeing a large police dog turn docile. This was the "attentive attitude" that Paul Veyne had noticed as characteristic of Foucault.[5] His body relaxed. His face seemed to broaden, as if to welcome ideas. He stared at me with an expression of utter candor. I had never met a distinguished scholar with such a capacity to put himself out to listen to others.

Tired by his lecture, Foucault was glad to speak in French. And speak we did. I think it was for two hours on end. There was not an aspect of his lecture on Cassian that we did not discuss. There was much that we touched on that seemed to be new to him. I suspect that he had never given sufficient thought to the role of Evagrius of Pontos (346–399)—and, behind Evagrius, to the giant figure of Origen of Alexandria (185–254)—as the source for Cassian's notion of the role of thoughts and the consequent need for self-scrutiny.

I urged Foucault to consider how those two figures, Origen and Evagrius, had made explicit the cosmic dimensions of the self that were only hinted at by Cassian. This implied a wider view of the person than that expounded with such force by Foucault. The monk was never alone with his thoughts: he was also wrapped in a cosmos filled with angels and demons.

For this reason, I suggested to him that Cassian's image of the monk was somehow depleted by being presented only in terms of the anxiety caused by the fluidity of his thoughts. In the monastic traditions of the East (if not so plainly in the West), the fear of the demonic had always been balanced by a sense of the warm presence of mighty angels who were as close to the soul as were the demons. They were personal protectors, based on a long and widespread tradition that viewed the Christian as a person perpetually surrounded by "Invisible Companions."

In such a view, there was room for warm, strong thoughts of joy and inspiration to bubble up in the monk. Such thoughts betrayed the touch of loving presences, angels who countered the monk's chill anxiety in the face of the Devil and his wiles. Without the imagined counterweight of warm angelic

5. Paul Veyne, *Foucault: His Thought, His Character* (Cambridge: Polity Press, 2010), 137.

powers, the "spiritual combat" of the monk, as Foucault presented it, seemed unnecessarily grim.

I do not know whether I persuaded Foucault. But we certainly came to agree on one thing—that to study attitudes to sexuality in Christian circles was not simply to trace the sad advance of sexual repression through the ages. It was a key that unlocked some of the essential features of the Christian and post-Christian West. A month later, in November, Foucault told the seminar of Richard Sennett at New York University that, "recently, Professor Brown stated to me that what we have to understand is why it is that sexuality became, in Christian circles, the seismograph of our subjectivity."[6]

Solemn words and suited to the mood of the early 1980s. Only time would tell how each of us would put this insight to work, each of us in our own way.

BRIEF ENCOUNTERS

I left next day for Chicago, so as to deliver lectures under the rubric of "Philosophers and Monks" at Seabury Western Theological Seminary (very much a summary of my work in the past two years); but not before leaving with Foucault a photocopy of the typescript of those lectures, along with *The Making of Late Antiquity*. It seems that what interested him most in that book were my remarks on the "watershed" between classical antiquity and the later world of Christian monasticism (represented by Cassian)—a watershed that he himself was exploring in terms of differing attitudes to the self.[7]

My next extensive contact with Foucault was very different from that evening in the Bear's Lair. I passed through Paris in February 1981 and had dinner at Foucault's apartment along with Paul Veyne, whom I met for the first time. The occasion was utterly unpretentious. Foucault served a stew based on a Poitevin recipe of his mother's. Purposive as ever, much of the conversation hinged on possible Anglophone authors in the field of late antiquity who might be translated in a new series edited by Gallimard.

6. Foucault, "Sexuality and Solitude," in *The Essential Works of Michel Foucault 1: Ethics*, ed. Paul Rabinow (New York: The New Press, 1997), 175–184, at 179.

7. Evidence for Foucault's reading of my *Making of Late Antiquity* and other papers by me that I sent him at a later time has been assembled by Professor Niki Clements of Rice University in her visits to the Foucault archive at the Bibliothèque nationale. See now Niki Clements, "Foucault and Brown: Disciplinary Intersections," *Foucault Studies* 22 (July 2022): 1–27.

Later, the conversation turned to the death of Saint Macrina—the sister of Gregory of Nyssa (ca. 335–395) and of Basil of Caesarea (ca. 330–379)—as I had described it in my *Cult of the Saints*: I had written of her as "sitting upright in bed, facing the setting sun." But this was wrong. I had been misled by memories of Schubert's *Der Jüngling und der Tod*: *Die Sonne sinkt, o könnt' ich mit ihr scheiden!* Macrina, however, was no Romantic. As a good early Christian she had turned, not to the setting sun, but to the East. Wherewith Veyne (who had spotted my mistake) launched out into a vivid disquisition on the notion of the "Mystic East" in Freemasonry. Then, a bit like the White Rabbit, he took his leave, to catch the last train from Paris that would take him back to his beloved Provence, to his house in Bédoin, at the foot of Mont Ventoux.

In the next few years, I met Foucault in Berkeley for the occasional coffee. Once again, there was no chitchat: just the same "attentive attitude," usually followed by a devastatingly simple question. Why, for instance, when speaking of intercourse in marriage, did Paul speak of the "marital debt"? Why did he use the commercial language of debt to speak of sexual relations? I was stumped. I had never thought of it that way. I gather that, a few years earlier, he had lobbed the same question at the Jesuits of Paris and, a little later, at members of the Philosophy Department at Berkeley. I hope their answers were more satisfactory than mine. I had seldom met somebody so skilled at putting himself in the learning position, and who gave so much in return, simply by being surprised at what he had learned.[8]

It was the Berkeley graduate students who experienced Foucault at his best. Only recently I was moved by the account that my Princeton colleague Steve Kotkin gave me of the relations between Foucault and the group of graduate students who took a seminar with him in 1982. In their company, Foucault settled down in an utterly unpretentious manner. He treated them with the absolute candor that was so striking a feature of his attentive moments— sharing his ideas with them, explaining his more opaque statements, telling them where he had been wrong. They had been the lucky ones. By the time that Foucault offered his famous Berkeley seminar on the Greek notion of *parrhésia*, in the fall of 1983,[9] I was already beyond the Sierras, far to the east, in Princeton.

---

8. For the importance of this concept for Foucault's interpretation of Augustine's views on marriage, see now *Les aveux de la chair* (Paris: Gallimard, 2018), 358–361; *Confessions of the Flesh*, 282–286.

9. M. Foucault, *Fearless Speech*, ed. J. Pearson (Los Angeles: Semiotext(e), 2001).

When, some five years later, I completed *Body and Society*, I summed up my debt to Foucault in a citation from his recent book on Greek attitudes to sex— *L'usage des plaisirs* (*The Use of Pleasures*):

> After all, what would be the value of the passion for knowledge if it resulted only in a certain knowingness . . . and not, in one way or another . . . in the knower's straying afield from himself? There are times in life when the question of knowing if one can think differently than one thinks, and perceive differently than one sees, is absolutely necessary if one is to go on thinking and reflecting at all.[10]

I did not know at the time that I wrote this (in 1987) that it was precisely this passage that had been read aloud at the small memorial service in honor of Michel Foucault that took place, on June 29, 1984, in the courtyard outside the mortuary of the Pitié-Salpêtrière Hospital.[11] I had chosen rightly.

Looking back, I ask myself what exactly it was that I owed to Foucault at this time. It is not an easy question. Since his death, the image of Foucault has swung wildly from having been for a time a cult figure in America to virtual silence, followed, now, by a more distant and scholarly return of interest. The publication of his many lectures—both those given at the Collège de France and those he gave in America—have revealed the fullness and cohesion of his thought far more extensively than I could have dreamed of when I first met him. Foucault the writer and thinker is now gathered into innumerable recent volumes.

What I got was a small part of Foucault. But it was sufficient to set me free from anachronistic approaches to sexuality in the ancient world. His interpretation of John Cassian, which appeared in print in 1982 as "Le combat de la chasteté," reassured me that I was on the right track in my own interpretation of the Desert Fathers. His other work on the Fathers of the Church, *Les aveux de la chair* (which included a chapter on Augustine) did not appear until 2018. But I did know that we shared a commitment to preserve the integrity of the past, disturbingly strange though it might appear to modern persons.

And I was fortunate to have known the living Foucault, even if only as briefly as a crackle of lightning, and to be touched by the freshness of his ever-questioning mind—the mind of a true philosopher, brought to bear on so many issues that had been blocked by intellectual inertia and false familiarity.

10. M. Foucault, *The Use of Pleasures* (New York: Pantheon, 1985), 8; P. Brown, *The Body and Society: Men, Women, and Sexual Renunciation in Early Christianity* (New York: Columbia University Press, 1988), xviii.

11. Macey, *The Lives of Michel Foucault*, 471.

VIRGINITY IN VENICE

Venice

In late 1980 and much of 1981, I began to work on the theme of virginity and society in late antiquity. This project eventually became a book called *Body and Society:. Men, Women, and Sexual Renunciation in Early Christianity*, which appeared in 1988.[1]

In many ways, this was a project that could have been done anywhere with a good library. Unlike my intended study of Sasanian Iran (which I had now abandoned), I was not dependent on access to a specific landscape. Nor did I need to go to a specific archive. Any major library with standard collections of classical and Christian texts in Greek and Latin (and, if possible, Syriac and Coptic) would do. This gave me a rare freedom to take my work wherever I wanted.

As it was, in those years, my wife Pat was working on her dissertation on the art and social setting of that most Venetian of Venetian painters, Vittore Carpaccio (1465–1520).[2] Her work tied her to the archives and artworks of Venice, while I was happy to make use of the abundant resources of the Marciana and of the other libraries scattered throughout the city. And so we lived in Venice from November 1980 to August 1981, and, then, for shorter periods each year up to 1986.

---

1. Peter Brown, *The Body and Society: Men, Women, and Sexual Renunciation in Early Christianity* (New York: Columbia University Press, 1988) and *Body and Society: Twentieth-Anniversary Edition with a New Introduction* (New York: Columbia University Press, 2008). I will cite from this more recent edition.

2. Patricia Fortini Brown, *Venetian Narrative in the Age of Carpaccio* (New Haven, CT: Yale University Press, 1988).

As anyone can imagine, it was a delight to live in Venice. But it was, at first sight, inappropriate for my project. Venice was one of the few cities of Italy without a Roman or an early Christian past. In the year 1000 it was still a brash new city, without an ancient past. The sense of the slow unbroken growth of Christianity from roots that plunged deep into Roman times, which was so very present in Rome, was almost entirely absent in Venice. My story would end five hundred years before the story of Venice began.

What Is Virginity? Images of the Virgin

Looking back, I think that this sense of a chasm between Venice and the ancient world had a salutary effect. It challenged me to define more sharply what virginity meant in early Christianity—that is, before the Middle Ages and before Venice came into existence. In that truly distant time, virginity was not what we mean now.

For this reason, Venice could not have been a better place to take the measure of the gulf between medieval and modern attitudes to virginity and those that had emerged in the world of late antiquity. The art of Venice condensed, with overwhelming beauty, the role of virginity in the Christian imagination of late medieval and early modern Europe. The Accademia gallery and the churches of Venice were filled with paintings from the days of the Renaissance and the baroque. For the artists of that time (as also for their pious patrons) virginity meant, above all, the Virgin Mary; and all other holy virgins were assumed to be women—female isomorphs of the Virgin herself.

Those splendid renderings of fully female, idealized women were the glory of Venetian painting, and for centuries they had exercised a powerful influence on our understanding of the Virgin and of women saints. Yet, looking at them in the churches of Venice, I had to remind myself that, a thousand years earlier, in late antiquity, virginity had not been gendered in that way. The virgin state had by no means been restricted to women: males had been just as prominent as women as advocates and exemplars of virginity. The early monks were often spoken of as "virgins"—and to such an extent that a medieval Armenian sculpture, in the monastery of Yovhannavank', even showed the Five Wise Virgins of the parable (Matthew 25:1) greeting the coming of Christ the Bridegroom as monks with full beards! Virginity was a charged option for both sexes to a degree that takes some effort of the imagination to recapture.

Byzantium: The Virgin of Murano

I came closer to the Christianity of the late antique world when I viewed the art of Venice in a more distant age, at a time when Venice (though a new city in itself) was closely linked to the ancient, eastern empire of Byzantium. Here were echoes of an older imaginative world, where virginity did not mean what it came to mean in western Europe.

I would go frequently to the church of San Donato on the island of Murano, so as to stand beneath the twelfth-century Byzantine mosaic of the Virgin in the apse. There I caught a hint of a more ancient notion of virginity. For what I saw was a human body perceptibly elongated, as it stretched from the top to the bottom of the dome of the apse—a thin, vertical figure set against a sky of gold. The physical contours and stance of the Virgin expressed a constant, insensible contraction of her whole person away from normal forms of human contact. This shrinking and elongation of the body marked out a virgin (not just the Virgin: but any virgin, male or female) as somehow standing alone as a joining point between Heaven and earth.

In this way, the Virgin ceased to be marked as either a man or a woman. She was what Byzantines called her—quite simply *ho anthrôpos*: the human being. She was not merely an exalted woman. Nor was she only a woman rendered both glorious and curious by the renunciation of sex. She had transcended the division of the sexes. She was humanity itself, as human persons were meant to be—men and women alike. In viewing such a mosaic, Byzantines, like late antique Christians, glimpsed the true order of the world, made palpable and present in a human body irrevocably detached from human society. It was a vision of the human person stripped of the conventional markers of social identity—free from sex, free from marriage, free from all the narrow boxes into which the life of the average person was divided. In late antiquity it was believed that anyone—male or female—could be like that. Indeed, it was more than hinted by many early Christian advocates of virginity that everyone *should* be like that—or, in a glorious future after the resurrection of the dead, that everyone *would* be like that.

The sense of representing a model for a new humanity, gained through dismantling the conventional building blocks of society, was caught in the apse mosaic of the Virgin in San Donato and in other Byzantine works of art in Venice. These works—and not the striking, idealized females of Renaissance and baroque art—were a faithful echo of the revolution implied in the late antique exaltation of virginity.

The Body Isolated

I sought the social and religious background to this radical notion in the volumes of the *Patrologia Graeca* and the *Patrologia Latina*, which stood on the shelves of the Marciana, the splendid public library of Venice that looked out on the busy waterfront of the Piazza di San Marco.

I began my work in the Marciana at the end of the story—I first immersed myself in the rich Latin and Greek hagiographical literature of the late fifth, sixth, and seventh centuries. I did this because the late antique notion of virginity was expressed at its most triumphant and most radical in those texts. They passed on dramatic notions of sexual renunciation and virginity in the form of legends that would haunt the Christian imagination in Byzantium and the West for the next thousand years.

What was the shape of those legends? The more I read, the more it struck me that the repression of sex was not their main theme. Rather, sexual renunciation was about liberation. It was about freeing the body from the dense network of prescribed social roles that tied it to marriage. Cut free from society in this way, the isolated human body jumped into sharp focus: the charged body of the virgin martyr, protected from violation by guardian angels (in the legend of Saint Agnes); the bodies of bride and bridegroom stripped for the first time in the privacy of their bedroom, as they decided never to join in intercourse (in the Acts of Judas Thomas and in the story of Amoun of Nitria, one of the first monks of Egypt); the son of a noble Roman family, once swaddled in marks of his high rank, reduced to nothing but his famished body as a beggar among the faceless poor (in the poignant legend of Saint Alexis, the "Man of God").

These bodies were not seen, primarily, as bodies subject to the repression of their sexual urges, as modern persons might expect. They were presented, rather, as bodies that had been prized loose from their conventional social identities as husbands and wives, noblemen and commoners. They were sacred—even uncanny—because they were the living bodies of the socially dead. It was society, not sex, over which the detached virgin body was thought to have triumphed.

Furthermore, the legends did not represent the bodies of their heroes and heroines as maimed by sexual repression. The very opposite was the case. They were presented as bodies set free to await a mighty transformation of the body itself.

At this time, making my way through the well-stocked new accessions shelf of the Marciana, I fell on an essay by the Russian aesthetician and historian of

Byzantine culture Sergei Averincev: "Gold in the Symbolic System of Byzantium."[3] Averincev reminded us that, for Byzantines (with their alchemical lore), gold was not a mere metal: it was corrupt matter "healed." In the same way, the bodies of virgins and ascetics were not seen as bodies repressed and mortified. They were bodies imagined to be turning slowly into pure gold as they were healed of their base matter. As I sat in the side chapels of San Marco, surrounded by domes and walls of liquid gold mosaic, it was indeed possible to imagine a higher destiny for the virgin body than the mere absence of sex. The virgin body was a body set free from the bonds of conventional society and sent on its way toward the luminous solidity of the Resurrection.

3. S. Averincev, "L'or dans le système des symboles de la culture byzantine," *Studi medievali* 20, no. 1 (1979): 47–67—taken from his *Poetika rannevizantijskoi literatury* [*The Poetics of Early Byzantine Literature*] (Moscow: Akademija Nauk, 1977).

BODY AND CITY

ANCIENT BODIES

So what did this progressive isolation of the body, associated with the elevation of virginity, mean in Greco-Roman society as it passed from the classical world to the world of late antiquity? In my next bout of reading in the Marciana, I returned to the doctors and moralists of the Roman Empire at its height, whom I had first read in Dow Library during my visit to Berkeley in 1975: the indefatigable writer on moral issues, Plutarch (ca. 50–ca. 120); the gynecological treatise of Soranus (98–138); and, above all, the works of Galen (129–?199/216). Through these authors, I gained a better idea of what pagans of the second century thought about sex and the body, before the rise of the more radical notions espoused by Christianity.

I found a body image profoundly different from our own. Roman doctors did not represent the body as a reservoir of instinctual drives that demanded fulfillment. Far from it. In matters of sex, the ancient body was thought to be subject to the restraints of a zero-sum game. Sexual energy was imagined to be in short supply. Intercourse required caution. It involved an expenditure of "heat" and vital energy that weakened the body. Galen could write that, if castration could only be performed in a less drastic fashion, then it was obvious that Olympic champions should be made eunuchs: "Men who remain chaste are stronger and bigger than the others and pass their time in better health" (Galen, *On Seed* 1.8).

Even if I allowed for the valetudinarian tendencies of ancient doctors and their clients, it was difficult to square such views with modern notions of Roman pagans as uninhibited children of nature, on whom Christianity came to impose sexual restraints from which they had once been free.

Rather, it seemed to me at the time that, in many circles in the late classical, pagan world, sex existed, as it were, on parole. It was made subservient to the needs of the ancient city. Sex was about supplying the city with generation after generation of citizens. Among the civic elites, the joys of sex were expected to take second place to this solemn mission. The concord of husband and wife was held to derive not from sexual pleasure but from a different source: marital concord echoed the concord of the city. It was an eminently decorous view, where even the bedroom could be spoken of by Plutarch as "a school of orderly deportment" (Plutarch, *Advice to a Bride and Groom* 47).

Looking back, I think that I may have exaggerated the rigidity of these codes. Enjoying easy sexual access to slaves, upper-class Roman males were a lot more permissive in sexual matters than were the doctors and philosophers who advised them.[1]

A double morality prevailed, in which men expected women of their own class to be chaste, while they themselves were promiscuous in their dealings with unfree persons. But, at the time, I was struck less by the puritanism of the upper-class codes of deportment than by the subservience of all thought on sexual matters to the needs of the city. Marriage, intercourse, and the relation between the sexes seemed to be engulfed in a strenuously asserted ideology of civic harmony.

Sex without the City

These attitudes to sex brought me up against a further problem. The Roman world itself changed in the course of the centuries. In AD 200, the imaginative grip of the city and its ideology still appeared to be dominant. But what happened when, by AD 400, this grip had slackened? Faced by this problem, I found myself following from a new perspective the intriguing lines of thought opened up by Évelyne Patalagean in her study of poverty in the Eastern Empire.

Évelyne had shown that, in matters of social relations, the mystique of the ancient city evaporated in late antiquity. In a brutally demystified world, people no longer saw their society in "civic" terms of the relations between citizens and noncitizens, but, more bleakly, in terms of a universal, economic relationship between rich and poor. What if the history of sexuality in the late

---

1. See now Kyle Harper, *From Shame to Sin: The Christian Transformation of Sexual Morality in Late Antiquity* (Cambridge, MA: Harvard University Press, 2013).

Roman world followed the same pattern? Closely tied to their civic status, the decorous couplings of the elites had gone unquestioned because they were thought to contribute, by reproduction, to the good of the city. But what if sex—even sex in marriage—came to be seen as in itself problematic ? Once the veil of civic ideology had been removed from the marriage bed, what remained? Mere bodies subject to sexual desire irrespective of their social status or usefulness to the city.

The tendency of classical moralists and doctors had always been to distinguish "good" sex from "bad" sex along civic lines. For them, marital intercourse was good sex: it produced heirs to carry on the traditions of their fathers. "Bad" sex was sex unmotivated and unrestrained by a sense of civic duty—it was the freewheeling sex of debauchees and of hotheaded young men.

In the pagan world, freewheeling sex was tolerated, especially in young males. This tolerance accounts for the widespread modern stereotype of classical pagans as being persons of enviably easy morals. But, in reality, sex was strictly corralled. It was kept in its place in a massively compartmentalized view of society. Hence a split image: two different kinds of sex—good or bad, civic or noncivic—were thought to belong each to a separate world. These worlds did not meet.

But what would happen if this cognitive split was removed: if sex could not be seen as safely compartmentalized in this way? Demystified, sex would be seen as sex wherever it occurred: it would emerge as a universal force, independent of the city. Just as there were no privileged citizens—only rich and poor—so there would be no privileged sex—sex for the sake of the city: only the universal libidinous stirring of bodies irrespective of their civic status and of the civic justifications for their sexual activity. All bodies were equal, and, in theory at least, all persons were equally free to do what they wished with their bodies. They could choose whether or not to have sex. Some men or women might say no, with dramatic results.

"The Ocean-Flood of the Messiah"

It was against the background of an unraveling civic world that I wanted to place the rise of the Christian ascetic movement. This movement produced heroes and heroines whose renunciation of marriage declared that society itself was as fragile as a spider's web. It could be abandoned. The exaltation of virginity showed that the body could resist the oceanic pressures of the ancient city. Human bodies no longer had to serve the city by marriage, intercourse, and childbearing.

In that way, the notions of sexual renunciation that circulated among radical Christians threatened to do a lot more than tamp down on sex. Virginity could be thought to act as a solvent of the social order. It vaporized the links between the individual and society, in a manner that often disturbed ordinary Christians quite as much as it disturbed Jews and pagans.

For this reason, there was a certain poignancy about the texts that I read in Venice at this time. Classical authors conveyed a massive sense of confidence that sex was really no problem: that it could always be subjected to the discreet discipline of the city. But already in the second century this consensus was at risk. The rise of radical forms of Christianity produced exponents who thought the exact opposite. These radicals believed that the proud mass of the ancient city (the work of so many centuries) would crumble like a sandcastle, touched by "the ocean-flood of the Messiah," as radical Christians said no to sex and marriage.[2]

There was a note of exhilaration in these radical statements that reminded me, in an odd way, of the enthusiasms of the sexual revolution of modern times. Just as the full expression of sex was expected to usher in, with almost magical ease, a new and happier society in the 1960s, so the fierce "boycott of the womb," advocated by many Christians in around the year 200, was held to mark the end of an evil age and the beginning of the kingdom of Christ.

In this way, my study of the more radical forms of sexual renunciation, as these were imagined or practiced by early Christians, showed that this renunciation had less to do with the fear of sex than might be expected. Instead, renunciation provided a language of hope, of the coming of new things.

Indeed, far from being only about sex, the issue of virginity and sexual renunciation was also part of a conflict about the nature of the ancient city, and about the rights of the civic community over the bodies of its members. Virginity meant freedom—the freedom of the individual to withdraw his or her body from the ever-present constraints of marriage in the interests of society. Hence the seriousness of the conflicts for and against sexual renunciation in the first centuries of Christianity. They were part and parcel of the grand debate of late antiquity on the nature of society, as the Mediterranean world passed from a very ancient, civic world to a new social order that would end in Byzantium and in the Catholic Middle Ages of the West.

2. Acts of Judas Thomas 31, cited in Peter Brown, *Body and Society: Men, Women and Sexual Renunciation in Early Christianity: Twentieth-Anniversary Edition* (New York: Columbia University Press, 2008), 32.

WINTER IN VENICE

WINTER

I came to Venice, in late 1980, in the grip of winter. The city was closed in on itself. Its lanes were no longer clogged with tourists. A damp cold settled on the ancient stones, turning them into ice pads. It was not simply in order to understand the Gnostics and the early monks of Egypt that I set about learning Coptic in these winter months. It was also from a wish to study a language that conjured up for me a hot and sunny land.

Making my way every day through narrow lanes, I began to yearn for a wide-open view. The one that I remember best was the widest of them all, and the saddest. It was a sunset view from the church of S. Elena, at the very tip of Venice, beyond the Arsenal and the Giardini Pubblici. From that point, the entire lagoon lay open. The light of the setting sun was diffused by a cold mist and by the smog of Mestre, and filled the sky with pure gold that was reflected in the water as in a mirror, turning the lagoon into a single spread of pale gold satin. Caught in the last rays of sunset, the windows on the Giudecca and even farther down the coast winked like light buoys. It was then, on the evening of January 24, 1981, that I sensed that my father had died.

IRELAND

My father had been battling prostate cancer, which had made itself increasingly manifest from October 1980 onward as it metastasized into his bones. With characteristic precision and dry humor, he narrated his symptoms—the "infernal triangle" of pain in his bladder and bowel, added to the occasional loss of balance. He chose his metaphors with care: "My illness still hits at me (yes, hits, and quite painfully at times; and with a quite maddening variety of method and timing, in the manner of a guerilla force 'teasing' an adversary large and creaking)." He advised me to keep healthy. I must not overwork: "You are now about exactly the same age as I was when I was invalided out from the Sudan—just think of what the auld wreck I was, and be warned. . . . Read only in good light . . . and hold on to your own faculties like a limpet!"

For three more months, he continued to care not only for my mother, but also for the family as a whole. He would drive into Dublin to visit Teedah and to make sure that she had a supply of coal for her fire (which meant that he lugged a heavy bucket up the long, wooden steps from the coalhouse in the garden). He also visited his sister, Norah, in an old persons' home on the other side of Dublin (no small drive for a man with an uncertain bladder). He would sit with her in the garden, as "this old bag of bones" could no longer make it up the stairs to her room. He would joke that, if a husband is defined as the man who takes tea with you and brings in the coals, then he was as polygamous, in his last years, as King Solomon himself.

When I visited my father in those months, it was his endurance of perpetual discomfort that amazed me. His humor remained. He drew support from a coral reef of habits carefully maintained. Buttons were slowly but surely fastened on trousers, jackets, and shirts—no Velcro for him.

I remember how I flew from America to see him, on November 13, 1980 (three weeks after my meeting with Foucault). First, I flew across the continent to join the Aer Lingus flight from JFK in New York to Dublin. Arriving at the great Lufthansa terminal in JFK, where Aer Lingus had a humble space, I walked past endless ice-blue desks cased in silver steel. Finally I saw my fellow countrymen gathered at the very end of the vast concourse—a gaggle of nuns, priests, and gentlemen with brown hats, tweed jackets, and rumpled woolen cardigans. I was home again.

Settling back in with my parents, I felt as if I had landed on a planet of crushing gravity, whose denizens moved in what was for me an agonizingly slow motion. Social custom seemed to rule their lives with a logic all of its own. On arrival, I suggested, brightly, that Dads should get a nurse to visit him every now and then to make him a little more comfortable—to wash him and to arrange his bedclothes. This was vetoed by both my parents—and for what, for them, were irrefragable reasons. Did I not know that the only shop in Glasthule where they were accustomed to buy biscuits had recently closed? The only other grocery shop in the neighborhood was out of walking range for my mother, so that she could not buy biscuits. And what had biscuits to do with a nurse? Everything. For how could my mother be expected to welcome a nurse to her home without offering her biscuits along with her cup of tea? It was an iron logic. No biscuits, no tea; no tea, no nurse.

Within a few days, these domestic rules and rituals came to make perfect sense to me. They bolstered the quiet courage with which my parents faced death. I came again in January. At the end of the visit, I left my father, having taken the Eucharist with him from the Reverend Linney, the local Church of Ireland clergyman. His clerical gown, put on for the occasion, (as my mother immediately noticed) failed to cover a pair of bright-red, most unclerical suspenders. Afterward my father said how happy he was that we could have Communion together. Then I had to leave for the airport. He died eight days later.

Later in the year, Roberta Chesnut, my old Hebrew teacher, heard of my father's death. She wrote to me about him. She had visited my parents in 1968 and had taken a great liking to them, but especially to my father:

> He was a fine man and a good man, too, a father to have loved and been proud of. I always remember him, natty, dressed in his rust wool suit in Dublin.

That was Dads.

DENIS BETHELL

I returned to Venice in early February after my father's funeral. I soon learned that I had lost yet another link to Ireland: my friend Denis Bethell had died, on February 15, 1981, of a swiftly moving cancer.

For over a decade, Denis had been my link to the medieval past of Ireland. Whenever I visited my parents, I would take time off to spend a long evening with Denis, talking about the Middle Ages in all aspects and in all countries, but mainly about Dark Age Ireland. His occasional vivid letters kept Ireland before my eyes. In 1971, I had sent him my *World of Late Antiquity*. He had read it "in one day under the mulberry tree in the garden of the archbishop's palace at Cashell." Returning to Dublin, he wrote to thank me, seated at the window of his apartment in Monkstown, overlooking Dublin Bay: he could watch

> the seagulls circle on the dull blue sea, the light catch the shore of Howth, and the children scamper down to the Martello tower at Seapoint. . . . It is a delightful place to live—but there, the Kish light is blinking at me, the Claude-like sunset has vanished. I must close.

Of all possible links to Ireland, Denis was the least likely. He was born in Gibraltar and educated in England. With his twill trousers, round, slightly flushed face, and little moustache, he looked what my mother would call threateningly "Anglo-English"—the image of Colonel Blimp. In fact, from the moment that he took up his post in University College Dublin (the National University), in 1966, Denis had entered with rare skill and sympathy into the intricacies and the sensitivities of the Irish medievalist scene, both as a scholar and as a teacher. He worked selflessly to establish an M.Phil. program in Medieval studies, which eventually drew students and scholars to Dublin from all over Europe and the English-speaking world, to benefit from Denis's extraordinarily diverse and humane learning.

In the Irish manner, Denis's apartment on Trafalgar Terrace in Monkstown was grand but had known better days. Its magnificent high ceiling was framed in elaborate plasterwork; wide windows, draped with velvet curtains, faced out onto Dublin Bay: but it was heated by only one turf fire. Professor János Bak, who was then a refugee from Hungary and a professor at the University of British Columbia in Vancouver, remembers "having my back froze off" as he worked with Denis on the translation of a basic introduction to medieval studies.[1]

This once-lordly apartment was the living heart of an extraordinary group of scholars of early Christian and medieval Ireland. It was there that I met Ludwig Bieler, the great authority on Saint Patrick, who, many years before, might have taught me Latin, when I was a boy in my gap year before going to Oxford, had my father's income and the complexities of the Dublin bus system permitted it.

These gatherings could stretch into the wee hours and beyond. One such legendary moment in Denis's apartment marked the end of a groundbreaking international conference on Visigothic Spain in May 1975.[2] As the sun rose over Dublin Bay on Whitsunday morning, Denis was heard to exclaim: "Glory be! On time as usual!"

Now deathly ill himself, Denis had, with his usual selflessness, driven me to the airport on my last visit to my father on January 16. When I saw him after my father's funeral, in late January, he was in bed, propped up by large pillows in his oversize, dimly lit bedroom. "You know, Peter," he said. "They say that one should prepare for death. But the fact is that it is Death that takes you."

1. J. Bak, in *Times of Upheaval: Four Medievalists in Twentieth-Century Central Europe*, ed. Pavlina Rychterová, Gábor Klaniczay, Pawel Kras, and Walter Pohl (Budapest: Central European University Press, 2019), 160.

2. *Visigothic Spain*, ed. E. James (Oxford University Press, 1980).

A lectureship was founded in his honor. In 1983, my mother reported to me the manner in which he was remembered on that occasion: "They said Denis was a beautiful man—gentle, scholarly, ever-polite, and infinitely patient." One would not wish for better virtues in a scholar and a friend.[3]

3. See now Marc A. Meyer, "Denis L. T. Bethell (1934–1981) Remembered," in *The Culture of Christendom. Essays in Medieval History in Memory of Denis L. T. Bethell*, ed. Marc A. Meyer (London: Hambledon Press, 1993), ix–xviii.

SURPRISED IN VENICE

Lellia Cracco Ruggini (1931–2021)

After those sad winter months, we stayed on in Venice until August 1981. At that time, Arnaldo Momigliano combined his professorship in London with an appointment at the Scuola Normale Superiore di Pisa. He encouraged me to get in touch with his many friends and with their students, who formed a network that stretched across northern Italy.

The most lasting friendship to emerge from those contacts was with Lellia Cracco Ruggini, the professor of Roman history in Turin. I had long known her work. Her *Economia e società nell' "Italia annonaria"*, which appeared in 1961, had immediately struck me as a breakthrough: it was the first successful attempt to write the economic history of a major Italian region in the late Roman period.[1] She invited me to lecture in Turin. I found a grande dame in the best Italian tradition, surrounded by the warm admiration of a cadre of enthusiastic and well-trained students, such as Domenico Vera, then at Trieste and now at Parma, with whom I have remained in contact ever since. (At a later time, I met a further generation of her students, most notably Rita Lizzi Testa of the University of Perugia.) This was the beginning of a lively relationship with a remarkable tradition of Italian scholarship on the institutional and social history of the later empire. It has proved as important for me as the one that I had already established with scholars in France.

---

1. Lellia Cracco Ruggini, *Economia e società nell' "Italia annonaria": Rapporti fra agricoltura e commercio dal IV al VI secolo d.C.* (Milan: Giuffrè, 1961), reprinted with an updated bibliography and a valuable introduction (Bari: Edipuglia, 1995), 1–16. See now Jean-Michel Carrié, "Lellia Cracco Ruggini," in *New Late Antiquity*, 77–110, and Rita Lizzi Testa, "In Memoriam. Omaggio a Lellia Cracco Ruggini," *Studi Medievali*, ser. 3, 62 (2021): 801–815.

I bonded instantly with Lellia's husband, Giorgio Cracco, a sweet soul, truly an *anima dulcis*. We realized that we shared a love of holy men. Giorgio had recently shown how the saints of the *Dialogues* of Gregory the Great were wilder figures, closer to the Syrian model of "my" holy men than we had thought. They brought a breath of charismatic power into the battered provinces of Gregory's Italy.[2] We were also surprised to find that we shared a curiosity about Marco Polo and the Mongol Empire, though I might have expected as much from someone born on the edge of the Veneto and deeply engaged with the politics of medieval Venice.[3]

Four years later, in November 1985, I was a visiting professor at Giorgio's Istituto di Storia Medioevale e Moderna in the University of Padua. The lectures that I gave there were a dress rehearsal for the last parts of *Body and Society*, especially on the long-term implications of the great debate between Augustine and Julian of Eclanum on sex, marriage, and original sin.[4]

A Surprise at the Mundial

When I returned to Venice in July and August 1982, I lived in an apartment on the waterfront of the Giudecca, close to the local sports club. On July 8 I was particularly aware of this proximity. The air shook with the roars of the nearby fans, gathered in front of the television in the bar of the sports club, as Italy beat Poland two to zero in the semifinal of the Mundial. I too was glued to the screen.

Then the telephone rang. It had to be an international call. No Italian would ring at such a sacred moment in the course of the Mundial. I answered rather coldly—yes, this is Peter Brown. It was an American male voice, with the heavy tone of someone who had settled down to the pleasant task (maybe, I liked to think, with a whiskey in hand) of telling a lot of people a lot of very good news. He was ringing from Chicago, in order to tell me that I had won a prize from the John D. and Catherine T. MacArthur Foundation. He asked me whether I had heard of the foundation. No, I'd never heard of it. So I did not know what this prize might be: in my case, it was $44,800 per year (virtually

---

2. G. Cracco, *Uomini di Dio e uomini di Chiesa nell'alto Medioevo* (Rome: Edizioni di storia e letteratura, 1977).

3. G. Cracco, *Società e stato nel Medioevo veneziano* (Florence: Olschki, 1967) and *Tra Venezia e Terraferma. Per la storia del Veneto regione del mondo* (Rome: Viella, 2009).

4. Peter Brown, *Sesso e persona tra antichità e Medioevo* (Padua: Nuova Vita, 1986).

a year's salary) for the next five years. This meant, in effect, that, if I wished, I could take the next five years off from teaching in order to pursue pure research.

Three days later, Italy beat Germany in the final of the Mundial, and the neighboring sports club exploded with joy, as half its members leaped into the lagoon with a huge splash and a wild yell of triumph.

SUMMERTIME

It was only when I returned to Berkeley that the full implications of my prize became clear to me. In the words of Larry Rosen, a fellow recipient of the prize:

> With businessmen, time is money; with academics, money is time.[5]

In an exacting and highly professional university system, the MacArthur Prize enabled scholars (and especially young scholars) to take time off from the burden of teaching and administration, to explore new fields and to find a voice of their own.

At the time, however, I was content to celebrate by treating myself to a coffee at a table in the ottocento splendor of Caffè Florian on the Piazza di San Marco. I did it only once—just to show that I could. I was glad to return to the brisk little bar beside the entrance to the Marciana, where (standing at the bar, of course: never at a table!) I would exchange banter with the barman with increasing confidence, and would listen to the scuttlebutt of fellow researchers in Venice.

I did much of my reading at home. In the full heat of summer, violent thunderstorms would explode over the Giudecca. A window of the apartment looked out onto the back of the dome of the church of *Il Redentore*—the magnificent church of Christ the Redeemer, built by Andrea Palladio as an ex-voto for the ending of the plague in Venice in 1575/76. A huge statue of Christ the Redeemer stood on top of the dome. As the storm clouds exploded at nighttime above the statue, lightning flashes threw the great figure of Christ into ever-sharper relief, so that it seemed, in the shimmering broken light of the storm, that he was walking ever closer to me, down from the dome of the church. It was in this sultry season that I settled down in the apartment to enjoy yet another surprise—twenty-nine hitherto unknown letters written by Augustine of Hippo in his old age.

---

5. Priscilla Van Tassell, "Rich but 'Embarassing' Prize," *New York Times*, November 7,' 1982.

"While We Groan in Vain and Are Unable to Help": Augustine in the *Divjak Letters*

Only a few years previously, a young Austrian scholar, Johannes Divjak, had discovered these letters, hidden at the back of a late medieval illuminated manuscript. Traveling on a low budget on behalf of the Austrian Academy of Sciences, (so I was told) Divjak was living in his trailer car in Le Camping de Paris when he went into town to announce his discovery to the Augustinian Institute.

Just before I left for Europe, I had been able to check Divjak's edition of the new letters out of Dow Library. I saw at once that many of these letters dealt with incidents in the life of Augustine as an old bishop of which we had known nothing previously; and—even better still—some dealt with incidents of which we had known only one side of the story. Photocopies of these letters were burning a hole in my luggage as I promised myself to read them at my leisure in Venice.

The letters bore the smell of the earth of Augustine's Roman Africa. They had plainly slipped out of the main collections of his correspondence because they contained little or no high theology. They were too down-to-earth for medieval tastes. Instead, they dealt primarily with Augustine's day-to-day business as a bishop in the last decade of his life.

This was a pure fragment of the past, fresh as the dawn, such as rarely comes the way of scholars of the ancient world. I have already referred to these letters, now known from their discoverer as the *Divjak Letters*.[6] Reading through them in Venice for the first time, I realized at once that I had to change my mind on many aspects of the portrait of Augustine that I had drawn in *Augustine of Hippo*.

Seen at ground level, through these letters, the old Augustine was a far less dominant figure as a Catholic bishop than I had once thought. When I wrote about Augustine in 1967, I had stressed the confidence with which he wrote (in his *City of God* and elsewhere) on the preordained expansion of the Catholic Church. The *Divjak Letters* showed that there was an element of wishful thinking in such claims. What I read in these letters revealed how little authority the Catholic bishops actually enjoyed on a day-to-day basis. Their wishes were frequently flouted by a robustly secular administration. Far from respecting

---

6. See chapter 40: "Writing Augustine of Hippo" and chapter 45: "Resonances."

the church, imperial officials had no hesitation about denying tax exemptions to the clergy and overriding the rights of church sanctuary by dragging fiscal debtors from the altar: "while we groan in vain and are unable to help."[7]

Nor did Augustine appear in these letters as a dominant theological authority. In 419, Consentius, a layman who had recently retired to the Balearic Islands, wrote to Augustine in a thoroughly offhand manner. He told Augustine that he had read a few pages of the *Confessions*. But he had put it aside. It was not to his taste. He preferred the "clear and elegantly ordered style" of Lactantius, the "Christian Cicero" and apologist for Christianity in the age of Constantine. At a time when Augustine was supposed to be at the height of his reputation during the Pelagian controversy, Consentius's letter was a shot across the bow: "even if we said that Augustine's writings are beyond reproach [he wrote], still we do not know what the judgment of posterity will be on his works. Neither did anyone rebuke Origen while he was alive—Origen who, there is no doubt, was condemned after two hundred years or so."[8]

I had never imagined that Augustine could have been treated in this dismissive way.

Nor did I expect the resilience that he showed in fighting a long uphill battle with corruption and violence on his own doorstep. In 428 (when seventy-four years old) Augustine mounted a campaign against a ring of local slave-traders who used the port of Hippo as their base so as to raid the mountain villages close to the city. Up until the discovery of the *Divjak Letters* we knew nothing of this incident: no mention of it was made in any of his surviving works or in any other text of the time. Yet here he was, interviewing the victims, consulting lawyers, and drafting a petition to the court of the distant emperor that is one of the noblest passages in his entire correspondence:

> Barbarians are resisted when the Roman armies are in good condition for fear that Romans will be held in barbarian captivity. But who resists these traders who are found everywhere, who trade, not in animals but in human beings. . . . Who resists when people everywhere and from every side, carried off by violence and ensnared by deception, are led into the hands of those who bid for them? Who will resist in the name of Roman freedom?[9]

7. *Letter* 22*. 2, trans. R. Eno, *Saint Augustine. Letters VI (1*-29*)* (Washington, DC: Catholic University of America Press, 1989), 151.

8. *Letter* 12*. 11, Eno, 105.

9. *Letter* 10*.5, Eno, 79.

"Our Little Greek"

Nor did I expect to come upon an urbane side of the old bishop. At the very end of his life, Augustine approached Firmus, a notable of Carthage, urging him to become baptized. He had even sent Firmus a copy of the *City of God*. Firmus had read as far as book 10 and remained unconvinced. Even though married to a Christian wife, he still held back.[10]

As part of their correspondence, Firmus had sent Augustine—of all things!—the school exercises of his son (probably little speeches composed by the boy), to ask the former rhetor for his opinion on them. Far from seeming bothered, Augustine was charm itself. He wrote back at once. How was "our little Greek"? He hoped that the boy would be a credit to the classical education that he was receiving in the schools of Carthage: "for you, of all people [Firmus], should know that these [rhetorical accomplishments] are good things, and of great advantage." Augustine did not condemn the classics. He simply urged the boy to be careful to use his education properly. He should remember his Cicero: "Eloquence combined with wisdom has proved to be of the greatest benefit to states: but eloquence without wisdom, harmful and of no good to anyone."[11]

This was one of the last letters that Augustine ever wrote, on the eve of the Vandal invasion of 429. It was an extraordinary experience to read for the very first time, in the damp heat of a Venetian summer, an interchange on Cicero between an old bishop and the father of a little boy in a Carthage still bathed in the late sunlight of the ancient world.

10. *Letter* 2*.3, Eno 20. On Firmus, see now Peter Brown, *Through the Eye of a Needle: Wealth, the Fall of Rome, and the Making of Christianity in the West, 350–550 AD* (Princeton, NJ: Princeton University Press, 2012), 357.

11. Cicero, *De inventione* 1.1, in *Letter* 2*.12, Eno, 28–29.

THE COLLÈGE DE FRANCE

PARIS 1982. *LE FAUTEUIL*: THE ARMCHAIR

In June 1982, I delivered lectures at the Collège de France in Paris. The invitation had been arranged by Paul Veyne and Michel Foucault. In many ways, those intense and happy days were like a homecoming. Ever since I had worked on Saint Augustine in the 1960s, visiting Marrou at Châtenay, sitting in on seminars, and seeking advice from the Augustinian Fathers on rue François 1er, Paris had been for me an alternative to Oxford.

My four lectures were entitled (in order) "Les Saints de la Paideia"; "Philosophes et Pouvoir au Bas-Empire"; "Le visage de la Pauvreté"; and "Vers une 'philosophie sociale.'" ("The Saints of Paideia"; "Philosophers and Power in the Later Empire"; "The Face of Poverty"; and "Toward a 'Social Philosophy'").

I remember a nervous walk from the Fondation Hugot, where I was lodged, past the church of Saint-Germain-des-Prés, and along the Boulevard Saint-Germain to the collège, at Place Marcellin Berthelot, in the heat of the early afternoon. It was the first time that I had ever lectured in French, and I was worried by the prospect of being derailed by my stammer on such a public occasion. I clutched a text of my lectures that was as heavily marked up as a musical score, hoping that the written words (carefully accented) would eventually turn into correctly spoken French.

I was saved by *le fauteuil*—by the professor's armchair. On arriving, I was told that it was customary for the lecturer to sit in a solid armchair behind a table, rather than to stand at a podium. To sit in the professor's *fauteuil* conveyed an almost late Roman sense of authority. I could imagine that I was an emperor and that my audience was my *consistorium*, standing before my throne. In fact, I found that the armchair was more comfortable and more intimate than standing at a podium. Most important of all, it enabled me to sit back, and to avoid the cramped breathing brought on by my stammer.

These lectures did not draw on my recent work on virginity. Instead, they reflected my preoccupations in my first years in Berkeley: the conflict between the philosopher and the monk in late antiquity, and the rise to power of the Christian bishop, in alliance with the monks and in the name of the poor, that brought an end to the ancient city. The lectures formed the basis of my subsequent book, *Power and Persuasion*, which would appear in 1992.[1]

Old Friends: Institut d'Études Augustiniennes, rue de l'Abbaye; Claude Lepelley (1934–2015)

In between lectures, I spent much time at the Institut d'Études Augustiniennes. I had last visited the Pères Augustiniens in their somewhat shabby office on rue François 1er. Now I found them handsomely installed as an institute on the rue de l'Abbaye, in the shadow of Saint-Germain-des-Prés.

I only needed to sit for a few hours in the reading room of the institute for the entire world of French Augustinian studies as I had known it since the 1960s to walk past my desk, as old friends and names long known to me came in and out. Among the very best of those friends was Claude Lepelley. I had first met Claude at the Oxford Patristics Conference of 1967. We had retired to the East Gate pub beside the Examination Schools, when the hectic business of the conference closed down for the night. He was a big man, with a heavy, square face and projecting chin like a Tough Guy in a cartoon. But he was the sweetest of men. A pious Catholic of Gallican leanings, he confessed to a huge admiration for the Anglican *Book of Common Prayer*. Whenever he came to Oxford, he said, he would go out of his way to attend evensong in Christ Church Cathedral.

In 1982, Claude had only recently made his name through a two-volume study of the cities of the Roman provinces of North Africa in the later empire. In an extraordinarily detailed mobilization of the epigraphic material, he made an impressive case for the permanence and for the essential Roman-ness of the urban life of Roman Africa throughout the fourth century and after.

Claude would defend this position fiercely up to the end of his life. In his opinion, the North African city of the later empire had managed to remain a

---

1. Peter Brown, *Power and Persuasion in Late Antiquity: Towards a Christian Empire* (Madison: University of Wisconsin Press, 1992).

precious oasis of neutral, civic values, at a time when these values were being swept aside in the rising tide of confessional intolerance. Here were men and women who (when it came to civic matters) thought of themselves as citizens first, and Catholics, Donatists, and pagans very much second. This emphasis on shared classical values echoed the insistence of Claude's exemplar, Henri-Irénée Marrou, on the continued strength of lay culture at a time of headlong religious change. It was a view thoroughly consistent with Claude's good nature and integrity.[2] From this time onward I have treasured his two volumes on the cities of Roman Africa. They set the life of Augustine against the background of a robust urban culture that had by no means succumbed to the otherworldly message of the bishop of Hippo.

DISCOVERIES

At just this time, Claude's instinct was proved right by an unexpected discovery. These were the *Divjak Letters*, which I mentioned in the previous chapter. Claude was among the first to get to study them and had instantly notified me of the discovery. I was thrilled to find myself once again on a new frontier in the study of Augustine.[3]

By way of return, I suggested to Claude that there might be similar letters from the province of Africa lying unnoticed in little-known collections. I urged him to look at the *Spuria*—the unidentified, spurious letters—attached to the works of Sulpicius Severus (the late fourth-century biographer of Saint Martin), which had struck me as having a distinctly local, African flavor. Sure enough, Claude looked at them carefully and immediately edited them with a full commentary.[4] Here was a rare voice—the voice of an unknown landowner from the very soil of Africa.

2. C. Lepelley, *Les cités de l'Afrique romaine au Bas-Empire* (Paris: Études Augustiniennes, 1977, 1981), and "Le lieu des valeurs communes: La cité terrain neutre entre paiens et chrétiens dans l'Afrique de l'Antiquité tardive," in *Idéologies et valeurs civiques dans le monde romain: Hommages à Claude Lepelley*, ed. H. Inglebert (Nanterre: Picard, 2002), 271–285. For a less positive view, see now M. Gassman, "A Feast in Carthage: Testing the Limits of 'Secularity' in Late Antiquity," *Journal of Roman Studies* 110 (2020): 199–219. See now Gareth Sears, "Transforming Late Antique Africa: Claude Lepelley," in *New Late Antiquity*, 551–565.

3. C. Lepelley, "La crise de l'Afrique romaine au début du Vᵉ siècle, d'après les lettres nouvellement découvertes de Saint Augustin," *Académie des Inscriptions et Belles-Lettres: Comptes Rendus*, July–October, 1981, 445–463.

4. C. Lepelley, "Trois documents méconnus sur l'histoire sociale et religieuse de l'Afrique romaine tardive," *Antiquités africaines* 25 (1989): 235–262.

New Friends: Aline Rousselle

I also made new friends. The one who impressed me most was Aline Rousselle. When working on the cult of saints, I had been struck by the manner in which Aline had applied her deep knowledge of Greco-Roman medicine to issues of late antique religion—to the miracles of Saint Martin and to the workings of his shrine compared with the former healing sanctuaries of pagan Gaul.[5] Here was a bridge between two worlds, the pre-Christian and the Christian.

Aline also pointed out the extent to which secular medicine converged on religious healing. Doctors and priests held similar views on the diagnosis and cure of illnesses. She showed, with great skill, how the two healing systems, far from being opposed to one another, converged on a similar view of the human body—so that religious actions, such as exorcism, shared the same body fantasies about the extrusion of disease as did the seemingly more "rational" writings of the doctors on purgative medicine. Her views were crucial to the last chapter of my *Cult of the Saints*.

We found that we were kindred souls in our fascination with the overlap of the rational and the irrational in late antiquity. She told me what it was like to grow up in Morocco, in daily contact with beliefs in djinns and with fully working healing shrines at the graves of Muslim *marabouts*. This shared interest had already led her to take on the translation of my *Cult of the Saints* and of *The Making of Late Antiquity*.[6]

Aline's own work on religion in late antiquity came to fruition a little later—with her prizewinning book, *Croire et guérir: la foi en Gaule dans l'Antiquité tardive*,[7] and brilliant chapters on the religious history of the third century in a volume that she wrote with Jean-Michel Carrié.[8]

I did not know, when I first met her in Paris, the extent to which Aline had carried her knowledge of ancient medicine into the study of the origins of Christian asceticism, and especially on the interrrelation of monastic diet, ancient medical knowledge, and the suppression of the sexual drive. It was she who noticed that John Cassian, of all people, had cited ancient medical lore

---

5. A. Rousselle, "Du sanctuaire au thaumaturge. La guérison en Gaule au ive siècle," *Annales* 31 (1976): 1085–1107.

6. Peter Brown, *Le culte des saints* (Paris: Le Cerf, 1984), and *La génèse de l'Antiquité tardive* (Paris: Gallimard, 1983).

7. A. Rousselle, *Croire et guérir: la foi en Gaule dans l'Antiquité tardive* (Paris: Fayard, 1990).

8. J.-M.Carrié and A. Rousselle, *L'empire romain en mutation: des Sévères à Constantin* (Paris: Le Seuil, 1999).

which had recommended that athletes should sleep with leaden plates on their genitals, so as to "cool" their sperm, thereby avoiding loss of energy through night emissions. I had not expected such medical precision in a Desert Father.

Aline Rousselle combined, to an impressive degree, a grasp of ancient medicine and of ascetic literature with a humane sense of the vast, silent pain brought to bear on women by the reproductive strategies advocated by late antique doctors, lawyers, and male intellectuals. These studies brought home to me the cost to women of the notion of service to the city through childbearing. At the same time, she played an important role in denouncing violence against women in her hometown, Montpellier. These qualities make her book *Porneia* one of the most serious contributions to feminist studies on the ancient world to appear in any language.[9]

Aline Rousselle shared with Évelyne Patlagean (whom I also met frequently at this time) an intense commitment to the social realities of the later empire and an acute compassion for the faceless millions—women, children, and the poor—who lived in the shade of a brilliant world. It was to this French tradition, where social history and the study of the body converged, that I would turn by preference when writing *Body and Society*, as a complement and a counterweight to the more literary approaches that had come to flourish among many historians of the early church.

At a time when early Christian studies tended to be dominated by textual approaches derived from New Testament scholarship, from postmodern literary criticism, and from the study of ancient rhetoric, I turned, for a sense of reality, to the more historically grounded work of Aline Rousselle and Évelyne Patlagean in France, and to the school of Lellia Ruggini in Italy. Among such scholars, I found the knowledge of law, of social institutions, and of archaeology that provided a solid context for the dazzling confections of Patristic and late classical literature.

PAUL VEYNE

The center of my life in Paris at that time was the group formed around the Collège de France. It was there that I linked up again with Paul Veyne, after our first meeting at dinner with Foucault in early 1981. Unlike many campuses

---

9. A. Rousselle, *Porneia. De la maîtrise du corps à la privation sensorielle* (Paris: Presses Universitaires de France, 1983), translated as *Porneia: On Desire and the Body in Antiquity* (Oxford: Blackwell, 1988).

I knew in America, where I would be passed from dinner to dinner and from power lunch to power lunch, the collège was not an absorptive host. Apart from one grand reception, I was left on my own to make whatever contacts I wished in Paris.

Veyne attended all my lectures, adding his usual puckish comments. After my third lecture on monks and poverty (where I had stressed the somewhat artificial identification of the monks with the poor) he dashed off a hilarious analysis of a similar play of identities by which Marxist militants claimed to represent the proletariat, based on his experiences as a Party member in the 1950s:

> When I was a young man, the relation between the militants of working class extraction (not the intellectuals!) was similar to the one between the monks and the poor. The communist militant symbolizes the proletariat. Each militant is reputed to be a proletarian, even if he becomes a professional politician and does not work in any factory.

These militants, Veyne continued, would pay back to the Party their salaries as members of Parliament (thirty thousand francs per week) and would get from the Party the minimum salary of a French worker (three thousand francs per month). But the payoff in prestige was worth it.

> For he [the militant] is assumed to be the *real* proletarian, and a proletarian who is *intéressant* [in one's interest] to visit, to be on visiting terms with—a reputable and not a tedious nor boring proletarian.

This was vintage Veyne, driven by his unfailing sense of the oddity of institutions.

PIERRE HADOT

My visit to Paris enabled me to link up again with one great friend—the unrivaled interpreter of ancient philosophy, Pierre Hadot. Our friendship went back for fifteen years. I first met Hadot at the Oxford Patristics Conference of 1967, when he and Frau Ilsetraut were a newly married couple. I brought roses from my garden for them, and we had supper together at a Chinese restaurant at the bottom of the Cowley Road. Hadot's gray-blue eyes flashed with intelligence, magnified in their effect by large glasses, as we discussed our various projects of research.

Many years before, I had met Hadot's mentor, the Jesuit scholar Paul Henry, who had written two groundbreaking studies: *Plotin et l'Occident*[1] and an essay on the Neoplatonic background to Augustine's account of the mystical experience that he had shared with his mother in Ostia—the famous "Vision of Ostia" recounted in the *Confessions*.[2] Henry had joined two hitherto distinct worlds by studying the reception of the pagan Neoplatonism of the Greek East by Christian thinkers in the Latin West. It was like the discovery of the missing link.

In the 1960s, Hadot collaborated with Paul Henry to edit the works of the Neoplatonic philosopher Marius Victorinus and eventually wrote a monograph on him.[3] Victorinus was a crucial figure in the transfer of ideas from East to West; and he had played a decisive role in the intellectual evolution of

1. P. Henry, *Plotin et l'Occident* (Louvain: Spicilegium Sacrum Lovaniense, 1934).
2. P. Henry, *La Vision d'Ostie* (Paris: J. Vrin, 1938).
3. P. Hadot, *Marius Victorinus. Recherches sur sa vie et ses oeuvres* (Paris: Études Augustiniennes, 1971).

Augustine. When teaching in Rome in the 350s, he had converted to Christianity in a fully public manner that impressed Augustine when he heard about it at the time of his own conversion in Milan in 386. More important yet, because Augustine knew no Greek, the only works of Plotinus that he was able to read were those that had been translated into Latin by Victorinus. These translations were Augustine's gateway to the Greek East.

I had met Paul Henry in 1957, when I was a young fellow at All Souls. He had come to Oxford to deliver a course of lectures on the philosophical background to the great Trinitarian controversies of the fourth century. He lectured to an almost empty room; but I was gripped. Like the lecture of Festugière on Libanius and his students, which I must have heard at roughly the same time, Henry's discussion of the role of Neoplatonism in Christian theology was one of those high moments that gave me the determination (at the age of twenty-three) to continue as a student of the later empire.

One late afternoon at the time of his visit, I was invited to meet Paul Henry at the home of Isobel Henderson (1906–1967) in Summertown in North Oxford. She was a brilliant classicist, an expert on ancient Greek music, and a good friend both of Paul Henry and of Arnaldo Momigliano.[4] I remember the late-afternoon light falling behind Henry, as he sat at a window in a small armchair, grasping a very full glass of whiskey. Isobel presided over the salon with a long black cigarette holder, wearing a pair of Chinese trousers in bright orange. It was a somewhat Proustian scene. On the strength of my memory of Henry's visit to Oxford, eleven years earlier, I introduced myself to Hadot at the Oxford Patristics Conference of 1967.

Spiritual Exercises

In 1967, I knew Hadot for his interventions in the debate on the Neoplatonic elements in the thought of Augustine, based on his study of Marius Victorinus, and for a brilliant little monograph (written, I now learn, in only one month!) on Plotinus—*Plotin ou la simplicité du regard*.[5] Although we had remained in contact, I had not followed very closely his other work in ancient philosophy. Hence my surprise when I came to Paris to the Collège de France, in June 1982, and found Hadot's new book, *Exercices spirituels et philosophie antique*, prominently displayed

---

4. See now Averil Cameron, her student, in *Past Masters*, October 27, 1994.

5. P. Hadot, *Plotin ou la simplicité du regard* (Paris: Plon, 1963; Gallimard, 1997), trans. M. Chase, *Plotinus, or the Simplicity of Vision* (Chicago: University of Chicago Press, 1993).

on the new accessions shelf of the Institute of Augustinian Studies. I realized immediately that this book would revolutionize our view of the aim of the ancient philosophers, and of the way in which they passed on their teachings.

Seated at a large table rendered golden by streaks of sunlight, with a view of the fresh green leaves of the trees that stood between the library of the institute and the gray roof of Saint-Germain-des-Prés, I began to read. I soon realized that I would never again read a text of ancient philosophy, or even the most banal ethical treatise, in the same way.

Hadot made clear that these written texts were meant to transform their readers. They were not treatises of abstract reasoning. They were the living voice of their authors, pleading, insisting, and, above all, arguing, that their readers should change their lives. For Hadot, ancient philosophy "did not consist in teaching an abstract theory . . . but rather in the art of living. . . . [It demanded] a concrete attitude and a determinate life-style, which engaged the whole of existence."[6]

At once, the world of the ancient philosophers took on a profound unfamiliarity. Our own practices in reading ancient philosophical texts seemed somehow trivial. As we sat in our armchairs or around a seminar table, leafing through the works of ancient thinkers in order to expound or to criticize their theories, we were doing the wrong thing. We should have been like the ancients, sitting at the feet of a guide who would show us how to use these theories so as to transform ourselves. The atmosphere of this guidance was totally different from that of a modern university. It was closer to the relation of master and disciple, of *pir* and *murshid* in Islam, or to Dante as he hung on the lips of Brunetto Latini:

La cara e buona imagine paterna
di voi, quando nel mondo ad ora ed ora
m'insegnavate come l'uom s'eterna.

The dear and kind, paternal image of you,
when, in the world, hour by hour,
you taught me how man makes himself eternal.

(*INFERNO* 15.83–85)

---

6. P. Hadot, *Exercices spirituels et philosophie antique* (Paris: Études Augustiniennes, 1981), trans. Arnold I. Davidson in *Pierre Hadot: Philosophy as a Way of Life* (Oxford: Blackwell, 1995), 83. I will use the translations of *Exercices spirituels* and of other articles and lectures by Hadot that are collected in Davidson's book. See, further, Matthew Sharpe and Federico Testa, *The Selected Writings of Pierre Hadot: Philosophy as Practice* (London: Bloomsbury Academic, 2020).

Elite men and women in the ancient world expected to get personal guidance of this kind on a regular basis. Hadot pointed out how even the texts themselves were deliberately written in a dialogic, rhetorical style: they were seen as no more than the fading echo of a master's voice. Put bluntly: people did not turn to a philosopher only for his theories. They turned to his theories (and there were many of them, often hotly debated) so as to give rational support to a slow therapy of the self. The principal aim was always "to steep ourselves in a rule for life," preferably under the guidance of a mentor.[7]

We moderns might no longer sit at the feet of a philosopher, as ancient persons had done. But we could at least recover something of the existential weight of the message behind the volumes that lined the shelves of our libraries:

> [For] we have forgotten how to read: how to pause, liberate ourselves from our worries, return to ourselves, and leave aside our search for subtlety and originality, in order to meditate calmly, ruminate, and let the texts speak to us. This, too, is a spiritual exercise.[8]

A lot of what Hadot wrote was not entirely new to me. As I have said, I had been increasingly struck by the very real seriousness with which many of my friends and colleagues at Berkeley decided on how they would live their lives. Their preoccupation with the proper use of freedom had already caused me to read the ancient moralists with greater sympathy than before. A lively interest in self-formation and self-fashioning had long preceded the appearance of Hadot's *Exercices spirituels* and Foucault's *Care of the Self.* The Berkeley conference on *adab* in the Islamic world in 1979, to which I had contributed, showed this clearly. But Hadot's *Exercices spirituels* offered something different. It was a presentation of the transformative nature of ancient philosophy by a towering scholar.

Philosophy as a Way of Living

Only twenty years later, in 2001, when reading the collection of Hadot's autobiographical interviews with Jeannie Carlier and Arnold Davidson, entitled *La philosophie comme manière de vivre*—Philosophy as a Way of Living—did I realize the extent to which the power of Hadot's book came from the fact that he had meditated on and lived every sentence of it. He had constantly battled

---

7. Hadot, *Philosophy as a Way of Life*, 85.
8. Hadot, *Philosophy as a Way of Life*, 109.

a heart condition. After four major operations, he spoke of himself, with irony, as "a great *habitué* of the hospitals of Paris." (In Paris, one is usually supposed to be an *habitué* of restaurants.) Maxims of the philosophers accompanied him into wards and operating rooms.[9]

Furthermore, Hadot's standards for public comportment were as unflinching as were those of any late antique man. He had been present when the future Pope John XXIII was papal nuncio in Paris and was solemnly entertained at Saint-Sulpice. A pious layman who was serving at table poured the nuncio's wine from the wrong side. The nuncio exploded at the gaffe. Looking back to this fit of rage, Hadot concluded that John XXIII, though now beatified, may not have been a saint by ancient standards.[10] *Exercices spirituels* was the work of a modern sage, based on years of personal meditation on the thought of the ancients. Every reading of an ancient text and every citation from an ancient author in it was just right: it could not have been chosen differently.

VERSAILLES

When we met again in Paris, in June 1982, it was a happy time for Hadot. He had recently been elected to the Collège de France, largely through the support of Michel Foucault. He would give his famous inaugural lecture— "Forms of Life and Forms of Discourse in Ancient Philosophy"—on February 18, 1983.[11]

We spent an entire Sunday together with Frau Ilsetraut at Versailles. We moved from pavilion to pavilion discussing everything from German Romanticism to the ancient cosmos. Still talking, we saw the *grands jets d'eau*. There was a lightness about Hadot as he discussed Goethe's maxim "The present is our only happiness," which showed that he practiced what he read. He really was a philosopher embracing a moment of intellectual contact with a fellow scholar—we were linked in the sheer, unassuming enjoyment of ideas.

After a long and happy lunch, he turned to me and said, "You know, Professor Brown, the more I study the ancient philosophers, the less Christianity means to me." My answer was the exact opposite: "No, as for me: the more I study ancient paganism, the more I have come to respect traditional religions such as Christianity, Judaism, and Islam."

9. Pierre Hadot, *La philosophie comme manière de vivre. Entretiens avec Jeannie Carlier et Arnold I. Davidson* (Paris: Albin Michel, 2001), 64 and 180.

10. Hadot, *La philosophie comme manière de vivre*, 188.

11. Now translated as "Ancient Philosophy," in *Philosophy as a Way of Life*, 49–70.

Hadot did not agree. He was a true philosopher. Religion, in his opinion, was a social creation—a clutter of culturally determined rituals and representations. This clutter had nothing whatsoever to do with that primal sense of oneness with the universe: that "shiver of divine delight" which Lucretius had once felt beneath the endless stars—an "oceanic" experience that Hadot himself had enjoyed on many occasions.[12] Indeed, as he recounted it to Jeannie Carlier in 2001, his life as a philosopher began in his teens with such an experience:

> Leaning with my back on the window-sill, I looked up into the night sky, feeling that I had taken a plunge into an immense world filled with stars.[13]

Hadot's religion was a true philosopher's religion, austerely shorn of mythic representations. A similar philosophic religion had once been professed by the Stoics and by some radical Platonists. It occasionally emerged in late antiquity and in Islam (much to the distress of the orthodox of all three religions—Jews, Christians, and Muslims alike), like a white peak towering above the clouds. Alas, from Hadot's point of view, I was a mere historian, congenitally tolerant of clutter.

FOUCAULT AND HADOT

The sense of joy through having broken out, for a moment, from the narrow confines of the self to the contemplation of an immensely wider world was what made Hadot so very different from Michel Foucault. He shared with the ancient sages whom he studied (if in a modern idiom) a sense of the thrill of kinship with the natural world that drew him always outside himself. For this reason, self-formation, the care of the self (*Le souci de soi,* to use the title of Foucault's book on the ethics of the Roman world) meant something very different to him from what it meant to Foucault.

Though they esteemed each other, the two men were not close, either in personality or in outlook.[14] It was a significant difference, which struck me at the time, when I had read Hadot's *Exercices spirituels* and then compared it with

---

12. Lucretius, *On the Nature of Things* 3.29; Hadot, *La philosophie comme manière de vivre,* 28 and 69.

13. Hadot, *La philosophie comme manière de vivre,* 24.

14. Hadot, *La philosophie comme manière de vivre,* 214–215, and "Reflections on the Idea of the 'Cultivation of the Self,'" in *Philosophy as a Way of Life,* 206–213.

Foucault's *Le souci de soi*, which appeared three years later. Both Hadot and Foucault were aware of the effort that educated persons in the ancient world put into ordering their lives through prolonged and carefully premeditated work on the self. For both, the philosophical literature of the classical world was not merely a gallery of theories. It drove serious endeavors at self-amendment.

But from then on they differed. Foucault's notion of the "self" was more narrow than that of Hadot. It lacked the cosmic dimension that the ancient sages took for granted. In his critique of Foucault, Hadot insisted that, for ancient philosophers, "care of the self" was never an end in itself. Simply to enjoy the pleasure of having established a carefully constructed lifestyle was not enough: that was mere dandyism—the creation of an eccentric persona. Rather, the soul was groomed so as to go beyond itself, to experience the leap of joy that came with realizing that it was somehow part of the supreme order and beauty of the universe.

Furthermore, it was this sense of working toward kinship with an ever-widening world that kept the ancient philosophers bound to society. Hadot rejected the current image of the ancient philosopher as a lonely practitioner of self-improvement. Still less were these philosophers otherworldly recluses. He resisted that view as firmly as I had done in "The Philosopher and Society in Late Antiquity." Far from it: the philosopher's activity reached out, in ever-wider circles, away from the narrow self, through lively networks of students, to the city; and finally, to the contemplation of the vibrant unity of the cosmos. Paradoxically, by withdrawing from society, which imposed such narrow confines on the self, ancient philosophers found that they were never alone.[15]

GETTING KNOWN IN THE 1980S

I returned to America with a copy of *Exercices spirituels*, which I photocopied regularly so as to educate my colleagues in classics and any interested graduate students. At that time, Hadot was totally eclipsed in America by Foucault, whose last books—*L'usage des plaisirs* and *Le souci de soi*: *The Use of Pleasures* and *The Care of the Self*—had been instantly translated into English in 1985. These two books, and not Hadot's *Exercices*, were assumed to contain all that anyone needed to know about spiritual guidance and self-formation in the ancient world.

15. Hadot, *Philosophy as a Way of Life*, 273.

I was sorry that the work of Hadot was ignored in this way. Looking back, however, I think that I should have remembered that academe, even in the 1980s (at the dawn of the internet and with no YouTube), was a lot more late antique in its structures than we realize. Access to entire bodies of thought still depended on the vivid presence of the scholar in person—as a visiting lecturer or as a teacher in a seminar.

Foucault had offered his presence most willingly in the United States. Not so Hadot. As soon as I arrived in Princeton, in late 1983, I had urged him to come to speak there. But he did not think that his English was up to the occasion. So Foucault was what we got. It was only in 1995 that Hadot's *Exercices* and other articles were edited and well translated by Arnold I. Davidson in *Philosophy as a Way of Life*. At long last, this precious flow of French classical culture at its best entered the veins of American and English academe.

As for myself, I remained in contact with Hadot, exchanging books and articles. I was always aware of his distinctive profile and lucidity of judgment in contemporary matters. He had no illusions about his own career. He had risen from a small Catholic seminary in Rheims to the Collège de France without any of the careful grooming and active patronage by leaders in the field that was usually necessary for the career of successful French academics. He viewed the system of examinations that regulated the advancement of young scholars in France (as analogous ones had regulated mine in England) as tests in rhetorical performance and not of real intellect.[16] This was the characteristically robust view of a philosopher and a shrewd judge of his times.

I last met the Hadots at Limours on June 1, 2008, for a characteristically generous and leisurely lunch and tea. Pierre died on April 24, 2010. To have known him—for so many years and through so many changes of interest on both our parts—was like living by the side of a quiet, deep river that was always in view, flowing serenely past the banks of my own varied engagements with late antiquity.

16. Hadot, *Philosophie comme manière de vivre*, 77–78.

A MIGHT-HAVE-BEEN

MICHEL FOUCAULT AND *LES AVEUX DE LA CHAIR*

I returned from Europe to Berkeley in late August 1982 and settled down to write a series of five lectures for the American Council of Learned Societies. These lectures were the first draft of *Body and Society*, which appeared in 1988. It is odd to think that, at almost exactly the same time, in 1982, Michel Foucault had finished an entire book on the same subject. This was the fourth volume of his *History of Sexuality*, called *Les aveux de la chair—The Confessions of the Flesh*.[1] In this volume, Foucault analyzed the attitudes to sex and marriage in Christian writers from Clement of Alexandria to Augustine. No book would have overlapped more perfectly with my own projected study, both in its subject matter and in its chronological range.

Yet this crucial last volume of Foucault's *History of Sexuality* did not appear until 2018. Foucault had handed in a typescript of *Les aveux* to Gallimard, his publisher, in the fall of 1982. At that time, he had been in no hurry to publish it. He was busy completing the other two books that had resulted from his *tournant antique*—his giant's stride across two millennia, from early modern Europe to the ancient world, which resulted in *L'usage des plaisirs*, on ancient Greece, and *Le souci de soi*, on classical Rome.[2] He wanted them to appear first. The Fathers of the Church could wait. Then he died, in June 1984. It was

1. Michel Foucault, *Histoire de la Sexualité 4: Les aveux de la chair* (Paris: Gallimard, 2018), trans. Robert Hurley, *Confessions of the Flesh: The History of Sexuality, Volume 4* (New York: Pantheon, 2021).

2. M. Foucault, *L'usage des plaisirs* (Paris: Gallimard, 1984): *The Use of Pleasures* (New York: Pantheon, 1985) and *Le souci de soi* (Paris: Gallimard, 1984): *The Care of the Self* (New York: Pantheon, 1985).

not until thirty-four years later that *Les aveux—The Confessions of the Flesh*—appeared.[3]

As a result of this delay, I now have on my desk a book that takes me back to the days when Foucault and I were working on the same themes, and very often reading the same texts. So what is it like to read *Les aveux* so many years later?

SOURCES CHRÉTIENNES

First and foremost, reading *Les aveux* today has brought me back to the Paris of the early 1980s. It reminded me that Foucault and I shared a debt to a common academic culture. We drew on the erudition of a remarkable generation. We both looked back to the recent Golden Age of French Patristic scholarship, associated with the liberal French Catholicism of the years before and after Vatican II. One of the greatest and most lasting scholarly ventures of this time had been the creation of a series that made the texts of ancient Christian authors fully available in reliable editions, accompanied (on the facing right page) with fine French translations, and with introductions and commentaries that were often complete essays in themselves.

The series was known as *Sources chrétiennes*. It had begun in Lyons in dire times—in 1942. Under the direction of Cardinal Jean Daniélou, Henri de Lubac (1896–1983), and Claude Mondésert (1906–1990), and with the warm encouragement of Henri-Irénée Marrou (who edited the *Paidagôgos* of Clement of Alexandria for the series), the *Sources chrétiennes* became both the symbol and the spearhead of the movement of *ressourcement*—of a return to the sources. Though we two came at it from very different angles, Foucault and I were the beneficiaries of that remarkable moment in French Catholic scholarship.

The editions of the *Sources chrétiennes* were, in many ways, products of the unsung heroes and heroines of the study of Christianity in late antiquity in the postwar years: Michel Aubineau (1921–2002), Claude Mondésert, Marguerite Harl, Anne-Marie Malingrey (1904–2002). I had known many of them from the Oxford Patristics Conferences of 1963 and 1967. Their patient work enabled readers like Foucault and many others to enter deeply, and with sane guidance, into masterpieces of early Christian thought on sex and marriage in a way that had not been possible previously.

---

3. Frédéric Gros, "Avertissment," *Les aveux de la chair*, iv–v; *Confessions of the Flesh*, ix–x. See also Stuart Elden, review of Michel Foucault, *Histoire de la Sexualité 4: Les aveux de la chair, Theory, Culture, and Society* 35 (2018): 293–311, at 293–297.

Among these Christian writers, Gregory of Nyssa (335–395) stood out for his ambitious treatise *On Virginity*, and for his touching study of virginity in action in the *Life of Macrina*—the life and tranquil death of his sister who became a nun. I still have a copy of the *Sources chrétiennes* edition of Gregory of Nyssa's *Life of Macrina*.[4] I notice that, at just this time, I wrote into the flyleaf a poem of Robert Frost, "Spring Pools," that seemed to catch Gregory's notion of virgin flesh as, somehow, a mirror of eternity:

> These pools that, though in forests, still reflect
> The total sky almost without defect.[5]

I note that Foucault's analysis of Gregory's *On Virginity* in *Les aveux* had reached a similar conclusion: here was a fragment of life on earth that already mirrored the world beyond death.[6]

I remember first reading Gregory of Nyssa's *On Virginity* in the capacious *Sources chrétiennes* edition of Michel Aubineau, in the dim cabin light of a plane that bounced up and down in the middle of a thunderstorm as it left Nashville, Tennessee, for San Francisco.[7] It is good to think that Michel Foucault may have been reading the same text, at much the same time, in the quiet of the library of the Dominican Order at Le Saulchoir (43 rue de la Glacière, Paris) to which he would retire to work in what, alas, proved to be his last years.

How New Was Christianity?

Reading *Les aveux* I also realize that Foucault was intervening on a topic that had long been a subject of debate among scholars of late antiquity: How original was the contribution of Christianity to the moral life of the Roman Empire in its last centuries? Can we speak of the victory of a novel "Christian morality" over the values of the pagan past? If so, should we acclaim the victory of this morality over the loose mores of a decadent empire; or should we regret this victory as the beginning of a moral ice age, characterized by the relentless suppression of sex?

---

4. Gregory of Nyssa, *Life of Macrina*, ed. Pierre Maraval, *Vie de Sainte Macrine*, Sources chrétiennes 178 (Paris: Le Cerf, 1971).

5. Robert Frost, *Selected Poems* (Harmondsworth: Penguin, 1973), 145.

6. Foucault, *Les aveux de la chair*, 196; *Confessions of the Flesh*, 150.

7. Grégoire de Nysse, *La Virginité*, ed. M. Aubineau, Sources chrétiennes 119 (Paris: Le Cerf, 1961).

In the early 1980s, this problem was being examined anew in many different ways. The tone had been set by Paul Veyne, Foucault's friend and mentor in ancient matters, in a provocative article entitled "Family and Love in the High Empire."[8] In this article, Veyne claimed that the spread of Christianity had contributed nothing whatsoever to the hardening of the moral tone of the later empire. This hardening had already happened in the age of Marcus Aurelius. At that time, Veyne argued, the elites of the Roman world had opted for a puritanical "morality of respectability" quite as repressive as any that developed in Christian, Jewish, or Muslim circles.

In Veyne's opinion, the emergence of this austere morality was the "great unnoticed event" that separated the freewheeling sexual mores of classical Greeks and Romans from the hard-bitten, ascetically inclined moralists of the second and third centuries. Far from being easygoing gentlemen (as they had usually been portrayed, with more than a hint of approval), the Romans of the Antonine Age were a somber lot. They passed on to the Christian church icy views on sex and marriage that would last in Europe until modern times.

OLD CODES IN A NEW KEY

Here Foucault made a brilliant intervention. He did not agree with Veyne. Sticking closely to a few well-known Christian texts, he pointed out that Christian writers had inherited these restrictive codes; but they played them out in a new key. The taboos and prohibitions imposed on sexual behavior, which Veyne presented as so prominent in pagan circles in the age of the Antonines, took on a new valence among Christians. He showed how Christian writings of the third and fourth centuries expressed new forms of experience not to be found among pagans.

Most scholars saw Christian advocacy of virginity as no more than the end result of a progressive tightening of the screws of prohibitions on sexual activity, with total rejection of sex as the ultimate form of repression. Foucault did not see it this way. He pointed out how the idea and practice of virginity appeared in a new light in Christian circles, freighted with significantly different, emancipatory meanings.[9]

8. Paul Veyne, "La famille et l'amour sous le Haut-Empire romain," *Annales* 33, no. 1 (1978): 35–63.

9. Foucault, *Les aveux de la chair*, 51; *Confessions of the Flesh*, 36.

To Be a Virgin

In *Les aveux*, Foucault dealt with the theme of virginity in a manner that paralleled my own approach in 1982. He rejected the notion that the Christian ideal of virginity could be explained by a growing taboo on sex. He argued that this explanation did not do justice to the novelty of the experience of continence itself. By this Foucault meant the expectations that the virgin state awoke in those who practiced or encouraged it, and the views on the person and on society that were condensed in this drastic choice of lifestyle.

Foucault summed up these expectations in a long chapter, "Être vierge"—To Be a Virgin:[10]

> The valorization of virginity is therefore something very different from and much more than the pure and simple disqualification or prohibition of sexual relations. It involves a substantial valorization of the individual's relation to their own sexual conduct, since it makes the relation a positive experience, which has a historical, metahistorical and spiritual meaning.[11]

In the third and fourth centuries, the practice of virginity was hailed, in Christian circles, as the sign of the beginning of a new age; and those who adopted it were acclaimed as pioneers carried forward by the march of history.

Had I read *Les aveux* in 1982, this chapter alone would have come as music to my ears. For this was exactly the message that I also had begun to draw from the same Christian writings on virginity as Foucault had read. Both of us were facing the same problem: How did a "mystique of virginity" develop in Christianity that would place sexual renunciation at the very top of the list of Christian virtues in a way that it was never placed in pagan, Jewish, and (later) Muslim circles?

Subjectivity or Society?

Despite this convergence, we went our separate ways. Foucault was a philosopher who wished to trace the stages by which a modern subjectivity—a sense of the self in relation to sexuality—emerged, somewhat surprisingly, among the Christians of late antiquity. For this reason, he studied early Christian texts very much with their future in mind. He turned to them because major figures

---

10. Foucault, *Les aveux de la chair*, 149–245; *Confessions of the Flesh*, 113–189.
11. Foucault, *Les aveux, de la chair*, 201–203; *Confessions of the Flesh*, 154–155.

such as Augustine and John Cassian had left the indelible imprint of their ideas on all subsequent generations of Western Catholics, and eventually on western Europe as a whole.

As a result, *Les aveux* presented a drastically simplified picture of early Christianity itself. Judaism did not concern Foucault. Nor did the world of the New Testament and the complicated story of early Christian origins. His interest in Christianity began two centuries after that time, when Christian authors such as Tertullian (ca. 160–ca. 240) and Clement of Alexandria (ca. 150–ca. 215) entered into a dialogue with the cultivated elites of the Roman world and struck up an alliance between Christianity and classical values that would eventually lead to the triumph of the Catholic Church in western Europe.

Tertullian, Clement, and their successors wrote the challenging texts (most of them available to French readers in the editions of the *Sources chrétiennes*) on which Foucault the philosopher set to work with his ever-questioning mind. But the tensions within the Christian communities themselves, which led to the writing of those texts, did not concern him greatly.[12]

By contrast, I was a historian. I wanted to understand the early Christians in their own time, regardless of the long-term future of their ideas. I wanted to know what exact circumstances caused these particular ideas to be discussed at a given time and place within the Christian churches. In *Body and Society*, I would follow how these ideas emerged, decade by decade and region by region, pushed to the surface through the ripple of tensions that ran throughout the Christian communities, scattered across the Roman world, from Mesopotamia to Carthage and beyond. While Foucault challenged modern readers to look back to the Christian past in order to understand the origins of many of their own notions of the human person in the present, I would invite the reader to listen in to a grand debate within early Christianity itself.

12. This is clearly seen by Johannes Zachhuber, "Sexuality and the Christian Self: Michel Foucault's Reading of the Church Fathers," *Toronto Journal of Theology* 36 (2020): 170–182, esp. 172–173.

THE NORTHEAST
CORRIDOR

Berkeley to Princeton

On May 22, 1983, I presented a paper, "Augustine and Sexuality," at a colloquy of the Center for Hermeneutical Studies at the Graduate Theological Union on Holy Hill. This was the center where I had presented "The Philosopher and Society in Late Antiquity" when I first arrived in California in 1978.

It was the last paper that I would give at Berkeley. My wife, Pat, having completed her dissertation on Venetian Renaissance art, had been offered a tenure-track appointment in the Art History Department in Princeton. I went with her. Here the good fortune of my MacArthur Prize was immediately apparent. I could take it anywhere I wanted. It left me free to apply for three years of unpaid leave from the University of California, so as to come to Princeton as a visiting professor in the History Department, to begin in the fall of 1983.

Hence a certain sadness surrounded my last Sunday evening colloquy on Holy Hill. With characteristic graciousness, Eric Gruen wound up the discussion, using phrases that were dear to Augustine's heart: "We want to wish you well at Princeton, but not too well. We hope that this will be a short sojourn, so that you will return to your true *amici*—your true friends—where your true *necessitudo socialis*—your bond of companionship—lies."[1]

We arrived at Princeton on a sultry evening in late August, having driven across America. The velvet darkness was occasionally lit up by the somewhat

---

1. Peter Brown, "Augustine and Sexuality," in *The Center for Hermeneutical Studies in Hellenistic and Modern Culture*, Colloquy no. 46, May 22, 1983 (Berkeley: Center for Hermeneutical Studies, 1983), 41.

eerie flash of fireflies, which I now saw for the first time—detonations of bright light without so much as a crackle. The air throbbed with the sound of lovesick cicadas. It seemed as if I had come to a Mediterranean place. I wondered whether a solemn *paseo* was taking place in the center of the town, in the warmth of the evening: a *paseo* such as I remembered it from Burgos many years before—groups of boys and girls, and solemn, well-dressed couples, accompanied by nannies in pure white dresses, pushing formidable perambulators. I found no such thing. Fully lit by powerful streetlights, Nassau Street seemed doubly empty. All that was to be seen was a slightly tiddly Princeton alumnus, in a bright-orange blazer, as he made his way out of Lahiere's Restaurant to his parked car. Plainly, I had not reached the Med.

A week or so later, I walked from the apartment on College Road toward the Institute for Advanced Study. Standing at the top of the great spread of open grass in front of Fuld Hall, I was struck by the sheer size and exuberance of the trees that surrounded the institute buildings. In these years, the treescapes of England (which consisted to a large degree of ancient elms) had been scythed by Dutch elm disease. To come upon a view of the enormous trees that surrounded the institute was like stepping into a Victorian landscape painted by John Constable. It was a time warp.

Setting off across the meadow, with grasshoppers buzzing at my feet like drops of water sizzling on a hot plate, I noticed another figure walking toward me. I recognized him from a short encounter at Berkeley: it was Clifford Geertz. As each of us advanced, we each became less certain of ourselves. Finally we met. Not a word was exchanged. We each smiled, bowed to each other in an amiable manner, and set off in the opposite direction, under a high fall sky.

On the East Coast: A New Geography

On my arrival at Princeton, Art Eckstein and Jeannie Rutenberg, my friends from my very first days at Berkeley, sent me a powerful memento—a few leaves from a eucalyptus tree as a reminder of those high groves of eucalyptus that filled the air of Berkeley campus with an unforgettable smell. Jeannie wrote:

> You will find enclosed a precious relic: a piece of eucalyptus leaf from the eucalyptus grove on Berkeley campus. When we first moved away from Berkeley, I longed for the smell of eucalyptus, and bought cough-drops and throat lozenges to sniff, hoping for a whiff of the familiar fragrance. . . .

This eucalyptus leaf was acquired through a spectacular athletic feat on Art's part (a miracle in itself, really): again and again, fearlessly, he hurled himself at the tree, trying to grasp at a branch.

There were no eucalyptus trees in Princeton. Instead, I was swept into the rapid changing of the seasons as we entered winter. Soon, the uncanny brightness of the Atlantic coast's winter skies made me forgive the snow and slush that lay all over the ground.

But the biggest change of all for me was the change in orientation. I was now on a northeast corridor, which stretched (in academic terms) from Harvard and Boston in the north to Dumbarton Oaks Byzantine Center and Washington, DC, in the south. I used to arrive at these places at the end of long flights—whether from Britain or from California. Now they were part of a busy corridor with Princeton almost at the center.

The most extraordinary change of all, of course, was the sudden proximity of New York. It was now a neighbor. I remember the solemn thrill of lingering in the Frick Collection long into the afternoon with no bus or cab waiting to take me to an airport. Instead, I felt that I could wait out the New York rush hour, whiling away my time in the palace of a millionaire, before New Jersey Transit took me home in little over an hour.

Dumbarton Oaks: A. P. Kazhdan

The moment I arrived at Princeton, "D.O."—the Byzantine Studies Program at Dumbarton Oaks, in Georgetown, Washington, DC—established itself on my horizon. At the time, my contact with D.O. was largely due to my Berkeley graduate student Paul Hollingsworth, who had won a visiting fellowship there for 1983–1984, to complete his dissertation on the Russian and Scandinavian elements in the legend of the child martyrs of eleventh-century Kiev, Boris and Gleb.[2] A gifted linguist and already well traveled in Eastern Europe and the Middle East, Paul found the atmosphere of D.O. heavy with a sense of privilege:

> Alas, I'm out of my element in not knowing every Byzantinist in the world (one has to pretend, even if one doesn't know them) and everything about

2. P. Hollingsworth, "Rulership and Suffering in Kievan Rus'" (PhD diss., University of California, Berkeley, 1987), and *The Hagiography of Kievan Rus'* (Cambridge, MA: Ukrainian Research Institute of Harvard University, 1992).

them (who's doing what, who's looking for a job, whose students are doing what, etc.). . . . Apparently, the one "out" from all this is to be eccentric, and being British helps that too . . . a lot of work is being done here, but not much thinking.

But Paul knew a great scholar when he saw one. That was Alexander Petrovich Kazhdan (1922–1997). Edged out of the Soviet historical community as a Jew and a scholar with startlingly unconventional opinions based on deep learning, Kazhdan had only recently come to Dumbarton Oaks. His work in the Soviet Union had already posed a major challenge to conventional views on the transition from late antiquity to the Byzantine Middle Ages. His definitive article on the cities of Byzantium between the seventh century and the ninth had appeared as early as 1954.[3]

It was only when Kazhdan began to publish in English (usually in harness with an Anglophone collaborator) that the originality of his views on the overall evolution of Byzantine culture and society became known to a wider world. It was the article entitled "Continuity and Discontinuity in Byzantium," which he published with Anthony Cutler in *Byzantion* in 1982, that made the ground shake for me when I first came across it in the new accessions shelf for periodicals in the Marciana library in Venice.[4]

For, in this article, I was confronted with the first consequential statement of the view that, in the seventh and eighth centuries, Byzantium had passed through a "Dark Age," a dislocation as drastic as any experienced in the West after the fall of the Roman Empire. Using archaeological and numismatic evidence, Kazhdan suggested that urban life had virtually collapsed throughout the empire, and with it the refined Greek culture associated with the civic elites—a culture that had apparently remained buoyant up to the reign of the emperor Justinian and a little beyond.

For Kazhdan, this drastic recession of urban life and of classical values was not due to the Muslim invasions alone. It was due to the inner collapse of an overcomplex urban civilization—a gigantic subsidence that opened a chasm between the medieval Byzantine world and its late antique past. At a stroke, the conventional view of the nature of Byzantine civilization had to be revised.

3. A. P. Kazhdan, "Vizantijskie goroda v vii--vv.," *Sovietskaya Arkheologija* 21 (1954): 164–188.

4. A .P. Kazhdan and A. Cutler, "Continuity and Discontinuity in Byzantium," *Byzantion* 52 (1982): 429–478.

Byzantium could no longer be treated as a miraculous, direct survival from the ancient world—somehow continuing, by sheer kinetic energy, the glories of the Greco-Roman past. Far from it. Quite as much as the barbarian kingdoms of western Europe, the medieval Byzantium that emerged from its own Dark Age was a new, rough-and-ready society, built from the ground up on the ruins of a former, very different classical and late antique world.

At the time, I was already in contact with Kazhdan on behalf of the University of California Press series with which I was involved, The Transformation of the Classical Heritage. In collaboration with Ann Wharton Epstein, Kazhdan had submitted a manuscript on social and cultural change in eleventh- and twelfth-century Byzantium. Though the period covered lay well outside the conventional limits of late antiquity, I urged Doris Kretschmer to bend the rules so as to include it in the series, as an exemplary study of the nature of change in a society ostensibly committed to making time stand still. The book appeared in 1985.[5]

It was Paul who brought us together in the early months of my arrival in Princeton:

> I told Kazhdan that I first became acquainted with his work through one of your bibliographies, and he said, "You know, I have never met Peter Brown. We should just get a car and go up and see him one of these days." At first glance you wouldn't think Kazhdan to be the kind of person who would do something like that, but the more I get to know him and that mischievous twinkle in his eye, the more I think we might do it.

Indeed, they did: and it was a great, relaxed occasion—a lunch that lasted well into the late afternoon. I had gone out of my way to buy the best, most authentically Russian vodka. But Kazhdan was not interested. "Give me no vodka. Rather, give me a Campari soda. For it is Campari soda which Gemingway [Ernest Hemingway] would drink at Harry's Bar in Venice. Is this not so?"

To know that such a towering scholar now lived "down the way," as it were, at the southern end of the northeast corridor, slowly brought a new flavor to my work on the late antique Roman Empire of the East in its last centuries, before the Dark Ages came, also, to Byzantium.

---

5. A. P. Kazhdan and A. W. Epstein, *Change in Byzantine Culture in the Eleventh and Twelfth Centuries* (Berkeley: University of California Press, 1985).

ACROSS THE POND

On the East Coast, only the Atlantic stood between America and Europe. I now understood how the Atlantic could be spoken of by Britons and Americans as "the Pond." By contrast, the flight from Heathrow to San Francisco had always had an epic quality for me. The plane chased the sunset across Greenland and northern Canada to drop down from a vast wilderness onto a golden landscape bathed in late-afternoon sunlight, as if we had come to another world.

No such romance attended flights to and from the East Coast. Whether from Heathrow or from Newark, the flight departed from and arrived at much the same grubby periphery of a sprawling city, usually under similar dull clouds. It was as if I had dropped off to sleep in the taxi that took me up the Cromwell Road to Heathrow only to wake up, a few hours later, in a cab on its way to Princeton.

I would soon be glad for this unromantic closeness. On February 20, 1984, Teedah—my aunt Freda Warren (my mother's sister)—died suddenly of a heart attack. She had held on to her apartment in the red-brick terrace houses of Morehampton Road, despite the high granite steps in front and the steep wooden staircase that led down to the garden and the shed that contained the coals which were her only source of heat. When she died, the apartment died. It was one of the coldest winters in memory. The moment the apartment became empty and heatless, it fell apart: a large chunk of the magnificent plaster cornice that ringed the high ceilings collapsed on her bed.

THE DEATH OF MEMORY

With Teedah, a large part of our family's memory died. I have noticed that in many families both in Ireland and in America, the daughters (and especially the unmarried daughters) were regarded as the guardians of family memory. It was they who could identify the figures on the paintings or photographs, who preserved the diaries or identified the wearer of this or that piece of jewelry.

This was certainly true of Teedah. My mother showed little interest in family mementoes. That was Teedah's business. Portraits from the early nineteenth century hung in the hall of Teedah's apartment in Morehampton Road. Some of these portraits even passed from the age of paint to the age of photography: a little girl holding a dolly, which had plainly been added to the painting at her insistence, reappeared as a full-grown woman in an early Victorian daguerreotype. But who were they? "Ach! Teedah knows . . . She knows everything." And now Teedah was dead. Worse than that: Teedah died at the wrong season of the year, in an unusually cold winter. Her empty flat was an icebox. My mother had little heart to rummage in family papers in such conditions. I suspect that whole closets full of bygones were simply thrown out.

Three months later, my mother wrote to tell me that a pile of family albums and scrapbooks had only recently been discovered by the painters who had been sent in to redo the apartment. They were hidden behind the great, heavy curtains of the dining room. These were saved. Now occupying little more than one small drawer of a bureau, they are the scraps—originally put together, I suspect, by Teedah as a young girl—that led me back to the Protestant Ireland of the late nineteenth century, when Bob Warren, my grandfather the rugby star, was the toast of Dublin; when, for most Protestants, Home Rule or Unionism (with no thought of an independent Republic) was the issue of the day; and when war had not yet come to scythe two generations of beloved cousins. In such a way, the past hangs on a filament as slender as a spider's thread.

HIGH GRAVITY

HIGH GRAVITY

My first years at Princeton had a certain dreamlike quality about them. My MacArthur Fellowship enabled me to be a visiting professor on a half-time basis in the History Department with minimal teaching and administrative duties.

In those first three years, I taught an outline course on late antiquity and the early Middle Ages: my Berkeley 4B became my Princeton 343A with very little change. The young of the athletic persuasion—the jocks—entered with gusto into a course that began with the barbarian invasions and ended with the Vikings. A little after midterm they learned, from *Beowulf*, that, had they lived in seventh-century northern Europe, they would have spent their teenage years shaping up to lead a war band, rather than getting ready for their SATs. They could relate to that. A preceptor (a teaching assistant) who once visited the bar of the Ivy Inn was surprised to find a happy company gathered around a long table, thumping their beer mugs to the chant of "Battle of Adrianople, 378 . . . boom, boom, boom." This was the famous battle where the Visigoths had trampled the Roman army and its emperor into the red dust on the plain near Edirne in European Turkey. The jocks were heartened by such events.

At that time, what I missed most in Princeton were the vivid conversations in coffeehouses, such as I had occasionally had with Michel Foucault and had frequently enjoyed with Tom Laqueur and other friends in Berkeley. As far as I could see, no one hung out at Princeton in 1983. Such leisurely habits did not seem to belong to a world where, in the university, the heavy gravity of the institution set the pace of social as well as intellectual life. I had moved from a large campus, like a gigantic low-gravity galaxy, to an incandescent star, throbbing with compressed energy. A strenuous mood prevailed, punctuated only by power lunches in Prospect House that ended strictly with the resumption of teaching at 1:30.

From Late Antiquity to Early Islam

But there were compensations for this weighty atmosphere. On March 10–11, 1984, I took part in a conference that made me realize the sheer critical mass of learning available at Princeton, and within a relatively short distance from Princeton along the northeast corridor. Entitled "From Late Antiquity to Early Islam," it was a conference on a topic that had been present to me for decades. Like a good dream, here were the authors of the books and articles that had long challenged and inspired me, all gathered together for two days in Betts Lecture Hall of the Architecture Building on Princeton campus, taking the podium, stirring their coffee cups, chatting over lunch. There was Oleg Grabar, author of *The Formation of Islamic Art* from Harvard.[1] There was also Michael Cook, the author, along with Patricia Crone, of *Hagarism*.[2] (This was the book whose bold arguments had jangled the world of Islamic historians, and which had both thrilled me and set my teeth on edge when I reviewed it for Bob Silvers in the *New York Review of Books*.) Irfan Shahid (1926–2016), the historian of the Christian Arabs, came up from Georgetown. My friend Fergus Millar, then a visiting fellow at the Institute for Advanced Study, spoke, along with Glen Bowersock, who wound up the conference in style.

The conference proved to be a landmark in the study of the continuity between the late antique and the Islamic Middle East. It also marked a turning point in my own views on the subject. It gave me the opportunity to revisit the thesis of the great Belgian historian Henri Pirenne, advanced in his *Mohammed and Charlemagne*. As we have seen, Pirenne had stressed the social and economic continuity of the late antique Mediterranean up to the end of the seventh century.[3] In his opinion, it was only when this benign continuum was fatally disrupted by the Muslim invasions that it could be said that the ancient world had ended and the Middle Ages had begun.

Pirenne's brilliant hypothesis had lasted for decades, largely because of the number of problems that it seemed to resolve. It explained why the barbarian

---

1. Oleg Grabar, *The Formation of Islamic Art* (New Haven, CT: Yale University Press, 1973).

2. Patricia Crone and Michael Cook, *Hagarism: The Making of the Islamic World* (Cambridge University Press, 1977).

3. Chapter 56: "To Muhammad" and chapter 59: "From the Mediterranean . . ."

invasions in the West, in the fifth century, seemed to have had little effect on the cultural and economic life of the Mediterranean. These invasions did not mark the end of an epoch. Instead, Pirenne reassigned the role of the violent invader to the Arabs of the seventh century. His view had lingered, almost as a default position, for students of late antiquity as an explanation of the change from the late antique to the medieval world.

I now realized that the Pirenne thesis had been proved wrong. A recent book by the archaeologists Richard Hodges and David Whitehouse, *Muhammed, Charlemagne, and the Origins of Europe*, showed that classical urban life and the commercial networks that went with it had collapsed around the western Mediterranean as early as the late sixth century.[4] Their views coincided to a remarkable degree with those that I had just learned from the work of Alexander Kazhdan on the cities of early Byzantium. It now seemed as if the ancient world had already died, almost a century before the appearance of Islam.

In the paper that I delivered at the conference, I suggested that scholars should find a new way of looking at the transition from late antiquity to early Islam in the Mediterranean and the Middle East. Put very briefly, the Muslims did not bring the ancient world to an end by imposing on it a totally new civilization based on a new religion. Far from it. They inherited a world that had already changed profoundly.

Above all, the cities had changed. Many had already taken on features that we tend to associate only with the Islamic Middle Ages. For instance, Hugh Kennedy, in a brilliant article entitled "From *Polis* to *Madina*," would soon show that a city such as Aleppo had lost its classical shape and taken on an "Islamic" look as early as 600. The *agora* had been abandoned, and the wide, classical streets had come to be cluttered with shops, like a *sûk*, reached through narrow, winding lanes.[5]

High culture lost its roots in the city. It did not vanish. It relocated. The cities were outflanked by a capillary system of great monasteries established in the countryside of Syria, Egypt, and the Holy Land, many of which became powerhouses of religious thought in Syriac and Coptic as well as proving to be active centers for the translation of Greek philosophy and theology into

---

4. Richard Hodges and David Whitehouse, *Muhammed, Charlemagne, and the Origins of Europe* (Ithaca, NY: Cornell University Press, 1983).

5. H. Kennedy, "From *Polis* to *Madina*: Urban Change in Late Antique and Early Islamic Syria," *Past and Present* 106 (1985): 3–27.

Syriac. These monasteries created the remarkable phenomenon of an "Oriental Hellenism": Greek thought expressed entirely in Syriac translation.[6]

These were the changes that eased the transition from a late antique to an Islamic world. The Muslim conquests and the formation of Islamic civilization took place in what was best called a "later late antiquity"—a further phase in the social and religious ferment of the Mediterranean and the Middle East, as much in need of study on its own terms as the brilliant centuries of the later empire proper.

For this reason, I concluded that studies of the continuity between late antiquity and early Islam should not begin by positing an abrupt transition from a full-blown late antique past to a brand-new Islamic present. Rather, scholars had to develop a sense of Middle Eastern society as a whole (Byzantine, eastern Christian, and Islamic alike) in constant, roiling motion from the days of Justinian to those of Harun al-Rashid. Brave words, and easier to say in twenty minutes than to follow up by detailed research. Yet subsequent decades of scholarship, along the lines suggested at this conference, have influenced my own work and teaching up until today.

The Group for the Study of Late Antiquity

Not long after, I experienced an unexpected change in my own situation that was paradigmatic of the weight of gravity (based on abundant financial resources) whose pull I had already sensed in the social and intellectual life of Princeton campus. To my complete surprise, as I had not even applied to them for funds, the Mellon Foundation offered me a budget to form an interdisciplinary group. It was called the Group for the Study of Late Antiquity. With this budget, the committee of the group ran up to four half-day seminars each term, and distributed small grants (mainly for travel) to undergraduates and graduate students studying late antique topics. It was a strange turn of events. I had come to Princeton as a visiting professor with a minimal workload in order to have the leisure to write. Now I found myself showered with money so as to be busy once again.

At the time I was struck by the contrast between the two campuses that this new venture revealed. At Berkeley, John Dillon and I had labored at writing

---

6. J. Tannous, *The Making of the Medieval Middle East: Religion, Society, and Simple Believers* (Princeton, NJ: Princeton University Press, 2018), sums up work that had only just begun in 1984.

proposals and filling out forms for the National Endowment for the Humanities for money to fund a late antique study group. I remember bending with John, late at night, over the large photocopier machine of the Classics Department in Dwinelle Hall, hurrying to meet a deadline. We labored in vain. No grant came our way.

Instead, a group of graduate students congealed to one side of campus in the informal manner that was typical of Berkeley. This was "Holy Men Incorporated." We met in the evening every two weeks. Fortified by six-packs of beer and a potluck supper, we would squat on the floor of my house and discuss hagiography in every period and region from Ireland to the Ganges. These were happy gatherings, which showed that late antiquity had come to stay on Berkeley campus. But they were a purely voluntary group, with no institutional recognition and no funding whatsoever to support them. At Princeton, by contrast, it was taken for granted that any intellectual endeavors worth pursuing must happen on campus, and that, once recognized, they could count on generous financial support.

As I look back, it surprises me that the formation of a late antique group was treated, at the time, as such a new departure. It takes some effort of the imagination to recall a Princeton where so few interdisciplinary joining points existed. It was a rather bleak scene. The History Department had its Davis Center, over which Lawrence Stone (1919–1999) presided with an iron hand, encouraging a cut and thrust of argument that invested its Friday morning sessions with the thrill of attendance at a public execution in early modern style. But for many classicists, ancient historians, historians of classical and Byzantine art, scholars in Judaism and Islam, and students of the classical tradition in its medieval and Renaissance forms, the Group for the Study of Late Antiquity was the only show in town at that time.

We met on Sundays in what amounted to a miniconference: lunch with the speaker, a three-hour session, and a reception often followed by supper. The speaker would not give a paper so much as act as a disk jockey, by introducing a set of texts and recent literature on a given subject that had been circulated in advance.

Those who attended quickly formed a remarkably stable and enthusiastic body of persons drawn from all over campus, from the Institute for Advanced Study, from the Theological Seminary, and from outside Princeton. I was impressed by how many of the faculty took part. While "Holy Men Incorporated" had been a venture for graduate students only, the Princeton group proved to be something of an urban lung for faculty members who were usually compartmentalized in strong departments with little connection with each other.

Late antiquity provided just what was needed to bring people together: it was a field where any number of disciplines converged so as to explore a civilization of unusual complexity. The group remained as open as possible to different themes and approaches. There was no single methodological agenda, and there was as much outreach as possible to fields beyond the Greco-Roman world. Judaism and Islam were very much part of the mix, along with archaeology and art history, beside the more usual themes of religious and cultural history. The art historians Danny Čurčić (1940–2017), newly arrived at Princeton, Dale Kinney of Bryn Mawr, and Archer Saint-Clair of Rutgers were regular attendants. Alan Cameron came from Columbia to talk about his work on the circus factions, and Simon Price (1954–2011), as a visiting fellow at the institute, spoke on the cities of Asia Minor, while Glen Bowersock introduced recent work on late antique Syria. Both Évelyne Patlagean and Aline Rousselle came from France to speak on campus and to lead a discussion of their books in the Sunday seminar of the group.

I recently discovered in my basement a mass of material that had been xeroxed for the meetings of the group. I realized how important these meetings had been for me, in maintaining for me a sense of the diversity of late antiquity. At a time when I was fully engaged in writing *Body and Society,* I was worried that I might be caught in a world of ethereal texts and high-pitched arguments on sexuality. I feared that I might lose contact with the more earthy realities of late antique life by entering the dimly lit tunnel of the history of the early church. It was the jolly mood of the Group for the Study of Late Antiquity that kept my feet on the ground. For here was a group where all aspects of the period—from Plotinus on the soul to urban thuggery in Byzantium—were thrashed out in regular meetings that showed the high gravity of Princeton at its very best.

Nonetheless, *Body and Society* had to get written. For this I turned to Speer Library (now Wright Library) of the Princeton Theological Seminary. In 1983, this was the old library, not the grand new building of today, whose wide central space resembles the concourse of a major hotel to such an extent that one expects to find bellhops in the elevator. The old library preserved a division between its floors that seemed to reflect the stern theological and moral worldview of the seminary's Presbyterian founders. Gnostics and Manichees lurked in the darkest reaches of the basement, along with somewhat dubious subjects (for good Protestants) such as monasticism and hagiography. At that time,

I worked mainly in the well-lit upper floor, surrounded by books on Judaism and the New Testament. Now, with such a collection to hand, was the time to write the final version of *Body and Society*—*BodSoc*, as I now called it. A book that was first conceived among the eucalyptus groves of Berkeley would be largely finished among the battleship-gray, steel shelves of Speer Library in Princeton.

WRITING *BODY AND SOCIETY*

LISTENING

I finished *Body and Society* in early 1987, and it was published a year later.[1] It was the first book that I had written from beginning to end in an American environment. I have always seen it as something of an ex-voto, an expression of gratitude for my freedom from the taxing workload of a British professor and for the intellectual stimulation that I had enjoyed in such abundance in Berkeley and Princeton. Not since I had written *Augustine of Hippo*, as a young fellow of All Souls College, was I so free to write at whatever length I wished.

In 1987, a nuanced book on sexual renunciation was not exactly in tune with the spirit of the age. The sexual revolution in America and elsewhere; the growing concern in the Catholic Church over the issue of celibacy among priests and members of relogous orders—monks and nuns alike; and the widespread tendency to blame the Christian churches in all ages for the ravages of sexual repression—all these made renunciation a hot topic. Scholars who wrote on the New Testament and on the early church were expected to offer a judgement—and usually a negative judgement—on the exaltation of virginity and celibacy in early Christian circles, and to derive from their work on the

---

1. P. Brown, *Body and Society: Men, Women, and Sexual Renunciation in Early Christianity* (New York: Columbia University Press, 1988). Readers should know that, in an introduction to the twentieth-anniversary edition, I have explained some of the difficulties that I faced in writing *Body and Society*, and how I have revised my views on many points: Peter Brown, introduction to *Body and Society: Twentieth-Anniversary Edition* (New York: Columbia University Press, 2008), xxi–lxvii. Throughout these two chapters I will cite from that edition as I have done previously.

distant past some message, some path of action for their own times. Activists and theologians of all denominations and shades of opinion were lavish in offering advice of this kind.

But I was neither an activist nor a theologian. Contemporary issues concerned me; but I wanted to avoid misrepresentations of the past in the interest of modern agendas. As a historian, I felt that my first duty was to listen carefully to the ancient Christian writers in order to make their views on the meaning and implications of sexual renunciation intelligible to modern readers. I wanted to catch those voices from a distant age, so as to understand what they had meant in their own time; what it meant to those who first read, heard, and debated them; and in what social and cultural circumstances these debates took place, and with what consequences: only then could I judge their effect on future ages and their relevance to modern times. So how did I go about it?

SMALL GROUPS

From the very beginning I faced an option as to the sort of history I would write. Put very briefly: I had to choose between what I might call macro-history (a history of broad movements) and micro-history (a history of small communities).

As an example of macro-history, Paul Veyne's challenging article "Family and Love in the High Empire" (which had appeared in 1978) intrigued me for a time, as it had intrigued Foucault. In this article, Veyne described what appeared to him to be a decisive, empire-wide mutation in attitudes to sex and marriage that took place in the second century. This was a study of a major change on the macro-level of Roman society as a whole. Following Veyne's lead, I had thought for a time that I would write a sequel to his history of sex and marriage in the classical Roman Empire, by tracing the growing influence of Christian asceticism and of Christian notions of virginity on sexual behavior in the late antique period.

Indeed, immediately after my return from my first stay in Venice, in 1981, I contributed a chapter on late antiquity to the *Histoire de la vie privée*, to accompany the essay on classical Rome written by Veyne himself.[2] But even

2. Peter Brown, "Antiquité tardive," in *Histoire de la vie privée*, ed. P. Ariès and G. Duby (Paris: Le Seuil, 1985), 1:226–299; *A History of Private Life: From Pagan Rome to Byzantium* (Cambridge, MA: Belknap Press of Harvard University Press, 1987), 237–311, and separately as *Late Antiquity* (Cambridge, MA: Belknap Press of Harvard University Press, 1998).

as I wrote that essay, I realized that I had told only half the story: the history of Christianity in its first centuries could not be written as a grand narrative, as if it were the story of a single, undivided movement (often spoken of, loosely, as "the expansion of Christianity") throughout the Roman world. There was no one-way traffic toward a single upshot that the reader might either deplore or acclaim in the light of present-day concerns.

Far from it: to write a history of early Christianity amounted to studying a series of micro-histories of the small, but surprisingly vocal, Christian communities that emerged as the new religion gradually gained a foothold in the Mediterranean and the Middle East. Vivid debates in any number of intense, face-to-face groups raised storms within Christianity itself that eventually came to touch Roman society at large.

CONTEXTS

Faced by this situation, I drew on a current in contemporary New Testament studies that was prominent in the 1980s. This was the attempt to "ground" the texts of first-century Judaism, of the New Testament, and of the early church by ascribing each to a precise social context and, if possible, to an identifiable community.

This search for a context was well represented by the work of Gerd Theissen and Wayne Meeks. Both scholars appeared to have explained the conflicting messages on marriage and sexual renunciation in the Gospels and in the writings of Saint Paul by placing them in contrasting social milieus. Some of the sayings of Jesus were deemed to have been addressed to settled village communities, while others (the more radical and ascetic) were held to have legitimated the activities of charismatic wanderers who roamed the rich countryside of Galilee and Syria.[3] Both Meeks and Theissen explained the mighty tensions in the letters of Paul, on whether or not to marry, by locating them in the stresses and strains of relatively well-to-do and articulate groups—the first urban Christians in Corinth and Ephesus.[4]

Nowadays, it takes some effort of the imagination to recapture the liberating effect of this approach to the world of the New Testament. It now seems

3. G. Theissen, *Sociology of Early Palestinian Christianity* (Philadelphia: Fortress Press, 1978).

4. W. A. Meeks, *The First Urban Christians: The Social World of the Apostle Paul* (New Haven, CT: Yale University Press, 1983); and G. Theissen, *The Social Setting of Pauline Christianity: Essays on Corinth* (Philadelphia: Fortress, 1982).

overconfident, even reductionist: texts themselves are now treated as more slippery, and the social background of early Christianity itself is now seen to be more complex than we had thought.[5] But, in the early 1980s, this approach offered a way to understand the conflicting views of early Christians on sex and marriage, such as had long perplexed theologians, by seeing them as the product of a variety of social situations.

I fastened on this small-group approach. It spoke to the historian in me, and especially to the anthropological tilt of much history written in the 1970s and 1980s—a tilt away from grand narratives toward the study of small, face-to-face communities. In this respect, the seminal article on Saint Paul by Henry Chadwick (1920–2008), which I had already read in Venice, was a model for me. Chadwick showed how Paul's rulings on marriage and virginity, which were to play such a crucial role in forming all future Christian attitudes, were not the magisterial pronouncements that many theologians took them to be. They were the result of unresolved social and cultural tensions within the Christian communities—tensions that it was the historian's business to identify and explain.[6]

Hence the shape of the first part of *Body and Society*. After a general introduction to attitudes to sex and society in the second-century Roman Empire, I settled down to reconstruct the social contexts in which different versions of the Christian notion of virginity emerged in different regions—on the roads of Syria, in the villages of upland Phrygia, in the complex urban environments of the Rome of Hermas, author of *The Shepherd* (around 120), or in the Carthage of Tertullian (160–220).

Throughout, I wanted the reader to listen in to the early Christians in their own, distant world. It was a world often revealed in small, vivid details that lay on the margins of well-known treatises—in stray inscriptions, graffiti, and papyri, and in evidence taken from texts in any number of languages: not only in Greek and Latin, but also in Syriac and Coptic. Whenever possible, I let the early Christians do the talking. Whereas Michel Foucault's *History of Sexuality* was tied to his own, distinctive philosophical agenda, and many treatments of sex in early Christianity were driven by contemporary issues, I took a different approach: I concentrated on catching those distant voices and the world in which they lived.

5. S. Friesen, "Poverty in Pauline Studies: Beyond the So-Called New Consensus," *Journal for the Study of the New Testament* 26 (2004): 323–361; P. Brown, *Treasure in Heaven: The Holy Poor in Early Christianity* (Charlottesville: University of Virginia Press, 2016), 1–16.

6. H. E. Chadwick, "All Things to All Men," *New Testament Studies* 1 (1955): 261–275.

At this time, my growing sense of the diversity of Christian regions owed much to the work of Robert Murray (1925–2018), whose groundbreaking study of Syriac Christianity—*Symbols of Church and Kingdom*—had appeared only recently (in 1975). Murray traced the manner in which sexual renunciation among the baptized "Sons and Daughters of the Covenant" in the Syrian churches took on distinctive meanings, different from those current in the Greco-Roman West

In the Syrian churches, the renunciation of sex was treated as a form of liberation. To abandon sex and marriage was hailed as a deliverance from the tyranny of "this world," and as the beginning of a new age—an age beyond sex. As a result, male and female ascetics were not segregated from each other. Rather they were thought of as complementing each other. They mingled, in the Christian communities, much as their mixed voices—in choirs made up of continent men and women—were joined, "across the aisle" as it were, in the beautiful chanting of Syriac hymns.

In regions where strict segregation of the sexes was the norm in daily married life, the notion of virginity as a gift of the Holy Spirit set a few men and women apart in every Christian community. Such groups were small but vibrant. They stuck out as the harbingers of a new age—an age beyond sex—brought in by Christianity.[7]

In this way, Syria continued to be a source of surprises to ascetics from other regions. For example: an outsider such as Jerome (342–420) was intrigued by what he found when he first visited the Middle East in the 370s. When he settled into a Syrian village near Antioch, he was surprised to find an elderly couple walking to church every day from the house in which they had lived together in continence for as long as the villagers remembered. Unfazed by this mixing of the sexes, the villagers simply told Jerome that the pious couple were known as "the Holy Ones"—they had got beyond sex. To Jerome, unused to such ease between the sexes in ascetic circles, the couple came as a challenge: he devoted an entire book to their adventures.[8]

I treasured this small nugget of evidence. For here was an encounter between two very different traditions of Christianity, of which most of us, in the West, had known only the darker side—the side represented by Jerome,

7. R. Murray, *Symbols of Church and Kingdom* (Cambridge University Press, 1975) and "The Exhortation to Candidates for Ascetical Vows at Baptism in the Ancient Syrian Church," *New Testament Studies* 21 (1974): 59–80.

8. Brown, *Body and Society*, 100–102.

the caricature of the repressed monk—without knowledge of a stranger, warmer, and more radical Christianity that was to be found in Syria and elsewhere.

The more I read, the more I was impressed by the diversity of Christian views on these issues. Far from following the fate of a single, unambiguous line of Christian doctrine, from which discordant voices were excluded as heretical—as extreme or downright dotty—I found that I was in a world of many voices.

To read myself into early Christian texts, with an eye to their diversity, century by century and region by region, was like learning a strange new language or picking up an exotic tune. I realized that I was listening in to a grand debate in which the very nature of society, of the human person, and of the material world was at stake. This debate, which pitted Christians against Christians quite as much as it pitted Christians against Jews and pagans, emerged as the central theme in my book.

FROM ORIGEN TO AUGUSTINE

FROM ORIGEN TO AUGUSTINE

In many ways, the later chapters of *Body and Society* were dominated by the contrast between two great Christian writers separated by two centuries—Origen of Alexandria (185–254) and Augustine of Hippo (354–430). I had long been acquainted with Augustine. But Origen was new to me. Here was a larger-than-life figure, both in his own days and in all later centuries. He emerged from a generation of great teachers and scholars as the greatest Christian teacher of all. From 203 to 215 he was head of the Catechetical School of Alexandria and later taught as a priest in Caesarea Maritima in Palestine, until his death in 254—brought about by the rigors of imprisonment at the time of the Decian persecution. Immensely productive, he created in Caesarea a library that formed the nucleus of what was, in its time, the equivalent of the first Christian university. Later generations of Greek and Syrian Christians looked back to him as a role model of the Christian scholar and as a seemingly inexhaustible source of erudition and of challenging ideas.

Origen was also a hotly debated figure. His daring speculations on the preexistence of the soul and his suggestion that even the Devil might be saved ensured that he would be formally condemned as a heretic in the sixth century. Even after this condemnation, he lingered on the edge of orthodoxy—a great Non-Person and an unspoken alternative to the less ambitious views of the average monk and churchman.

The recovery of the full profile of Origen as a scholar and theologian was one of the triumphs of French Patristic scholarship in postwar times. The work of Jean Daniélou, Pierre Nautin (1914–1997), Henri Crouzel (1919–2003), and

Marguerite Harl (to mention only a few) represented a triumph of the scholarly ideal of *ressourcement*—of the effort to enable the great figures of the Christian past (and especially the Greek Fathers of the Church) to speak to the present in their own voice.[1]

I remember reading Origen's commentaries and treatises in the bright, cool air of my garden in Berkeley, until I could almost hear his voice. Not since I had first read myself into the works of Augustine had I had so moving an experience. Here was an early Christian writer whose primary concern was with the growth of the soul, and with the soul's mysterious relation to the body, the sexual drive included.[2]

I warmed to Origen's vision of the seemingly unlimited potential for change in the individual. He insisted that the body was not a static prison of the soul. It was something more flexible: a finely calibrated vehicle for the soul—a light bed in which the soul rested. The body itself was a fluid thing, sensitive to the movements of the soul. It could be transformed along with the soul; and it even played a positive role in spurring on the soul to ever-greater effort to overcome its limitations.

Behind Origen's view of the fluidity of the person lay a sense of the immensity of the cosmos. He presented a boundless world where God had infinite time in which to bring each and every human being to perfection. He insisted that, even in this life, body and soul alike could change and expand in ways that went far beyond our cramped, socially bound imagination.

Origen placed sex against this vast horizon. For him, sexual renunciation was not a single, drastic act: it was only the beginning of a slow but sure process of transformation. Virginity and continence represented the start—but only the start—of the long journey of the self toward ever-widening horizons: to a state where even the restricting categories of gender might come to be shed by elect spirits.

This was a voice from the troubled but ambitious days of the third century, which had seen the emergence of so many religious leaders (pagan as well as

---

1. J. Daniélou, *Platonisme et Théologie mystique* (Paris: Aubin, 1944) and *L'être et le temps chez Grégoire de Nysse* (Leiden: Brill, 1970); Pierre Nautin, *Origène: sa vie et son oeuvre* (Paris: Beauchesne, 1977); Henri Crouzel, *Origène et la "connaissance mystique"* (Paris: Desclée de Brouwer, 1961); Marguérite Harl, *Origène et la fonction révélatrice du Verbe incarné* (Paris: Le Seuil, 1958). My other debt was to a scholar in a different tradition—W. Völker, *Das Vollkommenheitsideal des Origenes* (Tübingen: J.C.B. Mohr, 1931).

2. Brown, *Body and Society*, chapter 8: "I Beseech You: Be Transformed," 160–177.

Christian) who were believed to have been taken beyond themselves—to have been somehow transformed beyond their accustomed identity. For many who read Origen in later centuries, these speculations induced an unsettling sense of fluidity, of constant upward movement toward some barely imaginable goal. Origen's mighty synthesis came to be seen as a challenge and a danger—like the glimpse of a great prehistoric beast from a distant age.

ORIGEN: EAST AND WEST

A reviewer of *Body and Society* rightly observed that it was Origen who "haunts the book."[3] Origen's daring view of the human person's capacity for change was at the back of my mind when I moved a century later than Origen in order to study the Desert Fathers of Egypt. Here I did not find sweltering figures, obsessed with sex, such as were common in popular modern images of the monks of Egypt. Instead, I found figures who represented what has come to be known as a "Desert Origenism," devoted to the transformation of the self, body and soul together.

As they were described by contemporaries, the great monks of Egypt stood out against a desert landscape that seemed as boundless as the cosmos of Origen's imagination. Under the guidance of wise mentors, they were believed to have experienced transformations in their own souls that were clearly reflected in the poise and magnetic serenity of their bodies. The rise and fall, and the eventual dying away, of their sexual temptations registered the slow but sure workings of God's providence in the remaking of the human person.[4]

In contrast to his continued, almost subliminal, presence in the spiritual writers of the East, Origen fared less well at the hands of leading figures in the Latin world. This difference amounted to one of the most decisive partings of the way between East and West in early Christianity—between a Greek and Syrian world that continued to feel the magnetic power of Origen's cosmic synthesis, and a Latin West that found its own identity through *il gran rifiuto*[5]—"the great refusal" that took the form of an almost visceral rejection of his more daring ideas. It seemed to me that there was less room in the imagination of the Latin Fathers than in the East for his wide-open cosmic horizons, and for his daring speculations on the future transformation of bodies and souls.

3. Tom Morris, "Lust Beliefs," *Daily Telegraph*, April 8, 1989.
4. Brown, *Body and Society*, 223–232.
5. Dante, *Inferno* 3.60.

AUGUSTINE

In the ensuing debate concerning the views of Origen, in which Jerome and many others were heavily involved, Augustine was the odd man out. He pointedly ignored Origen's theories and, instead, created a vast system of his own.[6] Returning to Augustine, having spent many years with Origen and the Desert Fathers, I felt like a traveler returning to his hometown after a long absence abroad and finding it somehow shrunken. Origen's sense of constantly expanding horizons was absent. Instead, Augustine propounded a view of sexuality as an unchanging constant in human nature, a negative force singularly impervious to transformation.

This view became so well established in the medieval West that it takes no small effort to recapture how idiosyncratic Augustine must have appeared in his own time to many other Christians, and especially to the Christians of the East. In the first place, he treated sex as part of the original nature of human beings. Nowadays, this seems so obvious a fact that we forget that many of the Greek Fathers had followed Origen in thinking that sex was somehow peripheral to the human person. They believed that Adam and Eve had been sexless in Paradise. Sex was an afterthought, added to humans by God as a device by which human beings might be consoled for their loss of immortality by the gift of children. It was a sign of God's mercy in the face of death.

This was not Augustine's view. For him, sex was not an afterthought. He insisted that, if Adam and Eve had not rebelled against God, they could have had sex in Eden. Their intercourse, had it happened, would have been a serene—indeed, a joyful—encounter, barely imaginable to present-day, fallen humans.

These speculations by Augustine on the possibility of sex in Eden (in book 14 of the *City of God* and elsewhere) tend to evoke sniggers in the modern reader, as they already did in Augustine's opponents, the followers of Pelagius. But Augustine took this issue seriously. He insisted on the possibility of sex in Eden so as to underline the truly tragic nature of the Fall of Adam and Eve. They had been punished for their disobedience by losing control of what had once been an original, marvelous harmony of body and soul, in which sex was included.

---

6. See now Joseph W. Trigg, "Augustine's Reception of Origen," in *Augustine and Tradition: Influences, Contexts, Legacy. Essays in Honor of J. Patout Burns*, ed. David G. Hunter and Jonathan P. Yates (Grand Rapids, MI: Eerdmans, 2020), 233–260.

For Augustine, the loss of harmony between body and soul was irrevocable. As a result of God's punishment, Adam and Eve and all subsequent humans became mortal. Their bodies slipped out of their control in the supreme, obscene wrench of death. Their sexual drive also escaped their control: they were as little able to overcome frigidity or impotence as they were unable, by willpower alone, to master orgasm and sexual thoughts. In this way, intercourse was not seen as a benign remedy for death, as it had been among the Greek Fathers; the loss of control associated with intercourse was a small but faithful mirror image of death.

Above all, for Augustine, the sexual drive was there to stay. It was a permanent reminder of God's punishment for the rebellion of Adam and Eve. Something infinitely better could have happened if they had not rebelled. A touch of sadness—of Paradise lost—surrounded even the most pious Christian married couple. Their intercourse would never be like the untroubled intercourse that Adam and Eve might have enjoyed before the Fall, had they not rebelled against God.

And this would not change. As Augustine presented it, the sexual drive in its present form was a permanently deranged force, which needed to be continually kept under control even in the holiest of persons. There was no possibility that this drive might somehow be transformed and transcended—not even by a happy few. With Augustine, a great, half-expressed hope of the early church died.

JOHN CASSIAN

This bleak view brought down on Augustine the well-aimed critique of John Cassian (360–435). Cassian was a Latin-speaker from the mouth of the Danube (modern Romania). Equally fluent in Latin and Greek, he had traveled to Egypt and interviewed the Great Men of the Desert, before returning to the Latin-speaking world to settle in Marseilles around 415. He was an authentic representative of the wisdom of the Desert Fathers and of the "Desert Origenism" that remained such an important feature of the worldview of Eastern Christians. In many ways, he represented, in Provence, a perfect counterweight—a missing vitamin, as it were—to the somber synthesis that Augustine was in the process of elaborating in Africa.

In his *Conferences*—his monastic talk-ins—Cassian treated sex as a passing phase. Even though sexual temptation seemed ineradicable to the average person, this was not so. Strange things could happen in the desert: ascetic discipline, combined with the grace of God, could bring about a mighty transformation of soul and body alike. "The treasures of darkness" associated with sexual temptations could be thrown open, to allow the light of Christ to flood into the soul.

Cassian went on to insist that sexual fantasies which lingered in the mind were not signs of irremediable depravity. They would pass. God did not allow them to continue in the present only as a punishment. Rather, they served a purpose: to remind ascetics, who might be unduly proud of their chastity, that they were human. Their rise and fall acted as a sensor—as warning symptoms of the far more dangerous drives of pride and anger that lurked deeper in the psyche than did mere sex. It was with these sinister, inhuman drives, and not with the passing phase of sexual temptation, that the monks must wage their most bitter spiritual combat.

In this way, Cassian kept open the possibility of some profound mutation of the self that showed in the body in the form of a transformation of the sexual drive. Here I differed from the interpretation of Cassian that Michel Foucault had proposed in Berkeley. Foucault had concentrated on the temptations faced by the monk in the course of a lonely "battle of chastity" with his own thoughts. But this was not the whole story. I emphasized the other side of the picture—the hope of victory that was implied throughout Cassian's writings on the ascetic life. This hope of victory stood as a silent rebuke to the dour pessimism of Augustine's view of deranged sex as an immovable reminder of the Fall.

Cassian's guarded criticism of Augustine marked the ending of an age. For this reason, I lingered on the contrast between the two thinkers. They were almost exact contemporaries. Each of them wrote in seaports within easy sail of each other: Marseilles lay almost due north across the Mediterranean from Hippo. But they represented two very different traditions. Their clash of views showed that the ascetic traditions of the monks of Egypt (represented by Cassian's *Conferences*, written in clear Latin for the monks of Provence) could gain a foothold in the Latin world. But Cassian's critique of Augustine showed how far the traditions of the West (as interpreted by Augustine) differed from those of Egypt and the East.[7] In later generations, Cassian was sidelined. His works remained essential for monks and nuns; but on the general issue of sex and original sin, for good or ill, Augustine was allowed to have the last word throughout the West.

7. Brown, *Body and Society*, 420–423.

PERSON AND COSMOS

These comparisons with the ever-present thought of Origen reflected the last turn in my interests as I wrote *Body and Society*. Over the years of writing the book, I came to pay more attention to the differing images of the human person and of the cosmos that underlay the various attitudes to sexuality in Christian and non-Christian writers.

I owed this change, in part, to the series of seminars of the Group for the Study of Late Antiquity, which had begun in the academic year of 1985/86: "Images of the Person in Late Antiquity." This broad title, which included non-Christians as well as Christians, encouraged me to continue to think about the ideas and social setting of the last pagan philosophers, and about themes that I had raised in my conversations with John Dillon in Berkeley on Plotinus and the Neoplatonic tradition.

For this reason, in the later chapters of *Body and Society*, I attempted to set Christian notions of marriage and virginity against the wider framework of philosophical discourse in the late classical world. The pagans Plotinus and Porphyry now made their appearance, to highlight the difference between their treatment of sex and the views of their Christian contemporaries, Origen and Methodius of Olympus.

These were exciting comparisons. Because of the surprisingly rapid spread of Christianity among members of the intelligentsia of the Greek world, in the course of the third and fourth centuries, pagans and Christians now met each other as intellectual equals. Yet, on issues such as sexuality and marriage, persons who might seem, at first sight, to belong to the same milieu and to the same mental universe, emerged with very different perspectives. They could be worlds apart.

The lives of two upper-class women illustrated this point. The pagan philosopher Sosipatra had grown up on a family farm behind Ephesus in the mid-fourth century. Her younger contemporary Macrina (ca. 325–380), the pious sister of Gregory of Nyssa, had done much the same. She lived on a family estate at Annesi, outside Amaseia (Amasya, in northwestern Turkey), to which their formidable brother, Basil of Caesarea, had retired, in 358, to begin his monastic life.

A few years after finishing *Body and Society*, in 1990, I visited Annesi, now known as Kaleköy—the village of the castle. Close by, the river Iris (the Yeşilırmak) still swirled with the ominous vortices in which Macrina's brother

Naucratius had been drowned after he became entangled in his fishing nets. Fishermen still fished with the same nets.

But Annesi/Kaleköy was no desert. Macrina's formidable brother Basil of Caesraea (330–379) and his friends had implied (in their letters to each other) that Annesi was a remote mountain aerie, lost in the woods of Pontus—a heroically uncomfortable place for budding ascetics. In fact, it was a low hillock set in a smiling valley—a gentleman's villa or a well-appointed hunting lodge. It was probably little different from the country villa where Sosipatra had grown up.

Yet the lives of Sosipatra the pagan and Macrina the Christian took very different courses. Sosipatra married and had three children. She still thought of herself as embedded in a very ancient, civic world, which seemed to follow comfortably the rhythms of nature. Marriage and childbirth were part of those rhythms. They occurred to all persons in their due time; and they always would do so, like the solemn ticks of the clock of an eternal universe.

Macrina, by contrast, remained a virgin. For her, time stood still. Her life would not be broken up by marriage and the care of children. In this self-made suspension of the normal rhythms of a woman's life, she awaited with bated breath the Coming of Christ. For her, that Coming marked the end of a universe and of a social order which, to Sosipatra the pagan, still appeared to be immovable—part of a cosmos saturated with the golden light of eternity.[8]

Thinking of those two women—so similar in their social position and in much of their culture—I realized that, in late antiquity, the choice between marriage and virginity could be rooted in nothing less than two differing views of the natural world: Sosipatra saw her body as woven into the texture of a perpetual, ever-fertile universe, whose rhythms she must obey with quiet certainty in all the stages of her life; for Macrina, the same world (seemingly so solid) hung over an abyss, brought out of nothing by the power of God alone. It would soon be swept away to make the new heaven and the new earth for which her soul longed.

It was by such contrasts between striking individuals, each with a different worldview, as well as between different groups and churches, that I hoped to build up a fair and differentiated picture of a revolution that, in the name of sexual renunciation, helped to bring about the end of a very ancient world.

8. Brown, *Body and Society*, 301–303.

"Sex through the Celibate Centuries!" Reviews

I handed in the manuscript of *Body and Society* at the office of the Columbia University Press in early April 1987. It did not appear in print until late in 1988. It was also published by Faber in London. Faber had maintained their relation with Durant's press-cutting agency. The cuttings, which were sent to me, showed that British reviewers jumped at what they liked to think of as a risqué topic.

Many reviews approached the issue of sexual renunciation with a barely concealed snigger. The review in the *Daily Mail* was captioned "Sex through the Celibate Centuries!" The addition of the exclamation mark suggested that for sex to happen at all in late antiquity—still less to be discussed—was somehow rather naughty.[9]

Others were not amused. Writing in the *Glasgow Herald*, Stewart Lamont (for all I know, a fellow clansman) was truculent. This was the voice of the Protestant North, robust in its disapproval of the whole subject:

> It is this Pandora's box of piety, purity and prurience that Peter Brown has collected in an attempt to make sense of the dark obsessional and often brutal laws and behavior of the period from Paul to Augustine. It is difficult to read without a growing sense of revulsion. . . . a collection of peeps through bedroom curtains and monastery grilles.
>
> [After Constantine] when the monasteries acquired property from the Emperor along with their elite status they laid the foundations for the cancerous growth of medieval corruption which resulted in the Reformation.
>
> A survey such as this makes one wonder how normal, balanced people survived to carry Christianity forward to the next generation. I suppose we should be grateful for continence and celibacy in the Early Church, at least for the fact that it didn't permit all those "saints" with personality disorders to propagate themselves.[10]

"It Opens Many Doors": Margaret Mac Curtain

The review that I liked best was written in the *Irish Times* by Margaret Mac Curtain. She was a good judge of such matters. A Dominican nun and a lecturer in Irish history in University College Dublin from 1964 to 1994, she was

9. Peter Mullen, "Sex through the Celibate Centuries!" *Daily Mail*, March 9, 1989.
10. Stewart Lamont, "God's Virgins," *Glasgow Herald*, February 4, 1989.

a feminist determined to give women their proper place in the history of modern Ireland. Fully open to the tensions of the 1980s, she described better than most reviewers what had inspired me in writing *Body and Society*:

> Ten years ago Peter Brown could not have written this book. It was the combination of the new study of the religious world of women with the influence of Michel Foucault's thought which enabled him to bring early Christian society alive in its complex attitudes to human sexuality. As such it is a study which permanently alters our understanding of Late Antique men and women as they strove to achieve the daunting ideal of sexual renunciation. That "persistent sense of salutary vertigo" which for the author accompanied the writing of *The Body and Society* likewise affects the reader, for whom, as promised, it opens many doors.[11]

All that I can hope now, at a distance of over thirty years, is that it may still open doors in others, as it certainly did, over almost an entire decade, open doors in me.

11. Margaret Mac Curtain, "Discovery of the Body," *Irish Times,* March 11, 1989.

ARNALDO MOMIGLIANO

THREE HEARTS

In 1975, Arnaldo Momigliano had moved to the University of Chicago, where he would teach for two out of the three terms of the year until his death in 1987. In 1983, I contributed an article for him in the collection of writings in his honor organized by Emilio Gabba. The title of the collection was eminently appropriate. *Tria corda* referred to the "three hearts" of the first great Latin poet, Quintus Ennius (ca. 239–ca. 169 BC), which were the three different languages that offered entry into three different cultural worlds in the multilingual society of southern Italy—Latin, Greek, and Oscan. Arnaldo's third heart, his "Oscan," was his mastery of Hebrew, linked to the Jewish traditions of his family in Piedmont. It was this, the most private and local of his worlds, that emerged as the most tenacious in his time at Chicago.

My contribution to *Tria corda* was "Sexuality and Society in the Fifth Century A.D." I dealt with the debate between Augustine and Julian of Eclanum (a tenacious supporter of Pelagius) on sexuality and marriage. I presented this controversy as a Punic War of the mind, which involved the head-on collision of two worlds.

Julian of Eclanum (ca. 386–454), was a young southern Italian bishop with aristocratic connections. He defended sex as a neutral force, capable of being socialized in a manner not so very different from that proposed in the second century by the doctors of the Antonine Age: sex was "good" and basically unproblematic, provided that it served the family and—by implication—the city. This sunny view clashed with the profoundly destabilizing opinions of Augustine, for whom sex was a permanent reminder of a primeval dislocation: a dark, antisocial force incapable of ever being fully tamed and channeled so as to serve the needs of society—a matter of concern, not of delight, even on the marriage bed.

The opening paragraphs of the essay provided me with an opportunity to go back in time, almost thirty years, to when I first met Arnaldo as my supervisor for a dissertation on the senatorial Roman aristocracy of Italy, many of whose members had been involved, on one side or the other, in the confrontation between Augustine and Julian. I described my debt to him: "As a hesitant young student at Oxford, shamefully underequipped with the skills needed to perform the tasks of an ancient historian, [I found that] Arnaldo Momigliano's presence, in London, gave me, quite simply, the heart to persevere." At that time, Arnaldo's study of Cassiodorus and of the noble clan of the Anicii first introduced me to "those lords and ladies, who (in Arnaldo's words) 'moved with relative security in a world so far from secure.'"[1]

Arnaldo had approved of my move to the East Coast: "I am glad to have your good news from Princeton which, even if Calvinist, will probably be nearer your interest than Berkeley." But I am not so sure that he approved of what he may have suspected to be an undue engagement with the early church on my part. Religion was not for him. He remained throughout, despite his loyalty to the Judaism of his family, an unbeliever in the heroic mold of Spinoza.

> The more I study and respect those old Christians, the less I feel they have to tell me about myself or my contemporaries. . . .
>
> I am sceptic about monastic values—miracles included—in a world which desperately needs both rationality and distrust of charismatic leadership. . . .
>
> If there is something about early Christianity I would like to know [it] is how St. Paul emerged to defeat the Gospels.

When Arnaldo passed through Princeton, in late 1984, I was struck by how he had changed. Illness and personal sorrow had left him more frail. His intellectual energy was by no means diminished. His sharp and capacious mind was ready to confront eye-to-eye yet another major theme in the history of the ancient world, one that he had touched on only in passing in former years—the role of religion, and especially the role of religious biography, as this became ever more prominent in late antiquity. While declaring himself not to be

---

1. *Rivista storica italiana* 69 (1957): 282: P. Brown, "Sexuality and Society in the Fifth Century A.D.: Augustine and Julian of Eclanum," in *Tria corda. Scritti in onore di Arnaldo Momigliano*, ed. E. Gabba (Como: New Press, 1983), 49–70, at 49.

attracted, personally, to "monastic values," he fell with the full weight of his vast erudition and with his habitual lucidity on the novel genre of hagiography in late antiquity, and especially on Gregory of Nyssa's *Life of Macrina*.[2]

When I had almost completed writing *Body and Society*, I sent the entire manuscript to Arnaldo, asking for his permission to dedicate the book to him. He wrote back to me from London in early 1987:

> Now your book is read, and an exceptionally important book it is, which I shall be proud to have inscribed with my name. First of all it called my attention to so many texts which are never properly considered. It will open a new stage in the study of Christianity in its antique social setting. My only hesitation to say so is that I have the impression that Aids will soon make archaic our scholarly views about sex. The sort of exploitation bishops and rabbis (yes, rabbis of all people) try is for anyone to see on the pages of the London Times. . . .
>
> After all Italians are deserting bars for fear of badly washed espresso cups. . . .

Then he went on, in his usual manner, to open up yet another entire field for exploration—the contrast between Judaism and Christianity on the matter of the afterlife:

> If, as you rightly emphasize, sex replaced death as <u>the</u> menace in many Christian groups, there is probably a relation between this shift and the notion that there was no death, only hell for a sinful soul. . . . Paradise and hell have always played a relatively small part in Jewish life. . . . This made Jewish Civilization in the Middle Ages the sanest on the market, at least West of China. . . .

"HIS WISDOM IS MEDITATION ON LIFE"
(SPINOZA, *ETHICS* 4, PROPOSITION 72)

Arnaldo's letter ended on a troubling note. "So far my health has kept fairly stable, though a collapse is possible at any moment." His heart was giving out. In February 1986, he had fainted after a lecture. As I was later told, his

---

2. A. D. Momigliano, "The Life of Saint Macrina by Gregory of Nyssa," in *The Craft of the Ancient Historian: Essays in Honor of Chester G. Starr* (Lanham, MD: University Press of America, 1985), 443–458, also in *Ottavo contributo alla storia degli studi classici e del mondo antico* (Rome: Edizioni Storia e Letteratura, 1987), 333–347, at pp. 338 and 346.

condition worsened rapidly. He remained active, surrounded now by a team of devoted and solicitous friends; but, like a man on stilts, he feared that he might fall at any time. In May 1987, I flew in and out of Chicago on the same day to visit him in hospital. His last letter to me included condolences for the death of my mother, which had occurred in June 1987.

> My dear Peter,
>
>   I am so sorry for the death of your mother. Fortunately the mother is the mother for ever, and her particular beliefs as a Catholic [a good Italian, Arnaldo had difficulty in envisioning a mother who was not either a Catholic or Jewish!] must not count for you more than they counted before. It is already difficult enough to understand what the various religions do of this world, without taking into account the other (to my mind) most unlikely world. Apart from the Divine Comedy of my namesake [Dante: Arnaldo's second name] and the Jewish fancy that the good people like my grandfather and Moses Finley's ancestor The Maharal of Prague [it always gave Arnaldo great pleasure to point out the pious ancestry of his more secularist colleagues] would, in the afterlife, study the Torah for three hours with the Blessed Be He every evening (they are on the right side and free to contradict in this real Yeshiva)—there is nothing worth I know in the fancies about the alleged next world.
>
>   However, I may be near the next world or more precisely near death. There is no substantial or foreseeable improvement in my condition. Next Monday 20 July I return to London. . . .

Arnaldo then went on to comment on his recent award of a MacArthur Fellowship:

> The Mac Arthur Foundation was certainly providential. . . . The only story worth recounting is the entry of [Francis] Hope [the director of the Fellowships Program] in Hospital to announce to me the grant. "Are you still prepared to accept anything from us notwithstanding our quarrels?"

Arnaldo had been well known to the committee of the Fellowships Program as a vocal advocate of giving the grants only to young persons, and not to aging celebrities.

> "I thought I had made it clear [Arnaldo answered] that that I was defending my own interests."

Well, it was good to see you, very good. But my situation is what it is, no real progress, a sense of overwhelming tiredness.

In late August 1987, I flew to England to give the plenary lecture at the Oxford Patristics Conference. Knowing how much this congress had meant to me in 1963 and in 1967, I was touched to find myself lecturing in a slot once occupied by Cardinal Daniélou, Henri-Irénée Marrou, and Christine Mohrmann (1903–1988). More than that: the conference had grown so large that I had to give my lecture in the Sheldonian Theatre.

When I first accepted the invitation early in the year, I told this to my mother (who was then still alive). She reminded me that, in 1956, she and my father had come to see me receive my matriculation, along with a large crowd of fellow graduates, in the Sheldonian. I had caused her acute embarrassment (an embarrassment that, in fact, spiced the occasion for her) by failing to leave with the crowd. Instead, she reminded me, I had wandered around the emptying theater taking in its baroque ceiling and upper galleries. Now, on August 24, 1987, it was there that I gave my lecture: "Society and the Body: The Social Meaning of Asceticism in Late Antiquity."

Next day, I went to see Arnaldo, who had been taken to the Central Middlesex Hospital from his flat in Latymer Court in Hammersmith. To arrive at North Acton Tube station (near the hospital), where the lines ran aboveground in an open landscape near Wormwood Scrubbs, was like arriving at the end of the world. I found Arnaldo in a strange condition. The medications that kept his heart going had ruined his kidneys. He was both active and aware that he was sinking. A smile lit up his face when he was wheeled back to bed after yet another examination, impatient to get busy again on the proofs of yet another article. He was plainly angry at the failure of his body to support his ever-active mind. I reflected that, in such a state, the ancient dualism between the vivid spirit and the dull prison of the flesh (a dualism of body and soul that we, as scholars, had tended to brush aside as a legacy of ancient Greece and of Gnostic pessimism—a dark thought out of place in our sunnier world) made, alas, all too much sense. All one could wish, for Arnaldo, was in the verse of Psalm 124:7:

We have escaped as a bird
from the snare of the fowlers;
the snare is broken,
and we have escaped!

Arnaldo died on September 1, 1987. On October 22, I was back in Chicago. I spoke briefly at the memorial service.[3] It was then that I heard, for the first time, the words of Spinoza on the wise person, which Arnaldo had chosen for his memorial service, both in Chicago and in London:

And so he thinks of nothing less than death. Instead his wisdom is a meditation on life, q.e.d. (Spinoza, *Ethics* 4, proposition 72)

3. Peter Brown, "Remembering Arnaldo," in *The American Scholar* 57 (1988): 251–252.

REMEMBERING ARNALDO

An Intellectual Biography

At the end of 1987 I was asked by the British Academy to write the obituary memoir for Momigliano, to be published in the *Proceedings of the British Academy*. I wanted to do this in the way that Arnaldo might have wanted it—in other words, I wanted to write an intellectual biography that set his ever-unfolding scholarly agenda against the background of the thought of his times.

To do this, I read all Arnaldo's works in strict chronological order. This was a less heroic feat than it seems. Arnaldo was his own best historiographer. All his articles were printed, in the chronological order in which they were published, in a series of volumes, entitled *Contributi alla storia degli studi classici* published by Storia e Letteratura of Rome. By 1987, this series had reached the eighth volume. Also, owing to Arnaldo's spectacular generosity in keeping all his charges and friends up to date by lavishing offprints on them, his production after 1956 was, for me, almost a family matter. These offprints would come like the regular arrival of a favorite magazine. The difficulty was to place this extraordinary output against the shifting currents of Europe, Britain, and America from 1930 to 1987.

But I was determined to do this. The last thing I wanted was to produce a standard honorific portrait of Arnaldo—to paint an icon-like image of the successful scholar and public person. The result was a memoir of some thirty-seven pages.[1]

In July 1988, I flew to England in order to interview friends and colleagues of Arnaldo in Oxford and London, and then I went on to Italy—to Pisa, Turin,

---

1. Peter Brown, "Arnaldo Dante Momigliano 1908–1987," *Proceedings of the British Academy* 74 (1988): 405–442.

and Pavia. I had never conducted interviews of this kind before. I quickly learned one remarkable fact about the nature of such encounters. In the case of obituaries, when the dead person is still an object of grief and mourning, the interviewer takes on an almost shamanistic role: to a degree that I had never expected, I often *became* Arnaldo for a moment to those whom I interviewed. One did not have to be a very adroit psychologist to pick up the quality of the "vibes" that had only recently surrounded the living person. My interviews turned out to involve a lot more than gathering information. They enabled me to sense the nature of his presence to his various groups of friends and colleagues.

AMONG FRIENDS

I was struck by the differences of "temperature"—as one might call it—among the various circles on whom Arnaldo had impinged. Oxford was cool. In response to my request for help in finding persons who knew Arnaldo well, Peter Brunt (1917–2005)—the recently retired Camden Professor of Ancient History—was guarded:

> His deep interest in the modern historiography of the ancient world was little shared by British scholars, and his conviction that problems in history were best examined through the solutions that had been previously proposed involved an erudition that the rest of us could not match, and a procedure which in any case most of us would not have acknowledged to be of as much value as he believed.

Arriving at Oxford, among many interviews, I had a long and characteristically vivid conversation with Isaiah Berlin (1909–1997), in what I recognized were my own former rooms in All Souls. He later wrote to thank me for the draft of the obituary:

> I loved your article—it did not go beyond the limit to which he should be praised, it was beautifully eloquent, very moving and very true. What more can I say?

Reading this note, I had a flashback to a scene of the early 1970s. Arnaldo and Isaiah were standing beside the ironwork grille that closed the entrance from Radcliffe Square to the Hawksmoor Quadrangle of All Souls. To unlock the gate, each had taken out a key ring heavily loaded with keys that gave them personal access to any number of libraries, archives, and learned institutions that were closed to outsiders. In his jocose manner, Arnaldo challenged Isaiah, for all the world like a small boy, to show whether his equipment—his key ring—was bigger than his own. I had been present at a meeting of giants.

Later that afternoon, after my talk with Isaiah, I went up to North Oxford to interview Iris Murdoch (1919–1999), the philosopher and novelist. Iris had known Arnaldo from the very first days of his exile in Oxford, during the war years and after. The afternoon passed by. We were back in the 1940s, exploring the extraordinary friendship between Iris, a philosopher and magician of English prose, and this intense man of preternatural learning whose mouth, at that time, was still tied by lack of fluency in English. She dabbed her eyes for a moment: "You know, Professor Brown, now that Arnaldo is dead, there is no one from whom I can ask any questions any more."

Then we broke for a sherry. A little later, as we settled down to our conversation once again, Iris suddenly asked me: "Professor Brown, you who know about such things, what can I read to find out about the influence of Plato on the Christian doctrine of the Trinity?" To my amazement, I heard myself saying, with utter confidence and even in the thick Piedmontese accent with which Arnaldo always pronounced French: "Ah, of course! You must read Pierre Hadot, *Marius Victorinus. Recherches sur sa vie et ses oeuvres.*" I had brought Arnaldo to her quite as much as she had brought to me the edgy exile of the 1940s. A little later, in August 1988, she wrote to me: "I loved and revered Arnaldo so much and keep 'seeing' him and thinking about him and his particular Jewishness and funniness and sweetness and wisdom and that vast learning."

When I went to London, I had the same sense that I was in the middle of a group of friends, feeling their affection for him as we sat together (as Arnaldo must have done with them, in the seat that I now occupied), at the cafeteria in University College, and discussed Arnaldo's inspired chases for hitherto unconsidered evidence for the complex interrelations of Jewish scholars in Renaissance and in modern times.

Memories of Exile

It was with a similar sense of intimacy with Arnaldo that Carlo Dionisotti (1908–1998), the distinguished former professor of Italian at Bedford College, handed me a box full of the letters that Arnaldo had written to him from the very beginning of his exile in England, in 1939. I read them deep into the night. Next morning, I woke up convinced that I had had a nightmare. No: it was not a nightmare; it was the memory of what I had read in Arnaldo's lucid, regular descriptions of the small humiliations of starting life from scratch in a foreign country—the cold, cramped accommodations with a kitchen shared with the landlady; the uncertainty of funding; right down to the vulnerability (in a prewar Europe, where travel was less frequent) to flus and colds carried by local germ pools against which the Momiglianos had developed no immunity. It was, indeed, the world of Dante's days of exile:

> Tu proverai sì come sa di sale
> lo pane altrui, e com' è duro calle
> lo scendere e salir per l'altrui scale

> You shall make trial of how another's bread
> tastes like salt,
> and how hard is the path to descend and mount
> upon another's stair.[2]

In the same way, in Italy, over slow and generous meals with Emilio Gabba in Pavia—as the frogs in the neighboring lakes (frankly advertised for sale by the bucket to the local epicures) honked triumphantly, and the mosquitoes rose around the hotel in such swarms that I had to cover myself from head to foot with aftershave for lack of an insect repellent—I relived the difficulties that Arnaldo had suffered on his return to Italy immediately after the war.

Chicago and Peterhouse

In Chicago, which I visited a little later, I found myself at the center of the many circles of Arnaldo's friends. There I met Edward Shils, whose redefinition of charisma had made him the hero of my early contacts with American sociology in my first years at Berkeley. He now became a friend through his devotion to Arnaldo, whom we discussed all day, in Shils's apartment in a skyscraper overlooking Lake Michigan, so high up as to look down on every bird.

Among the abundant memories of Arnaldo's Chicago friends, I was surprised to find how many of these concerned his later visits to England. He had plainly regaled his friends at the Quadrangle Club in Chicago with anecdotes of solemn ceremonies and high table life in Oxford and Cambridge. He spoke with particular affection of his days in Peterhouse, Cambridge, in the early

---

2. Dante, *Paradiso* 17.58–60.

1980s. He had enjoyed the atmosphere of the college feasts. He had been touched when the college porter wished him "Happy birthday." He had invariably found something interesting to talk about at high table, even with scientists.

This was a side of Arnaldo that I had not expected. But it made sense. He had been made a fellow of Peterhouse for two years at the behest of the master, Hugh Trevor-Roper (later Lord Dacre). Trevor-Roper (1914–2003) had hoped to be cheered up by Arnaldo's presence. From being a highly contested Regius Professor of History in Oxford, Trevor-Roper had become master of Peterhouse in 1980. As he recounted it, the change from Oxford to Peterhouse was a disaster. He found himself blocked by a morose cabal of ultraconservative fellows.[3] When I was still in Berkeley, I received a letter from Hugh canvassing my support for a protégé of his. He added, with characteristic acerbity: "How are you enjoying Berkeley? Is it as strange as Peterhouse? I feel that I might as well be in Basutoland."

AFFECTION

What no purely intellectual biography could quite capture was that sense of affection which I picked up in those charged weeks in July 1988. My friend Averil Cameron reminded me of this when I showed her the draft of my memoir:

> I think I might have wanted to include the extreme <u>affection</u> felt for him by his circle of devoted younger friends in his various places—London, Pisa, Chicago. I myself more and more felt that I could simply not live up to the tremendous faith he obviously had in me. . . . When he died I really realized that he had simply <u>always</u> been there for me and never failed me. . . . In his turn he had terrific respect for one's separateness and intellectual integrity— usually a much higher conception of it than one had one's self.

At the end of a book that is devoted, in large part, to my own intellectual itinerary, it is good to remember Arnaldo, and the qualities of scholar, mentor, and friend, for which he was not only held in awe, but loved.

3. Adam Sisman, *Hugh Trevor-Roper: The Biography* (London: Weidenfeld and Nicolson, 2010), 454–474.

MUMS

"Better to Live the Life of a Slug"

Ever since my father's death, in January 1981, my mother (Mums to me) faced a great loneliness. Her diary in her last years often makes painful reading.

> Tea. Got dinner—usual lonely evening and it will always be the same.
>
> (DIARY 2/19/81)

> Washed up supper. Glad that Easter is over. I missed Jim so much
>
> (DIARY 4/19/81)

It did not get better. As she wrote to me, in 1983, about her visit to Dean's Grange cemetery where my father was buried:

> I brought out bits and pieces from the garden, including some Christmas roses and some iris stylosa. People say how quickly the two years have gone. I'm afraid I don't agree—they have just crawled.
>
> (LETTER 1/27/83)

But at least in the first years, until 1984, she had her sister Freda—my aunt Teedah. My mother could not drive, but Freda had a car—an Austin Mini, a little mouse of a car that made Teedah herself seem even rounder and smaller as she rolled out of it on her arrival in front of my mother's house. Every Monday she drove down from Dublin to have tea with my mother. Often, on those Mondays, Freda would drive my mother to the local shops at Glasthule, in order to do heavy shopping, and, occasionally, to Dean's Grange cemetery. After that, they would settle down to a "grand chat"—a precious exchange of news and excitements over tea. It was then that they could joke about themselves, and the jokes would be passed on to me in my mother's letters: "So here we are, two elderly ladies, and never a man to darken our doors!! Oh yes, [there is] Bolton Thom [a plump and ceremonious church warden] but he is certainly not a Thom cat" (*Letter* 10/2/81).

When, as we have seen, Freda died suddenly in February 1984 of a heart attack (probably the result of a spell of hypothermia in her grand, unheated flat in Morehampton Road), my mother lost half her world. Mondays, now, were always sad days for her: "I still miss Freda so much. No one to chat with or have a laugh with" (*Letter* 5/22/85).

Yet despite this slow but sure narrowing of her horizon, as relatives and friends died, or became less mobile—unable to visit her or even, at last, no longer available even on the telephone—my mother stayed put. The one thing she would not consider was to leave her house for some more comfortable and sociable place to live—an apartment or a retirement home. My phone calls from California, in the depths of the worst Irish winter for ninety-three years, were welcome: "an aura of sanity seems to enter the room, you were speaking from a warm country with flowers" (*Letter* 12/12/81). But my mother never dreamed of moving.

> And I think to myself that it is not worth going to a place to be miserable—it's much wiser to carry on in this boring way of living—shopping, R.D.S. [the Royal Dublin Society Library in Ballsbridge] hair do!: it is better to live the life of a slug as I do.
>
> (*LETTER* 1/25/82)

Slugs throve in the dank atmosphere of the Irish summers. They were well-established denizens of the little walled-in garden at the back of my mother's house. Occasionally they would gather at the kitchen door, like a group of tiny carol-singers. Those who found their way into the kitchen itself would be picked up with care by my mother, on a piece of paper, and deposited, in their proper home near the compost heap. They were not thought of as disgusting creatures. They were symbols of tenacity in a dim world.

SANDYCOVE AVENUE EAST

Reading my mother's diaries and her letters to me, I cannot resist the feeling that the Ireland of the 1980s was a hard place for old persons like my mother. This was not yet the Ireland of only ten years later, when the Celtic Economic Tiger began to swish its tail. It was a time of hectic government expenditure, high taxes, inflation, and rising unemployment. Above all, the services on which the elderly depended were as unreliable as the Irish weather. The telephone, for instance, often failed: "This is the year of 'No Summer'. But all I want is the phone—though I never use it!! . . . Still no phone, but its making queer sounds" (*Letter* 9/1/85).

The buses also failed. Her diaries and letters were full of accounts of half-hour waits, of strikes and rumors of strikes. Yet the running of the buses was essential to my mother. I talk of her world becoming "narrower" with the deaths of my father and of Freda. In fact, it grew exponentially *wider* without a car. Everything became that much farther away. Pulling a trolley for her regular shopping, she could go only as far as her legs, and then the bus, could carry her. Fortunately, the number 8 bus ran past the top of Sandycove Avenue all the way into Dublin. This was her lifeline. It took her, in a few minutes, to Glasthule, to do her shopping. But it continued like a magic carpet to the library of the Royal Dublin Society at Ballsbridge. Often the magic worked: she would be back home from the Royal Dublin Society with four books in her trolley bag by the end of the morning. But frequently it did not. Hence the accounts of the kindness of strangers—drivers who stopped to offer her a lift—that light up the diary: "Hair done. Was petrified waiting for bus, but kind woman offered me a lift. Another wait of ½ hour coming home. How Jim would have taken care of me!" (*Diary* 1/6/82).

In the unusually cold winter of 1981/82, these kindnesses stand out in my mother's letters to me:

A knock at 7.20 p.m. I saw someone peering in at the letter box—I was a bit scared but decided it was too early for a robbery! Guess who it was? You couldn't. It was one of the three young men from next door [asking if they could do shopping for her] . . . that offer of help has solved one of my dreads—a bulb "going" and not being able to stand on a ladder to put one in. He smokes 10 to 20 cigs a day, and quite understands that I missed my two. It really was a lovely surprise.

(*LETTER* 12/23/81)

But despite these kindnesses, a dark stain of violence seemed to be spreading. In her diary, she noted the renewed terrorist activities of the Provisional IRA. The bomb attack on Harrods of London disturbed her: "Harrods' bomb. 5 killed. Dreadful business. I hope they won't start now" (*Diary*, 12/17/82). "Start now" had an ominous ring.

Sandycove was no Belfast. But the undertows of a depressed economy were there. I was appalled to learn, from my mother's diaries, that she had been burgled on many occasions, and had told me about only the worst of them. Neighbors were burgled too. Mr. Doyle, up the road, was robbed of three hundred pounds just taken out of the bank; and Mrs. Doyle's diamond ring was also stolen. Plainly the Doyles had been watched.

My mother suffered seriously on only one occasion: she returned home from church one day to find that all her jewelry except for her engagement ring had been stolen from her bedroom. The other occasions were, in many ways, more disturbing—pointless acts of vandalism rather than cold robbery. The house in Sandycove was all too open to such violence. It had once been a one-story fisherman's cottage. A spare room had been fitted under the roof, with a window. It was easy to shin up the low granite wall of the garden, onto the roof and through the window into the spare room. This happened more than once. On the last occasion, just before my mother's death, she found mud stains all over the sheets, and family papers scattered all over the floor. I wonder how much of my past went, literally, out the window on that occasion. Indeed, when I returned to Sandycove in 1990, the new owners of the house handed me a little attaché case that they had found in the garden—among the slugs, no less! It contained all my school reports from Aravon, half washed away by the damp. Plainly the thief had discarded it, having found nothing of value.

"Where Can You Get a Germ in Your Own House?"

It was here that my mother settled down to endure, for six years, the siege of her widowhood. The two principal rooms of the house—the sitting room and the bedroom—were kept spotless. Carpets were brushed and vacuumed well beyond necessity. The brass knobs and letter slot on the front door always shone, as did the silverware, even though it was tucked away where nobody could see it. The daily chores were carefully recorded in soft pencil on each page of my mother's pocket diary. This diary was not about my mother's thoughts or feelings. Written every evening, it brought the day to order, by recording the household tasks that she had successfully performed. Hence the few occasions in which she expressed her feelings of loss for my father and for Freda in her diary were that much more poignant.

What kept her going? I think it was a huge sense of order and an equally sharp desire to present a neat front in public. She kept up her appearance as fiercely as she kept up the shine of her silverware and polished wood. Tiffin, a ladies' dress store, lay at the extreme outward edge of her walking range to

Glasthule. But she made the distance. Tiffin therapy always did her a world of good:

> I felt I needed a bit of attention so, after lunch, I went down to Tiffin and bought a lovely shade of dark red—not really red, but a very subdued jumper and skirt. I just walked into it.
>
> I am sure you will be glad to hear this news, and that I'm not getting really shabby!
>
> (LETTER 10/4/84)

Such things meant much to her because she was a supremely social creature. She had always combined huge charm with a fear of disgrace in social situations. It was a fear that sprouted around her like icicles at the very thought of an awkward encounter. My father had been, in many ways for many years, her bridge to the outside world—a minister of foreign affairs. A Dublin gentleman and a model of politeness, he took people as they came. Now that he was gone, my mother had to handle these encounters on her own. Her diaries and letters showed all too clearly the sharp pendulum swings between dread of others and a capacity to turn what, only a moment before, had seemed to be an occasion of acute shame into the most friendly and humorous "grand chat." Her charm never left her, any more than did the rock-firm handwriting with which she would describe these encounters in her letters to me every week.

But she had few overriding interests to fall back upon. She had no good causes to which she was devoted. She could not drive a car nor could she type. When in danger of being roped into a neighborhood association, she declared herself, with a touch of sarcasm, to be a "Useless Female" (*Letter* 1/27/83).

Nor were the clergy very welcome. Mums was pious—she enjoyed going to church and said her prayers regularly at night, maybe along with a daily scripture reading. But "religion" was not for her. The Reverend Linney, rector of St. Paul's Church, Glenageary, was a conscientious visitor. But "I do wish he could talk about something besides religion. I fear he has come to the wrong person for that" (*Letter* 4/20/1981). A devout cousin (probably an Evangelical) whose family went out of their way to take care of my mother—regularly driving her to church, and bringing her home for Sunday lunch (where she exercised her charm on all the children, who adored her)—seems to have cut no ice on matters of religion: "Had a good chat. Had lunch. Then read about sense of sin. Had a snooze" (*Diary*, 4/1/82).

Nor did any doctor darken her door. The medical system then prevailing in the area ensured that she experienced a magnificently (though, nowadays, some might say—criminally) unmonitored approach to death. Dr. Robin Benson was a general practitioner of the old school. He came (or his stand-in came) only when called. He occasionally brought a pill. Far from being unsympathetic or neglectful (he looked after my father day by day in his last illness), he treated his elder patients with a robust laissez-faire that kept them cheerful. His advice was simple: "Put on all your woollies." My mother complied: "I now wear (1) two vests (2) 4 pairs of knickers (3) 1 jumper (4) 3 cardigans (5) 1 dressing gown!!" (*Letter* 12/23/81). It was that cold when the sea wind blew.

This regime might appall us. But it slid into place with my mother's deepest wish to stand siege in her own house on her own terms. She was told once that she might have caught a cold from a germ. But how could she have done so, having never gone out for days? "The doctor says it can only be caught by a germ—where can you get a germ in your own house?!" (*Letter* 2/24/83). That was my mother.

SHIFTING BOUNDARIES

BOUNDARIES

As I reread my mother's letters to me, I increasingly realized that they were historical documents in a manner that I had not expected. Her letters were more revealing than the impersonal, clocklike entries in her diaries. She wanted to bond with me through shared memories, and (my mother being my mother, with a wicked sense of humor) through shared, long-standing family jokes. These memories reached back directly to our days together in wartime Bray. Reading her letters from the late 1980s, I realize that I was being taken back by my mother to the sadder, more rigid Ireland that we had both known in the 1940s and 1950s.

For this reason, the social map of Ireland that my mother expected me to take for granted in her letters was still a map marked strongly in religious colors—Protestant, Roman Catholic. No description of any encounter or piece of news was quite complete without ticking one of the two most important boxes—Prot or R.C. In 1982, she voted for Garrett Fitzgerald (later to become the fourth president of Ireland) in the general election: "I voted for Garrett Fitzgerald, but he is too good to get in! His mother was a Protestant" (*Letter* 4/27/82). Settling into Princeton, I had praised to her an Irish stonemason with the name of Murphy. My mother wrote back: "I wonder if he is a Prot." (*Letter* 11/17/83). For my mother, this was not a sign of intolerance. It was simply a matter of knowing where one stood. This meant that there was also room for delicious surprises, noted in her diary: "Went for bus and a very nice young man offered me a lift! I took it. He was very nice and knew the Frenches in church [a Protestant family who came regularly to St. Paul's Glenageary], but was an R.C." (*Diary* 7/18/84).

Yet, at long last, things were changing. Even Aravon, once the all-Protestant realm of "the Boss," had crumbled. Not everyone was pleased. "Marjorie [a Bray friend of my mother's, of long standing] hates Aravon now—she says its nearly all girls and R.C.s, and not a bit what it was . . . [and] it's the same with St. Columba's [the Protestant public school]" (*Letter* 10/12/83).

Despite the changing mood of Ireland, the old conundrums still worried my mother. She wrote to ask me why, in an interview that I had sent her, did I need to point out that I was a *Protestant* Irishman? "Does that mean that most people only connect being Irish with Roman Catholic?" But, no matter whether they were Protestant or Catholic, "there is no doubt about it. The Irish are, indeed, liked much better than the English" (*Letter* 6/6/81).

"I Prefer to Be a Warren and Irish"

What struck me in these letters was a distinct shift in favor of an Irish identity. My mother never became an anti-British nationalist. But she was capable of unusually strong reactions to what she called "Englishness." To her, "Englishness" was not a national marker; it was a social vice. It conjured up snobbery, assertiveness, and condescension. She had experienced it at first hand as a young wife in Sudan. And she didn't like it. She commiserated with me when I described to her an awkward dinner with English expatriates in Venice: "How I know and hate those loud-mouthed English women! I met many in the Sudan and it is due to them that I (and many others) have such a hatred of the English as a whole" (*Letter* 2/26/81). Even to sound a bit "English" over the phone was a warning sign. Yet some of her firmest friends from Sudan were English. This was because they had dropped their "Englishness." They had become, as it were, honorary Irish and could be spun into a "grand chat."

This mental map, which contrasted English high-handedness and snobbery with a more authentic "Irish" identity, was put on display when I sent to my mother a postcard of a Tudor portrait of Lady Jane Grey. In my second chapter, I have already mentioned the importance that some members of the Grey family (from which my mother's mother came) attached to a tenuous link to Lady Jane Grey, the Protestant would-be queen of England, executed by Mary Tudor in 1554. My mother responded instantly:

The post came with lovely PCs of my ancestor (or should it be ancestress) Lady Jane Grey! As a rule I laugh at all this family snobbishness, but it really does impress me when I see someone like Lady Jane and realize that there must be <u>some</u> connection with us—I suppose. . . . But the real snag is that Lady Jane and all her family were very English indeed, so I prefer to be a Warren and Irish!

(<small>LETTER</small> 10/12/81)

I do not remember Lady Jane ever being discussed in this way when I grew up. Slowly, over the years, a shift in the family mythology had taken place in favor of Ireland.

ROBERT DE WARREN / BOBBY WARREN

This game of identities based on genealogies was played to the full on the occasion of the unexpected appearance, in Dublin, of a real live Warren. We have already met Robert de Warren as the *maître de ballet* of the shah of Iran.[1] As I wrote there, I had dismissed him as an almost mythological character, belonging, perhaps, to an earlier generation of Warrens. Far from it. I could have met him in Tehran; and, as far as I know, he is still living in Sarasota, Florida, where he wrote a memoir, *Destiny's Waltz: In Step with Giants*, that included treasured memories of the court of Shah Reza in the 1960s and 1970s. I like to think of him as something of a doppelgänger.

In 1984 my mother wrote to tell me that Bobby Warren in person had come over to Dublin. He came as director of the Northern Ballet Company, in order to direct *Sleeping Beauty* for the opening of the refurbished and upgraded Gaiety Theatre—a long way from the very "Dublin" pantomime humor of Jimmie O'Dea! He declared that he wanted to meet my mother so as to find out more about the Warren family from which he was descended. He had been encouraged to do so by Cousin Aileen, a relative settled in Taunton, England, who was, in many ways, the guardian of the memories of his branch of the Warrens.

Like many members of dispersed Irish Protestant families, Bobby was buoyed up by the thought of illustrious and energetic ancestors. On entering the world of ballet in Europe, he changed his name to Robert *de* Warren—in honor of Earl William de Warenne, a companion of William the Conqueror, from whom the Warrens of county Meath traditionally claimed descent. For my mother, this name change was the last straw—a sign of egregious snobbery.

Bobby's letter announcing his arrival fell on my mother like a meteorite from outer space. She was furious with Aileen for having sent her way a virtual

---

1. Chapter 69: "To the Top of the World."

stranger and, she feared, an ultra-English snob. Cousin Aileen was fifteen years older than my mother: a handsome lady, seeming to last forever, she brought out all my mother's ambivalences. She was "religion" personified: an ardent Christian and Spiritualist, she longed (poor woman) to hear the voices from the other world of her dead husband, a clergyman, and her son killed in the war. My mother held her both in awe and in ridicule. She would never mention Aileen's intense religiosity without adding some catty remark that brought her down to earth.

> Christian and all as she is, she is a bloody snob and Dads always agreed with me. My leanings are not towards the "Upper Classes" (as they call themselves) but my own class which rings me up and says he has an appointment at "Half Eight"!!
>
> (*LETTER* 12/12/81)

My mother, in fact, would never herself have said "half eight," which was an Irish turn of phrase. She always said "half past eight," in the most proper English manner: but the right sort—such as gardeners—did say "half eight." And that was good enough for her.

When Bobby Warren's visit finally materialized, in late 1984, the encounter dreaded by my mother turned, almost instantly, into a "grand talk." But that was not what my mother had expected. She kept me posted with regular letters on this oncoming meeting. First there was the usual ice storm of social anxiety:

> You'll never guess who I heard from today, Robert de Warren—"Bobby", Mervyn Warren's son. You know he was head of the Iranian Ballet, and the Shah never took the smallest notice of him. He has always kept in with Aileen and I suppose wrote and told her he was coming over to the big opening of the Gaiety Theatre. . . . He wrote a letter "Dear Mrs Brown" and wondered would I come to the Ballet, with a friend. If not, he would like to come down and see me! Ending the letter "with affectionate greetings—Bobby—Robert de Warren! . . . I'll have to write and ask him down, only tea or drinks (I hope he doesn't bring his wife—Aileen says she has <u>two</u> fur coats). . . .
>
> Sunday 14th. Just written to "Bobby"—I did not call him Robert de Warren! Said I didn't go out at night, but would love to see him and when he rang me, we could make plans.
>
> (*LETTER* 10/11/84)

Just been rung up by Bobby Warren! He and his wife are over. . . . He and his wife had driven down to Duleek [the church where the Warren family were buried, in county Meath], to see all the old places. It won't be much fun, really, I think. He sounded a bit "English" . . . and the wife will be a "drawback".

(LETTER 10/29/84)

Then the storm blew over:

Well, Bobby Warren and wife came to tea and we had a great talk. They were dressed in jumpers!

It was these unpretentious sweaters ("jumpers" in English usage) that did it:

He hadn't even a tie, so it was really cheery. He is about 56. I don't know her age—she may be the same but looks years younger—longish fair hair and blue eyes, and she is French. . . . The whole talk was about the Warren family—we talked of nothing else, and he had maps of everywhere. He had been to Duleek. Disastrous. The lovely little church pulled to bits by van-dals and now never used—he took photos and showed me them, monu-ments broken and all the people who were buried there pulled out of their graves and left there—all our grandmothers—every one. They do it every-where. So that was the end of Drummin [the family house]—there's no one in the house and it's all falling down. I asked him about the "de". He said everyone had it when they came to England first [Bobby meant, of course, with William the Conqueror in 1066!] and he decided to use it! He had thick black hair, and quite nice looking. She was pretty fat. They gave me a pound box of Terry's chocolates—beautiful box. . . . .

(LETTER 11/12/84)

Bobby returned next year to a more relaxed occasion.

Sunday. They are coming to tea! He needs to go on a drive to Drummin! They were to come here on their way home to tea. I had only one cake, so cut brown bread and will have biscuits. Later I sat from 4 o'c to 5.30 p.m, not a sign of them !! Phone rang and it was Bobby. He lost his way and has just arrived back at the Shelbourne [their Dublin hotel]. Could he come down? So they were here having tea at 6 and didn't go till after 7. But we had a great chat. She is very nice too. And we talked about the Shah and how much she liked him and Bobbie talked about Drummin. . . . He brought me a box of chocolates—good of him—(He is really quite plain, because he has his mother's nose—not a Warren one!)

(LETTER 11/18/85)

"'Abroad' . . . but I Am Irish to the Backbone"

Just before Bobby Warren made his last appearance, my mother committed herself to what was for her a most unaccustomed tea party. Mrs. Cardan was a retired civil servant who had moved into Sandycove Avenue East. She and her two friends represented the new, bureaucratic Ireland. "She was a civil servant and you never heard such a common accent (and yet, its not really common, just Dublin)." That "not really common, just Dublin," was a revealing concession on my mother's part.

> She has a good sense of humour, but I can't imagine having any of these three people in the old days. And yet they couldn't be nicer and they loved their tea and admired my blue suit. She said I had an English accent, and where did it get it? So I said "Abroad . . . but I am Irish to the backbone!"
>
> So we all enjoyed ourselves.

(LETTER 9/1/85)

Despite her time "abroad" among the English, Mums belonged to Ireland.

"Brought Me Strawberries. Were Very Nice"

My mother lived for almost another two years. Given the near total absence of medical monitoring, there was no telling when she might die. Chances for her to display her charm in a "grand chat" still came her way. Of all people, Lellia Ruggini of Turin—a scholar whom I had admired for many years and came to know when I was in Venice—gave her a phone call on my urging when she attended a conference at Trinity College Dublin. "She spoke good English. We had a good talk, and I found out she is Italian. Aren't people clever about the different languages? I wonder if she really understood me at all?" (*Letter* 3/13/86).

Most intriguing, for my mother, was a telephone call from a Princeton undergraduate, Michael Meckler, whom the Group for the Study of Late Antiquity had sent to Dublin to do research that led to a significant article on the links between Saint Columba and the O'Neill dynasty in Ulster and Scotland.[2]

> Just been having a talk with Michael Meckler! We must have talked nearly an hour. He seems so friendly. He seems such a nice 21 year old (I asked him his age!). . . . We had a grand chat. Is he good looking, I wonder? Not that it matters one way or the other, but I just wondered. Its very nice to have a chat, and as we can't see each other, it makes it all the easier.
>
> (LETTER 4/23/86)

In those years, my mother herself noticed that she had changed. She was no longer an avid reader. Back in 1981, when a major Dublin bus strike had ended, this had been a great event for her: it meant that the way to the Royal Dublin Society Library was open at last: "4 weeks since I smelt the smell of books!" (*Letter* 7/31/81). And these were no trash novels: they included George Eliot's *Daniel Deronda* and William Faulkner, whom she had been encouraged to read by Roberta Chesnut, almost twenty years earlier, in 1968. Now, in 1987, that zest had ebbed: "Funny the way the love of reading has gone—except in bed. There is always some paper to read. I never take up a book and yet, when I was young, I was always reading. I suppose it was to discover what the world was really like! Now I seem to know!" (*Letter* 3/31/87).

Only in the last days of May did the handwriting in my mother's diaries weaken and lose its shape.

> Not feeling so good. Nancy came by. Brought me strawberries. Were very nice.
>
> (DIARY 5/28/87)

Nancy lived two houses up the road: I never knew her surname. She had come close to my mother as she also had lost a sister and understood what it felt like.

I found my mother's last letter to me on her bedside table. It was the only time that her writing was incoherent. Though now confused, the determination to get her jobs done was still there:

> I am not really very well, and am really quite all right, and so its very awkward to have to think of everything being all right!! I saw Robin Benson yesterday, and all seemed well, and I am going to give up my well prepared

---

2. M. Meckler, "Colum Cille's Ordination of Aedán Mac Gabráin," *Innes Review* 41 (1990): 139–150.

plan of campaign, and start to work again. . . . There's a new kind of campaign now which will be most effective and quite easy to do. May 27ᵗʰ Robin Benson will be here yesterday and to do what he said to do, I'm to do it. . . . But do not expect your room to look your best when you arrive! So there we are, I must try and go out tomorrow, and do some shopping, if I can.

Mums died on June 9, 1987. Her death was unexpected. I was in Rome at the time, at an international conference in honor of Richard Krautheimer, which took place in Trastevere. I had intended to fly to Ireland the next week. After I heard the news of her death, I left the conference for a long walk, up the steep slope of the Aventine near Sant'Alessio. I remember that I went out of my way to help an old lady by carrying her shopping bag up the hill.

Soon I was in the spare bedroom beneath the roof of my mother's house in Sandycove Avenue East. It was there, in the drawer of a bureau in the adjoining lumber room, that I found two newspaper cuttings from the *Irish Times* and the *Khartoum Times*. One side of each announced my birth. On the other side of each, a major politician—Éamon de Valera and Air Marshal Italo Balbo—told their hearers with the greatest confidence what the future would be. Both were proved entirely wrong. It was a salutary lesson in the tragic blindness of those we study in the past. It set me thinking. It made me determined, at some time, to write this book.

POSTSCRIPT

SINCE THEN

Princeton

It has been almost thirty-five years since 1987. Those years have been a time of extraordinary creativity for the entire field of late antiquity. When I began to study it, in the 1950s, it was a marginal field, barely recognized as a field at all. Over the past decades it has attracted a remarkable range of young and gifted scholars. Once based on a handful of European countries, it is now studied all over the world.

I have been fascinated and delighted to watch this flowering of the field. But if I were to trace its progress in the detail that it deserves, I would need to write an entire new book, and it would be a long one. So, instead, let me conclude with a brief sketch of my life and work as they have evolved over the past thirty-five years.

Since 1987, I have remained in Princeton. I found that its high gravity challenged me to widen yet further my field of interests, and that the campus provided a perfect balance between teaching and research. To this I should add that my friendship with Glen Bowersock, who came from Harvard to the Institute for Advanced Study in 1980, has kept me in touch with that remarkable institution and with the constant succession of scholars from Britain and Europe who have passed through the institute as visiting fellows.

On Princeton campus itself, the dynamic presence of Dimitri Gondicas (now the director of the Seeger Center for Hellenic Studies) brought me into contact with all that was best and most adventurous in the study of the Byzantine and modern Greek world. From 2001 onward, my involvement, through Dimitri, in the Hellenic Studies Program has given me new, rich air to breathe, and an invaluable experience of the day-to-day workings of an unusually happy academic project.

TURKEY

This widening of my field of interest coincided with a notable widening of my travels. As early as 1986, I decided to pick up again my Middle Eastern interests by learning Ottoman and modern Turkish from Cemal Kafadar, now at Havard, who was then in the Department of Near Eastern Studies in Princeton. This was not only because travel to the rich remains of late antiquity—and of all other periods of the ancient world—was relatively easy and safe in Turkey. It was also because I decided that, if I was to engage in a serious study of the problems of empire in late antiquity, I would need some traditional empire— such as the Ottoman Empire at its height—to compare with the workings of the autocracy of East Rome.

As a result, I spent many months in Istanbul, in 1989–1990. Later (from 1996 to 2001) I directed an archaeological survey in the region of Beypazarı that led to the discovery of the ruins of the monastery and church of Sykeon, the home village of none other than Theodore of Sykeon (died 613), one of the most notable holy men in the early Byzantine world.[1]

I journeyed from one end of Turkey to the other, often in the footsteps of the indomitable Ottoman traveler Evliya Çelebi (1611–1682). This remarkable gentleman, a mixture of globe-trotter, courtier, and master raconteur, had traveled the full extent of the Ottoman Empire at its height—from the walls of Vienna to Sudan.[2] I followed Evliya's journeys along the old Roman road, which led from Constantinople to Antioch and the East, and which had been the spine of the East Roman Empire (now known to the locals as the Bağdat Yolu—the Baghdad Road).

There I caught a glimpse, as it were, of two superimposed empires—that of the Ottomans and that of East Rome. Each empire had left its imprint on a vast and ancient land: the well-preserved ruins of classical and late Roman cities, with their marble colonnades, theaters, and great Christian basilicas, often standing, strangely untouched, as if they had gone to sleep in the age of Justinian, only to be reawakened by the modern archaeologist; and (for Evliya) the reassuring succession of Ottoman towns, with their caravansaries, their elegant

---

1. Peter Brown, "Chorotope: Theodore of Sykeon and His Sacred Landscape," in *Ierotopiia: sozdanie sakral'nych prostranstv v Vizantii i Drevneï Rusi* [Hierotopy: the Creation of Sacred Spaces in Byzantium and Old Russia], ed. A. Lidov (Moscow: Indrik 2006), 117–124.

2. See now *An Ottoman Traveller: Selections from the Book of Travels of Evliya Çelebi*, ed. Robert Dankoff and Sooyong Kim (London: Eland, 2020).

mosques and attached soup kitchens for the poor, and their quiet central squares, where the local intelligentsia conversed at ease in the shade of ancient plane trees. Such journeys across heart-stretching landscapes, in the alert company of Evliya, gave me a sense of what Braudel had called *la mesure du siècle*—a sense of the possible in two great empires.

This experience has lingered in my memory. Evliya's description of his visit to the great mosques of Edirne formed the basis of my introduction to the exquisite volume of photographs—*Sacred Spaces: Turkish Mosques and Tombs*—by my friend Mary Cross (1936–2016), a brilliant star in the firmament of the town of Princeton, for whose hospitality this essay was a small return.[3]

I returned from those travels (as from later ones in Syria, Jordan, Israel, Egypt, Tunisia, and Algeria) with a greater sense of the social structure of the late Roman Empire, and especially of the nature of the cities whose ruins were scattered throughout these regions. In this way, I benefited from the archaeological revolution that had revealed the richness and complexity of rural and urban life in East Rome. This revolution reached its peak in a fragile moment of relative peace—peace, at least, for field archaeologists—between the playing out of the Iranian Revolution and the disastrous rise of ISIS in 2014.

WEALTH, POVERTY, AND POWER: *POWER AND PERSUASION* AND *POVERTY AND LEADERSHIP*

My next two books—*Power and Persuasion* (1992) and *Poverty and Leadership* (2002)—are what I would call my first Princeton books.[4] They were based on frequent travel and on access to state-of-the-art archaeological publications in the Marquand Library of Art and Archaeology and in the library of the Institute for Advanced Study.

Both books touched on a raw nerve in the conscience of late antique Christians that has remained sensitive up to this day: what to do with wealth; what to do with the poor. Wealth and poverty (like the issue of sexual renunciation) were themes that concerned the very basis of late Roman society, and that have

---

3. Peter Brown, "The Garden and the Dome," introduction to Mary Cross, *Sacred Spaces: Turkish Mosques and Tombs* (New York: W. W. Norton, 2013), 13–20.

4. Peter Brown, *Power and Persuasion in Late Antiquity: Towards a Christian Empire*, Merle Curti Lectures (Madison: University of Wisconsin Press, 1992); *Poverty and Leadership in the Later Roman Empire*, Menahem Stern Jerusalem Lectures (Hanover, NH: University of New England Press, 2002).

attracted the attention both of historians of the ancient world and of polemicists anxious to draw a moral from the fate of Rome.

I wanted to show how the issue of the care of the poor got underway, in practice, as the poor came to be mobilized as part of the constituency of the Christian bishops in the clergy's bid for control of the cities, through the creation of new institutions—poorhouses, hospitals, and regular food doles. At the same time, all over the Roman world, Christian preaching on almsgiving presented the relations between rich and poor with an intensity and a pathos that posed the issue of the solidarity of late Roman society. Far from being the story of a few, idealistic ventures in Christian charity, the emergence of the notion of the poor as objects of concern with a claim on the rich brought to a head the anxieties of an entire, hard-driven society. To listen to debates on wealth and poverty throughout the Roman world was like listening to the creaking of a great ship on the high seas.

Rome and After in the West:
Through the Eye of a Needle

And nowhere were some Christians so rich, some Christian writers so radical and so articulate, and society seemingly so much under threat as in the Latin West at the time of the fall of Rome, the barbarian invasions, and the formation of a postimperial society. Not surprisingly, therefore, *Through the Eye of a Needle* (2012) was my longest book. It was the result of a decade of work, much of it involving a reassessment of the nature of late Roman society in the West. It described the dilemmas of the very rich, whose vast villas (many of which had only recently been discovered) had dominated the landscape in many parts of Britain, Gaul, Spain, and Italy, and whose old-world lifestyle had once seemed so secure. It followed the way in which these aristocrats adjusted to a world after Rome, in which the little big men of the provinces— not so rich, regional figures—won out at the expense of the grandees of the Roman ancien régime. And they did this, largely, because they sought careers as bishops, clergymen, and administrators of the properties of an ever-richer church.[5]

5. *Through the Eye of a Needle: Wealth, the Fall of Rome, and the Making of Christianity in the West, 350–550 AD* (Princeton, NJ: Princeton University Press, 2012). For the next stage in this development, see now Ian Wood, *The Christian Economy in the Early Medieval West: Towards a Temple Society* (Binghamton, NY: Gracchi Books, 2022).

When working, for almost a decade, on *Through the Eye of a Needle*, I was heartened by the emergence of Spain (along with Portugal) as a major center of late antique studies. Until then, Spain had been somewhat peripheral to the study of the late Roman West—Italy, Gaul, and Rome's northern frontier with the barbarian world had held the center of attention. Now a new generation of ancient historians and archaeologists began to give a voice to the Iberian Peninsula—an immense and hitherto silent land.

To mention only those whom I knew personally, I found that the work of Kim Bowes (originally a graduate student at Princeton) on the villa churches of Spain and Portugal, and the studies of Javier Arce and Gisela Ripoll, added an entire new dimension to the study of religion and society in the Roman and post-Roman West. In this way, a cohort of young scholars (including gifted Argentinians and Brazilians) joined their French and Italian colleagues as equals in the study of late antiquity and the early Middle Ages.[6]

CHRISTIANIZATION

Though working, mainly, on wealth and poverty, I also found myself confronting problems of which I had little or no inkling in 1987. This often happens to scholars. Like a swimmer on an unknown beach, I learned that it is quite possible to set off in one direction and to find oneself carried, by an invisible riptide, to an entirely different part of the seashore.

My riptide, in the 1990s and early 2000s, was the problem of Christianization. It may seem strange that this problem was new to me. After all, my very first articles were written on the Christianization of the Roman aristocracy, and on the role of religious coercion in securing the victory of Catholic Christianity in Augustine's North Africa and elsewhere.[7] But this was different. I now wanted to understand not what happened but what was said to have happened: how the piecemeal and ambiguous process of change by which a pagan society was replaced, over a period of centuries, by a new Christian order, was represented—written about, talked about, remembered, and celebrated—by Christians

---

6. For a sample of work on the Iberian Peninsula, see Kim Bowes, *Private Worship, Public Values, and Religious Change in Late Antiquity* (Cambridge University Press, 2008); Javier Arce, *Bárbaros y romanos en Hispania* (Madrid: Marcial Pons, 2005); G. Ripoll and I. Velázquez, *La Hispania visigoda* (Madrid: Temas de Hoy, 1997); and Damián Fernández, *Aristocrats and Statehood in Western Iberia, 300–600 C.E.* (Philadelphia: University of Pennsylvania Press, 2017).

7. See chapter 38: "Religious Dissent" and chapter 39: "Religious Coercion."

themselves. It was this Christian "representation" of the end of paganism and the triumph of the church that held my attention in those years.[8]

There was a growing awareness, among scholars of late antiquity (such as Françoise Thélamon and Averil Cameron) of the skill with which Christian authors presented accounts of the end of paganism in such a way as to make the triumph of Christianity seem inevitable.[9] This was only natural in a once-persecuted religious group tasting the fruits of victory. But what struck me was something rather different. As I read accounts of Christianization from all over the Roman world and beyond, I realized that these accounts varied from region to region; and that, paradoxically, the victory of Christianity over paganism was often remembered in narratives based on pre-Christian imaginative patterns.

In Egypt, the end of the temples was presented as if it were the last, abrupt round in a long series of clashes between rival gods that was a common theme in pharaonic myth. In Armenia, it was the opposite: Christianization was treated as a long-drawn-out process, subject to dramatic reversals, like the eternal wrestling of the powers of good with the powers of evil in Zoroastrian apocalyptic thought. In Ireland, accounts of the coming of Saint Patrick took the form of a battle of wits between the saint and local pagan landowners, in which Patrick played the role of a trickster god, offering mere Latin words of blessing in return for solid food, rich land, and a portion of their daughters as nuns. In each of these cases we are listening in to a rare phenomenon—traditional societies reflecting, in their own terms, on one of the great changes of their times.

TRIUMPH AND DIVERSITY:
THE RISE OF WESTERN CHRISTENDOM

It was this new interest in the process of Christianization that led me to write *The Rise of Western Christendom: Triumph and Diversity, A.D. 200–1000*.[10] As early as 1988, I had agreed with Jacques LeGoff to contribute a volume on

8. See Peter Brown, "The Problem of Christianization," Raleigh Lecture, 1992, *Proceedings of the British Academy* 82 (1993): 89–106, and *Authority and the Sacred: Aspects of the Christianisation of the Roman World*, Tanner Lectures (Cambridge University Press, 1995).

9. Françoise Thélamon, *Paiens et chrétiens au ive siècle: l'apport de l'Histoire ecclésiastique de Rufin d'Aquilée* (Paris: Études Augustiniennes, 1981); and Averil Cameron, *Christianity and the Rhetoric of Empire: The Development of Christian Discourse*, Sather Lectures (Berkeley: University of California Press, 1991).

10. Peter Brown, *The Rise of Western Christendom: Triumph and Diversity, A.D. 200–1000* (Oxford: Blackwell, 1996).

divided Christendoms to his series called Faire l'Europe. It seemed to me that such a book gave me the chance to highlight the distinctive qualities of each region, as these were revealed by the different ways in which they had become Christian. Instead of the story of a single, unified Catholic Church, advancing triumphantly in the West, I would try to present a history of late antique and early medieval Christianity as a whole, including the Christian East, like a great chain of distinctive regions, which stretched from Ireland, through the Mediterranean and the Middle East, to the churches scattered along the Silk Road from Central Asia to China.

Each of these regions formed what I called a "micro-Christendom." Each was convinced that its practices and doctrines were a microcosm that reflected faithfully the worldwide macrocosm of Christian truth. Instead of a conventional history of conflicting churches—of heresies and schisms—I would offer a history of the interaction of different Christian regions in terms of the rise and fall of different "micro-Christendoms," as they withdrew into themselves, or reached out to absorb others, like amoebic cells contracting and expanding beneath a microscope. Eventually, in Europe, a distinctive cluster of "micro-Christendoms" came together to form the more uniform world of the medieval Catholic West. But this was not how things had been in late antiquity and in the early Middle Ages: at that time, Western Christendom was only one cluster of regions among many, perched at the northwestern tip of a vast and variegated Christian world. Hence the importance, for me, of including in a book, whose title promised a study of *Western* Christendom, many chapters devoted to Byzantium, Islam, and the Christianities of the East. These chapters on non-Western forms of Christianity further emphasized the theme of the subtitle—"Triumph *and Diversity*."

The Rise got off to a hesitant start. It was first published in 1996 as little more than an extended essay. It did not even have footnotes; and this for a very down-to-earth reason: I had broken my wrist and found that pulling books from shelves and turning over their pages to find references was exquisitely painful. It was only in 2003 that Blackwell brought out a completely rewritten version, accompanied by an introduction and ample notes. Ten years later, Wiley-Blackwell reprinted the 2003 edition with a further long preface.[11]

---

11. Peter Brown, *The Rise of Western Christendom: Triumph and Diversity, A.D. 200–1000*, 2nd ed. (Oxford: Blackwell, 2003) and tenth-anniversary rev. ed. (Malden, MA: Wiley-Blackwell, 2013).

I wanted to do this rewriting for two reasons. First: I had felt the need to return yet again to western Europe, having spent so much time and travel on understandng the East. It seeemed to me, looking back, that *The World of Late Antiquity* had skimped on the post-Roman West, by concentrating on the Eastern Empire and the Middle East. I needed to redress the balance by writing on the Christianization of western Europe, as an example of the general problem of the methods and meaning of Christianization, to which I was giving much attention in my reading and in my teaching. Furthermore, I had come to take a second look at my own work in the previous decades, with an eye to where it needed to go forward.[12] It was time to put all this together in a work of synthesis.

Second: I was struck by the veritable dam burst of studies of postimperial western Europe, partly fostered by a European Science Foundation project, the Transformation of the Roman World, under the guidance of Walter Pohl. This Europe-wide breakthrough challenged me to set the spread of Christianity against a very different background from what had been conventional hitherto. Instead of the story of a unified Catholic Church impinging on solidly "ethnic" barbarian kingdoms—Goths, Franks, Anglo-Saxons, and Irish—each with their own, closed culture and static institutions, we find a fluid situation, where regional elites engaged in a process of state formation in which the Christian clergy collaborated with enterprising kings to build, from a wide variety of traditions, the network of "micro-Christendoms" that dotted the Latin West.

All this time, I was encouraged and inspired by my Princeton friends and colleagues, each in a different way. To mention only a few: early on, Judith Herrin, the Byzantinist in the History Department, provided, in her adventurous book, *The Formation of Christendom* (1987), a model for my own treatment of the interrelated Christianities of East and West.[13] Slobodan Čurčić (1940–2017)—Danny Čurčić—was a gentle giant in the field of the art and architecture of the Byzantine and early modern Balkans. His *Architecture in the Balkans from Diocletian to Süleyman the Magnificent* (2010) was a masterpiece.[14] I read

12. Peter Brown, "The World of Late Antiquity Revisited," *Symbolae Osloenses* 72 (1997): 5–90; "The Rise and Function of the Holy Man in Late Antiquity, 1971–1997," *Journal of Early Christian Studies* 6 (1998): 353–376; and *Augustine of Hippo* (2000), 441–520.

13. Judith Herrin, *The Formation of Christendom* (Princeton, NJ: Princeton University Press, 1987, reedited with a new preface, 2022).

14. Slobodan Čurčić, *Architecture in the Balkans from Diocletian to Süleyman the Magnificent* (New Haven, CT: Yale University Press, 2010).

every chapter in draft, and discussed them over long breakfasts replete with learning. With his unfailingly fresh eye, his vast range—from the age of Constantine to early modern Muscovy—and his unflinching academic integrity in the midst of so much ethnic strife within his field, Danny stood for the best in Balkan and Byzantine studies. In the Department of Classics, Brent Shaw's immense learning, his humanity, and his capacity always to be amazed made him a model of what it is to be an ancient historian.[15] Throughout, I was fortunate to find myself teaching a succession of graduate students (as well as class after class of undergraduates) whose diverse interests and enthusiasms kept my horizons stretched to the limits.

The End of the Ancient Other World:
The Ransom of the Soul

My last two books—*The Ransom of the Soul: Afterlife and Wealth in Early Western Christianity* (2015) and *Treasure in Heaven: The Holy Poor in Early Christianity* (2016)—make plain the pendulum swing from East to West and back again that has always made the field of late antiquity so challenging to me.

The Ransom of the Soul (which I delivered in Vienna at the Institut für die Wissenschaften vom Menschen) was the story of what one might call the Christianization of death and the Other World in the Latin West. It showed how the care of the dying, and the rituals connected with the fate of the souls of the departed, alongside representations of the Other World, changed over time. They slowly took on the clarity that we associate with the medieval Catholic Church, characterized by a threefold division of Heaven, Hell, and Purgatory. This change took place over the centuries, in an unbroken arc that reached from the homely symbiosis of living and dead in the catacombs of Rome, in the third century, to the great monasteries—formidable power-houses of prayer for the dead—founded by wandering Irishmen in northern Gaul, in the seventh century.[16]

A long-term change, seemingly unrelated to the dramatic events of the period (the sack of Rome, the barbarian invasions, the formation of kingdoms), but as powerful as a long ocean roller, enveloped the populations of Christian

15. Peter Brown, "Brent Shaw: An Intellectual Profile," in *Empire and Religion in the Roman World*, ed. Harriet Flower (Cambridge University Press, 2021), 241–251.

16. Peter Brown, *The Ransom of the Soul: Afterlife and Wealth in Early Western Christianity* (Cambridge, MA: Harvard University Press, 2015).

Europe in a new imaginative world beyond this world, centered, as never before, on the tremulous journey of the soul.

Syria, Egypt, and the Meaning of Work: *Treasure in Heaven*

Treasure in Heaven (the James W. Richards Lectures at the University of Virginia, Charlottesville) took me to a very different part of the world. It studied the clash between two major Christian regions of the East. It describes how the ascetics of Egypt and the holy men of Syria came to differ on the role of work in the monastic life. Far from being a squabble among monks alone, the debate on work involved the very definition of the human person and of human society. Could Christian ascetics live the life of the angels by opting out of society to such an extent as to live without working, supported by the alms of the faithful, as in the "Lands of the Begging Bowl"—the vast expanse of Buddhist countries to the east of Iran? Or must they accept a common humanity, defined by the cry of the stomach and the ache of the hands at work?

The monasteries of Egypt, and with them, those of the West, tended to opt for solidarity with human toil. By contrast, the holy men of Syria and neighboring regions dared the human condition. As they swayed in constant prayer on top of pillars, in caves, and on the untilled edges of the settled world, their radical stance summed up a yearning to be free from the long pain of labor that went back to the origins of civilization in the Middle East.[17]

"Not by One Avenue Alone"

As I look back now, after seventy years, on the study of late antiquity, what strikes me is the sheer diversity of institutional settings, of scholarly backgrounds, and of individual intellectual trajectories that have gone into making it so vibrant a field. It is too large a field to be tied to any one discipline, methodology, or learned tradition. Something of the awe of the last pagans faced by the majesty of the stars is not out of place. *Uno itinere non potest perveniri*

---

17. *Treasure in Heaven: The Holy Poor in Early Christianity* (Charlottesville: University of Virginia Press, 2016). For a splendid development of these themes, see now Daniel Caner, *The Rich and the Pure: Philanthropy and the Making of Christian Society in Early Byzantium* (Berkeley: University of California Press, 2021).

ad tam grande secretum: "Not by one avenue alone can we make our way to so vast a mystery."[18]

As for myself, I have become, at the age of eighty-seven, a creature of regular habits. I wake up early every morning, which gives me time to say my prayers and to turn, before dawn's early light, to reading ancient languages. Lately, I have returned, in my mind, to the sources of the Nile, to Ethiopia—the Ethiopia from whence Martha, my nanny in Khartoum, had come as a refugee, in 1938.[19] I have begun to read in Ge'ez (in Classical Ethiopic) texts that still echo, at a vast distance of time and space, the controversies and ascetic legends of Syria and Egypt of the fifth and sixth centuries, which had trickled down the Nile and the Red Sea to Ethiopia, to yet another "micro-Christendom," founded in late antiquity and still surviving in the Horn of Africa. There is room, in late antiquity, for many more such journeys of the mind.

18. Symmachus, *Relatio* 3.10, in *Prefect and Emperor: The Relationes of Symmachus A.D. 384,* ed. R. H. Barrow (Oxford: The Clarendon Press, 1973), 40 (my translation).

19. Chapter 8: "Atbara: Life Abroad."

INDEX